Data Mining and Machine Learning with Applications

Data Mining and Machine Learning with Applications

Editor

Wei Fang

Basel • Beijing • Wuhan • Barcelona • Belgrade • Novi Sad • Cluj • Manchester

Editor
Wei Fang
Nanjing University of Information
Science & Technology
Nanjing, China

Editorial Office
MDPI
St. Alban-Anlage 66
4052 Basel, Switzerland

This is a reprint of articles from the Special Issue published online in the open access journal *Mathematics* (ISSN 2227-7390) (available at: https://www.mdpi.com/si/mathematics/Data_Mining_Mach_Learn).

For citation purposes, cite each article independently as indicated on the article page online and as indicated below:

Lastname, A.A.; Lastname, B.B. Article Title. *Journal Name* **Year**, *Volume Number*, Page Range.

ISBN 978-3-0365-9807-9 (Hbk)
ISBN 978-3-0365-9818-5 (PDF)
doi.org/10.3390/books978-3-0365-9818-5

© 2024 by the authors. Articles in this book are Open Access and distributed under the Creative Commons Attribution (CC BY) license. The book as a whole is distributed by MDPI under the terms and conditions of the Creative Commons Attribution-NonCommercial-NoDerivs (CC BY-NC-ND) license.

Contents

About the Editor vii

Jing Lu, Hongjun Chai and Ruchun Jia
A General Framework for Flight Maneuvers Automatic Recognition
Reprinted from: *Mathematics* 2022, *10*, 1196, doi:10.3390/math10071196 1

Wei Fang, Yu Sha and Victor S. Sheng
Survey on the Application of Artificial Intelligence in ENSO Forecasting
Reprinted from: *Mathematics* 2022, *10*, 3793, doi:10.3390/math10203793 17

Yousef Almaghthawi, Iftikhar Ahmad and Fawaz E. Alsaadi
Performance Analysis of Feature Subset Selection Techniques for Intrusion Detection
Reprinted from: *Mathematics* 2022, *10*, 4745, doi:10.3390/math10244745 39

Pan Zheng, Wenqin Zhao, Yaqiong Lv, Lu Qian and Yifan Li
Health Status-Based Predictive Maintenance Decision-Making via LSTM and Markov Decision
Process
Reprinted from: *Mathematics* 2023, *11*, 109, doi:10.3390/math11010109 65

Adel A. Ahmed, Sharaf J. Malebary, Waleed Ali and Ahmed A. Alzahrani
A Provable Secure Cybersecurity Mechanism Based on Combination of Lightweight
Cryptography and Authentication for Internet of Things
Reprinted from: *Mathematics* 2023, *11*, 220, doi:10.3390/math11010220 79

**Ali Raza, Sharjeel Adnan, Muhammad Ishaq, Hyung Seok Kim, Rizwan Ali Naqvi and
Seung-Won Lee**
Assisting Glaucoma Screening Process Using Feature Excitation and Information Aggregation
Techniques in Retinal Fundus Images
Reprinted from: *Mathematics* 2023, *11*, 257, doi:10.3390/math11020257 103

**Gaeithry Manoharam, Mohd Shareduwan Mohd Kasihmuddin, Siti Noor Farwina
Mohamad Anwar Antony, Nurul Atiqah Romli, Nur 'Afifah Rusdi, et al.**
Log-Linear-Based Logic Mining with Multi-Discrete Hopfield Neural Network
Reprinted from: *Mathematics* 2023, *11*, 2121, doi:10.3390/math11092121 123

Tariq Ahamed Ahanger, Usman Tariq, Fadl Dahan, Shafique A. Chaudhry and Yasir Malik
Securing IoT Devices Running PureOS from Ransomware Attacks: Leveraging Hybrid Machine
Learning Techniques
Reprinted from: *Mathematics* 2023, *11*, 2481, doi:10.3390/math11112481 153

Juan Laborda, Sonia Ruano and Ignacio Zamanillo
Multi-Country and Multi-Horizon GDP Forecasting Using Temporal Fusion Transformers
Reprinted from: *Mathematics* 2023, *11*, 2625, doi:10.3390/math11122625 177

Yifen Li and Yuanyang Chen
NSNet: An N-Shaped Convolutional Neural Network with Multi-Scale Information for Image
Denoising
Reprinted from: *Mathematics* 2023, *11*, 2772, doi:10.3390/math11122772 203

**Sebastián Vázquez-Ramírez, Miguel Torres-Ruiz, Rolando Quintero, Kwok Tai Chui and
Carlos Guzmán Sánchez-Mejorada**
An Analysis of Climate Change Based on Machine Learning and an Endoreversible Model
Reprinted from: *Mathematics* 2023, *11*, 3060, doi:10.3390/math11143060 223

Jamolbek Mattiev, Monte Davityan and Branko Kavsek
ACMKC: A Compact Associative Classification Model Using K-Modes Clustering with Rule Representations by Coverage
Reprinted from: *Mathematics* **2023**, *11*, 3978, doi:10.3390/math11183978 . . . . **249**

About the Editor

Wei Fang

Wei Fang is a Professor in the School of Computer Science at Nanjing University of Information Science & Technology, China, and Director of the Institute of Artificial Intelligence and Meteorological Big Data (AIMB). He was a visiting scholar at the University of Florida from 2015 to 2016. Currently, Prof. Fang also serves as a senior member of the China Computer Federation (CCF), an executive member of the Committee of Computer Applications of CCF, a member of the Chinese Artificial Intelligence Society, a Program Reviewer of the National Natural Science Foundation of China, a Program Reviewer of the Ministry of Science and Technology, and a Dissertation Reviewer of the Ministry of Education Expert, a Reviewer of the National Postdoctoral Innovation and Entrepreneurship Competition, and a member of the JiangSu Association of Artificial Intelligence. Prof. Fang has presided over one top-level project of the National Natural Science Foundation of China, four provincial and ministerial projects, and three municipal projects, and has participated in nine national, provincial and ministerial research projects. He has published more than 30 academic papers indexed in SCI and EI, authorized 12 national invention patents, and been granted 10 software copyrights. He has served as the chair of ICAIS International Conference Workshops, TURC_AIS 2019, a TPC Member of the MLAI2022 International Conference, a guest editor of many SCI journals, and a reviewer of numerous international academic journals.

A General Framework for Flight Maneuvers Automatic Recognition

Jing Lu [1,2,*], Hongjun Chai [2] and Ruchun Jia [3]

1. College of Computer Science and Technology, Nanjing University of Aeronautics and Astronautics, Nanjing 211106, China
2. College of Computer Science, Civil Aviation Flight University of China, Guanghan 618307, China; chaihongjun@cafuc.edu.cn
3. Wangjiang Campus, Sichuan University, Chengdu 610065, China; ruchunjia@zaibei.org.cn
* Correspondence: lujing_cafuc@nuaa.edu.cn

Abstract: Flight Maneuver Recognition (FMR) refers to the automatic recognition of a series of aircraft flight patterns and is a key technology in many fields. The chaotic nature of its input data and the professional complexity of the identification process make it difficult and expensive to identify, and none of the existing models have general generalization capabilities. A general framework is proposed in this paper, which can be used for all kinds of flight tasks, independent of the aircraft type. We first preprocessed the raw data with unsupervised clustering method, segmented it into maneuver sequences, then reconstructed the sequences in phase space, calculated their approximate entropy, quantitatively characterized the sequence complexity, and distinguished the flight maneuvers. Experiments on a real flight training dataset have shown that the framework can quickly and correctly identify various flight maneuvers for multiple aircraft types with minimal human intervention.

Keywords: Flight Maneuver Recognition (FMR); unsupervised clustering; phase space reconstruction

1. Introduction

Flight Maneuver, according to the standard definition given by the Federal Aviation Administration (FAA) [1], refers to a series of flight patterns of an aircraft under the control of the pilot. FMR as a key technology for automatic evaluation of flight technology is the focus of research on the application of artificial intelligence in the field of flight training. In the 1970s, for one-on-one, air-to-air combat training, NASA developed an adaptive maneuvering logic computer program (AML) [2,3], which provides an virtual competitor for human pilots at NASA Langley Research Center's (LRC) Differential Maneuvering Simulator (DMS). As AI, AML recognizes the maneuvers and intentions of the opponent and makes the right decisions to drive the next maneuvers. In addition, the study of flight maneuvers' aircraft loads is an important issue in the field of flight safety involving aircraft design, flight certification, and accident investigation, and FMR is the basic technology for this study. Barndt G. [4] examined how the Navy could process raw parameter data generated by HUMS to identify the maneuvers flown so as to support the structural monitoring function in 2007. Many studies in this area have been generated since then.

Although there is also a wide demand for FMR in the field of UAV and air combat research, due to the limitation of data sources and author's concentration, this paper only focuses on manned fixed-wing civil aviation training flight.

The raw data of FMR is multivariate time-series data generated from nonlinear aircraft power system, which has typical chaotic characteristics and cannot be directly applied to common time series analysis methods. As an artificial mechanical operating system, the data performance of the same flight maneuver of different pilots of different types of aircraft is very different, not to mention the influence of environmental factors such as weather variation.

Essentially, FMR is a multiple nonlinear time-series pattern-recognition problem [5]. Pattern-recognition problems mainly include classification and clustering.

Classification-based FMR

In the time-series classification problem, feature volume construction and classifier design are the core problems. Time-series classification aims to take the whole time series as input to assign a discrete label. In FMR, different maneuvers often have different lengths due to differences in aircraft types, and the same maneuvers have different lengths due to differences in pilot operating habits. It is more difficult than the general classification problem owing to the inequational length of the classified time-series data, which makes it impossible to apply the general classification algorithm directly.

In order to solve these difficulties, there are usually two approaches. First, define the appropriate distance degree using a distance-based pattern-recognition method, such as Dynamic Time Warping (DTW) distance [6–8], Locality Sensitive Hash (LSH) distance [9], and Approximate Entropy [10]. The advantages of these methods are that they conform to the basic principles of pattern recognition; the more similar the patterns are, the smaller their distances are; and the algorithms are simple and easy to implement, do not limit the length of the time series between patterns, and can analyze nonlinear time series. The significant disadvantages are expensive calculation and inability to identify subtle differences between patterns.

Second, using knowledge rules or context-dependent modeling, each sequence is represented by an equal-length and same-dimension feature vector of model parameters and then trained and classified by a conventional classification algorithm, which is a domain-related approach called the model-based method. In general, model-based FMR methods can be divided into four categories: (1) feature extraction-based [11–14], (2) expert knowledge rule-based [15–27], (3) probabilistic graphical model-based [28–31], and (4) neural network-based [32–36].

(1) The main methods for feature extraction are SVD and SVM methods, combined with least squares or hierarchical classification methods, which reduce the computational effort by reducing the number of dimensions and compressing the data. The models are simple and easy to train but are not complete, and they are sensitive to temporal length and require manual prior knowledge. (2) The expert knowledge rule model method needs to establish the artificial rule knowledge database first, then use the pattern-matching query method to achieve recognition. The knowledge rule extraction method includes Natural Language Processing, Genetic Algorithm, and Swarm Optimization. This type of method is very widely used, with high recognition efficiency and correct rate, but the unavoidable disadvantages are high labor cost; the fact that a certain model only corresponds to a certain type of aircraft type or flight task; and the inability of the method be generalized. (3) The probabilistic graphical model-based mainly uses hidden Markov model (HMM), Kalman filtering, and dynamic Bayesian methods, which can not only identify but also predict and only need a few parameters to form a complete model but cannot handle nonlinear time series. (4) The model based on neural network work uses deep neural network with fully supervised training method to constitute the model, with high recognition rate and good model maturity but also with high cost of integration with labeled data and computational complexity. Different aircraft types correspond to different models and need to be completely retrained.

Naturally, hybrid methods combining multiple methods have also been proposed [37,38]; these methods have better recognition performance but still do not have the ability to generalize.

Clustering-based FMR

In addition, some scholars have also conducted FMR from the perspective of clustering [39–42]. These methods do not require prior knowledge with the ability to generalize. However, the clustering results rely heavily on good temporal segmentation, and most of the papers appearing now use manual segmentation without automatic segmentation capability, and the clustered results still need to be interpreted by human experts and cannot correspond automatically.

In summary, it can be found that the existing literature methods all perform FMR for a certain task of a certain aircraft model and generally have the significant disadvantages of relying on manual expert knowledge, being unable to automatically segment, and being difficult to generalize.

To the best of our knowledge, there is no general framework that can automatically segment sequences and quickly discriminate between maneuvers with minimal human intervention.

This paper proposes a new general framework; the general idea is to integrate the automatic segmentation capability of unsupervised clustering and the ability of information entropy to distinguish sequence complexity.

This paper is organized as follows. Section 2 introduces the automatic segmentation method of flight maneuver sequence. Section 3 introduces the automatic recognition method of maneuver segments. Section 4 completely elaborates the overall framework of automatic FMR processing. Section 5 covers the experimental process and experimental results, and the conclusion is given in Section 6.

2. Sequence Segmentation

2.1. The Trend Fragmentation Algorithm

In this paper, a key parameter is selected for trend identification, and the index of all trend segments is obtained using the slope method combined with a height change threshold, using a sliding model with a double window.

The slope method is based on the least square method, where the sequence to be segmented is fitted to a straight line, and the main trend of the sequence is determined by comparing the slope of the line with a threshold size.

Set $D = (y_1, y_2, \cdots, y_m)^T$ is a sample set, $X = (x_1, x_2, \cdots, x_m)^T$ is the time sequence set, D_i is a subset of the samples, $i = (1, 2, \cdots, L)$, and L is the number of trend segments. The model parameters are obtained by fitting the least squares method as in Equation (1).

$$\omega_i = (k_i, b_i)^T = \left(D_i^T D_i\right)^{-1} D_i^T \cdot X_i, \ i = (1, 2, \cdots, L) \tag{1}$$

The height-change threshold is used to determine long, slow-climbing, or circling maneuvers in flight, which have small slopes and long durations and can be misjudged based on the slope alone. The algorithm is described in Algorithm 1.

The core of Algorithm 1 is to use the sliding double window method to fit the slope to the original data and determine the flight attitude as ascending, leveling, or descending at that time based on the slope and use the change in attitude as the signal for automatic sequence segmentation. The k_s is slope threshold, Δ_s is height-change threshold, ω is fitting matrix, F is the fixed window, S is the sliding window, O_j is the output subsequence, f is the flag bit, and takes values in the range {'U', 'L', 'D'}.

2.2. The Clustering Algorithm

With Algorithm 1, we obtain the trend segments, and this section will use the dynamic clustering method ISODATA (Iterative Self Organizing Data Analysis Techniques Algorithm) to complete the segment classification. ISODATA algorithm automatically selects a number of samples as cluster centers and adjusts the class centers by sample mean iteration in subsEquationuent calculations and realizes the adjustment of cluster center data by merging and splitting of patterns. However, the input data are time series, so the algorithm cannot be used directly; therefore, this paper improves the algorithm to TS-ISODATA, and the algorithm is described as follows Algorithm 2.

For input raw data $X = \begin{bmatrix} x_{11} & \cdots & x_{1n} \\ \vdots & \ddots & \vdots \\ x_{m1} & \cdots & x_{mn} \end{bmatrix}$, n parameters, m data points of the fragment, normalized as

$$x_{ij} = \frac{x_{ij} - x_{j,min}}{x_{j,max} - x_{j,min}} - 0.5 \tag{2}$$

calculate its statistics as

$$\bar{x}_i = \frac{1}{m}\sum_{j=1}^{m} x_{ij},\ s_i = \frac{1}{m}\sqrt{\sum_{j=1}^{m}(x_{ij}-\bar{x}_i)^2}\ (i=1,2,\cdots,n) \qquad (3)$$

Algorithm 1 The Trend Fragmentation Algorithm.

Input : sample set $D = (y_1, y_2, \cdots, y_m)^T$; time sequence set $X = (x_1, x_2, \cdots, x_m)^T$;

1. Set slope threshold k_s and height-change threshold Δ_s;
2. Initial value of fitting parameter $\omega = (k, b)^T$;
3. Initialize the fixed window $F = (x_{F_{start}}, x_2, \cdots, x_{F_{end}})^T$, $F_{start} = 1$, $F_{end} = h$;
4. Initialize the sliding window $S = (x_{S_{start}}, x_2, \cdots, x_{S_{end}})^T$, $S_{start} = 1$, $S_{end} = h$;
5. Initialize the output sequence $O_j = (x_{F_{start}}, x_{F_{end}}, f)$;
6. Read a samples subset $D_i = (y_{S_{start}}, \cdots, y_{S_{end}})^T$; time sequence set $X_i = S$;
7. Least squares fitting model to obtain parameters: ω_i;
8. If $k \geq k_s$, identifies X_i as an upward trend, set $f = $ 'U';
9. Otherwise, if $-k_s < k < k_s$ identifies X_i as a level trend, set $f = $ 'L';
10. Otherwise, identifies X_i as a downward trend, set $f = $ 'D';
11. If X_i is not a level trend, and k's signs are unchanged, set
    $F_{start} = F_{start}$, $F_{end} = F_{end} + 1$, $S_{start} = S_{start} + 1$, $S_{end} = S_{end} + 1$;
12. Otherwise, if k's signs are changed, set $O_j = (x_{F_{start}}, x_{F_{end}}, f)$,
    $F_{start} = S_{start}$, $F_{end} = F_{start} + h$, $S_{start} = S_{start} + 1$, $S_{end} = S_{end} + 1$;
13. If X_i is a level trend, set $F_{start} = F_{start}$, $F_{end} = F_{end} + 1$, $S_{start} = S_{start} + 1$, $S_{end} = S_{end} + 1$;
14. Least squares fitting model to obtain parameters: $\omega_l = (D_l^T D_l)^{-1} D_l^T \cdot X_l$;
15. Calculate fixed window height change $\Delta = |k_l \cdot (F_{end} - F_{start})|$;
16. If $|k_l| > k_s$, set $f = $ 'L', set $O_j = (x_{F_{start}}, x_{F_{end}}, f)$,
    $F_{start} = S_{start}$, $F_{end} = F_{start} + h$, $S_{start} = S_{start} + 1$, $S_{end} = S_{end} + 1$;
17. If $|k_l| < k_s$, and $\Delta > \Delta_s$, set $f = $ 'U' ($k_l > 0$) or 'D' ($k_l < 0$), set $O_j = (x_{F_{start}}, x_{F_{end}}, f)$,
    $F_{start} = S_{start}$, $F_{end} = F_{start} + h$, $S_{start} = S_{start} + 1$, $S_{end} = S_{end} + 1$;
18. Otherwise, if $|k_l| < k_s$, and $\Delta < \Delta_s$, set
    $F_{start} = F_{start}$, $F_{end} = F_{end} + 1$, $S_{start} = S_{start} + 1$, $S_{end} = S_{end} + 1$;
19. If $S_{end} \geq m$, end iterations; otherwise, go back to 7.

Output : O.

Algorithm 2 TS-ISODATA Algorithm.

Input : X, trend sequence O;

1. Normalized processing x_{ij};
2. Statistics calculation $\bar{x}_i, s_i$;
3. Construct feature vectors $y = (\bar{x}_1, s_1, \bar{x}_2, s_2, \cdots, \bar{x}_n, s_n)^T$;
4. Randomly select k_0 samples as initial clustering centers $C = \{c_1, c_2, \cdots, c_{k_0}\}$;
5. Calculate the distance from each sample x_i to the cluster center of the k_0 cluster centers and assign it to the class with the min distance;
6. Determine whether the number of elements in each class above is less than N_{min}. If so, discard the class, make $k = k - 1$, and reassign the samples to the class with the min distance;
7. For each category c_i, recalculate the clustering centers $c_i = \frac{1}{|c_i|}\sum_{x \in x_i} x$;
8. If the current k $\leq \frac{1}{2}k_0$, split operation;
9. If the current k $\geq 2k_0$, merge operation;
10. Terminate if the maximum number of iterations is reached; otherwise, go back to 2.

Output: Clustering results

3. Flight Maneuver Recognition

Algorithm 2 assigns the fragment to a specific class without knowing which flight maneuvers it is. In this section, the algorithm will use phase reconstruction to reconstruct the feature space and identify specific classes of flight maneuvers based on the principle that different maneuvers have different approximate entropy.

3.1. Phase Space Reconstruction

Due to the superiority of PSR (phase space reconstruction) for chaotic time-series computation [43], this paper adopts a multivariate data fusion reconstruction method based on Bayesian estimation theory, and the main calculation steps are as follows.

3.1.1. Reconstruction Parameters

The phase space reconstruction technique has two key parameters: the dimension of the embedding m and the delay time τ, which are determined here using the C-C method.

1. Define the correlation integral corresponding to each point y of the embedded time series in the reconstructed phase space as in Equation (4).

$$C(m, N, r, t) = \frac{2}{M(M-1)} \sum_{1 \leq i \leq j \leq m} \theta(r - d_{ij}) \quad (4)$$

$$d_{ij} = \|Y_i - Y_j\|_\infty, \ \theta(z) = \begin{cases} 0, & z < 0 \\ 1, & z > 0 \end{cases} \quad (5)$$

where Y_i is the reconstructed phase space vector, M is the number of vectors $M = N - (m-1)\tau$, m is the embedding dimension, N is the number of points of the original time series, t is time, and $\theta(z)$ is the associative integral, a cumulative distribution function that expresses the probability that the distance between any two points in the phase space is less than the radius r. Here, the distance between points is expressed as an infinite number of parameters of the difference of vectors.

2. Split the given time series into t equationual and disjoint subsequences as Equation (6), where t is the reconstruction time delay.

$$x^1 = \{x_1, x_{t+1}, \cdots, x_{N-t+1}\}, x^2 = \{x_1, x_{t+2}, \cdots, x_{N-t+2}\}, \cdots, x^t = \{x_1, x_{2t}, \cdots, x_N\} \quad (6)$$

3. Calculate the original sequence's S_1 and each sequence's S_2:

$$S_1(m, N, r, t) = C(m, N, r, t) - C^m(1, N, r, t) \quad (7)$$

$$S_2(m, r, t) = \frac{1}{t} \sum_{s=1}^{t} [C_s(m, N, r, t) - C_s^m(1, r, t)] \quad (8)$$

4. Select the two radiuses r with the max and min values and define the increments ΔS_2:

$$\Delta S_2(m, t) = \max\{S_2(m, r_j, t)\} - \min\{S_2(m, r_j, t)\} \quad (9)$$

5. Calculate the statistics:

$$\overline{S}_2(t) = \frac{1}{16} \sum_{m=2}^{5} \sum_{j=1}^{4} S_2(m, r_j, t) \quad (10)$$

$$\Delta \overline{S}(t) = \frac{1}{4} \sum_{m=2}^{5} \Delta S(m, t) \quad (11)$$

$$S_{2cor}(t) = \Delta S_2(m, t) + |S_2(m, r, t)| \quad (12)$$

6. Take the value corresponding to the first zero point of $\overline{S}_2(t)$ or the first minimal value of $\Delta \overline{S}(t)$ as the optimal time delay τ.

7. Let the t corresponding to the global minimum of $S_{2cor}(t)$ be the length of the time series window and the embedding dimension m.

3.1.2. Fusion Phase

As previously stated, the single variable delay time is τ, and the embedding dimension is m. To ensure that the multivariate is fully expanded in the same phase space without distortion, each variable's $\tau = \min(\tau_i)$, and $m = \max(m_i)$, $(i = 1, 2, \cdots, r)$. Each reconstructed sequence expression X_i as in Equation (13).

$$X_i = \begin{bmatrix} x_{i,1} & x_{i,1+\tau} & \cdots & x_{i,1+(m-1)\tau} \\ x_{i,2} & x_{i,2+\tau} & \cdots & x_{i,2+(m-1)\tau} \\ \vdots & \vdots & \vdots & \vdots \\ x_{i,M} & x_{i,M+\tau} & \cdots & x_{i,M+(m-1)\tau} \end{bmatrix}, i = 1, 2, \cdots, r \quad (13)$$

Extract the r reconstructed sequences of the same position k out of phase points in Equation (13) to form the fusion set $D_k = [x_1, x_2, \cdots, x_r]$. The specific expression is given in Equation (14).

$$\begin{cases} x_1 = \begin{bmatrix} x_{1,k} & x_{1,k+\tau} & \cdots & x_{1,k+(m-1)\tau} \end{bmatrix} \\ x_2 = \begin{bmatrix} x_{2,k} & x_{2,k+\tau} & \cdots & x_{2,k+(m-1)\tau} \end{bmatrix} \\ \vdots \\ x_r = \begin{bmatrix} x_{r,k} & x_{r,k+\tau} & \cdots & x_{r,k+(m-1)\tau} \end{bmatrix} \end{cases} \quad (14)$$

Let the expression of the phase point at position k after fusion be z_k, and the optimal fusion phase point at k is obtained according to Equation (15).

$$p(z_k|x_1, x_2, \cdots, x_r) = \frac{p(x_1, x_2, \cdots, x_r|z_k)}{p(x_1, x_2, \cdots, x_r)} \cdot p(z_k) \quad (15)$$

Let $p(z_k|x_1, x_2, \cdots, x_r)$ obey a normal distribution with mean z and variance δ^2. According to (16) and (17), the calculation gives (18).

$$\begin{cases} \frac{1}{\sigma^2} = \sum_{i=1}^{r} \frac{1}{\sigma_i^2} + \frac{1}{\sigma_0^2} \\ \frac{z}{\sigma^2} = \sum_{i=1}^{r} \frac{x_i}{\sigma_i^2} + \frac{z_0}{\sigma_0^2} \end{cases} \quad (16)$$

$$\gamma \exp\left[-\frac{1}{2}\sum_{i=1}^{r}\left(\frac{x_i - z_k}{\sigma_i}\right)^2 - \frac{1}{2}\left(\frac{z_k - z_0}{\sigma_0}\right)^2\right] = \frac{1}{\sqrt{2\pi}\sigma}\exp\left[-\frac{1}{2}\left(\frac{z_k - z}{\sigma}\right)^2\right] \quad (17)$$

$$z = \frac{\sum_{i=1}^{r} \frac{x_i}{\sigma_i^2} + \frac{z_0}{\sigma_0^2}}{\sum_{i=1}^{r} \frac{1}{\sigma_i^2} + \frac{1}{\sigma_0^2}} \quad (18)$$

The final Bayesian estimate of the optimal fusion phase point at position k is obtained as in Equation (19), where the upper and lower limits of ω are the maximum and minimum values of the phase point, and the PSR can be completed after finding all M position phase points.

$$\hat{z}_k = \int_\omega z_k \frac{1}{\sqrt{2\pi}\sigma}\exp\left[-\frac{1}{2}\left(\frac{z_k - z}{\sigma}\right)^2\right] dz_k, \forall k = 1, 2, \cdots, M \quad (19)$$

3.2. Recursion Graphs and Approximate Entropy

Recursion graphs (RP) is an effective method for qualitative analysis of nonlinear dynamical systems, which can reveal the internal state evolution process of the system by using the image-change pattern. It is generally implemented using the Heaviside function.

The black dots in the RP diagram indicate that the attractor trajectories reach the same region of the orbit at different moments and vice versa for the white dots.

Approximate entropy can quantitatively analyze the structural complexity of nonlinear systems [44] as defined in Equation (20). Different flight maneuvers generally have different complexity and have different approximate entropy. By calculating the approximate entropy and combining with the maneuvers entropy library, we can know which maneuver it is.

$$ApEn(m,r) = \lim_{N \to \infty} \left[\Phi^m(r) - \Phi^{m+1}(r) \right], \Phi^m(r) = \frac{1}{N-m+1} \sum_{i=1}^{N-m+1} \ln C_i^m(r) \tag{20}$$

$$C_i^m(r) = \frac{1}{N-m} \{ d[X_i, X_j] < r \} \tag{21}$$

$$d[X_i, X_j] = \max_{k=0,1,\cdots,m-1} \left| x_{i+k} - x_{j+k} \right| \tag{22}$$

where $i = (1, 2, \cdots, N-m+1)$, $j = (1, 2, \cdots, N-m+1)$, and $i \neq j$.

4. The FMR General Framework

The general idea of the generic framework proposed in this paper is to integrate the automatic segmentation capability of unsupervised clustering and the information entropy capability of distinguishing sequence complexity.

First, the original input data are processed using a dynamic clustering method such as ISODATA, and the algorithm outputs the segmented, unknown kinds of maneuver sequences. Second, the multivariate phase space reconstruction calculation is applied to establish the complete phase space of the dynamical system. Then, the recurrence map and approximate entropy are calculated in the new phase space to analyze the complexity of the sequences qualitatively and quantitatively. Finally, according to the principle that the complexity of different kinds of maneuver sequences is different, the specific kind of the sequence is determined based on the calculation results so as to complete the FMR. The specific flow chart is shown in Figure 1.

In the flow chart, the raw flight data are first preprocessed to extract some of the parameter columns. The speed, altitude, roll angle, and pitch angle form a parameter matrix, which is involved in the unsupervised clustering calculation. Using the double-window algorithm, the trend identification is completed by using the normal load as the slope primitive, and the trend is used to segment the whole raw sequence into subseries and output the index values. Based on the index values of subsequences in the previous step, parameter fragments are extracted for each of the four parameter sequences. The extracted four parameter fragments are fed into the C-C algorithm, and the phase space reconstruction is performed according to the calculated minimum delay time and maximum embedding dimension, respectively, and the phase points at the same position in these four spaces are fused to extract the action fragments. After a comprehensive analysis of the qualitative values of the recurrence map and the quantitative values of the approximate entropy, the action recognition results are finally obtained.

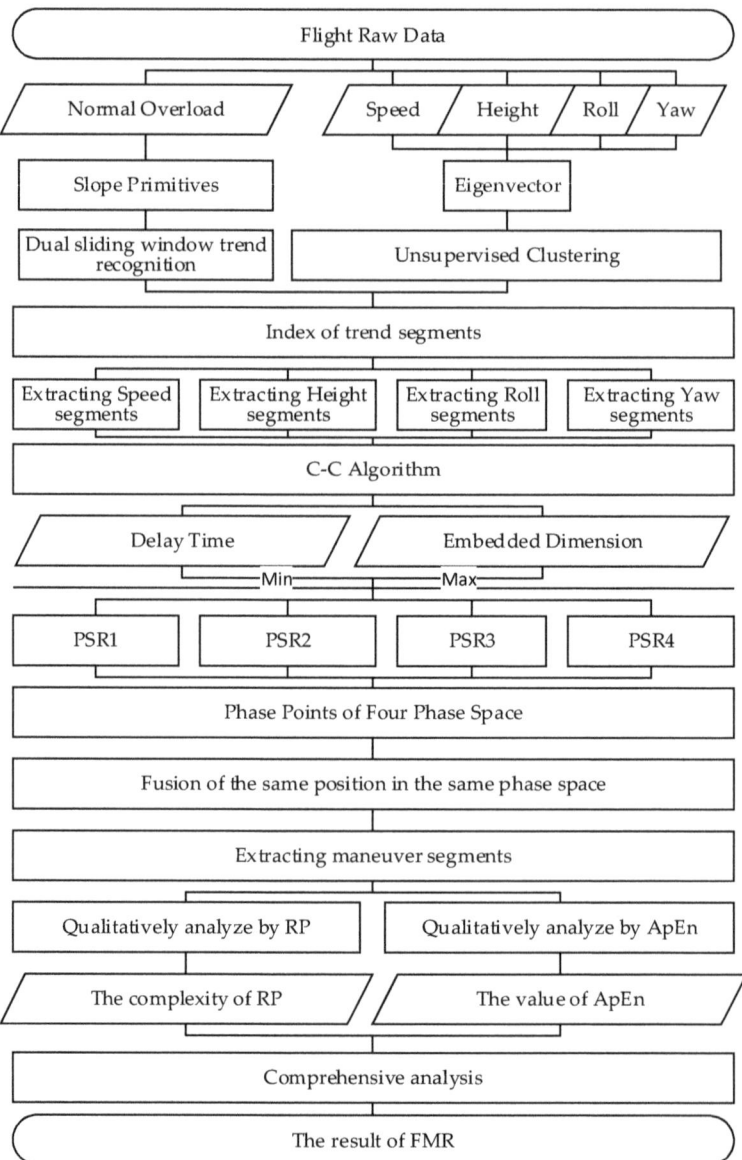

Figure 1. A general framework for FMR.

5. Experiments

The experimental environment is Windows 10 operating system, Anaconda development environment, python language, and Matlab7.1 simulation platform. The visualization tool is the three-dimensional flight path recovery system (3D-FPRS) developed by the author's team. The system is based on the open-source CesiumJS platform and implemented using WebGL, HTML5 technology, which can reduce the input flight raw data into 3D dynamic visualization of flight trajectory.

The experimental raw data were obtained from CAFUC real flight training records: the aircraft type is C172R, file name 1 log_210721ZUCK, 5724 lines; file name 2 log_210316ZUUU, 6445 lines. Due to the problem of data accuracy, 1104 rows of data in log_210721ZUCK and

4626 rows of data in log_210316ZUUU were used during the experiment, with six columns of data in each row, totaling 34,380 pieces of data. The total length of the experimental sequence was 5730. The whole raw flight data are visualized as Figure 2.

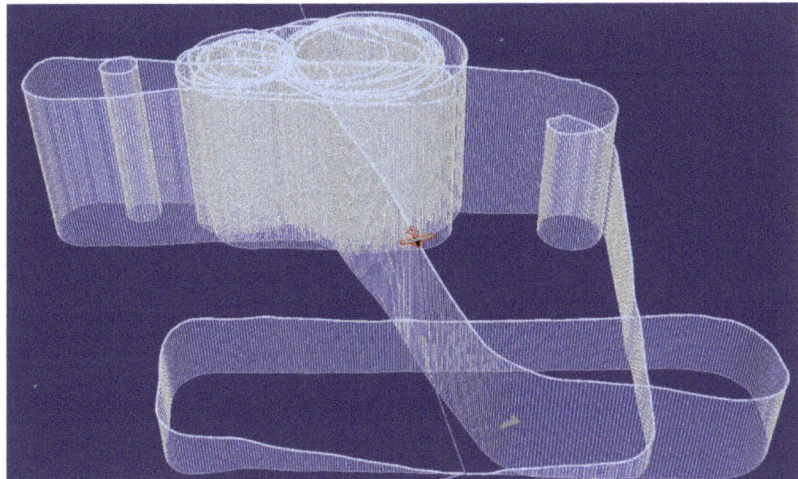

Figure 2. The visualization of whole raw flight data (file 1 and file 2).

The speed, sideslip angle, altitude, pitch angle, roll angle, and normal overload are considered as key data during the experiment, with other multi-column flight parameter data participating in the feature dataprocessing.

TS-ISODATA model has six clustering parameters, and $K = 7$, $L = 1$, and $I = 100$ were selected in the experiment, and the genetic algorithm was used to find $\theta_n, \theta_S, \theta_C$. The final optimal parameter setting values obtained are $\theta_n = 1$, $\theta_S = 0.0373$, and $\theta_C = 0.0043$, and the evaluation result using this set of parameter values is 6.3823. The input raw sequence is segmented into 96 maneuver segments. The segmentation calculation process takes an average of 76 s.

The index of the extracted motorized fragment for a particular experiment was (0, 54, 108, 162, 216, 270, 378, 432, 486, 540, 594, 648, 702, 756, 810, 864, 918, 972, 1026, 1080, 1134, 1188, 1242, 1296, 1350, 1404, 1458, 1512, 1566, 1674, 1728, 1782, 1836, 1890, 1944, 1998, 2052, 2160, 2214, 2268, 2322, 2376, 2430, 2484, 2538, 2592, 2646, 2700, 2754, 2808, 2862, 2916, 3024, 3078, 3132, 3186, 3240, 3294, 3348, 3402, 3456, 3510, 3564, 3618, 3672, 3726, 3780, 3834, 3888, 3942, 3996, 4050, 4104, 4158, 4212, 4266, 4320, 4374, 4428, 4482, 4536, 4590, 4644, 4698, 4752, 4806, 4860, 4914, 4968, 5022, 5076, 5130, 5184, 5238, 5292, 5346, 5368), where each index number represents the specific moment when the file was imported,

The feature vector extracted according to this was (1:{−0.131, 0.108, 0.203, 0.090, −0.039, 0.057, 0.176, 0.099, 0.203, 0.101, 0.472, 0.017},2:{0.018, 0.096, −0.042, 0.091, 0.034, 0.029, 0.074, 0.050, −0.094, 0.109, 0.164, 0.055}, . . . ,96:{0.018, 0.096, −0.042, 0.091, 0.034, 0.029, 0.074, 0.050, −0.094, 0.109, 0.164, 0.055}). The result of clustering is shown in Table 1. The clustering calculation process takes an average of 121 s.

Table 1. TS-ISODATA clustering results.

Categories	Corresponding Maneuver Segments
1	8,9,16,18,23,24,31,34,35,42,45,48,52,55,60,63,67,74,77,82,19,28,37,40,49,58,69,79
2	1,87,92,94
3	3,5,12,14,15,20,27,33,36,39,41,51,54,57,62,81,84,88,95,96,11,25,38,43,65,68,71,72,
4	4,6,22,53,50,66,73,89,91,2,7,10,13,17,21,26,29,30,44,47,32,46,56,59,61,64,70,75,83,85,76,78,80,86,90,93

After preliminary expert analysis, category 4 are all transitional-level flights between complex maneuvers, which are not significant, so this paper uses PSR method to study the recurrence graph and approximate entropy of category 1, 2, and 3. The ApEn results are given in Table 2.

Table 2. The ApEn value for categories 1–3.

Categories	1	2	3	4	5	6	7	8	9	10	Average
1	0.3937	0.3148	0.4985	0.3512	0.2881	0.4112	0.3309	0.2490	0.3989	0.4117	0.3648
2	0.3166	0.3594	0.4252	0.0870	0.2491	0.0408	0.0870	0.0741	0.1295	0.1922	0.1961
3	0.1346	0.0941	0.2007	0.1178	0.0953	0.1457	0.1178	0.0953	0.1419	0.0344	0.1177

Experimental results show that the dataset as a multivariate time series does fit the chaotic nonlinear dynamical system characteristics. Similar maneuvers show similar characteristics on the recurrence graph, with close values of approximate entropy (ApEn), while different maneuvers vary widely. Thus, the phase space reconstruction recognition method based on approximate entropy can distinguish the recognition of flight maneuvers, especially complex maneuvers.

Three samples of the trace recovery visualization and recurrence map experiment are given in Figures 3–5.

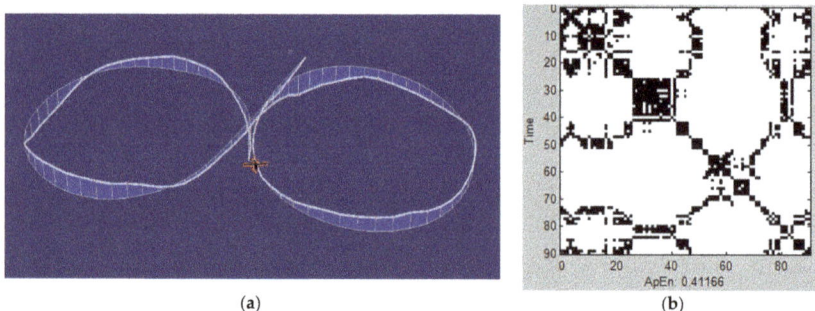

Figure 3. (**a**) Category 1 maneuver visualization reduction; (**b**) the maneuver's RP and ApEn value.

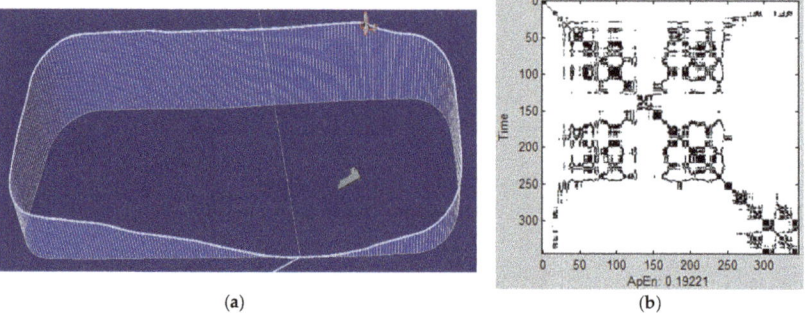

Figure 4. (**a**) Category 2 maneuver visualization reduction; (**b**) the maneuver's RP and ApEn value.

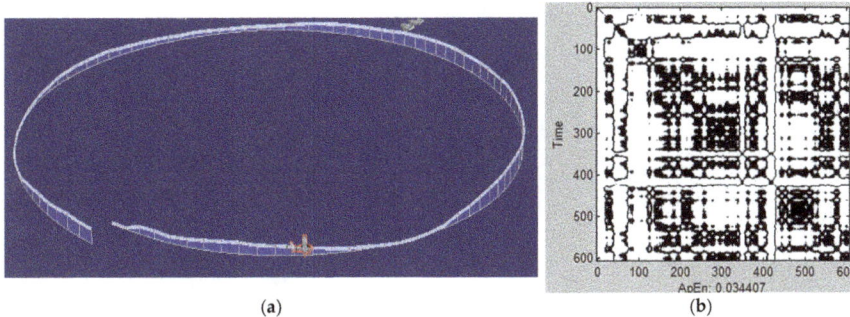

Figure 5. (**a**) Category 3 maneuver visualization reduction; (**b**) the maneuver's RP and ApEn value.

In order to study what exactly these three categories of maneuvers are, this paper uses the recurrence diagrams of these three categories of maneuvers in conjunction with the visual flight path recovery system to be able to clearly distinguish the categories of maneuvers. As shown in Figures 3a, 4a and 5a, category 1 is Eight maneuver, category 2 is RectangularCourse maneuver, and category 3 is Spin maneuver. Not only do these three categories of maneuvers have different ApEn value, but their RPs also have significant differences, which perfectly match the complexity level given by flight experts as shown in Figures 3b, 4b and 5b. The RP and ApEn calculation process takes an average of 88 s.

The overall average time of the whole framework automatic FMR calculation process is 285 s with 5730 raw input data.

In order to verify that the framework can be applied to multiple aircraft types, we selected two other datasets to complete the validation experiments, which are also from CAFUC real flight training records: aircraft types SR20 and DA42, file 3 name log_210521_ZHCC (13,750 lines), and file 4 name log_210531_ZUUU (13,018 lines); the raw flight data are visualized as Figure 6.

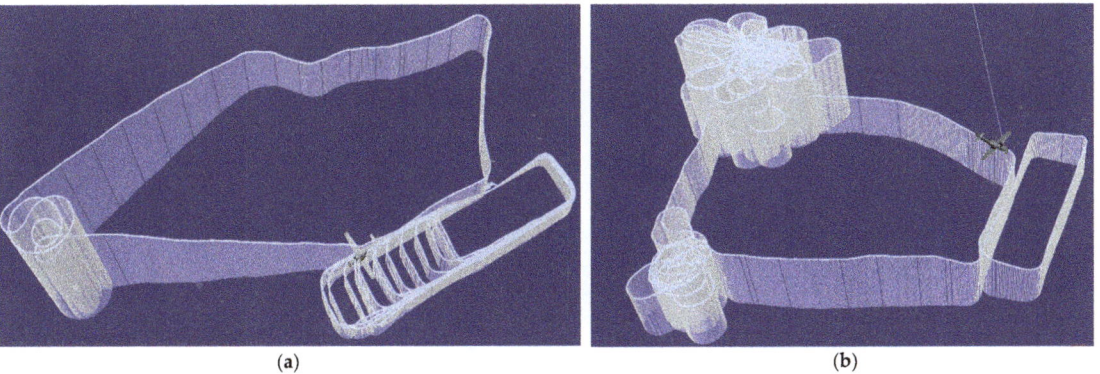

Figure 6. (**a**) File 1 visualization; (**b**) file 2 visualization.

In addition, in order to do comparison experiments, the project team developed an expert validation aid tool (EVAT) as shown in Figure 7.

The system is also based on the CesiumJS platform, which can not only be reduced to 3D dynamic visualization of flight trajectory but also can display each second of temporal parameters and mark them in sequence, helping flight experts to judge flight movements with the naked eye.

With this tool, three flight experts made flight maneuvers judgments on the above two experimental files and two validation files, frame by frame, respectively, and the complete comparison results are shown in Table 3 below.

Figure 7. Expert validation aid tool (EVAT).

Table 3. The overall experimental results.

Categories		File 1 + File 2 C172, 5730 Lines			File 3 SR20, 13,750 Lines			File 4 DA32, 13,018 Lines			Average
Number		FMR	Expert	Accuracy (%)	FMR	Expert	Accuracy (%)	FMR	Expert	Accuracy (%)	Accuracy
1		28	26	92.3	6	5	80	49	50	98.2	90.2
2		4	4	100	20	24	83.3	7	5	60	81.1
3		28	26	92.3	10	8	75	15	17	88.2	85.2
Time (seconds)		285	15,675	Ratio 55	382	17,569	Ratio 45.9	349	21,638	Ratio 62	Ratio 54.3

The experimental results in Table 3 show that the method in this paper can perform FMR for three types of aircraft and different file lengths, with the highest accuracy rate for category 1 (Eight maneuver), and the lowest accuracy rate for category 2 (Rectangular-Course maneuver), with an overall average accuracy rate of 85.5%. The reason why the Eight maneuver accuracy is the highest is because the maneuver is significantly different from others, and the RectangularCourse maneuver accuracy is the lowest because the maneuver is generally time-consuming, which is accompanied by a half-spin maneuver, and the number of such maneuvers is small, so the recognition is not effective.

In terms of time consumption, the consumption time is related to the document length, and overall, the recognition speed of this paper is 54.3 times faster than human flight experts.

The comparison experiments were difficult to design and implement because none of the other papers disclosed the datasets used, and some of the papers corresponded to aircraft types that were fighter jets or UAVs, which differed greatly from the temporal nature of this paper; neither did any of the other methods cover temporal segmentation and automatic recognition. However, we still completed the recognition experiments using the same datasets provided in this paper, files 1 and 2, and the experimental results are shown in the following Table 4.

Table 4. The comparison experiments results.

Methods	DTW [4]	RF-SVM [10]	Expert System [15]	DBM [29]	CNN-LSTM [33]	Ours
Accuracy (%)	79.6	61	89.6	77	71	85.5
Time (Seconds)	314	276	656	295	489	285

From the results, we can see that under the same flight-type condition, the accuracy of this paper's method is second only to the expert system, and the speed is second only to SVM, which is better than other methods in the comprehensive evaluation. More importantly, if we want to follow the aircraft model, except for this paper, all other methods have to retrain the model or redesign the knowledge rules, which does not have generalization ability in practical application scenarios.

6. Conclusions

In this paper, a general framework was constructed for the first time for automated FMR based on dynamic clustering and phase space reconstruction. The framework decomposes the FMR task into two parts, which are automatic maneuver sequence segmentation and automatic maneuver class identification. The automatic maneuver sequence segmentation was implemented by the improved dynamic clustering method TS-ISODATA, which solves the problem of self-organized iterative clustering of multivariate time series and successfully segments the input data into multiple segments and automatically clusters them into four classes. Due to the chaotic nature of the flight dynamics system, the automatic recognition of maneuver categories partially reconstructs the phase space of multivariate fusion, transforms the representational dimensional change patterns of flight maneuvers that are difficult to organize into attractive subsequences that are easy to identify, and generates recursive graphs from them to calculate ApEn values that can characterize the complexity of maneuvers. With the help of a visual 3D flight-track reduction system, the flight maneuver categories are easily identified. With an input sequence of 5000 s, the entire framework computation process takes an average of 285 s, which is 54 times faster than human expert recognition, with an overall accuracy rate of 85.5%.

In the next step, the entropy corresponding to different flight actions can be solidified so as to form an automatic identification library for fast and automatic classification output. This step requires collecting a large number of samples of a particular flight maneuver and deriving a reasonable range of approximate entropy values through a large number of experiments, and the range of values among the maneuvers should not overlap to avoid duality. According to different entropy value ranges corresponding to different aircraft maneuvers categories, automatic identification rules were established to realize the final automatic output of flight maneuvers. For maneuvers with close approximate entropy values and little difference, the complexity of the recurrence graph should be considered, and the difference enhancement of information entropy should be designed to further strengthen the difference between maneuvers. In addition, as a pattern-recognition category, although the method in this paper has better generalization ability and does not require pre-training, it is computationally intensive and time-consuming and cannot realize online real-time recognition. At this stage, it can only be used for post-flight analysis to support the next application, such as flight technology scoring based on a specific flight maneuver and post-accident investigation after a flight accident. In the future, the principle of the method can be explored in depth to simplify the computation process.

Author Contributions: Conceptualization, J.L.; methodology, J.L.; software, J.L. and H.C.; formal analysis, J.L.; investigation, J.L. and H.C.; resources, J.L., H.C. and R.J.; data curation, J.L.; writing—original draft preparation, J.L.; writing—review and editing, J.L. and R.J.; visualization, J.L. and H.C.; supervision, J.L.; project administration, J.L.; funding acquisition, J.L. All authors have read and agreed to the published version of the manuscript.

Funding: This research was funded by the Civil Aviation Flight Technology and Flight Safety Key Laboratory of China research projects, NO: FZ2020ZZ02; The CAFUC Research Project, NO: CJ2021-01; National Natural Science Foundation of China, NO: U2033213; Sichuan Science and Technology Program, NO: 2022YFG0027.

Institutional Review Board Statement: Not applicable.

Informed Consent Statement: Not applicable.

Data Availability Statement: Not applicable.

Acknowledgments: The authors would like to thank Xiaodong Liu and graduate students Zhe Cao and Lu Pang for their contributions.

Conflicts of Interest: The authors declare no conflict of interest.

References

1. The United States Department of Transportation; Federal Aviation Administration; Airman Testing Standards Branch. *Pilot's Handbook of Aeronautical Knowledge*; The United States Department of Transportation: Oklahoma City, AK, USA, 2016.
2. Burgin, G.H.; Owens, A.J. *An Adaptive Maneuvering Logic Computer Program for the Simulation of One-to-One Air-to-Air Combat. NASA Contractor Report (CR), Volume 2: Program Description*; NASA: San Diego, CA, USA, 1975.
3. Burgin, G.H. Improvements to the Adaptive Maneuvering Logic Program. 1986. Available online: https://ntrs.nasa.gov/404?original=%2Fcitations%2F19880002266 (accessed on 2 March 2022).
4. Barndt, G.; Sarkar, S.; Miller, C. Maneuver regime recognition development and verification for H-60 structural monitoring. In Proceedings of the Annual Forum Proceedings-American Helicopter Society, Virginia Beach, VA, USA, 1–3 May 2007; American Helicopter Society, Inc.: Fairfax, VA, USA, 2007; Volume 63, p. 317.
5. Zhang, J.Y. *Time Series Analysis Method of Flight Data and Its Application*; National Defense Industry Press: Beijing, China, 2013.
6. Li, Z.-X.; Zhang, F.-M.; Li, K.-W. A multivariate time series indexing structure supporting DTW distance. *J. Softw.* **2014**, *25*, 560–575.
7. Li, H.; Shan, Z.; Guo, H. MDTW-based flight action recognition algorithm. *Comput. Eng. Appl.* **2015**, *51*, 267–270.
8. Shen, Y.; Ni, S.; Zhang, P. A similar subsequence query method for flight data. *J. Air Force Eng. Univ.* **2019**, *20*, 7–12.
9. Tang, C.; Dong, J. LSH-based time subsequence query algorithm. *J. Comput. Sci.* **2012**, *35*, 2228–2236.
10. Qu, J.; Lv, M.; Yang, Y. Flight Motion Recognition Method Based on Multivariate Phase Space Reconstruction and Approximate Entropy. In Proceedings of the 2021 40th Chinese Control Conference (CCC), Shanghai, China, 26–28 July 2021; IEEE: Piscataway, NJ, USA, 2021; pp. 7247–7253.
11. Mao, H.; Zhang, F.; Feng, H. Research on flight maneuver evaluation method based on singular value decomposition. *Comput. Eng. Appl.* **2008**, *44*, 240–242.
12. Mao, H.; Zhang, F.; Feng, H. Similar pattern query for multivariate flight data. *Comput. Eng. Appl.* **2011**, *47*, 151–155.
13. Yang, J.; Duan, C.; Xie, S. Fuzzy least squares support vector machine based aircraft flight maneuver recognition. *J. Ballist. Arrow Guid.* **2004**, *S6*, 395–398.
14. Jia, Z.; Fan, X.; Xue, M. Online identification method for tactical maneuvers of enemy aircraft based on maneuver elements. *J. Beijing Univ. Technol.* **2018**, *38*, 820–827.
15. Kendrick, J.D.; Maybeck, P.S.; Reid, J.G. Estimation of aircraft target motion using orientation measurements. *IEEE Trans. Aerosp. Electron. Syst.* **1981**, *2*, 254–260. [CrossRef]
16. Kou, Y.; Jiang, L.; Wang, D. High-order reconstruction of the decision process of close air com-bat maneuver. *J. Syst. Simul.* **2019**, *31*, 2085.
17. Molkenthin, J. Determination and Verification of Operational Maneuver Parameters and Time Histories. *Loads Requir. Mil. Aircr.* **1997**, *6*, 3–11.
18. Wang, Y.; Dong, J.; Liu, X. Identification and standardization of maneuvers based upon operational flight data. *Chin. J. Aeronaut.* **2015**, *28*, 133–140. [CrossRef]
19. Xie, C.; Ni, S.; Zhang, Z. A knowledge-based method for fast recognition of aerobatic maneuvers. *Comput. Eng.* **2004**, *30*, 116–118.
20. Ni, S.; Shi, Z.; Xie, C. Establishment of a knowledge base for maneuvering flight maneuvers recognition of military warplanes. *Comput. Simul.* **2005**, *22*, 23–26. [CrossRef]
21. Travert, J.H. Flight Regime and Maneuver Recognition for Complex Maneuvers. Master's Thesis, Embry-Riddle Aeronautical University, Daytona Beach, FL, USA, 2009.
22. Chunmei, G.; Lili, Z.; Yu, B. Recognition of Flight Operation Action Based on Expert System Inference Engine. In Proceedings of the 2019 11th International Conference on Intelligent Human-Machine Systems and Cybernetics (IHMSC), Hangzhou, China, 24–25 August 2019; IEEE: Piscataway, NJ, USA, 2019; Volume 1, pp. 17–20.
23. Tian, H.; Xie, S.; Wang, L. Flight trajectory identification based on rough set theory. *Firepower Command Control* **2015**, *40*, 29–33.
24. Zhou, D.Y.; Li, F. Genetic algorithm-based tactical flight maneuver decision for aircraft. *J. Northwest. Polytech. Univ.* **2002**, *20*, 109–112.
25. Wei, Z.; Ding, D.; Zhou, H. A flight maneuver recognition method based on multi-strategy affine canonical time warping. *Appl. Soft Comput.* **2020**, *95*, 106527. [CrossRef]
26. Wang, L.; Huang, C.Q.; Wei, Z.L. Automatic extraction of flight action rules based on SSA algorithm. *Comput. Eng. Appl.* **2019**, *14*, 203–208.
27. Wang, Y.W.; Gao, Y. A flight action recognition rule extraction method based on whale optimization algorithm. *J. Nav. Aviat. Eng. Coll.* **2019**, *33*, 447–451.
28. He, D.; Wu, S.; Bechhoefer, E. Development of Regime Recognition Tools for Usage Monitoring. In Proceedings of the 2007 IEEE Aerospace Conference, Big Sky, MT, USA, 3–10 March 2007; IEEE: Piscataway, NJ, USA, 2007; pp. 1–11.
29. He, D.; Wu, S.; Bechhoefer, E. A Regime Recognition Algorithm for Helicopter Usage Monitoring. *Aerosp. Technol. Adv.* **2010**, 391–404. Available online: https://books.google.co.jp/books?hl=en&lr=&id=bQWQDwAAQBAJ&oi=fnd&pg=PA391&dq=A+regime+recognition+algorithm+for+helicopter+usage+monitoring.+&ots=4Kgn_R61wO&sig=I6atHzxhI1AC8YqD9Tw1cNbI_ZQ&redir_esc=y#v=onepage&q=A%20regime%20recognition%20algorithm%20for%20helicopter%20usage%20monitoring.&f=false (accessed on 2 March 2022).

30. Rajnicek, R.E. Application of Kalman Filtering to Real-Time Flight Regime Recognition Algorithms in a Helicopter Health and Usage Monitoring System. Master's Thesis, Embry-Riddle Aeronautical University, Daytona Beach, FL, USA, 2008.
31. Meng, G.-L.; Zhang, H.-M.; Park, H.-Y. Maneuver recognition of warplanes in automated flight training evaluation. *J. Beijing Univ. Aeronaut. Astronaut.* **2020**, *46*, 1267–1274.
32. Li, Y.F.; Ni, S.H.; Zhang, Z.L. A fuzzy Kohonen network-based intelligent processing method for flight data. *Syst. Eng. Electron. Technol.* **2002**, *24*, 53–55.
33. Xu, W. A fuzzy neural network-based approach for shipboard aircraft landing maneuvers recognition. *Appl. Sci. Technol.* **2013**, *2*, 26–29.
34. Hanyang, F.; Hongming, F.; Ruiyuan, G. Research on air target maneuver recognition based on LSTM network. In Proceedings of the 2020 International Workshop on Electronic Communication and Artificial Intelligence (IWECAI), Shanghai, China, 12–14 June 2020; IEEE: Piscataway, NJ, USA, 2020; pp. 6–10.
35. Fang, W.; Wang, Y.; Yan, W.J.; Gong, Y. Flight action recognition based on differential ideas and convolutional neural net-works. *J. Chin. Acad. Electron. Sci.* **2021**, *16*, 347–353.
36. Fang, W.; Wang, Y.; Yan, W.; Lin, C. Symbolic flight action recognition based on neural networks. *Syst. Eng. Electron.* **2021**, *1*, 13.
37. Zhang, Y.Y.; Wang, Y.Y.; Wang, C.H.X. Analysis of parametric correlation and temporal features for flight action recognition method. *Comput. Eng. Appl.* **2016**, *52*, 246–249.
38. Shen, Y.; Ni, S.; Zhang, P. A Bayesian network-based approach for flight action recognition. *Comput. Eng. Appl.* **2017**, *53*, 161–167.
39. Zhang, X.; Yin, Z.; Liu, F.; Huang, Q. Data mining method for aircraft maneuvering division. *J. Northwest. Polytech. Univ.* **2016**, *34*, 33–40.
40. Zhang, L. A non-supervised automatic method of aircraft maneuver partition. *J. Comput. Methods Sci. Eng.* **2021**, *21*, 383–395. [CrossRef]
41. Kang, Z.; Shang, J.; Feng, Y. A deep sequence-to-sequence method for accurate long landing prediction based on flight data. *IET Intell. Transp. Syst.* **2021**, *15*, 1028–1042. [CrossRef]
42. Li, X.; Shang, J.; Zheng, L. CurveCluster+: Curve Clustering for Hard Landing Pattern Recognition and Risk Evalua-tion Based on Flight Data. *IEEE Trans. Intell. Transp. Syst.* **2021**. [CrossRef]
43. Tou, J.T.; Gonzalez, R.C. *Pattern Recognition Principles*; Addison-Wesley Publishing Company: Reading, MA, USA, 1974.
44. Pincus, S.M. Approximate entropy as a measure of system complexity. *Proc. Natl. Acad. Sci. USA* **1991**, *88*, 2297–2301. [CrossRef] [PubMed]

Review

Survey on the Application of Artificial Intelligence in ENSO Forecasting

Wei Fang [1,2,3,*], Yu Sha [1] and Victor S. Sheng [4]

[1] School of Computer and Software, Engineering Research Center of Digital Forensics, Ministry of Education, Nanjing University of Information Science and Technology, Nanjing 210044, China
[2] State Key Laboratory of Severe Weather, Chinese Academy of Meteorological Sciences, Beijing 100081, China
[3] Jiangsu Collaborative Innovation Center of Atmospheric Environment and Equipment Technology (CICAEET), Nanjing University of Information Science and Technology, Nanjing 210044, China
[4] Department of Computer, Texas Tech University, Lubbock, TX 79409, USA
* Correspondence: hsfangwei@sina.com or fangwei@nuist.edu.cn

Citation: Fang, W.; Sha, Y.; Sheng, V.S. Survey on the Application of Artificial Intelligence in ENSO Forecasting. *Mathematics* **2022**, *10*, 3793. https://doi.org/10.3390/math10203793

Academic Editors: Jonathan Blackledge, Christophe Guyeux and Jakub Nalepa

Received: 15 August 2022
Accepted: 11 October 2022
Published: 14 October 2022

Publisher's Note: MDPI stays neutral with regard to jurisdictional claims in published maps and institutional affiliations.

Copyright: © 2022 by the authors. Licensee MDPI, Basel, Switzerland. This article is an open access article distributed under the terms and conditions of the Creative Commons Attribution (CC BY) license (https://creativecommons.org/licenses/by/4.0/).

Abstract: Climate disasters such as floods and droughts often bring heavy losses to human life, national economy, and public safety. El Niño/Southern Oscillation (ENSO) is one of the most important inter-annual climate signals in the tropics and has a global impact on atmospheric circulation and precipitation. To address the impact of climate change, accurate ENSO forecasts can help prevent related climate disasters. Traditional prediction methods mainly include statistical methods and dynamic methods. However, due to the variability and diversity of the temporal and spatial evolution of ENSO, traditional methods still have great uncertainty in predicting ENSO. In recent years, with the rapid development of artificial intelligence technology, it has gradually penetrated into all aspects of people's lives, and the climate field has also benefited. For example, deep learning methods in artificial intelligence can automatically learn and train from a large amount of sample data, obtain excellent feature representation, and effectively improve the performance of various learning tasks. It is widely used in computer vision, natural language processing, and other fields. In 2019, Ham et al. used a convolutional neural network (CNN) model in ENSO forecasting 18 months in advance, and the winter ENSO forecasting skill could reach 0.64, far exceeding the dynamic model with a forecasting skill of 0.5. The research results were regarded as the pioneering work of deep learning in the field of weather forecasting. This paper introduces the traditional ENSO forecasting methods and focuses on summarizing the various latest artificial intelligence methods and their forecasting effects for ENSO forecasting, so as to provide useful reference for future research by researchers.

Keywords: climate disasters; ENSO forecasting; artificial intelligence; machine learning; deep learning

MSC: 68-xx; 68-11

1. Introduction

Climate change is a difficult problem facing the world today, and it affects people's production and life to a large extent. The most prominent El Niño-Southern Oscillation (ENSO) phenomenon is the most important interannual signal of short-term climate change on the earth [1]. It will have a great impact on the climate, environment, and socio-economics on a global scale.

ENSO is wind and sea surface temperature oscillations that occur in the equatorial eastern Pacific. In 1969, Bjerknes [2] proposed that El Niño and the Southern Oscillation are two different manifestations of the same physical phenomenon in nature, which is reflected in the ocean as the El Niño phenomenon and in the atmosphere as the Southern Oscillation phenomenon. El Niño refers to the phenomenon of abnormal warming of the ocean every two to seven years (every four years on average) in the equatorial eastern Pacific Ocean, and the opposite cold phenomenon is called La Niña [3]. The Southern Oscillation refers to the mutual movement of the atmosphere between the eastern tropical Pacific and the western tropical Pacific, and the cycle is also approximately four years. El Niño and La Niña are closely related to the Southern Oscillation. When the Southern Oscillation index has a persistent negative value, an El Niño phenomenon will occur in that year, and on the contrary, a La Niña phenomenon will occur in that year.

Since ENSO is a global ocean–atmosphere interaction, it has a huge impact on crop yields, temperature, and rainfall on Earth. In 1997-1998, fires triggered by an unusual drought caused by ENSO destroyed large swathes of tropical rainforest worldwide [4]. Hurricanes caused considerable damage in the United States from 1925-1997, with an average annual loss of $5.2 billion [5]. In ENSO years, flood risk anomalies exist in basins spanning almost half of the Earth's surface [6]. The World Health Organization estimates that over the past 30 years, anthropogenic warming and precipitation have claimed 150,000 lives each year [7]. In order to deal with the threat of such climate disasters, knowing and understanding the laws of climate change and making effective climate predictions in advance are crucial to reducing disaster losses around the world.

ENSO prediction is one of the most important issues in climate science, affecting both interannual climate predictions and decadal predictions of near-term global climate change. Since the 1980s, scientists from all over the world have been working on ENSO prediction research [8]. Since the relevant time scale of SST variability in most of the tropical Pacific Ocean is about 1 year, the ENSO event dominates the SST variability [9], and the occurrence of ENSO is reflected by the sea surface temperature anomaly (SSTA); therefore, ENSO is predicted. The phenomenon is equivalent to predicting SSTA. In addition, among all the indices, Niño3.4 is the most commonly used index to measure ENSO phenomena, and the Niño3.4 index is the mean sea temperature in the range of 5° N~5° S 170° W~120° W.

ENSO projections are by far the most successful of short-term climate predictions. Traditional ENSO prediction models are mainly divided into two categories: statistical models and dynamic models. Statistical models analyze and predict ENSO through a series of statistical methods, such as the linear transpose model (LIM), nonlinear canonical correlation analysis (NLCCA), singular spectrum analysis (SSA), etc. Essentially, this is accidental, they do not take full advantage of the laws of physics. The dynamic models are mainly based on the dynamic theory of atmosphere–ocean interaction, such as the intermediate coupled model (ICM), the hybrid coupled model (HCM), and the coupled circulation model (CGCM) [10]. It is successful in short-term prediction, but it does not make full use of the large amount of existing real historical data. For long-term prediction, the pure dynamic method is difficult to work. Practice has shown that both dynamic methods and statistical methods have a certain accuracy, and both can reflect some of the laws of atmospheric motion [11–13], but due to the variability and diversity of ENSO spatiotemporal evolution, traditional methods of predicting ENSO still have great deficiencies, especially in the 21st century; the intensified influence of the extratropical atmosphere on the tropics makes ENSO more complex and unpredictable.

The concept of artificial intelligence first came from the Dartmouth Conference on Computers in 1956, and its essence is to hope that machines can think and respond similarly to human brains. Machine learning is an important way to realize artificial intelligence. As the most important branch of machine learning, deep learning has developed rapidly in recent years and is now widely used in image recognition, natural language processing, and other fields.

The concept of deep learning, which refers to the machine learning process of obtaining a deep network structure containing multiple levels through a certain training method based on sample data, was first proposed by Hinton et al. [14] at the University of Toronto in 2006. Figure 1 shows the relationship among artificial intelligence, machine learning, artificial neural networks and deep learning. Unlike machine learning, the deep learning feature extraction process is performed automatically through deep neural networks. The features in the neural network are obtained through learning. Under normal circumstances, when the network layer is shallow, the extracted features are less representative of the original data. When the number of network layers is deep, the features extracted by the model will be more representative. When the task to be solved is more complex, the parameter requirements of the model are also higher, and the number of network layers at this time is often deeper, which means that more complex tasks can be solved. Therefore, it can be considered that the deeper the network layer, the stronger the feature extraction ability. Currently, the commonly used deep neural network models mainly include CNN, recurrent neural network (RNN), deep belief network (DBN), and the deep autoencoder and generative adversarial network (GAN).

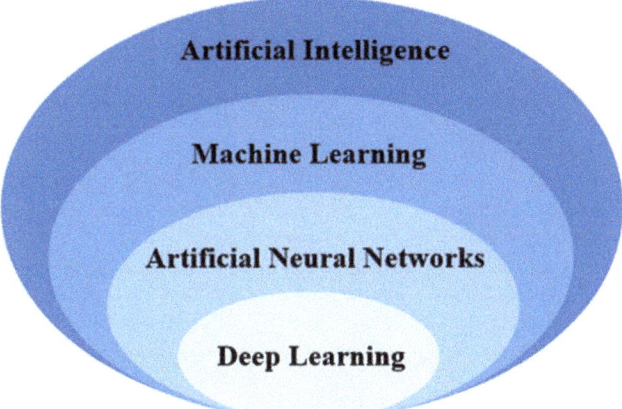

Figure 1. The relationship between artificial intelligence, machine learning, artificial neural networks, and deep learning.

With the wide application of machine learning and deep learning in various fields in recent years, some scholars have begun to use machine learning or deep learning technology to predict meteorological elements (wind speed, temperature, etc.) or climate phenomena, such as ENSO, and have obtained better results. This paper will summarize the previous research results and make a more complete summary of ENSO predictions combined with deep learning.

This paper is organized as follows: Section 1 outlines the main learning knowledge and development status in ENSO forecasting; Section 2 focuses on traditional ENSO forecasting methods; Section 3 is the key part of this paper, introducing the related models and theories of deep learning in artificial intelligence and the existing ENSO prediction methods and applications of deep learning in artificial intelligence; Section 4 summarizes the ENSO forecasting methods in tabular form and discusses the existing deficiencies and future development directions of ENSO predictions; finally, Section 5 provides a summary of the full text.

2. Traditional Methods

In this section, we will focus on the existing theories or conclusions of traditional ENSO forecasting methods. There are generally two methods for traditional ENSO prediction, namely, the statistical model and the dynamic model. The following will list the currently commonly used ENSO forecast methods and related ENSO forecast knowledge.

2.1. Climate Dynamics Methods

The dynamic method uses dynamic equations to model the ocean, atmosphere, land, and other spheres and their interactions and uses the computer to gradually integrate to simulate the evolution of the atmosphere. Since the first coupled ENSO model was developed [15,16], various types of coupled models have been designed and used for ENSO simulation and prediction. The coupling models mainly include the simple coupled model

(SCM) [17], intermediate coupled model (ICM) [16], hybrid coupled model (HCM) [18], and fully coupled circulation models (GCMs) [19]. Dynamical models have become the main tool for studying the mechanism, simulation, and prediction of ENSO, and the prediction time reaches 6–12 months. Ref. [17] identified several free equatorial modes for simple coupled ocean–atmosphere models and found that they included unstable and damped modes at large regional scales and long periods, systematically exploring the effects of ocean thermodynamics on the behavior of unstable modes. Ref. [16] developed an atmosphere–ocean coupled model to study the ENSO phenomenon. In the absence of anomalous external forcing, the coupled model reproduces some key features of the observed phenomenon. The results show that the mean sea surface temperature, wind, and ocean current field determine the characteristic spatial structure of the ENSO anomaly. Ref. [18] conducted a series of hindcast and prediction experiments using the HCM of the tropical ocean–atmosphere system. It shows real skills in forecasting fall/winter tropical Pacific SST up to 18 months in advance. Ref. [19] used an integrated ocean–atmosphere circulation model (OAGCM) for climate prediction. Both model performance and data assimilation schemes for climate simulations were improved to yield better forecasting skills. Most OAGCMs can now proficiently predict the Indian Ocean Dipole (IOD) 1–2 seasons in advance, with ENSOs up to 6–9 months ahead.

In recent years, many forecasting systems have been put into use. The National Climate Center of China Meteorological Administration (BCC/CMA) developed the ENSO Monitoring, Analysis and Prediction System (SEMAP2) [20]. The system consists of five subsystems: real-time monitoring of tropical atmosphere and ocean, dynamic diagnosis, physical-based statistical prediction, model ensemble prediction, and simulation-based model prediction [21] correction, which can realize the feedback process of ENSO changes and dynamics in the recent year real-time monitoring and can provide users with forecasts of the ENSO index and related main variable processes in the coming year. Since the spring of 2013, SEMAP2 has been applied to ENSO business meetings organized by the National Climate Center several consecutive times and given forecast opinions, with good results and was adopted by forecasters many times. Especially in the spring of 2014, the prediction of the evolution trend of El Niño in summer and autumn was basically in line with reality and more accurately predicted the weak central El Nino event in the winter of 2014/15 and accurately predicted the development of El Niño since the spring of 2015. Trends and Type Conversions. The forecasting system is still in use to this day. The fifth-generation seasonal forecast system SEAS5 was put into use in November 2017 by the European Centre for Medium-Range Weather Forecasts. It is a coupled dynamical model that includes higher resolution models of the atmosphere, ocean, and sea ice. An important improvement in SEAS5 is the weakening of the cold tongue bias in the equatorial Pacific, while the amplitude of El Niño is closer to the actual value and improves the prediction ability of El Niño in the central and western Pacific, making it show particular advantages in ENSO predictions. When the forecast period is 9 months, the correlation coefficient of SEAS5 to ENSO forecast reaches more than 0.7 [22].

If the starting time of the prediction model is advanced by more than 6 months, the prediction ability of the traditional method model will be greatly reduced due to the phenomenon of the spring predictability barrier (SPB) [1]. The SPB phenomenon was discovered by Webster et al. [23] in the dynamic prediction model. Wang et al. [24] proposed that the largest vertical temperature gradient and the weakest east–west thermal difference in spring are conducive to the growth of the coupled system disturbance, which in turn makes the spring sea-air coupling the most unstable, which is conducive to the generation of the SPB phenomenon. Chen et al. [25] proposed a novel ENSO prediction model (EPM) that combines tropical states and extratropical ocean–atmosphere interactions, which can significantly improve ENSO forecasting skills beyond the spring-predictable barriers. Although dynamical models are successful in short-term predictions, pure dynamical methods are ineffective for long-term predictions.

2.2. Mathematical Statistical Methods

The statistical ENSO prediction method is to realize the analysis and prediction of ENSO phenomenon by sorting, summarizing, and analyzing historical ENSO indicators. Statistical models include linear statistical models and nonlinear statistical models. The former is constructed using linear methods such as multiple linear regression, canonical correlation, and Markov chains, while the latter is mainly constructed using machine learning methods such as Bayesian and neural networks.

2.2.1. Traditional Linear Statistical Methods

Among the traditional linear statistical methods, there are two outstanding classical methods, Holt Winters (HW) method and autoregressive integrated moving average (ARIMA) method. The HW method is a short-term statistical method [26] that proposes a forecasting expression for exponentially weighted moving averages for forecasting time series with seasonal patterns and repeating forms, using a technique called "exponential smoothing", reducing the volatility of time-series data, allowing for a clearer understanding of its rationale [27]. In 2014, Mike et al. used the HW model to predict the SST index in the Niño3 region from 1933 to 2012 by 1 month and 12 months in advance, with a root mean square error of 0.303 and 1.309. To address the shortcoming that the HW model is not suitable for periodically stationary time series, they proposed an improved HW model called the dynamic seasonal model (DSM). Experiments show that this model predicts monthly Nino3 in sample analysis Area, and is better than the deterministic seasonal model and HW model in terms of sea surface temperature index and intraday stock return changes [28].

ARIMA, also known as the integrated moving average autoregressive model, is one of the time series forecasting analysis methods. In 2011, Matthieu et al. [29] developed a time-series analysis method using ARIMA to investigate the temporal correlation between monthly *P. falciparum* case numbers and ENSO measured by SOI at Cayenne General Hospital from 1996 to 2009. Results showed that an El Niño lag of 3 months had a positive effect on *P. falciparum* cases ($p < 0.001$), and adding SOI data to the ARIMA model reduced the Akaike information criterion (AIC) [30] by 4%. However, ARIMA cannot return estimates of seasonal components [31]. In addition, Penland et al. [32] proposed to represent the Indo-Pacific SSTAs as a stable linear process driven by spatially coherent stochastic forcing, obtain the relevant parameters that best fit the stable linear process through observations, and then make assumptions about stability and linearity. The experimental results show that the optimal model can achieve a sample correlation of 67% between two time series predicted 7 months in advance. The multiple linear regression model proposed by Tseng et al. [33] only relies on five evolutions of thermocline depth anomalies and zonal surface wind modulation over a 25-day period. It successfully post-reported all ENSOs except the 2000/01 La Niña. Xue et al. [34] established a forecast model using the linear Markov model, using sea surface temperature, sea level height, and wind stress as predictors. When the forecast period is 6 months, its forecast-related skill reaches 0.8. Kondrashov et al. [35] obtained the stochastic forcing model of ENSO by polynomial regression analysis. When the forecast period is 6 months, the correlation coefficient exceeds 0.6.

The ENSO phenomenon is a highly complex and dynamic pattern whose trend over time is nonlinear. Traditional statistical methods have poor fitting effect on nonlinear data sets, and are not ideal for complex pattern recognition and knowledge discovery.

2.2.2. Machine Learning Methods

The ML-based ENSO prediction method is realized by learning and mining historical ENSO index features and establishing an ENSO prediction model. In 1998, Tangang et al. [36] and Jiang Guorong et al. [37] found that the combination of the neural network algorithm and empirical orthogonal function analysis method can have unexpected effects on ENSO forecasting. In 2009, Silvestre and William [38] proposed two nonlinear regression models,

Bayesian neural network (BNN) and support vector regression (SVR). Temperature can be used as a predictor of SST anomalies in the tropical Pacific for 3–15 months. The results show that the BNN model has better overall prediction performance than the SVR model. Liu Kefeng et al. [39] also found that the multi-step hierarchical prediction method based on the combination of support vector machine and wavelet decomposition method can effectively predict the time series of sea temperature anomalies. Feng et al. [40] proposed a toolbox "climatelearn", combined with some machine learning methods, to predict the occurrence of El Niño and Niño3.4 indices. In 2016, in terms of ENSO forecasting, the zero-mean random error model of ICM was proposed [41], called the ensemble-mean model, which showed better results than the deterministic ICM on ENSO forecasting. Peter D et al. [42] combined the classic autoregressive synthetic moving average technique with an artificial neural network to predict the ENSO index. In addition, Li Chentong used the decision tree algorithm to establish a multi-modal ENSO prediction result intelligent consultation system. He used four decision tree model methods (boosting-based GBDT, XGBoost, lightGBM, and bagging-based RF), respectively, and established a multi-modal ENSO forecasting result intelligent consultation system according to different advance forecasting times.

ML-based methods, especially those based on deep networks, tend to be more complex, take longer to compute, and have poor predictive ability for very long sequences of ENSO indices. In addition, for the long-time series Niño 3.4 index and SOI data, they not only have approximately periodic interannual variation characteristics but also have a large amount of high-frequency random noise due to seasonal variation, which seriously reduces the predictive ability of numerical simulation models. Therefore, ENSO events are still difficult to predict with a lead time of more than one year.

3. Deep Learning Methods

With the rapid development of big data and deep learning methods in recent years, prediction methods based on deep learning have been widely used in various fields, and some scholars have begun to use deep learning to improve ENSO forecasting skills. This section mainly introduces the related models and theories of spatiotemporal sequences in deep learning and the application of deep learning in ENSO prediction, including shallow neural networks, CNNs, RNNs, and graph neural networks (GNN).

3.1. Shallow Neural Networks

In 1986, Rumelhar and Hinton [43] proposed the back-propagation algorithm, which solved the complex calculation problem of the two-layer neural network, which led to the research upsurge of the two-layer neural network in the industry. In addition to an input layer and an output layer, a two-layer neural network also includes an intermediate layer, where both the intermediate layer and the output layer are computational layers. Its matrix change formula is:

$$\left(W^{(1)} * a^{(1)}\right) = a^{(2)}$$

$$g\left(W^{(2)} * a^{(2)}\right) = z \quad (1)$$

In each layer of the neural network, except for the output layer, there will be a bias unit. As in linear regression models and logistic regression models. The matrix operation of the neural network after considering the bias is as follows:

$$g\left(W^{(1)} * a^{(1)} + b^{(1)}\right) = a^{(2)}$$

$$g\left(W^{(2)} * a^{(2)} + b^{(2)}\right) = z \quad (2)$$

Different from the single-layer neural network, it is theoretically proven that the two-layer neural network can approximate any continuous function infinitely, that is to say, in the face of complex nonlinear classification tasks, the two-layer neural network can better classify.

The multi-layer neural network continues to add layers after the output layer of the two-layer neural network. Its advantage is that it can represent features in a deeper way and has a stronger ability to simulate functions. The BP neural network is a concept proposed by scientists headed by Rumelhart and McClelland in 1986. It is a multi-layer feedforward neural network trained according to the error back-propagation algorithm. In other words, it is a feedforward multi-layer perceptron (MLP) trained using the BP algorithm. The BP neural network is widely used in meteorological forecasting. The classic BP neural network is generally divided into three layers, namely, the input layer, the hidden layer, and the output layer. The main idea of its training is: input data, use the back-propagation algorithm to continuously adjust and train the weights and thresholds of the network, adjust the weights and thresholds according to the prediction error, and output the results that are close to the expectations until the predicted results can reach the expectations. The topology of the BP neural network is shown in Figure 2.

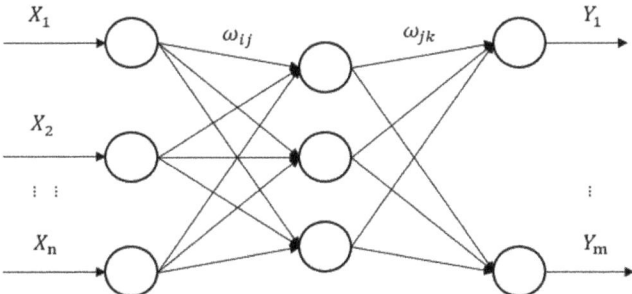

Figure 2. BP neural network topology diagram.

When the BP neural network processes data, the network should be initialized first and the network parameters should be set; The second step is to calculate the output of the hidden layer, the output formula is shown in Formula (3), where X represents the input variable, ω_{ij}, a are the input connection weight of the layer and the hidden layer and the threshold of the hidden layer, l is the number of nodes in the hidden layer, f is the activation function of the hidden layer; then the output layer is calculated, and the predicted output Y of the BP network is shown in formula (4), Among them, H is the output of the hidden layer, ω_{ij}, b are the connection weights and thresholds, respectively; The formula for calculating the error is shown in (5), where Y_k is the predicted value of the network, O_k is the actual expected value; We update the weights and update the network connection weights ω_{ij}, ω_{jk} through the prediction error e. The formula is shown in (6), and η is the learning rate; the network thresholds a and b are updated according to the prediction error e, and the formula is shown in (7); Finally, determine whether the iteration can end. If the algorithm iteration does not end, we return to the second step until the algorithm ends.

$$H_j = f\left(\sum_{i=1}^{n} \omega_{ij} x_i + a_j\right), j = 1, 2, \ldots, l \tag{3}$$

$$Y_k = \sum_{j=1}^{l} H_j \omega_{jk} + b_k, k = 1, 2, \ldots, m \tag{4}$$

$$e_k = Y_k - O_k, k = 1, 2, \ldots, m \tag{5}$$

$$\begin{aligned}\omega_{ij} &= \omega_{ij} + \eta H_j(1 - H_j) x_i \sum_{k=1}^{m} \omega_{jk} e_k, i = 1, 2, \ldots, n; j = 1, 2, \ldots, l \\ \omega_{jk} &= \omega_{jk} + \eta H_j e_k, j = 1, \ldots, l; k = 1, \ldots, m\end{aligned} \tag{6}$$

$$a_j = a_j + \eta H_j(1-H)x_i \sum_{k=1}^{m} \omega_{jk}e_k, \; j = 1,\ldots,l$$
$$b_k = b_k + \eta e_k, \; k = 1,\ldots,m \tag{7}$$

Many researchers initially tried to apply shallow neural networks to ENSO prediction and achieved good results. Jiang Guorong et al. [37] used the back-propagation (BP) algorithm for ENSO forecasting, which could better predict the changing trend of SST in key areas. However, forecast skill assessment depends on forecast time, which is inversely proportional. Baawain et al. [44] designed a three-layer multi-layer perceptron model, and the hidden layer and output layer were trained using a logical activation function through an error back-propagation algorithm. Ravi et al. [45] used the ANN model to select the Niño1+2, Niño3, Niño3.4, and Niño4 indices as the predictors of the Indian summer monsoon rainfall index (ISMRI) for prediction. The results show that the neural network model has better predictive power than all linear regression models. Mekanik et al. [46] found through experiments that using the lagged ENSO-DMI index combined with ANN to predict spring rainfall can achieve a 96.96% correlation. This method can be used in areas of the world where there is a relationship between rainfall and large-scale climate patterns that cannot be established by linear methods. Petersik and Dijkstra et al. [47] used an ensemble of Gaussian density neural networks and quantile regression neural networks to train ENSO indices and ocean heat content with a small amount of data to predict ENSO. For 1963–2017 assessments, these models are highly correlated with longer lead times. However, the shallow neural network has limited ability to represent complex functions, and its generalization ability for complex classification problems is restricted to a certain extent, and the shallow neural network tends to fall into a local minimum during training, which is prone to overfitting during testing. The multi-layer neural network can represent complex functions with fewer parameters by learning a deep nonlinear network structure and has strong feature learning ability. A multi-layer neural network has great potential to solve complex nonlinear stochastic problems with many influencing factors such as climate prediction.

3.2. Convolutional Neural Networks

Research on CNNs began in the 1980s and 1990s, and time delay networks and LeNet-5 were the first CNNs. Yann LeCun et al. [48] proposed a CNN algorithm based on gradient learning in 1998 and applied it to handwritten digit recognition. In 2012, Hinton et al. [49] won the classification competition, which opened the prelude to the gradual domination of CNNs in the field of computer vision.

As a type of neural network, CNN can effectively extract features contained in images, so it is widely used in fields involving image processing (such as image recognition, object detection, etc.) [49,50]. For meteorological data, the distribution field of a certain element at a certain time can be regarded as an image, and it can be used as the input of CNN. Using CNN to solve it is actually a nonlinear regression of the global ocean element field and the Nino3.4 regional SST in the next few months.

The main structure of CNN includes input layer, convolution layer, pooling layer, fully connected layer, and output layer. The main function of the convolution layer is to enhance the original signal features and reduce noise through convolution operations. The expression for convolution in calculus is:

$$S(t) = \int x(t-a)w(a)da \tag{8}$$

The discrete form is:

$$s(t) = \sum_a x(t-a)\omega(a) \tag{9}$$

This formula can be expressed as a matrix:

$$(t) = (X * W)(t) \tag{10}$$

Among them, ∗ represents the convolution operation; if it is a two-dimensional convolution, it is represented as:

$$s(i,j) = (X * W)(i,j) = \sum_m \sum_n x(i-m, j-n)w(m,n) \tag{11}$$

The convolution formula in CNN is slightly different from the definition in mathematics. For example, for two-dimensional convolution, it is defined as:

$$s(i,j) = (X * W)(i,j) = \sum_m \sum_n x(i+m, j+n)w(m,n) \tag{12}$$

Among them, W is the convolution kernel, and X is the input. If X is a two-dimensional input matrix, then W is also a two-dimensional matrix. However, if X is a multidimensional tensor, then W is also a multidimensional tensor.

The main purpose of the pooling layer is to reduce the amount of data processing and speed up network training while retaining useful information. Commonly used pooling operations include average pooling and maximum pooling. The results of max pooling and average pooling are as follows:

$$y_{i^{l+1}, j^{l+1}, d} = \frac{1}{HW} \sum_{0 \leq i \leq H, 0 \leq j \leq W} x^l_{i^{l+1} \times H + i, j^{l+1} \times W + j, d^l} \tag{13}$$

$$y_{i^{l+1}, j^{l+1}, d} = \max_{0 \leq i \leq H, 0 \leq j \leq W} x^l_{i^{l+1} \times H + i, j^{l+1} \times W + j, d^l} \tag{14}$$

The activation function layer is also called the nonlinear mapping layer. The purpose is to increase the expressive ability (nonlinearity) of the entire network. The main activation functions include the sigmoid function, the tanh function, and the relu function. The formula of the activation function is shown in (15). After several layers of convolution and pooling operations, the obtained feature maps are expanded row by row, connected into vectors, and input into the fully connected network. The fully connected layer integrates the features in the feature map to obtain the high-level meaning of the image features, which is then used for image classification.

$$sigmoid(x) = \frac{1}{1+e^{-x}}$$

$$\tanh(x) = \frac{1-e^{-2x}}{1+e^{-2x}} \tag{15}$$

$$relu(x) = \begin{cases} 0 \ (x \leq 0) \\ x \ (x > 0) \end{cases}$$

CNNs are applied in many fields of weather forecasting, and they are also helpful for ENSO forecasting. In September 2019, Ham et al. [51] first proposed using a CNN for ENSO prediction. The model structure is shown in Figure 3. CNN requires a large number of images for training in order to improve the accuracy of prediction. Despite the large scale of meteorological data, the use of CNNs in ENSO forecasting has encountered difficulties with data shortages. Ham et al. proposed to combine climate models with artificial intelligence methods, using dozens of global climate models from CMIP5 to generate a series of simulated data based on historical ocean data. As a result, scientists not only have a set of actual historical observations but also thousands of simulation results for training. The research results show that when the prediction time is more than 6 months, the prediction ability of the CNN method for the Nino3.4 index is significantly higher than that of the current international best dynamic prediction system. When tested on real data from 1984 to 2017, CNN was able to predict El Niño events 18 months in advance. At the time, the research results were regarded as the pioneering work of deep learning in the field of weather forecasting.

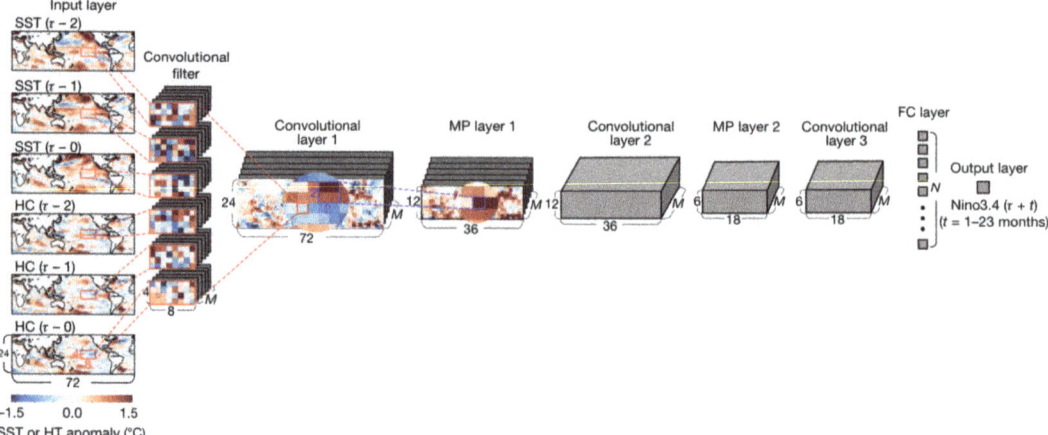

Figure 3. Structure of the CNN model for ENSO prediction [51].

However, the defects of CNN itself, including fixed input vector size and inconsistent input and output size, limit its application in time-series forecasting. In 2020, Yan et al. [52] proposed the ensemble empirical mode decomposition-temporal convolutional network (EEMD-TCN) hybrid method, which decomposes the variable Niño3.4 exponent and SOI into relatively flat subcomponents; then, The TCN model is used to predict each subcomponent in advance, and finally, the sub-prediction results are combined to obtain the final ENSO prediction result. The TCN residual module diagram is shown in Figure 4. TCN is a variant of CNN that uses random convolution and dilation for sequential data with temporality and large receptive fields. Empirical mode decomposition can decompose high-frequency time series Niño 3.4 index and SOI data into multiple adaptive orthogonal components, improving the prediction accuracy of the model. The experimental results show that the TCN method has a good effect in the advance prediction of ENSO, which has important guiding significance for the research into ENSO. In response to the problem of data shortage, in addition to [51] using climate models to generate a large amount of simulated data, in 2021, Hu [53] et al. used dropout and transfer learning to overcome the problem of insufficient data during model training and proposed a model based on a deep residual convolutional neural network. The model effectively predicts the Niño 3.4 index with a lead time of 20 months during the 1984–2017 evaluation period, three months more than the existing optimal model. In addition, they also use heterogeneous transfer learning. This model achieved 83.3% accuracy for forecasting the 12-month-lead El Niño type. However, many forecasts only consider temporality and the lack of spatial features in ENSO. In 2022, Zhao [54] et al. proposed an end-to-end spatial temporal semantic network, named STSNet, which consists of three main modules: (1) Geographic semantic enhancement module (GSEM) distinguishes various latitude and longitude through a learnable adaptive weight matrix; (2) A novel spatiotemporal convolutional module(STCM) is designed specially to extract the multidimensional features by alternating the execution of temporal and spatial convolution and temporal attention; (3) Combining and exploiting multi-scale temporal information in a three-stream temporal scale module (3sTSM) to further improve performance. Figure 5 illustrates the pipeline of the proposed STSNet. The results show that STSNet can simultaneously provide effective ENSO predictions for 16 months with higher correlation and lower bias compared to other deep learning models.

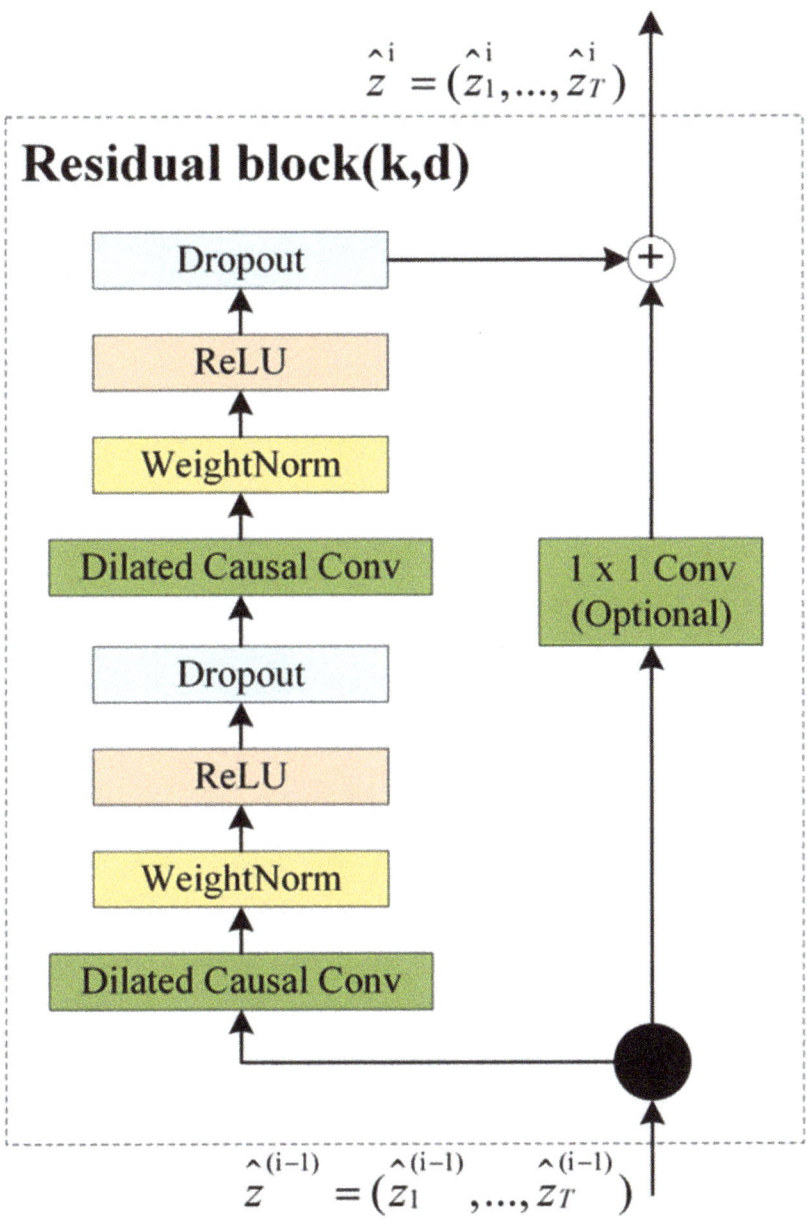

Figure 4. The TCN residual module [52].

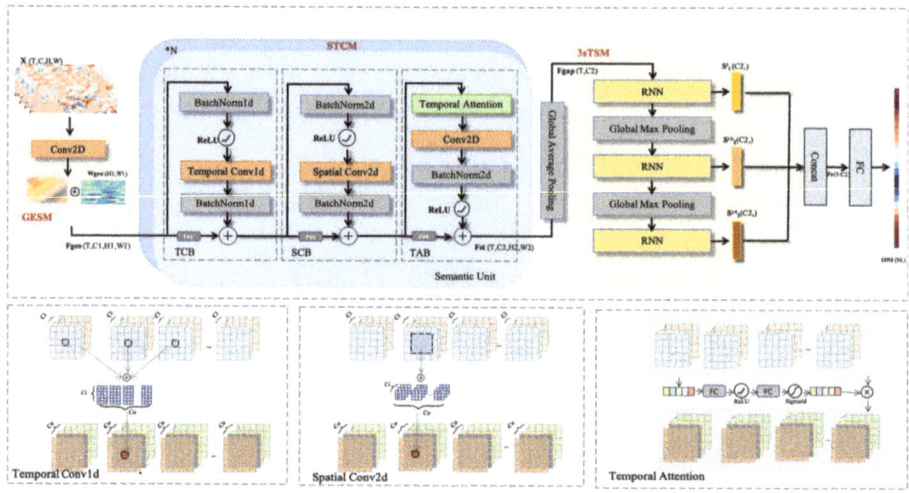

Figure 5. The pipeline of the proposed STSNet [54].

3.3. Recurrent Neural Network

When the input data has dependencies and is a sequential pattern, the results of CNNs are generally not very good, because there is no correlation between the previous input of the CNN and the next input. In 1982, Hopfield [55] proposed RNN. RNN is used to solve the problem that the training sample input is a continuous sequence, and the length of the sequence is different, such as the problem based on the time series. RNNs enable deep learning models to make breakthroughs in solving problems in NLP domains such as speech recognition [56], language models [57], machine translation [58], and time series analysis. In 1997, Jurgen Schmidhuber et al. [59] proposed long short-term memory (LSTM), a novel RNN variant structure that uses gating units and memory mechanisms to capture long-term temporal dependencies, and successfully solves gradient disappearance and the explosion problem, which controls the flow of information through learnable gates. The structure comparison of RNN and LSTM is shown in Figure 6. Among them, LSTM introduces the concepts of the forgetting gate, input gate, and output gate, thus, modifying the calculation method of the hidden state in RNN. The formula is as follows:

$$I_t = \sigma(X_t W_{xi} + H_{t-1} W_{hi} + b_i) \tag{16}$$

$$F_t = \sigma\left(X_t W_{xf} + H_{t-1} W_{hf} + b_f\right) \tag{17}$$

$$O_t = \sigma(X_t W_{xo} + H_{t-1} W_{ho} + b_o) \tag{18}$$

Among them, W_{xi}, W_{xf}, W_{xo} and W_{hi}, W_{hf}, W_{ho} are all learnable weight parameters, and b_i, b_f, b_o are learnable offset parameters. The candidate cell in long short-term memory $\widetilde{C}_t$ uses the hyperbolic tangent function tanh in the range $[-1, 1]$ as the activation function:

$$\widetilde{C}_t = \tanh(X_t W_{xc} + H_{t-1} W_{hc} + b_c) \tag{19}$$

The flow of information in the hidden state can be controlled by input gates, forgetting gates, and output gates with element values in the range [0, 1]: this can usually be performed with the element-wise multiplication operator $\odot$. The calculation of the cell $\widetilde{C}_t$ at the current moment combines the information of the cell at the previous moment and the candidate cell at the current moment, and controls the flow of information through the forgetting gate and the input gate:

$$C_t = F_t \odot C_{t-1} + I_t \odot \tilde{C}_t \tag{20}$$

Next, the information flow from the cell to the hidden layer variable H_t can be controlled by the output gate:

$$H_t = O_t \odot \tanh(C_t) \tag{21}$$

In 2017, Zhang, Wang [60], and others defined the SST prediction problem as a time-series regression problem and used LSTM as the main layer of the network structure to predict the Bohai Sea temperature. The experimental results compared with SVR show that the LSTM network has better prediction performance. In 2018, Clifford et al. [61] used the "climate complex network" to extract meteorological data features, used the extracted features as predictors, and used LSTM to predict the Nino3.4 index. Experiments show that training LSTM models on network metric time series datasets has great potential for predicting ENSO phenomena many steps ahead. In 2021, Zhou et al. [62] used LSTM to build a tropical Pacific Niño3.4 index forecast model and analyzed the seasonal forecast error of the model. The results show that for the 1997/1998 and 2015/2016 strong eastern-type El Niño events, the model can more accurately predict the trends and peaks of the events, and the anomalous correlation coefficient (ACC) reaches more than 0.93. However, for the 1991/1992 and 2002/2003 weak central El Niño events, it did not perform well in peak forecasting.

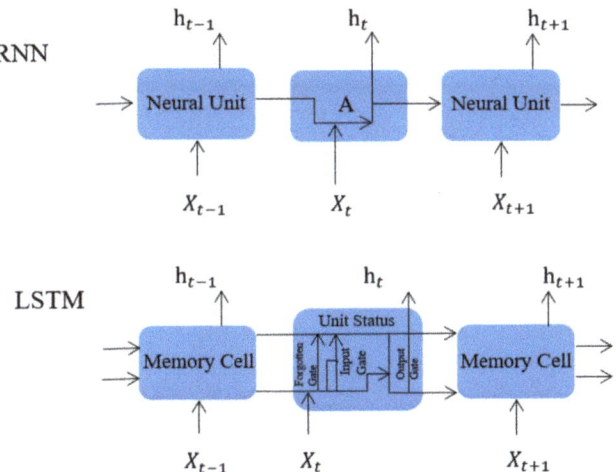

Figure 6. Comparison of the RNN and LSTM structure.

Shi X et al. [63] proposed the concept of convolutional long short-term memory (ConvLSTM) and established an end-to-end trainable for the precipitation now-prediction problem by stacking multiple ConvLSTM layers to form an encoder–decoder structure The model diagram is shown in Figure 7. ConvLSTM is designed to solve the problem of 3D data prediction; the unit can receive 2D matrices and even higher dimensional inputs at each time step. The key improvement is that the Hadamard product between the weights and the input is replaced by a convolution operation, as shown in Equation (22). It can not only establish temporal relationships similar to LSTM but also describe local spatial features by extracting features similar to CNN.

$$i_t = \sigma(W_{xi} * X_t + W_{hi} * X_{t-1} + b_i)$$

$$f_t = \sigma\left(W_{xf} * X_t + W_{hf} * H_{t-1} + b_f\right)$$
$$o_t = \sigma(W_{xo} * X_t + W_{ho} * H_{t-1} + b_o) \quad (22)$$
$$\tilde{C}_t = \tanh(W_{xc} * X_t + W_{hc} * H_{t-1} + b_c)$$
$$C_t = f_t \odot C_{t-1} + i_t \odot \tilde{C}_t$$
$$H_t = o_t \odot \tanh(C_t)$$

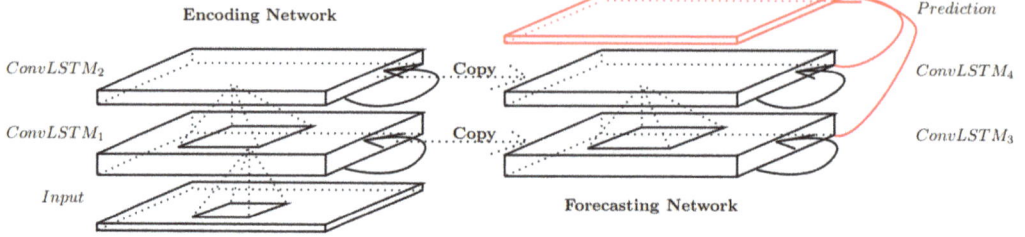

Figure 7. Encoding-forecasting ConvLSTM network [63].

Among them, "∗" represents the convolution operation, "⊙" represents Hadamard product. The difference between ConvLSTM and LSTM is only that the input-to-state and state-to-state parts are replaced by fully connected calculations with convolution calculations.

In 2019, Dandan He et al. [64] established a deep learning ENSO prediction model (DLENSO) using ConvLSTM to predict ENSO by directly predicting SST in the tropical Pacific. DLENSO is a sequence-to-sequence model. Its encoder and decoder are both ConvLSTM, and the input and prediction targets are both spatiotemporal sequences. DLENSO is superior to the LSTM model and the deterministic prediction model and is almost equivalent to the ensemble average in the medium and long-term prediction models. To capture both spatial and temporal correlations in SST and improve prediction skills over longer time horizons, Mu [65] et al. proposed the ConvLSTM-RM model, which is a hybrid of convolutional LSTM and rolling mechanism, and used it to build an end-to-end trainable model for the ENSO prediction problem. Their experiments on historical SST datasets show that ConvLSTM-RM outperforms seven well-known methods on multiple time horizons (6 months, 9 months, and 12 months). The deep learning methods used above are all supervised learning, the training data are all labeled, and the cost of data labeling is often huge. In recent years, unsupervised learning has been mined and gradually developed. The biggest advantage of unsupervised learning is that it does not need to label the data so it can save a lot of manpower and resources. At the same time, compared with the limited labels marked by supervised learning, the features that can be learned by unsupervised learning are more adaptive and rich. In 2021, Geng et al. [66] regarded ENSO prediction as an unsupervised spatiotemporal prediction problem and designed a dense convolution–long short-term memory (DC-LSTM). The model diagram is shown in Figure 8. To obtain a more adequately trained model, they added historical simulated data to the training set. The experimental results show that the DC-LSTM method is more suitable for large area and single factor prediction. During the 1994–2010 validation period, the full-season correlation ability of the Nino3.4 index of DC-LSTM was higher than that of the existing dynamic models and regression neural networks, and the prediction effect for a lead time of up to 20 months was much higher than [51]. In 2022, Lu et al. [67] developed a new hybrid model, POP-Net, to predict SST in Niño 3.4 regions by combining POP analysis procedures with CNN and LSTM. POP-Net achieved a high correlation of 17-month lead-time predictions (correlation coefficient over 0.5) during the 1994–2020 validation period. In addition, POP-Net also mitigates SPB.

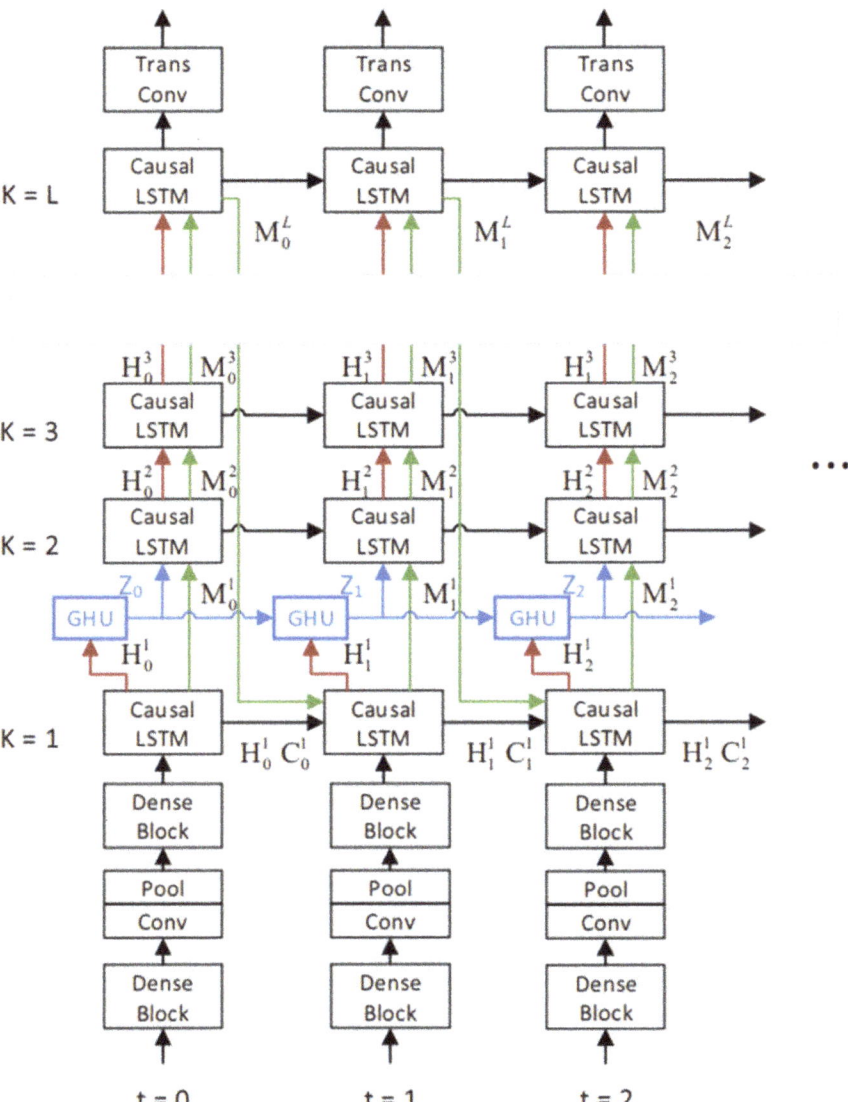

Figure 8. Model structure diagram of DC-LSTM [66].

RNNs also have their own flaws. The RNN is often used to process sequence data, but the disadvantage is that it is not suitable for long sequences, and the gradient is easy to vanish. LSTM is proposed to deal with the problem of gradient disappearance. It is especially suitable for long sequences, but the disadvantage is the large amount of calculation; GRU is proposed to simplify the calculation of LSTM; obviously, GRU lost a gate in LSTM. Obviously, if the parameters are less, the natural calculation will be faster. When the training set is large, the performance is naturally not as good as LSTM.

3.4. Graph Neural Networks

The concept of GNN was first proposed by Gori [68] and others in 2005. The RNN framework was used to deal with undirected graphs, directed graphs, labeled graphs, and cyclic graphs. The feature map and node aggregation of the method generate a vector representation for each node, which cannot well deal with the complex and changeable graph data in reality. Bruna et al. [69] proposed to apply CNN to graphs, and through clever transformation of convolution operators, they proposed the graph convolutional network (GCN) and derived many variants. The proposal of GCN is the "pioneering work" of the graph neural network. For the first time, the convolution operation in image processing is simply used in the processing of graph structure data, which reduces the computational complexity of the graph neural network model. The calculation of the Laplacian matrix in the calculation process has since become past tense. Supposing we have a batch of graph data, which has N nodes and each node has its own characteristics, we let the characteristics of these nodes form an N × D-dimensional matrix X, and then the relationship between each node will also form an N × D. An N-dimensional matrix A is called an adjacency matrix. X and A are the inputs to our model, and the formula for GCN is as follows:

$$H^{(l+1)} = \sigma \left(\tilde{D}^{-\frac{1}{2}} \tilde{A} \tilde{D}^{-\frac{1}{2}} H^{(l)} W^{(l)} \right) \tag{23}$$

Among them, $\tilde{A} = A + I$, I is the identity matrix; $\tilde{D}$ is the degree matrix of $\tilde{A}$; H is the feature of each layer; for the input layer, H is X; σ is the nonlinear activation function. The model of GCN is shown in Figure 9.

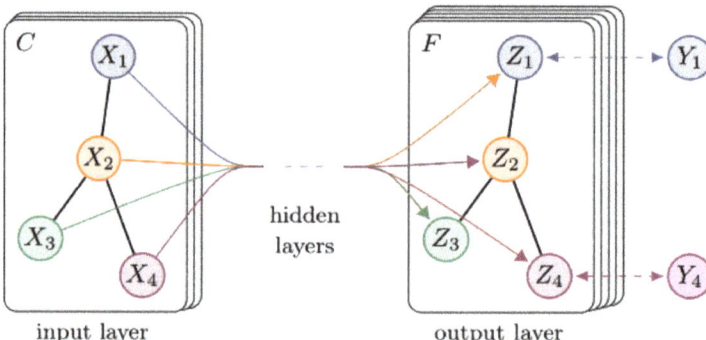

Figure 9. Graph convolutional neural networks [68].

In 2021, Cachay et al. [70] first proposed the application of a graph neural network in seasonal forecasting and published it in NIPS. They advocated defining the ONI prediction problem as a graph regression problem and modeled it using GNNs that generalized convolutions to non-Euclidean data, thus, allowing us to model large-scale global connections as edges of the graph, except in graph convolutional neural networks, and they also designed a new graph-connected learning module to enable GNN models to learn large-scale spatial interactions together with practical ENSO prediction tasks. The model surpasses the state-of-the-art deep learning-based CNN model in ENSO prediction, and is also more effective than the LSTM model and the dynamic model, and its correlation coefficients in ENSO predictions 1 month, 3 months, and 6 months ahead of time reach 0.97, 0.92, and 0.78. The heat map of its effect is shown in Figure 10. Simply using the graphical model can achieve such excellent results. If the graphical model is combined with the power coupler, will there be new gains? Practice brings true knowledge. Bin [71] et al. designed a graph-based multivariate air–sea coupler (ASC) using the features of multiple physical variables to learn multivariate synergy through graph convolution. Based on this coupler, an ENSO deep learning prediction model, ENSO-ASC, was proposed, which uses stacked ConvLSTM layers as the skeleton of the encoder to extract spatiotemporal features, and the decoder consists of stacked transform convolutional layers and upsampling layers. The model structure diagram is shown in Figure 11. The experimental results show that

ENSO-ASC outperforms other models; sea surface temperature and zonal wind are two important predictors; and the Niño 3.4 index has correlations of over 0.78, 0.65, and 0.5 for lead times of 6, 12, and 18 months, respectively. Through this case, we can see that combining deep learning models with multivariate air–sea couplers or other dynamical models can improve the effectiveness and superiority of predicting ENSO and analyzing underlying dynamical mechanisms in a complex manner.

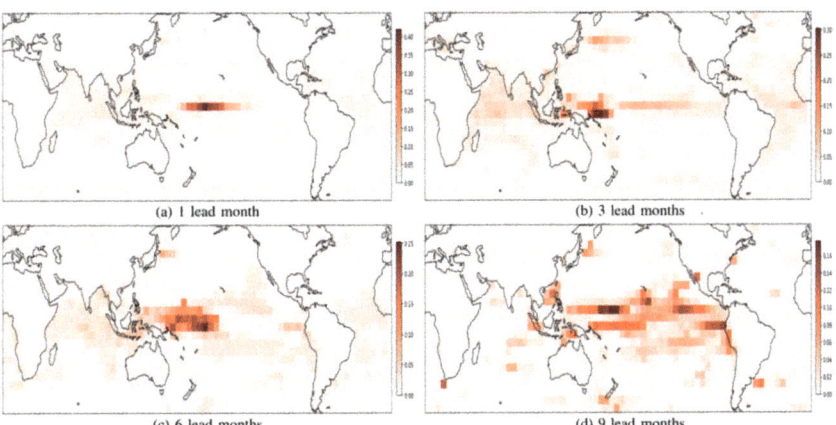

Figure 10. Heatmap of the effect of GNN predicting ENSO [70]. (**a**–**d**) respectively represent the heat map of GNN's prediction of ENSO on a time scale of 1, 3, 6 and 9 months in advance.

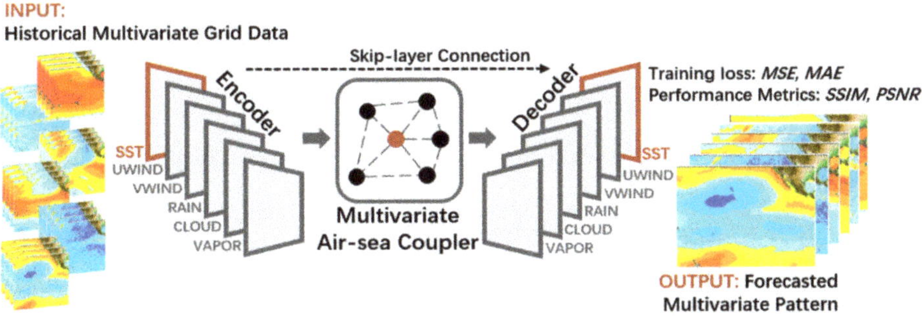

Figure 11. The structure of ENSO-ASC [71].

However, many recent cross-domain studies have found that GNN models do not provide the expected performance. When the researchers compared them to simpler tree-based baseline models, GNNs could not even outperform the baseline models. GNN can only perform feature denoising and cannot learn nonlinear manifolds. GNNs can, therefore, be viewed as a mechanism for graph learning models (e.g., for feature denoising) rather than as a complete end-to-end model. It has to be said that GNN, as an emerging neural network, has great prospects for development.

4. Discussion

We summarize the traditional and deep learning methods for ENSO prediction listed in this paper in Table 1. More than half a century of ENSO research has achieved significant results, especially the possibility of real-time prediction of its advance month–season scale, such as the current linear statistical models or the dynamic models based on mathematical equations can predict ENSO at least 6 months in advance. We have achieved better real-time forecasting, but there are still large errors and uncertainties in forecasting skills. On the other hand, deep learning methods were put into use in ENSO forecasting and have greatly improved our forecasting ability for ENSO. The experimental indicators show that most spatiotemporal neural networks are suitable for ENSO prediction. Although deep learning methods can improve the accuracy of ENSO forecasting, artificial intelligence methods are not developed for the field of science, and research using neural networks to predict climate phenomena is still in its infancy, so there are still many problems.

Table 1. Summary of deep learning and its application in ENSO forecasting.

Method	Specific Method		Generalize	Features
Traditional Method	Dynamic Methods		Using dynamic equations, the ocean, atmosphere, land, and other spheres and their interactions are modeled, and the computer is gradually integrated to simulate the evolution of the atmosphere. Ranging from relatively simple physical models to comprehensive fully coupled models.	The averaging skills of dynamic models are generally better than statistical models, but in practice, it is difficult to simulate the interannual average variation of sea surface temperature due to uncertainty in initial conditions. The emergence of SPB phenomenon.
	Statistical Methods	Linear Statistical Methods	Realize the analysis and prediction of ENSO phenomenon by sorting, summarizing, and analyzing historical ENSO indicators.	Statistical models require past long-term forecast data to discover potential relationships, but observations of the tropical Pacific did not begin until the 1990s. Compared to complex dynamic models, statistical models reduce cost and are easier to develop.
		Machine Learning Methods	Nonlinear statistical method, by learning and mining historical ENSO index features, using machine learning models to capture the nonlinear features of ENSO for prediction.	
Deep Learning Methods	Convolutional Neural Network		CNN is a kind of feed-forward neural network with convolution calculation and deep structure from inputting original information, self-learning features, as the network goes from front to back, combining features from shallow to deep.	The forecasting skills of CNN are much higher than the current state-of-the-art dynamic models and can also better predict the detailed regional distribution of SST, overcoming the weaknesses of the dynamic prediction models. CNN is less affected by SPB, but it is not suitable for time-series forecasting.
	Recurrent Neural Network		RNNs are a pattern for text, sequence data recognition. Its input includes more than just the currently seen input example. It also includes information that the network perceives at the last minute. Using this property, information can circulate in the network for any length of time. Including LSTM, ConvLSTM, ConvGRU, etc.	RNN is suitable for solving sequence problems with continuous and different length of training sample input, such as time-series-based problems. The model can more accurately predict the trend and peak of strong El Niño events, but it is not good for weak El Niño peaks.
	Graph Neural Network		GNN is a deep learning method based on a graph structure, where data is represented in the form of a graph, and information flow is explicitly modeled through edge connections.	The gridded climate data can be naturally mapped to the nodes of GNN, and the prediction effect of GNN in the first 6 months exceeds the current state-of-the-art CNN model. However, there are still problems such as difficulty in predicting extreme ENSO events and limited training samples.

First, deep learning has better modeling capabilities on the basis of big data, while the number of climate observation samples is small, especially for extreme events. In this case, the self-learning ability of deep learning methods is greatly limited, so the development of deep learning methods for small sample events is a current development direction. Second, in recent years, deep learning models have become more and more complex. Generally speaking, the more complex the model, the better its learning ability, but the problem is that the interpretability of the model results is worse.

In addition, when making long-term predictions, the prediction of ENSO event peaks has the problem of underestimation and prediction lag. We could try to introduce some random disturbance mechanisms so that the model can predict greater intensity. ENSO will also have the SPB problem in long-term forecasting, which is a difficult point in dynamic forecasting. More in-depth parameter adjustment work can be performed on the learning rates of different optimizers in the deep learning model, perhaps by finding hyperparameters that mitigate SPB in the training set. In addition, in order to improve the accuracy and length of ENSO predictions, we could try the spatiotemporal prediction model and graph neural network model recently proposed by AI, and use observation data and simulated data for training to increase the amount of training data. With sufficient data, we may be able to train a better model. At present, most of the research on artificial intelligence to improve ENSO prediction and other aspects mainly stays on the direct application of related artificial intelligence technology. Considering that phenomena such as ENSO in earth science research have clear temporal and spatial structures and evolution laws of physical processes, the ability to organically combine the temporal and spatial evolution characteristics of ENSO based on physical analysis methods with artificial intelligence methods based on big data to further improve ENSO Forecasting skills is a hot topic in the field of climate change. It is also worth continuing to explore how to combine deep learning with meteorology and climate in the future.

5. Conclusions

The severe cold and heat caused by the climate change caused by ENSO affect people's daily life, and improving the accuracy of ENSO prediction is still a direction that researchers need to work on. This paper summarizes the main knowledge and development status of ENSO forecasting, including traditional ENSO forecasting methods and the application of artificial intelligence in ENSO forecasting. In this paper, artificial intelligence methods are divided into machine learning methods and deep learning methods. In the section on machine learning, the main methods such as decision tree, Bayesian, support vector machine and ARIMA are reviewed in ENSO forecasting. In the deep learning section, we summarized convolutional neural networks, recurrent neural networks, graph neural networks and their variants, focusing on the performance of these models in ENSO prediction. Table 1 provides an overview of various ENSO prediction methods and compares the advantages and disadvantages of each method. From the introductions in Sections 2 and 3, it can be seen that the application of deep learning in ENSO prediction is widely effective and has great potential to further improve the prediction accuracy and length. By combining deep learning and meteorological science, researchers have drawn more conclusions, contributing to better climate predictions in the future. Finally, we analyzed the problems and research directions of artificial intelligence in ENSO prediction for future researchers' reference and further development and better use of deep learning to expand more ways to help predict ENSO and even other climate problems.

Author Contributions: Conceptualization, W.F. and Y.S.; methodology, W.F.; investigation, Y.S.; resources, W.F.; writing—original draft preparation, W.F. and Y.S.; writing—review and editing, W.F. and V.S.S. All authors have read and agreed to the published version of the manuscript.

Funding: This work was supported by the National Natural Science Foundation of China (Grant No. 42075007), the Open Grants of the State Key Laboratory of Severe Weather (No. 2021LASW-B19).

Institutional Review Board Statement: Not applicable.

Informed Consent Statement: Not applicable.

Data Availability Statement: Not applicable.

Acknowledgments: The author would like to thank the researchers in the field of ENSO forecasting and other related fields. This paper cites the research literature of several scholars. It would be difficult for me to complete this review without being inspired by their research results. Thank you for all the help we have received in writing this article.

Conflicts of Interest: The authors declare that they have no conflict of interest to report regarding the present study.

References

1. McPhaden, M.J.; Zebiak, S.E.; Glantz, M.H. ENSO as an integrating concept in earth science. *Science* **2006**, *314*, 1740–1745. [CrossRef] [PubMed]
2. Bjerknes, J. Atmospheric teleconnections from the equatorial Pacific. *Mon. Weather Rev.* **1969**, *97*, 163–172. [CrossRef]
3. Lin, J.; Qian, T. Switch between El Nino and La Nina is caused by subsurface ocean waves likely driven by lunar tidal forcing. *Sci. Rep.* **2019**, *9*, 13106.
4. Siegert, F.; Ruecker, G.; Hinrichs, A. Increased damage from fires in logged forests during droughts caused by El Nino. *Nature* **2001**, *414*, 437–440. [CrossRef] [PubMed]
5. Pielke, R.A.; Landsea, C.N. La Nina, El Nino, and Atlantic Hurricane Damages in the United States. *Bull. Am. Meteorol. Soc.* **1999**, *80*, 2027–2034. [CrossRef]
6. Ward, P.J.; Jongman, B.; Kummu, M. Strong influence of El Niño southern oscillation on flood risk around the world. *Proc. Natl. Acad. Sci. USA* **2014**, *111*, 15659–15664. [CrossRef] [PubMed]
7. Patz, J.A.; Campbell-Lendrum, D.; Holloway, T. Impact of regional climate change on human health. *Nature* **2005**, *438*, 310–317. [CrossRef]
8. Tang, Y.; Zhang, R.H.; Liu, T. Progress in ENSO prediction and predictability study. *Natl. Sci. Rev.* **2018**, *5*, 826–839. [CrossRef]
9. Masson, S.; Terray, P.; Madec, G. Impact of intra-daily SST variability on ENSO characteristics in a coupled model. *Clim. Dyn.* **2012**, *39*, 681–707. [CrossRef]
10. Wang, Y.; Jiang, J.; Zhang, H. A scalable parallel algorithm for atmospheric general circulation models on a multi-core cluster. *Future Gener. Comput. Syst.* **2017**, *72*, 1–10. [CrossRef]
11. Jin, E.K.; Kinter, J.L.; Wang, B. Current status of ENSO prediction skill in coupled ocean-atmosphere models. *Clim. Dyn.* **2008**, *31*, 647–664. [CrossRef]
12. Ren, F.M.; Yuan, Y.; Sun, C.H. Review of progress of ENSO studies in the past three decades. *Adv. Meteorol. Sci. Technol.* **2012**, *2*, 17–24.
13. Clarke, A.J. El Niño physics and El Niño predictability. *Annu. Rev. Mar. Sci.* **2014**, *6*, 79–99. [CrossRef] [PubMed]
14. Hinton, G.E.; Osindero, S.; The, Y.W. A fast learning algorithm for deep belief nets. *Neural Comput.* **2006**, *18*, 1527–1554. [CrossRef]
15. Cane, M.A.; Zebiak, S.E.; Dolan, S.C. Experimental forecasts of EL Nino. *Nature* **1986**, *321*, 827–832. [CrossRef]
16. Zebiak, S.E.; Cane, M.A. A model El Niñ-southern oscillation. *Mon. Weather Rev.* **1987**, *115*, 2262–2278. [CrossRef]
17. Hirst, A.C. Unstable and damped equatorial modes in simple coupled ocean-atmosphere models. *J. Atmos. Sci.* **1986**, *43*, 606–632. [CrossRef]
18. Barnett, T.P.; Graham, N.; Pazan, S. ENSO and ENSO-related predictability. Part I: Prediction of equatorial Pacific sea surface temperature with a hybrid coupled ocean-atmosphere model. *J. Clim.* **1993**, *6*, 1545–1566. [CrossRef]
19. Luo, J.J.; Yuan, C.; Sasaki, W.; Behera, S.K.; Masumoto, Y.; Yamagata, T.; Masson, S. Current status of intraseasonal-seasonal-to-interannual prediction of the Indo-Pacific climate. In *Indo-Pacific Climate Variability and Predictability*; World Scientific Publishing Company: Singapore, 2016; pp. 63–107.
20. Ren, H.L.; Liu, Y.; Zuo, J.Q. The new generation of ENSO prediction system in Beijing climate centre and its predictions for the 2014/2016 super El Niño event. *Meteorology* **2016**, *42*, 521–531.
21. Liu, Y.; Ren, H.L. Improving ENSO prediction in CFSv2 with an analogue-based correction method. *Int. J. Climatol.* **2017**, *37*, 5035–5046. [CrossRef]
22. Johnson, S.J.; Stockdale, T.N.; Ferranti, L. SEAS5: The new ECMWF seasonal forecast system. *Geosci. Model Dev.* **2019**, *12*, 1087–1117. [CrossRef]
23. Webster, P.J.; Yang, S. Monsoon and ENSO: Selectively interactive systems. *Q. J. R. Meteorol. Soc.* **1992**, *118*, 877–926. [CrossRef]
24. Wang, B.; Fang, Z. Chaotic oscillations of tropical climate: A dynamic system theory for ENSO. *J. Atmos. Sci.* **1996**, *53*, 2786–2802. [CrossRef]
25. Chen, H.C.; Tseng, Y.H.; Hu, Z.Z. Enhancing the ENSO predictability beyond the spring barrier. *Sci. Rep.* **2020**, *10*, 984. [CrossRef]
26. Holt, C.C. Forecasting seasonals and trends by exponentially weighted moving averages. *Int. J. Forecast.* **2004**, *20*, 5–10. [CrossRef]
27. Chang, V.; Wills, G. A model to compare cloud and non-cloud storage of Big Data. *Future Gener. Comput. Syst.* **2016**, *57*, 56–76. [CrossRef]
28. So, M.K.P.; Chung, R.S.W. Dynamic seasonality in time series. *Comput. Stat. Data Anal.* **2014**, *70*, 212–226. [CrossRef]

29. Hanf, M.; Adenis, A.; Nacher, M.; Carme, B. The role of El Niño Southern Oscillation (ENSO) on variations of monthly Plasmodium falciparum malaria cases at the Cayenne General Hospital, 1996-2009, French Guiana. *Malar J.* **2011**, *22*, 10–100. [CrossRef]
30. Li, X.; Shang, X.; Morales-Esteban, A. Identifying P phase arrival of weak events: The akaike information criterion picking application based on the empirical mode decomposition. *Comput. Geosci.* **2017**, *100*, 57–66. [CrossRef]
31. Dietrich, B.; Goswami, D.; Chakraborty, S. Time series characterization of gaming workload for runtime power management. *IEEE Trans. Comput.* **2013**, *64*, 260–273. [CrossRef]
32. Penland, C. A stochastic model of IndoPacific sea surface temperature anomalies. *Phys. D Nonlinear Phenom.* **1996**, *98*, 534–558. [CrossRef]
33. Tseng, Y.; Hu, Z.Z.; Ding, R. An ENSO prediction approach based on ocean conditions and ocean-atmosphere coupling. *Clim. Dyn.* **2017**, *48*, 2025–2044. [CrossRef]
34. Xue, Y.; Leetmaa, A.; Ji, M. ENSO prediction with Markov models: The impact of sea level. *J. Clim.* **2000**, *13*, 849–871. [CrossRef]
35. Kondrashov, D.; Kravtsov, S.; Robertson, A.W. A hierarchy of data-based ENSO models. *J. Clim.* **2005**, *18*, 4425–4444. [CrossRef]
36. Tangang, F.T.; Tang, B.; Monahan, A.H. Forecasting ENSO events: A neural network-extended EOF approach. *J. Clim.* **1998**, *11*, 29–41. [CrossRef]
37. Jiang, G.R.; Zhang, R.; Sha, Y.W. Research on ENSO prediction using EOF unfolding and artificial neural network methods. *Mar. Forecast.* **2001**, *18*, 1–11.
38. Aguilar-Martinez, S.; Hsieh, W.W. Forecasts of tropical Pacific sea surface temperatures by neural networks and support vector regression. *Int. J. Oceanogr.* **2009**, *2009*, 167239. [CrossRef]
39. Liu, K.F.; Zhang, J.; Chen, Y.D. ENSO prediction experiment based on wavelet decomposition and support vector machine. *J. PLA Univ. Sci. Technol. Nat. Sci. Ed.* **2011**, *12*, 531–535.
40. Feng, Q.Y.; Vasile, R.; Segond, M. ClimateLearn: A machine-learning approach for climate prediction using network measures. *Geosci. Model Dev. Discuss.* **2016**, *10*, 1–18.
41. Zheng, F.; Zhu, J. Improved ensemble-mean forecasting of ENSO events by a zero-mean stochastic error model of an intermediate coupled model. *Clim. Dyn.* **2016**, *47*, 3901–3915. [CrossRef]
42. Nooteboom, P.D.; Feng, Q.Y.; López, C. Using network theory and machine learning to predict El Niño. *Earth Syst. Dyn.* **2018**, *9*, 969–983. [CrossRef]
43. Rumelhart, D.E.; Hinton, G.E.; Williams, R.J. Learning representations by back-propagating errors. *Nature* **1986**, *323*, 533–536. [CrossRef]
44. Baawain, M.S.; Nour, M.H.; El-Din, M.G.G. Applying artificial neural network models for ENSO prediction using SOI and Nino3 as onset indicators. In Proceedings of the Canadian Society for Civil Engineering-31st Annual Conference, 2003 Building our Civilization, Moncton, NB, Canada, 4–7 June 2003; pp. 858–867.
45. Shukla, R.P.; Tripathi, K.C.; Pandey, A.C. Prediction of Indian summer monsoon rainfall using Niño indices: A neural network approach. *Atmos. Res.* **2011**, *102*, 99–109. [CrossRef]
46. Mekanik, F.; Imteaz, M.A. Forecasting Victorian spring rainfall using ENSO and IOD: A comparison of linear multiple regression and nonlinear ANN. In Proceedings of the International Conference on Uncertainty Reasoning and Knowledge Engineering, Jalarta, Indonesia, 14–15 August 2012; pp. 86–89.
47. Petersik, P.J.; Dijkstra, H.A. Probabilistic forecasting of El Niño using neural network models. *Geophys. Res. Lett.* **2020**, *47*, e2019GL086423. [CrossRef]
48. LeCun, Y.; Bottou, L.; Bengio, Y. Gradient-based learning applied to document recognition. *Proc. IEEE* **1998**, *86*, 2278–2324. [CrossRef]
49. Krizhevsky, A.; Sutskever, I.; Hinton, G.E. ImageNet classification with deep convolutional neural networks. *Adv. Neural Inf. Processing Syst.* **2012**, *1*, 1097–1105. [CrossRef]
50. Simonyan, K.; Zisserman, A. Very deep convolutional networks for large-scale image recognition. *arXiv* **2014**, arXiv:1409.1556.
51. Ham, Y.G.; Kim, J.H.; Luo, J.J. Deep learning for multi-year ENSO forecasts. *Nature* **2019**, *573*, 568–572. [CrossRef]
52. Yan, J.; Mu, L.; Wang, L. Temporal convolutional networks for the advance prediction of ENSO. *Sci. Rep.* **2020**, *10*, 8055. [CrossRef]
53. Hu, J.; Weng, B.; Huang, T.; Gao, J.; Ye, F.; You, L. Deep residual convolutional neural network combining dropout and transfer learning for ENSO forecasting. *Geophys. Res. Lett.* **2021**, *48*, e2021GL093531. [CrossRef]
54. Zhao, J.; Luo, H.; Sang, W.; Sun, K. Spatiotemporal semantic network for ENSO forecasting over long time horizon. *Appl. Intell.* **2022**, 1–17. [CrossRef]
55. Hopfield, J.J. Neural networks and physical systems with emergent collective computational abilities. *Proc. Natl. Acad. Sci. USA* **1982**, *79*, 2554–2558. [CrossRef] [PubMed]
56. Graves, A.; Jaitly, N. Towards end-to-end speech recognition with recurrent neural networks. In Proceedings of the International Conference on Machine Learning, JMLR, Beijing, China, 21–26 June 2014; pp. 1764–1772.
57. Mikolov, T.; Karafiát, M.; Burget, L. Recurrent neural network based language model. *Interspeech* **2010**, *2*, 1045–1048.
58. Cho, K.; Van Merriënboer, B.; Gulcehre, C. Learning phrase representations using RNN encoder-decoder for statistical machine translation. *arXiv* **2014**, arXiv:1406.1078.
59. Hochreiter, S.; Schmidhuber, J. Long short-term memory. *Neural Comput.* **1997**, *9*, 1735–1780. [CrossRef]
60. Zhang, Q.; Wang, H.; Dong, J. Prediction of sea surface temperature using long short-term memory. *IEEE Geosci. Remote Sens. Lett.* **2017**, *14*, 1745–1749. [CrossRef]

61. Broni-Bedaiko, C.; Katsriku, F.A.; Unemi, T. El Niño-Southern Oscillation forecasting using complex networks analysis of LSTM neural networks. *Artif. Life Robot.* **2019**, *24*, 445–451. [CrossRef]
62. Pei, Z.; Yingjie, H.; Bingyi, H. Spring predictability barrier phenomenon in ENSO prediction model based on LSTM deep learning algorithm. *Beijing Da Xue Bao* **2021**, *57*, 1071–1078.
63. Shi, X.; Chen, Z.; Wang, H. Convolutional LSTM network: A machine learning approach for precipitation nowcasting. *Adv. Neural Inf. Process. Syst.* **2015**, *28*, 802–810.
64. He, D.; Lin, P.; Liu, H. Dlenso: A deep learning ENSO forecasting model. In *Proceedings of the Pacific Rim International Conference on Artificial Intelligence*; Springer: Cham, Switzerland, 2019; pp. 12–23.
65. Mu, B.; Peng, C.; Yuan, S.; Chen, L. ENSO forecasting over multiple time horizons using ConvLSTM network and rolling mechanism. In Proceedings of the International Joint Conference on Neural Networks, Budapest, Hungary, 14–19 July 2019; pp. 1–8.
66. Geng, H.; Wang, T. Spatiotemporal model based on deep learning for ENSO forecasts. *Atmosphere* **2021**, *12*, 810. [CrossRef]
67. Zhou, L.; Zhang, R.H. A hybrid neural network model for ENSO prediction in combination with principal oscillation pattern analyses. *Adv. Atmos. Sci.* **2022**, *39*, 889–902. [CrossRef]
68. Scarselli, F.; Gori, M.; Tsoi, A.C. The graph neural network model. *IEEE Trans. Neural Netw.* **2008**, *20*, 61–80. [CrossRef] [PubMed]
69. Kipf, T.N.; Welling, M. Semi-supervised classification with graph convolutional networks. *arXiv* **2016**, arXiv:1609.02907.
70. Cachay, S.R.; Erickson, E.; Bucker, A.F.C. The World as a Graph: Improving El Ni\~no Forecasts with Graph Neural Networks. *arXiv* **2021**, arXiv:2104.05089.
71. Mu, B.; Qin, B.; Yuan, S. ENSO-ASC 1.0.0: ENSO deep learning forecast model with a multivariate air-sea coupler. *Geosci. Model Dev.* **2021**, *14*, 6977–6999. [CrossRef]

Article

Performance Analysis of Feature Subset Selection Techniques for Intrusion Detection

Yousef Almaghthawi, Iftikhar Ahmad * and Fawaz E. Alsaadi

Faculty of Computing and Information Technology, King Abdulaziz University, Jeddah 21589, Saudi Arabia
* Correspondence: iakhan@kau.edu.sa

Abstract: An intrusion detection system is one of the main defense lines used to provide security to data, information, and computer networks. The problems of this security system are the increased processing time, high false alarm rate, and low detection rate that occur due to the large amount of data containing various irrelevant and redundant features. Therefore, feature selection can solve this problem by reducing the number of features. Choosing appropriate feature selection methods that can reduce the number of features without a negative effect on the classification accuracy is a major challenge. This challenge motivated us to investigate the application of different wrapper feature selection techniques in intrusion detection. The performance of the selected techniques, such as the genetic algorithm (GA), sequential forward selection (SFS), and sequential backward selection (SBS), were analyzed, addressed, and compared to the existing techniques. The efficiency of the three feature selection techniques with two classification methods, including support vector machine (SVM) and multi perceptron (MLP), was compared. The CICIDS2017, CSE-CIC-IDS218, and NSL-KDD datasets were considered for the experiments. The efficiency of the proposed models was proved in the experimental results, which indicated that it had highest accuracy in the selected datasets.

Keywords: intrusion detection; genetic algorithm; greedy search; backward elimination learning; NSL-KDD; CIC-IDS-2017; CIC-IDS2018

MSC: 68M25

1. Introduction

Currently, the internet is necessary for storing and transferring the diverse information of users, companies, and governments. Protecting and securing systems and information is necessary. One of the most efficient existing systems used to secure systems and control intrusion activities is the intrusion detection system (IDS). In recent years, several IDSs have been proposed. These security systems have many problems such as an increasing processing time, high false positive rate (FPR), and low detection rate (DR), which are caused by the large amount of data containing various irrelevant and redundant features [1,2]. Feature selection (FS) can solve these problems by reducing the number of features and selecting only useful features. Several feature selection methods are available, but the task of finding which one is suitable for IDS that provides the minimum number of features with the maximum accuracy is a major challenge [2,3]. This challenge motivated us to investigate the application of different FS techniques in intrusion detection. The performance of the selected techniques, such as the GA [4], SFS [5], and SBS [3] were analyzed, addressed, and compared with existing techniques. This study used the recent CICIDS2017 and CSE-CIC-IDS218 [6] datasets as well as the NSL-KDD [7] dataset.

1.1. Intrusion Detection System

IDS is a software or hardware that monitors activities inside and outside the network to detect abnormal ones [3]. It is one of the most important mechanisms that protect

systems and networks against malicious activities [6,8]. This system generates alarms if any abnormal pattern is recognized. IDSs have two types: host-based IDS, which focuses on individual computers, and network-based IDS, which focuses on the traffic between computers. Based on the detection method, IDS can be classified into two categories, namely signature-based and anomaly-based detection [1,9].

1.1.1. Signature-Based Detection

This detection method is also known as misuse detection. It uses the attack signature database to identify intrusions or abnormal activities. When a packet signature matches with a signature in the database, IDSs detect that packet as an intrusion. This detection type can detect known attacks only [1].

1.1.2. Anomaly-Based Detection

In this detection type, IDSs build profiles of the normal network packets. They then analyze and monitor the network packets. When there is any deviation from the normal profile, IDSs detect the abnormal activity. This detection type can detect known and unknown attacks [1].

1.2. Feature Selection Methods

Feature selection methods select the relevant and useful features from a dataset. The goal of FS techniques is to increase the accuracy and detection rate and decrease the execution time and false positive rate. To achieve this goal, FS measures the importance of features and only allows the most important features to enter the classification. The number of features is then reduced as well as the classification time. There are two types of FS methods based on evaluation criteria [8,10]. The first type is the filter method, which it is independent of the classifier. It analyzes each single feature and decides which features are useful and should be trained based on statistical measures [8,11,12]. The second type is the wrapper method, which is dependent on the classifier. In contrast to filter methods, wrapper methods use machine learning algorithms to determine the best feature subset to provide a high classification performance [8,10–12]. The filter and wrapper FS methods are based on two components: a search strategy (e.g., GA, SFS, and SBS) and an objective function or fitness function (e.g., classifier performance in wrapper methods and statistical measure in filter methods). The search strategy determines the optimal subset of features that provide high accuracy and low false alarms results based on the classifier's performance (in wrapper methods) or statistical measures such as information gain (in filter methods) [13]. The search strategy can be made up of exhaustive, heuristic, and random searches [14]. Exhaustive searches are time consuming and impractical because of the large number of combinations to evaluate. For example, a search of an 2^{n-1} possible feature subsets in n features dataset becomes an NP-hard problem as the number of features grow [13]. Heuristic searches such as the forward sequential search and fuzzy systems and random searches such as the GA perform better in large datasets [15–17].

Filter selection methods are faster and have a lower level of complexity than wrapper methods, but the latter are more accurate [18]. Therefore, we used wrapper methods in our study to build an efficient IDS model that provides a low FPR and high ACC with the minimum number of features.

Several features selection methods are available such as the GA, SBS, and SFS, but the problem is to find which one is more suitable for an intrusion detection system (IDS) that provides a minimum number of features with maximum accuracy [2,3].

1.2.1. Sequential Forward Selection (SFS) and Sequential Backward Selection (SBS)

SFS and SBS are simple search techniques that run in iterations and make a greedy decision to select the best local solution in each iteration based on the objective function.

The SFS algorithm starts with an empty set and adds one feature to the subset at each iteration until a stopping criterion is met such as the search is completed or the desired number of subset features is reached. After that, it returns the local optimal solution among iterations or the solution in the desired number of subset features. Figure 1a shows an SFS methodology in which a dataset has three features: F1, F2, and F3. In the first iteration, SFS generates and evaluates several subsets that contain only one feature from the complete set of features. The feature that has the maximum objective function is selected as a local optimal solution in this iteration. In the second iteration, it also generates and evaluates several subsets, in which one feature is added to the selected feature from the previous iteration. Subsequently, each subset is evaluated to select the best local optimal solution. In the third iteration, a feature is added to the selected features from the previous iteration; in this case, the complete set of features is evaluated. Finally, it returns the best local optimal solution among these iterations as the output. By contrast, the SBS algorithm starts from a complete set of features and iteratively removes one feature until a stopping criterion is met. After that, it returns the local optimal solution among iterations or the solution in the desired number of subset features. Figure 1b shows an SBS methodology in which a dataset has three features: F1, F2 and F3.

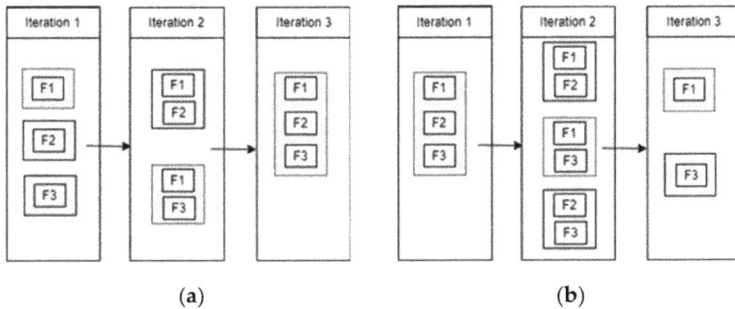

Figure 1. (**a**) An example of SFS; (**b**) an example of SBS.

1.2.2. Genetic Algorithm

The GA is a metaheuristic search and work algorithm based on a direct Darwinian natural selection analogy and genetics in biological systems [12,13]. It is composed of four components: a population of individuals, a fitness function, a selection function, and a genetic operator (e.g., crossover and mutations). The GA randomly generates a population of individuals or chromosomes in which each chromosome represents a solution to the problem [12,13]. The fitness function determines the chromosome's chance of being chosen to create the offspring or the next generation individuals. The selection function selects the parents of the offspring from the current generation, and then the crossover and mutation are applied to the selected parents to generate the offspring or the next generation of individuals. Several selection functions are available, such as the tournament selection method, roulette wheel, and rank selection [13]. Crossover and mutation operators are then applied to the selected individuals or chromosomes to create offspring or the generation of new individuals. Crossover is the exchange of individual bits between two randomly selected parents. Mutation is the alteration of individual bits to generate new individuals. New and different individuals are generated from the current generation after applying crossover and mutation operators. The evaluation of individuals, selection, crossover, and mutation are repeated in a predefined number of generations until a stopping criterion is met.

2. Related Work

Sarvari et al. [19] used the wrapper cuckoo search algorithm (CSA) as an FS technique to build an efficient IDS model. They applied the FS method and trained an artificial neural network (ANN) using a multiverse optimizer (MVO). The proposed model, called MCF &

MVO-ANN, was evaluated using the NSL-KDD dataset. As a result, their model achieved a high ACC (98.16%), a high DR (96.83%), and a low FPR (0.03%).

Saleh et al. [8] presented an IDS approach based on the wrapper NBFS technique to select the best feature subsets. The proposed model combines optimized support vector machines (OSVMs) and prioritized k-nearest neighbors (PKNN) techniques. They used OSVM for rejecting outliers and PKNN to detect attacks. The experimental results indicate that NBFS achieves a higher DR (approximately 90.28%) than other techniques using an NB classifier with 18 selected features. The proposed model also gives a higher DR (95.77% using the NSL-KDD dataset and 93.28% using KDD Cup99) than other techniques.

Ates et al. [5] used the greedy search (GS) algorithm and SVM to detect distributed denial of service (DDoS) attacks. They used GS for FS and SVM as a classifier. The proposed model calculates the distances between the probability distributions of header information using the GS algorithm and Kullback–Leibler divergence. In the testing phase, they used a dataset collected from the MIT Darpa 2000 dataset and a university network and achieved a high AC of 99.99% and a low FPR of 0.001% for the MIT Darpa 200 dataset. However, the proposed model needs to be evaluated using a standard dataset to compare its performance results with recent models.

Asdaghi et al. [20] proposed a new backward elimination (BE) method called Smart-BT for web spam detection. They used index of balance accuracy values as a performance metric. The proposed model uses the chi-square as a pre-processing process. Afterward, Smart-BT selects the relevant and useful features by eliminating a set of features from the initial set. The experimental results show that the Smart-BT gives better classification results than other existing FS techniques such as the ranker search algorithm and particle swarm optimization (PSO) techniques.

Tao et al. [4] introduced an FS technique based on the GA and SVM to improve the IDS. They presented a new fitness function for the chosen FS method to determine the optimal feature subset. The experimental results indicate that their model succeeds in minimizing the number of features to 19 features and achieves a high DR and low FPR using the KDD Cup99 dataset. However, the determination of the weight values for the TPR and selected feature number is carried out manually.

Thakkar and Lohiya [3] presented a performance analysis of FS techniques in IDSs. Chi-square, IG, and recursive feature elimination (REF) were implemented separately as FSs with several ML classifiers such as SVM and ANN. For determining the best combination performance in terms of FS technique and machine learning classifier using the NSL-KDD dataset, they conducted several experiments and reported that the combination of SVM and REF performs well compared with other techniques. The average ACC, precision, recall, and F-score rates were 98.95%, 99.2%, 99.75%, and 98.40%, respectively, for the SVM-REF model.

G Suseendran and T. Nathiya [10] presented a GS FS method to increase the accuracy and decrease the false alarm rate in IDSs. They used correlation feature selection (CFS) to evaluate the selected feature subsets. The RF classifier is used in their model. The experiments showed that their model achieves 98.32% in terms of ACC and 0.40% in terms of the false alarm rate using the NSL-KDD dataset.

Aslahi et al. [21] used the GA for FS and SVM as a classifier for building a new IDS model. Their model reduces the amount of features to 10 features from the original 41 features. The KDD dataset was used in their experiments. Their model achieves 97.30% in terms of accuracy and 1.70% in terms of false alarm rate.

J. Lee et al. [22] proposed a sequential forward floating search (SFFS) method to increase the ACC and decrease the false alarm rate in IDSs. They used a SFFS to select the optimal feature set and RF classifier for the evaluation. The NSL-KDD dataset was used in the experiments for the proposed model. The experiments proved that their model achieves a 0.40% false alarm rate and 99.89% ACC with 10 selected features.

Li et al. [15] proposed a modified random mutation hill climbing (MRMHC) method as a wrapper FS technique. They used a modified linear SVM as an evaluation criterion.

MRMHC generates an initial subset from the complete set of features. Then, the MLSVM evaluates the selected subset and select the best subset. Their experiments on the KDD Cup dataset showed that their approach has a high ACC and low detection time.

Li Y et al. [23] used a gradual feature removal method to select the important features in IDSs. This method deletes the less important features gradually. They used SVM classifier as an objective function in their proposed model. Their model selected 19 features from the KDD Cup dataset, which was used in the experiments. The results obtained an ACC of 98.62%.

Raman et al. [24] proposed a hypergraph-based GA (HG-GA) to build an adaptive IDS with a high ACC and low false alarm rate. HG-GA is used for FS in their proposed model, and SVM is used for classification. In their experiments, they used the NSL-KDD dataset. The proposed model achieves an ACC of 97.14% and a false alarm rate of 0.83%.

Khammassi and Krichen [13] used the GA for FS and linear regression as a classification algorithm. This wrapper approach selects the important features from the original datasets (KDD99 and UNSW-NB15). Then, the DT classifier uses the selected features to measure the efficiency of the selected features. An accuracy of 99.90% and false alarm rate of 0.11% were obtained in their experiments for the KDD99 dataset with 18 features.

Zhou and Cheng [25] developed an IDS model based on correlation-based FS (CSF) and the bat algorithm (BA). They combined RF, C4.5, and forest attributes to build an ensemble approach. The proposed model was evaluated using several IDS datasets such as the CICIDS2017 and NSL-KDD datasets. Their model obtains 94.04% in terms of the detection rate, 2.38% in terms of the FPR and 96.76% in terms of ACC.

Hua Y. [26] developed a hybrid filter and wrapper FS method based on IG and LightGBM. An under-sampling technique was used to balance the used CICIDS2017 dataset. The proposed model achieves an ACC of 98.37%, a precision of 98.17%, and a recall of 98.37% with 10 selected features.

Sugandh Seth et al. [27] used random forest (RF) and principal component analysis (PCA) as a hybrid feature selection method. A light gradient boosting machine (LightGBM) classifier was used to classify the instances of the CIC-IDS-2018 dataset. The authors used an under-sampling technique to balance the dataset. Their model achieves 97.73% in terms of accuracy and a 97.57% F1-Score with 24 selected features.

Alazzam et al. [28] used the pigeon inspired optimizer (PIO) technique. They designed two models of the POI such as the sigmoid PIO and binary cosine PIO to determine the optimal number of features. In the binary PIO, the calculation of the velocity of pigeons is based on the cosine similarity. Their models were evaluated using the decision tree (DT) technique. Through experiments, the models were evaluated using the UNSW-NB15, NSL-KDD, and KDDCUP99 datasets. The result indicate that the proposed model (cosine PIO) outperforms several proposed FS algorithms in terms of AC, F-score, FPR, and TPR.

Mazini et al. [29] used the wrapper artificial bee colony (ABC) algorithm for FS to build an efficient anomaly IDS. The AdaBoost classifier is used for evaluation and classification. Through simulation, the model was evaluated using the ISCXIDS2012 and NSL-KDD datasets. As a result, the proposed model achieves a high DR (99.61%), low FPR (0.01%), and high ACC (98.90%). However, the parameter settings for FS are determined manually.

Aween Saeed and Noor Jameel [30] used the particle swarm optimization algorithm with a decision tree (DT) to build a wrapper feature selection model for IDS. The authors trained and tested their model using a DT classifier. Their model selected 19 features from the CIC-IDS-2018 dataset, which was used in the experiments. The results obtained an ACC of 99.52%.

Jahed Shaikh and Deepak Kshirsagar [31] used information gain (IG) and a correlation attribute evaluation as a feature selection method to select the optimal number of features from the CIS-IDS-2017 dataset. A PART rule-based machine learning classifier was used to evaluate the proposed model. An accuracy of 99.98% and false alarm rate of 1.35% were obtained in their experiments with 56 features.

Patil and Kshirsagar [32] presented an IDS model based on information gain (IG) and ranker method as a feature selection method. The J48 classifier was used to evaluate the selected features. Their model selected 75 features from the CIC-IDS-2017 dataset, which was used in the experiments. The results obtained an ACC of 87.44%.

Many of the above FS techniques have not been evaluated on high-dimension datasets such as CICI-IDS-2017 and CSE-CIC-IDS-2018, which contain more features (80 features) compared with KDD Cup99 and NSL-KDD, which contain 41 features [17]. In addition, certain researchers did not mention the obtained number of selected features, which affects the execution time in terms of classification [2]. Moreover, BE, GA, and GS techniques achieved high results in previous works [3–5,31]. Hence, the present study investigated these FS techniques using several standard datasets to determine the most appropriate technique that provides the minimum number of relevant features with maximum accuracy. A summary of the literature review is shown in Table 1.

Table 1. Summary of the literature review.

Ref.	Feature Selection Algorithm	Classification Algorithm	Dataset	Number of Features	Result (%)
[3]	REF	SVM	NSL-KDD	-	ACC: 98.95 F-score: 99.75
[4]	GA	SVM	KDD Cup99	19	
[5]	Greedy Search	SVM	MIT Darpa 2000	-	ACC: 99.99 FPR: 0.001
[8]	NBFS	PKNN + OSVMs	NSL-KDD	-	DR: 95.77
[10]	Greedy Search + CFS	RF	NSL-KDD	-	ACC: 98.32 FPR: 0.40
[13]	GA	DT	KDD99	18	ACC: 99.90 FPR: 0.11
[15]	MRMHC	MLSVM	KDD Cup	4	TPR: 80.00 FPR: 3.65
[19]	CSA	MCF & MVO-ANN	NSL-KDD	22	ACC: 98.81 DR: 97.25 FPR: 0.03
[21]	GA	SVM	KDD Cup	10	ACC: 97.30 FPR: 1.70
[22]	SFFS	RF	NSL-KDD	10	ACC: 99.89 FPR: 0.40
[23]	Gradual feature removal	SVM	KDD Cup	19	ACC: 98.62
[24]	HG-GA	SVM	NSL-KDD	-	ACC: 97.14 FPR: 0.83
[25]	CSF + BA	RF + C4.5 + FOREST ATTRIBUTE	NSL-KDD CICIDS2017	-	ACC: 96.76 DR: 94.04 FPR: 2.38
[26]	IG	LightGBM	CICIDS2017	10	ACC: 98.37
[27]	Hybrid Feature Selection (RF + PCA)	Light GBM	CICIDS2018	24	ACC: 97.73
[28]	Sigmoid POI	DT	NSL-KDD	18	ACC: 86.90 FPR: 6.40
[28]	Cosine POI	DT	NSL-KDD	5	ACC: 86.90 FPR: 8.80

Table 1. Cont.

Ref.	Feature Selection Algorithm	Classification Algorithm	Dataset	Number of Features	Result (%)
[29]	ABC	AdaBoost	NSL-KDD	25	ACC: 98.90 FPR: 0.01
[30]	Binary-particle swarm optimization	Decision tree	CICIDS2018	19	ACC: 99.52
[31]	IG and correlation attribute evaluation methods	PART	CICIDS2017	56	ACC: 99.98 FPR: 1.35
[32]	Information gain and ranker algorithm	J48	CICIDS2017	75	ACC: 87.44

3. Methodology

Figure 2 shows the methodology which includes: database selection, pre-processing, feature selection, classification, evaluation, as well as the analysis and comparison of results steps. We will explain these steps in the following subsections.

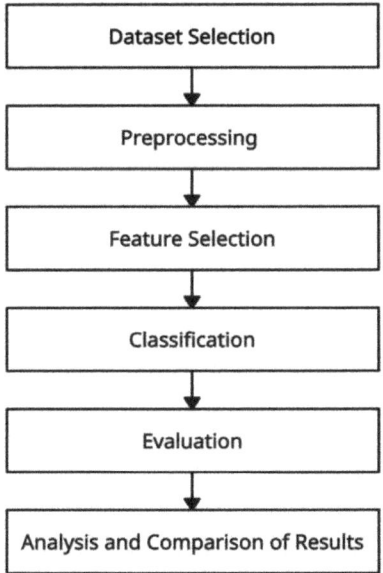

Figure 2. The methodology.

3.1. Dataset Selection

New cybersecurity datasets are available, so this work used three different datasets, namely NSL-KDD, CIC-IDS-2017, and CIC-IDS-2018, for the experiments. All of these datasets were explored to determine which was the most suitable dataset for building an efficient IDS.

3.1.1. NSL-KDD

The NSL-KDD dataset is one of the most widely used benchmarks for IDSs [8,19,28]. It is an upgraded version of the old KDD Cup99 dataset [7]. It has four attack categories: user to root attack (U2R), denial of service attack (DoS), probing attack, and remote to local attack (R2L). The full NSL-KDD training dataset contains 125,973 records, whereas the full

NSL-KDD testing dataset contains 22,254 records. There are 41 features in the NSL-KDD dataset: three of them are nominal or symbolic features, and the rest are numeric features.

3.1.2. CIC-IDS-2017

The CIC-IDS-2017 dataset is a network traffic dataset that consists of both normal and a variety of attack data developed by the Faculty of Computer Science, University of New Brunswick and the Canadian Institute of Cybersecurity (CIC) in 2017. This dataset was captured over a duration of five days, and it uses a large variety of attack types [25,33,34]. In the CIC 2017 dataset, the attack simulation is divided into seven categories namely, botnet, brute force attack, DoS attack, DdoS attack, infiltration attack, web attack, and heart bleed attack [25,34]. This dataset contains over 2.5 million records and 78 features, including the label column, and 19.70% of CIC-IDS-2017 is attack traffic. The dataset has a class imbalance. An unequal distribution between majority and minority classes in databases is known as class imbalance, which affects the performance of classification [34].

3.1.3. CIC-IDS-2018

The CIC-IDS-2018 dataset is a network traffic dataset consisting of both normal and a variety of attack data developed by the Faculty of Computer Science, University of New Brunswick, the CIC, and the Communications Security Establishment (CSE) in 2018 [6]. The structure of this dataset is similar to the previous dataset, and both have a class imbalance. Roughly 17% of the total number of records, which is 16,233,002 records, is attack traffic.

3.2. Preprocessing

The datasets must be preprocessed to avoid inconsistent, irrelevant, and missing data that affect the performance of the IDS. This step may include several tasks such as removing null or missing values, resampling, and scaling.

Certain datasets have missing, null, or symbolic values. These types of data structures make the classification algorithms difficult to handle. Therefore, missing values or null values are removed, and symbolic values are mapped to numeric values. Duplicated records and features should be removed to prevent the classifiers from being biased to the most frequent records [28]. Certain machine learning classifiers such as SVM and MLP are sensitive to feature scaling and require the scaling of a dataset because these classifiers provide weights to the input features according to their data points and inferences for output. Therefore, scaling all the used datasets before the FS, training, and testing phases is highly recommended.

The highly unbalanced datasets in the CIC-IDS-2017 and CIC-IDS-2018 datasets affect the performance of the classifier. The random under-sampling (RUS) technique is used to balance the class distribution. The RUS technique, in which specific majority instances are removed to balance a dataset, provides a good result compared with other sampling methods in the context of the CIC-IDS-2017 dataset [35].

3.3. Feature Subset Selection

This work focused on FS techniques and considered different wrapper FS techniques such as SFS, SBS, and the GA. Different machine learning techniques such as MLP and SVM were applied as the objective functions for the chosen FS techniques.

Not all features of the NSL-KDD, CIC-IDS-2017, and CIC-IDS-2018 datasets are important to build an efficient IDS. A subset of these features can achieve high a ACC and low FPR. Moreover, eliminating certain features using FS techniques is necessary to build an efficient IDS with a high accuracy and low false alarms. In this study, the performance of SFS, SBS, and GA FS techniques were explored. We used the wrapper FS approach. This approach is based on three components: a search strategy, a classifier, and an evaluation function [13,14]. We used three search strategies (SFS, SBS, and the GA). In each search strategy, we used SVM and MLP as classifiers. The evaluation of the feature subsets was a fitness function based on a custom score of the cross-validation of the previous classifiers. Cross-validation is a resampling technique that divides the dataset into equal different portions to train and test a model on different iterations. Cross-validation gives an insight on how the model can be generalized to an unknown dataset, and it is a useful technique to identify the overfitting of a model. In the FS phase, two-fold, five-fold, and ten-fold cross validation are used. Our goal in this study was to propose an FS method that increases the ACC and decreases the false alarm rate with the minimum number of features. Therefore, our objective function or fitness function was based on three criteria: the classification accuracy of SVM or MLP, the false alarm rate or FPR, and the number of selected features. Hence, the subset having the smallest number of features, the highest ACC, and the lowest FPR produces the highest objective function.

Several objective functions are available. Hence, we investigated several objective functions in the FS phase. Bamakan et al. [36] proposed an objective function based on the detection rate, the false alarm rate of the classifier, and the number of selected features, as shown in Equation (1). Hang and Wang [37] proposed an objective function based on the accuracy and the number of selected features, as shown in Equation (2).

$$Objective\ Function(X) = DR(X)*WA + (1-FPR)*WF + (1-N*WN) \quad (1)$$

$$Objective\ Function(X) = ACC(X)*WA + (1-N*WN) \quad (2)$$

where N is the number of selected features in the subset, WA is a predefined weight for the accuracy score of the subset, WF is a predefined weight for the FPR of the subset, WD is a predefined weight for the DR of the subset, and WN is a predefined weight for the number of selected features in the subset. All the weights should be in range [0–1].

In the following, we explain the selected FS techniques in this study, which were the SFS, SBS, and GA feature methods.

3.3.1. Sequential Forward Selection (SFS)

SFS is a wrapper FS that selects k features from an initial d features dataset where k < d through a number of iterations. It selects the best feature subset by starting from an empty dataset and adding one feature at a time based on the classifier performance in an iterative process until a stopping criterion is met, such as a feature subset of the specified size k being reached. If the desired number of features is in a range (e.g., 1–40), SFS selects the feature subset that contains the highest objective function (e.g., accuracy) in that range. SFS flowchart is shown in Figure 3.

3.3.2. Sequential Backward Selection (SBS)

This method is essentially the reverse of the above method. It selects the best feature subset by starting from the original full feature dataset and removes one feature at a time based on the classifier performance in an iterative process until a stopping criterion is met, such as a feature subset of the specified size k being reached. If the desired number of features is in a range (e.g., 1–40), SBS selects the feature subset that contains the highest objective function (e.g., accuracy) in that range. SBS flowchart is shown in Figure 4.

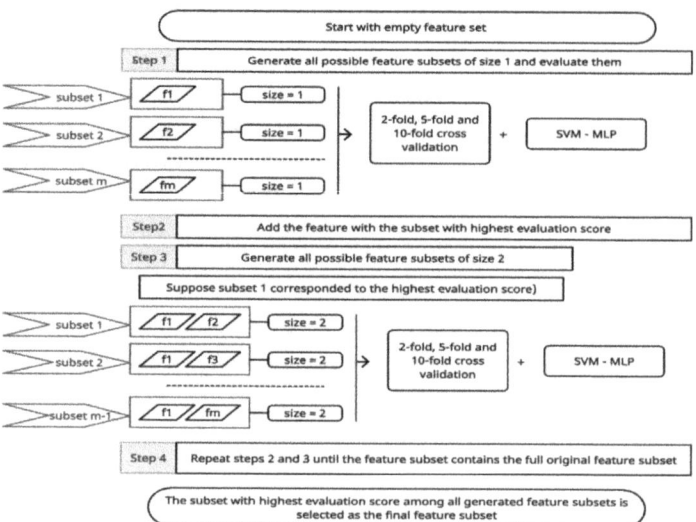

Figure 3. SFS flowchart.

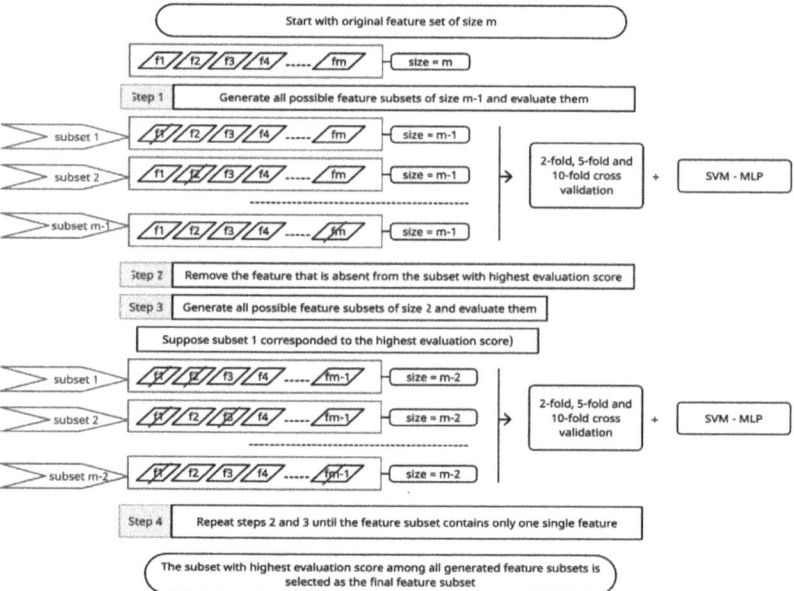

Figure 4. SBS flowchart.

3.3.3. Genetic Algorithm (GA)

The GA is composed of five components: the initiation of the population, a fitness function, a selection function, genetic operators (e.g., crossover and mutations), and stopping criteria. Below, we explain each component in a separate section.

Population Initiation

First, the GA randomly generates a population of individuals or chromosomes in which each chromosome represents a solution for the problem [12,13]. Each chromosome or individual is encoded as binary; a feature is either included or not in the subset. The number of individuals or the population size is defined by the user (n_population). A large population size provides a large search space to the GA but it increases the required time to evaluate all the individuals of the population. In contrast, a small population size provides a small search space to the GA but the required time to evaluate all the individuals of population is less than in the first situation.

Fitness Function

The fitness function determines the chromosome's chance of being chosen to create the offspring or the next generation. The fitness function can be any metric of the classifier performance, such as accuracy. For example, if the classifier accuracy is chosen to be the fitness function, the chromosome having the highest accuracy produces the highest fitness value [13].

Selection Function

The selection function selects the parents of offspring or the next generation of individuals from the current generation. In this study, we used the tournament selection method that selects the best individuals from a population of individuals. It randomly selects a predefined number of individuals (tournament_size) and runs a tournament among them. The individual or chromosome with the best fitness is the winner of the tournament and it is selected for generating the next generation. The tournament selection is repeated several times, as specified by the user. The best induvial with the highest fitness function among other individuals in each generation is added to the population of the next generation. Hence, each generation in the GA has an individual that has the highest fitness function among its previous generations.

Crossover Process

The crossover operator is used to generate new offspring or solutions from the current solutions (the parents). For each two randomly selected individuals or chromosomes, a crossover is performed with a predefined probability in a range [0–1]. Several crossover operators are available, such as one-point, two-point, and uniform crossovers. In this study, we used a uniform crossover in which each bit in a parent's chromone is swapped based on a predefined probability and a random number in a range [0–1]. For instance, if the predefined probability is 0.5 and the random number is 0.7, in this case the random number is equal to or greater than the predefined probability. Therefore, bit swapping occurs. This process is repeated for all bits in the parents' chromosome. Hence, we have two probabilities: a probability for applying crossover between two individuals and a probability for exchanging the bit value between two individuals.

Mutation Process

Mutation, which is applied after the crossover process, is the alteration of individual bits to generate new individuals from the current individuals. Several mutation operators are available, such as inversion mutation, insertion mutation, and flip-bit mutation [38]. In this study, we used flip-bit mutation, which switches certain bits from 1 to 0 or vice versa. Two probabilities are used in mutation: the probability of applying mutation on the individual and the probability of mutation or flipping the bit value of the individual. New different individuals are generated from the current generation after applying crossover and mutation operators.

Stopping Criteria

The evaluation of individuals, selection, crossover, and mutation are repeated in a predefined number of generations until a stopping criterion is met (e.g., the maximum number of generation or a specified number of generations is reached when the objective function cannot improve).

3.4. Classification

The selected feature subsets are then fed to a classifier such as MLP and SVM to classify the inputs as normal or attack traffic. Different classifiers are investigated to identify the most suitable one for training and testing the IDS model.

3.4.1. Support Vector Machine (SVM)

SVM is a supervised learning model that provides a good level of accuracy in classification problems [4,8,10,21,33]. SVM builds one or more hyperplanes by using the nearest training data points of each data (called support vectors). Then, it tries to maximize the margin between the data points. In the implementation of SVMs, there are certain kernel functions such as polynomial, sigmoid, and radial kernel functions (RBF). Making the trade-off between constant C and the type of kernel function is crucial to achieve a good result for the classification [8].

3.4.2. Artificial Neural Network Multi Perceptron (ANN-MLP)

MLP is also a supervised learning model. It is a class of feedforward ANN. There are at least three layers in MLP: an input, hidden, and output layer [19]. Each layer contains one or more neurons. Each neuron connects with a specific weight to every neuron in the following layer [19]. The learning in MLP occurs by changing the weights after each input of data.

3.5. Evaluation

The performance of each FS technique is evaluated on the basis of performance measures such as ACC, FPR and F1 score as well as the number of selected features. Several metrics are available for evaluating feature selection algorithms such as accuracy, false positive rate, detection rate, and precision. These metrics can be calculated using the confusion matrix that is represented by the following four main parameters:

- True positive (TP): represents number of attack samples classified correctly.
- True negative (TN): represents number of normal samples classified correctly.
- False positive (FP): represents number of normal samples classified wrongly.
- False negative (FN): represents number of attack samples classified wrongly.

In binary classification, a confusion matrix is a table or matrix of size 2×2 that is used to describe the performance of machine learning classifiers. A confusion matrix is shown in Table 2, where each column represents the predictive records and each row represents the actual records.

Table 2. Confusion matrix.

	Predictive Records	
Actual records	TP	FP
	FN	TN

The definition and formulas of the performance metrics are as follows [28]:
- Accuracy: represents the proportion of correct classified instances to the total number of classifications, as in Equation (3).

$$Accuracy = (TP + TN)/(TP + TN + FP + FN) \qquad (3)$$

- FPR (a.k.a. false alarms): represents the proportion of the normal instances that are identified as attack or abnormal instances, as in Equation (4).

$$FPR = FP/(TN + FP) \qquad (4)$$

- Precision: represents the ratio of correctly predicted positive instances to the total predicted positive instances, as in Equation (5).

$$Percision = TP/TP + FP \qquad (5)$$

- Recall (a.k.a. detection rate (DR)): represents the ratio of correctly predicted positive instances to the overall number of actual positive instances, as in Equation (6).

$$Recall = TP/TP + FN \qquad (6)$$

- F1 score: represents the weighted average of precision and recall values, as in Equation (7).

$$F1\ score = 2 * \frac{percision * recall}{percision + recall} \qquad (7)$$

3.6. Analysis and Comparison of Results

The results obtained from the previous step were analyzed and compared with one another to select an efficient IDS model with a high accuracy, low false alarm, and a small number of features.

4. Implementation

In this section, the experimental settings are presented, and the effectiveness of the SFS, SBS, and GA methods are illustrated. The experimental environment was set up as follows: a desktop computer running Windows 10 on an Intel Core i9-12th Gen with 48 GB RAM, Anaconda 3 with Python 3 distribution, the Scikit-learn library, and the Jupyter notebook [39]. Figure 5 illustrates and summarizes the steps of implementation, which are presented in detail.

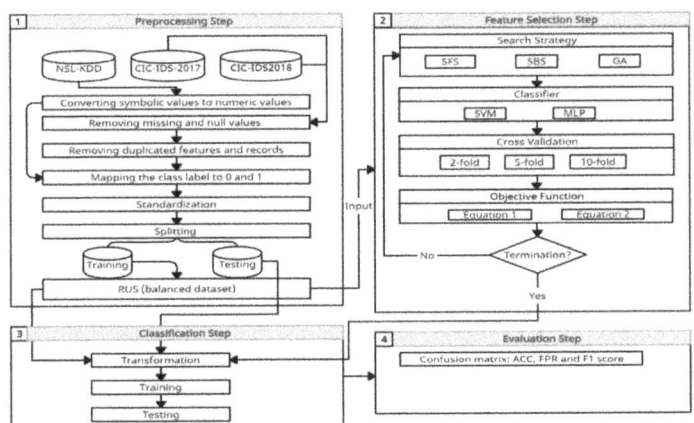

Figure 5. Implementation flowchart.

4.1. Preprocessing

The processing phase we used consist of eight steps which are:

1. In the NSL-KDD dataset, three categorical features, which are flag, service, and protocol_type features, are mapped to numeric values ranging from 0 to $N-1$, where N is the number of symbols in the feature.
2. Missing values or null values are removed from the CIC-IDS-2017 and CIC-IDS-2018 datasets. A script written in Python is used for removing these records.

3. A duplicate feature in CIC-IDS-2017, namely Fwd Header Length, is removed manually. The timestamp feature is removed manually in CIC-IDS-2018. In addition, ten features are removed manually in CIC-IDS-2017 and CIC-IDS-2018, as they have zero values.
4. Duplicated records are removed in all datasets. A script written in Python is used for removing these records.
5. The class label is mapped to 0 for normal class and 1 for attack. As we use binary classification in this study, all the sub-category attack labels are mapped to 1. The resulted label feature contains 0 for normal records and 1 for attack records.
6. The StandardScaler method from the sklearn library in Python is applied to standardize the feature variance in all the used datasets.
7. All datasets are split into 70% training and 30% testing datasets.
8. The random under-sampling (RUS) technique is applied in all training datasets.

4.2. Feature Selection

The scikit-learn library and Jupyter notebook are used to implement SFS, SBS, and GA FS methods. The performance evaluation of the selected features of the subsets in each iteration in SFS, SBS, and the GA is carried out using the cross-validation technique in which the dataset is randomly divided into several K subsets. One subset is used for testing the model, and the remaining subsets are used for training. This process is iterated K times, and the testing subset is different in each iteration [13]. Table 3 shows the selected weights in the selected fitness functions.

Table 3. Parameters of fitness functions.

Objective Function	Parameter	Value
Equation (1)	WD	0.45
	WF	0.45
	WN	0.1
Equation (2)	WA	0.94
	WN	0.06

Implementation of SFS, SBS and the GA

The MLxtend library in Python is used to implement SFS and SBS, while the Sklearn-genetic, which is a genetic FS module for scikit-learn, is used to implement the GA [40,41]. SVM and MLP are used separately as estimators in SFS, SBS and the GA. To evaluate the subsets of selected features in each iteration, two-fold, five-fold, and ten-fold cross validation are used separately in the implementation of SFS, SBS and the GA. The parameters of SFS and SBS are configured as shown in Table 4, while the parameters of the GA are configured as shown in Table 5.

Table 4. Parameters of SFS and SBS.

Parameter	Value	Parameter	Value
Estimator	SVM	n_jobs	−1
	MLP	floating	False
Scoring	Equation (1)	cv	2
	Equation (2)		5
k_features	NSL-KDD (1,40)		10
	CIC-IDS-2017 (1,66)	forward	True (SFS)
	CIC-IDS-2018 (1,67)		False (SBS)

Table 5. Parameters of GA.

Parameter	Value	Parameter	Value
Estimator	SVM	crossover_proba	0.6
	MLP	crossover_independent_proba	0.6
Scoring	Equation (1)	mutation_proba	0.1
	Equation (2)	mutation_indenpdent_proba	0.1
Max_features	NSL-KDD (40)	caching	True
	CIC-IDS-2017 (66)	n_gen_no_change	NSL-KDD (50)
	CIC-IDS-2018 (67)		CIC-IDS-2017 (65)
n_population	NSL-KDD (60)		CIC-IDS-2018 (65)
	CIC-IDS-2017 (80)	n_jobs	−1
	CIC-IDS-2018 (80)	verbose	1
n_generations	NSL-KDD (50)	cv	2
	CIC-IDS-2017 (65)		5
	CIC-IDS-2018 (65)		10

4.3. Training and Testing

For each selected subset, we transform the original training dataset to have the same number of selected features from the FS phase. The selected feature subsets from the previous FS methods are fitted into the same used classifier in the FS phase to determine and evaluate the performance of the selected feature subset. Hence, SVM is used to evaluate the selected feature subsets selected from the FS phase when SVM is used as an objective function. MLP is used to evaluate the selected feature subsets selected from the FS phase when MLP is used an objective function.

4.4. Results and Discussion

The experimental results of the chosen feature selection methods are presented in this section.

Table 6 shows the result of SFS, SBS and the GA based on SVM and MLP in the NSL-KDD dataset using an objective function based on accuracy and the number of selected features. As shown in the table, the results are presented and compared using different cross validations such as two-fold, five-fold, and ten-fold cross validation for each combination of FS method and classifier. The highest accuracy among all these combinations is 99.23% with the GA+SVM, with a 0.77% false alarm rate and 29 selected features using two-fold cross validation in the feature selection phase. This model also has the highest F1 score, of 99.20%, among the models. The lowest false alarm rate among these combinations is 0.73% with the GA+SVM, with an accuracy of 99.06%. SBS+SVM performs well with a different number of folds. It obtained 98.92%, 98.95%, and 98.99% in terms of accuracy and 1.20%, 1.36%, and 1.16% in terms of FPR, respectively, with the same selected number of features (10 features). A graphical illustration of Table 6 is shown in Figure 6.

Table 7 shows the result of SFS, SBS, and the GA based on SVM and MLP in the CIC-IDS-2017 dataset using an objective function based on accuracy and the number of selected features. As shown in the table, the highest accuracy among all these combinations is 99.96% with the GA+MLP, with a 0.03% false alarm rate and 40 selected features using five-fold cross validation in the feature selection phase. The lowest false alarm rate among all these combinations is 0.01% with SFS+MLP and the GA+SVM, with accuracies of 88.74% and 99.9%, respectively. SBS+SVM performs well with a different number of folds. It obtained 99.65%, 99.81%, and 99.75% in terms of accuracy and 0.50%, 0.13%, and 0.27% in terms of FPR, with the six, five, and five selected features, respectively. An illustration of Table 7 is shown in Figure 7.

Table 6. Performance of SFS, SBS and the GA using objective function based on accuracy and number of selected features in NSL-KDD.

Metric	Fold	SFS+SVM	SFS+MLP	SBS+SVM	SBS+MLP	GA+SVM	GA+MLP
Accuracy (%)	2	98.94	97.83	98.95	98.25	99.23	99.01
	5	98.80	97.66	98.82	98.81	99.16	99.02
	10	98.89	98.78	98.88	98.16	99.06	99.06
Number of selected features	2	10	9	10	16	29	38
	5	9	9	10	14	27	35
	10	10	13	10	13	29	36
FPR (%)	2	1.14	2.51	0.99	1.50	0.77	0.95
	5	1.44	2.84	1.18	1.26	0.84	1.20
	10	1.39	1.59	1.26	1.84	0.73	1.16
F1 (%)	2	98.90	97.75	98.81	98.17	99.20	98.98
	5	98.76	97.59	98.77	98.77	99.13	98.98
	10	98.85	98.83	98.84	98.09	99.03	99.02

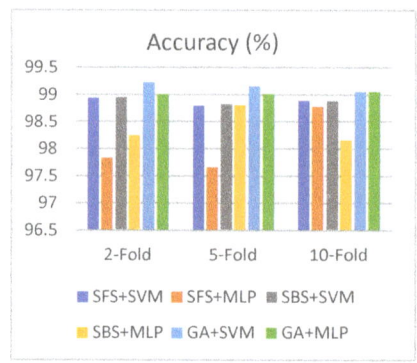

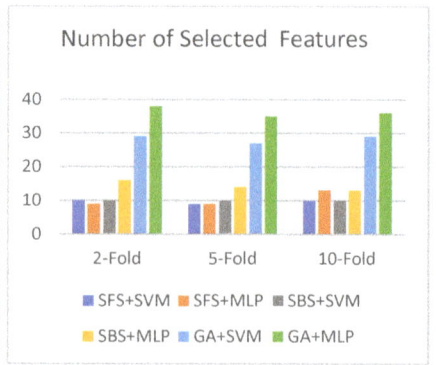

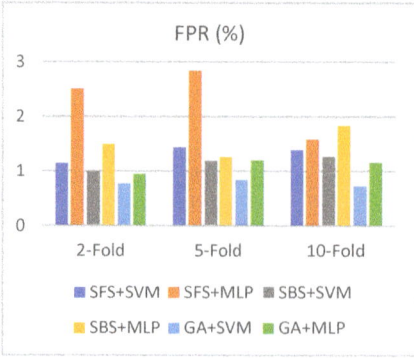

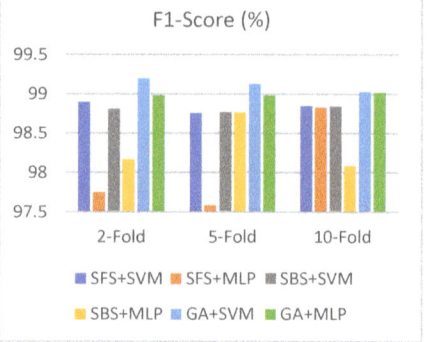

Figure 6. Performance of SFS, SBS and GA using objective function based on accuracy and number of selected features in NSL-KDD.

Table 7. Performance of SFS, SBS, and GA using objective function based on accuracy and number of selected features in CIC-IDS-2017.

Metric	Fold	SFS+SVM	SFS+MLP	SBS+SVM	SBS+MLP	GA+SVM	GA+MLP
Accuracy (%)	2	99.75	99.83	99.65	94.79	99.94	99.93
	5	99.78	89.61	99.81	99.84	99.94	99.96
	10	99.28	88.74	99.75	99.83	99.9	99.91
Number of selected features	2	5	7	5	6	42	44
	5	5	5	6	5	39	40
	10	5	5	5	6	45	38
FPR (%)	2	0.27	0.04	0.5	1.12	0.02	0.02
	5	0.22	0.03	0.13	0.17	0.02	0.03
	10	1.44	0.01	0.27	0.12	0.01	0.03
F1 (%)	2	99.78	99.86	99.69	95.24	99.95	99.96
	5	99.81	89.93	99.83	99.86	99.93	99.94
	10	99.36	89.00	99.78	99.85	99.93	99.39

Figure 7. Performance of SFS, SBS, and GA using objective function based on accuracy and number of selected features in CIC-IDS-2017.

Table 8 shows the result of SFS, SBS, and the GA based on SVM and MLP in the CIC-IDS-2018 dataset using an objective function based on accuracy and the number of selected features. As shown in the table, the highest accuracy among all these combinations is 99.87% with the SFS+MLP and SBS+MLP models. SFS+MLP obtains a lower FPR, of 0.1%, than SBS+MLP with eight selected features using five-fold cross validation in the feature selection phase. Three models, which are SFS+MLP, SBS+SVM, and the GA+MLP obtain the lowest false alarm rate, of 0.1%, among the models. A demonstration of Table 8 is shown in Figure 8.

Table 8. Performance of SFS, SBS, and GA using objective function based on accuracy and number of selected features in CIC-IDS-2018.

Metric	Fold	SFS+SVM	SFS+MLP	SBS+SVM	SBS+MLP	GA+SVM	GA+MLP
Accuracy (%)	2	99.46	99.87	99.78	99.87	99.71	99.69
	5	97.67	99.87	99.64	99.51	99.82	99.83
	10	97.72	99.80	99.69	99.67	99.8	99.78
Number of selected features	2	21	11	7	8	18	23
	5	6	8	7	10	21	26
	10	6	8	8	11	24	25
FPR (%)	2	0.32	0.90	0.10	0.90	0.16	0.21
	5	0.18	0.10	0.10	0.84	0.16	0.10
	10	0.30	0.30	0.20	0.90	0.19	0.17
F1 (%)	2	99.46	99.88	99.77	99.88	99.71	99.69
	5	97.61	99.85	99.64	99.51	99.82	99.80
	10	97.63	99.80	99.71	99.74	99.80	99.75

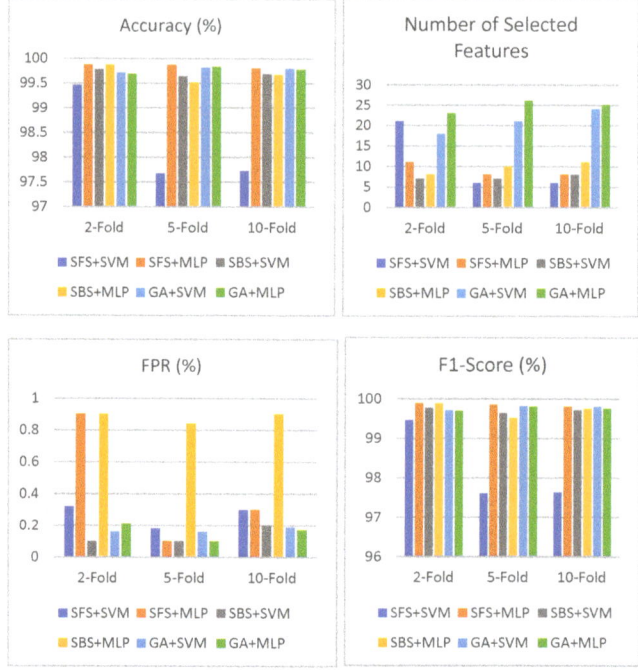

Figure 8. Performance of SFS, SBS, and GA using objective function based on accuracy and number of selected features in CIC-IDS-2018.

Table 9 shows the result of SFS, SBS, and the GA based on SVM and MLP in the NSL-KDD dataset using an objective function based on detection rate, false positive rate, and number of selected features. As shown in the table, the GA+SVM obtains the highest accuracy and lowest false alarm rate among all these combinations. It obtains an accuracy of 99.21% and an FPR of 0.83% with 30 selected features using 10-fold cross validation in the feature selection phase. In addition, this model obtains an accuracy of 99.19% and an FPR of 0.81% with 33 selected features using five-fold cross validation in the feature selection phase. Table 9 is depicted in Figure 9.

Table 9. Performance of SFS, SBS, and GA using objective function based on DR, FPR, and number of selected features in NSL-KDD.

Metric	Fold	SFS+SVM	SFS+MLP	SBS+SVM	SBS+MLP	GA+SVM	GA+MLP
Accuracy (%)	2	98.77	97.83	97.76	97.7	99.18	99.11
	5	98.19	97.66	98.82	97.99	99.19	98.98
	10	98.19	98.82	98.65	97.93	99.21	98.93
Number of selected features	2	9	9	6	9	27	37
	5	7	9	10	10	33	28
	10	7	12	8	10	30	39
FPR (%)	2	1.46	2.51	1.94	2.76	0.89	0.85
	5	1.85	2.84	1.81	1.76	0.81	1.17
	10	1.85	1.65	1.82	2.64	0.83	1.28
F1 (%)	2	98.72	97.96	97.66	97.63	99.15	99.08
	5	98.12	97.59	98.78	97.91	99.16	98.92
	10	98.12	98.09	98.61	98.01	99.18	98.88

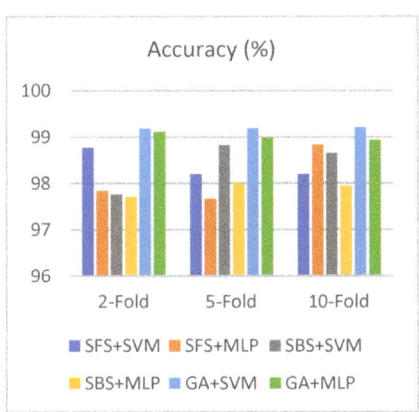 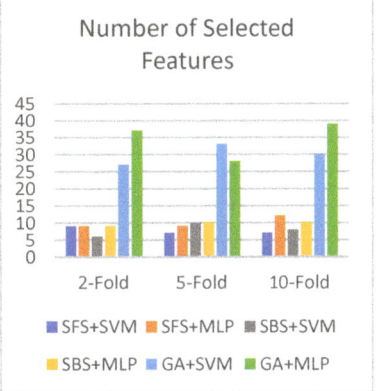

Figure 9. Cont.

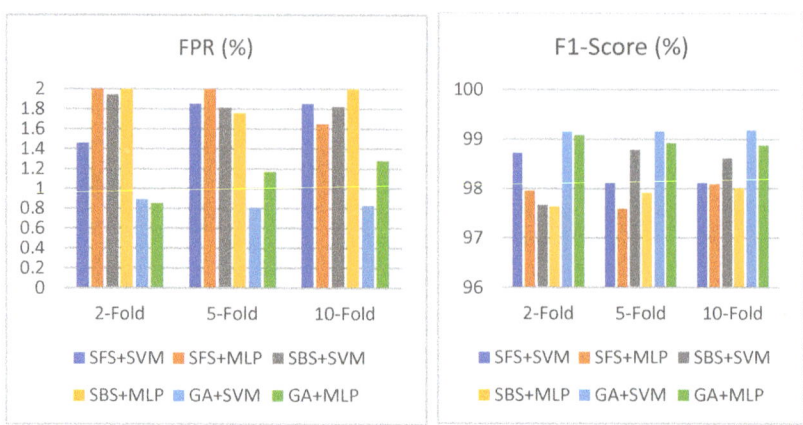

Figure 9. Performance of SFS, SBS, and GA using objective function based on DR, FPR, and number of selected features in NSL-KDD.

Table 10 shows the results of SFS, SBS, and the GA based on SVM and MLP in the CIC-IDS-2017 dataset using an objective function based on the detection rate, false positive rate, and number of selected features. As shown in the table, GA+MLP obtains the highest accuracy, of 99.95%, among all these combinations and a low false alarm rate of 0.007% with 35 selected features using two-fold cross validation in the feature selection phase. The GA models obtain a higher accuracy than the SFS and SBS models and give a low false alarm rate (less than 0.035%) in all their combinations. Figure 10 displays Table 10 in its entirety.

Table 10. Performance of SFS, SBS, and GA using objective function based on DR, FPR, and number of selected features in CIC-IDS-2017.

Metric	Fold	SFS+SVM	SFS+MLP	SBS+SVM	SBS+MLP	GA+SVM	GA+MLP
Accuracy (%)	2	97.86	98.07	99.86	96.41	99.94	99.95
	5	99.87	97.9	99.9	98.17	99.93	99.91
	10	99.87	97.62	99.89	94.72	99.94	99.93
Number of selected features	2	27	17	16	10	38	35
	5	31	24	14	14	42	40
	10	29	24	19	9	41	33
FPR (%)	2	0.06	0.05	0.03	0.03	0.003	0.007
	5	0.09	0.003	0.05	0.05	0.03	0.01
	10	0.06	0.05	0.04	0.04	0.02	0.005
F1 (%)	2	98.08	98.28	99.88	96.74	99.93	99.92
	5	99.89	98.12	99.92	98.36	99.93	99.93
	10	99.89	97.86	99.91	95.12	99.92	99.89

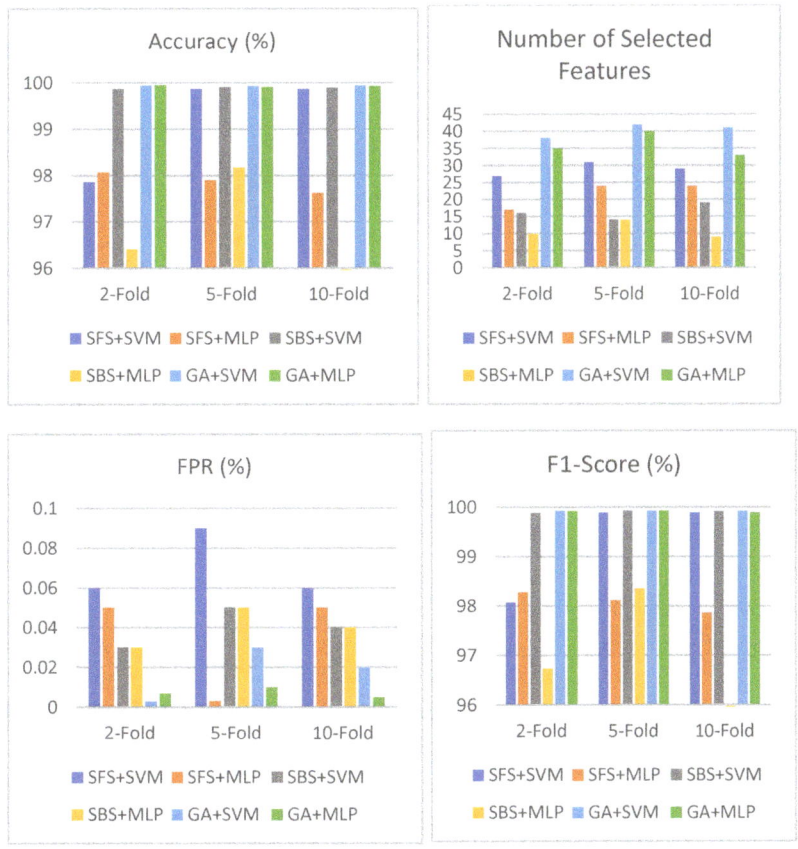

Figure 10. Performance of SFS, SBS, and GA using objective function based on DR, FPR, and number of selected features in CIC-IDS-2017.

Table 11 shows the result of SFS, SBS, and the GA based on SVM and MLP in the CIC-IDS-2018 dataset using an objective function based on the detection rate, false positive rate, and number of selected features. As shown in the table, the GA+MLP obtains the highest accuracy, of 99.92%, and lowest false alarm rate, of 0.07%, with 47 selected features using two-fold cross validation in the feature selection phase. The GA models obtain a higher accuracy than the SFS and SBS models and give a low false alarm rate (less than 0.20%) in all their combinations. Figure 11 depicts Table 11 in detail.

Table 11. Performance of SFS, SBS, and GA using objective function based on DR, FPR, and number of selected features in CIC-IDS-2018.

Metric	Fold	SFS+SVM	SFS+MLP	SBS+SVM	SBS+MLP	GA+SVM	GA+MLP
Accuracy (%)	2	97.41	97.57	98.2	99.56	99.56	99.92
	5	97.41	99.78	99.6	99.09	99.8	99.89
	10	97.38	98.21	99.01	99.16	99.74	99.82

Table 11. Cont.

Metric	Fold	SFS+SVM	SFS+MLP	SBS+SVM	SBS+MLP	GA+SVM	GA+MLP
Number of selected features	2	6	8	6	8	14	47
	5	4	7	5	7	15	41
	10	6	7	6	9	17	38
FPR (%)	2	0.35	0.19	0.36	0.15	0.13	0.07
	5	0.30	0.16	0.19	1.31	0.19	0.11
	10	0.33	0.19	0.20	1.22	0.15	0.19
F1 (%)	2	97.35	97.51	98.91	99.55	99.56	99.93
	5	97.34	99.78	99.60	99.07	99.80	99.89
	10	98.85	98.83	98.84	98.09	99.03	99.02

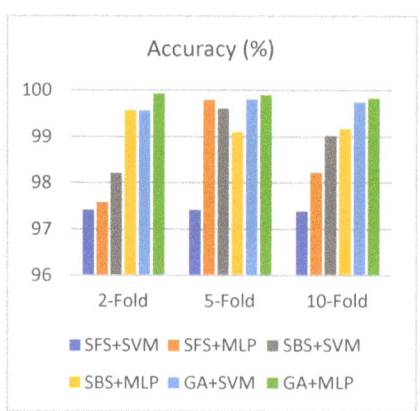
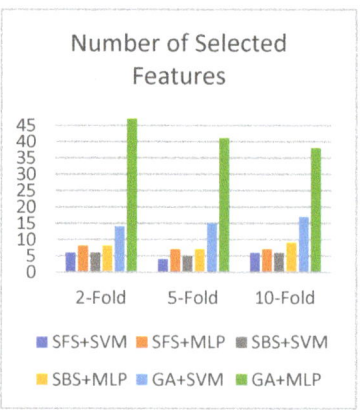
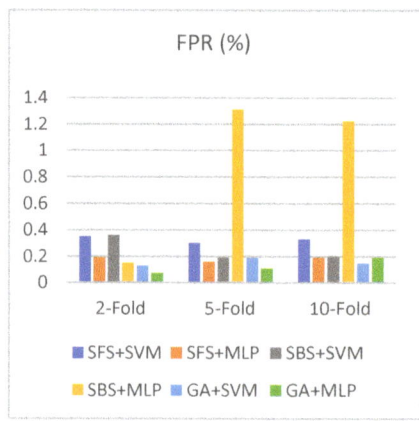
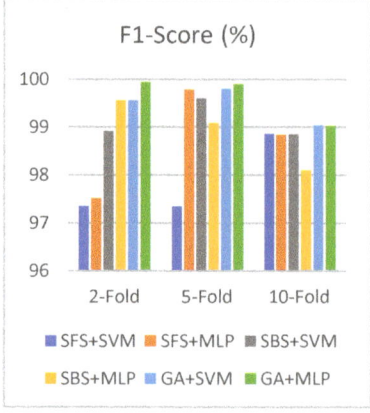

Figure 11. Performance of SFS, SBS, and GA using objective function based on DR, FPR, and number of selected features in CIC-IDS-2018.

4.5. Performance Comparison with the Recent Methods

Tables 12–14 show the comparison between our best obtained results and those of other recent methods in the NSL-KDD, CIC-IDS-2017, and CIC-IDS-2018 datasets.

Table 12. Performance comparison with recent methods in NSL-KDD.

Ref.	FS Tech.	Classifier	Number of Selected Features	ACC (%)	FPR (%)
[19]	CSA	MCF+MVO-ANN	22	98.81	0.02
[28]	Sigmoid POI	DT	18	86.90	6.40
[28]	Cosine POI	DT	5	88.30	8.80
[29]	ABC	AdaBoost	25	98.90	0.01
Proposed model	GA	SVM	29	99.23	0.77

Table 13. Performance comparison with recent methods CIC-IDS-2017.

Ref.	FS Tech.	Classifier	Number of Selected Features	ACC (%)	FPR (%)
[31]	IG and correlation attribute evaluation methods	PART	56	99.98	1.35
[32]	Information gain and ranker algorithm	J48	75	87.44	-
[26]	IG	LightGBM	10	98.37	-
Proposed model	GA	MLP	35	99.95	0.007
Proposed model	GA	SVM	38	99.94	0.003

Table 14. Performance comparison with recent methods in CIC-IDS-2018.

Ref.	FS Tech.	Classifier	Number of Selected Features	ACC (%)	FPR (%)
[27]	Hybrid feature selection (RF + PCA)	Light GBM	24	97.73	-
[30]	Binary-particle swarm optimization	Decision tree	19	99.52	-
Proposed model	SFS	MLP	11	99.87	0.90
Proposed model	SBS	MLP	8	99.87	0.90
Proposed model	GA	MLP	47	99.92	0.07

5. Conclusions

This paper has presented a comparative study of sequential forward selection, sequential backward selection, and genetic algorithm feature selection methods in intrusion detection systems to select an efficient IDS model that provides a high accuracy and low false alarm with a minimum number of features. The efficiencies of the three feature selection techniques with two classification methods, namely SVM and MLP, were compared. These methods were applied to three publicly available intrusion detection system data sets, namely NSL-KDD, CICIDS2017, and CICIDS2018. This paper has presented an assessment of these datasets, identifying their limitations and providing solutions to overcome these limitations.

The performance of the proposed models was analyzed, addressed, and compared to existing techniques. The efficiencies of the proposed models were proven in the experimental results, which indicated that the highest accuracy in the NSL-KDD dataset was 99.23%, achieved using the GA+SVM, with a 0.77% false alarm rate and 29 selected features using two-fold cross validation in the feature selection phase. This model also has the highest F1 score, of 99.20%, among the models. In the CICIDS2017 dataset, the highest accuracy among the proposed models is 99.96%, achieved with the GA+MLP, with a 0.03% false alarm rate and 40 selected features using five-fold cross validation in the feature selection phase. The lowest false alarm rate among the proposed models is 0.01% in the case of SFS+MLP and the GA+SVM, with accuracies of 88.74% and 99.9%, respectively. In the CSE-CIC-IDS218 dataset, SFS+MLP and SBS+MLP achieved an accuracy of 99.87%. SFS+MLP obtains a lower FPR, of 0.10%, than SBS+MLP with eight selected features using five-fold cross validation in the feature selection phase.

Author Contributions: Conceptualization, I.A. and Y.A.; methodology, I.A.; software, Y.A.; validation, I.A., Y.A. and F.E.A.; formal analysis, I.A. and Y.A.; investigation, Y.A.; resources I.A. and F.E.A.; data curation, I.A.; writing—original draft preparation, Y.A.; writing—review and editing, I.A., Y.A. and F.E.A.; visualization, I.A.; supervision, I.A. and F.E.A.; project administration, I.A.; funding acquisition, I.A. All authors have read and agreed to the published version of the manuscript.

Funding: This research work was funded by Institutional Fund Projects under grant no. (IFPRC-076-611-2020). The authors acknowledge technical and financial support from the Ministry of Education and King Abdulaziz University, DSR, Jeddah, Saudi Arabia.

Institutional Review Board Statement: Not applicable.

Informed Consent Statement: Not applicable.

Data Availability Statement: Not applicable.

Acknowledgments: This research work was funded by Institutional Fund Projects under grant no. (IFPRC-076-611-2020). Therefore, the authors gratefully acknowledge technical and financial support from the Ministry of Education and King Abdulaziz University, DSR, Jeddah, Saudi Arabia.

Conflicts of Interest: There is no conflict of authors.

References

1. Thakkar, A.; Lohiya, R. A survey on intrusion detection system: Feature selection, model, performance measures, application perspective, challenges, and future research directions. *Artif. Intell. Rev.* **2022**, *55*, 453–563. [CrossRef]
2. Alhakami, W.; Alharbi, A.; Bourouis, S.; Alroobaea, R.; Bouguila, N. Network Anomaly Intrusion Detection Using a Nonparametric Bayesian Approach and Feature Selection. *IEEE Access* **2019**, *7*, 52181–52190. [CrossRef]
3. Thakkar, A.; Lohiya, R. Attack classification using feature selection techniques: A comparative study. *J. Ambient. Intell. Humaniz. Comput.* **2020**, *12*, 1249–1266. [CrossRef]
4. Tao, P.; Sun, Z.; Sun, Z. An Improved Intrusion Detection Algorithm Based on GA and SVM. *IEEE Access* **2018**, *6*, 13624–13631. [CrossRef]
5. Ates, C.; Ozdel, S.; Anarim, E. A New Network Anomaly Detection Method Based on Header Information Using Greedy Algorithm. In Proceedings of the 6th International Conference on Control, Decision and Information Technologies (Codit 2019), Paris, France, 23–26 April 2019; IEEE: New York, NY, USA, 2019; pp. 657–662. [CrossRef]
6. Sharafaldin, I.; Lashkari, A.H.; Ghorbani, A.A. Toward generating a new intrusion detection dataset and intrusion traffic characterization. In Proceedings of the International Conference on Information Systems Security and Privacy, Funchal, Portugal, 22–24 January 2018; pp. 108–116.
7. Tavallaee, M.; Bagheri, E.; Lu, W.; Ghorbani, A. A detailed analysis of the KDD CUP 99 data set. In Proceedings of the Second IEEE Symposium on Computational Intelligence for Security and Defence Applications, Ottawa, ON, Canada, 8–10 July 2009; pp. 1–6. [CrossRef]
8. Saleh, A.I.; Talaat, F.M.; Labib, L.M. A hybrid intrusion detection system (HIDS) based on prioritized k-nearest neighbors and optimized SVM classifiers. *Artif. Intell. Rev.* **2019**, *51*, 403–443. [CrossRef]
9. Leevy, J.L.; Khoshgoftaar, T.M. A survey and analysis of intrusion detection models based on CSE-CIC-IDS2018 Big Data. *J. Big Data* **2020**, *7*, 104. [CrossRef]
10. Wang, W.; Du, X.; Wang, N. Building a Cloud IDS Using an Efficient Feature Selection Method and SVM. *IEEE Access* **2019**, *7*, 1345–1354. [CrossRef]
11. Guyon, I.; Elisseeff, A. An Introduction to Variable and Feature Selection. *J. Mach. Learn. Res.* **2003**, *3*, 1157–1182.
12. Thangavel, N.S.G. Building an Efficient Feature Selection Using Greedy Search Method for HNIDS in Cloud Computing. *J. Adv. Res. Dyn. Control Syst.* **2019**, *11*, 307–316.
13. Khammassi, C.; Krichen, S. A GA-LR wrapper approach for feature selection in network intrusion detection. *Comput. Secur.* **2017**, *70*, 255–277. [CrossRef]
14. Kohavi, R.; John, G.H. Wrappers for feature subset selection. *Artif. Intell.* **1997**, *97*, 273–324. [CrossRef]
15. Li, Y.; Wang, J.-L.; Tian, Z.-H.; Lu, T.-B.; Young, C. Building lightweight intrusion detection system using wrapper-based feature selection mechanisms. *Comput. Secur.* **2009**, *28*, 466–475. [CrossRef]

16. Mohammadzadeh, A.; Taghavifar, H. A robust fuzzy control approach for path-following control of autonomous vehicles. *Soft Comput.* **2020**, *24*, 3223–3235. [CrossRef]
17. Varma, P.R.K.; Kumari, V.V.; Kumar, S.S. Feature Selection Using Relative Fuzzy Entropy and Ant Colony Optimization Applied to Real-time Intrusion Detection System. *Procedia Comput. Sci.* **2016**, *85*, 503–510. [CrossRef]
18. Mohammadi, S.; Mirvaziri, H.; Ghazizadeh-Ahsaee, M.; Karimipour, H. Cyber intrusion detection by combined feature selection algorithm. *J. Inf. Secur. Appl.* **2019**, *44*, 80–88. [CrossRef]
19. Sarvari, S.; Sani, N.F.M.; Hanapi, Z.M.; Abdullah, M.T. An Efficient Anomaly Intrusion Detection Method with Feature Selection and Evolutionary Neural Network. *IEEE Access* **2020**, *8*, 70651–70663. [CrossRef]
20. Asdaghi, F.; Soleimani, A. An effective feature selection method for web spam detection. *Knowl.-Based Syst.* **2019**, *166*, 198–206. [CrossRef]
21. Aslahi-Shahri, B.M.; Rahmani, R.; Chizari, M.; Maralani, A.; Eslami, M.; Golkar, M.J.; Ebrahimi, A. A hybrid method consisting of GA and SVM for intrusion detection system. *Neural Comput. Appl.* **2016**, *27*, 1669–1676. [CrossRef]
22. Lee, J.; Park, O. Feature Selection Algorithm for Intrusions Detection System using Sequential forward Search and Random Forest Classifier. *KSII Trans. Internet Inf. Syst.* **2017**, *11*, 5132–5148. [CrossRef]
23. Li, Y.; Xia, J.; Zhang, S.; Yan, J.; Ai, X.; Dai, K. An efficient intrusion detection system based on support vector machines and gradually feature removal method. *Expert Syst. Appl.* **2012**, *39*, 424–430. [CrossRef]
24. Raman, M.G.; Somu, N.; Kirthivasan, K.; Liscano, R.; Sriram, V.S. An efficient intrusion detection system based on hypergraph—Genetic algorithm for parameter optimization and feature selection in support vector machine. *Knowl.-Based Syst.* **2017**, *134*, 1–12. [CrossRef]
25. Zhou, Y.; Cheng, G.; Jiang, S.; Dai, M. Building an efficient intrusion detection system based on feature selection and ensemble classifier. *Comput. Netw.* **2020**, *174*, 107247. [CrossRef]
26. Hua, Y. An Efficient Traffic Classification Scheme Using Embedded Feature Selection and LightGBM. In Proceedings of the Information Communication Technologies Conference (ICTC), Nanjing, China, 29–31 May 2020; pp. 125–130. [CrossRef]
27. Seth, S.; Singh, G.; Chahal, K.K. A novel time efficient learning-based approach for smart intrusion detection system. *J. Big Data* **2021**, *8*, 1–28. [CrossRef]
28. Alazzam, H.; Sharieh, A.; Sabri, K.E. A feature selection algorithm for intrusion detection system based on Pigeon Inspired Optimizer. *Expert Syst. Appl.* **2020**, *148*, 113249. [CrossRef]
29. Mazini, M.; Shirazi, B.; Mahdavi, I. Anomaly network-based intrusion detection system using a reliable hybrid artificial bee colony and AdaBoost algorithms. *J. King Saud Univ.-Comput. Inf. Sci.* **2019**, *31*, 541–553. [CrossRef]
30. Saeed, A.A.; Jameel, N.G.M. Intelligent feature selection using particle swarm optimization algorithm with a decision tree for DDoS attack detection. *Int. J. Adv. Intell. Inform.* **2021**, *7*, 37. [CrossRef]
31. Shaikh, J.M.; Kshirsagar, D. Feature Reduction-Based DoS Attack Detection System. In *Next Generation Information Processing System*; Springer: Berlin/Heidelberg, Germany, 2021; pp. 170–177. [CrossRef]
32. Patil, A.; Kshirsagar, D. Towards Feature Selection for Detection of DDoS Attack. *Comput. Eng. Technol.* **2019**, 215–223. [CrossRef]
33. Ahmad, I.; Hussain, M.; Alghamdi, A.; Alelaiwi, A. Enhancing SVM performance in intrusion detection using optimal feature subset selection based on genetic principal components. *Neural Comput. Appl.* **2014**, *24*, 1671–1682. [CrossRef]
34. He, H.; Garcia, E.A. Learning from Imbalanced Data. *IEEE Trans. Knowl. Data Eng.* **2009**, *21*, 1263–1284. [CrossRef]
35. Ho, Y.B.; Yap, W.S.; Khor, K.C. The effect of sampling methods on the cicids2017 network intrusion data set. In *IT Convergence and Security*; Springer: Singapore, 2021; pp. 33–41.
36. Bamakan, S.M.H.; Wang, H.; Yingjie, T.; Shi, Y. An effective intrusion detection framework based on MCLP/SVM optimized by time-varying chaos particle swarm optimization. *Neurocomputing* **2016**, *199*, 90–102. [CrossRef]
37. Huang, C.-L.; Wang, C.-J. A GA-based feature selection and parameters optimization for support vector machines. *Expert Syst. Appl.* **2006**, *31*, 231–240. [CrossRef]
38. Gen, M.; Cheng, R. *Genetic Algorithms and Engineering Optimization*; John Wiley & Sons: Hoboken, NJ, USA, 1999; Volume 7.
39. Pedregosa, F.; Varoquaux, G.; Gramfort, A.; Michel, V.; Thirion, B.; Grisel, O.; Blondel, M.; Prettenhofer, P.; Weiss, R.; Dubourg, V.; et al. Scikit-learn: Machine learning in python. *J. Mach. Learn. Res.* **2011**, *12*, 2825–2830.
40. Raschka, S. Mlxtend: Providing machine learning and data science utilities and extensions to python's scientific computing stack. *J. Open Source Softw.* **2018**, *3*, 638. [CrossRef]
41. Calzolari, M. Manuel-Calzolari/Sklearn-Genetic: Sklearn-Genetic 0.5.1 (0.5.1). Zenodo. 2022. Available online: https://zenodo.org/record/5854662#.Y5knyH1ByUk (accessed on 18 January 2022).

Health Status-Based Predictive Maintenance Decision-Making via LSTM and Markov Decision Process

Pan Zheng, Wenqin Zhao, Yaqiong Lv *, Lu Qian * and Yifan Li

School of Transportation and Logistics Engineering, Wuhan University of Technology, Wuhan 430063, China
* Correspondence: y.q.lv@whut.edu.cn (Y.L.); qianlu@whut.edu.cn (L.Q.)

Abstract: Maintenance decision-making is essential to achieve safe and reliable operation with high performance for equipment. To avoid unexpected shutdown and increase machine life as well as system efficiency, it is fundamental to design an effective maintenance decision-making scheme for equipment. In this paper, we propose a novel maintenance decision-making method for equipment based on Long Short-Term Memory (LSTM) and Markov decision process, which can provide specific maintenance strategies in different degradation stages of the system. Specifically, the LSTM model is firstly applied to predict the remaining service life of equipment to distinguish its health state quantitatively. Then, based on the bearing residual life prediction curve, the degradation process model is constructed, and the corresponding parameters of the model are identified. Finally, the bearing degradation curve is obtained by the degradation process model, based on which the Markov decision process model is constructed to provide accurate maintenance strategies for different health conditions of system. To demonstrate the effectiveness of the proposed method, an experimental study with the full life cycle data set of rolling bearings is carried out. The experimental results show that the proposed method can achieve efficient maintenance decisions for bearings under different health states, which provides a feasible solution for the maintenance of bearing systems.

Keywords: Markov decision process; maintenance decision-making; rolling bearing; LSTM

MSC: 90C40

1. Introduction

With the continuous improvement in modern industrialization, as well as the progress of society and the rapid development of science and technology, mechanical equipment is becoming more intelligent, systematic and modular. The functions of mechanical equipment have become increasingly diversified to meet the growing requirements of industrial production. In the process of long-term operation, mechanical equipment will be gradually aging, along with gradually declining operating performance and remaining life, the possibility of failure will increase. Once the failure occurs, it may cause costly industrial downtime, casualties or even serious social impact. Therefore, how to design effective maintenance decision-making scheme, in order to ensure the long-term safe and stable operation of the mechanical equipment is an urgent problem to be solved.

To ensure the reliable and safe operation of equipment, the existing research paid a lot of attention to fault detection and diagnosis for different equipment via various means [1–4]. Actually, further study on effective maintenance decision-making method is also of great importance. Due to the crucial role in mechanical equipment, maintenance decisions for bearings have drawn increasing attention of many scholars [5,6]. The maintenance decision-making scheme for the bearing system is also our focus in this paper.

To attain safe and reliable operation with high performance of equipment and achieve the lowest possible maintenance costs at the same time, a novel maintenance decision-making method for equipment based on LSTM and Markov decision process is proposed in this paper. To this end, the prediction curve of the bearing remaining life is firstly obtained by applying the LSTM model. Then, the degradation process model is constructed, and the corresponding parameters are estimated based on the bearing remaining life prediction curve. Finally, based on the bearing degradation curve acquired by the degradation process model, the Markov decision process model is applied to provide optimal maintenance strategies for different health conditions of the system. The main contributions of this paper are given as follows.

(1) A novel maintenance decision-making method is developed for rotating mechanical system.
(2) An LSTM model is adopted to predict the remaining life of system, and the remaining life prediction data are used as the input of the following degradation process model to identify the model parameters.
(3) A maintenance decision-making model is constructed based on Markov decision process to provide an effective maintenance solution for equipment. Furthermore, the revenue of maintenance decisions under different health conditions is designed for the instruction of maintenance strategies. Moreover, the maintenance decision-making model is tested on the experimental platform of rolling bearings, and the effectiveness of the proposed method has been validated.

The remainder of this paper is organized as follows. In Section 2, the related work is reviewed, which summarizes the main research progress in the field of maintenance decision-making. Section 3 presents the framework of the proposed method in detail, including the prediction of remaining life based on LSTM and maintenance decision-making model for bearings. The effectiveness of the proposed method is verified by the experimental study in Section 4. Finally, the conclusions of this paper are summarized in Section 5.

2. Literature Review

With the development of science and technology, as well as increasing demand for economic and healthy operation of equipment, autonomous decision-making and equipment maintenance decision-making has drawn increasing attention from the academy [7–9]. In the past decades, the research topic of maintenance decision-making has been widely studied [10]. The existing methods can be mainly divided into two categories: time-based maintenance (TBM) and condition-based maintenance (CBM).

Many scholars have made in-depth research on TBM strategy optimization. Buchholz, Peter et al. [11] proposed a general model of partially observable states and non-exponential fault, maintenance and repair time based on phase distribution. D.E. Ighravwe et al. [12] proposed a fuzzy objective programming model and used it to establish a single objective function of maintenance optimization considering random constraints, so as to generate reliable information for fault maintenance plan. Considering the time-based preventive maintenance scheduling problem under the uncertainty of unit life distribution, De Jonge et al. [13] evaluated the long-term benefits of initially delaying preventive maintenance and made the benefits maximization through the numerical research. Yiming Chen et al. [14] proposed two optimization problems by taking the static availability or expected performance capacity of the system as the goal.

The condition-based maintenance (CBM) is based on the methods of integrating current state prediction, plan diagnosis and future state prediction. These methods can be classified into physical model-based methods, data-driven methods and hybrid methods. Guang Zou [15] developed a probabilistic maintenance optimization method using information value (VOI) calculation and Bayesian decision optimization. The VOI based approach explicitly quantifies the added value of future inspections and gives the best decision by directly modeling decision alternatives and evaluating their expected results.

In the field of CBM, more and more scholars use the Markov decision process to study the degradation process of equipment. Paté-Cornell et al. [16] applied Markov chains with four states to simulate the degradation process of production system, where time-based maintenance and three condition-based maintenance strategies are considered. The latter is based on product inspection, machine signals and signals provided by product in service. Minou C.A. Olde Keizer et al. [17] constructed a parallel system, which is subject to both fault dependence and economic dependence by maintenance cost through load sharing. The system is formulated as a Markov decision process, where the optimal replacement decision is obtained to minimize the long-term average cost per unit time. Yaqiong Lv and Qianwen Zhou et al. [9] proposed an intelligent predictive maintenance system for production equipment multi granularity fault based on BP neural network and fuzzy decision-making, which successfully realized the automatic predictive maintenance decision-making. Renny Arismendi et al. [18] explored the application of piecewise deterministic Markov process (PDMP) to cover different modeling assumptions, such as non-ignorable maintenance delay and inspection-based status monitoring.

In addition, some researchers consider the combination of the two types of methods in applications. Mckone and Weiss [19] combined CBM with TBM methods. The available status information is limited to potential fault signals that may be received before the actual fault. Therefore, the performance of CBM depends on the prediction accuracy. In some cases, TBM or the combination of CBM and TBM is preferred.

From the state of art and development of the study on equipment maintenance decision-making, existing research has been demonstrated by relatively ideal research results in some respects. However, in the field of equipment maintenance decision-making, less efforts have been reported to systematically map out the specific maintenance strategies in different degradation stages of the system, which is worthy to be further explored. Due to the superior ability to find a strategic solution with maximum return and broad application prospects in automatic control and recommendation systems, the Markov decision process has great potential in the field of equipment maintenance decision-making. Motivated by the aforementioned studies, this paper develops a novel maintenance decision-making scheme based on LSTM and Markov decision process, which can provide effective maintenance strategies in different degradation stages of the equipment.

3. Methodology

The framework of the maintenance decision-making method proposed in this paper is shown in Figure 1. Specifically, the LSTM model is applied to predict the remaining life curve of the equipment. Then, based on the bearing remaining life prediction curve, the degradation process model is constructed, and the parameters of the model are identified. Finally, the bearing degradation curve is obtained by the degradation process model, based on which the Markov decision process model is constructed to provide accurate maintenance strategies for different health conditions of system.

3.1. Prediction of Remaining Life Based on LSTM

LSTM is a special type of Recurrent Neural Network (RNN) that can learn long-term dependent information, which has been demonstrated by many successful applications [20,21].

The specific structure of LSTM is shown in Figure 2, where Xt is the input of cell state at time t and Ht is the output of cell state at time t. LSTM realizes information protection and control through three gate unit structures, including input gate, forgetting gate and output gate.

(1) Forgetting gate

The first step in LSTM is to decide what information will be discarded from the cellular state. The decision is made through the forgetting gate. The gate will read the output of the hidden layer at the last moment and the input of the current cell, and then output a value between 0 and 1, where 1 means "completely preserved", 0 means "completely discarded".

(2) Input gate

The next step is to decide how much new information will be added to the cellular state. To this end, there are two steps to be performed: first, the input gate determines which information needs to be updated. A tanh layer generates a vector, which is the alternative content for updating. In the second step, the two parts are combined to update the cell state.

(3) Output gate

Finally, we need to determine the output value. This output will be based on the cell state. Firstly, we run a sigmoid layer to determine which part of the cell state will be output. Then, we deal with the cell state through tanh (get a value between -1 and 1) and multiply it with the output of the sigmoid gate. Finally, we just output the part of the output we determined.

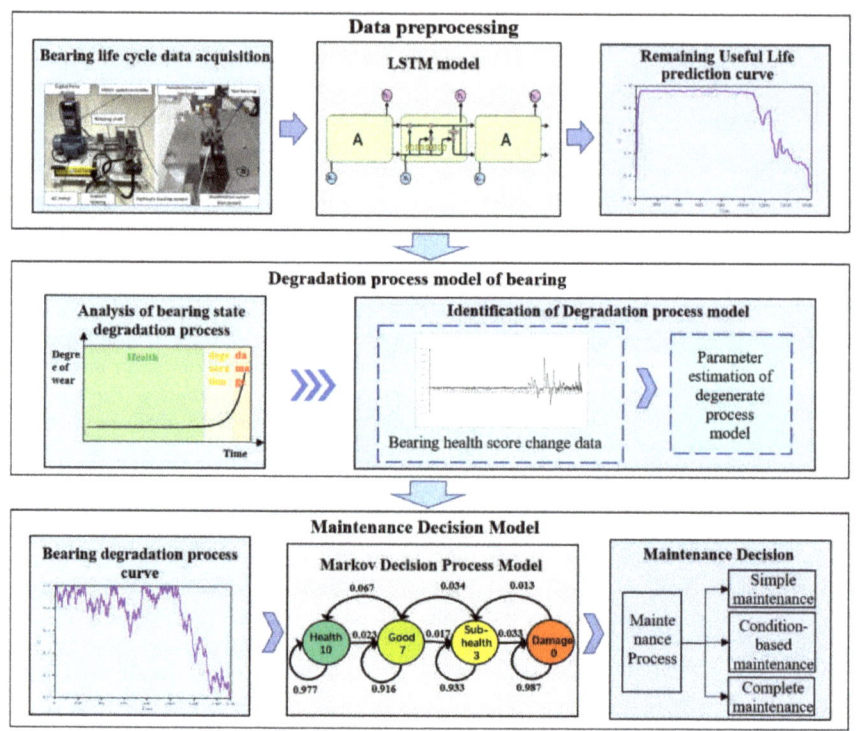

Figure 1. Framework of the proposed approach.

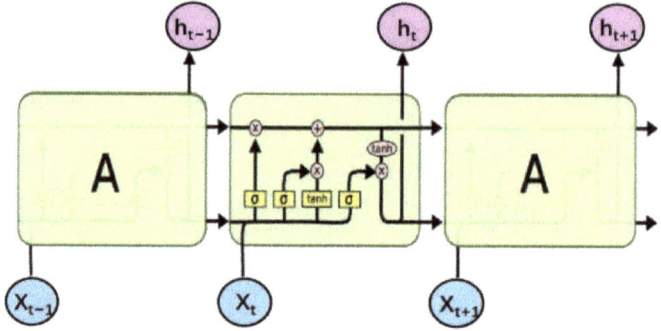

Figure 2. LSTM Structure.

Through the above three gating units, LSTM realizes the selective retention and output of information, and meanwhile solves the problem of gradient disappearance of RNN.

The remaining life prediction based on LSTM can integrate the original learning samples with the new learning mode to realize the re-training of samples. It can not only improve the accuracy of remaining life prediction, but also has the characteristics of fast convergence and high stability. Due to the great advantages in the processing of serial data, LSTM is applied for remaining life prediction of bearings by making use of the vibration signals in operation, which also have serial characteristics.

In what follows, the remaining life prediction data obtained by LSTM model will be used to quantify the health status of the bearing.

3.2. Degradation Process Model

The bearing degradation curve in ideal conditions is shown in Figure 3. According to the curve, the trend of the bearing degradation has the following characteristics [22]:

(1) The normal operation time of bearing is long, accounting for 80–90% of the whole life cycle of the bearing.
(2) When a small crack appears on the surface of the bearing rolling elements or raceways, the bearing begins to enter the degradation stage.
(3) When the degree of bearing degradation accumulates to a certain extent, the probability of bearing damage and equipment failure will increase significantly

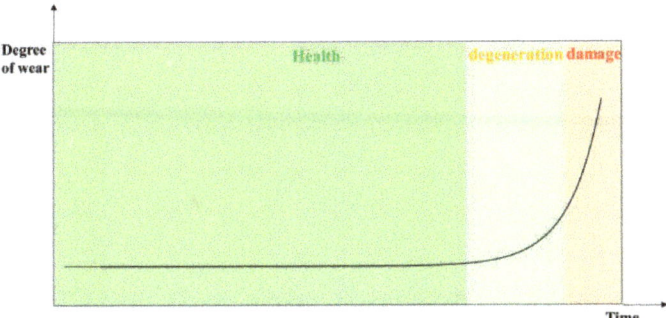

Figure 3. Bearing degradation curve.

The degradation quantity of rolling bearing in a certain period Δt is expressed as $Z(\Delta t)$, including both continuous degradation quantity and sudden degradation quantity in the process of bearing degradation. The degradation process of bearing follows the Gauss–Poisson process:

$$Z(\Delta t) = X(\Delta t) + \beta Y(\Delta t) \qquad (1)$$

where $X(\Delta t)$ denotes the continuous degradation of bearings, and $X(\Delta t) \sim N(\mu, \sigma^2)$. $Y(\Delta t)$ represents the quantity of degradation due to sudden factors, and $Y(\Delta t) \sim \text{Poisson}(\lambda)$. β is the average degradation amount generated by each sudden degradation.

In order to evaluate the health state of the system, the health score is introduced in the construction of degradation process model. The initial health score of the bearing is set to be 1. After operation time t, the normal continuous degradation of the bearing is denoted by $X(t)$, and the quantity of sudden degradation is $Y(t)$, then the health score of the bearing is given by:

$$Ht = 1 - \sum_{t=0}^{t}(X(t) + \beta Y(t)) \qquad (2)$$

The parameters of the health state degradation process can be identified by the historical health score degradation data, which is discussed in the following.

After obtaining the remaining life prediction data, the bearing health score degradation data can be obtained from the following formula:

$$H_t(n) = H(t) - H(t+1) \tag{3}$$

Assume that $H_N(n)(n = 1, 2, 3, ..., N)$ is a group of historical degradation data of health score, where n represents the state number. According to the health score degradation data $H_N(n)$, the parameters in Equation (2) are estimated by calculating the central moments of each order of $H_N(n)$. The estimation of parameters is given as follows:

$$E(H_N) = \mu + \lambda\beta \tag{4}$$

$$D(H_N) = \sigma^2 + \lambda\beta^2 \tag{5}$$

$$E(H_N - E(H_N))^3 = \beta^3 \lambda \tag{6}$$

$$E(H_N - E(H_N))^4 = 3\sigma^2 + 3\beta^4\lambda^2 + \beta^4\lambda + 6\sigma^2\beta^2\lambda \tag{7}$$

where $\mu, \sigma, \lambda, \beta$ are the parameters of rolling bearing degradation process. The central moments of each order of the group of data are calculated by the health score degradation data, which can be recorded as $H_1, H_2, H_3, \ldots, H_n$. The obtained central moments are expressed as a_1, a_2, a_3, a_4 respectively, which can be calculated as follows:

$$a_1 = E(H_N) = \frac{1}{n}\sum_{N-1}^{n} H_N \tag{8}$$

$$a_2 = D(H_N) = \frac{1}{n}\sum_{N-1}^{n} (H_N - a_1)^2 \tag{9}$$

$$a_3 = E(H_N - E(H_N))^3 = \frac{1}{n}\sum_{N-1}^{n} (H_N - a_1)^3 \tag{10}$$

$$a_4 = E(H_N - E(H_N))^4 = \frac{1}{n}\sum_{N-1}^{n} (H_N - a_1)^4 \tag{11}$$

Based on the above equations, each parameter of the Gauss–Poisson process model is given by:

$$\lambda = \frac{a_3^4}{(a_4 - 3a_2^2)^3} \tag{12}$$

$$\sigma = \sqrt{a_2 - \frac{a_3^2}{a_4 - 3a_2^2}} \tag{13}$$

$$\mu = a_1 - \frac{a_3^3}{(a_4 - 3a_2^2)^2} \tag{14}$$

$$\beta = \frac{a_4 - 3a_2^2}{a_3} \tag{15}$$

According to the above discussions, the parameters of the bearing degradation process are completely identified.

3.3. Maintenance Decision-Making Model

3.3.1. Markov Decision Process Model

The health score (0–1) of the system can be obtained in Section 3.2. Higher health score indicates better system health state. Health score 1 means that the system is completely healthy, and health score 0 indicates that the system is failed.

The health score can effectively represent the deterioration of the system, motivating us to use to evaluate the health status of the system. The health score is divided into four intervals: [1, 0.8), [0.8, 0.6), [0.6, 0.4) and [0.4, 0], corresponding to four different health states of the bearing:

Healthy (that is, the bearing is under a completely healthy state with only slight degradation),

Good (the bearing begins to deteriorate but is not obvious),

Sub-health (the bearing has been seriously degraded and its performance has been obviously reduced),

Damaged (the bearing is completely damaged and cannot be used).

Their health states are recorded as 1, 2, 3, 4 respectively. Therefore, the health state set of rolling bearing can be defined as S = {1, 2, 3, 4}, which is a continuous Markov process. Since the bearing degradation process is continuous, the rolling bearing must be in a certain state (health, good, sub-health, damage) at any time in its full life cycle [23]. The health state transition process of rolling bearing is shown in Figure 4, where each circle represents different health states, and the value in the circle represents the benefit of remaining in each state.

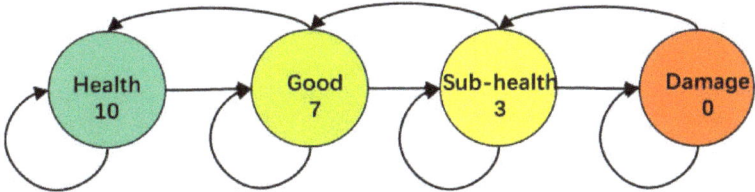

Figure 4. State transition process model.

3.3.2. Transition Probability

In this paper, the Monte Carlo method is used to calculate the transition probability of the Markov process [24]. The transition probability can be calculated as follows:

$$P_{ij} = \frac{M_{ij}}{M_i} \quad (16)$$

where P_{ij} is the transition probability of state from i to j; M_{ij} is the number of samples transferring from state i at the last moment to state j at the next moment, and M_i is the total number of samples in state i.

3.3.3. Maintenance Effect

According to the impact of different maintenance modes on bearing service life, the maintenance effect of different maintenance modes can be represented, as well as the impact of different maintenance modes on the health status of the bearing.

In this paper, the effect of different maintenance modes in this paper is given as follows. Simple maintenance applied to rolling bearings can prolong the bearing service life by 10% on average. If the bearings are repaired by complete maintenance, the health score can directly change to 1. If we apply state maintenance to repair rolling bearings, the bearing service life can be extended by 40% on average. The health states transition probability matrix under different maintenance states can be obtained through the health score represented by the life extension.

3.3.4. Cost Analysis

Different maintenance modes of bearings under different health conditions brings different cost, which has significant impact on the decision-making process. The cost includes three parts:

(1) Maintenance costs (the maintenance costs incurred by various maintenance activities);
(2) Continuous maintenance costs (the costs incurred from continuous care and maintenance of rolling bearings to keep them healthy and effective);
(3) Signal detection costs (the costs caused by the vibration signal detection of the bearing to identify the current health status).

At present, there is no uniform standard for the maintenance mode and cost of mechanical equipment, and the maintenance mode setting in this paper is only to verify the effectiveness of this method. Therefore, this paper formulates the maintenance cost based on some maintenance experience. To sum up, the costs of each simple maintenance, state maintenance and complete maintenance are 15, 40 and 300, respectively, where the relative value is selected to facilitate the calculation of the total reward.

For a Markov decision process, G_t is defined as the cumulative reward of the system, which can be expressed as:

$$G_t = R_{t+1} + R_{t+2} + R_{t+3} + \cdots = \sum_{k=0}^{\infty} \gamma^k R_{t+k+1} \tag{17}$$

where γ represents the discount factor, which is set as 1. Rt denotes the income at time t.

4. Experiment Analysis

4.1. Bearing Data Acquisition

The data used in this paper are the life cycle experimental data of bearings from Xi'an Jiaotong University [25]. The experimental platform is shown in Figure 5 [26]. The accelerated life tests for various types of bearings (including rolling bearings and sliding bearings) under different working conditions can be carried out on the experimental platform, where the life cycle data of the test bearings can be collected. The main bearing operating parameters, including the radial force and the rotating speed, which can be adjusted by the test-bed. The test bearing type is LDK UER204 rolling bearing, whose parameters are shown in Table 1.

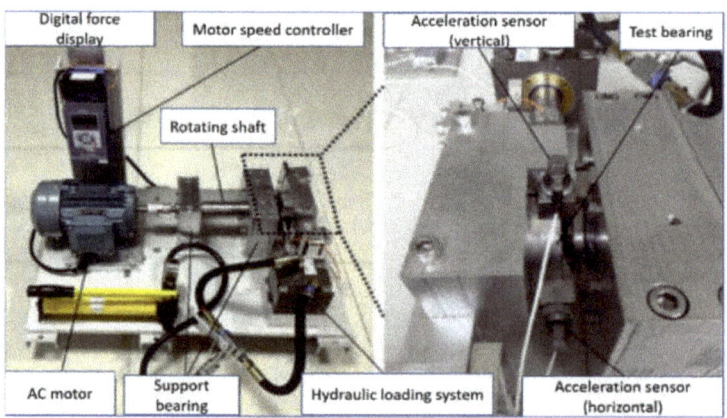

Figure 5. Bearing acceleration experimental platform [26].

Table 1. LDK UER204 Bearing parameters.

Parameters	Numerical Value
Diameter of inner race/mm	29.30
Outer ring raceway diameter/mm	39.80
Bearing pitch diameter/mm	34.55
Basic dynamic load rating/N	12,820
Ball diameter/mm	7.92
Number of balls	8
Contact angle/(°)	0
Basic static load rating/kN	6.65

4.2. Prediction of the Remaining Useful Life of Bearings

The aforementioned data are used for the verification of the proposed method. Several groups of data samples are selected as the training set from the bearing life cycle data of Xi'an Jiaotong University, including Bearing 1_1, earing1_2 and Bearing1_4. While Bearing1_5 is selected as the test set. (Operating condition: speed 2100 r/min, radial force 12 kN, sampling frequency 25.6 kHz, sampling interval 1 min, sampling duration 1.28 s).

The actual remaining life of the bearing is used as the training and testing label value y. The process of label construction is discussed as follows. label 1 represents the bearing state that it is in good condition, and label 0 means that the bearing is in complete failure. For example, Bearing1–2 dataset has a total of 2496 groups of data, which means the total life of the bearing is 2496 min. If the current sample is the 1000th datum, then the remaining life of the bearing is 1496 min, and the value of the corresponding label y under the sample is 1496/2496 = 0.599358. According to the remaining life of the rolling bearing, the data samples, are labeled in the same manner.

The LSTM model is designed based on the Python open-source deep learning framework. In the experiment, the Adam optimizer is selected to optimize the training loss of LSTM model. Adam is a popular optimizer in the current architecture. Compared with other optimizers, it can learn parameters adaptively, which has the advantages of fast convergence, small memory requirements, and better processing of noise samples. The obtained life prediction curve of Bearing1_5 is shown in Figure 6, and the prediction accuracy rate is 96.7%.

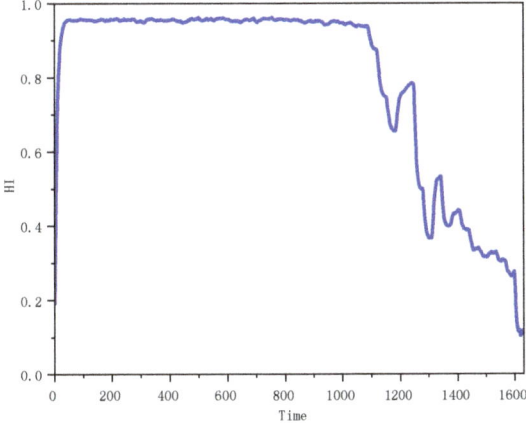

Figure 6. Bearing life prediction curve.

To illustrate, the status of bearing is provided. As shown in Figure 7, at time point 400, the bearing status is shown as the left bearing, while at time point 1400, the bearing status is shown as the right bearing. It can be seen that the left bearing is in good condition, while the right bearing has been severely worn, which is consistent with the life prediction results by the LSTM model. Therefore, the method in this paper can fit well with the whole life degrading trend of the bearing so as to predict the remaining life of it.

Figure 7. Bearings in two different states.

4.3. Parameters Estimation

At present, we have obtained the predicted value of the remaining life of the bearing. Based on this, we subtract the predicted value of the remaining life of the bearing at adjacent time points to obtain the deterioration of the bearing health score ($H_N(n)$), then we can calculate the relevant parameters of the model.

Based on the health score of bearing life prediction curve obtained in Figure 6, which represents the degradation quantity of bearings, the parameters of the bearing degradation process model are identified as follows:

$$\mu = 0.000243, \ o = 0.0208 \ \beta = 0.000596, \ \lambda = 0.400$$

According to the obtained bearing degradation process model, we can estimate the bearing degradation curve as shown in Figure 8.

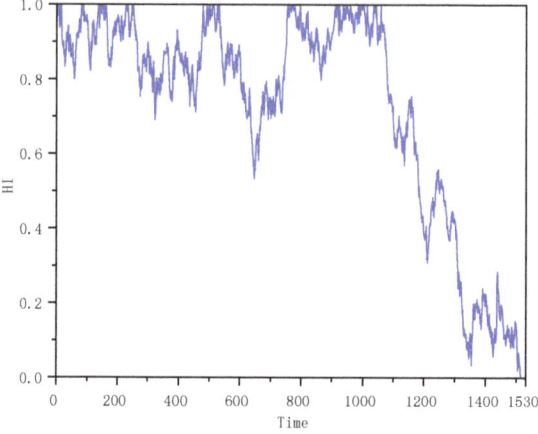

Figure 8. Curve of Bearing Degradation Process.

Based on the bearing degradation curve, the transition probability of Markov decision process can be calculated. According to the maintenance effect in Section 3.3, the impact of each maintenance mode on the bearing health state transition is discussed as follows:

The state transition probability matrix after simple maintenance is:

$$A1 = \begin{bmatrix} 1 & 0 & 0 & 0 \\ 0.64 & 0.36 & 0 & 0 \\ 0 & 0.27 & 0.63 & 0 \\ 0 & 0 & 0.09 & 0.91 \end{bmatrix}$$

The state transition probability matrix after condition-based maintenance is:

$$A2 = \begin{bmatrix} 1 & 0 & 0 & 0 \\ 1 & 0 & 0 & 0 \\ 0.14 & 0.71 & 0.15 & 0 \\ 0 & 0 & 0.29 & 0.71 \end{bmatrix}$$

The state transition probability matrix after complete maintenance is:

$$A3 = \begin{bmatrix} 1 & 0 & 0 & 0 \\ 1 & 0 & 0 & 0 \\ 1 & 0 & 0 & 0 \\ 1 & 0 & 0 & 0 \end{bmatrix}$$

According to Equation (16), the health state transition probability matrix of the rolling bearing can be obtained as:

$$A4 = \begin{bmatrix} 0.977 & 0.023 & 0 & 0 \\ 0.067 & 0.916 & 0.017 & 0 \\ 0 & 0.034 & 0.933 & 0.033 \\ 0 & 0 & 0.013 & 0.987 \end{bmatrix}$$

The row of the above matrix represents the original state, and the column is the state after transition. The value means the probability of transition from the original state to the new state. Finally, the Markov decision process model of the entire bearing degradation process is obtained as shown in Figure 9. Each circle of the figure represents the different health states of the bearing, in which the value represents the benefit of remaining in each state, and the value on the line of circles represents the transition probability of each state.

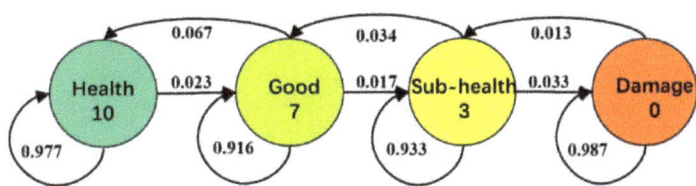

Figure 9. Markov Decision Model.

To calculate the value of each maintenance decision on each state, the Bellman equation is used to iteratively calculate the value function of each state, and the following results are obtained: Revenue in healthy state R1 = 4631.84, revenue in good state R2 = 4195.92, revenue in sub-health state R3 = 2141.21, and revenue in damaged state R4 = 0.

The benefits of different maintenance modes under different conditions are obtained by combining the effects of the above maintenance decisions on different health status, as shown in Table 2.

Table 2. Revenue from different maintenance decisions.

Maintenance Modes	Health	Good	Sub-Health	Damage
Simple maintenance	4616.84	4429.91	2466.86	177.71
Condition-based maintenance	4591.84	4591.84	3908.72	580.95
Complete maintenance	4331.84	4331.84	4331.84	4331.84

4.4. Summary

It can be seen from Table 2 that when the rolling bearing is in healthy state, and simple maintenance is applied, i.e., routine maintenance, the maximum benefit can be obtained. While the benefit of condition-based maintenance is only slightly lower than that of simple maintenance. When the rolling bearing is under good condition, the maximum benefit can be obtained by carrying out appropriate condition maintenance according to its condition, and considerable benefit can be gained by carrying out simple maintenance or complete maintenance under this condition. If the rolling bearing is under sub-health state, the benefit of complete maintenance, i.e., directly replacing the bearing, is the largest, which is far greater than that of the other two maintenance modes. However, if the rolling bearing has been damaged, only when the bearing is completely repaired, that is to say, the replacement of the bearing can obtain greater benefits.

Our conclusions obtained above are consistent with the historical experience of bearing maintenance, verifying that the proposed maintenance decision-making method can provide effective guidance for the maintenance strategy of rolling bearings under different states.

5. Conclusions

In this paper, a maintenance decision-making scheme for equipment is proposed based on LSTM and Markov decision process, which can provide effective maintenance decisions for system under different degradation stages. First, the LSTM model is adopted to predict the remaining service life to distinguish the health state quantitatively. Then, the degradation process model is constructed, and the parameters of the model are identified. With the aid of the degradation curve obtained from the degradation process model, the maintenance decision-making model is established based on the Markov decision process. Moreover, to facilitate more appropriate maintenance strategy identification, the revenue of maintenance decisions under different health conditions is analyzed. Experimental study with the full life cycle data set of bearings is carried out to demonstrate the effectiveness of the proposed method. Besides the rotating mechanical systems, the application of the proposed method can be further extended to other industrial fields.

Author Contributions: Conceptualization, Y.L. (Yaqiong Lv) and L.Q.; methodology, P.Z. and Y.L. (Yaqiong Lv); software, P.Z. and W.Z.; validation, Y.L. (Yaqiong Lv), L.Q. and Y.L. (Yifan Li); data curation, P.Z. and W.Z.; writing—original draft preparation, P.Z.; writing—review and editing, L.Q. and Y.L. (Yaqiong Lv); project administration, Y.L. (Yifan Li); funding acquisition, Y.L. (Yaqiong Lv). All authors have read and agreed to the published version of the manuscript.

Funding: This research was sponsored by the Humanities and Social Science Foundation of Ministry of Education of China (Project No. 20YJC630096) and partially sponsored by the National Natural Science Foundation of China (Project No. 72101194).

Data Availability Statement: Not applicable.

Acknowledgments: The authors would like to thank all the editors and reviewers for their invaluable comments on this manuscript.

Conflicts of Interest: The authors declare no conflict of interest.

References

1. Ainapure, A.; Siahpour, S.; Li, X.; Majid, F.; Lee, J. Intelligent robust cross-domain fault diagnostic method for rotating machines using noisy condition labels. *Mathematics* 2022, *10*, 455. [CrossRef]
2. Chen, H.; Jiang, B. A review of fault detection and diagnosis for the traction system in high-speed trains. *IEEE Trans. Intell. Transp. Syst.* 2019, *21*, 450–465. [CrossRef]
3. Wu, J.; Lin, M.; Lv, Y.; Cheng, Y. Intelligent fault diagnosis of rolling bearings based on clustering algorithm of fast search and find of density peaks. *Qual. Eng.* 2022, *11*, 1–14.
4. Khan, A.; Hwang, H.; Kim, H.S. Synthetic Data Augmentation and Deep Learning for the Fault Diagnosis of Rotating Machines. *Mathematics* 2021, *9*, 2336. [CrossRef]
5. Lv, Y.; Zhao, W.; Zhao, Z.; Li, W.; Kam, K.H.N. Vibration signal-based early fault prognosis: Status quo and applications. *Adv. Eng. Inform.* 2022, *52*, 101609. [CrossRef]
6. Qian, L.; Pan, Q.; Lv, Y.; Zhao, X. Fault Detection of Bearing by Resnet Classifier with Model-Based Data Augmentation. *Machines* 2022, *10*, 521. [CrossRef]
7. Wang, T.; Wu, Q.; Zhang, J.; Wu, B.; Wang, Y. Autonomous decision-making scheme for multi-ship collision avoidance with iterative observation and inference. *Ocean. Eng.* 2020, *197*, 106873. [CrossRef]
8. Arzaghi, E.; Abaei, M.M.; Abbassi, R.; Garaniya, V.; Chin, C.; Khan, F. Risk-based maintenance planning of subsea pipelines through fatigue crack growth monitoring. *Eng. Fail. Anal.* 2017, *79*, 928–939. [CrossRef]
9. Lv, Y.; Zhou, Q.; Li, Y.; Li, W. A predictive maintenance system for multi-granularity faults based on AdaBelief-BP neural network and fuzzy decision making. *Adv. Eng. Inform.* 2021, *49*, 101318. [CrossRef]
10. La Fata, C.M.; Giallanza, A.; Micale, R.; La Scalia, G. Improved FMECA for effective risk management decision making by failure modes classification under uncertainty. *Eng. Fail. Anal.* 2022, *135*, 106163. [CrossRef]
11. Buchholz, P.; Dohndorf, I.; Scheftelowitsch, D. Time-Based Maintenance Models under Uncertainty. *Lect. Notes Comput. Sci.* 2018, *10740*, 3–18.
12. Ighravwe, D.E.; Oke, S.A. A machine survival time-based maintenance workforce allocation model for production systems. *Afr. J. Sci. Technol. Innov. Dev.* 2016, *8*, 457–466. [CrossRef]
13. De Jonge, B.; Dijkstra, A.S.; Romeijnders, W. Cost benefits of postponing time-based maintenance under lifetime distribution uncertainty. *Reliab. Eng. Syst. Saf.* 2015, *140*, 15–21. [CrossRef]
14. Chen, Y.; Liu, Y.; Jiang, T. Optimal Maintenance Strategy for Multi-State Systems with Single Maintenance Capacity and Arbitrarily Distributed Maintenance Time. *Reliab. Eng. Syst. Saf.* 2021, *211*, 107576. [CrossRef]
15. Guang, Z.; Havbro, F.M.; Arturo, G.; Kian, B. Fatigue inspection and maintenance optimization: A comparison of information value, life cycle cost and reliability based approaches. *Ocean. Eng.* 2020, *220*, 108286.
16. Paté-Cornell, M.E.; Lee, H.L.; Tagaras, G. Warnings of Malfunction: The Decision to Inspect and Maintain Production Processes on Schedule or on Demand. *Manag. Sci.* 1987, *33*, 1277–1290. [CrossRef]
17. Keizer, M.C.O.; Teunter, R.H.; Veldman, J.; Babai, M.Z. Condition-based maintenance for systems with economic dependence and load sharing. *Int. J. Prod. Econ.* 2018, *195*, 319–327. [CrossRef]
18. Renny, A.; Anne, B.; Antoine, G. Piecewise deterministic Markov process for condition-based maintenance models-Application to critical infrastructures with discrete-state deterioration. *Reliab. Eng. Syst. Saf.* 2021, *212*, 107540.
19. McKone, K.E. Guidelines for implementing predictive maintenance. *Prod. Oper. Manag.* 2002, *11*, 109–124. [CrossRef]
20. Greff, K.; Srivastava, R.K.; Koutník, J.; Steunebrink, B.R.; Schmidhuber, J. LSTM: A Search Space Odyssey. *IEEE Trans. Neural Netw. Learn. Syst.* 2016, *28*, 2222–2232. [CrossRef]
21. Zhao, X.; Lu, H.; Yu, W.; Tao, B.; Ding, H. Robotic Grinding Process Monitoring by Vibration Signal Based on LSTM Method. *IEEE Trans. Instrum. Meas.* 2022, *71*, 1–10. [CrossRef]
22. Lei, Y.; He, Z.; Zi, Y.; Hu, Q. Fault diagnosis of rotating machinery based on multiple ANFIS combination with Gas. *Mech. Syst. Signal Process.* 2007, *21*, 2280–2294. [CrossRef]
23. Sun, Q.; Zhou, J.; Zhong, Z.; Zhao, J.; Duan, X. Gauss-Poisson Joint Distribution Model for Degradation Failure. *IEEE Trans. Plasma* 2004, *32*, 1864–1868. [CrossRef]
24. Zhou, D.; Yu, Z.; Zhang, H.; Weng, S. A novel grey prognostic model based on Markov process and grey incidence analysis for energy conversion equipment degradation. *Energy* 2016, *109*, 420–429. [CrossRef]
25. Lei, Y.; Han, T.; Wang, B.; Li, N.; Yan, T.; Yang, J. XJTU-SY Rolling Element Bearing Accelerated Life Test Datasets: A Tutorial(Article). *J. Mech. Eng.* 2019, *55*, 1–6.
26. Wang, B.; Lei, Y.; Li, N.; Li, N. A Hybrid Prognostics Approach for Estimating Remaining Useful Life of Rolling Element Bearings. *IEEE Trans. Reliab.* 2018, *69*, 401–412. [CrossRef]

Disclaimer/Publisher's Note: The statements, opinions and data contained in all publications are solely those of the individual author(s) and contributor(s) and not of MDPI and/or the editor(s). MDPI and/or the editor(s) disclaim responsibility for any injury to people or property resulting from any ideas, methods, instructions or products referred to in the content.

Article

A Provable Secure Cybersecurity Mechanism Based on Combination of Lightweight Cryptography and Authentication for Internet of Things

Adel A. Ahmed [1,*], Sharaf J. Malebary [1], Waleed Ali [1] and Ahmed A. Alzahrani [2]

[1] Information Technology Department, Faculty of Computing and Information Technology-Rabigh, King Abdulaziz University, Jeddah 25729, Saudi Arabia
[2] Information Technology Department, Faculty of Computing and Information Technology, King Abdulaziz University, Jeddah 21589, Saudi Arabia
* Correspondence: aaaabdullah1@kau.edu.sa; Tel.: +966-563-884-738

Citation: Ahmed, A.A.; Malebary, S.J.; Ali, W.; Alzahrani, A.A. A Provable Secure Cybersecurity Mechanism Based on Combination of Lightweight Cryptography and Authentication for Internet of Things. *Mathematics* **2023**, *11*, 220. https://doi.org/10.3390/math11010220

Academic Editor: Wei Fang

Received: 30 November 2022
Revised: 23 December 2022
Accepted: 28 December 2022
Published: 1 January 2023

Copyright: © 2023 by the authors. Licensee MDPI, Basel, Switzerland. This article is an open access article distributed under the terms and conditions of the Creative Commons Attribution (CC BY) license (https://creativecommons.org/licenses/by/4.0/).

Abstract: Internet of Things devices, platform programs, and network applications are all vulnerable to cyberattacks (digital attacks), which can be prevented at different levels by using cybersecurity protocol. In the Internet of Things (IoT), cyberattacks are specifically intended to retrieve or change/destroy sensitive information that may exceed the IoT's advantages. Furthermore, the design of a lightweight cybersecurity mechanism experiences a critical challenge that would perfectly fit resource-constrained IoT devices. For instance, identifying the compromised devices and the users' data and services protection are the general challenges of cybersecurity on an IoT system that should be considered. This paper proposes a secure cybersecurity system based on the integration of cryptography with authentication (ELCA) that utilizes elliptic curve Diffie–Hellman (ECDH) to undertake key distribution while the weak bits problem in the shared secret key is resolved. In this paper, three systems of integration are investigated, while ELCA proposes secure integration between authentication and encryption to facilitate confidentiality and authenticity transfer messages between IoT devices over an insecure communication channel. Furthermore, the security of ELCA is proven mathematically using the random oracle model and IoT adversary model. The findings of the emulation results show the effectiveness of ELCA performance in terms of a reduced CPU execution time by 50%, reduced storage cost by 32–19.6%, and reduced energy consumption by 41% compared to the baseline cryptographic algorithms.

Keywords: IoT; ECDH; symmetric cryptographic; authentication

MSC: 68M25

1. Introduction

The Internet of Things (IoT) enables communication between various items and things that have internetworking devices as well as technological devices. An IoT device is configured with a unique IP address to perform various smart applications without human intervention. Moreover, IoT devices are extremely heterogeneous, differ in their capabilities, and have very limited resources in terms of storage capacity and processing complexity, input/output hardware features, and sources of energy [1]. The cybersecurity mechanism remains a significant challenge for IoT implementation and deployment due to the software and hardware vulnerability against cyberattacks. Moreover, cybersecurity has become a transversal discipline to guarantee the confidentiality, authenticity, and integrity of the generated data, transmitted and/or stored on IoT devices. Privacy and security must be ensured by the cybersecurity mechanism to generate trust in data, which is a decisive factor in making critical decisions for the development of all areas involved in this interconnected world. Generally, cyberattacks utilize the internet to gain unauthorized access to disable

IoT devices, and destroy and disrupt the critical information of the IoT [2–6]. Regardless of the network structure layers, the IoT is susceptible to numerous kinds of attacks at the application, network, and sensing layers. The access control mechanism can effectively monitor the access activities of resources by legitimate users [3]. For instance, cyberattacks cause dangerous compromises on the IoT the strengths of which include sensor imprisonment, known key security, stolen-verifier and controlled information, denial of service (DoS), link sniffing, man-in-the-middle, forced delay, session hijacking, brute force, and dictionary attacks [7–10]. Furthermore, key distribution is the predicament of the symmetric cryptography, and it represents the essential challenge task in a resource-constrained system such as the IoT. One of the practical solutions is using ECDH, which is considered an appropriate solution for secret key distribution among IoT devices. This is primarily due to ECDH having a smaller key size with higher security strength compared to an RSA cryptosystem [11]. Furthermore, ECDH requires fewer CPU resources, which causes less power consumption and processing delay compared to RSA.

Figure 1 illustrates the scenario of a cyberattack that can compromise the channel communication between the sensor devices and the IoT gateway or compromise the IoT cloud networks. The standard cryptosystem solutions (e.g., RSA, AES, DES) require the imperative computation overhead, long key size, high memory capacity, and long processing delay. As a result, they cannot be applied immediately to the technology or sensors with the lowest resource requirements, such as the IoT. Therefore, it is a difficult task to build effective, quick, small, and safe cryptographic techniques for the IoT. Additionally, the IoT networks should put in place a minimal cybersecurity system to guard against unauthorized attackers disclosing sensitive information and to confirm that users are permitted to use IoT services (e.g., authentication and access control) [12–19].

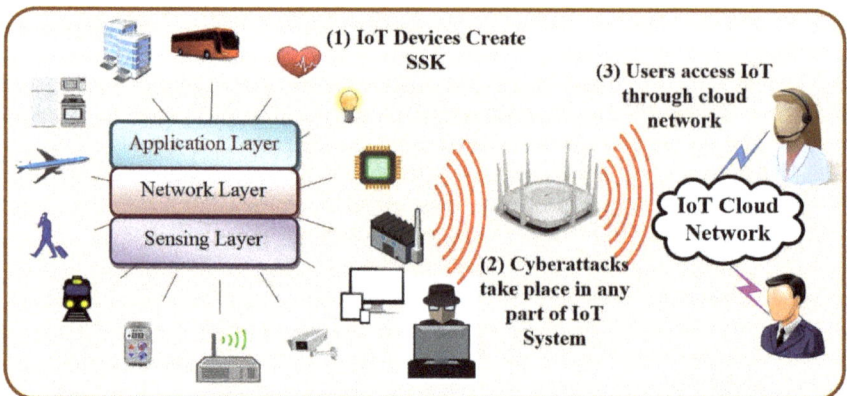

Figure 1. Scenario of cyberattacks on the IoT network.

Cryptography, digital signature, and authentication are the essential solutions to defend against cyberattacks on the IoT. One of the two widely used encryption techniques symmetric (private key) or asymmetric (public key) encryption can be used with IoT cryptography. The same key is used for the cryptographic operation in symmetric encryptions at both the source and the destination. The distribution of the private key among IoT devices determines how strong the symmetric encryption is. As opposed to symmetric encryptions, asymmetric encryptions use two distinct keys: the public key and the private key. The public key can be communicated across a secure channel to the authorized devices, while the private key is kept hidden and never shared.

While encryption can guarantee privacy, message authentication can guarantee authenticity/integrity of the received data. Nevertheless, IoT systems need both authentication and confidentiality. It may be attractive to integrate encryption and authentication; however, not all combinations will provide both privacy and authentication. Certainly, it is a very difficult task to combine cryptographic tools securely, which means that, sometimes, outstanding cryptographic tools can be integrated in a way that produces an insecure combination. Consequently, without proven security of a specific combination, it is risky to use it. The popular methods to merge message authentication and encryption can be described as follows [11]:

- **Method 1**: Encrypt-and-authenticate (EAT), which means the original data should be encrypted using K_1 as $C = E_{k1}(M)$ and the message authentication code should be calculated using K_2 as $T = MAC_{k2}(M)$. The sending message is the pair (C, T), which should be sent separately as shown in Figure 2a.
- **Method 2**: Authenticate-then-encrypt (ATE), which means the tag T is first calculated, and then the original data and T are encrypted together. The sending message is $C = E_{k1}(M+T)$ where $T = MAC_{k2}(M)$ as illustrated in Figure 2b.
- **Method 3**: Encrypt-then-authenticate (ETA), which means the original data M is first encrypted using K_1 as $C = E_{k1}(M)$, and then the tag T is calculated over C. The sending message is the pair (C, T) where $T = MAC_{k2}(C)$ as illustrated in Figure 2c.

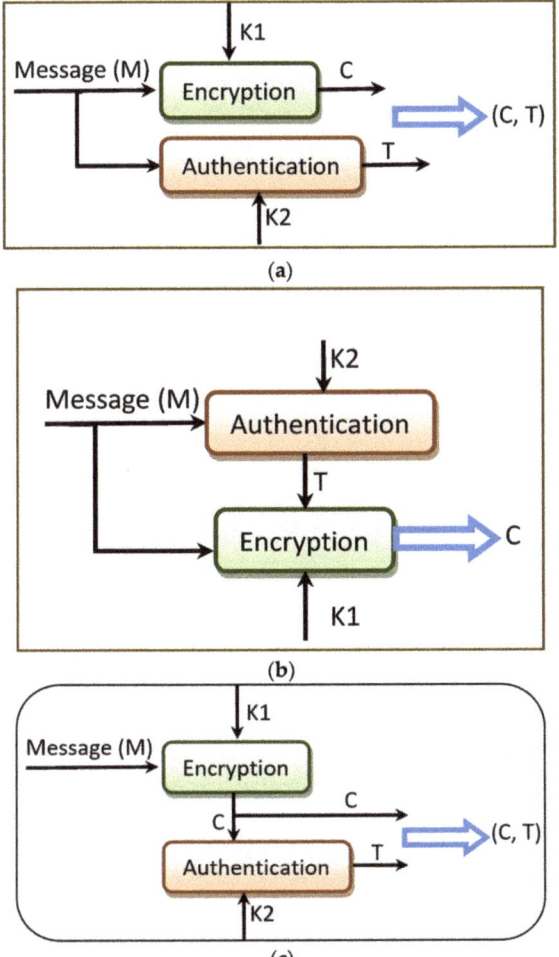

Figure 2. Integration methods between encryption and authentication: (**a**) Encrypt-and-authenticate; (**b**) authenticate-then-encrypt; (**c**) encrypt-then-authenticate.

1.1. Adversary Model on IoT

The main goal of an adversary cyberattack against the IoT is to disrupt its control function by taking advantage of one or more weaknesses that a malicious adversary could use to penetrate the IoT environment's security system [20–22]. The adversary is presumptively capable of reading, transmitting, and faking IoT network traffic, which could raise concerns about sensed data, IoT device privacy, and IoT gateway control management. The most crucial adversary attacks on ELCA are described as follows:

- **Spoofing attack.** To obtain the IoT device credential needed to access the sensed data, the attacker intercepts or eavesdrops on the IoT network traffic.
- **A man-in-the-middle.** In this attack, the malicious adversary has the ability to connect to any IoT device and listen to any network data. Additionally, the adversary can alter the captured messages before they are transmitted to the receiver if it engages in active man-in-the-middle behavior [8].
- **A replay attacks.** A replay attack creates a replica of the message to be used later, as opposed to transmitting it directly to the recipient. An opponent does this by intercepting the data and delaying, replaying, or retransmitting it.
- **A brute force.** Even though the domain parameters that both parties use for ECDH are adequately robust, the malicious adversary in this attack tries every possible combination of letters, digits, and characters to crack the shared secret key.
- **A sensor capture attack.** In this attack, the impostor adversary seizes a sensor node and takes the shared secret key and shared domain parameters in order to carry out unethical activities on the Internet of Things network.
- **A stolen-verifier attack.** If the imposter attacker has obtained the shared secret key from an IoT device, they can pretend to be an authorized device to launch attacks against other IoT devices, steal data, or get around access controls.

1.2. Research Motivation

The motivation of the proposed method is to develop a cybersecurity mechanism that securely combines a lightweight cryptography with authentication to prevent a cyberattack and fit the resource-constrained IoT system. In addition, the proposed solution protects IoT messages from modification, and spoofing attacks.

1.3. Research Contribution

The following contributions are reported in this research:

- It proposes a lightweight symmetric encryption based on the scalar multiplication of the hash function and the base point of the elliptic curve. The modular multiplicative based on order of base point has been used to create the final ciphertext. Additionally, the proposed ELCA confidentially distributes a shared secret key between IoT parties over an insecure communication channel using the ECDH method. Indeed, the secure shared key is an ephemeral that resolves the weak bits problem and is recommended by RFC8442 to provide perfect forward secrecy.
- It proposes an efficacious secure combination between authentication and encryption to facilitate confidentiality and authenticity transfer messages between IoT devices over an insecure communication channel.
- A comprehensive cryptanalysis based on the random oracle model mathematically proves the security of the proposed combination between authentication and encryption on the IoT.
- The well-known IoT adversary model is also exploited to verify the security strength and to prove the security of the proposed scheme.
- Finally, the performance of the suggested ELCA is also evaluated in terms of CPU execution time, power consumption, and storage cost through a number of emulation experiments.

The rest of this paper is organized as follows: the related works on authentication and encryption over an IoT platform is presented in Section 2. The algorithm of the proposed ELCA is explained in Section 3. Additionally, Section 4 describes the cybersecurity analysis for the ELCA mechanisms. The implementation and evaluation of ELCA on the IoT is presented in Section 5. Finally, Section 6 presents the conclusion and future work. All notations used in ELCA are summarized in Table 1.

Table 1. Frequently used notation.

Notation	Meaning	Notation	Meaning
C	Ciphertext	m	Converting M to the integer number
CCA	Chosen-ciphertext attack	MAC	Message authentication code
CPA	Chosen-plaintext attack	n	Order of G
CMA	Chosen-message attack	O	An extra point at infinity of the curve
d	Private key	P	Modular prime
D	Destination node	Pb	Random point in the curve
ECC	Elliptic curve cryptography	Pb.X1	X coordinate of Pb
ECDH	Elliptic curve Diffie–Hellman	PPT	Probabilistic polynomial time
ELCA	Effective, lightweight cryptographic and authentication	PRF	pseudorandom function
EU-CMA	Existentially unforgeable under chosen-message attack	Q	Public key
G	Base point generator	ROM	Random oracle model
h	Subgroup cofactor	S	Source node
IND-CPA	Indistinguishability chosen-plaintext attack	SSK/X_K	Shared secret key
M	Plaintext message	T	Authentication tag

2. Related Works on Cryptographic and Authentication Algorithms

A small number of studies have previously been established to fit resource-constrained devices, particularly for sensors and actuators on IoT networks, despite the fact that many academics have investigated the security algorithms on the IoT. In our earlier work [23], the digital certificate authority was used to link a public key to its owner using a digital certificate, thereby authenticating the sender's genuine identity. Therefore, the related efforts in this research focus on creating simple cryptographic algorithms and lightweight authentication across IoT networks.

Elliptic curve integrated encryption (ECIES), which is combined with advanced standard encryption and is known as ECIES AES, was proposed by V. Shoup. Additionally, ECIES includes rabbit encryption, known as ECIES Ra, in accordance with the specifications in RFC4503. NIST proposed a lightweight authenticated encryption with associated data (AEAD) that can operate with a device that has limited resources, such as an Internet of Things system [24]. The encryption and tag provided by AEAD can be used as a message authentication code (MAC). AEAD provides data authentication, confidentiality, and integrity as a result. To match an IoT resource-constrained system, Byoungjin Seok et al. [25] created secure device-to-device communication using the concepts of AEAD and ECC.

A secure data sharing mechanism for device-to-device communication on the 5G mobile system was presented by Atefeh et al. [26]. The virtual check concept was used in this study as a system of encouragement to encourage manipulators' involvement in the development of data sharing. In the study suggested by Adeel et al. [27], a public key infrastructure (PKI)-based lightweight authentication method was combined with elliptic ElGamal encryption. Additionally, Yasir et al. [28] created a small cryptographic system that relies on ECC and ElGamal over public key infrastructure (EEoP). Additionally, Adel et al. [29] proposed a powerful multifactor authentication (CMA) system that makes use of the concept of combining various hash functions with geolocation authentication over the IoT. In order to verify the key generation, Sciancalepore et al. [30] integrated ECDH exchange with a digital certificate. In order to enhance user authentication, Mohammad Ayoub et al. [31] created a secure ECC-based authentication and encryption system that makes use of user credentials and biometric parameters. Secure IoT (SIT), which makes use of a 64-bit key of Feistel and a consistent substitution–permutation, was proposed by Muhammad U. et al. [32]. Shah et al. [33] presented the integration of Diffie–Hellman-based cryptography and authentication. To share a secret key through the Internet of Things, multifactor authentication is used. One-time passwords (OTPs) that rely on ECC and isogeny to ensure IoT security were proposed by Badis Hammi et al. [34]. The OTP based on ECC's unpredictability is not guaranteed though. A safe system with privacy and authentication based on three factors was proposed by Rangwani, D. et al. [35].

The limitations of the previous literature studies [23–35] are summarized in Table 2. In this table, the main limitations can be specified in four facts: First, the integration between authentication and encryption has not been proven to be secure. Second, the outstanding construction of the IoT and the resource constraints have not been considered. Third, the vulnerabilities of ECDH (i.e., weak bits and chosen-ciphertext attack) have not been resolved and recovered. Finally, the cryptanalysis under a random oracle model has not been investigated.

Table 2. Summary of Related Works.

Approaches	Date Published	Methodology and Features	Limitations
AEAD [24]	2020	It provided the cipher and the tag that offers data confidentiality, integrity, and authentication.	It does not provide secure integration.
B. Seok et al. [25]	2020	In order to accommodate an IoT system with limited resources, it developed a secure device-to-device communication using the concepts of AEAD and ECC.	The cryptanalysis was not studied.
Adeel et al. [27]	2019	In order to manage the public key infrastructure (PKI), it combined the two algorithms ElGamal and ECC.	It lacks the adversary mode analysis.
Yasir et al. [28]	2017	It created a small-scale cryptography system that utilizes ECC and ElGamal.	The cryptanalysis was not studied.
Adel et al. [29]	2019	It proposed a secure multifactor authentication (CMA) that uses robust combiners of the hash functions and geolocation authentication over IoT.	The time processing complexity is high.
KMP [30]	2017	To verify the key generation, ECDH exchange and a digital certificate were included.	Due to the implicit certificate's power consumption, it does not fit IoT resource constraints.

Table 2. Cont.

Approaches	Date Published	Methodology and Features	Limitations
M. Ayoub et al. [31]	2020	It created a secure ECC-based authentication and encryption system that strengthens user authentication by using personal information and biometrics.	Due to the vulnerability of biometric parameter mistake, it does not fit IoT resource constraints.
SIT [32]	2017	It used the idea of combination 64-bit key of Feistel and a uniform substitution–permutation.	Due to power consumption, it does not fit the IoT resource limitations.
Shah et al. [33]	2017	To share a secret key via an IoT network, it integrated authentication and cryptography based on Diffie–Hellman.	It does not prove the security for integration.
B. Hammi et al. [34]	2020	It proposed OTP that relies on ECC and isogeny to guarantee IoT security.	The randomness of the OTP based on ECC is not ensured.
Rangwani, D [35]	2021	It suggested a safe, private, and three-factor authentication mechanism for the Internet of Things.	It does not study the effect of three-factor authentication on the operating system.

3. System Design of ELCA Algorithm

The system design of the proposed ELCA algorithm mainly consists of key management based on ECDH, symmetric encryption algorithm with a random padding system, and message authentication based on multifactor hash function. This research proposes secure integration between symmetric cryptography and authentication based on method 3 (e.g., encrypt-then-authenticate). The three algorithms are organized to guarantee cyberattack protections on the IoT. The three proposed functions in this study were created under the following presumptions:

- The IoT gateway has a robust security mechanism and hence cannot be compromised.
- The shared secret key (SSK) is calculated based on ECDH and it is considered as the private key of the ELCA cryptography.
- SSK in all IoT devices uses the preinstalled two secure keys: the public key, which is calculated at all involved IoT devices, and the private key, which is not known publicly.
- All keys in the proposed system are ephemeral (dynamic), which means they must be changed in each new session.
- The domain parameters of the ECDH are inserted and programmed into all IoT devices during the initialization session.
- The detail of ELCA is explained in the following sections.

3.1. Key Management Algorithm Based on ECDH

The exchange of the common secret key between the IoT devices is the essential concern in traditional symmetric cryptography. This is primarily due to the insecure communication channel that makes IoT devices susceptible to many cyberattacks. Consequently, the proposed encryption mechanism utilizes the ECDH to securely calculate rather than distribute a new SSK for each transmission session between IoT devices (i.e., forward secrecy). The elliptic curve is a set of points identified by solving the following equation:

$$E = \{(x,y)|y^2 = x^3 + ax + b\} \cup \{O\}, \text{ where } a,b \in K(\mathbb{Z}/P\mathbb{Z}) \text{ satisfy } (4a^3 + 27b^2) \neq 0 \quad (1)$$

where K presents an integer finite field over a modular prime P. An extra point at infinity (e.g., O) has been added to the equation to add any point to itself. Let us assume that S and D are the IoT source and the IoT destination, respectively. The domain parameters of elliptic curve consist of p, G, n, h which are the prime number, the base point generator, the order of G, and the subgroup cofactor that is usually 1. These parameters demonstrate the agreed information between S and D to utilize the ECDH key exchange protocol. In each new session, the private key at S and D is generated using the random function, which is selected between 1 and n-1. The public key is a point in the curve, namely Q, which is produced using scalar multiplication of d and G (e.g., $Q = d \times G$) as shown in Figure 3. In this figure, S has a key pair (d_S, Q_S) and D (d_D, Q_D), which represent the private and public keys at each node. Each S and D should receive the public key from the other party prior to implementing the ECDH protocol. Later, S computes its SSK point as $K(X_K, Y_K) = d_S \times Q_D$ and D computes its SSK point as $K(X_K, Y_K) = d_D \times Q_S$. As a result, the agreed SSK is the x coordinate of the point K, which is $k_1 = X_K$. Moreover, $k_2 = Y_K$ represents the agreed SSK for authentication. It is interesting to note that the SSK that is calculated by both parties is equal because $d_S \times Q_D = d_S \times d_D \times G = d_D \times d_S \times G = d_D \times Q_S$, where " $\times$ " denotes elliptic curve scalar multiplication.

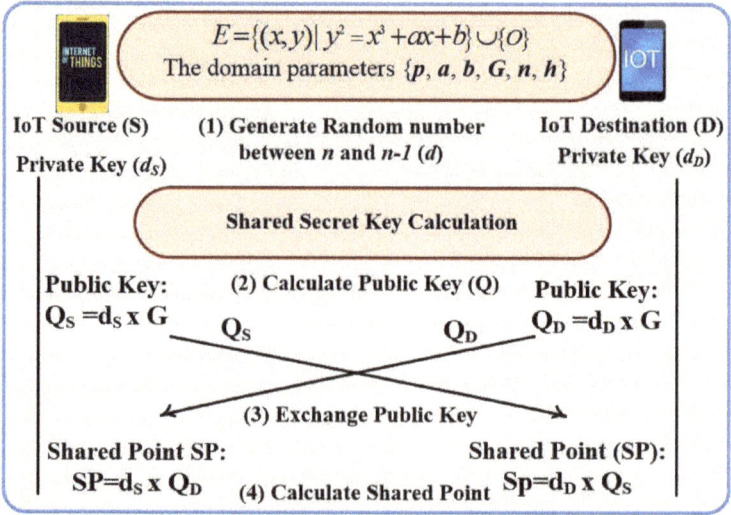

Figure 3. ECDH key management.

3.2. Secure Integration between Encryption and Authentication

The combination between encryption and authentication should be carefully designed because it is very hard to combine cryptographic tools correctly to provide both privacy and authenticity. This means that excellent cryptographic tools can sometimes be applied in a way so that the result is not secure. This research proposes secure integration between symmetric cryptography and authentication based on the encrypt-then-authenticate method called ELCA. In order to fit the maximum transmission unit in the IoT network, the message M is parsed into several chunks based on Secp192r1 elliptic curve domain parameters [36]. Hence, the maximum size of each chunk is 127 bytes, and the minimum size is 24 bytes. The cryptographic steps of ELCA at the source node are implemented as follows:

- Calculate $E = \text{StrToInt}(\text{Hash}(X_K))$; the Hash is a secure cryptographic hash function such as CMA [29] or SHA-256 [37].
- Calculate the curve point $Pb(X_1, Y_1) = E \times G$; the ECC scalar multiplication has a one-way function property, which means it is hard to reverse.
- Calculate the ciphertext $C_i = (m_i \times X_1) \mod n$; where i represents the chunk number. The padding scheme is used to convert the chunk (M_i) to the integer number m_i, which should be agreed upon in reversible protocol.

- Calculate a hash function for C_i as $Z = \text{StrToInt}(\text{Hash}(C)) \mod n$.
- Calculate the authentication code as $T_s = (Y_K \times Z) \mod n$;
- The transmitted message is the pair (C_i, T_s).

The cryptographic steps of ELCA at the destination node upon receiving the pair (C_i, T_s) are performed as follows:

- Calculate a hash function of the integer number m as $Z = \text{StrToInt}(\text{Hash}(C_i)) \mod n$ where Hash() represents the similar cryptographic hash function that is used in the encryption process.
- Calculate $T_d = (Y_K \times Z) \mod n$.
- If $T_d = T_s$, the message is accepted (e.g., message is authentic, and integrity checked). Otherwise, the message is rejected.
- If the message is accepted, calculate $E = \text{StrToInt}(\text{Hash}(X_K))$.
- Calculate the curve point $Pb(X_1, Y_1) = E \times G$.
- Calculate $m_i = (C_i \times X_1^{-1}) \mod n$ where $X_1^{-1} \mod n$ can be resolved using a modular multiplicative inverse.
- Convert the m_i to string M_i and recover the plaintext $M =$ where L is the number of chunks.

Figure 4 shows the flow phases and Algorithm 1 presents the pseudo code of the ELCA algorithm. In these figures, the source node and the destination must use the same domain parameters of the ECDH equation. Upon the public key being calculated at the two parties, it is sent to the other party, which can calculate the shared secret key. Finally, the combination of encrypt-then-authenticate in ELCA is utilized as explained above.

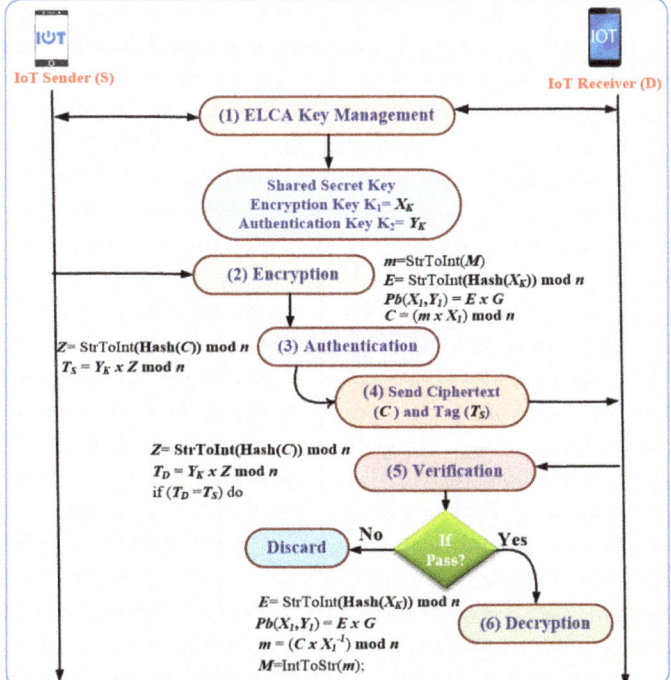

Figure 4. Flow diagram of ELCA algorithm.

Algorithm 1 Pseudo code of ELCA algorithm

ELCA at IoT Sender (S)
Input: Secp192r1 domain parameters p, a, b, G, n, h;
Output: Q_S, T, C; // Q_S: Public key of S, T: authentication tag C: Ciphertext
Start Algorithm (ELCA)

1. | While (new session start) do
2. | Determine the private key (d_S); // $1 \leq d_S \leq n$
3. | $Q_S = (d_S \times G)$; // Q_S: the public key of S
4. | Send_Public_key (Q_S); // Send the public key to destination
5. | Receive_Public_key(Q_D); // Receive the public key of D
6. | $K(X_K, Y_K) = d_S \times Q_D$; // calculate the shared key
7. | For ($i = 0; i<L; i++$) // L: number of chunks
8. | m_i = StrToInt(M_i); // convert the plaintext to an integer.
9. | E = StrToInt(Hash(X_K)) mod n; // E: the hash fun. of key X_K
10. | $Pb(X_1, Y_1) = E \times G$;
11. | $C_i = (m_i \times X_1)$ mod n; // C_i: the ciphertext of message m_i
12. | Z = StrToInt(Hash(C_i)) mod n; // hash fun. for integer m.
13. | $T_S = Y_K \times Z$ mod n; // T_S: Authentication code at the sender
14. | Send("C_i"+" T_S"); // The source sends "C_i"+" T_S" to D
15. | End; // For Loop *Statement*
16. | End; // While loop
17. End; // Algorithm

ELCA at IoT Receiver (D)
Input: the domain parameters p, a, b, G, n, h;
Output: Q_D, T_S, C; // Q_D: Public key of D

18. Start Algorithm (ELCA)
19. | While (new session start) do
20. | Determine the private key (d_D); // $1 \leq d_D \leq n$
21. | $Q_D = (d_D \times G)$; // Q_D: the public key of D
22. | Send_Public_key (Q_D); // Send the public key to source node
23. | Receive_Public_key(Q_S); // Receive the public key from source
24. | $K(X_K, Y_K) = d_D \times Q_S$; // if Q_S is a valid curve point, the shared key will be calculated
25. | Foreach (msg received; i++) do
26. | Get(T_S, C_i); // Receive the message pair (T_S, C_i)
27. | Z = StrToInt(Hash(C_i)) mod n; // hash fun. for C
28. | $T_D = Y_K \times Z$ mod n; // T_D: Authentication code at the destination
29. | If $T_d = T_s$, the message is accepted. Otherwise, the message is rejected.
30. | E = StrToInt(Hash(X_K)) mod n;
31. | $Pb(X_1, Y_1) = E \times G$;
32. | $m_i = (C_i \times X_1^{-1})$ mod n; // Recover the padded message
33. | For ($i = 0; i<L; i++$) // L: number of chunks
34. | M_i = Convert_IntToStr(m_i); // convert integer to plaintext.
35. | $M = M + M_i$ // concertante all chunks.
36. | End; // for loop
37. | End; // While loop
38. End; // Algorithm

4. Cybersecurity Analysis

In order to measure the security level of ELCA, the cryptanalysis for ELCA on the IoT was developed and analyzed.

4.1. Cryptanalysis of ELCA

Let us imagine that, even if the shared secret key is unknown, the adversary may decrypt encrypted messages and bypass the authentication and encryption of the ELCA mechanism. The following are some examples of the most typical cryptanalysis attacks that have been studied using the random oracle model:

- **Chosen-plaintext attack (CPA).** It is expected that the adversary will obtain the ciphertexts for any plaintexts of its choosing. Additionally, the adaptive CPA (CPA2) allows the adversary to select a fresh input for ELCA ($ELCA_E$) encryption based on an analysis of the plaintext queries he previously selected and the accompanying ciphertexts [38]. By assuming that an advertiser A has access to an encryption oracle with any pair of equal-length messages (m1, m2) as input, we can describe the definition of CPA mathematically [20–22].

Definition 1. *Let $ELCA_E$ = (K, E, D) be an encryption mechanism in ELCA, E is encryption, D is decryption, and K is the space of all keys. The advantage of indistinguishability of chosen-plaintext attack (IND-CPA) of A is defined as:*

$$Adv^{in-cPa}_{ELCA_E}(A) = P_r[k \leftarrow K; C \leftarrow E_k(m_1) : A(C) = 1] \\ - P_r[k \leftarrow K; C \leftarrow E_k(m_2) : A(C) = 1] \quad (2)$$

- If the advantage of IND-CPA is negligible, which indicates that A is struggling, the aforementioned equation demonstrates that ELCA is secure. Contrarily, ELCAE is not stable if the IND-advantage of CPA is non-negligible, indicating that A is performing well.
- **Chosen-ciphertext attack (CCA).** It is expected that the adversary will obtain the decryption of any ciphertext(s) of its choosing. A further benefit of the adaptive CCA (CCA2) is that the adversary can select a fresh input for the decryption of ELCA ($ELCA_D$) based on the analysis of his previously chosen queries [39].

Definition 2. *Let $ELCA_E$ = (K, E, D) be an encryption mechanism in ELCA, and A is an adversary who can access the encryption (E) and decryption (D) oracle. The advantage of IND-CCA of A is defined as:*

$$Adv^{in-cca}_{ELCA_E}(A) = P_r[k \leftarrow K; C \leftarrow E_k(m_b); b \leftarrow \{0,1\}; \\ b' \leftarrow A(E_k(.), D_k(.)) : b' = b] \quad (3)$$

According to the aforementioned definition, the adversary is free to access the decryption oracle at any time and with any ciphertext C, with the exception of the previously answered queries from its encryption oracle. Therefore, if the adversary who was provided access to the oracles may find little benefit in differentiating the two occurrences of b (0/1), then ELCAE can be regarded secure against IND-CCA.

4.1.1. Cryptanalysis of Combination between Cryptographic Tools

The combination cryptanalysis will use an all or nothing approach to validate both message confidentiality and authentication for every possible combination between them. This does not mean that the combination is not always secure for every encryption and authentication; however, it means there exists even one case where the combination is not secure. The security level that should be considered in the analysis is IND-CPA for encryption and existentially unforgeable under chosen-message attack (EU-CMA) for authentication. The two attacks (e.g., IND-CPA and EU-CMA) meet the requirement for gaining chosen-ciphertext security together with existential unforgeability. Generally, the proposed cryptanalysis approach to prove the security for the combination is to prove that a given combination meets the definition of the secure communication channel [11]. Let tuple of algorithms ($\overline{K}$, $\overline{ET}$, $\overline{D}$, $\overline{V}$) be a combination of (K, E, D) and (K, T, V), where $\overline{K}$ represents the ECDH key-generation algorithm and produces shared secret keys ($k_1 = X_K$, $k_2 = Y_K$). The combination algorithm in ELCA is represented by $\overline{ET}$, which receives a pair of keys (k_1, k_2) and a message m as input and outputs C and authentication tag T. Furthermore, $\overline{V}$ represents the verification procedure in ELCA, which applies a combination of $E(X_K)$ and

$T(Y_K)$ upon receiving a pair of keys (k_1, k_2) and a value C and/or T. Latterly, $\overline{V}$ outputs 1 or 0. The $\overline{D}$ represents the decryption algorithm in ELCA, which applies a combination of $E(X_K)$ and $T(Y_K)$ upon receiving a pair of keys (k_1, k_2) and a value C. Finally, $\overline{D}$ recovers the original message m.

The satisfactory requirement is that for every $k_1 = X_K$, $k_2 = Y_K$, and for every value m, $\overline{D}_{k1,k2}(\overline{ET}_{k1,k2}(m)) = m$ and $\overline{V}_{k1,k2}(\overline{ET}_{k1,k2}(m)) = 1$. The combination $(\overline{K}, \overline{ET}, \overline{D}, \overline{V})$ is required to satisfy both a CCA-security and authentication security for $\overline{ET}_{k1,k2}$ as defined in the following:

Definition 3. *ELCA = $(\overline{K}, \overline{ET}, \overline{D}, \overline{V})$ is considered as a secure combination of encryption and authentication if (K, E, D) has IND-CPA and the scheme (K, T, V) is EU-CMA.*

Next we analyze the three combination approaches that are illustrated in Figure 2.

- **Encrypt-and-authenticate** (EAT). This combination can reveal the original message m for any encryption mechanism. For instance, if (K, T, V) provides a secure message authentication code and $\overline{T}_k(m) = (m, T_k(m))$, it does not necessarily imply privacy. Hence, the combination $(E_{k1}(m), \overline{T}_{k2}(m))$ completely reveals m and is therefore not IND-CPA. As a result, the EAT does not yield a secure combination of encryption and message authentication.
- **Authenticate-then-encrypt** (ATE). Let us discuss the contrived encryption example that suffices to show that the ATE method is not always secure.
  - ➤ Let us assume that there exists an encryption $(E_k(m))$ mechanism that works as follows: any 0 in m is changed to 00, and any 1 in m is changed randomly to 01 or 10. The decryption of C $(D_k(C))$ in this scheme works as follows: change 00 back to 0, and 01 and 10 back to 1. Nevertheless, a pair of bits 11 will result in $\perp$.
  - ➤ Define $\overline{E}_k(m) = PRF \oplus E_k(m)$ and PRF is a pseudorandom function that creates a new number for each message to encrypt.
  - ➤ Let us study the cryptanalysis of the ATE combination based on $\overline{E}_k(m)$ with any message authentication in the presence of a CCA attack. Let A be an adversary who implements the CCA attack as follows. Given a challenge $C = \overline{E}_{k1}((m, T_{k2}(m))$, A basically complements the first two bits of C and verifies if the resulting ciphertext is valid. If the new C is valid, then A decides that the first bit of m was 1. This is primarily due to the fact that if the first bit of m equals 1, then the first two bits of $\overline{E}_{k1}(m)$ can be 01 or 10. Therefore, the complement of these two bits still yields the same bit 1. However, if the new C is not valid, then A decides that the first bit of m equals 0. This is mainly due to the fact that 0 is mapped to 00 and so flipping these bits yields 11, which means an incorrect C. Accordingly, m is null ($\perp$), which contradicts with the assumption that T_{k2} is still computed over m.

4.1.2. Proven Security of ETA Combination in ELCA Using ROM

The ETA combination in the proposed ELCA is proven secure based on the following security analysis.

Theorem 1. *Let $ELCA_E = (K, E, D)$ be the encryption of ELCA that is secure under IND-CPA, and let $ELCA_M = (K, T, V)$ be the authentication of ELCA that is EU-CMA. Then, ELCA = $(\overline{K}, \overline{ET}, \overline{D}, \overline{V})$ created by the encrypt-then-authenticate is a secure combination of $ELCA_E$ and $ELCA_M$.*

Methodology of Proof. The contradiction methodology is used to prove Theorem 1. Since $ELCA_M$ is *EU-CMA*, all queries (except that obtained from encryption oracle) to the decryption oracle can be assumed to be invalid. Thus, the cryptanalysis of *ELCA* can be reduced to *IND-CPA* of $ELCA_E$ because the decryption oracle is effectually useless. At the beginning, this paper proves that, except with negligible probability, the only valid queries made by A were C that were previously obtained from the encryption oracle. Therefore, if

ELCA is proven as not secure under CCA, then it should be that $ELCA_E$ is not secure under IND-CPA, which contradicts the assumption in Theorem 1.

Proof. Let A be any PPT adversary that implements CCA attack on ELCA, which can be denoted as $PrivK_{A,ELCA}^{CCA}$ (n). Additionally, let us define $VQuery_{A,ELCA}$ (n) to be the event that A inputs a valid query (C,T) to its decryption oracle, which does not reply $\bot$. Generally, if we prove that the $P_r[VQuery_{A,ELCA}$ (n)] is at most negligible, then that will be sufficient to prove Theorem 1. This is because if the decryption oracle does not reply $\bot$, then T is a valid tag for C. Consequently, if (C,T) is a valid input for the decryption oracle, this means that A essential forged a message authentication. If the probability that VQuery occurs is non-negligible, A_{mac} can be constructed to break the message $ELCA_M$ as follows: Let us define $q(\cdot)$ to be a polynomial that represents the upper bounds of queries that are issued from A. The $Mac - forge_{A_{mac},ELCA_M}$(n) is interacted by A_{mac}, which calls the A with chosen random k_i for encryption where $i \leftarrow \{1, \ldots \ldots q(n)\}$. Moreover, A_{mac} uses k_1 and its MAC oracle to simulate the encryption and decryption oracle for A. Let us assume that all queries to the decryption oracle are invalid except the ith query, which is hoped to be valid. This means if A queries the encryption oracle with M, A_{mac} computes $C = E_{k1}(M)$ and calls its MAC oracle to obtain a hope forged T for C. Finally, A_{mac} returns the pair (C,T) to A as its oracle reply. On the other hand, if A sends any decryption oracle query (C,T) except i^{th}, A_{mac} will review if (C,T) has been created before, then A_{mac} returns M. Otherwise, A_{mac} returns $\bot$. However, A_{mac} returns (C,T) as its message authentication forgery and halts upon receiving i^{th} decryption oracle query from A. We remark that since $ELCA_M$ provides a unique tag, this means that the query C was never requested by A_{mac} to its MAC-tag oracle. This is primarily due to (C,T) not being gained from an encryption query, which means there is only a single likelihood that T is a valid tag for C. The probability that the ith query is the first valid query by A is at least $1/q(n)$ since A makes at most $q(n)$. Consequently, the probability that A_{mac} does well in $Mac - forge_{A_{mac},ELCA_M}$(n) is at least $1/q(n)$ times the probability that the VQuery event occurs. Subsequently, the probability of A_{mac} to do well in $Mac - forge_{A_{mac},ELCA_M}$(n) is at most negligible probability; this means VQuery occurs with at most negligible probability, which proves the first part of Theorem 1. As a result, for some negligible function $negl(n)$, the probability of VQuery can be written as:

$$P_r[VQuery_{A,ELCA}(n)] < negl(n)$$

Given that the probability of VQuery happens at most negligible probability, the combination of encrypt-then-authenticate in ELCA will be proven to be CCA-secure. For simplicity, if we prove the security of $ELCA_E$ against IND-CPA attack, then ELCA is proven secure. Let an adversary A_{enc} be created using A for the CPA experiment with $ELCA_E$. A_{enc} selects a key k_2 and calls A. Each time A requests an encryption query for M, A_{enc} calls its encryption oracle with M and receives back C. After that, A_{enc} calculates $T = T_{k2}(C)$ and returns the pair (C,T) to A. In contrast, when A requests a decryption query for the pair (C,T), A_{enc} will search about the pair (C,T) in its history table, which was previously generated from its encryption query, and returns M to A if it is available. Otherwise, A_{enc} returns $\bot$. It is clear to conclude that if A_{enc} succeeds in $PrivK^{CPA}$ when VQuery does not happen, then this equals the success of A in $PrivK^{CCA}$ when VQuery does not happen, which can be defined as follows [11]:

$$\begin{aligned} P_r[PrivK_{A_{enc},ELCA_E}^{CPA}(n) &= 1 \cap \neg VQuery_{A,ELCA}^{CPA}(n)] \\ &= P_r[PrivK_{A,ELCA}^{CCA}(n) = 1 \cap \neg VQuery_{A,ELCA}^{CPA}(n)] \end{aligned} \qquad (4)$$

Implying that:

$$\begin{aligned} P_r[PrivK_{A_{enc},ELCA_E}^{CPA}(n) &= 1] \\ &\geq P_r[PrivK_{A_{enc},ELCA_E}^{CPA}(n) = 1 \cap \neg VQuery_{A,ELCA}(n)] \\ &= P_r[PrivK_{A,ELCA}^{CCA}(n) = 1 \cap \neg VQuery_{A,ELCA}(n)] \end{aligned} \qquad (5)$$

Let us use the contradiction by assuming a non-negligible function ε exists such that:

$$P_r[PrivK^{CCA}_{A,ELCA}(n) = 1] = \frac{1}{2} + \varepsilon(n) \tag{6}$$

Using the fact that $P_r[VQuery_{A,ELCA}(n)]$ is negligible, this means it is smaller than $\varepsilon(n)/2$. As a result, we can conclude the following:

$$P_r[PrivK^{CCA}_{A,ELCA}(n) = 1 \cap VQuery_{A,ELCA}(n)] < \frac{\varepsilon(n)}{2} \tag{7}$$

This means:

$$\begin{aligned} &P_r[PrivK^{CCA}_{A,ELCA}(n) = 1] = \\ &\begin{pmatrix} P_r[PrivK^{CCA}_{A,ELCA}(n) = 1 \cap VQuery_{A,ELCA}(n)] \\ + P_r[PrivK^{CCA}_{A,ELCA}(n) = 1 \cap \neg VQuery_{A,ELCA}(n)] \end{pmatrix} \\ &< \left(P_r[PrivK^{CCA}_{A,ELCA}(n) = 1 \cap \neg VQuery_{A,ELCA}(n)] + \frac{\varepsilon(n)}{2} \right) \end{aligned} \tag{8}$$

By means that A succeeds in $PrivK^{CCA}$ with probability $1/2 + \varepsilon(n)$, then Equation (8) can be expressed as:

$$\begin{aligned} P_r[PrivK^{CCA}_{A,ELCA}(n) &= 1 \cap \neg VQuery_{A,ELCA}(n)] > \\ P_r[PrivK^{CCA}_{A,ELCA}(n) &= 1] - \frac{\varepsilon(n)}{2} \\ &= \frac{1}{2} + \varepsilon(n) - \frac{\varepsilon(n)}{2} = \frac{1}{2} + \frac{\varepsilon(n)}{2} \end{aligned} \tag{9}$$

Equations (5) and (9) can be combined as:

$$P_r[PrivK^{CPA}_{A_{enc},ELCA_E}(n) = 1] > \frac{1}{2} + \frac{\varepsilon(n)}{2} \tag{10}$$

Equation (10) shows that the advantage of A_{enc} to succeed in $PrivK^{CPA}$ is non-negligible over $1/2$. As a result, this contradicts IND-CPA of $ELCA_E$ and we conclude that the combination of encrypt-then-authenticate in ELCA is CCA-secure. □

4.2. ELCA Cybersecurity Analysis

ELCA contains important security features such as impersonation resilience against key compromise and perfect forward secrecy (PFS). ELCA employs a hash function to produce a pseudorandom function (PRF) since it may be thought of as a random oracle function. As stated in Section 3, the ELCA's (i.e., CMA's) hash function uses the shared secret key (X_K) as an input to create the secure random parameter ($H(X_K)$), which is then multiplied by the base point (G) in a scalar manner to obtain the random point Pb(). To protect against IND-CPA and replay attacks, Pb.X1 (i.e., the x coordinate of Pb) is a random value that is periodically modified.

Proven Security of ELCA in ROM

The length of the shared secret key $X_K \in \{0,1\}^L$ can be represented as $L = |X_K| = |n| = |p|$, which is equals the length of the used elliptic curve Secp192r1 (e.g., 192 bits). The hash function is instantiated in ROM using the established security in ELCA as $H(.) : \{0,1\}^* \to \{0,1\}^L$.

Theorem 2. *If Pb is a (t,ϵ)-pseudorandom function (PRF), then the ELCA cryptographic is secure against IND-CPA.*

Methodology of Proof. The second theorem is proven using the contradiction methodology. Let us assume that A runs in PPT exist and that they compromise $ELCA_E$'s security. With non-negligible cost, algorithm A creates a PPT distinguisher B that separates the output of Pb from a random number. Since Pb is a PRF, the prior conclusion that Pb is a random function is incorrect. As a result, the initial hypothesis is incorrect, and the $ELCA_E$ needs to be secure.

Proof. Let us assume A attacks $ELCA_E$ in the sense of IND-CPA and two messages M_0, M_1 are used as follows:

$$\left| \begin{array}{l} P_r[H(X_K) \leftarrow \mathbb{Z}_n^*; Pb \leftarrow H(X_K) \times G; C \leftarrow M_0 \times Pb.X1 : A(C) = 0] \\ -P_r[H(X_K) \leftarrow \mathbb{Z}_n^*; Pb \leftarrow H(X_K) \times G; C \leftarrow M_1 \times Pb.X1 : A(C) = 0] \end{array} \right| = \gamma(L) \quad (11)$$

where $\gamma(L)$ is non-negligible. The algorithm B was constructed to distinguish Pb from the random function. This can be accomplished by determining if Pb is a PRF or a totally random function utilizing B's ability to call Pb. B functions as follows: (1) Pick a random b between 0 and 1, (2) B computes $C = Pb.X1 \times M_b \mod n$, (3) Run the experiment $A(C)$ to obtain A's guess as to the encrypted message. A correctly predicted if $b=$, $\bar{b}$ then B estimates the PRF and the result is "1" as indicated by B. However, A guessed incorrectly if $b \neq \bar{b}$ if B guesses random function and this can be represented by B resulting as "0". The algorithm B distinguishes the output of $Pb.X1$ as:

$$\left| \begin{array}{l} P_r[H(X_K) \leftarrow \mathbb{Z}_n^*; Pb \leftarrow (H(X_K) \times G); y \leftarrow Pb.X1 : B(y) = 1] \\ -P_r[y \leftarrow \mathbb{Z}_n^* : B(y) = 1] \end{array} \right| \quad (12)$$

We will study each of these terms separately as: $P_1 \stackrel{\text{def}}{=} P_r[H(X_K) \leftarrow \mathbb{Z}_n^*; Pb \leftarrow (H(X_K) \times G); y \leftarrow Pb.X1 : B(y) = 1]$, and $P_2 \stackrel{\text{def}}{=} P_r[y \leftarrow \mathbb{Z}_n^* : B(y) = 1]$. In step 3, the algorithm B obtained the following:

$$P_1 = P_r[H(X_K) \leftarrow \mathbb{Z}_n^*; Pb \leftarrow (H(X_K) \times G); y \leftarrow Pb.X1 : \\ b \in \{0, 1\}; b' \leftarrow A(Pb.X1 \times M_b) : b' = b] \quad (13)$$

By using the condition on b gives:

$$P_1 = P_r[H(X_K) \leftarrow \mathbb{Z}_n^*; y \leftarrow Pb.X1 : A(Pb.X1 \times M_0) = 0] \times P_r[b = 0] \\ + P_r[H(X_K) \leftarrow \mathbb{Z}_n^*; y \leftarrow Pb.X1 : A(Pb.X1 \times M_1) = 0] \times P_r[b = 1] \quad (14)$$

With applying the fact:

$$P_r[b = 0] = P_r[b = 1] = \frac{1}{2}$$

and

$$P_r[H(X_K) \leftarrow \mathbb{Z}_n^*; y \leftarrow Pb.X1 : A(Pb.X1 \times M_1) = 1] = \\ 1 - P_r[H(X_K) \leftarrow \mathbb{Z}_n^*; y \leftarrow Pb.X1 : A(Pb.X1 \times M_1) = 0] \quad (15)$$

gives:

$$P_1 = \frac{1}{2} + \left[\frac{1}{2} \times \left(\begin{array}{l} P_r[H(X_K) \leftarrow \mathbb{Z}_n^*; y \leftarrow Pb.X1 : A(Pb.X1 \times M_0) = 0] \\ -P_r[H(X_K) \leftarrow \mathbb{Z}_n^*; y \leftarrow Pb.X1 : A(Pb.X1 \times M_1) = 0] \end{array} \right) \right] = \frac{1}{2} + \left(\frac{1}{2} \times \gamma(L) \right) \quad (16)$$

P_2 is calculated as:

$$P_2 = P_r[y \leftarrow \mathbb{Z}_n^* : b \in \{0, 1\}; b' \leftarrow A(Pb.X1 \times M_b) : b' = b] \quad (17)$$

As before, we eventually obtain:

$$P_2 = \frac{1}{2} + \left[\frac{1}{2} \times \left(\begin{array}{c} P_r[y \leftarrow \mathbb{Z}_n^* : A(Pb.X1 \times M_0) = 0] \\ -P_r[y \leftarrow \mathbb{Z}_n^* : A(Pb.X1 \times M_1) = 0] \end{array}\right)\right] \tag{18}$$

Since y is completely random and $Pb = H(X_K) \times G$, the probability of A wins when breaking the one-time pad is 0. Therefore, P_2 is $1/2$. The final result after using all parameters together gives:

$$\left|\begin{array}{c} P_r[H(X_K) \leftarrow \mathbb{Z}_n^*; Pb \leftarrow (H(X_K) \times G); \\ y \leftarrow Pb.X1 : B(y) = 1] - P_r[y \leftarrow \mathbb{Z}_n^* : B(y) = 1] \\ = \left|\frac{1}{2} + \frac{\gamma(L)}{2} - \frac{1}{2}\right| = \frac{\gamma(L)}{2} \end{array}\right| = |P_1 - P_2| \tag{19}$$

Since the term $\gamma(L)$ was non-negligible, the term $\frac{\gamma(L)}{2}$ is also non-negligible. As a result, A has a non-zero advantage in breaking $ELCA_E$ and hence B has a non-negligible advantage in breaking the PRF (i.e., distinguishing result of Pb from random). However, this contradicts the fact that Pb is a (t, ϵ)-PRF. Since no such A may exist, the assumption must be incorrect, thus $ELCA_E$ is secure *against IND-CPA*. □

4.3. Countermeasures Spoofing Attacks

ELCA can prevent spoofing attacks (e.g., replay attacks and the man-in-the-middle attacks) using the secure combination integration between encryption and authentication. Moreover, ELCA drops the reply packet from the intruders because of the following reasons:

- The MAC should be checked before performing the decryption process.
- The ephemeral shared secret key is computed at the source and destination.
- The three stages must be carried out by replay attacks before resending the intercepted communication. These steps—calculating the shared secret key, encrypting messages, and calculating the authentication tag—make it incredibly difficult to access information without compromising the shared secret key and hash function.

4.4. Countermeasures against Brute Force Attacks

ELCA addresses the weak bits issue and offers perfect forward secrecy because the shared secret key must change with each communication session. Additionally, the elliptic curve discrete logarithm problem (ECDLP), which requires $0.886 * \sqrt{k}$ steps, must be solved by the brute force attacker. This indicates that the security strength is 96, which will probably require a lot of computer power [37,40].

4.5. Countermeasures against Session Hijacking Attack

Secure hash functions such as SHA-2 and CMA are applied using the shared secret key in ELCA [29]. This method produces a random integer that can be used to create the session identification, such as the digest of a shared secret key after it has been hashed. In order to obtain access to the communication channel between the IoT parties, the attacker must determine the authentication code if he is successful in cracking the session ID. This is mostly because the verification process between the IoT sender and receiver of the session requires the authentication code.

4.6. Countermeasures against IoT Device Capture and Stolen-Verifier Attacks

The ELCA cryptographic system uses the built-in multifactor hash functions (e.g., CMA [29]) that are burned during programming sessions inside all IoT devices to protect against IoT device capture and stolen-verifier attacks. As stated in the assumption, the multifactor hash functions used in ELCA are flashed and transformed into low level source code language. Therefore, the stolen key will not function without disabling the hash algorithms, preventing the hacker from accessing any safe data in the IoT device.

5. Implementation and Performance Evaluation of ELCA on IoT

Based on the resource constraints in terms of computing cost, storage utilization, and power consumption, the security software in IoT platforms should be assessed. Therefore, ELCA adopted the concept of ECDH for exchanging the secret key advised by SECG/NIST (such as Secp192r1) [37]. Following are some reasons why utilizing the Secp192r1 standard elliptic curve in ELCA is advantageous:

- The size of the encryption and authentication keys is 24 bytes (192 bits), and the processing latency for the ECDH to generate and exchange the secret key has been assessed to be 0.576 s through experimental testing [31].
- It takes $0.886 * \sqrt{k}$ steps to determine the k-size of the acknowledged ideal algorithm for the ECDLP. In general, if the security system employs at least 2*k-bit key size, a k-bit security strength can be attained. Because of this, ELCA chose to employ the Secp192r1 curve, which can offer 96-bit security strength [37,40].
- The 6LowPAN protocol, which uses a 40-byte header to establish connections between IoT devices and sensor nodes, can be used to construct IoT devices with messages up to 127 bytes in size [41].

Since Mininet-IoT can replicate the IoT hardware and communication description, it is used in the assessment scenarios to implement and verify the performance of ELCA [42]. As can be shown in Figure 5, one IoT gateway (BaseST1), eight static IoT devices (sensors 1 through 8), two intruders (Intrudr6 and Intrudr7), and one mobile IoT device (IoTDev5) make up the experiment's IoT network topology. The adversary model that was covered in the previous part is mostly implemented by intruders. Each IoT hardware board includes two network interface cards, one for IPv4 and one for IPv6 communications with the IoT base station (i.e., 6LowPAN). Additionally, all sensors, IoTDev5, and BaseST1 have the suggested ELCA software uploaded. Additionally, all legitimate IoT devices exchange public keys and secure packets utilizing client–server socket programming in combination with ELCA code. BaseST1 implements the server code, and IoTDev5 and all sensors run the client code. The settings and setup of the experiment are shown in Table 3. In Mininet-IoT, the 6LowPAN protocol is implemented on the TCP/IP model using the 802.15.4 hwsim and 802.11 hwsim wireless models. Additionally, the wireless signal's propagation model is set up using a shadowing model, which depicts the actual signal degradation brought on by signal impairments including attenuation, noise, and interference. In the experiment, the grid network area measures 1000 m by 900 m, and random movement is used to construct the mobility model of mobile devices. To investigate the effectiveness of ELCA against intruders using dictionary and brute force attacks, the operating time of every experimental program is set to 1000 s.

Table 3. Experiment Configuration.

Parameter	Values
MAC and PHY	802.15.14_hmsim and 802.11_hmsim
Propagation Model	Shadowing
Path loss exponent	3.0
Shadowing deviation (dB)	3.0
Event area	(1000 m × 900 m)
Number of IoT devices	12
Coverage of IoT device	150 m
Cover range of BaseST1	250 m
Traffic Emulator	TCP Socket client/server; 1000 messages.
Performance metrics	CPU execution time, storage cost, and energy consumption
ECDH curve	Secp192r1
Message Size	127 bytes
Key size	192 Bits
Emulation duration	1000 s

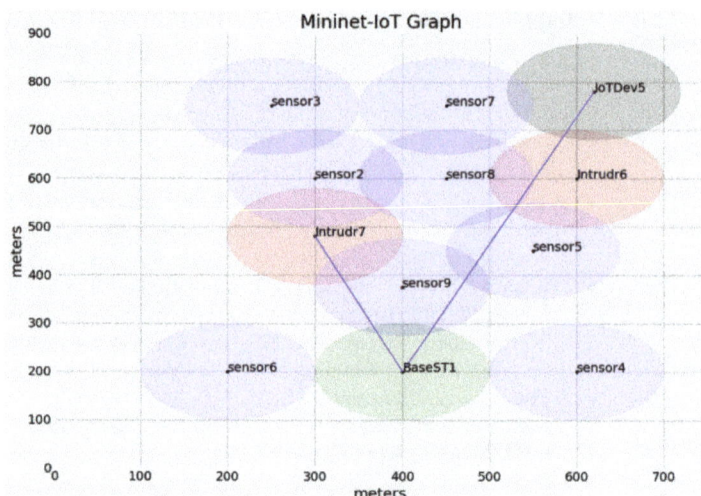

Figure 5. IoT mesh topology.

5.1. Performance Evaluation and Results Discussion

In terms of CPU execution time, memory utilization, and power consumption expenses, the suggested integration of encryption and authentication (for example, ELCA) was evaluated in terms of performance. For the three combinations of authentication and encryption shown in Figure 2, a comparison of performance analysis was investigated. Additionally, ECIES AES and ECIES Ra (RFC4503), two benchmark security algorithms, were used to compare ELCA's performance. Python is used throughout the source code and is implemented in the Mininet-IoT emulator. Additionally, all baseline algorithms' primary source codes can be downloaded from the security website [43]. Numerous scenarios were run, and each testbed was repeated ten times while exchanging 1000 packets. Finally, using the mean and standard deviation as inputs and accepting 5% variation errors in the sample, the average findings were determined with a confidence interval that exceeds 95%. Furthermore, the memory profiler and cProfile programs offer deterministic cost profiling of the baseline methods and ELCA. Memory profiler can be used to calculate an algorithm's execution time, storage expense, and energy usage. The product of CPU execution time and the quantity of steps per execution (s/e) can be used to evaluate the entire cost of CPU execution time. Additionally, the total cost of communication (send/received message) data, sensed data, and the cost of the source code in a time unit can be used to calculate the storage cost in each IoT device. Additionally, the total energy required by IoT devices (mJ) can be calculated as the total energy used to carry out the security algorithm's source code plus any packet overhead [44].

5.1.1. Comparison between Integration Methods of Authentication and Encryption

In this experiment, the performance of using ELCA in three methods of integration between authentication and encryption was evaluated. ELCA was implemented using the three combination approaches (e.g., ATE, EAT and ETA) illustrated in Figure 2. Generally, the results in Figure 6 show that the performance cost of BaseST1 in three combination is higher than IoTDev5. This is mainly due to the type of connection in the IoT system is many-to-one that means all sensor devices send the environment data to the sink (BaseST1). The sink in Figure 6 manipulated the security for all data in the IoT system. As shown in Figure 6a, the ELCA with ETA experiences on average 30.74% less CPU execution time compared to ELCA with ATE, and it experiences on average 15% less CPU execution time compared to ELCA with EAT. Moreover, Figure 6b illustrates that ELCA with ETA experiences on average 22.5% less memory usage compared to ELCA with ATE, and it experiences on average 32.63% less memory usage compared to ELCA with EAT. Moreover, Figure 6c shows that ELCA with ETA consumes on average 68.7% less energy consumption compared to ELCA with ATE, and it consumes on average 52.5% less energy consumption compared to ELCA with EAT. The results presented in Figure 6 show that the impressive performance of the ELCA with ETA algorithm is mainly achieved due to the following reasons: Firstly, ELCA with ETA uses fewer steps of call functions due to the verification of authentication being implemented before the decryption, which causes a reduced CPU execution time, less memory to be used, and reduced power consumption. However, ATE and EAT must implement decryption and verification of authentication with all received ciphertexts and tags, which consumes more resources in term of energy consumption, storage cost, and CPU execution time. Finally, ATE and EAT consume higher call functions, execution time, and communication overheads due to the frequent uses of scalar multiplication and the inverse modular multiplicative in the decryption process.

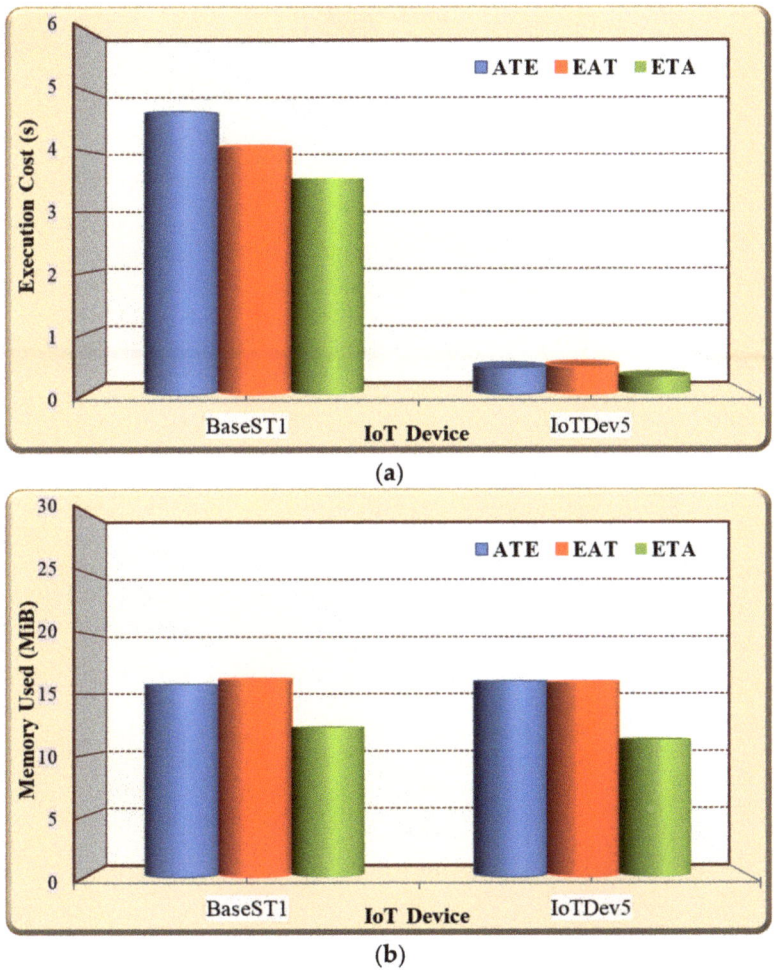

Figure 6. Cont.

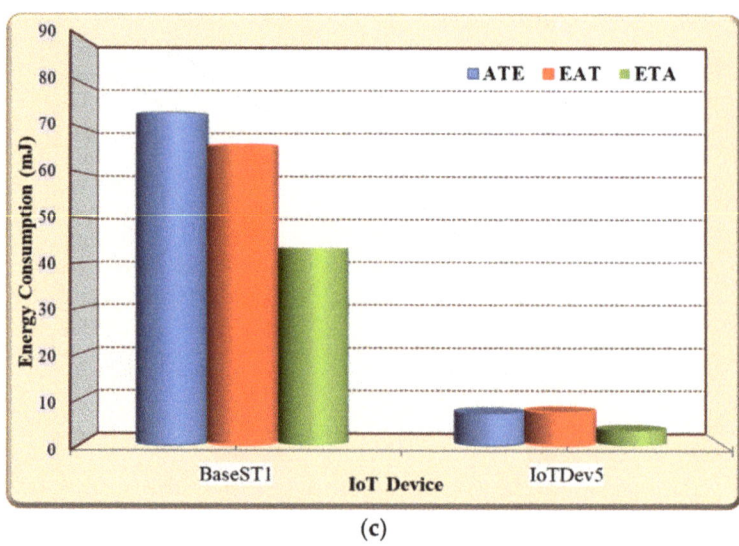

(c)

Figure 6. Comparison between integration methods of authentication and encryption. (**a**) Execution cost; (**b**) storage cost; (**c**) energy consumption.

5.1.2. Performance of Cryptographic Algorithms

It has been determined how well ELCA encryption (ELCA_E) performs in comparison to ECIES_Ra and ECIES_AES. As can be seen in Figure 7a, ELCA_E executes with an average execution time that is 50% lower than that of EDIDS_AES and averages 39.4% lower than that of ECIES_Ra. Additionally, Figure 7b shows that ELCA_E uses memory on average 19.6% and 32% less efficiently than ECIES_AES and ECIES_Ra. Additionally, Figure 7c demonstrates that ELCA_E uses an average of 32.6% less energy than ECIES_Ra and there is a difference of 41.2% between ECIES_AES and ELCA_E. The aforementioned results show that ELCA E outperforms ECIES_AES and ECIES_Ra in terms of CPU time execution, storage cost, and energy usage. This is mostly because of the following factors: Firstly, ELCA_E uses less computing power and energy during encryption and decryption because it is based on an effective mathematical random function. For each session between IoT devices, ELCA_E generates an overall shared secret key that ensures perfect forward secrecy of the encrypted message. Second, because fewer functions are called and there are fewer execution steps for each function, ELCA_E uses less storage space. Finally, ECIES_AES and ECIES_Ra employ more difficult and inefficient encryption and decryption techniques than ELCA_E. In conclusion, the experimental findings demonstrate that the suggested integration of authentication and encryption in ELCA is efficient, lightweight, and offers exceptional performance in terms of CPU execution time, storage cost, and energy consumption. More crucially, it fixes the issues with symmetric cryptography's key distribution and the verification of the sender's identity in digital signatures.

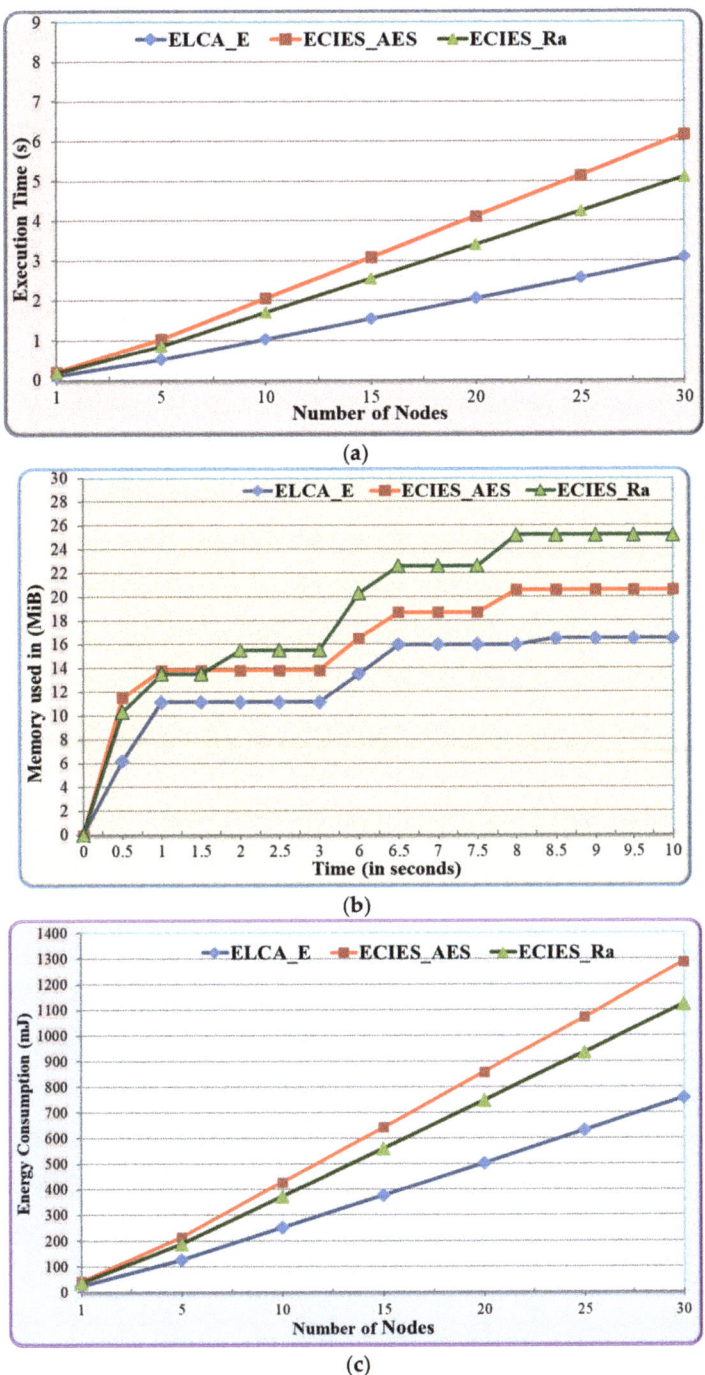

Figure 7. Comparison between ELCA encryption (ELCA_E) and baseline cryptographic algorithms on IoT. (**a**) Execution cost; (**b**) storage cost; (**c**) energy consumption.

6. Conclusions and Future Work

The proposed secure integration between encryption and authentication (e.g., ELCA) algorithm was presented and compared with standard lightweight cryptographic schemes. ELCA utilized ECDH to implement key distribution, while the weak bits problem in the shared secret key is resolved. The security of ELCA was proven mathematically using the IoT adversary model and the random oracle model. The finding in the experimental results shows the efficiency and effectiveness of ELCA performance in terms of a reduced CPU execution time by 50%, reduced storage cost by 32–19.6%, and reduced energy consumption by 41% compared to the baseline cryptographic algorithms. The future work of this research will focus on developing an unforgeable digital signature based on the three steps of hash function inspections for IoT networks. Moreover, the weak bit problem will be resolved using advanced key generation without concerns about the IoT key selection.

Author Contributions: Conceptualization, A.A.A. (Adel A. Ahmed) and W.A.; methodology, A.A.A. (Adel A. Ahmed); software, A.A.A. (Adel A. Ahmed); validation, S.J.M., A.A.A. (Ahmed A. Alzahrani) and W.A.; formal analysis, S.J.M.; investigation, W.A.; resources, A.A.A. (Adel A. Ahmed); data curation, A.A.A. (Ahmed A. Alzahrani); writing—original draft preparation, A.A.A. (Adel A. Ahmed); writing—review and editing, W.A.; visualization, A.A.A. (Ahmed A. Alzahrani); supervision, A.A.A. (Adel A. Ahmed); project administration, A.A.A. (Adel A. Ahmed); funding acquisition, A.A.A. (Adel A. Ahmed). All authors have read and agreed to the published version of the manuscript.

Funding: This research work was funded by institutional Fund Projects under grant no. (IFPIP:324-830-1443). The authors gratefully acknowledge technical and financial support provided by the Ministry of Education and King Abdulaziz University, DSR, Jeddah, Saudi Arabia.

Data Availability Statement: Not applicable.

Acknowledgments: This research work was funded by institutional Fund Projects under grant no. (IFPIP:324-830-1443). The authors gratefully acknowledge technical and financial support provided by the Ministry of Education and King Abdulaziz University, DSR, Jeddah, Saudi Arabia.

Conflicts of Interest: The authors declare no conflict of interest.

References

1. Malina, L.; Hajny, J.; Fujdiak, R.; Hosek, J.J. On perspective of security and privacy-preserving solutions in the internet of things. *Comput. Netw.* **2016**, *102*, 83–95. [CrossRef]
2. Hussain, S.; Ullah, S.S.; Ali, I.; Xie, J.; Inukollu, V.N. Certificateless signature schemes in Industrial Internet of Things: A comparative survey. *Comput. Commun.* **2022**, *181*, 116–131. [CrossRef]
3. Qiu, J.; Tian, Z.; Du, C.; Zuo, Q.; Su, S.; Fang, B. A survey on access control in the age of internet of things. *IEEE Internet Things J.* **2020**, *7*, 4682–4696. [CrossRef]
4. Li, S.; Zhang, T.; Yu, B.; He, K. A Provably Secure and Practical PUF-Based End-to-End Mutual Authentication and Key Exchange Protocol for IoT. *IEEE Sens. J.* **2021**, *21*, 5487–5501. [CrossRef]
5. Arne, B.; Le, N.; Dominik, S.; Stephan, S.; Lars, C.W. Security Properties of Gait for Mobile Device Pairing. *IEEE Trans. Mob. Comput.* **2019**, *19*, 697–710.
6. Attarian, R.; Hashemi, S. An anonymity communication protocol for security and privacy of clients in IoT-based mobile health transactions. *Comput. Netw.* **2021**, *190*, 107976. [CrossRef]
7. Almajed, H.N.; Almogren, A.S. SE-Enc: A Secure and Efficient Encoding Scheme Using Elliptic Curve Cryptography. *IEEE Access* **2019**, *7*, 175865–175878. [CrossRef]
8. Bu, L.; Isakov, M.; Kinsy, M.A. A secure and robust scheme for sharing confidential information in IoT systems. *Ad Hoc Netw.* **2019**, *92*, 101762. [CrossRef]
9. Hendaoui, F.; Eltaief, H.; Youssef, H. UAP: A unified authentication platform for IoT environment. *Comput. Netw.* **2021**, *188*, 107811. [CrossRef]
10. Vidya, R.; Prema, K.V. Lightweight hashing method for user authentication in Internet-of-Things. *Ad Hoc Netw.* **2019**, *89*, 97–106.
11. Katz, J.; Yehuda, L. *Introduction to Modern Cryptography*; CRC Press: Boca Raton, FL, USA, 2007.
12. Barker, E. Recommendation for Key Management. In *Computer Security*; NIST Special Publication 800-57 Part 1, Revision 5; USA, Department of Commerce: Washington, DC, USA, 20 May 2020. [CrossRef]
13. Chuang, Y.-H.; Lo, N.-W.; Yang, C.-Y.; Tang, S.-W. A Lightweight Continuous Authentication Protocol for the Internet of Things. *Sensors* **2018**, *18*, 1104. [CrossRef] [PubMed]

14. Alaba, F.A.; Othman, M.; Hashem, I.A.T.; Alotaibi, F. Internet of Things security: A survey. *J. Netw. Comput. Appl.* **2017**, *88*, 10–28. [CrossRef]
15. Riad, K.; Huang, T.; Ke, L. A dynamic and hierarchical access control for IoT in multi-authority cloud storage. *J. Netw. Comput. Appl.* **2020**, *160*, 102633. [CrossRef]
16. Alexander, J.M.; Kueffer, C.; Daehler, C.; Edwards, P.J.; Pauchard, A.; Seipel, T.; Arévalo, R.J.; Cavieres, L.A.; Dietz, H.; Jakobs, G.; et al. NETRA: Enhancing IoT Security Using NFV-Based Edge Traffic Analysis. *IEEE Sens. J.* **2019**, *19*, 4660–4671. [CrossRef]
17. Hellaoui, H.; Koudil, M.; Bouabdallah, A. Energy-efficient mechanisms in security of the internet of things: A survey. *Comput. Netw.* **2017**, *127*, 173–189. [CrossRef]
18. Magdich, R.; Jemal, H.; Ayed, M. A resilient Trust Management framework towards trust related attacks in the Social Internet of Things. *Comput. Commun.* **2022**, *191*, 92–107. [CrossRef]
19. Liu, X.; Yu, W.; Liang, F.; Griffith, D.; Golmie, N. On deep reinforcement learning security for Industrial Internet of Things. *Comput. Commun.* **2021**, *168*, 20–32. [CrossRef]
20. Li, X.; Niu, J.W.; Ma, J.; Wang, W.D.; Liu, C.L. Cryptanalysis and improvement of a biometrics-based remote user authentication scheme using smart cards. *J. Netw. Comput. Appl.* **2011**, *34*, 73–79. [CrossRef]
21. Al-Karaki, J.N.; Gawanmeh, A.; Almalkawi, I.T.; Alfandi, O. Probabilistic analysis of security attacks in cloud environment using hidden Markov models. *Trans. Emerg. Telecommun. Technol.* **2022**, *33*, e3915. [CrossRef]
22. Wang, Y.; Yang, G.; Li, T.; Li, F.; Tian, Y.; Yu, X. Belief and fairness: A secure two-party protocol toward the view of entropy for IoT devices. *J. Netw. Comput. Appl.* **2020**, *161*, 102641. [CrossRef]
23. Ahmed, A.A. Lightweight Digital Certificate Management and Efficacious Symmetric Cryptographic Mechanism over Industrial Internet of Things. *Sensors* **2021**, *21*, 2810. [CrossRef] [PubMed]
24. NIST Computer Security Resource Center. Lightweight Cryptography Project. Available online: https://csrc.nist.gov/projects/lightweight-cryptography (accessed on 13 March 2022).
25. Seok, B.; Sicato, J.C.S.; Erzhena, T.; Xuan, C.; Pan, Y.; Park, J.H. Secure D2D Communication for 5G IoT Network Based on Lightweight Cryptography. *Appl. Sci.* **2020**, *10*, 217. [CrossRef]
26. Mohseni-Ejiyeh, A.; Ashouri-Talouki, M.; Mahdavi, M. An Incentive-Aware Lightweight Secure Data Sharing Scheme for D2D Communication in 5G Cellular Networks. *ISeCure* **2018**, *10*, 15–27.
27. Abro, A.; Deng, Z.; Memon, K.A. A Lightweight Elliptic-Elgamal-Based Authentication Scheme for Secure Device-to-Device Communication. *Future Internet* **2019**, *11*, 108. [CrossRef]
28. Javed, Y.; Khan, A.S.; Qahar, A.; Abdullah, J. EEoP: A lightweight security scheme over PKI in D2D cellular networks. *J. Telecommun. Electron. Comput. Eng.* **2017**, *9*, 99–105.
29. Ahmed, A.A.; Ahmed, W.A. An Effective Multifactor Authentication Mechanism Based on Combiners of Hash Function over Internet of Things. *Sensors* **2019**, *19*, 3663. [CrossRef]
30. Sciancalepore, S.; Piro, G.; Boggia, G.; Bianchi, G. Public Key Authentication and Key Agreement in IoT Devices with Minimal Airtime Consumption. *IEEE Embed. Syst. Lett.* **2017**, *9*, 1–4. [CrossRef]
31. Khan, M.A.; Quasim, M.T.; Alghamdi, N.S.; Khan, M.Y. A Secure Framework for Authentication and Encryption Using Improved ECC for IoT-Based Medical Sensor Data. *IEEE Access* **2020**, *8*, 52018–52027. [CrossRef]
32. Muhammad, U.; Ahmed, I.; Imran, M.A.; Shujaat, K.; Usman, A.S. SIT: A lightweight encryption algorithm for secure internet of things. *Int. J. Adv. Comput. Sci. Appl.* **2017**, *8*, 402–411.
33. Shah, R.H.; Salapurkar, D.P. A multifactor authentication system using secret splitting in the perspective of Cloud of Things. In Proceedings of the International Conference on Emerging Trends & Innovation in ICT (ICEI), Pune, India, 3–5 February 2017; pp. 1–4.
34. Hammi, B.; Fayad, A.; Khatoun, R.; Zeadally, S.; Begriche, Y. A Lightweight ECC-Based Authentication Scheme for Internet of Things (IoT). *IEEE Syst. J.* **2020**, *14*, 3440–3450. [CrossRef]
35. Rangwani, D.; Sadhukhan, D.; Ray, S.; Khan, M.K.; Dasgupta, M. A robust provable-secure privacy-preserving authentication protocol for Industrial Internet of Things. *Peer-to-Peer Netw. Appl.* **2021**, *14*, 1548–1571. [CrossRef]
36. Lochter, M.; Merkle, J. *RFC 5639: Elliptic Curve Cryptography (ECC) Brainpool Standard Curves and Curve Generation*; IETF: Felemon, CA, USA, 2010; ISSN 2070-1721.
37. NIST. *Fips Publication 180-2: Secure Hash Standard*; Technical Report; National Institute of Standards and Technology (NIST): Gaithersburg, MD, USA, 2003.
38. Biryukov, A. Adaptive Chosen Plaintext Attack. In *Encyclopedia of Cryptography and Security*; Van Tilborg, H.C.A., Jajodia, S., Eds.; Springer: Boston, MA, USA, 2011.
39. Biryukov, A. Related Key Attack. In *Encyclopedia of Cryptography and Security*; Van Tilborg, H.C.A., Jajodia, S., Eds.; Springer: Boston, MA, USA, 2011.
40. Silverma, J.H. *An Introduction to the Theory of Elliptic Curves, Summer School on Computational Number Theory and Applications to Cryptography*; Brown University: Providence, RI, USA, 2006.
41. IPv6 over Low-Power Wireless Personal Area Networks (6LoWPANs): Overview, Assumptions, Problem Statement, and Goals. Available online: http://www.ietf.org/rfc/rfc4919.txt (accessed on 27 November 2022).
42. Mininet-IoT Emulator of Internet of Things. Available online: https://github.com/ramonfontes/mininet-iot (accessed on 27 November 2022).

43. A Security Site. Available online: https://asecuritysite.com/encryption (accessed on 27 November 2022).
44. Ahmed, A.A. An optimal complexity H. 264/AVC encoding for video streaming over next generation of wireless multimedia sensor networks. *Signal Image Video Process.* **2016**, *10*, 1143–1150. [CrossRef]

Disclaimer/Publisher's Note: The statements, opinions and data contained in all publications are solely those of the individual author(s) and contributor(s) and not of MDPI and/or the editor(s). MDPI and/or the editor(s) disclaim responsibility for any injury to people or property resulting from any ideas, methods, instructions or products referred to in the content.

Article

Assisting Glaucoma Screening Process Using Feature Excitation and Information Aggregation Techniques in Retinal Fundus Images

Ali Raza [1,†], Sharjeel Adnan [1], Muhammad Ishaq [1], Hyung Seok Kim [2], Rizwan Ali Naqvi [3,*,†] and Seung-Won Lee [4,*]

1   Department of Primary and Secondary Healthcare, Lahore 54000, Pakistan
2   Department of Intelligent Mechatronics Engineering, Sejong University, Seoul 05006, Republic of Korea
3   Department of Unmanned Vehicle Engineering, Sejong University, Seoul 05006, Republic of Korea
4   School of Medicine, Sungkyunkwan University, Suwon 16419, Republic of Korea
*   Correspondence: rizwanali@sejong.ac.kr (R.A.N.); swlsejong@sejong.ac.kr (S.-W.L.)
†   These authors contributed equally and are co-first authors.

Abstract: The rapidly increasing trend of retinal diseases needs serious attention, worldwide. Glaucoma is a critical ophthalmic disease that can cause permanent vision impairment. Typically, ophthalmologists diagnose glaucoma using manual assessments which is an error-prone, subjective, and time-consuming approach. Therefore, the development of automated methods is crucial to strengthen and assist the existing diagnostic methods. In fundus imaging, optic cup (OC) and optic disc (OD) segmentation are widely accepted by researchers for glaucoma screening assistance. Many research studies proposed artificial intelligence (AI) based decision support systems for glaucoma diagnosis. However, existing AI-based methods show serious limitations in terms of accuracy and efficiency. Variations in backgrounds, pixel intensity values, and object size make the segmentation challenging. Particularly, OC size is usually very small with unclear boundaries which makes its segmentation even more difficult. To effectively address these problems, a novel feature excitation-based dense segmentation network (FEDS-Net) is developed to provide accurate OD and OC segmentation. FEDS-Net employs feature excitation and information aggregation (IA) mechanisms for enhancing the OC and OD segmentation performance. FEDS-Net also uses rapid feature downsampling and efficient convolutional depth for diverse and efficient learning of the network, respectively. The proposed framework is comprehensively evaluated on three open databases: REFUGE, Drishti-GS, and Rim-One-r3. FEDS-Net achieved outperforming segmentation performance compared with state-of-the-art methods. A small number of required trainable parameters (2.73 million) also confirms the superior computational efficiency of our proposed method.

Keywords: assisting glaucoma screening; convolutional neural network; deep learning; fundus image analysis; information aggregation

MSC: 68T07

Citation: Raza, A.; Adnan, S.; Ishaq, M.; Kim, H.S.; Naqvi, R.A.; Lee, S.-W. Assisting Glaucoma Screening Process Using Feature Excitation and Information Aggregation Techniques in Retinal Fundus Images. *Mathematics* **2023**, *11*, 257. https://doi.org/10.3390/math11020257

Academic Editor: Wei Fang

Received: 5 December 2022
Revised: 23 December 2022
Accepted: 26 December 2022
Published: 4 January 2023

Copyright: © 2023 by the authors. Licensee MDPI, Basel, Switzerland. This article is an open access article distributed under the terms and conditions of the Creative Commons Attribution (CC BY) license (https://creativecommons.org/licenses/by/4.0/).

1. Introduction

Ophthalmic diseases have a significant impact on the well-being of human lives. Retinal diseases are increasing at a rapid pace, worldwide [1]. Therefore, modern diagnostic solutions need to be introduced for fast and accurate ophthalmic diagnosis. Glaucoma is a publicly very common neurodegenerative disease that can cause permanent vision loss [2]. Early and accurate glaucoma screening is highly desirable for its effective treatment [2]. Typically, manual procedures and assessments are carried out by ophthalmologists for glaucoma diagnosis. These manual procedures are usually time-consuming, subjective, tedious, and error-prone. Hence, automatic methods are crucially required to assist the existing approaches.

Artificial intelligence (AI) is providing robust automation solutions to automate manual procedures [3]. AI-based models significantly contributed to the biomedical and diagnostic industry by introducing intelligent methods for delivering computer-assisted diagnosis [4]. Deep learning solved many complex diagnostic problems using convolutional neural networks (CNNs). Specifically, CNN-based semantic segmentation has a proven record in ophthalmic diagnostic support [5]. Fundus imaging is widely accepted by experts for glaucoma screening [6]. Optic cup (OC) and optic disc (OD) segmentation are performed for glaucoma detection. Glaucoma produces some morphological and structural changes in OC and OD. Segmentation of both OC and OD provides exact area and boundaries which consequently helps in glaucoma screening. Vertical cup-to-disc-ratio (V-CDR) is also a widely accepted biomarker by researchers to help in glaucoma diagnosis [7]. The ratio between the vertical diameter of OC and OD is calculated for computing V-CDR. Higher values of V-CDR refer to a high chance of glaucoma occurrence. A high-performance OC and OD segmentation is the preliminary step to obtain accurate V-CDR measures. Similarly, enlargement in the OC size which is termed cupping is also a biomarker for glaucoma diagnosis. Areas of OC and OD are computed to provide area-cup-to-disc-ratio (A-CDR) [8]. A-CDR computations also assist ophthalmologists in the glaucoma screening process. Pixel-wise segmentation of OC and OD enables the frameworks to obtain all the above-mentioned computations for assisting the glaucoma diagnosis process. Hence, accurate segmentation of OC and OD provides a solid foundation for supporting medical experts in glaucoma screening.

Many research studies proposed OC and OD segmentation for glaucoma screening. However, OC and OD segmentation is challenging because of the extensive variations in the images. This variation includes different background effects, pixel intensity values, sizes, and shapes. Specifically, the size of OC is usually quite small with unclear boundaries that make its segmentation much more challenging. Therefore, existing methods exhibited serious limitations in OC boundary predictions. Lastly, the OC and OD regions are very small compared with those of the background class and it creates a class imbalance problem that negatively impacts the learning of the network. To mitigate these challenges, a novel feature excitation-based dense segmentation network (FEDS-Net) is developed for the semantic segmentation of OC and OD. FEDS-Net is a novel development and it is not based on any other network. FEDS-Net uses feature excitation and aggregation to obtain accurate predictions for OC and OD classes. FEDS-Net also introduced abrupt feature downsampling and aggregation mechanism for expanded learning.

Many research works proposed CNNs for glaucoma diagnosis using OC and OD segmentation. Nevertheless, most of the methods employ expensive frameworks which use a large number of parameters for training. A large number of parameters' requirements not only increases the training time but also enhances the memory requirements. To address this problem, FEDS-Net designed an efficient depth mechanism to minimize the number of parameters. FEDS-Net is evaluated using three open databases namely; REFUGE, Drishti-GS, and Rim-One-r3. The proposed network showed excellent segmentation without leveraging computational efficiency. FEDS-Net needs only 2.73 million parameters for its training.

The contribution of this work is summarized as follows:

- A novel architecture, FEDS-Net, is developed for accurate OC and OD segmentation to assist the existing glaucoma screening procedures. FEDS-Net uses feature excitation and information aggregation (IA) to significantly improve prediction accuracy.
- In FEDS-Net, rapid feature downsampling (RFD) and efficient convolutional depth (ECD) are also introduced for diverse and efficient learning, respectively.
- The proposed architecture is evaluated using three open databases: REFUGE[1], Drishti-GS[2], and Rim-One-r3[3]. FEDS-Net showed excellent performance compared with state-of-the-art methods. In addition, outperforming results are obtained with a superior computational efficiency having a requirement of only 2.73 million parameters for full training.

The remaining paper is organized as follows. In Sections 2 and 3 proposed methods and results are presented, respectively. Discussion is provided in Section 4 whereas a conclusion of the study is given in Section 5.

2. Related Work

Automatic glaucoma screening is a topic of vast interest. Many research studies conducted to automate and assist the glaucoma diagnosis procedure. Existing studies can be broadly divided into handcrafted and deep feature-based methods.

2.1. Methods Based on Handcrafted Features

Many research studies used handcrafted feature-based methods for automatic glaucoma screening purposes. In this study [9], OD pixel-wise segmentation is performed using the blood vessels inpainting mechanism. Initially, a region growing approach is used and then a blood inpainting scheme is employed to detect OD region. Evaluation of the proposed model is performed using multiple databases to analyze the effectiveness of the method. Preprocessing employed in this method can be attributed as the limitation of this study [9].

Similarly, another method [10] uses texture features for the glaucoma assessment. Features were selected based using a proper feature selection structure. The proposed method of this study includes preprocessing to obtain the region of interest (ROI) [10]. In a work [11], pixels belonging to OD are detected by combining edge detection with a deformable model and Hough transform [11]. Preprocessing requirements to remove retinal vessels can be considered the limitation of this work [11].

In a study [12], pixels of OD boundary were predicted by reconstructing the morphology in fundus images. A convex hull estimation was carried out as the final step to extract the boundary of OD [12]. A dataset that needs to be used for the preprocessing of this method can be attributed as the limitation of this work [12]. Another method [13] uses principal component analysis (PCA) for the conversion of original images to a grayscale images. In this method, OD is automatically detected using mathematical morphology in combination with PCA [13]. The proposed method in [14] eliminated peripapillary atrophy for segmenting the OD area. A three-stage process pipeline based on ROI detection, edge filtering, and Hough transform is used for eliminating peripapillary atrophy [14]. Approaching the obtained results using this method requires postprocessing [14].

In [15], OD region candidates are first selected using k-means clustering. Secondly, OD area selection is finalized based on the maximum saliency. Preprocessing requirements can be attributed as the limitation of this method [15]. Similarly in [16], an expert system using an active contour approach is proposed for the OC and OD segmentation. Although this method achieves a high sensitivity in performance, however, it needs preprocessing [16]. Another study [17] proposes a combination of level set and clustering for pixel-wise OC and OD segmentation. At first, OD boundaries are roughly predicted using clustering, and segmentation results were refined with the help of a level set approach [17].

2.2. Methods Based on Deep Features

Deep learning has a vital contribution to providing robust and intelligent solutions. In many research works, deep feature-based solutions are presented almost in every field of life [18]. Deep learning-based methods are usually accepted as an effective and efficient choice for dealing with complex patterns in images and videos. Several methods are also introduced for performing segmentation tasks to detect desired features or patterns from medical images [19]. Segmentation networks provide pixel-wise predictions that help in pixel-level image analysis. Deep feature-based segmentation algorithms are extensively applied to retinal images for different disease quantification [20]. A recent study [5] presented a prompt deep light-weight vessel segmentation network (PLVS-Net) to diagnose diabetic retinopathy. PLVS-Net is based on prompt blocks that contain separable, standard, and asymmetric convolutional layers. These prompt blocks ensure improved retinal vessels segmentation with enhanced computational efficiency [5]. However, the evaluation of their method with datasets having less number of images can be attributed as the limitation of this work. Subsequently, many image processing-based automated methods used OC and OD segmentation to assist the glaucoma screening process [6]. In this work [6], a double threshold method is employed; initially, background and retinal vessels are removed and then super intensity pixels in OC and OD are segmented. Preprocessing requirements of this method can be considered as the weakness of their proposed method [6]. In ref [7], several deep feature-based methods associated with glaucoma are discussed. Along with glaucoma screening, this study also emphasizes detecting glaucoma progression [7].

Although OC and OD segmentation is considered a gold standard for computer-aided glaucoma diagnosis. Nevertheless, few methods use other features of fundus imaging to strengthen the automated diagnosis [8]. In this work [8], OD and OC segmentation process is followed by focal notch analysis of the neural rim to aid glaucoma screening. Evaluation of the proposed method with a single dataset can be attributed as the limitation of this work [8]. In a study [21], an encoder-decoder fashion architecture is used for segmenting OC and OD, simultaneously. The framework used in this study provides both image classification and segmentation outputs [21]. Comparatively poor segmentation performance for OC can be attributed as the limitation of this study [21]. Similarly in [22], optic disc segmentation is performed using a particle swarm optimization network. The segmentation performance of mask R-CNN is improved using transfer learning combined with optimization frameworks [22]. This method is limited to OD (not OC) segmentation only [22].

The method proposed in [23] refers to an attention-based mechanism for the efficient training process of the network. In this method, OD and OC refined segmentation is also achieved using a cascading approach [23]. Cascading itself can be the limitation of this method considering the case of transferring false prediction to the next stage [23]. Similarly in [24], a combination of DenseNet and a fully convolutional network is employed for segmenting fundus images for glaucoma screening. The computational efficiency of this framework is also enhanced using the feature reuse approach [24]. Limitation of this method includes preprocessing requirement and inefficient training [24]. Another method [25] employed different CNNs with DeepLabv3+ at the encoder end for segmenting OD pixels. Moreover, image-level predictions (classification) are also generated using transfer learning and pre-trained models [25]. This work shows several limitations in terms of prior requirements such as transfer learning, preprocessing, and pretrained models [25].

A few methods also used adversarial learning for assisting the glaucoma screening process [26]. In this method, the domain-shifting problem is addressed using a patch-based adversarial framework [26]. The limitation of this study can be attributed to its preprocessing and postprocessing requirements [26]. Subsequently, another method [27] based on adversarial learning is used to segment retinal vessels and OD. In this study, the famous U-Net [28] is used as the generator whereas multiple models serve for discrimination purposes in adversarial learning [27]. In another study [29], a recurrent fully convolutional mechanism is developed to overcome the problem of feature loss in CNNs. High-level information along with edge information is processed to improve the pixel-wise OC and OD segmentation performance [29]. Evaluation with a single database can be considered the limitation of this study [29].

U-Net [28] is considered a benchmark architecture, especially for medical image segmentation. Few studies reproduced and implemented U-Net on a computer for performing OC and OD segmentation [30]. The effectiveness of U-Net with limited time was analyzed in OC and OD segmentation tasks. Subsequently, another method [31] made some modifications to the standard U-Net [28] and evaluated for OC and OD segmentation. Channels used in the convolutional layers of this network were optimized for an efficient training process [31]. Preprocessing requirements can be attributed as the limitation of this work [31].

3. Material and Methods

3.1. Datasets

In our work, the proposed method is evaluated using three datasets containing fundus images for OC and OD segmentation. All three datasets, namely; REFUGE[1], Drishti-GS[2], and Rim-One-r3[3] [26] have original images with corresponding expert annotations. Sample images for the REFUGE dataset are shown in Figure 1. Rows 1 and 2 in Figure 1 represent original and groundtruth images, respectively. Pixels shown in black and gray colors of groundtruth images represent OD and OC whereas white color shows the background class. REFUGE has equally divided (400 images for each category) images for training, validation, and testing purposes. REFUGE is among the latest and most challenging datasets because of the extensive intra-dataset variations.

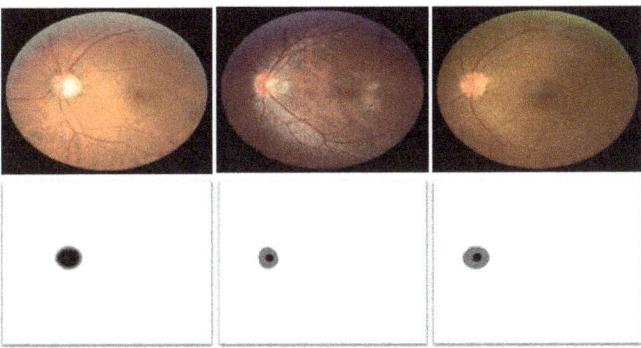

Figure 1. Sample images from the REFUGE dataset along with expert annotation images.

In Figure 2, sample images from Rim-One-r3 and Drishti-GS datasets are shown in rows 1 and 2, respectively. Rim-One-r3 is collected by MIAG group (Spain) and it has a total of 159 fundus images with expert annotations. The Drishti-GS dataset is also one of the benchmark datasets for OC and OD segmentation. It has a total of 101 images with 50 training and 51 testing images. The OD and OC annotations for both Rim-One-r3 and Drishti-GS are provided in Figure 2b,c. Black pixels in the groundtruth images represent the background class whereas white pixels refer to desired classes (OC and OD). It is worth noting that all three datasets have extensive variations in background effects, pixel intensity values, objects (OC and OD) sizes, and illumination effects which makes its segmentation challenging. In addition, most of the images have a small-sized OC with unclear boundaries; therefore, accurate segmentation becomes even more challenging.

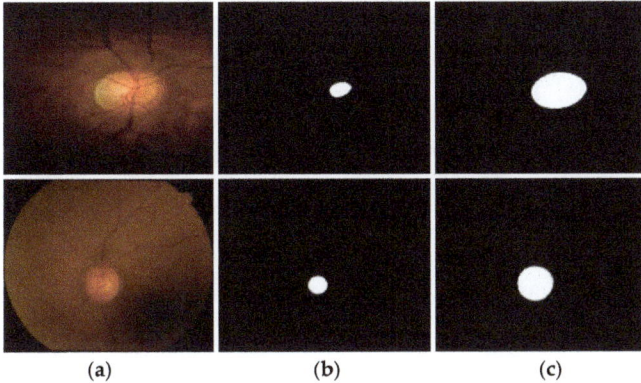

Figure 2. Sample images from row 1: Rim-One-r3; row 2: Drishti-GS databases. (**a**) Original image (**b**) groundtruth image with OD annotation (**c**) groundtruth image with the OC annotation.

3.2. Proposed Method

3.2.1. Overview of the Proposed Method

OC and OD pixel-wise segmentation provides valuable analysis for glaucoma diagnosis and prognosis. Accurate segmentation of OC and OD is challenging because of the high inter and intra-datasets variations along with an indistinct area of OC. A novel architecture, FEDS-Net, is developed to overcome these challenges. An overview of the proposed framework is shown in Figure 3. Input images are fed to the network and after feature processing, the network provides a prediction mask for OC and/or OD at the output. Networks usually require a large amount of training data for optimal learning of the network. To fulfill this need, training images are resized and augmented to produce a sufficient amount of training data. FEDS-Net uses feature excitation and IA mechanism to boost the segmentation accuracy. Moreover, RFD and ECD ensure a diversified and efficient learning of the network (details are provided in the subsequent subsection). The trained model of FEDS-Net generates a prediction mask and predictions are compared with groundtruth images for results generation. Resizing the prediction mask back to the original size is carried out for a valid evaluation. Training images are used for training purposes whereas testing is performed only for unseen test split. In the prediction mask, white and black pixels represent desired (OC and/or OD) and undesired (background) classes, respectively, whereas FEDS-Net provides segmented OC and/or OD at the output.

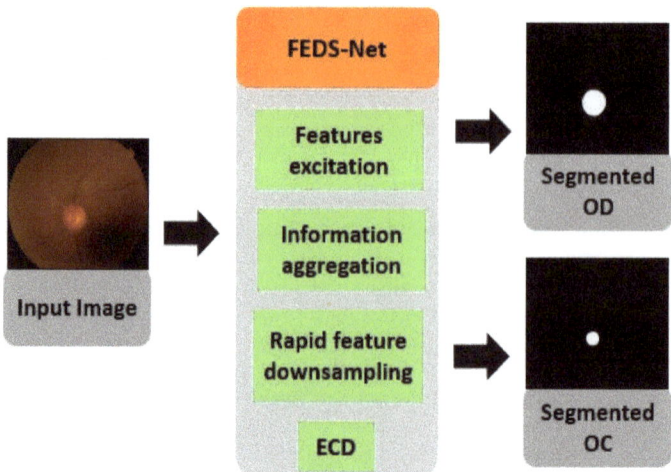

Figure 3. The overview diagram of the proposed method.

3.2.2. Explanation of the Proposed Method

Existing methods are usually based on some famous networks or use pre-trained models as a backbone. In the case of OD and OC segmentation, famous segmentation architectures such as U-Net [28] and SegNet [32] cannot deliver convincing results because of the small object size with unclear boundaries. Both U-Net and SegNet architectures exhibit vanishing gradient problems because of the excessively small final featuremap size. FEDS-Net is developed from scratch, and it is not based on other architecture. The detailed network architecture of FEDS-Net is shown in Figure 4. Training images from the training split are resized for an efficient training process. Input images are provided to the network using the image input layer. Image features are extracted and activations are produced using convolutional layers. In FEDS-Net, spatial information from different stages of the network is aggregated with spatial features at different IA points. FEDS-Net has a total of five IA points almost at every stage of the network.

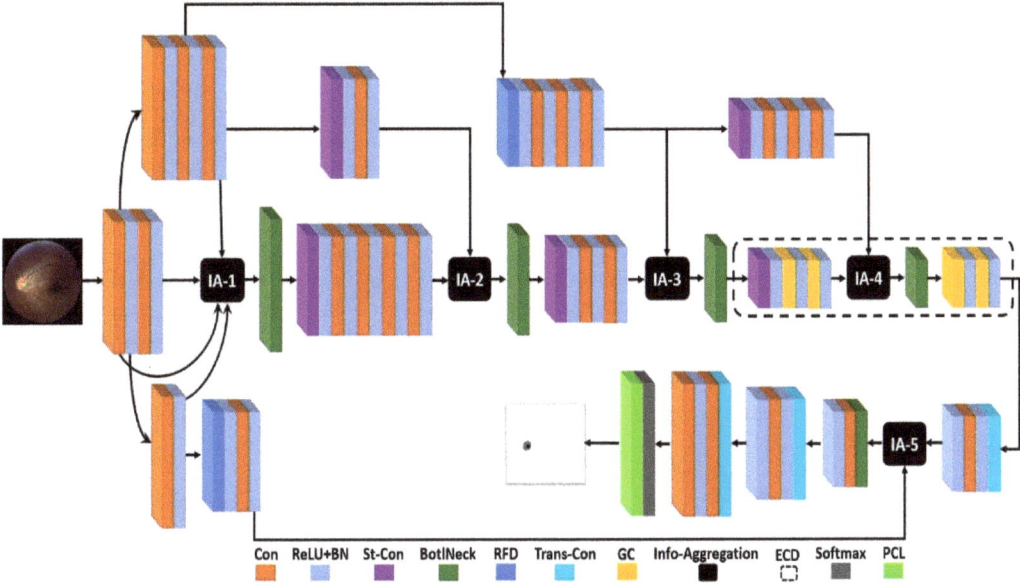

Figure 4. The architecture of the proposed FEDS-Net (Con: Convolutional layer; BN: Batch normalization layer; St-Con: Strided convolutional layer; BotlNeck: Bottleneck layer; RFD: Rapid feature downsampling; Trans-Con: Transposed convolutional layer; GC: Grouped convolutional layer; ECD: Efficient convolutional depth; PCL: Pixel classification layer; IA: Information aggregation).

In CNNs, the initial spatial feature has the potential to improve the prediction accuracy of the network [33]. Therefore, initial spatial feature excitation is obtained by aggregating features with different process levels and channels at IA-1. In IA-1, initial spatial features from three different convolutional effects along with identity mapping from the first convolutional layer are aggregated for initial feature excitation. The output of IA-1 is provided to the strided convolutional (St-Con) layer via a bottleneck (BotlNeck) layer. Furthermore, St-Con reduces the featuremap size and processes the spatial information from a series of four convolution layers for further activations. Activated information from the series of convolutional layers is further aggregated with the downsampled spatial feature using St-Con at IA-2. It is notable that FEDS-Net architecture does not include maximum pooling or unpooling layers to change the featuremap dimensions to avoid spatial loss caused by these layers. Instead, FEDS-Net uses St-Con and transposed convolutional (Trans-Con) layers to reduce and increase the featuremap size, respectively.

In CNNs, a relatively high stride value of St-Con results in more efficient learning of the network [34]. Therefore, FEDS-Net uses RFD using a high stride of 4 in two St-Con layers. The spatial information from IA-2 is further activated through a couple of convolutional layers via a BotlNeck layer followed by a Str-Con. In IA-3, rapid downsampled features are aggregated with spatial information from a couple of convolutional layers. This aggregated information is provided to ECD. The ECD has valuable semantic information with the maximum number of channels and minimum featuremap dimension. ECD is based on one St-Con, four grouped convolutional layers, one IA point, and a BotlNeck layer. In CNNs, the maximum depth of the network is the most expensive part of the network which strongly hit the computational efficiency of the network. Nevertheless, FEDS-Net used four grouped convolutional layers to contain the required number of parameters in maximum depth. In ECD (IA-4), aggregated spatial information is further aggregated with downsampled and activated spatial features through three convolutional layers. Feature aggregation in ECD helps in learning semantics and consequently enhance prediction accuracy.

Subsequently, the spatial information dimension is increased using a Trans-Con layer and fed to IA-5 via a single convolutional layer. As earlier mentioned, initial features have the potential to improve the overall learning of the network. These initial features underwent RFD and were provided to IA-5 for aggregation with upsampled features from ECD. The spatial dimension of final aggregated features, from IA-5, is increased using two Trans-Con layers one after the other. The final spatial feature from the last Trans-Con layer is refined using a couple of convolutional layers before providing to the softmax and pixel classification layers (PCL) for pixel-wise predictions. PCL produces a prediction mask with the marking of each pixel belonging to the respective class.

Key parts of the aggregation process are further explained using a schematic diagram in Figure 5. Spatial information (I_s) is fed to IA (x) via convolutional layers and it becomes I'_s. Similarly, initial features are represented with F_i and after undergoing RFD become the rapid downsampled initial features (F'_{rdi}). In IA (x), I'_s is aggregated with F'_{rdi} and it provides aggregated spatial features (F_{ax}), as follows.

$$F_{ax} = I'_s \; F'_{rdi} \tag{1}$$

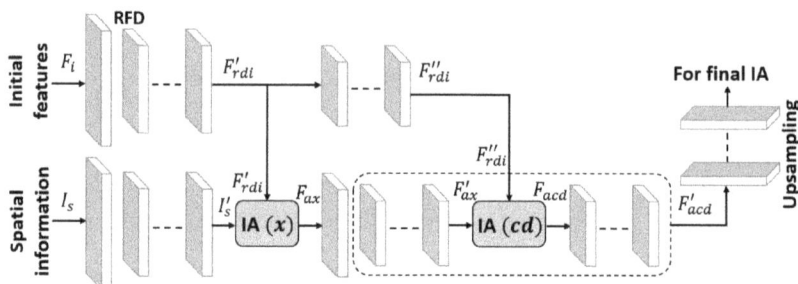

Figure 5. Schematic diagram showing information aggregation in FEDS-Net.

Because information aggregation is based on concatenation; therefore, aggregation is represented with symbol ©. after activations through convolutional layers F_{ax} become F'_{ax}. Subsequently, F'_{rdi} is further refined through a series of convolutional layers and it is represented with F''_{rdi}. In convolutional depth, F'_{ax} is aggregated with F''_{rdi} and finally, it provides aggregated features from convolutional depth (F_{acd}) as given below

$$F_{acd} = F'_{ax} \; F''_{rdi} \tag{2}$$

F_{acd} are further activated using convolution layers and final features out of convolution depth (F'_{acd}) are provided for upsampling before the prediction stage. This feature aggregation in general and in the maximum depth, in particular, improves the overall segmentation performance.

3.2.3. Training, Testing, and the Experimental Environment of the Proposed Method

In this study, experimentation is performed on three publicly available databases. The data split of REFUGE and Drishti-GS databases are pre-defined by the dataset providers and we followed the same official splits in our experiments. For the experimental work of Rim-One-r3, the same data split used by [26] is followed for a fair comparison. Images from the training split are resized using nearest neighbor interpolation for fast training of the network. The limited availability of annotated medical data is a common limitation, worldwide. Therefore, training images are augmented to create artificial images. In this work, arithmetic and geometric operations such as cropping, flipping, and rotation are randomly used for augmentation. No preprocessing is involved for the training of FEDS-Net.

As shown in sample images (Figures 1 and 2), pixels of desired classes (OC and OD) are significantly dominated by undesired class (background) pixels and this scenario triggers a class-imbalance problem. In the experimental work of this study, dice loss (DL) is employed as the loss function for the training of the network. DL mitigates the class-imbalance problem and minimizes the metric while backpropagation and ensures convergence of the network for effective training. Mathematically, DL is expressed as follows

$$\text{DL} = 1 - \left(\frac{2 \times \sum_k^A P_{\text{Pro}-k} G_{\text{Truth}-k}}{\sum_k^A P_{\text{Pro}-k}^2 + \sum_k^A G_{\text{True}-k}^2} \right) \quad (3)$$

In the above mathematical expression, A symbolizes all pixels which are available whereas k represents the current pixel. The probability of prediction for k pixel is referred by $P_{\text{Pro}-k}$ and the true groundtruth label is represented by $G_{\text{Truth}-k}$. P represents generated label after prediction whereas G denotes the groundtruth.

The proposed method is comprehensively evaluated on three publicly available databases. Testing was conducted only on the unseen testing split of the respective database for a fair evaluation. A trained model by FEDS-Net is applied to the testing images and a pixels-level prediction mask is generated for each image. The pixels of the prediction mask are compared with those of the groundtruth pixels to compute results on the bases of evaluation measures. In semantic segmentation, accuracy (AC), sensitivity (S), specificity (SPE), dice similarity coefficient (DSC), and Jaccard index (JCI) are the commonly accepted measures for evaluation [35]. In evaluation measures, true positive (tp), true negative (tn), false positive (fp), and false negative (fn) pixels are computed for the evaluation purposes. Mathematically evaluation measures can be given, as follows

$$AC = \frac{tp + tn}{tp + fn + fp + tn} \quad (4)$$

$$S = \frac{tp}{tp + fn} \quad (5)$$

$$SPE = \frac{tn}{tn + fp} \quad (6)$$

$$DSC = \frac{2\, tp}{2\, tp + fp + fn} \quad (7)$$

$$JCI = \frac{tp}{tp + fp + fn} \quad (8)$$

FEDS-Net is developed from scratch and all the experimental work is performed using MATLAB 2021a [36] framework. In addition, Intel® Core™ i7 CPU950@3.7 GHz processor (Intel Corporation, Seoul, Republic of Korea) with an NVIDIA GeForce GTX 1080 graphics processing unit (GPU) [37] (NVIDIA Corporation, Seoul, Republic of Korea) having 8 GB graphics memory is used for experiments. Computational details related to trainable parameters and inference time are presented in Tables 4 and 5, respectively in Section 5.

4. Results

The proposed method is evaluated using three open databases containing retinal fundus images. FEDS-Net delivered excellent segmentation results. Both qualitative and quantitative results for all three databases are given in subsequent subsections.

4.1. FEDS-Net Evaluation Using REFUGE Database

REFUGE is one of the latest and most challenging datasets for OD and OC segmentation. Images in REFUGE datasets are entirely different from the other two databases. Nonetheless, FEDS-Net provided superior segmentation performance for both OC and OD classes. Many images in the testing split have a very small OC area with indistinct boundaries. However, FEDS-Net delivered a better segmentation accuracy even for such challenging cases. Qualitative good and poor segmentation results using FEDS-Net on the

REFUGE database are shown in Figures 6 and 7, respectively. Poor results are perhaps because of the unclear objects' boundaries along with the small size of OC.

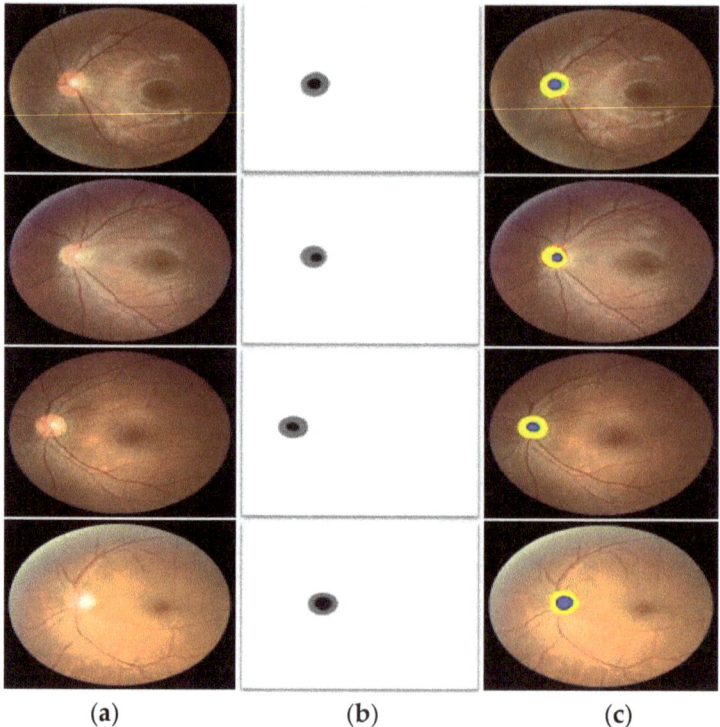

Figure 6. Good OC and OD segmentation qualitative results on the REFUGE database, attained by applying FEDS-Net. (**a**) Input image, (**b**) corresponding groundtruth image, and (**c**) segmented output images (tp pixels for OD and OC are indicated in yellow and blue, respectively. Likewise, red and green show fn and fp pixels, respectively).

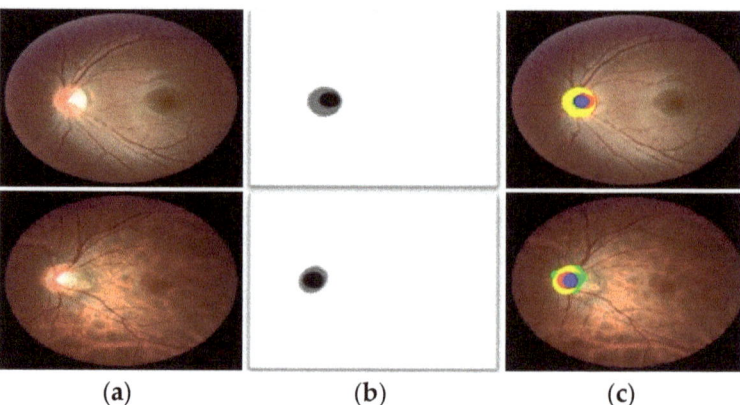

Figure 7. Poor OC and OD segmentation qualitative sample results on the REFUGE database, attained by applying FEDS-Net. (**a**) Input image, (**b**) corresponding groundtruth image, and (**c**) segmented output images (tp pixels for OD and OC are indicated in yellow and blue, respectively. Likewise, red and green show fn and fp pixels, respectively).

Quantitative OC and OD segmentation results are further compared with those of the state-of-the-art methods to confirm the effectiveness of the proposed method. The listed results in Table 1 show a better segmentation performance of FEDS-Net compared with existing methods. It is worth notable that most of the methods require extensive preprocessing to achieve the desired performance. Instead, the proposed method did not employ any preprocessing to keep the method straightforward.

Table 1. Segmentation quantitative results comparison of FEDS-Net with state-of-the-art methods using the REFUGE database. "-" indicates that no result is available (unit: %). (OC: optic cup; OD: optic disc; AC: accuracy; S: sensitivity; SPE: specificity; DSC: dice similarity coefficient; JCI: jaccard index).

Methods	OC					OD				
	AC	S	SPE	DSC	JCI	AC	S	SPE	DSC	JCI
Variational auto-encoder [38]	-	-	-	88.91	-	-	-	-	95.81	-
Patch-based pOSALseg-T [26]	-	-	-	88.2	-	-	-	-	96.0	-
M-Ada [21]	-	-	-	88.25	-	-	-	-	95.85	-
SLSR-Net [39]	99.90	94.70	99.90	89.50	81.50	99.80	96.90	99.90	96.50	93.30
U-Net + VGG16 encoder [40]	-	-	-	-	-	99.8	95.7	-	94.0	89.0
Mask-RCNN [41]	-	-	-	85.4	-	-	-	-	94.7	-
ET-Net [42]	-	-	-	89.1	-	-	-	-	95.2	-
U-Net [28]	-	-	-	85.4	-	-	-	-	93.0	-
Self-attention [23]	-	-	-	85.36	-	-	-	-	95.09	-
Team masker [43]	-	-	-	88.3	-	-	-	-	94.6	-
Cascaded network [25]	-	-	-	88.04	-	-	-	-	93.31	-
Team BUCT [43]	-	-	-	87.2	-	-	-	-	95.2	-
Segtran (eff-B4) [44]	-	-	-	87.2	-	-	-	-	96.1	-
Multi-modal approach [45]	-	-	-	-	79.02	-	-	-	-	92.25
Conditional GAN [46]	-	-	-	-	80.0	-	-	-	-	88.4
FEDS-Net (Proposed method)	99.91	90.40	99.96	89.80	82.13	99.89	96.62	99.94	96.53	93.39

4.2. FEDS-Net Evaluation Using Drishti-GS Database

Evaluation of FEDS-Net is extended to benchmark Drishti-GS database. Images in the Drishti-GS database are entirely different from those of the other two databases of this study. Nevertheless, the proposed method provided superior segmentation accuracies for the Drishti-GS database too. Qualitative results of OD and OC segmentation on the Drishti-GS database are presented in Figures 8 and 9, respectively. Figure 8 (rows 1–3), shows good OD segmentation visual results whereas Figure 8 (row 4) shows sample visual result of relatively poor segmentation. Similarly, good segmentation qualitative results for OC segmentation of the Drishti-GS database are shown in Figure 9 (rows 1–3) whereas the relatively poor visual result is shown in Figure 9 (row 4). Poor segmentation cases can be attributed to indistinct object boundaries.

In Table 2, quantitative results produced by FEDS-Net are compared with state-of-the-art methods on the Drishti-GS database. Results confirm a convincing performance by FEDS-Net using its feature excitation and IA mechanism. FEDS-Net ensures a high segmentation performance without disregarding the training parameters' overheads. FEDS-Net used a small number of training parameters to achieve outperforming results.

4.3. FEDS-Net Evaluation Using Rim-One-r3 Database

The proposed method is further evaluated using the Rim-One-r3 database with challenging pixel intensity variations. FEDS-Net effectively deals with these variations using its architectural strengths. Qualitative results produced by FEDS-Net for the OD and OC segmentation are provided in Figures 10 and 11, respectively. Qualitative results confirm that FEDS-Net provides excellent segmentation accuracy for different pixel intensity variations and illumination effects. Good segmentation performance's qualitative results are presented in Figures 10 and 11 (rows 1–3) whereas relatively poor segmentation is shown in Figures 10 and 11 (row 4). Poor segmentation cases can be attributed to indistinct objects' boundaries along with variations in pixel intensity values and illumination effects.

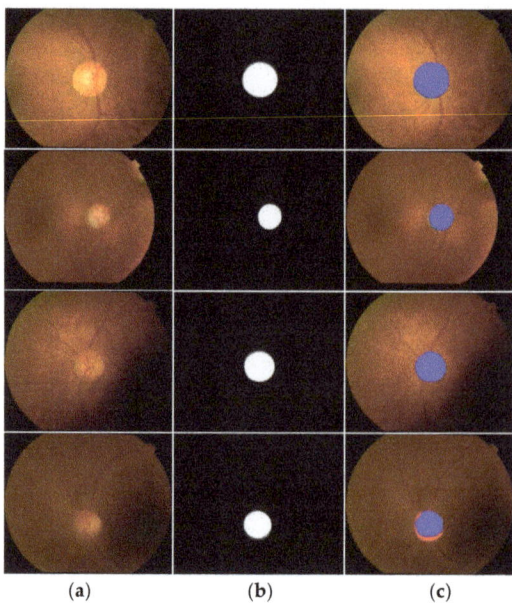

Figure 8. Good OD segmentation qualitative results on the Drishti-GS database, attained by applying FEDS-Net. (**a**) Input image, (**b**) corresponding groundtruth image, and (**c**) segmented output images (tp and fn pixels for OD are indicated in blue and red, respectively. Whereas, fp pixels are presented with green color) (Rows 1–3: good segmentation results; Row 4: poor segmentation result).

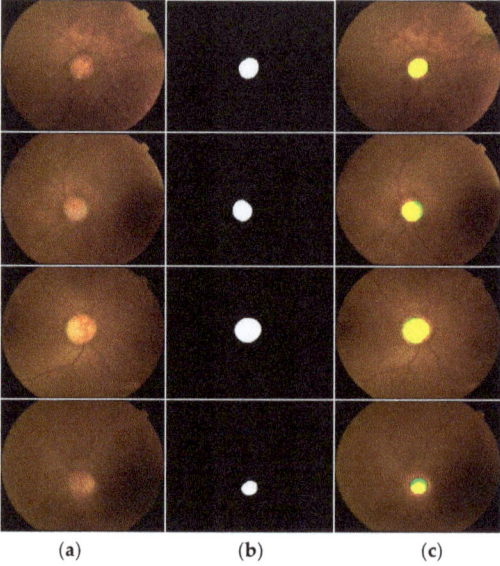

Figure 9. Good OC segmentation qualitative results on the Drishti-GS database, attained by applying FEDS-Net. (**a**) Input image, (**b**) corresponding groundtruth image, and (**c**) segmented output images (tp and fn pixels for OD are indicated in yellow and red, respectively, whereas fp pixels are presented in green color) (Rows 1–3: good segmentation results; Row 4: poor segmentation result).

Table 2. Segmentation quantitative results comparison of FEDS-Net with state-of-the-art methods using the Drishti-GS database. "-" indicates that no result is available (unit: %). (OC: optic cup; OD: optic disc; AC: accuracy; S: sensitivity; SPE: specificity; DSC: dice similarity coefficient; JCI: jaccard index).

Methods	OC					OD				
	AC	S	SPE	DSC	JCI	AC	S	SPE	DSC	JCI
U-Net with VGG16 encoder [40]	-	-	-	-	-	99.79	97.54	-	96.5	93.1
Mod U-Net [47]	-	-	-	88.7	80.4	-	-	-	97.3	94.9
RACE-Net [48]	-	-	-	87.0	-	-	-	-	97.0	-
RetinaGAN [27]	-	-	-	-	-	-	-	-	96.7	-
Entropy sampling [49]	-	-	-	87.1	-	-	-	-	97.3	-
FC-DenseNet [24]	99.4	-	-	82.8	71.1	99.6	-	-	94.9	90.4
Depth estimation [50]	-	-	-	83.0	-	-	-	-	97.0	-
FCN and adversarial [51]	-	-	-	85.0	75.0	-	-	-	-	-
Edge smoothing approach [52]	-	-	-	81.0	-	-	-	-	95.0	-
Modified U-Net [31]	-	-	-	85.0	-	-	-	-	-	-
Shape regression [53]	-	-	-	85.0	-	-	-	-	95.0	-
Multi-Stage framework [54]	-	-	-	84.0	-	-	-	-	97.0	-
Drishti-GS Challenge [55]	-	-	-	79.0	-	-	-	-	96.0	-
Edge TPU [30]	-	-	-	88.0	-	-	-	-	90.0	-
U-Net [28]	98.1	86.5	98.3	70.2	57.8	99.2	92.8	99.4	91.3	85.8
NAS-U2-Net [56]	-	-	-	87.69	-	-	-	-	96.95	-
FEDS-Net (Proposed method)	99.66	93.28	99.81	90.40	83.38	99.86	97.64	99.94	98.01	95.99

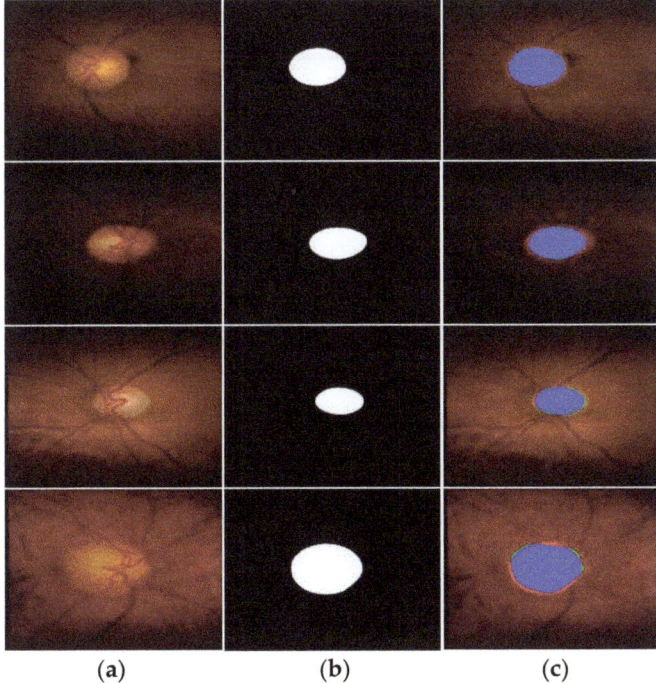

Figure 10. Good OD segmentation qualitative results on the Rim-One-r3 database, attained by applying FEDS-Net. (**a**) Input image, (**b**) corresponding groundtruth image, and (**c**) segmented output images (tp and fn pixels for OD are indicated in blue and red, respectively. Whereas fp pixels are presented with green color) (Rows 1–3: good segmentation results; Row 4: poor segmentation result).

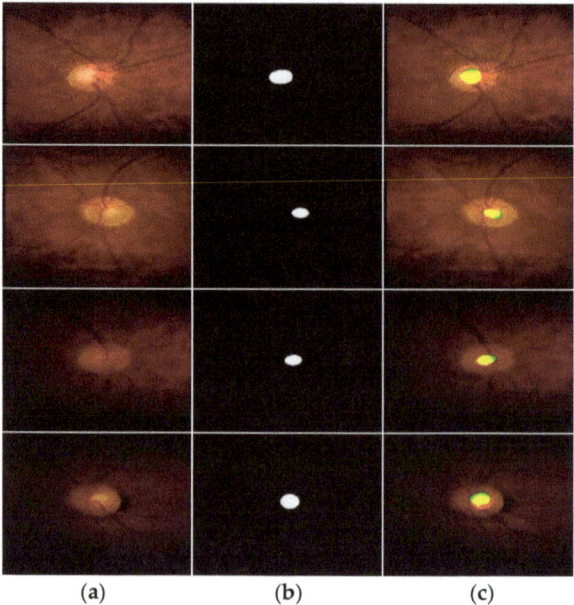

(a) (b) (c)

Figure 11. Good OC segmentation qualitative results on the Rim-One-r3 database, attained by applying FEDS-Net. (**a**) Input image, (**b**) corresponding groundtruth image, and (**c**) segmented output images (tp and fn pixels for OD are indicated in yellow and red, respectively. Whereas fp pixels are presented in green color) (Rows 1–3: good segmentation results; Row 4: poor segmentation result).

FEDS-Net quantitative results are listed in Table 3 for comparison with existing methods. Results exhibit a competitive and convincing performance by the proposed method. Aggregation of features results in effective training; therefore, FEDS-net maintains its better performance even dealing with challenging variations.

Table 3. Segmentation quantitative results comparison of FEDS-Net with state-of-the-art methods using Rim-One-r3 database. "-" indicates that no result is available (unit: %). (OC: optic cup; OD: optic disc; AC: accuracy; S: sensitivity; SPE: specificity; DSC: dice similarity coefficient; JCI: jaccard index).

Methods	OC					OD				
	AC	S	SPE	DSC	JCI	AC	S	SPE	DSC	JCI
Patch-based pOSALseg-T [26]	-	-	-	85.6	-	-	-	-	96.8	-
DRIU [57]	-	-	-	-	-	-	-	-	95.5	-
U-Net with modification [31]	-	-	-	-	-	-	-	-	95.0	-
RetinaGAN [27]	-	-	-	-	-	-	-	-	95.5	-
Entropy sampling [49]	-	-	-	82.4	-	-	-	-	94.2	-
Auto-encoder [58]	-	-	-	-	-	99.45	87.30	99.81	90.2	88.24
Edge TPU [30]	-	-	-	84.0	-	-	-	-	85.0	-
FEDS-Net (Proposed method)	99.60	87.67	99.80	86.20	76.20	99.73	96.97	99.86	97.01	94.13

5. Discussion

The trend of ophthalmic diseases is on the rise, worldwide. Ophthalmologists have to examine many glaucoma-suspected patients daily. Typically, glaucoma-related examinations are conducted manually which is subjective, time-consuming, and prone to error procedure. Therefore, the need of the time is to assist ophthalmologists with AI-based automated solutions. Hundreds of research studies accepted that OC and OD segmentation can assist the glaucoma diagnosis process. However, OC and OD segmentation task has many associated challenges. Fundus images have a high variation in pixel intensity values, backgrounds, OC/OD sizes, and illuminations that makes the segmentation tricky. In addition, OC size is usually very small and its boundary is too indistinct to accurately segment. Nevertheless, FEDS-Net overcomes these challenges using feature excitation, IA, RFD, and ECD in its architecture. Computational efficiency is another serious criterion for modern AI-based frameworks. In most cases, existing methods show serious limitations in computational efficiency and require a large number of parameters for the complete training of their model. FEDS-Net not only provides excellent segmentation accuracies but also maintains computational efficiency. FEDS-Net requires only 2.73 million parameters which turns out to confirm its computational strength. The comparison of FEDS-Net with existing methods in terms of required trainable parameters is listed in Table 4. Parameters' comparison exhibits that the proposed method requires a smaller number of parameters compared with those of the state-of-the-art methods. In addition, inference time (per image) for all three datasets using FEDS-Net is also computed and presented in Table 5. A considerably less inference time is also because of the computational effectiveness of the proposed method.

Table 4. Comparison of trainable parameters with those of the existing methods. (OC: optic cup; OD: optic disc; DSC: dice similarity coefficient).

Methods	Number of Parameters (Million)	DSC (%)	
		OC	OD
Team masker [43]	1224	88.3	94.6
Mask-RCNN [41]	127	85.4	94.7
Segtran (eff-B4) [44]	93.1	87.2	96.1
pOSAL (Xception) [26]	41.3	88.5	95.3
U-Net [28]	31.03	85.4	93.0
U-Net with VGG16 encoder [40]	16.8	-	94.0
pOSAL (MobileNetV2) [26]	5.8	88.5	95.6
FEDS-Net (Proposed)	2.73	89.80	96.53

Table 5. Inference time (per image) computation using FEDS-Net.

Sr.	Dataset	Inference Time (Seconds)
1	REFUGE	0.11
2	Rim-One-r3	0.091
3	Drishti-GS	0.097

5.1. Assisting the Glaucoma Screening Process

Automated glaucoma diagnosis methods are required to strengthen existing traditional glaucoma screening methods. The OC and OD segmentation can provide valuable computational and morphological details that can work as parallel support for ophthalmologists [26]. Accurate OC and OD segmentation can lead to providing precise *V-CDR* value and *V-CDR* is an important biomarker for ophthalmologists in glaucoma diagnosis and prognosis. Glaucoma usually causes cupping, which refers to an increase in the size of OC. The increased size of OC increases the *V-CDR* value which consequently reflects a high risk of glaucoma [53]. *V-CDR* is mathematically expressed as

$$V - CDR = \frac{vD_c}{vD_D} \qquad (9)$$

In the above mathematical expression, vD_c represents the vertical diameter of the cup area whereas vD_D symbolizes disc area. The ratio between both vertical diameters of the cup and disc provides a V-CDR value. A sample *V-CDR* computation from the REFUGE database is presented in Figure 12. The CDR value of groundtruth image is represented by

CDR_{gt} whereas predicted CDR by FEDS-Net is shown with CDR_{pr}. The computed CDR by FEDS-Net is quite closer to that of the CDR_{gt} value that confirms the effectiveness of FEDS-Net in accurately segmenting the OC and OD.

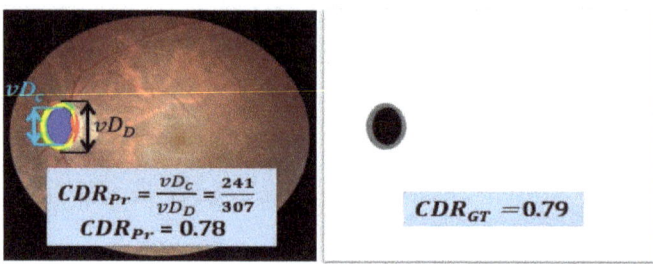

Figure 12. Sample CDR computation using the REFUGE dataset.

Although *V-CDR* computation provides potential insight for assisting the glaucoma screening process, nevertheless; segmentation-based glaucoma screening is not limited to only *V-CDR* computations. The area-cup-to-disc-ratio (Ar-CDR) is another measure to assess the glaucoma occurrence [8]. Ar-CDR is the ratio between the area of the cup region and the disc region. Glaucoma occurrence and progression bring changes in the area of OC and OD (mainly OC); therefore; Ar-CDR can also provide considerable assistance in glaucoma diagnosis and prognosis [8]. *V-CDR* has a limitation in selecting a reference center point for calculating vertical diameters whereas Ar-CDR is an area-based approach and does not require any reference point. Moreover, glaucoma progression can also be assessed by analyzing the change in the area of only OC during patients' multiple visits [17]. The rim area between OD and OC is termed a neural rim. The notching phenomenon is the shrinkage of the neural rim, it can be also analyzed for glaucoma screening. Similarly, the disc damage likelihood scale (DDLS) is calculated for the estimation and quantification of this disease [59]. The DDLS can be computed by taking the ratio between the thinnest part of the neural rim and disc diameter [59]. Subsequently, the inferior superior nasal and temporal (ISNT) rule also provides a solid basis to discriminate between glaucomatous and non-glaucomatous cases [60]. According to the ISNT rule, the width of the neural rim should be biggest to smallest for the inferior, superior, nasal, and temporal regions, respectively [60]. Cases satisfying the ISNT rule are classified as non-glaucomatous cases otherwise vice-versa.

5.2. OC and OD Segmentation for the Diagnosis of Other Diseases

Accurate segmentation of OC and OD not only assists in glaucoma screening but also helps in the diagnosis of some other diseases. Alzheimer's disease (AD) is a neurodegenerative problem that can be assessed using OC and OD segmentation [61]. Similar to glaucoma suspects, a high *V-CDR* value refers to a high risk of AD. Subsequently, poor cognitive function is common among postmenopausal women [62]. Medical experts consider *V-CDR* for cognitive assessment of the patient. Hence, accurate OC and OD segmentation is also crucial for assisting in the diagnosis of numerous diseases.

5.3. Demonstrating Learning of the Network using Heat Activation Maps

Understanding the learning process or feature selection of a CNN is very hard to visually explain. Gradient-weighted class activation mapping (Grad-CAM) [63] is used for the visual demonstration of network learning. In Figure 13, heat activation maps of OD and OC using the Rim-One-r3 database are presented in rows 1 and 2, respectively. As shown in Figure 13c–f, heat activation maps are extracted from different layers of the network to assess the learning process. Grad-CAM refers to the main features selected by the CNN during training and marks them with distinguished colors. Figure 13 (last column) is taken from the last layers of the network, and it confirms that FEDS-net rightfully focuses on desired classes without any biases.

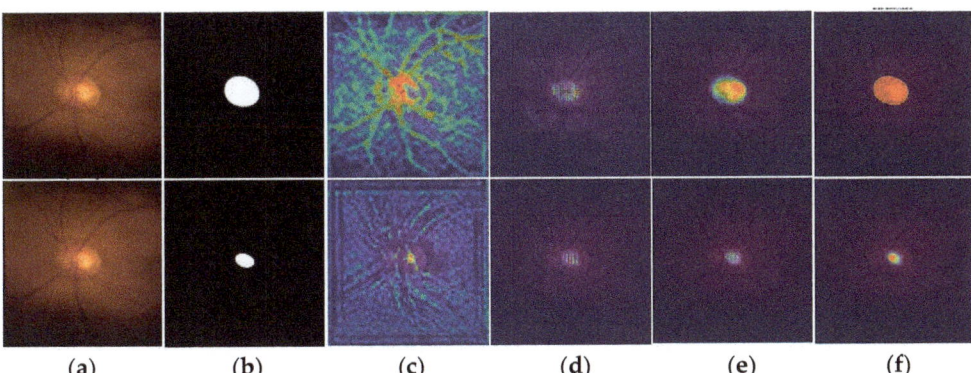

Figure 13. Visual explanation of FEDS-Net learning process using heat activation maps with Rim-One-r3 database. Activation maps for the OD and OC are provided in rows 1 and 2, respectively. (**a**) Input image. (**b**) groundtruth image. Heat activation maps extracted from (**c**) Initial layer, (**d**) first convolutional layer after IA-2, (**e**) convolutional layer after ECD, and (**f**) final convolutional layer of the network.

6. Conclusions

Glaucoma is one of the most critical ophthalmic diseases that can lead to irreversible vision loss. Glaucoma is typically diagnosed with manual assessments which is a time-consuming, error-prone, and inefficient procedure. Therefore, AI-based automatic methods are desirable to assist ophthalmologists in glaucoma diagnosis. Most of the existing AI-based methods require complex preprocessing, lack segmentation performance, and show serious limitations in terms of computational efficiency. To address all these problems, a novel architecture FEDS-Net is developed for accurate segmentation of OC and OD. FEDS-Net uses feature excitation and IA mechanism to enhance the prediction accuracies. Moreover, FEDS-Net employs ECD and RFD blocks for diverse and efficient learning of the network. The proposed method is evaluated on three challenging databases; REFUGE, Drishti-GS, and Rim-One-r3. FEDS-Net showed outperforming segmentation performance without disregarding the computational requirements of the network. FEDS-Net requires only 2.73 million training parameters for its complete training. FEDS-Net produced better results compared with those of state-of-the-art methods. Hence, the proposed method can be used as second-level support for ophthalmologists in glaucoma diagnosis and prognosis.

Relatively low segmentation accuracies for OC because of its indistinct boundaries can be attributed as the common limitation for all methods. Although FEDS-Net delivered a better performance for OC, still more techniques can be researched for further improvement. In the future, we intend to explore more techniques for enhancing OC segmentation performance.

Author Contributions: A.R., S.A. and M.I. Conceptualization, Methodology, Software, Visualization, Writing Original Draft.; H.S.K. and R.A.N. Data Curation, Resources, Software, Editing; R.A.N. Resources, Validation, Methodology; S.-W.L. Project administration. Investigation, Funding acquisition, Supervision. All authors have read and agreed to the published version of the manuscript.

Funding: This work was supported by a national research foundation (NRF) grant funded by the Ministry of Science and ICT (MSIT), Republic of Korea through the Development Research Program (NRF2022R1G1A1010226) and (NRF2021R1I1A2059735).

Institutional Review Board Statement: This study is based on publicly available datasets mentioned in Section 3.1. The datasets are public for research purposes, therefore it is not applicable. Weblinks for used datasets of this study are as follows. REFUGE: https://ai.baidu.com/broad/download?dataset=gon. (accessed on 10 August 2022) Drishti-GS: http://cvit.iiit.ac.in/projects/mip/drishti-gs/mip-dataset2/Home.php. (accessed on 10 August 2022) Rim-One-r3: http://medimrg.webs.ull.es/rim-one-release-3-is-finally-here/ (accessed on 10 August 2022).

Informed Consent Statement: Not applicable.

Data Availability Statement: Not applicable.

Conflicts of Interest: The authors declare no conflict of interest.

References

1. Troy, J.B. Visual prostheses: Technological and socioeconomic challenges. *Engineering* **2015**, *1*, 288–291. [CrossRef]
2. Shanmugam, P.; Raja, J.; Pitchai, R. An automatic recognition of glaucoma in fundus images using deep learning and random forest classifier. *Appl. Soft Comput.* **2021**, *109*, 107512. [CrossRef]
3. Haider, A.; Arsalan, M.; Choi, J.; Sultan, H.; Park, K.R. Robust segmentation of underwater fish based on multi-level feature accumulation. *Front. Mar. Sci.* **2022**, *9*, 1010565. [CrossRef]
4. Arsalan, M.; Haider, A.; Cho, S.W.; Kim, Y.H.; Park, K.R. Human blastocyst components detection using multiscale aggregation semantic segmentation network for embryonic analysis. *Biomedicines* **2022**, *10*, 1717. [CrossRef]
5. Arsalan, M.; Khan, T.M.; Naqvi, S.S.; Nawaz, M.; Razzak, I. Prompt deep light-weight vessel segmentation network (PLVS-Net). *IEEE/ACM Trans. Comput. Biol. Bioinform.* **2022**, 1–9. [CrossRef]
6. Dutta, M.K.; Mourya, A.K.; Singh, A.; Parthasarathi, M.; Burget, R.; Riha, K. Glaucoma detection by segmenting the super pixels from fundus colour retinal images. In Proceedings of the International Conference on Medical Imaging, m-Health, and Emerging Communication Systems, Greater Noida, India, 7–8 November 2014; pp. 86–90.
7. Thompson, A.C.; Jammal, A.A.; Medeiros, F.A. A review of deep learning for screening, diagnosis, and detection of glaucoma progression. *Transl. Vis. Sci. Technol.* **2020**, *9*, 42. [CrossRef]
8. Dasgupta, S.; Mukherjee, R.; Dutta, K.; Sen, A. Deep learning based framework for automatic diagnosis of glaucoma based on analysis of focal notching in the optic nerve head. *arXiv* **2021**, arXiv:2112.05748.
9. Sarathi, M.P.; Dutta, M.K.; Singh, A.; Travieso, C.M. Blood Vessel inpainting based technique for efficient localization and segmentation of optic disc in digital fundus images. *Biomed. Signal Process. Control* **2016**, *25*, 108–117. [CrossRef]
10. Septiarini, A.; Harjoko, A.; Pulungan, R.; Ekantini, R. Automated detection of retinal nerve fiber layer by texture-based analysis for glaucoma evaluation. *Healthc. Inf. Res* **2018**, *24*, 335–345. [CrossRef]
11. Yin, F.; Liu, J.; Ong, S.H.; Sun, Y.; Wong, D.W.K.; Tan, N.M.; Cheung, C.; Baskaran, M.; Aung, T.; Wong, T.Y. Model-based optic nerve head segmentation on retinal fundus images. In Proceedings of the IEEE on International Conference on IEEE Engineering in Medicine and Biology Society, Boston, MA, USA, 30 August–3 September 2011; pp. 2626–2629.
12. Roychowdhury, S.; Koozekanani, D.D.; Kuchinka, S.N.; Parhi, K.K. Optic disc boundary and vessel origin segmentation of fundus images. *IEEE J. Biomed. Health Inform.* **2016**, *20*, 1562–1574. [CrossRef]
13. Morales, S.; Naranjo, V.; Angulo, J.; Alcañiz, M. Automatic detection of optic disc based on PCA and mathematical morphology. *IEEE Trans. Med. Imaging* **2013**, *32*, 786–796. [CrossRef] [PubMed]
14. Cheng, J.; Liu, J.; Wong, D.W.K.; Yin, F.; Cheung, C.; Baskaran, M.; Aung, T.; Wong, T.Y. Automatic optic disc segmentation with peripapillary atrophy elimination. In Proceedings of the IEEE International Conference on IEEE Engineering in Medicine and Biology Society, Boston, MA, USA, 30 August–3 September 2011; pp. 6224–6227.
15. Xue, L.-Y.; Lin, J.-W.; Cao, X.-R.; Zheng, S.-H.; Yu, L. Optic disk detection and segmentation for retinal images using saliency model based on clustering. *J. Comput.* **2018**, *29*, 66–79. [CrossRef]
16. Mittapalli, P.S.; Kande, G.B. Segmentation of optic disk and optic cup from digital fundus images for the assessment of glaucoma. *Biomed. Signal Process. Control* **2016**, *24*, 34–46. [CrossRef]
17. Thakur, N.; Juneja, M. Optic disc and optic cup segmentation from retinal images using hybrid approach. *Expert Syst. Appl.* **2019**, *127*, 308–322. [CrossRef]
18. Arsalan, M.; Haider, A.; Choi, J.; Park, K.R. detecting blastocyst components by artificial intelligence for human embryological analysis to improve success rate of in vitro fertilization. *J. Pers. Med.* **2022**, *12*, 124. [CrossRef]
19. Haider, A.; Arsalan, M.; Lee, Y.W.; Park, K.R. Deep features aggregation-based joint segmentation of cytoplasm and nuclei in white blood cells. *IEEE J. Biomed. Health Inform.* **2022**, *26*, 3685–3696. [CrossRef]
20. Arsalan, M.; Haider, A.; Koo, J.H.; Park, K.R. Segmenting retinal vessels using a shallow segmentation network to aid ophthalmic analysis. *Mathematics* **2022**, *10*, 1536. [CrossRef]
21. Hervella, Á.S.; Rouco, J.; Novo, J.; Ortega, M. End-to-end multi-task learning for simultaneous optic disc and cup segmentation and glaucoma classification in eye fundus images. *Appl. Soft Comput.* **2022**, *116*, 108347. [CrossRef]
22. Zhang, L.; Lim, C.P. Intelligent optic disc segmentation using improved particle swarm optimization and evolving ensemble models. *Appl. Soft Comput.* **2020**, *92*, 106328. [CrossRef]

23. Bian, X.; Luo, X.; Wang, C.; Liu, W.; Lin, X. Optic disc and optic cup segmentation based on anatomy guided cascade network. *Comput. Methods Programs Biomed.* **2020**, *197*, 105717. [CrossRef]
24. Al-Bander, B.; Williams, B.M.; Al-Nuaimy, W.; Al-Taee, M.A.; Pratt, H.; Zheng, Y. Dense fully convolutional segmentation of the optic disc and cup in colour fundus for glaucoma diagnosis. *Symmetry* **2018**, *10*, 87. [CrossRef]
25. Sreng, S.; Maneerat, N.; Hamamoto, K.; Win, K.Y. Deep learning for optic disc segmentation and glaucoma diagnosis on retinal images. *Appl. Sci.* **2020**, *10*, 4916. [CrossRef]
26. Wang, S.; Yu, L.; Yang, X.; Fu, C.-W.; Heng, P.-A. Patch-based output space adversarial learning for joint optic disc and cup segmentation. *IEEE Trans. Med. Imaging* **2019**, *38*, 2485–2495. [CrossRef] [PubMed]
27. Son, J.; Park, S.J.; Jung, K.-H. Towards accurate segmentation of retinal vessels and the optic disc in fundoscopic images with generative adversarial networks. *J. Digit. Imaging* **2019**, *32*, 499–512. [CrossRef]
28. Ronneberger, O.; Fischer, P.; Brox, T. U-Net: Convolutional networks for biomedical image segmentation. In Proceedings of the International Conference on Medical Image Computing and Computer-Assisted Intervention, Munich, Germany, 5–9 October 2015; pp. 234–241.
29. Gao, J.; Jiang, Y.; Zhang, H.; Wang, F. Joint disc and cup segmentation based on recurrent fully convolutional network. *PLoS ONE* **2020**, *15*, e0238983. [CrossRef]
30. Civit-Masot, J.; Luna-Perejón, F.; Corral, J.M.R.; Domínguez-Morales, M.; Morgado-Estévez, A.; Civit, A. A study on the use of edge TPUs for eye fundus image segmentation. *Eng. Appl. Artif. Intell.* **2021**, *104*, 104384. [CrossRef]
31. Sevastopolsky, A. Optic disc and cup segmentation methods for glaucoma detection with modification of U-net convolutional neural network. *Pattern Recognit. Image Anal.* **2017**, *27*, 618–624. [CrossRef]
32. Badrinarayanan, V.; Kendall, A.; Cipolla, R. SegNet: A deep convolutional encoder-decoder architecture for image segmentation. *IEEE Trans. Pattern Anal. Mach. Intell.* **2017**, *39*, 2481–2495. [CrossRef] [PubMed]
33. Hosseinzadeh Kassani, S.; Hosseinzadeh Kassani, P.; Wesolowski, M.J.; Schneider, K.A.; Deters, R. Deep transfer learning based model for colorectal cancer histopathology segmentation: A comparative study of deep pre-trained models. *Int. J. Med. Inform.* **2022**, *159*, 104669. [CrossRef] [PubMed]
34. Kong, C.; Lucey, S. Take it in your stride: Do we need striding in CNNs? *arXiv* **2017**, arXiv:1712.02502. [CrossRef]
35. Bengani, S.; Jothi, J.A.A.J.; Vadivel, S. Automatic segmentation of optic disc in retinal fundus images using semi-supervised deep learning. *Multimed. Tools Appl.* **2021**, *80*, 3443–3468. [CrossRef]
36. MATLAB R2021a. Available online: https://www.mathworks.com/products/matlab.html (accessed on 5 March 2022).
37. GeForce GTX. Available online: https://www.nvidia.com/en-gb/geforce/products/10series/geforce-gtx-1070/ (accessed on 5 March 2022).
38. Cheng, P.; Lyu, J.; Huang, Y.; Tang, X. Probability distribution guided optic disc and cup segmentation from fundus images. In Proceedings of the IEEE International Conference in Medicine & Biology Society, Montreal, QC, Canada, 20–24 July 2020; pp. 1976–1979.
39. Haider, A.; Arsalan, M.; Lee, M.B.; Owais, M.; Mahmood, T.; Sultan, H.; Park, K.R. Artificial Intelligence-based computer-aided diagnosis of glaucoma using retinal fundus images. *Expert Syst. Appl.* **2022**, *207*, 117968. [CrossRef]
40. Sarhan, A.; Al-KhazÁly, A.; Gorner, A.; Swift, A.; Rokne, J.; Alhajj, R.; Crichton, A. Utilizing transfer learning and a customized loss function for optic disc segmentation from retinal images. *arXiv* **2020**, arXiv:2010.00583.
41. Almubarak, H.; Bazi, Y.; Alajlan, N. Two-stage mask-RCNN approach for detecting and segmenting the optic nerve head, optic disc, and optic cup in fundus images. *Appl. Sci.* **2020**, *10*, 3833. [CrossRef]
42. Zhang, Z.; Fu, H.; Dai, H.; Shen, J.; Pang, Y.; Shao, L. ET-Net: A generic edge-attention guidance network for medical image segmentation. In Proceedings of the Medical Image Computing and Computer Assisted Intervention, Shenzhen, China, 13–17 October 2019; pp. 442–450.
43. Orlando, J.I.; Fu, H.; Barbosa Breda, J.; van Keer, K.; Bathula, D.R.; Diaz-Pinto, A.; Fang, R.; Heng, P.-A.; Kim, J.; Lee, J.; et al. REFUGE challenge: A unified framework for evaluating automated methods for glaucoma assessment from fundus photographs. *Med. Image Anal.* **2020**, *59*, 101570. [CrossRef] [PubMed]
44. Li, S.; Sui, X.; Luo, X.; Xu, X.; Liu, Y.; Goh, R. Medical image segmentation using squeeze-and-expansion transformers. *arXiv* **2021**, arXiv:2105.09511.
45. Hervella, Á.S.; Ramos, L.; Rouco, J.; Novo, J.; Ortega, M. Multi-modal self-supervised pre-training for joint optic disc and cup segmentation in eye fundus images. In Proceedings of the IEEE International Conference on Acoustics, Speech and Signal Processing, Barcelona, Spain, 4–9 May 2020; pp. 961–965.
46. Liu, S.; Hong, J.; Lu, X.; Jia, X.; Lin, Z.; Zhou, Y.; Liu, Y.; Zhang, H. Joint optic disc and cup segmentation using semi-supervised conditional GANs. *Comput. Biol. Med.* **2019**, *115*, 103485. [CrossRef]
47. Yu, S.; Xiao, D.; Frost, S.; Kanagasingam, Y. Robust optic disc and cup segmentation with deep learning for glaucoma detection. *Comput. Med. Imaging Graph.* **2019**, *74*, 61–71. [CrossRef]
48. Chakravarty, A.; Sivaswamy, J. RACE-Net: A recurrent neural network for biomedical image segmentation. *IEEE J. Biomed. Health Inform.* **2019**, *23*, 1151–1162. [CrossRef]
49. Zilly, J.; Buhmann, J.M.; Mahapatra, D. Glaucoma detection using entropy sampling and ensemble learning for automatic optic cup and disc segmentation. *Comput. Med. Imaging Graph.* **2017**, *55*, 28–41. [CrossRef]

50. Chakravarty, A.; Sivaswamy, J. Joint optic disc and cup boundary extraction from monocular fundus images. *Comput. Methods Programs Biomed.* **2017**, *147*, 51–61. [CrossRef] [PubMed]
51. Shankaranarayana, S.M.; Ram, K.; Mitra, K.; Sivaprakasam, M. Joint optic disc and cup segmentation using fully convolutional and adversarial networks. In Proceedings of the International Workshop on Fetal and Infant Image Analysis, Québec City, QC, Canada, 10 September 2017; pp. 168–176.
52. Haleem, M.S.; Han, L.; van Hemert, J.; Li, B.; Fleming, A.; Pasquale, L.R.; Song, B.J. A novel adaptive deformable model for automated optic disc and cup segmentation to aid glaucoma diagnosis. *J. Med. Syst.* **2017**, *42*, 20. [CrossRef] [PubMed]
53. Sedai, S.; Roy, P.K.; Mahapatra, D.; Garnavi, R. Segmentation of optic disc and optic cup in retinal fundus images using shape regression. In Proceedings of the International Conference of the IEEE Engineering on Medicine and Biology Society, Orlando, FL, USA, 16–20 August 2016; pp. 3260–3264.
54. Joshi, G.D.; Sivaswamy, J.; Krishnadas, S.R. Optic disk and cup segmentation from monocular color retinal images for glaucoma assessment. *IEEE Trans. Med. Imaging* **2011**, *30*, 1192–1205. [CrossRef] [PubMed]
55. Sivaswamy, J.; Krishnadas, S.R.; Datt Joshi, G.; Jain, M.; Syed Tabish, A.U. Drishti-GS: Retinal image dataset for optic nerve head (ONH) segmentation. In Proceedings of the IEEE International Symposium on Biomedical Imaging, Beijing, China, 29 April–2 May 2014; pp. 53–56.
56. Sun, J.-D.; Yao, C.; Liu, J.; Liu, W.; Yu, Z.-K. GNAS-U2Net: A new optic cup and optic disc segmentation architecture with genetic neural architecture search. *IEEE Signal Process. Lett.* **2022**, *29*, 697–701. [CrossRef]
57. Maninis, K.-K.; Pont-Tuset, J.; Arbeláez, P.; Van Gool, L. Deep retinal image understanding. In Proceedings of the Medical Image Computing and Computer-Assisted Intervention, Athens, Greece, 17–21 October 2016; pp. 140–148.
58. Salehi, S.S.M.; Erdogmus, D.; Gholipour, A. Tversky loss function for image segmentation using 3d fully convolutional deep networks. In Proceedings of the International Workshop on Machine Learning in Medical Imaging, Québec City, QC, Canada, 10 September 2017; pp. 379–387.
59. Thakur, N.; Juneja, M. Survey on segmentation and classification approaches of optic cup and optic disc for diagnosis of glaucoma. *Biomed. Signal Process. Control* **2018**, *42*, 162–189. [CrossRef]
60. Pathan, S.; Kumar, P.; Pai, R.M.; Bhandary, S.V. Automated segmentation and classifcation of retinal features for glaucoma diagnosis. *Biomed. Signal Process. Control* **2021**, *63*, 102244. [CrossRef]
61. Malik, F.H.; Batool, F.; Rubab, A.; Chaudhary, N.A.; Khan, K.B.; Qureshi, M.A. Retinal disorder as a biomarker for detection of human diseases. In Proceedings of the IEEE International Conference on Multitopic, Bahawalpur, Pakistan, 5–7 November 2020; pp. 1–6.
62. Vajaranant, T.S.; Hallak, J.; Espeland, M.A.; Pasquale, L.R.; Klein, B.E.; Meuer, S.M.; Rapp, S.R.; Haan, M.N.; Maki, P.M. An association between large optic nerve cupping and cognitive function. *Am. J. Ophthalmol.* **2019**, *206*, 40–47. [CrossRef]
63. Selvaraju, R.R.; Cogswell, M.; Das, A.; Vedantam, R.; Parikh, D.; Batra, D. Grad-CAM: Visual explanations from deep networks via gradient-based localization. In Proceedings of the IEEE International Conference on Computer Vision, Venice, Italy, 22–29 October 2017; pp. 618–626.

Disclaimer/Publisher's Note: The statements, opinions and data contained in all publications are solely those of the individual author(s) and contributor(s) and not of MDPI and/or the editor(s). MDPI and/or the editor(s) disclaim responsibility for any injury to people or property resulting from any ideas, methods, instructions or products referred to in the content.

Article

Log-Linear-Based Logic Mining with Multi-Discrete Hopfield Neural Network

Gaeithry Manoharam [1], Mohd Shareduwan Mohd Kasihmuddin [1,*], Siti Noor Farwina Mohamad Anwar Antony [1], Nurul Atiqah Romli [1], Nur 'Afifah Rusdi [1,2], Suad Abdeen [1] and Mohd. Asyraf Mansor [3]

[1] School of Mathematical Sciences, Universiti Sains Malaysia, Gelugor 11800, Penang, Malaysia; gaeithry@student.usm.my (G.M.); farwina@usm.my (S.N.F.M.A.A.); nurulatiqah_@student.usm.my (N.A.R.); afifahrusdi@student.usm.my (N.'A.R.); suadabdeen@student.usm.my (S.A.)

[2] Institute of Engineering Mathematics, Universiti Malaysia Perlis, Kampus Pauh Putra, Arau 02600, Perlis, Malaysia

[3] School of Distance Education, Universiti Sains Malaysia, Gelugor 11800, Penang, Malaysia; asyrafman@usm.my

* Correspondence: shareduwan@usm.my; Tel.: +60-4-6534769

Abstract: Choosing the best attribute from a dataset is a crucial step in effective logic mining since it has the greatest impact on improving the performance of the induced logic. This can be achieved by removing any irrelevant attributes that could become a logical rule. Numerous strategies are available in the literature to address this issue. However, these approaches only consider low-order logical rules, which limit the logical connection in the clause. Even though some methods produce excellent performance metrics, incorporating optimal higher-order logical rules into logic mining is challenging due to the large number of attributes involved. Furthermore, suboptimal logical rules are trained on an ineffective discrete Hopfield neural network, which leads to suboptimal induced logic. In this paper, we propose higher-order logic mining incorporating a log-linear analysis during the pre-processing phase, the multi-unit 3-satisfiability-based reverse analysis with a log-linear approach. The proposed logic mining also integrates a multi-unit discrete Hopfield neural network to ensure that each 3-satisfiability logic is learned separately. In this context, our proposed logic mining employs three unique optimization layers to improve the final induced logic. Extensive experiments are conducted on 15 real-life datasets from various fields of study. The experimental results demonstrated that our proposed logic mining method outperforms state-of-the-art methods in terms of widely used performance metrics.

Keywords: logic mining; data mining; log-linear analysis; reverse analysis; statistical classification; evolutionary computation; discrete Hopfield neural network

MSC: 68T07

1. Introduction

Data mining is the process of discovering patterns, relationships, and insights from large datasets using various mathematical and computational techniques. It involves extracting valuable information from data and transforming it into an understandable structure for further use. Data mining is commonly used in various fields, such as business, healthcare, and science, to make informed decisions and predictions [1–4]. In theory, data mining enables us to make an informed decision or to explore the outcome of a decision without making the decision itself. Thus, this method of handling data can be used in a multitude of real-life applications, including those in the medical [5], water research [6], stock market [7], data mining [8], landslide prediction [9], education [10], and diagnostics [11] fields, among others [12,13]. With the rapid advancement of science and technology, it is vital to return to the fundamentals of data mining. Typically, data are converted into a certain rule and processed by an AI platform [14]. The AI platform is then used to explore the behavior of the dataset and to provide the end user with interpretable rules. In this context, the data must be easily interpreted by both AI and humans, so that the AI system governing the outcome can be well understood [15]. This leads us to the main issue with data mining: most of the rules extracted from datasets are not optimally interpreted by early and end users. To overcome this problem, instead of extracting rules from the data using the black box model, the data can be represented in terms of logic that is supported by mathematics. Therefore, one must understand how logic can be applied to represent data in artificial neural networks.

One of the most challenging tasks in creating an optimal logic mining method is choosing the right logic to represent the dataset. The logic is then learned using intelligent systems, such as a discrete Hopfield neural network (DHNN) [16]. The first implementation of logic in an ANN was pioneered by Abdullah [17], where logic was implemented in a DHNN. In that paper, the synaptic weight of a neuron was obtained by comparing the cost function of a logic with the Lyapunov energy function. By computing the synaptic weight of the network, the optimal final neuron state corresponding to the learned logic could be obtained. Following the introduction of logic into the DHNN, several variants of logic from the literature were implemented into DHNNs. Kasihmuddin et al. [18] proposed incorporating 2-satisfiability logic (2SAT) into a DHNN with exactly two neurons per clause. With the aid of a mutation operator during the retrieval phase, the proposed logic in the DHNN was reported to outperform all existing state-of-the-art DHNNs in governing 2SAT logic. In [19], the first non-systematic logic, random 2-satisfiability logic (RAN2SAT), was implemented into a DHNN. The first and second clauses of the RAN2SAT formulation were connected by a disjunction. Despite facing learning problems during the learning phase, RAN2SAT was still compatible with a lower number of neurons. Interestingly, this study attracted a large number of studies in the field of non-systematic logic. Recently, Zamri et al. [20] proposed weighted random 2-satisfiability (r2SAT) logic in a DHNN as an extension of RAN2SAT. The proposed logic required an additional phase, the logic phase, to ensure that each logic embedded into the DHNN had a certain ratio of negated literals. Thus, the DHNN had more search space to represent the neuron in terms of the logical rule. Gao et al. [21] proposed Y-type random 2-satisfiability logic (YRAN2SAT), which randomly generates a first- and second-order clause. This logic exhibits an interesting behavior because YRAN2SAT can be represented in terms of systematic and non-systematic logical rules. Despite the rapid development of logic in DHNNs, the use of higher-order systematic logic in DHNNs is limited to a single-unit DHNN. For example, the work by Mansor et al. [22] demonstrated the use of a single-unit DHNN that has limited storage information, which leads to a potential overfitting issue when the data are represented in the form of logic.

DHNN, which is governed by logic, plays a pivotal role in creating an optimal logic mining method. Logic mining is a subset of data mining where the information from the dataset is extracted in the form of logical rules. Logic mining was first proposed by Sathasivam and Abdullah [23], namely a reverse analysis that extracted logical rules from real-life datasets. In that paper, Wan Abdullah's method was utilized to find the synaptic weight of the neuron responsible for the final induced logic. The induced logic was verified using support and confidence metrics. The main issue with that study was the absence of general induced logic that represents the behavior of the dataset. To tackle this problem, Kho et al. [24] proposed a novel logic mining method called 2-satisfiability reverse analysis (2SATRA) to extract information from the dataset in the form of 2SAT. Compared with the previous method, 2SATRA has the capability to produce induced logic that can classify the outcome of the dataset. The proposed 2SATRA was reported to be useful in extracting logical rules in E-games in terms of error and accuracy. Zamri et al. [25] proposed a higher-order logic mining method by representing data in the form of 3SAT. With the aid of the clonal selection algorithm (CSA), the proposed logic mining method (3SATRA) managed to extract optimal induced logic from data on Amazon employees' resource access. Despite reporting huge success in obtaining the best induced logic for the dataset, the quality of the logic learned by DHNN was far from optimal. Jamaludin et al. [26] argued that the logic used during logic mining can be further optimized by applying a permutation to change the configuration of the attribute in the 2SAT. This argument led to the development of permutations 2SATRA and P2SATRA, where all possible 2SAT containing the attributes of the datasets were embedded into a DHNN. The proposed P2SATRA was reported to outperform the state-of the art logic mining methods in extracting the best induced logic from the benchmark dataset. In another study, Jamaludin et al. [27] ensured that each induced logic produced by logic mining must be derived from the final neuron state that achieved the global minimum energy. This led to the introduction of an energy-based 2-satisfiability reverse analysis method (E2SATRA), where the proposed logic mining method was utilized to extract a logical rule from E-recruitment data. By using the induced logic, the behavior of the potential recruits could be optimally classified. Although the proposed E2SATRA was reported to obtain global induced logic, there is a high chance that the selected attribute is an insignificant variable for the logical rule. In this context, the insignificant attribute makes the final induced logic uninterpretable.

Due to the potential pitfall of unsupervised logic mining, Kasihmuddin et al. [28] proposed the first supervised logic mining, the supervised 2-satisfiability-based reverse analysis method (S2SATRA). In this model, the calculation for each attribute is computed with respect to the outcome of the datasets. The proposed S2SATRA has outperformed all the state-of-the-art logic mining models in various performance metrics. After supervised learning was introduced, Jamaludin et al. [29] proposed another interesting logic mining model by capitalizing on the log-linear model (A2SATRA) to extract significant attributes with respect to the outcome of the dataset. The proposed A2SATRA uses the k-Way interaction to ensure only significant attributes represent the 2-satisfiability logic. After obtaining the best logic, the DHNN learns the logic and produces the induced logic for dataset classification. Despite the usefulness of supervised learning in the context of logic mining, previous studies only utilized only a single objective function, which leads to potential overfitting during the learning phase of a DHNN. Another possible issue with current logic mining is the lack of higher-order logic to represent the induced logic. Higher-order logic, such as 3SAT logic, is crucial to ensure that more attributes fit into each logical clause. In other words, each attribute allows for more than one attribute to be connected, which we believe will improve the generalizability of the induced logic. Although the work of Zamri et al. [25] shows some development in terms of higher-order logic, the selection of attributes from the datasets was still poorly executed and prone to potential overfitting.

According to the existing literature [29], the log-linear model has been found to be effective in representing data classification. By utilizing a multi-unit discrete Hopfield neural network governed by higher-order logic and a permutation operator, our proposed logic mining method is able to obtain optimal induced logic for a real-life dataset. Therefore, these are the contributions of this paper:

(a) A log-linear approach is formulated by selecting significant attributes with respect to the final logical outcome. The log-linear approach removes insignificant attributes from datasets before being translated into a higher-order logical rule (3-satisfiability), which reduces the complexity of the logic mining to select the best attribute to represent the dataset.

(b) A novel objective function that utilizes both true positives and true negatives when deriving optimal 3-satisfiability logic is formulated. In this context, the logic mining method selects the top and best logic before entering the learning phase of the discrete Hopfield neural network. Using multi optimal logical rules that maximize the objective function, that the search space of the network can be expanded in one direction.

(c) A multi-unit discrete Hopfield neural network that is governed by the best logic obtained from the datasets is proposed. The multi-unit discrete Hopfield neural network independently learns the logic from the datasets and derives respective synaptic weights using Wan Abdullah's method. Using the multi-unit network, the number of induced logics that represent the behavior of the datasets can be increased.

(d) A permutation operator of 3-satisfiability logic is proposed in a discrete Hopfield neural network. In this case, the chosen attribute from the log-linear analysis undergoes permutation to ensure that the optimal attribute configuration in each logical clause can be obtained. By allowing logical permutation, logic mining has the capability to identify the highest performing induced logic in terms of a confusion matrix.

(e) An extensive analysis of the proposed hybrid logic mining is performed in real-life datasets. The performance of the proposed hybrid logic mining is compared with state-of-the-art logic mining methods. In this context, various performance metrics are analyzed to validate the performance of the proposed logic mining method. A nonparametric test is performed to validate the superiority of the proposed logic mining.

This paper is organized as follows: Section 2 presents the motivation behind the paper. Then, in Section 3, we introduce the higher-order 3-satisfiability representation. Next, in Section 4, we explain how 3-satisfiabilty is implemented into a DHNN. Section 5 described the integration of a log-linear model into 3SATRA. Section 6 outlines the experimental setup. The most important parts of the paper are presented in Section 7 where we discuss the simulation of log-linear model in a 3-satisfiability-based reverse multi-unit. Section 8, we reveal the limitation of our research and in Section 9 discussed future work. Finally, we conclude with the results of our findings in Section 10.

2. Motivation

In this section, we discuss the motivation behind our work. Each motivation addresses the problem with existing logic mining and how our proposed logic mining can fill these gaps in the field.

2.1. Lack of Higher-Order Logic to Represent Selected Attributes

Logical rules play a pivotal role in representing the information in a dataset. In the conventional paradigm, attributes with more connection to the logical rule have the capacity to store more information. In current methods of logic mining, such as 2SATRA [26] and E2SATRA [27], logic is limited to the second order, where only two attributes are embedded into the clause. In this context, each attribute connects with only one attribute to satisfy the clause. This causes problems in satisfying the interpretation of the logic during the learning phase because the probability of the 2SAT being satisfied is less than that of a higher-order clause [29]. There are two potential issues with lower-order logic in logic mining. Firstly, obtaining the wrong synaptic weight can lead to a wrong final neuron state during the retrieval phase of a DHNN, which can impact the performance of the induced logic. Secondly, lower-order logic has a smaller search space, which may not be sufficient to accurately represent the behavior of the dataset. On the other hand, higher-order logic can represent more attributes, which can improve the generalizability of the induced logic. Furthermore, the permutation operator can be implemented to explore more possible combinations of attributes, which can lead to the discovery of better solutions. The work by Jamaludin et al. [30] demonstrated that a permutation operator can reveal possible induced logical rules. However, if the number of attributes is low, the performance of logic mining will not improve. This will result in a huge loss in potential optimal induced logic. Although there are some attempts to realize higher-order logic mining, such as the work proposed by Zamri et al. [25], where 3SAT was utilized to represent logic in logic mining, there has not been any attempts to represent the "right" 3SAT logic because all attributes in the dataset have equal probability of being chosen. In this paper, we propose a higher-order logic mining by capitalizing on the use of 3-satisfiability logic to represent attributes in a dataset. In this context, our proposed logic mining. will utilize log-linear models to extract the most optimal attribute with respect to the logical outcome.

2.2. Limited Single-Unit DHNN

Due to its simplicity and effective synaptic weight management, a DHNN governed by logic has good potential in learning the behavior of a dataset. Given the simplicity of DHNNs such as content addressable memory (CAM) and effective synaptic weight management, a DHNN has the capability to retain information about the dataset and to retrieve any necessary rules during the retrieval phase. Despite demonstrating stellar performance in simulated learning [20,21], DHNNs have been shown to be ineffective at extracting information from real-life datasets. This is due to only one logic being translated into CAM, which leads to a single outcome, because only one set of synaptic weights was learned during the learning phase of the DHNN. In this context, the possibility of logic mining obtaining the most optimal induced logic is reduced drastically. For instance, the logic mining method proposed by Kho et al. [24] embedded the single best logic into DHNN. Since each DHNN can only learn one type of logic, the final induced logic obtained from logic mining was limited to the direction of the local field. When the number of induced logical rules was small, the performance of the logic mining deteriorated. A similar observation was found in the work by Alway et al. [31], where a single-unit DHNN reduced the probability of the network arriving at the optimal induced logic. To remedy this matter, this paper proposes a multi-unit DHNN to increase the solution space for logic mining. After obtaining a few logical rules with high fitness values, each logic is learned by the DHNN. In this context, each DHNN learns the logic independently and recommends their own induced logic without any interaction between other CAMs. This perspective helps the logic mining method achieve optimal induced logic [32].

2.3. Issue with Single Objective Function

In addition to the multi-unit DHNN discussed in Section 2.2, the quality of the best logic must be improved to reduce potential overfitting of the DHNN. Generally, the objective function of logic mining during the pre-processing phase is to maximize the number of true positives. For example, the logic mining proposed by Zamri et al. [25] depends solely on the number of positive outcomes from the learning phase and does not consider the number of true negatives although both outcomes are consistent with the learned logic. In the event of all outcomes achieving all true negatives, the proposed logic mining is reduced to a random classifier because the DHNN is unable to obtain the most optimal synaptic weight. A similar observation was reported in the work by Kasihmuddin et al. [26]. Despite achieving optimal induced logic using S2SATRA, the induced logic could learn data that led to true positives. This is the major limitation of the proposed S2SATRA because most of the logic from the dataset that yields true negatives are ignored. In this context, the learning data embedded into the DHNN is reduced drastically, which reduces the sensitivity of the logic mining towards more specialized datasets. To address the root of this problem, the best logic obtained from the pre-processing phase must be flexible enough without sacrificing valuable information about the learning data. In this way, the objective function of the best logic must accommodate the frequency of the true negative outcome. In this paper, we propose a logic mining that maximizes any logical outcomes that are both true positives and true negatives before being learned by the DHNN. Therefore, the proposed logic mining contributes to enhancing the search ability of induced logic in extracting more accurate logical rules from a dataset.

3. Higher-Order 3-Satisfiability Representation

The systematic 3SAT is a logical rule that strictly comprises three variables in each clause with disjunction between the clauses. This logic was popularized in several prominent studies, such as [22], where each variable represented information about the application or problem. Since 3SAT was proven in NP by [33], there was no efficient method to guarantee that a consistent assignment that satisfies 3SAT can be found by the algorithm. Based on [25], 3SAT consists of the following features:

(a) A set of n variables, $L_1, L_2, L_3, \ldots \ldots L_n$;
(b) A set of literals, where a literal is a variable L or a negation of variable L;
(c) A set of m distinct clauses, which are connected with the logical AND ($\wedge$) and in which each M_i consists of exactly three literals variables forming the k-SAT clause

and every logical clause normally has exactly k variables that are linked with the OR ($\wedge$) operator.

The general formula for 3SAT can be defined as follows:

By considering features (a)–(c), the formulation for 3SAT can be generalized as follows:

$$L_{3SAT} = \wedge_{i=j}^{m} C_i \quad \text{where} \quad C_i = \vee_{i=j}^{3}(x_{ij}, y_{ij}, z_{ij}) \tag{1}$$

where each clause contains exactly three literals. Note that each variable in the clause can be 1, which represents true, or -1, which represents false. The goal of Equation (1) is to align all the states of the variable so that $L_{3SAT} = 1$.

The suggested logical formula of L_{3SAT} is shown in Equation (2):

$$L_{3SAT} = (A \vee B \vee C) \wedge (D \vee E \vee F) \wedge (G \vee H \vee I) \tag{2}$$

As presented in Equation (2), L_{3SAT} is satisfiable when $(A, B, C, D, E, F, G, H \,\&\, I)$ in the initial neuron state are $\{-1, -1, -1, -1, -1, -1, 1, 1, 1\}$, which represents true. On the other hand, if $(A, B, C, D, E, F, G, H \,\&\, I)$ in the initial neuron state is $\{-1, -1, -1, -1, -1, -1, 1, 1, 1\}$, it is not satisfied. This logical structure does not consider redundant literals. The dimensionality feature, which permits only three decisions to affect the outcome of the datasets, is another benefit of suggesting three variables per clause. When a logical rule is embedded into an artificial neural network, the choice of three-dimensional model remains interpretable based on the logical rule. Furthermore, we need to save the interaction between the variables in the sentence. Optimizing the value of k is necessary as reaching $k = 3$ is the primary goal. This study also utilized a permutation operator in the logical structure. The basic definition of the L_{3SAT} is as follows:

$$L^i_{3SAT} = \wedge_{u=1}^{n} C_u \quad \text{where} \quad C_u = \vee_{v=1}^{k}\left(X^a_{uvw}, Y^b_{uvw}, Z^c_{uvw}\right), k = 3 \tag{3}$$

where a, b, and c are the arrays of attributes and $a \neq b \neq c$. Then, X^a_{uvw}, Y^b_{uvw} is the selected attributes a and b, respectively. The 3SAT logical structure is a higher-order logical structure that is probably satisfied and compatible into the DHNN. The logical structure obtains the correct synaptic weight in order to achieve the global minimum value. The possible logical structure after the permutation is shown in Equations (4) and (5).

$$L^1_{3SAT} = (C \vee E \vee H) \wedge (G \vee F \vee I) \wedge (D \vee B \vee A) \tag{4}$$

$$L^2_{3SAT} = (G \vee D \vee C) \wedge (F \vee V \vee H) \wedge (E \vee A \vee B) \tag{5}$$

Equation (4) has a difference in the arrangement of the literals in each clause in the logical structure. The logical permutation in both equations gives a higher accuracy for the logical structure.

4. 3-Satisfiability (L_{3SAT}) in Discrete Hopfield Neural Network

The discrete Hopfield neural network (DHNN) consists of interconnected neurons that have input and output patterns in the form of discrete vectors. The network's weights are symmetrical, and there are no self-connections [17]. The symmetrical synaptic weights are connected by interconnected neurons in a conventional recurrent network. Low computation, high convergence, and good content addressable memory (CAM) are all elements of this network [24]. Furthermore, in this study, the HNN is compatible with the bipolar neuron representation, and the fundamental neuron update can be expressed using

Equation (6), and the fundamental neuron update can be expressed using Equation (6). HNN's general asynchronous updating rule is as follows:

$$S_i = \begin{cases} 1, & \sum_{j}^{N} W_{ij} S_j \geq \varepsilon \\ -1, & otherwise \end{cases} \quad (6)$$

where S_i is the weight for units a to b, and ε refers to the threshold of the HNN.

To incorporate L3SAT into a DHNN, a neuron is assigned to each variable in Equation (3). Each neuron is defined in [−1,1], which stands for false and true, respectively. To model neurons collectively, the cost function associated with the L3SAT must be minimized. In general, the cost function, δL_{3SAT}, is formulated as follows:

$$\delta L_{3SAT} = \sum_{u=1}^{NC} \prod_{v=1}^{NV} w_{uv} \quad (7)$$

where NV denotes the number of variables, whereas NC denotes the number of clauses, and Equation (8) presents the definition of the L3SAT inconsistency:

$$w_{uv} = \begin{cases} \frac{1}{2}(1-S_x), & if\ x \\ \frac{1}{2}(1+S_x), & Otherwise \end{cases} \quad (8)$$

Before identifying any inconsistencies in the L3SAT, the first step is to identify the cost function of the L3SAT. In the learning phase, the αL3SAT must be able to produce at least the minimum cost function so that the synaptic weight results can guarantee that the proposed L3SAT can be modelled into the DHNN. The final neuron state of the DHNN will be sequentially updated in the retrieval phase using the local field $H_{\alpha L3SAT}$, shows in Equation (9):

$$h_L(t) = \sum_{c=1, c\neq b}^{n} \sum_{b=1, b\neq c}^{n} W_{abc}^{(3)} S_b S_c + \sum_{b=1, b\neq a}^{n} W_{ab}^{(2)} S_b + W_c^{(1)} \quad (9)$$

where the synaptic weights are connected at the third order $W_{abc}^{(3)}$, second order $W_{ab}^{(2)}$, and first order $W_c^{(1)}$. The most recent final neuron state S_i, is as followed by Equation (10):

$$S_i = \begin{cases} 1, & \tanh h_L(t) \geq 0 \\ -1, & Otherwise \end{cases} \quad (10)$$

The hyperbolic tangent activation function (HTAF), abbreviated as $h_L(t)$, is shown in Equation (11):

$$\tanh(h_i) = \frac{e^{h_L(t)} - e^{h(t)L}}{e^{h_L(t)} + e^{h(t)L}} \quad (11)$$

It is important that, according to [23], HTAF capacity is non-linearly classified and that the optimal solution is differentiated by minimizing neuron oscillation during the retrieval phase in the DHNN. The final neuron state generated by DHNN-L3SAT denotes the L3SAT performance. The properties of DHNN, as described by Theorem 1 in [17], include its tendency to converge, which is also corroborated by [18].

Theorem 1. *Assume that N = (W, θ), where θ is the model's threshold for the DHNN. Assume that W is a symmetric matrix with nonnegative diagonal components and that N operates in an asynchronous mode. DHNN will then always reach a stable state.*

Since the suggested 3SAT into DHNN does not contain a hidden layer, the network must be examined before transferring into the ideal neuron state. It will be simple to evaluate the optimality as Lyapunov energy in this scenario that be instantly identify if the final neuron state was captured in a suboptimal condition. The following is the formulation of the $H_{\delta L3SAT}$ Lyapunov energy function, which relates to the DHNN-L3SAT.

$$H_{L3SAT}(t) = -\frac{1}{3}\sum_{a=1,a^1b^1c}^{n}\sum_{b=1,a^1c}^{n}\sum_{c=1,a^1b^1c}^{n}W_{abc}^{(3)}S_aS_bS_c \\ -\frac{1}{2}\sum_{a=1,a^1}^{n}\sum_{b=1,a^1b}^{n}W_{ab}^{(2)}S_aS_b - \sum_{a=1}^{n}W_a^{(1)}S_a \quad (12)$$

The value of $H_{\delta L3SAT}$ is the absolute final energy, and $H_{\delta L3SAT}$ is monotonically reduced to produce the minimum energy $H_{\delta L3SAT}^{min}$. According to [17] and [22], the number of clauses can be used to predict the absolute minimum energy of any logical rule. The lowest energy of the L3SAT is presented in Equation (13) as this paper addresses logical rules that include three variables per phase. $H_{\delta L3SAT}^{min}$ is calculated using Equation (13).

$$H_{\delta L3SAT}^{min} = -\frac{1}{8}n\left(\chi_i^3\right) \quad (13)$$

Meanwhile, χ_i^3 and a represent the third order and three literal clauses in $H_{\delta L3SAT}$.

Finally, to identify the global and local minimum solutions, Equation (14) can be used. Significantly, the final neuron states will reach the global minimum solution if it is satisfied; if not satisfied, they become the local minimum solution. v is the tolerance value, which is an indicator of a satisfied solution.

$$\left|H_{\delta L3SAT} - H_{\delta L3SAT}^{min}\right| \leq v \quad (14)$$

Figure 1 presents a schematic 3SAT outline, and Figure 2 presents a flow chart of the DHNN-3SAT steps using the following pseudocode. $G3SATRA\mu$ then updates the neuron at time $t+1$. In Figure 1, the main block represented by the black dotted lines shows the higher-order logic based on the number of clauses. Inside the higher-order logic block, the blue, red, and green lines indicate the connections between the neurons labelled $w^2{}_{ij} = w^2{}_{ji}$, $w^3{}_{ijk} = w^3{}_{kji} = w^3{}_{jki}$, and $w^1{}_i = w^1{}_j$, respectively.

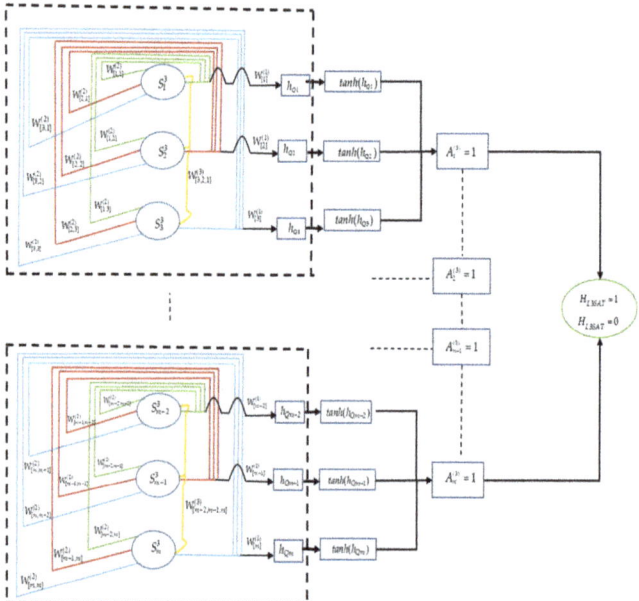

Figure 1. Schematic diagram for DHNN-L3SAT.

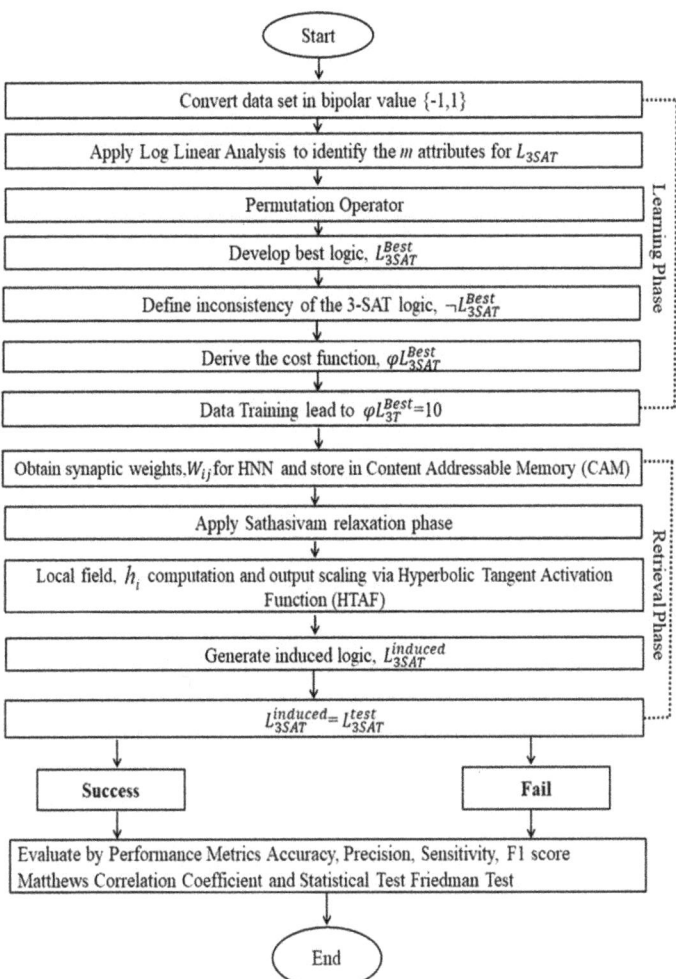

Figure 2. Flow chart of the workflow of $G3SATRA\mu$.

The methodology used in this study is illustrated in Figure 2 and comprises a logic phase and a training phase. The flow chart shows that the pre-processing method is involved in the learning phase, making it a critical step. Therefore, the quality and appropriateness of the pre-processing method can significantly influence the performance of the logic mining model. To evaluate the performance of the induced logic after completing the training phase, performance metrics were utilized. These metrics were used to determine whether the $G3SATRA\mu$ model accurately predicted the outcome or if it required improvement.

5. Proposed Higher-Order Log-Linear Model in Logic Mining

This paper discusses the method of a higher-order log-linear analysis and the objective function of a multi-unit DHNN. The following section explores the formulation of a log-linear model, including the selection of significant attributes, and the creation of a multi-unit DHNN. Furthermore, in each section, the log-linear formula is well explained according to the objective function.

5.1. Log-Linear Analysis to Represent 3-Satisfiability Logic

One of the significant applications of logic in DHNN is logic mining. Logic mining is used to extract logical rules from real-life datasets. Logic mining is different from data mining methods in the literature [23–31] because the end product for logic mining is a classification model based on SAT rules. The main goal of logic mining is to extract a logical rule that explains the behavior of the dataset. Note that logic mining that utilizes 3SAT in a DHNN was first proposed by Zamri et al. [25] and can be abbreviated as 3SATRA. In this context, it is imperative for logic mining to have a more effective DHNN model that is governed by higher-order logic. However, a real-life dataset might consist of hundreds of attributes and often contributes to the "curse of dimensionality" [32] in logic mining. One of the possible solutions to this problem is choosing the right attribute to be processed by logic mining.

One of the possible methods of extracting the right attributes is through a log-linear analysis. In this paper, we propose a log-linear analysis using 3SATRA or $G3SATRA\mu$. Let N be the quantity of variables that represents the attribute $P_i = (P_1, P_2, P_3, \ldots \ldots P_N)$ in bipolar form $P_i = \{-1, 1\}$. Before proceeding to the DHNN, we are required to extract the best r attributes from the total of N from the datasets. The log-linear model is used to examine whether there is a significant difference between the proportion of categories with two or more group variables [33]. This model expresses the log of an expected frequency in a contingency table as a summation of the function for all parameters involved in the datasets. Note that the two-way table with respect to the expected frequency, L_{ij}, for a column is given as follows if each of the neurons is independent from each other [34].

$$L_{ij} = nr_{ij} = nr_{i+}r_{+j} \tag{15}$$

where n is the sum of entries, while ρ_i and ρ_j stand for partial distributions for the variables in the i-th row (row probabilities) and j-th column (column probabilities), respectively. The outcome of performing a linear regression on Equation (15) is shown in Equation (16):

$$\ln L_{ij} = \ln n + \ln \rho_{i+} + \ln \rho_{+j} \tag{16}$$

The frequency for the cross-tabulation cell is predicted using a linear model for the log-linear function. The margins and interaction between the variables should be measured in a two-way table known as a saturated model. Equation (17) shows the formulation for the saturation model:

$$\ln L_{ij} = \rho + \rho_{i+} + \rho_{+j} + \rho_{ij}, \quad i \neq j \tag{17}$$

where $\rho = \ln n$ is the true outcomes, while $\rho_{i+} = \ln \rho_{i+}$, $\rho_{+j} = \ln \rho_{+j}$ are the basic outcomes of neurons S_i and S_j, respectively. According to [29], the association parameter that represents the ability to adapt the log expected cell frequency is expressed using only the partial distribution of each variable and k_{ij}. Equation (18) reproduces the observed frequencies f_{ij} perfectly, known as a saturated model. G^2 and the Pearson chi square χ^2 are used to evaluate the goodness of fit to acquire the likelihood ratio.

$$G^2 = 2 \sum_{i=1}^{i} \sum_{j=1}^{j} f_{ij} \ln \left(\frac{f_{ij}}{L_{ij}} \right) \tag{18}$$

$$\chi^2 = \sum_{i=1}^{i} \sum_{j=1}^{j} f_{ij} \left[\ln(f_{ij} - L_{ij})^2 - \ln(L_{ij}) \right]$$
$$= \sum_{i=1}^{i} \sum_{j=1}^{j} f_{ij} \ln \frac{(f_{ij} - L_{ij})^2}{L_{ij}} \tag{19}$$

Equations (18) and (19) are employed to identify the results based on both the statistical sample size and targeted model [35]. Additionally, the values of these two statistics are computationally the same. In the log-linear analysis, determination of the significance level requires assessing both the parameter and the goodness of fit. In $G3SATRA\mu$ model, the significance of the parameters is evaluated using a partial association test, which calculates the difference in values for the relevant degrees of freedom (df) in the model. Essentially, this means that if there is a relationship between a pair of variables, the null hypothesis test can be selected [36]. Additionally, the null hypothesis is rejected when the parameter values of each individual variable are found to be significantly associated. The alternative hypothesis assumes that there is a significant difference between the observed data and the population parameter. In hypothesis testing, the goal is to reject the null hypothesis in favor of the alternative hypothesis based on statistical evidence [37]. The outcomes of the variables are shown by the generated parameter, by indicating the both P_i and P_j values. $G3SATRA\mu$ is then embedded into the DHNN and can be formulated using the P_i and P_j values, whereas P_i and P_j are significant p-values for attributes S_i and S_j, respectively. Additionally, $\min|P_i|$ represents the lowest significant p-value between S_i and S_j. To guarantee the final model of L3SAT, this work implemented a log-linear analysis and embedded it into a DHNN model according to [38]. It is important to note that neither neuron was considered in the L3SAT formulation when evaluating the performance of each neuron. Another consideration in this suggested method is the changes in traditional k-SATRA proposed by [24,25] if Equation (20) for all variables cannot reach the threshold variable when $0 \leq P_i \leq \alpha$. Furthermore, determining the neuron negativity presents the biggest problem in Equation (15). The essence of a log-linear analysis is to remove any weak neurons, as indicated by Equations (18) and (19). In this study, we apply a log-linear analysis in the 3-satisfiability-based reverse analysis multi-unit approach or $G3SATRA\mu$ in order to determine which attributes in the dataset will be selected to represent specific variables in the $G3SATRA\mu$. In particular, $G3SATRA\mu$ utilizes a log-linear analysis to select the best nine attributes that have the strongest interactions among the dataset outcomes. To apply higher-order logic, the selected nine attributes are randomly permuted. The selected ideal attribute will then be represented as an induced logic in the form of a 3SAT, which will be embedded into the DHNN. This method was also implemented by [30], in work on the 2SAT logical rule based on a six-attribute selection. This method obtains the optimal solution when we compare the logic mining method introduced by [30] with 2SAT logical rules.

5.2. New Objective Function with Multi-Unit DHNN

In previous studies, such as [24–29], the objective function of the pre-processing phase is to find the best logic L_{3SAT}^{best} that maximizes the true positive TP. After obtaining the most optimal L_{3SAT}^{best}, the DHNN will learn this logic and obtain the optimal synaptic weight, which leads to the final induced logic. The main issue with this procedure is the lack of consideration of another important variable, which is the true negative TN. A previous study [39] failed to consider the TN, which plays a pivotal role in obtaining a negative variable in the induced logic. In this paper, we propose a new objective function that considers L_{3SAT} and maximizes the summation of TP and TN. The formulation of the objective function is as follows:

$$\max\{|P_{ij} = 1| + |Q_{ij} = -1|\}, j \in \mathbb{N} \quad (20)$$

where $|TP_{ij} = 1|$ is the cardinality of TP in set j that has a state equal to 1. Note that j represents the DHNN unit. In other words, L_{3SAT}^{best} represents the initial behavior of the dataset before being learned by the DHNN. Equation (20) is different from the work by Zamri et al. [25], where only L_{3SAT}^{best} with the highest frequency was chosen. In this paper, the top k logic that satisfies the condition in Equation (20) is chosen to proceed to the learning phase.

5.3. L_{3SAT}^{best} in Multi-Unit DHNN

The next strategy to learn L_{3SAT}^{best} through the DHNN is proposing a multi-unit DHNN that processes several L_{3SAT}^{best} independently. This strategy ensures that the proposed $G3SATRA\mu$ can cover more search space during the retrieval phase. This can be implemented by capitalizing on the synaptic weight from different types of L_{3SAT}^{best}, which leads to different directions in the final neuron state. Kasihmuddin et al. [18] proposed a mutation DHNN to address a similar concern by increasing the search space by mutating the final neuron state. However, due to the limited number of synaptic weights produced by the Wan Abdullah method, the final neuron state tends to converge towards a similar neuron state. From this perspective, we can obtain different types of final neuron states just by obtaining different logic during the learning phase of the DHNN [40]. The equation that governs the multi-unit DHNN is given as follows:

$$\mu_j = \wedge_{j=1}^{NC} (A_i \vee B_i \vee C_i), \quad j \in R$$
$$\max_{j=1}^{N} |n\left[(p=1) \vee (Q=-1)\right]| \tag{21}$$

where μ_j refers to a multi-unit DHNN in which the structure leads to $L_{3SAT}^{Learn} = \ell$. After obtaining a satisfactory interpretation, the synaptic weight of L_{3SAT}^{best} can be obtained and is stored as CAM in each multi-unit DHNN. During the retrieval phase of the DHNN, the final neuron state S_i^B is obtained using Equation (9) and is transformed into the following induced logic.

$$S_i^{Induced} = \begin{cases} S_i, & S_i^B = 1 \\ S_j, & S_i^B = -1 \end{cases} \tag{22}$$

Next, using the obtained induced logic, the outcome of the induced logic is compared with the testing data. In this context, the comparison is only made with all of the proposed L_{3SAT}^{best} from different DHNN units. Algorithm 1 shows the pseudocode of the proposed work.

Algorithm 1: pseudocode of $DHNN - L3SAT$.

Input
Set all attributes $L_1, L_2, L_3, \ldots\ldots L_n$ with respect to $L_{3SAT}^{Learn} = \ell$ GC, and *trial*
Output
The best induced logic $L_{3SAT}^{Induced}$
Begin
  Initialize algorithm parameters;
  Define the attribute for $L_1, L_2, L_3, \ldots\ldots L_n$ with respect to L_{3SAT}^{Best}
  Search the *p*-value for each Attribute;
  for $(\alpha < p)$ do
  if Equation (7) is satisfied then
  Assign L_i as S_i and continue;
  while $(i \leq GC)$ do
    Using Equation (21) to find the L_{3SAT}^{Best}
    Check the clause satisfaction for L_{3SAT}^{Best}
    Compute $H_{\delta L3SAT}$ using Equation (12)
    Compute the synaptic weight associated with L_{3SAT}^{Best} by using WA approach:
    Store the synaptic weight and L_{3SAT}^{Best} in CAM;
    Initialize the final neuron state;
  for $(k \leq trial)$
      Compute h_i using Equation (9);
      Convert S_i^B to the logical from using Equation (22);
      Combine S_i^B to form induced logic $L_{3SAT}^{Induced}$
      Compare the outcome of the $L_{3SAT}^{Induced}$ with the L_{3SAT}^{Test} continue; -
  $k \leftarrow k+1$
  end for
    $i \leftarrow i+1$
  end for
End

6. Experimental Setup

To validate the performance of the proposed $G3SATRA\mu$, the experiment setup must be performed according to the following setup:

6.1. Benchmark Dataset

The $L_i^{induced}$ for 15 datasets is extracted using the log-linear analysis in Section 5.1. These datasets and their assigned labels are retrieved from the UCI machine learning repository (https://archive.ics.uci.edu/ml/datasets.php) and Kaggle open set (https://www.kaggle.com/datasets). The dataset was downloaded on 6 November 2022 from the respective website. To avoid possible bias, we chose datasets from different fields of studies (refer to Table 1). Table 1 shows the details of each selected dataset.

Table 1. Details of each selected dataset.

Code	Dataset	Data Link	Attribute	Instances	Missing Value	Field	Outcomes
L1	Horse Colic	UCI Machine Learning Repository: Horse Colic Data Set	27	300	Yes	Zoology	Surgery
L2	Credit Approval	https://achive.ics.uci.edu/ml/datasets/credit+approval	15	690	Yes	Finance	Class
L3	Absenteeism	https://achive.ics.uci.edu/ml/datasets/Absenteeism+at+work	21	740	No	Business	Time in hours
L4	Early-Stage Diabetes	https://achive.ics.uci.edu/ml/datasets/Early+stage+diabtes+risk+prediction+dataset.	17	520	Yes	Medical	Class
L5	Chronic Kidney Disease	https://achive.ics.uci.edu/ml/datasets/chronic_kidney_disease	24	400	yes	Medical	Classification
L6	Spec heart	https://achive.ics.uci.edu/ml/datasets/SPECT+Heart	22	267	No	Medical	Diagnosis
L7	Congressional Voting Records	https://achive.ics.uci.edu/ml/datasets/congressional+voing+records	16	435	Yes	Social	Class
L8	Hepatitis	https://achive.ics.uci.edu/ml/datasets/Hepatitis	19	155	Yes	Medical	Class
L9	Autistic disorder for children	https://achive.ics.uci.edu/ml/datasets/Autistic+Spectrum+Disorder+Screeing+Data+for+Children++	21	292	Yes	Medical	Class
L10	Automobile	https://achive.ics.uci.edu/ml/datasets/Automobilee	26	205	Yes	Automotive	Price
L11	Primary Tumor	https://achive.ics.uci.edu/ml/datasets/primary+tumor	17	339	Yes	Medical	Classification
L12	Facebook metrics	https://arhive.ics.uci.edu/ml/datasets/Facebook+metrics	19	500	Yes	Business	Total Interactions
L13	Hungarian Chicken Pox	UCI Machine Learning Repository: Hungarian Chicken pox Cases Data Set	20	521	No	Life	Country
L14	Alcohol effect on math study	https://www.kaggle.com/datasets/whenamancodes/alcohol-effects-on-study?select=Maths.csv	33	395	No	Educational	Grade
L15	Soybean-Large	UCI Machine Learning Repository: Soybean (Large) Data Set	35	307	Yes	Life	Overall Diagnosis

There are two main criteria for choosing datasets. First, each dataset must contain at least 15 attributes. This is important for validating the capability of the log-linear model in extracting the best attributes during the pre-processing phase. In other words, if we choose datasets that have less than 10 attributes, the proposed model $G3SATRA\mu$ would provide the same results as the work by Zamri et al. [25]. Second, the number of instances must be more than 200 to avoid overfitting in $G3SATRA\mu$. When the number of instance is very low, there is a high chance that the learning data will consist only of FP and FN, which leads to random L_{3SAT}^{Best} selection. In addition, k-means clustering [30] will be used to convert the value of the dataset into bipolar form $S_i = \{-1, 1\}$. This conversion is crucial to ensure that the proposed $G3SATRA\mu$ can be compared with other existing work. Since each attribute is represented in bipolar form, the missing data are assigned randomly to 1 or -1. According to Sathasivam [38], the CAM dismisses the outlier data in the bipolar form as being the fault tolerance of the DHNN.

The continuous attribute values in the dataset are standardized using k-means clustering by converting them into bipolar representations. The method used for k-means clustering was inspired by the work of [24,25,31]. To address the issue of missing values, they are replaced with a random bipolar state (either 1 or -1), but the selected datasets should have very few missing values to ensure that the learning phase is not affected.

In addition, all simulations utilize the train-split [30] method, where the training phase contains 60% of instances and the testing phase contains 40% of instances. This method has been used in various studies [24–31], where a further testing percentage was used to confirm the effectiveness of the $L_i^{induced}$. This study used k cross validation on the limited sampling instances to estimate how the dataset is expected to perform in the testing phase; those same instances are not used during the training phase for the model.

6.2. Performance Metrics

Based on popular classification metrics such as accuracy (Acc), precision (PREC), sensitivity (SEN), F_1 score (F_1), and Matthews correlation coefficient (MCC), the effectiveness of the suggested model can be assessed. Acc is applied to figure out the percentage of true-positive and true-negative predictions over the total number of instances. The numbers of instances accurately anticipated a positive and negative cases are known as the true positive (TP) and true negative (TN), respectively, whereas false-positive (FP) and false negative (FN) instances are the sum of the number of falsely anticipated negative and positive outcomes, respectively. The Acc value can be measured using Equation (23), as shown in [41]:

$$ACC = \frac{TP + TN}{TP + TN + FP + FN} \quad (23)$$

SEN examines the positive tendencies of the instances accurately anticipated in a particular situation, as mentioned by [42].

$$SEN = \frac{TP}{TP + FN} \quad (24)$$

According to [43], PREC is used to analyze the number of positive outcomes among the false-positive outcomes from the predicted outcomes. The PREC can be formulated as follows:

$$PREC = \frac{TP}{TP + FP} \quad (25)$$

F_1 is also one of the metrics used to measure accuracy. F_1 is the modulation index of the sensitivity and precision parameters. The F_1 formula is presented in the following equation:

$$F_1 = \frac{2TP}{2(TP + FP)} \quad (26)$$

The effectiveness of the logic mining process is evaluated in the Matthews correlation coefficient (MCC), which considers all the elements of a confusion matrix. According to [44], MCC is a valid indicator for evaluating the quality of the proposed model and may be applied in various sizes of classes.

$$MCC = \frac{TPTN - FPFN}{\sqrt{(TP + FP)(TP + FN)(TN + FP)(TN + FN)}} \quad (27)$$

6.3. Baseline Methods

The performance of the $G3SATRA\mu$ model is compared with numerous well-known current works to confirm the efficiency of the suggested methodology. Even though there are numerous classification algorithms that have been introduced, including those proposed by [43–47], none of these studies have demonstrated that induced logical rules can effectively categorize and extract patterns from a dataset.. Note that the authors of [48] have proposed logic mining that utilizes a log-linear model, but the order of the logic is lower than what we propose in this paper. In addition, our proposed $G3SATRA\mu$ model is incomparable with the work in [49] due to the structure of the radial basis function neural network (RBFNN), which only produced a single $L_i^{induced}$. Thus, our proposed $G3SATRA\mu$ model is compared with the following state-of-the-art logic mining methods:

(a) 2SATRA [24] was the first attempt at extracting the best $Q_i^{induced}$ from datasets. This logic mining method utilizes systematic Q_{2SAT} as a logical rule during training and testing phase. As for the preprocessing phase, 2SATRA uses random selection to choose the best attribute. In terms of the best logic Q_{2SAT}^{best}, 2SATRA uses the objective function that maximizes the number of TP. In addition, 2SATRA only uses a single-unit DHNN.

(b) E2SATRA [27] utilizes energy-based logic mining to ensure that the $Q_i^{induced}$ always follows the dynamic of the Lyapunov function. During the retrieval phase of the DHNN, the neuron state that achieves the local minimum energy is discarded. In this context, the number of $Q_i^{induced}$ is theoretically lower than those of 2SATRA and P2SATRA. E2SATRA uses similar objective functions to that of 2SATRA and only utilizes a single-unit DHNN.

(c) L2SATRA was inspired by the work of [50], which employed the log-linear method to extract a model for an ovarian cyst dataset. This standard selection method utilized characteristics and incorporated conventional 2SATRA based on a log-linear analysis. Although the log-linear method was utilized to extract the best attributes, L2SATRA does not contain a permutation operator. L2SATRA uses a similar objective function to that of 2SATRA and only utilizes a single-unit DHNN.

(d) P2SATRA [26] is an extension of the work by [51], where Q_{2SAT} was formulated with a permutation operator and took into consideration various configurations for the literals in $C_i^{(2)}$. The permutation operator determines all the possibility search spaces of the $Q_i^{induced}$ and leads to the highest accuracy value. P2SATRA uses similar objective functions to that of 2SATRA and only utilizes a single-unit DHNN.

(e) RA [23] is the earliest logic mining that utilizes HornSAT when extracting a logical rule from a dataset. The initial RA does not contain any pre-processing phases and generalized induced logic. In this paper, the RA is the systematic second-order logic during the preprocessing phase. During the retrieval phase, only a $Q_i^{induced}$ that has the property of HornSAT is chosen. RA uses a similar objective function to that of 2SATRA and only utilizes a single-unit DHNN.

(f) A2SATRA was inspired by [30], and its permutation operator investigates every conceivable search space that is connected only to the selected attributes. Attributes are selected by focusing only on a log-linear analysis by selecting significant attributes in the form of a contingency table. In the context of the learning and testing phases, A2SATRA uses a similar objective function to that of 2SATRA and only utilizes a single-unit DHNN.

6.4. $G3SATRA\mu$ Configuration Model

The configuration model of $G3SATRA\mu$ was built based on a log-linear analysis, which consists of a multidimensional examination dataset in the form of a contingency table that presents the relationship between the qualitative and discrete scales. However, $G3SATRA\mu$ concentrates on only one-way interactions to identify the minor qualities that could potentially cause the logic to overfit. Equation (16) is used to measure the likelihood ratio to detect any significant effects and to carry out a primary interaction analysis. Significant attributes are determined using Equation (18) and the permutation attributes are determined using Equation (19). The permutation operator in Equation (20) is used to expose all the interconnections among the variables of $G3SATRA\mu$. Equation (21) determines the significant attribute applied. We incorporate the configuration of the L_{3SAT}^{Best} into DHNN-3SAT using the optimal attribute which leads to $L_i^{induced}$ via Equation (2).

Table 2 shows the k-Way model and higher-order effects component for $k = 1$, whereby the saturated model yields the significant effect components. We want to understand how the variables interact with one another rather than with all the attributes; hence, $k = 1$ is the most important value to observe how using $G3SATRA\mu$ into DHNN can create interactions between variables by concentrating just on one specific variable at a time. Due to the p-value of the Pearson chi square being less than 0.05, it is possible to infer that the number of iterations representing the trial variable stops at one point significantly more often than expected by chance. Table 2 shows that the first-order effects have a substantial impact on the model. Even though in Table 2 it was indicated that the first-order effect had a significant impact on the analysis, we still need to consider partial relationships among all the variables. As a result, to obtain the partial association findings, the variables selected before being expressing in the 3SAT logical structure are analyzed. The parameters are selected based on the p-value by excluding unimportant qualities from the datasets (p-$value = 0.05$).

Table 2. Contingency table with significant values.

Dataset Code	df	Likelihood Ratio		Pearson		Number of Iterations
		Chi Square	Sig.	Chi Square	Sig.	
L1	6560	2577.08	>0.05	29,311.98	>0.05	2
L2	6560	6177.97	>0.05	83,385.89	>0.05	2
L3	2186	6232.99	<0.05	66,353.66	>0.05	2
L4	59,048	6659.89	>0.05	716,016.90	>0.05	2
L5	59,048	5162.86	>0.05	511,554.83	>0.05	2
L6	59,048	3575.83	>0.05	461,730.61	>0.05	2
L7	59,048	6027.20	>0.05	1,159,233.06	>0.05	2
L8	59,048	2037.78	>0.05	144,991.25	>0.05	2
L9	59,048	3460.08	>0.05	150,161.62	>0.05	2
L10	59,048	2944.39	>0.05	352,648.78	>0.05	2
L11	59,048	4531.92	>0.05	402,552.85	>0.05	2
L12	59,048	6618.33	>0.05	791,465.19	>0.05	2
L13	59,048	1635.73	>0.05	780,527.78	>0.05	2
L14	59,048	4592.94	>0.05	181,834.70	>0.05	2
L15	59,048	1448.48	>0.05	177,047.00	>0.05	2

6.5. Experimental Design

In this experiment, we used IBM SPSS Statistics version 27 to perform a log-linear analysis on each dataset in Table 1. The specific concentrations used are listed in Table 3, which provides a comprehensive overview of the experimental parameters and their respective values. We used cross-validation to identify the most important attribute, which we then used for logic mining in DEV C++ Version 5.11. The simulation ran on a device with an AMD Ryzen 5 3500U processor, Radeon Vega Mobile Gfx, and 8 GB of RAM running on Windows 10. To ensure consistent results, we ran all trials on the same device to avoid any potential errors during the simulation.

Table 3. The parameters for each standard logic mining method.

Parameter	G3SATRAμ	E2SATRA	RA(HornSat)	L2SATRA	A2SATRA	2SATRA	P2SATRA	3SATRA
Number of Variable	9	6	6	6	6	6	6	9
Number of Clauses	3	3	3	3	3	3	3	3
Neuron Combination [52]	100	100	100	100	100	100	100	100
Attribute Selection	Log Linear	Random	Random	Log Linear	Log Linear	Random	Random	Random
Energy Tol	0.001	0.001	-	0.001	0.001	-	-	-
Learning Iteration	100	100	100	100	100	100	100	100
Learning Method [26]	ES	ES	ES	ES	ES	ES	ES	ES
Selection rate	0.1	0.1	0.1	0.1	0.1	0.1	0.1	0.1
Trial [40]	100	100	100	100	100	100	100	100
CPU time [49]	24 h	24 h	24 h	24 h	24 h	24 h	24 h	24 h
Logical Permutation (GC)	100	100	100	100	100	100	100	100
Activation Function [53]	HTAF	HTAF	HTAF	HTAF	HTAF	HTAF	HTAF	HTAF
p-value	0.05	-	-	0.05	0.05	-	-	-

7. Results and Discussion

The primary aim of this study is to assess the performance of logic mining when using a pre-processing structure to select attributes. In this section, we evaluate its performance by comparing $G3SATRA\mu$ with existing work. The results of each performance metric for $G3SATRA\mu$ (the existing logic mining = $G3SATRA\mu$), where + is the existing logic mining *loss* in $G3SATRA\mu$ and - is the existing *surplus* by $G3SATRA\mu$, compared with existing methods, showed good results and are discussed in this section.

7.1. Accuracy for Current and G3SATRAμ Logic Mining Models

Table 4 shows the *ACC* results for the selected logic mining model. There are several variations in the performances for $G3SATRA\mu$. The bold values indicate that the logic mining method achieved the maximum value. *Diff* refers to the differences between the proposed logic mining method ($G3SATRA\mu$) and the selected existing logic mining method. Table 4 also displays the average value and minimum, maximum, and average ranks of the Friedman test. The accuracy values were recorded following computing using Equation (23).

Table 4. *Acc* value for $G3SATRA\mu$ in comparison with state-of-the-art logic mining methods.

Code	G3SATRAμ	E2SATRA		RA(HornSAT)		L2SATRA		A2SATRA		2SATRA		P2SATRA		3SATRA	
		ACC	Diff	ACC	Diff	ACC	Diff	ACC	Diff	ACC	Diff	ACC	Diff	ACC	Diff
L1	0.655	0.567↓	0.088	0.475↓	0.180	0.423↓	0.232	0.602↓	0.053	0.453↓	0.202	0.600↓	0.055	0.602↓	0.053
L2	0.720	0.474↓	0.246	0.442↓	0.278	0.564↓	0.155	0.686↓	0.033	0.519↓	0.201	0.845↑	−0.125	0.670↓	0.050
L3	0.666	0.566↓	0.100	0.484↓	0.182	0.461↓	0.205	0.597↓	0.070	0.502↓	0.164	0.571↓	0.095	0.566↓	0.101
L4	0.823	0.534↓	0.289	0.619↓	0.204	0.595↓	0.228	0.855↑	−0.032	0.574↓	0.249	0.778↓	0.045	0.677↓	0.146
L5	0.939	0.763↓	0.176	0.509↓	0.430	0.770↓	0.169	0.923↓	0.016	0.454↓	0.485	0.980↑	−0.041	0.576↓	0.363
L6	0.757	0.553↓	0.204	0.703↓	0.054	0.564↓	0.193	0.665↓	0.092	0.619↓	0.138	0.759↑	−0.002	0.684↓	0.073
L7	0.868	0.431↓	0.437	0.421↓	0.447	0.686↓	0.182	0.869↑	−0.001	0.440↓	0.428	0.778↓	0.090	0.786↓	0.082
L8	0.858	0.384↓	0.474	0.539↓	0.319	0.432↓	0.426	0.826↓	0.032	0.387↓	0.471	0.829↓	0.029	0.671↓	0.187
L9	0.776	0.723↓	0.053	0.485↓	0.291	0.617↓	0.159	0.762↓	0.014	0.747↓	0.029	0.754↓	0.022	0.651↓	0.125
L10	0.812	0.737↓	0.076	0.400↓	0.412	0.471↓	0.341	0.671↓	0.141	0.776↓	0.037	0.873↑	−0.061	0.739↓	0.073
L11	0.690	0.557↓	0.132	0.619↓	0.071	0.576↓	0.113	0.613↓	0.076	0.619↓	0.071	0.676↓	0.013	0.572↓	0.118
L12	0.910	0.497↓	0.413	0.468↓	0.442	0.345↓	0.565	0.771↓	0.139	0.467↓	0.443	0.970↑	−0.060	0.567↓	0.343
L13	0.751	0.646↓	0.105	0.376↓	0.375	0.530↓	0.222	0.708↓	0.043	0.652↓	0.100	0.751	0.000	0.641↓	0.110
L14	0.695	0.547↓	0.148	0.544↓	0.151	0.466↓	0.229	0.638↓	0.057	0.547↓	0.148	0.589↓	0.106	0.668↓	0.027
L15	0.724	0.607↓	0.117	0.521↓	0.203	0.623↓	0.101	0.624↓	0.099	0.623	0.101	0.707↓	0.016	0.626↓	0.098
+/=/−	9/0/6	15/0/0		15/0/0		15/0/0		13/0/2		15/0/0		10/0/5		15/0/0	
Avg	0.776	0.572		0.507		0.542		0.721		0.559		0.764		0.646	
Min	0.655	0.384		0.376		0.345		0.597		0.387		0.571		0.566	
Max	0.939	0.763		0.703		0.770		0.923		0.776		0.980		0.786	
Avg Rank	1.600	6.170		6.430		6.500		3.070		5.700		2.230		4.300	

Note: The symbol ↑ indicates that the logic mining has a higher *accuracy* value, while ↓ indicates a lower *accuracy* value. The bold numbers under diff are comparison values for $G3SATRA\mu$ vs. current logic mining methods.

(a) Several decent performances resulted from the $G3SATRA\mu$. The application of the log-linear analysis is assumed to be highly effective in pre-processing methods, as it identifies significant attributes with a p-value of $p \leq 0.05$. This results in optimal synaptic weight values associated with the resulting attributes for L3SAT [50]. Furthermore, since the logical rules embedded in the $G3SATRA\mu$ model are well-structured, the outcomes have the potential to achieve higher values for the true positives (TPs) and true negatives (TNs).

(b) The dataset L11 (Facebook Metric) was significant because its accuracy rating was almost 1. Therefore, we can conclude that the induced logic obtained an accuracy that was very close to 1 for all TP and TN. However, a study by [26] found that, when compared with the log-linear integration method using the nine-attribute permutation method, the P2SATRA method with restrictions improved identification of the best induced logic and produced more satisfactory results based on true data. This indicates that, in terms of the performance of the dataset, the local field can extract the best induced logic [54].

(c) According to Table 4, there are several values for our proposed logic in which an accuracy of Acc > 0.8 was achieved. Therefore, we can deduce that the proposed logic mining method $G3SATRA\mu$ separate true positives from true negative for datasets. Therefore, our work applied Wan Abdullah's approach to obtain optimal synaptic weight stands [17] to decrease the false negative values that can be produced in clauses [23].

(d) The induced logic retrieved for L8 is $L = A \leftarrow B \leftarrow C \wedge D \wedge E$. L8 refers to symptoms of hepatis disorder, with attribute A, B, C, D, E, F, G, H, and I representing steroid, antivirals, fatigue, malaise, anorexia, liver big, liver firm, spleen palpable, ascites, and varices, respectively. According to the induced logic, the symptoms of hepatis disorder increase when bilirubin increases by about 60% for factors A, C, E, and G.

(e) The Friedman rank test was performed on each dataset with $\alpha = 0.05$ and degree of freedom $(df = 7)$. The Acc p-value is less than 0.05 ($\chi^2 = 69.269$). The null hypothesis, which claimed that all logic mining models perform identically, was rejected. As mentioned by [30], the highest average rank is evidence of the superior performance of a logic mining model. In this research, the proposed $G3SATRA\mu$ model achieved a mean rank of approximately 1.6 among the other logic mining models. However, the second-highest rank was achieved by P2SATRA [21], which closely competed with our model, with an average rank of approximately 2.23.

As shown in Figure 3, we can conclude that the high ACC value is due to the effective training phase, which leads to an optimal synaptic weight for the 3SAT logical rule. This enables the network to retrieve the optimal induced logic through a local field (Equation (9)). By using a log-linear analysis to select the best attribute, we can further improve the accuracy by obtaining optimal synaptic weights, which leads to higher true positive (TP) and true negative (TN) values. Additionally, the log-linear model can eliminate non-significant attributes, resulting in lower false positive (FP) and false negative (FN) values. Comparing our work with RA(HornSAT) [18], we observe that the non-flexible synaptic weight of their logical structure results in lower TP and TN values. The suboptimal synaptic weight also leads to suboptimal induced P, which is further exacerbated when attributes are randomly selected in RA(HornSAT). This feature contributes to the lower TP and TN values in RA(HornSAT).

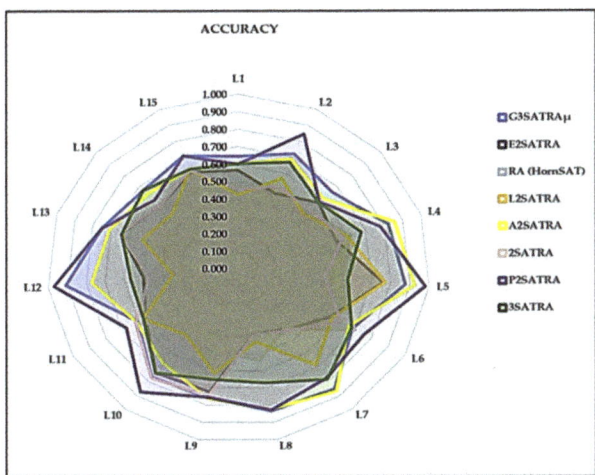

Figure 3. Accuracy of logic mining models.

7.2. Precision for Current and G3SATRAμ Logic Mining Models

The *PREC* values for the chosen logic mining model are displayed in Table 5 below. *G3SATRAμ* shows several variations in performance for each dataset. The values in bold show that the specific logic mining method reached its maximum value. *Diff* denotes the differences between the chosen current logic mining and the proposed logic mining (*G3SATRAμ*). Table 5 also shows the Friedman test's average value, minimum and maximum ranks, and range for ranks. The *precision* values here were predicated based on Equation (25).

Table 5. *PREC* value for *G3SATRAμ* in comparison with state-of-the-art logic mining methods.

Code	G3SATRAμ	E2SATRA		RA(HornSAT)		L2SATRA		A2SATRA		2SATRA		P2SATRA		3SATRA	
		PREC	Diff	PREC	Diff	PREC	Diff	PREC	Diff	PREC	Diff	PREC	Diff	PREC	Diff
L1	0.693	0.659↓	0.034	0.610↓	0.083	0.518↓	0.175	0.674↓	0.019	0.537↓	0.156	0.628↓	0.065	0.634↓	0.059
L2	0.628	0.440↓	0.188	0.444↓	0.185	0.451↓	0.177	0.611↓	0.017	0.461↓	0.167	0.751	−0.123	0.604↓	0.024
L3	**0.547**	0.410↓	0.137	0.372↓	0.175	0.355↓	0.192	0.286↓	0.261	0.371↓	0.176	0.391↓	0.156	0.443↓	0.105
L4	0.883	0.634↓	0.250	0.655↓	0.229	0.751↓	0.132	0.910	−0.027	0.648↓	0.235	0.823↓	0.060	0.687↓	0.196
L5	0.917	0.901↓	0.016	0.606↓	0.311	0.703↓	0.213	0.864↓	0.053	0.568↓	0.348	0.938	−0.021	0.614↓	0.303
L6	0.916	0.745↓	0.171	0.787↓	0.129	0.850↓	0.066	0.937	−0.021	0.793↓	0.123	0.906↓	0.010	0.788↓	0.128
L7	0.888	0.442↓	0.446	0.590↓	0.297	0.838↓	0.050	0.915	−0.028	0.552↓	0.335	0.815↓	0.073	0.861↓	0.026
L8	**0.898**	0.867↓	0.030	0.842↓	0.055	0.889↓	0.009	0.866↓	0.031	0.718↓	0.180	0.880↓	0.018	0.800↓	0.097
L9	0.720	**0.732**	−0.012	0.495↓	0.225	0.580↓	0.140	0.710↓	0.010	0.687↓	0.033	0.700↓	0.020	0.609↓	0.112
L10	0.700	0.606↓	0.094	0.379↓	0.321	—	—	0.599↓	0.102	0.671↓	0.029	0.815	−0.115	0.603↓	0.097
L11	**0.676**	0.469↓	0.207	0.462↓	0.214	0.542↓	0.134	0.573↓	0.103	0.462↓	0.214	0.634↓	0.042	0.525↓	0.151
L12	0.790	—	—	0.264↓	0.527	0.279↓	0.512	0.612↓	0.178	0.287↓	0.503	0.950	−0.160	0.405↓	0.386
L13	0.639	0.521↓	0.118	0.336↓	0.303	0.448↓	0.192	0.582↓	0.058	0.554↓	0.085	0.644	−0.005	0.541↓	0.099
L14	**0.668**	0.542↓	0.125	0.545↓	0.122	0.422↓	0.246	0.605↓	0.063	0.542↓	0.125	0.571↓	0.097	0.631↓	0.036
L15	**0.739**	0.636↓	0.102	0.581↓	0.157	0.648↓	0.090	0.649↓	0.089	0.650↓	0.089	0.699↓	0.040	0.654↓	0.084
'+/=/−'		6/0/9		13/0/2		15/0/0		14/0/1		12/0/3		15/0/0		10/0/5		15/0/0
Avg	0.753	0.615		0.531		0.591		0.693		0.567		0.743		0.627	
Min	0.547	0.410		0.264		0.279		0.286		0.287		0.391		0.405	
Max	0.917	0.901		0.842		0.889		0.937		0.793		0.950		0.861	
Avg Rank	1.6	5.330		6.200		5.470		3.270		5.600		2.530		6.000	

Note: The symbol ↑ indicates that the logic mining method has higher *precision* values, while ↓ indicates lower *precision* values. The bold number under *diff* is a comparison value for *G3SATRAμ* vs. the current logic mining method.

(a) *PREC* shows that *G3SATRAμ* performs better than other logic mining models across all 15 datasets. This demonstrates the capability of *G3SATRAμ* to extract a high value for true positives. *G3SATRAμ* improved the performance of the 3SATRA proposed by [20] by embedding optimal attributes in the 3SAT and retrieving optimally induced logic that is important to the dataset. As a result, *G3SATRAμ* is more capable than other current logic mining models at producing successful outcomes.

(b) $G3SATRA\mu$ achieved a *PREC* that is very close to 1 (*Precision* = 1) in two datasets, L5 and L6. There, it shows that the induced L_{3SAT}^{Best} retrieved by $G3SATRA\mu$ can predict positive outcomes with certainty. Every dataset output from the induced L_{3SAT}^{Best} equals 1. The proposed logic mining model $G3SATRA\mu$ yields a precision that is almost equal to 1 in datasets L5 and L6. Therefore, the final neuron states obtained from the local field provide a satisfactory interpretation as a result [25].

(c) In comparison with A2SATRA proposed by [30], the proposed $G3SATRA\mu$ in this paper is able to more accurately predict positive instances, with the exception of three datasets (L4, L6, and L7). While P2SATRA suggested by [21] may still predict the best induced logic for five datasets (L2, L5, L10, L12, and L13), the $G3SATRA\mu$ model can achieve higher positive values for these specific datasets.

(d) This proposed $G3SATRA\mu$ model outperforms other logic mining models such as E2SATRA, RA, 2SATRA, 3SATRA, and L2SATRA in terms of achieving higher values of true positives (TPs) and true negatives (TNs). It has been demonstrated that using a log-linear analysis for attribute selection and multi-unit theory in 3SAT leads to more accurate TP values.

(e) The average rank of the proposed $G3SATRA\mu$ logic mining model is 1.600, which is higher than the average rank of other models. The closest competing method is P2SATRA, with an average rank of 2.530. The statistical analysis confirms that our proposed model $G3SATRA\mu$ is superior to the other methods. This means that our model is very good at identifying both positive and negative results.

In Figure 4, the precision value is higher compared with other existing logic mining methods such as RA(HornSAT), E2STRA, 2SATRA, and A2SATRA. The proposed model using a log-linear analysis achieved a higher P_{best} value by selecting the perfect attribute from the whole dataset. The permutation operated within a very large searching space to reduce the cost function. The multidimensional solution in the proposed systematic logical structure led to obtaining more TNs and less FPs. The existing logic mining methods L2SATRA [50] and A2SATRA [30] obtained sup-optimal performances in the testing phase, obtaining more FPs that reduce the precision value for their model.

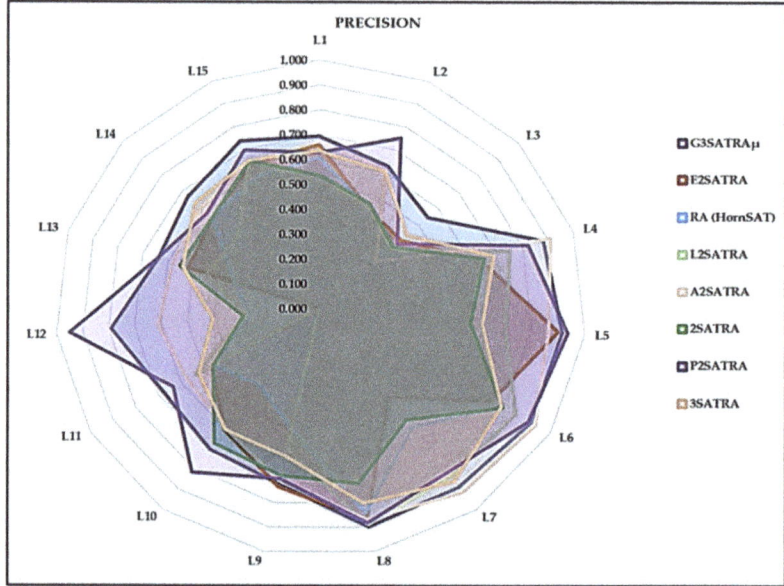

Figure 4. Precision of logic mining models.

7.3. Sensitivity for Current and G3SATRAµ Logic Mining Models

Table 6 shows the *SEN* results for the selected logic mining model. There are variations in the performances of the $G3SATRA\mu$. Whereas the bold values indicate that the particular logic mining achieved the maximum value, *diff* refers to the differences between the proposed logic mining method ($G3SATRA\mu$) and the selected existing logic mining method. Table 6 also displays the average value and minimum, maximum, and average ranks from the Friedman test. These *SEN* values were obtained using Equation (24).

Table 6. SEN values for $G3SATRA\mu$ in comparison with state-of-the-art logic mining methods.

Code	G3SATRAµ	E2SATRA		RA		L2SATRA		A2SATRA		2SATRA		P2SATRA		3SATRA	
		SEN	Diff	SEN	Diff	SEN	Diff	SEN	Diff	SEN	Diff	SEN	Diff	SEN	Diff
L1	0.769	0.586↓	**0.183**	0.389↓	**0.380**	0.514↓	**0.255**	0.670↓	0.099	0.562↓	0.207	0.843↑	−0.074	0.784↑	−0.015
L2	0.643	0.663↑	−0.021	0.522↓	0.121	0.596↓	0.047	0.513↓	0.130	0.809↑	−0.167	0.914↑	−0.271	0.648↑	−0.006
L3	0.516	0.436↓	**0.080**	0.610↑	−0.094	0.515↓	0.001	0.185↓	**0.330**	0.506↓	0.010	0.339↓	0.177	0.720↑	−0.204
L4	0.777	0.505↓	**0.272**	0.774↓	0.003	0.554↓	0.223	0.838↑	−0.061	0.524↓	0.253	0.736↓	0.041	0.792↑	−0.015
L5	0.937	0.720↓	**0.217**	0.834↓	0.104	0.923↓	0.015	0.947↑	−0.009	0.676↓	0.262	0.956↑	−0.019	0.876↓	0.062
L6	0.755	0.667↓	**0.088**	0.859↑	−0.104	0.575↓	0.180	0.613↓	0.141	0.678↓	0.076	0.778↑	−0.023	0.811↑	−0.056
L7	0.901	0.195↓	**0.705**	0.384↓	**0.516**	0.608↓	**0.293**	0.867↓	0.034	0.516↓	**0.385**	0.831↓	0.070	0.784↓	0.116
L8	0.921	0.260↓	**0.661**	0.522↓	**0.398**	0.353↓	**0.568**	0.918↓	0.003	0.428↓	**0.492**	0.895↓	0.026	0.807↓	0.113
L9	0.921	0.754↓	0.168	0.700↓	0.221	0.940↑	−0.019	0.907↓	0.014	0.926↑	−0.004	0.894↓	0.027	0.893↓	0.029
L10	0.860	0.711↓	0.148	0.900↑	−0.040	0.299↓	**0.561**	0.455↓	**0.405**	0.802↓	0.058	0.887↑	−0.027	0.926↑	−0.067
L11	0.596	0.668↑	−0.072	0.507↓	0.089	0.602↓	−0.006	0.443↓	0.153	0.507↓	0.089	0.578↓	0.018	0.801↑	−0.205
L12	0.933	0.537↓	**0.396**	0.519↓	**0.414**	0.862↓	0.071	0.496↓	**0.437**	0.586↓	**0.347**	0.941↑	−0.008	0.654↓	0.279
L13	0.759	0.585↓	0.175	0.727↓	0.032	0.832↑	−0.072	0.773↑	−0.014	0.755↓	0.004	0.694↓	0.066	0.779↑	−0.020
L14	0.855	0.958↑	−0.102	0.814↓	0.041	0.588↓	0.267	0.903↑	−0.048	0.958↑	−0.102	0.887↑	−0.031	0.904↑	−0.048
L15	0.852	0.695↓	0.157	0.697↓	0.156	0.822↓	0.031	0.854↑	−0.001	0.827↓	0.026	0.912↑	−0.060	0.810↓	0.043
'+/=/−'	2/0/13	12/0/3		12/0/3		12/0/3		10/0/5		12/0/3		8/0/7		6/0/9	
Avg	0.800	0.596		0.651		0.639		0.692		0.671		0.806		0.799	
Min	0.516	0.195		0.384		0.299		0.185		0.428		0.339		0.648	
Max	0.937	0.958		0.900		0.940		0.947		0.958		0.956		0.926	
Avg Rank	2.97↑	5.87		5.33		5.2		4.53		4.8		3.13		4.17	

Note: The symbol ↑ indicates that the logic mining method has a higher *sensitivity* value, while ↓ indicates a lower *sensitivity* value. The bold number under *diff* is a comparison value for $G3SATRA\mu$ vs. current logic mining methods.

(a) Our proposed logic mining method $G3SATRA\mu$ outperformed the 3SATRA and P2SATRA. This demonstrates the importance of the log-linear-approach-chosen features for a given dataset not being significant for the dataset. The random selection proposed by [26] successfully retrieved $Q^{test}_{2SAT} = 1$ for all outcomes.

(b) Our $G3SATRA\mu$ model achieved a *SEN* close to 1 (0.937), indicating its ability to predict positive outcomes in the retrieval phase of the DHNN for the L5 dataset. For the other datasets, our model demonstrated high TN and TP values compared with other logic mining models. In fact, for the L7 and L8 datasets, our proposed model achieved higher TN and TP values than other models.

(c) There are some instances where the sensitivity was not recorded due to the lack of a positive outcome for that dataset in the logic mining methods E2SATRA and L2SATRA. Furthermore, there is a good likelihood that the dataset represents an actual situation and that the testing data only contains negative classes. It follows that the induced Q^{Best} is bias towards to the negative class.

(d) For all of the datasets, the Friedman rank test was performed with $\alpha = 0.05$ and $df = 7$. The *p*-value for Sen is <0.05, and $(\chi^2 = 18.698)$. As a result, the null hypothesis that all logic mining models perform equally well was rejected. According to Table 6, $G3SATRA\mu$'s performance still displays a competitive Sen value when compared with other published work such as 3SATRA, P2SATRA, and A2SATRA. The lowest statistical average rank achieved in the logic mining method E2SATRA was 5.80. This statical test can predict that A3SATRA can still reach the $L^{induced}_{Best}$ when adding another optimization layer, which would increase the DHNN's complexity.

Similarly, to the *precision* metrics, the confusion metric for *sensitivity* also achieves a higher *TP* value in the proposed logical structure $G3SATRA\mu$ when compared with other logical structures, except P2SATRA [26]. Figure 5 shows the selection of random attributes and the permutation operator obtaining an accurate local field to achieve the best optimal solution. The $G3SATRA\mu$ is not bad in terms of the optimal solution when we used the Friedman rank test. Its ranking value was still of a higher order compared with the other current logic mining methods.

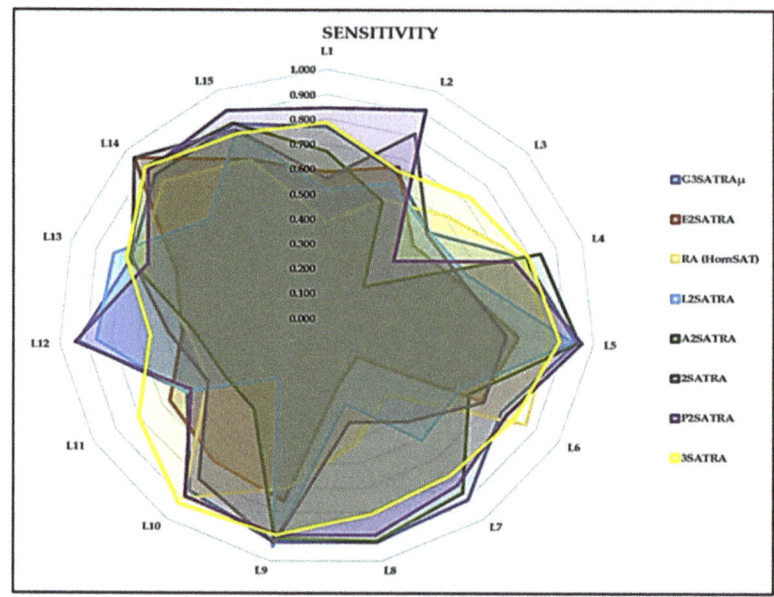

Figure 5. Sensitivity of logic mining models.

7.4. F_1 for Current and $G3SATRA\mu$ Logic Mining Models

Table 7 shows the F_1 result for the selected logic mining model. There is variation in the performances for the $G3SATRA\mu$. Whereas the bold values indicate that the particular logic mining method achieved the maximum value, *diff* refers to the differences between the proposed logic mining method ($G3SATRA\mu$) and the selected existing logic mining method. Table 7 also displays the average value and minimum, maximum, and average ranks from the Friedman test. These F_1 values were computed using Equation (26).

Table 7. F_1 value for $G3SATRA\mu$ in comparison with state-of-the-art logic mining methods.

Code	$G3SATRA\mu$ F_1 Score	E2SATRA F_1 Score	Diff	RA(HornSAT) F_1 Score	Diff	L2SATRA F_1 Score	Diff	A2SATRA F_1 Score	Diff	2SATRA F_1 Score	Diff	P2SATRA F_1 Score	Diff	3SATRA F_1 Score	Diff
L1	0.726	0.610↓	**0.116**	0.461↓	**0.265**	0.512↓	**0.214**	0.666↓	**0.060**	0.549↓	**0.178**	0.712↓	**0.014**	0.700↓	**0.026**
L2	0.630	0.504↓	**0.127**	0.423↓	**0.207**	0.508↓	**0.122**	0.546↓	**0.085**	0.569↓	**0.061**	0.820↑	**−0.190**	0.607↓	**0.023**
L3	0.529	0.415↓	**0.114**	0.455↓	**0.074**	0.411↓	**0.118**	0.195↓	**0.334**	0.425↓	**0.104**	0.354↓	**0.175**	0.547↑	−0.018
L4	0.826	0.548↓	**0.278**	0.684↓	**0.142**	0.625↓	**0.202**	0.870↑	−0.044	0.569↓	**0.257**	0.776↓	**0.050**	0.722↓	**0.104**
L5	0.919	0.759↓	**0.160**	0.617↓	**0.303**	0.739↓	**0.181**	0.886↓	**0.034**	0.553↓	**0.366**	0.947↑	−0.027	0.663↓	**0.257**
L6	0.827	0.698↓	**0.129**	0.816↓	**0.011**	0.667↓	**0.160**	0.741↓	**0.086**	0.722↓	**0.105**	0.835↑	−0.008	0.796↓	**0.031**
L7	0.893	0.259↓	**0.634**	0.448↓	**0.445**	0.702↓	**0.191**	0.890↓	**0.003**	0.522↓	**0.371**	0.820↓	**0.073**	0.817↓	**0.075**
L8	0.909	0.392↓	**0.517**	0.635↓	**0.274**	0.467↓	**0.442**	0.891↓	**0.018**	0.509↓	**0.400**	0.886↓	**0.022**	0.787↓	**0.122**
L9	0.807	0.735↓	**0.072**	0.577↓	**0.230**	0.716↓	**0.091**	0.795↓	**0.012**	0.788↓	**0.019**	0.785↓	**0.023**	0.723↓	**0.084**
L10	0.770	0.639↓	**0.130**	0.531↓	**0.239**	0.250↓	**0.520**	0.504↓	**0.266**	0.727↓	**0.043**	0.839↑	−0.069	0.726↓	**0.044**
L11	0.618	0.515↓	**0.103**	0.463↓	**0.155**	0.554↓	**0.064**	0.410↓	**0.208**	0.463↓	**0.155**	0.539↓	**0.079**	0.626↑	−0.008
L12	0.854	0.302↓	**0.552**	0.334↓	**0.520**	0.419↓	**0.435**	0.546↓	**0.308**	0.348↓	**0.506**	0.946↑	−0.092	0.479↓	**0.374**
L13	0.686	0.511↓	**0.175**	0.456↓	**0.230**	0.564↓	**0.122**	0.655↓	**0.031**	0.621↓	**0.065**	0.665↓	**0.021**	0.619↓	**0.067**
L14	0.747	0.690↓	**0.056**	0.652↓	**0.095**	0.464↓	**0.283**	0.724↓	**0.023**	0.690↓	**0.056**	0.694↓	**0.053**	0.740↓	**0.007**
L15	0.787	0.633↓	**0.154**	0.622↓	**0.164**	0.719↓	**0.068**	0.728↓	**0.059**	0.722↓	**0.065**	0.789↑	−0.002	0.723↓	**0.064**
'+/=/−'	6/0/9		15/0/0		15/0/0		15/0/0		14/0/1		15/0/0		8/0/7		13/0/2
Avg	0.769	0.547		0.545		0.555		0.670		0.585		0.760		0.685	
Min	0.529	0.259		0.334		0.250		0.195		0.348		0.354		0.479	
Max	0.919	0.759		0.816		0.739		0.891		0.788		0.947		0.817	
Avg Rank	1.53	5.930		6.330		5.870		3.800		5.000		2.400		5.130	

Note: The symbol ↑ indicates that the logic mining method has a higher F_1 Score, while ↓ indicates a lower F_1 score. The bold number under *diff* is a comparison value for $G3SATRA\mu$ and current logic mining methods.

(a) The multi-unit $G3SATRA\mu$ forms quite a good number of positive outcomes when learning from all the datasets [41]. When we compare P2SATRA with the proposed $G3SATRA\mu$, performance is lacking in terms of retrieved positive outcomes. Therefore, the authors of [29] stated that the optimal value for synaptic weight is kept in the content addressable memory, and L_{3SAT}^{Best} can enhance the local field when computing the ideal final neuron state.

(b) One dataset, L5, obtained an F_1 score of 0.921, which is close to 1, in the proposed model $G3SATRA\mu$. This shows that our proposed $G3SATRA\mu$ produced the correct number of TPs during the retrieval phase of the DHNN, and as we know through previous work [43], if $F_1 = 1$, the model has perfect precision and recall (correct positive predictions relative to total actual positives) efficiency.

(c) There is no instance where our data return an F_1 score = 0; therefore, our proposed logic was able to produce TPs. The $L_{Best}^{induced}$ that was determined by computing the local field is sensitive to correctly forecasted positive situations. The majority of $L_{Best}^{induced}$ leaned towards $L_{3SAT}^{test} = 1$, reaching the value of F1. The induced logic led to $L_{3SAT}^{Learn} = 1$

(d) All datasets with $\alpha = 0.05$ and seven degrees of freedom underwent the Friedman test accurately. The F_1 p-value is $\alpha \leq 0.05$, and $(\chi^2 = 54.089)$. Thus, the null hypothesis that all logic mining models will perform equally well was rejected. However, compared with the other works, $G3SATRA\mu$ obtained a great average rank equal to 1.53. This is the outcome of $G3SATRA\mu$'s ability to anticipate which attributes maximise TP during the DHNN retrieval phase.

In Figure 6, we continue analyzing the F_1 value with all of the higher-order logical structures; 3SAT has a higher probability of being a satisfied logic. Its higher-order logical rule obtains the correct synaptic weight to achieve an ideal local field, which increases accuracy. $G3SATRA\mu$ is still has the highest FI value compared to other logic mining methods, which are second-order logical structures with a high probability of being an unsatisfied condition. A successfully selected random attribute obtains more FP values in the 15 selected datasets. As we can see, the 3SATRA proposed by [25] still can achieve an optimal value close to that of $G3SATRA\mu$ due to both being higher-order logical structures.

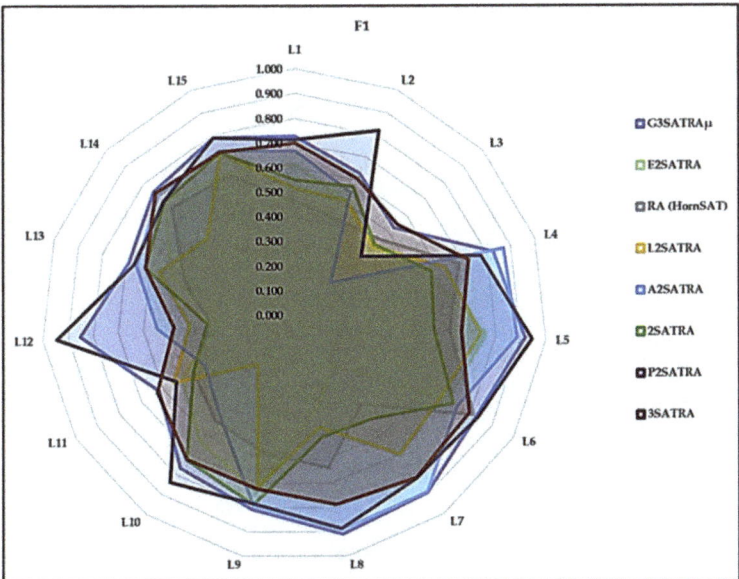

Figure 6. F_1 Score of logic mining models.

In Figure 6, we continue analyzing the F_1 value with all of the higher order logical structures; 3SAT has a higher probability of being a satisfied logic. It higher-order logical rule obtain the correct synaptic weight to achieve an ideal local field, which increases its accuracy. $G3SATRA\mu$ is still in the lead in terms of F_1 value compared with the other logic mining methods that are second-order logical structures with very high chances of being an unsatisfied condition. A successfully selected random attribute obtains more FP values in the 15 selected datasets. As we can see, the 3SATRA proposed by [25] can still achieve an optimal value close to that of $G3SATRA\mu$ due to both being higher-order logical structures.

7.5. Matthews Correlation Coefficient for Current and $G3SATRA\mu$ Logic Mining Models

The MCC result for the chosen logic mining model can be seen in Table 8. $G3SATRA\mu$ displays a variety of linear capabilities. The bold numbers, on the other hand, show that a given logic mining approach has reached its maximum value. $Diff$ represents the differences between the chosen existing logic mining method and the suggested logic mining method ($G3SATRA\mu$). The average value and minimum, maximum, and average ranks of the Friedman test are shown in Table 8. These MCC values were obtained using Equation (27).

Table 8. MCC value for $G3SATRA\mu$ in comparison with state-of-the-art logic mining methods.

Code	G3SATRAμ	E2SATRA		RA(HORNSAT)		L2SATRA		A2SATRA		2SATRA		P2SATRA		3SATRA	
	MCC	MCC	Diff	MCC	Diff	MCC	Diff	MCC	Diff	MCC	Diff	MCC	Diff	MCC	Diff
L1	0.272	0.102↓	0.170	−0.010↓	0.282	−0.196↓	0.468	0.154↓	0.118	−0.145↓	0.417	0.076↓	0.196	0.114↓	0.158
L2	0.337	−0.018↓	0.356	−0.016↓	0.353	0.005↓	0.332	0.257↓	0.080	0.074↓	0.263	0.623↑	−0.286	0.298↓	0.039
L3	0.267	0.065↓	0.201	0.022↓	0.245	−0.078↓	0.345	−0.004↓	0.271	0.005↓	0.262	0.042↓	0.225	0.189↓	0.077
L4	0.530	0.045↓	0.485	0.148↓	0.382	0.211↓	0.319	0.611↑	−0.081	0.069↓	0.461	0.441↓	0.089	0.214↓	0.316
L5	-	-	-	-	-	-	-	-	-	-	-	-	-	-	-
L6	-	-	-	-	-	-	-	-	-	-	-	-	-	-	-
L7	0.724	−0.060↓	0.784	−0.144↓	0.868	0.413↓	0.310	0.730↑	−0.006	−0.186↓	0.910	0.535↓	0.189	0.567↓	0.157
L8	0.486	0.054↓	0.432	0.071↓	0.415	0.146↓	0.340	0.331↓	0.155	−0.177↓	0.662	0.354↓	0.132	0.062↓	0.424
L9	0.573	0.461↓	0.113	−0.051↓	0.624	0.269↓	0.304	0.541↓	0.032	0.523↓	0.050	0.523↓	0.050	0.327↓	0.246
L10	0.624	0.454↓	0.170	−0.002↓	0.625	-	-	0.269↓	0.355	0.547↓	0.077	0.750↓	−0.126	0.546↓	0.078
L11	0.284	−0.049↓	0.334	−0.074↓	0.359	0.057↓	0.228	0.060↓	0.225	−0.074↓	0.359	0.078↓	0.207	0.090↓	0.194
L12	0.797	-	-	−0.054↓	0.851	-	-	0.400↓	0.397	-	-	0.925↑	−0.128	0.186↓	0.611
L13	0.497	0.290↓	0.207	−0.116↓	0.613	-	-	0.434↓	0.062	0.360↓	0.136	0.467↓	0.030	0.361↓	0.136
L14	0.404	-	-	0.073↓	0.330	−0.107↓	0.510	0.299↓	0.105	-	-	0.180↓	0.223	0.372↓	0.032
L15	0.399	-	-	−0.016↓	0.415	-	-	-	-	-	-	0.361↓	0.038	0.141↓	0.258
'+/=/−	13/0/2	13/0/2		15/0/0		14/0/1		12/0/3		15/0/0		10/0/5		15/0/0	
Avg	0.476	0.134		−0.013		0.080		0.340		0.100		0.412		0.267	
Min	0.267	−0.060		−0.144		−0.196		−0.004		−0.186		0.042		0.062	
Max	0.797	0.461		0.148		0.413		0.730		0.547		0.925		0.567	
Avg Rank	1.87↑	5.670		6.130		5.900		3.430		5.800		2.800		4.400	

Note: The symbol ↑ indicates that the logic mining method has a higher MCC value, while ↓ indicates a lower MCC value. The bold number under $diff$ is a comparison value for $G3SATRA\mu$ vs. current logic mining methods.

(a) Our proposed logic mining method, the multi-unit $G3SATRA\mu$, managed to obtain optimal results for MCC, about 10 out of 15, for all datasets. The authors of [51] mentioned that as the MCC value approaches 0, the values are able to predict which attributes will be randomly selected. In this aspect, the MCC value analysis assists in determining the effectiveness of the confusion matrix derived from the induced logic extracted by $G3SATRA\mu$.

(b) The log-linear analysis proposed by [30] is able to produce the best attribute selection in A2SATRA and $G3SATRA\mu$ to obtain instances of positive outcomes, with $MCC => > 0.5$ in this research analysis. As a result, the MCC values of the five datasets in the $G3SATRA\mu$ model are more than 0.5 among the 15 dataset (L4, L7, L9, L10, and L12).

(c) Datasets L5 and L6 obtained values of zero, as the MCC was not registered because no positive outcome was registered throughout the dataset. This indicates in the $G3SATRA\mu$ model, L_{3SAT}^{test} is not reliable. In some the other logic mining methods, the false values of zero in logic mining methods E2SATRA, L2SATRA, and 2SATRA L_{3SAT}^{test} are not reliable in certain datasets.

(d) All datasets with $\alpha = 0.05$ and $df = 7$ were subjected to a Friedman rank test. The MCC p-value is $\alpha \leq 0.05$, and $(\chi^2 = 51.854)$. As a result, the null hypothesis that all logic mining models perform equally well was rejected. The highest average rank among the currently used methods is 1.87, for $G3SATRA\mu$. At the same time, notice that P2SATRA, with an average rank of 2.800, is the method that most closely rivals $G3SATRA\mu$. As a result, it indicates that all the confusion matrices proposed in this study statistically support $G3SATRA\mu$'s superiority over those in previous studies.

According to the findings in Figure 7, $G3SATRA\mu$ has a greater MCC value than the other available methods. This model capitalizes on higher-order k-satisfiability logic as opposed to the model put forth by [26], where only second-order logic was used to represent the dataset. Throughout this condition, $G3SATRA\mu$ has a greater logical capacity to reflect the dataset's dimensionality. The proposed log-linear analysis in Equation (20) can filter a greater number of non-significant attributes using higher values of k, which results in well-balanced TPs and TNs. For learning in the HNN, $G3SATRA\mu$ additionally obtains more than one L^{Best}_{3SAT}, preventing the network from becoming overfit with a single $L^{Induced}_{3SAT}$. As a result, the L^{Best}_{3SAT} in the $G3SATRA\mu$ has a greater MCC value, preventing it from becoming a random classifier. E2SATRA was found to have several drawbacks E2SATRA uses 2SAT poor capacity in a satisfied logical rule. The lower-order logical structure retrieves worse CAM than higher-order logic, which can minimize the energy ($P_{Best} = P_{induced}$). $L^{Induced}_{3SAT}$ significantly achieves a smaller search space. There is a higher chance that only one induced logic was discovered during the learning phase, which caused the MCC value to be close to zero, converging to the random classifier.

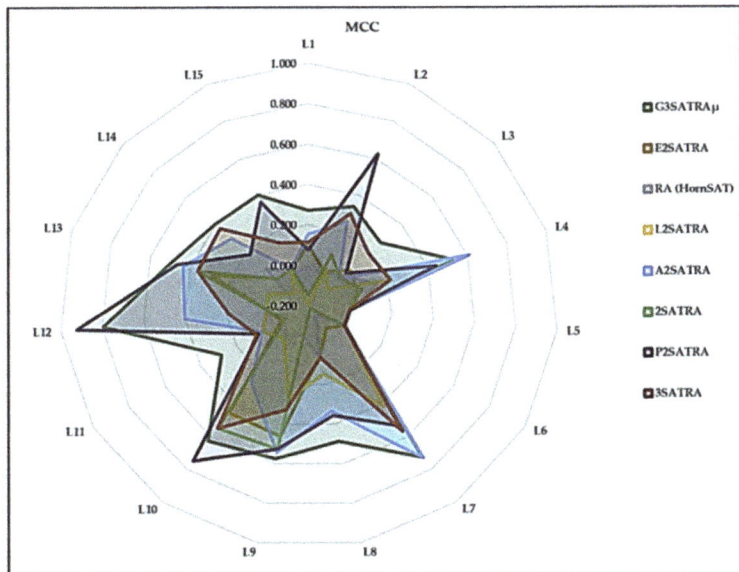

Figure 7. MCC of logic mining models.

From Figure 8, we can conclude that the Friedman test is a statistical test that does not rely on specific assumptions about the data, and it is commonly used to compare three or more related groups or conditions. This test is preferred when the data do not meet the criteria needed for parametric tests, such as a normal distribution or homogeneity of variances. In the Friedman test, the highest rank refers to the logic mining method with the highest median rank across all the logic mining included in the study, which indicates that it performed the best or had the most favorable outcome compared with all the other logic mining methods compared. Similarly, the lower ranking is a crucial element in interpreting the results of the Friedman test as it helps to identify which treatment or condition performed the worst and suggests that it may require improvement or elimination in future studies.

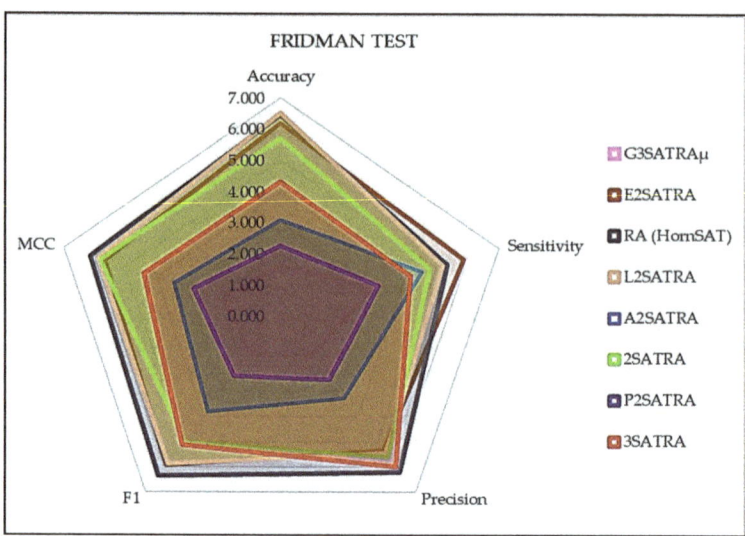

Figure 8. *Friedman test* results for logic mining models.

According to the results of the test, the $G3SATRA\mu$ model achieved the highest average rank among all the logic mining models that were discussed. This means that the $G3SATRA\mu$ model performed better than the other models. The second highest average rank among the logic mining models was achieved by the P2SATRA model. The permutation operator used in the P2SATRA model had a significant impact on its performance during the statistical test. Overall, the results of the Friedman test indicate that the $G3SATRA\mu$ model is the best performing logic mining model among those evaluated. However, it is important to note that the test only evaluated a specific set of models and may not necessarily generalize to other models or scenarios. In contrast, the RA(HornSAT) achieved the lowest rank in a Friedman test result. This indicates that it had the lowest median rank among all the proposed logic mining approaches in the study and performed the worst or had the least favorable outcome among all the logic mining methods compared.

In summary, the proposed logical structure $G3SATRA\mu$ demonstrates superior performance compared with other logic mining methods, according to the technical analysis. The $G3SATRA\mu$ uses a log-linear analysis to select the best attributes, which results in optimal synaptic weights, leading to higher true positives and true negatives and lower false positives and false negatives. The different performance metrics such as accuracy, precision, sensitivity, MCC, and F1 score showed that the proposed method outperforms the other logical mining methods, except for P2SATRA in sensitivity, which achieved more true positives. Additionally, the statistical test results ranked the proposed method as the best among the other methods. The goal of this study was to assess the effectiveness of the proposed method relative to other logic mining techniques using a range of performance metrics and statistical tests. This evaluation aimed to determine whether the proposed method performs better than other methods and, if so, to what degree.

8. Limitation of $G3SATRA\mu$

The aim of logic mining is to extract rules and patterns from data that can be used to make predictions or to gain insights into the underlying structure of the data. However, like any other scientific method, logic mining has its limitations. There may be cases where the data are too noisy or where the patterns are too complex for the method to effectively identify useful rules. There may also be situations where the method is too computationally expensive or requires too much data to be practical.

Therefore, in this study, we aim to explore these limitations in more detail. By identifying and understanding the limitations of logic mining, we can find ways to enhance the effectiveness of logic mining techniques.

(a) Only focusing the log-linear approach on selecting significant attributes. Firstly, by removing insignificant attributes from the dataset before translation into higher-order logical rules, the complexity of the logic mining process can be reduced, which can lead to a faster and more efficient $G3SATRA\mu$ model in the training phase. The selected attribute that best represents the dataset can improve the overall accuracy and performance of the logic mining model and can reduce the risk of overfitting, which can improve the generalizability and applicability of the $G3SATRA\mu$.

(b) Selecting multi-unit optimal 3-satisfiability logical rules is dependent on the selection of true positive and true negative values. Relying on a single set of values for true positives and true negatives may not be sufficient in capturing the intricacies of the dataset, thus resulting in suboptimal solutions. However, using multi-unit optimal logical rules may lead to a substantial expansion of the search space for the discrete Hopfield neural network, particularly when dealing with highly complex or noisy datasets.

(c) The multi-unit discrete Hopfield neural network may not always be effective in learning and deriving the best logic from the dataset. The accuracy and performance of the network may be affected by the quality and quantity of the data used in the analysis. Therefore, the use of Wan Abdullah's method to derive synaptic weights can be effective for highly complex or noisy datasets. Using a multi-unit neural network, the amount of induced logic that represents the behavior of the datasets increases.

(d) The proposed permutation operator for 3-satisfiability logic in a discrete Hopfield neural network enables the identification of the optimal attribute configuration for each logical clause, which can lead to the generation of more accurate and efficient induced logic. Additionally, the use of permutation provides flexibility in the identification of the highest performing induced logic in terms of a confusion matrix, which can improve the overall accuracy and performance of the model. Moreover, the ability to identify the highest performing induced logic through permutation enables the selection of the most relevant and significant attributes, which can lead to more meaningful and interpretable results.

9. Future Work

In selecting a network for our needs, we opted for DHNN over RBFNN and others due to the need for an additional optimization layer when adjusting parameters. The RBFNN requires multiple training phases (no-training, half-training, and full training) to evaluate relevant parameters such as width and center. Even with the right parameters, the feedforward RBFNN only creates a single piece of induced logic, which is usually a simplified linear classifier with no utility. However, this work does not compare DHNN options, such as the one presented by [48]. Instead, this experiment examines the impact of attribute selection on logic mining. It is important to note that in the $G3SATRA\mu$ method, the interaction indicated by a log-linear analysis only depends on the integration of the attributes and the solution. The method is biologically inspired and based on the premise that the human brain is effective at removing unwanted details when the outcome is visible.

Selecting true positive and true negative values from the performance of the logic mining and discrete Hopfield neural network involves experimenting with various selection strategies, such as using different thresholds or weights for each value and evaluating their impact on the quality of the induced logics and the overall performance of the network [55,56]. Another idea could be to explore the use of other machine learning techniques in conjunction with the proposed hybrid logic mining approach, such as deep learning or reinforcement learning. This could involve investigating how these techniques can be integrated with the discrete Hopfield neural network to further enhance the accuracy and efficiency of the logic mining process, particularly when dealing with large and complex datasets. Finally, other potential studies can apply the proposed hybrid logic mining method to specific real-world problems or applications, such as fraud detection or medical diagnoses. This could involve adapting the approach to the specific requirements and characteristics of the problem domain and evaluating its performance and effectiveness in comparison with existing solutions.

10. Conclusions

In this paper, we proposed a new logic mining $G3SATRA\mu$ that utilizes several fresh perspectives. First, we formulated a log-linear approach by selecting significant higher-order attributes with respect to the final logical outcome. Using this approach, we reduced the number of insignificant attributes in the datasets. Second, a new objective function that utilizes both true positives and negatives during the pre-processing phase was proposed. The new objective function considers negative outcomes, which were not considered in previous state-of-the-art methods. Third, this paper proposed the first multi-unit DHNN where each unit learns from individual L_{3SAT}^{Best}, which leads to diversification of the induced logic. Fourth, the proposed logic mining in this paper utilizes a permutation operator to ensure the optimal arrangement of the attribute was used during the learning phase of a DHNN. Finally, extensive experimentation using various real-life datasets was performed in $G3SATRA\mu$ and was compared with other state-of-the-art logic mining methods. Based on these results, our proposed $G3SATRA\mu$ was observed to outperform the state-of-the-art logic mining methods in terms of various performance metrics and statistical validation. Ultimately, this signifies the robustness of the $G3SATRA\mu$ in extracting the most optimal logical rule. As for future work, the proposed $G3SATRA\mu$ can be implemented using non-satisfiable logic such as maximum satisfiability. This study provides a new perspective in extracting datasets that have negative outcomes in nature. In addition, metaheuristics algorithms such as reinforcement learning and simulated annealing can be implemented during the learning phase of a DHNN to ensure only that correct synaptic weights are obtained.

Author Contributions: Conceptualization, methodology, software, writing—original draft preparation, G.M.; formal analysis; S.N.F.M.A.A.; validation, N.'A.R.; supervision and funding acquisition, M.S.M.K.; writing—review and editing, S.A.; visualization, N.'A.R.; project administration, M.A.M. All authors have read and agreed to the published version of the manuscript.

Funding: This research is fully funded and supported by Universiti Sains Malaysia, Short Term Grant, 304/PMATHS/6315655.

Data Availability Statement: Not applicable.

Acknowledgments: The authors express special thanks to all researchers in the Artificial Intelligence Research Development Group (AIRDG) for their continued support. We also acknowledge "Universiti Sains Malaysia, Short Term Grant, 304/PMATHS/6315655" for the support and funding.

Conflicts of Interest: The authors declare no conflict of interest.

References

1. Witten, I.H.; Frank, E. Data mining: Practical machine learning tools and techniques with Java implementations. *Acm Sigmod Rec.* **2002**, *31*, 76–77. [CrossRef]
2. Li, H.; Li, T. A review of data mining techniques and their applications in healthcare. *Int. J. Med. Inform.* **2022**, *158*, 104618.
3. Wu, X.; Zhu, X.; Wu, G.Q.; Ding, W. Data mining with big data. *IEEE Trans. Knowl. Data Eng.* **2014**, *26*, 97–107.
4. Wang, X.; Yao, X.; Sun, Y. Application of data mining techniques in the field of business: A systematic review. *Electron. Commer. Res. Appl.* **2019**, *34*, 100827.
5. Aslani, N.; Galehdar, N.; Garavand, A. A systematic review of data mining applications in kidney transplantation. *Inform. Med. Unlock.* **2023**, *37*, 101165. [CrossRef]
6. Da Silveira Barcellos, D.; de Souza, F.T. Optimization of water quality monitoring programs by data mining. *Water Res.* **2022**, *221*, 118805. [CrossRef]
7. Kaur, J.; Dharni, K. Application and performance of data mining techniques in stock market: A review. *Intell. Syst. Account. Financ. Manag.* **2022**, *29*, 219–241. [CrossRef]
8. Sunhare, P.; Chowdhary, R.R.; Chattopadhyay, M.K. Internet of things and data mining: An application orient-ed survey. *J. King Saud Univ. Comput. Inf. Sci.* **2022**, *34*, 3569–3590. [CrossRef]

9. Miao, F.; Xie, X.; Wu, Y.; Zhao, F. Data Mining and deep learning for predicting the displacement of "Step-like" landslides. *Sensors* **2022**, *22*, 481. [CrossRef]
10. Shafiq, D.A.; Marjani, M.; Habeeb, R.A.A.; Asirvatham, D. Student Retention Using Educational Data Mining and Predictive Analytics: A Systematic Literature Review. *IEEE Access* **2022**, *10*, 72480–72503. [CrossRef]
11. Izonin, I.; Tkachenko, R.; Shakhovska, N.; Ilchyshyn, B.; Singh, K.K. A Two-Step Data Normalization Approach for Improving Classification Accuracy in the Medical Diagnosis Domain. *Mathematics* **2022**, *10*, 1942. [CrossRef]
12. Wang, Y.; Yang, L.; Wu, J.; Song, Z.; Shi, L. Mining Campus Big Data: Prediction of Career Choice Using Interpretable Machine Learning Method. *Mathematics* **2022**, *10*, 1289. [CrossRef]
13. Montisci, A.; Porcu, M.C. A Satellite Data Mining Approach Based on Self-Organized Maps for the Early Warn-ing of Ground Settlements in Urban Areas. *Appl. Sci.* **2022**, *12*, 2679. [CrossRef]
14. Ferandez, D.M.; Cernadas, E.; Barro, S.; Amorim, D. Explainable artificial intelligence (XAI): Concepts, taxonomies, opportunities, and challenges toward responsible AI. *Inf. Fusion* **2020**, *58*, 82–115.
15. Kumar, A.; Tanwar, S. Explainable AI for data-driven decision-making in healthcare. *J. Ambient. Intell. Humaniz. Comput.* **2021**, *2021*, 1–13.
16. Hopfield, J.J.; Tank, D.W. "Neural" computation of decisions in optimization problems. *Biol. Cybern.* **1985**, *52*, 141–152. [CrossRef]
17. Abdullah, W.A.T.W. Logic programming on a neural network. *Int. J. Intell. Syst.* **1992**, *7*, 513–519. [CrossRef]
18. Mohd Kasihmuddin, M.S.; Mansor, M.A.; Md Basir, M.F.; Sathasivam, S. Discrete mutation Hopfield neural network in propositional satisfiability. *Mathematics* **2019**, *7*, 1133. [CrossRef]
19. Sathasivam, S.; Mansor, M.A.; Ismail, A.I.M.; Jamaludin, S.Z.M.; Kasihmuddin, M.S.M.; Mamat, M. Novel random k satisfiability for $k \leq 2$ in hopfield neural network. *Sains Malays* **2020**, *49*, 2847–2857. [CrossRef]
20. Zamri, N.E.; Azhar, S.A.; Mansor, M.A.; Alway, A.; Kasihmuddin, M.S.M. Weighted random k satisfiability for k= 1, 2 (r2SAT) in discrete Hopfield neural network. *Appl. Soft Comput.* **2022**, *126*, 109312. [CrossRef]
21. Guo, Y.; Kasihmuddin, M.S.M.; Gao, Y.; Mansor, M.A.; Wahab, H.A.; Zamri, N.E.; Chen, J. YRAN2SAT: A novel flexible random satisfiability logical rule in discrete hopfield neural network. *Adv. Eng. Softw.* **2022**, *171*, 103169. [CrossRef]
22. Mansor, M.A.; Kasihmuddin, M.S.M.; Sathasivam, S. Artificial Immune System Paradigm in the Hopfield Network for 3-Satisfiability Problem. *Pertanika J. Sci. Technol.* **2017**, *25*, 1173–1188.
23. Sathasivam, S.; Wan Abdullah, W.A.T. Logic mining in neural network: Reverse analysis method. *Computing* **2011**, *91*, 119–133. [CrossRef]
24. Kho, L.C.; Kasihmuddin, M.S.M.; Mansor, M.; Sathasivam, S. Logic Mining in League of Legends. *Pertanika J. Sci. Technol.* **2020**, *28*, 211–215.
25. Zamri, N.E.; Mansor, M.A.; Mohd Kasihmuddin, M.S.; Alway, A.; Mohd Jamaludin, S.Z.; Alzaeemi, S.A. Amazon employees resources access data extraction via clonal selection algorithm and logic mining approach. *Entropy* **2020**, *22*, 596. [CrossRef]
26. Jamaludin, S.Z.M.; Mansor, M.A.; Baharum, A.; Kasihmuddin, M.S.M.; Wahab, H.A.; Marsani, M.F. Modified 2 satisfiability reverse analysis method via logical permutation operator. *Comput. Mater. Contin.* **2023**, *74*, 2853–2870.
27. Mohd Jamaludin, S.Z.; Mohd Kasihmuddin, M.S.; Md Ismail, A.I.; Mansor, M.A.; Md Basir, M.F. Energy based logic mining analysis with hopfield neural network for recruitment evaluation. *Entropy* **2020**, *23*, 40. [CrossRef]
28. Li, S.; Li, Y.; Li, R.; Li, X.; Liu, Y. A novel hybrid algorithm for solving large-scale 2-SAT problems. *Appl. Soft Comput.* **2021**, *100*, 106997.
29. Kasihmuddin, M.S.M.; Jamaludin, S.Z.M.; Mansor, M.A.; Wahab, H.A.; Ghadzi, S.M.S. Supervised learning perspective in logic mining. *Mathematics* **2022**, *10*, 915. [CrossRef]
30. Jamaludin, S.Z.M.; Romli, N.A.; Kasihmuddin, M.S.M.; Baharum, A.; Mansor, M.A.; Marsani, M.F. Novel logic mining incorporating log linear approach. *J. King Saud Univ. Comput. Inf. Sci.* **2022**, *34*, 9011–9027. [CrossRef]
31. Alway, A.; Zamri, N.E.; Mohd Kasihmuddin, M.S.; Mansor, A.; Sathasivam, S. Palm Oil Trend Analysis via Logic Mining with Discrete Hopfield Neural Network. *Pertanika J. Sci. Technol.* **2020**, *28*, 967–981.
32. Wu, X.; Zhang, X.; Wei, X. A dynamic Hopfield neural network for constrained optimization problems. *Neural Netw.* **2017**, *87*, 43–54.
33. Cook, S.A. Short propositional formulas represent non-deterministic computations. *Inf. Process. Lett.* **1988**, *26*, 269–270. [CrossRef]
34. Zollanvari, A.; James, A.P.; Sameni, R. A theoretical analysis of the peaking phenomenon in classification. *J. Classif.* **2020**, *37*, 421–434. [CrossRef]
35. Gardini, F.; Trivisano, C.; Lanciotti, R.; Maffei, M.; Guerzoni, M.E. Suitability of log-linear models to evaluate the microbiological quality of baby clams (*Chamelea gallina* L.) harvested in the Adriatic Sea. *Int. J. Food Microbiol.* **2000**, *54*, 63–74. [CrossRef] [PubMed]
36. Haque, M.M.; Chin, H.C.; Debnath, A.K. An investigation on multi-vehicle motorcycle crashes using log-linear models. *Saf. Sci.* **2012**, *50*, 352–362. [CrossRef]
37. Cumming, G. The new statistics: Why and how. *Psychol. Sci.* **2014**, *25*, 7–29. [CrossRef]
38. Sathasivam, S.; Mamat, M.; Kasihmuddin, M.S.M.; Mansor, M.A. Metaheuristics approach for maximum k satisfiability in restricted neural symbolic integration. *Pertanika J. Sci. Technol.* **2020**, *28*, 545–564.
39. Lloyd, S. Least squares quantization in PCM. *IEEE Trans. Inf. Theory* **1982**, *28*, 129–137. [CrossRef]
40. Sathasivam, S. Upgrading logic programming in Hopfield network. *Sains Malays.* **2010**, *39*, 115–118.
41. Jha, K.; Saha, S. Incorporation of multimodal multi objective optimization in designing a filter-based feature selection technique. *Appl. Soft Comput.* **2021**, *98*, 106823. [CrossRef]

42. Ahmad, S.; Ullah, T.; Ahmad, I.; Al-Sharabi, A.; Ullah, K.; Khan, R.A.; Ali, M.A. Novel hybrid deep learning model for metastatic cancer detection. *Comput. Intell. Neurosci.* **2022**, *2020*, 8141530. [CrossRef] [PubMed]
43. Luque, A.; Carrasco, A.; Martin, A.; Heras, A. The impact of class imbalance in classification performance metrics based on the binary confusion matrix. *Pattern Recognit.* **2019**, *91*, 216–231. [CrossRef]
44. Chicco, D.; Starovoitov, V.; Jurman, G. The benefits of the Matthews correlation coefficient (MCC) over the diagnostic odds ratio (DOR) in binary classification assessment. *IEEE Access* **2021**, *9*, 47112–47124. [CrossRef]
45. Shi, J.; Li, Z.; Zhao, H. Feature Selection via Maximizing Inter-class Independence and Minimizing Intra-class Redundancy for Hierarchical Classification. *Inf. Sci.* **2023**, *626*, 1–18. [CrossRef]
46. Shang, R.; Kong, J.; Wang, L.; Zhang, W.; Wang, C.; Li YJiao, L. Unsupervised feature selection via discrete spectral clustering and feature weights. *Neurocomputing* **2023**, *517*, 106–117. [CrossRef]
47. Wang, P.; Xue, B.; Liang, J.; Zhang, M. Feature Selection Using Diversity-Based Multi-objective Binary Differential Evolution. *Inf. Sci.* **2023**, *626*, 586–606. [CrossRef]
48. Jeon, Y.; Hwang, G. Feature selection with scalable variational gaussian process via sensitivity analysis ased on L2 divergence. *Neurocomputing* **2023**, *518*, 577–592. [CrossRef]
49. Alzaeemi, S.A.S.; Sathasivam, S. Examining the forecasting movement of palm oil price using RBFNN-2SATRA metaheuristic algorithms for logic mining. *IEEE Access* **2021**, *9*, 22542–22557. [CrossRef]
50. Jamaludin, S.Z.M.; Ismail, M.T.; Kasihmuddin, M.S.M.; Mansor, M.A.; Antony, S.N.F.M.A.; Makhul, A.A. Modelling benign ovarian cyst risk factors and symptoms via log-linear model. *Pertanika* **2021**, *29*, 99–2216. [CrossRef]
51. Singh, N.; Singh, P. A hybrid ensemble-filter wrapper feature selection approach for medical data classification. *Chemometr. Intell. Lab. Syst.* **2021**, *217*, 104396. [CrossRef]
52. Sidik, S.S.M.; Zamri, N.E.; Mohd Kasihmuddin, M.S.; Wahab, H.A.; Guo, Y.; Mansor, M.A. Non-systematic weighted satisfiability in discrete hopfield neural network using binary artificial bee colony optimization. *Mathematics* **2022**, *10*, 1129. [CrossRef]
53. Mansor, M.A.; Sathasivam, S. Accelerating activation function for 3- satisfiability logic programming. *Int. J. Intell. Syst. Appl.* **2016**, *8*, 44–50. [CrossRef]
54. Karim, S.A.; Zamri, N.E.; Alway, A.; Kasihmuddin, M.S.M.; Ismail, A.I.M.; Mansor, M.A.; Hassan, N.F.A. Random sat-1125 isfiability: A higher-order logical approach in discrete Hopfield Neural Network. *IEEE Access* **2021**, *9*, 50831–50845. [CrossRef]
55. Kudenko, D.; Kazakov, D. Logic-based reinforcement learning. *Mach. Learn.* **2009**, *75*, 47–88.
56. Chen, J.; Chen, Y.; Hu, Y. Improved discrete Hopfield neural network for solving optimization problems. *Neurocomputing* **2018**, *312*, 257–267.

Disclaimer/Publisher's Note: The statements, opinions and data contained in all publications are solely those of the individual author(s) and contributor(s) and not of MDPI and/or the editor(s). MDPI and/or the editor(s) disclaim responsibility for any injury to people or property resulting from any ideas, methods, instructions or products referred to in the content.

Article

Securing IoT Devices Running PureOS from Ransomware Attacks: Leveraging Hybrid Machine Learning Techniques

Tariq Ahamed Ahanger [1,*], Usman Tariq [1,*], Fadl Dahan [2], Shafique A. Chaudhry [3] and Yasir Malik [4]

1 Management Information System Department, College of Business Administration, Prince Sattam Bin Abdulaziz University, Al-Kharj 16278, Saudi Arabia
2 Department of Management Information Systems, College of Business Administration-Hawtat Bani Tamim, Prince Sattam Bin Abdulaziz University, Al-Kharj 11942, Saudi Arabia; f.naji@psau.edu.sa
3 Reh School of Business, Clarkson University, Potsdam, NY 13699, USA; schaudhr@clarkson.edu
4 Department of Computer Science, Faculty of Science, Bishops University, 2600 Rue College, Sherbrooke, QC J1M 1Z7, Canada; ymalik@ubishops.ca
* Correspondence: t.ahanger@psau.edu.sa (T.A.A.); u.tariq@psau.edu.sa (U.T.); Tel.: +966-(11)-5887080 (T.A.A. & U.T.)

Abstract: Internet-enabled (IoT) devices are typically small, low-powered devices used for sensing and computing that enable remote monitoring and control of various environments through the Internet. Despite their usefulness in achieving a more connected cyber-physical world, these devices are vulnerable to ransomware attacks due to their limited resources and connectivity. To combat these threats, machine learning (ML) can be leveraged to identify and prevent ransomware attacks on IoT devices before they can cause significant damage. In this research paper, we explore the use of ML techniques to enhance ransomware defense in IoT devices running on the PureOS operating system. We have developed a ransomware detection framework using machine learning, which combines the XGBoost and ElasticNet algorithms in a hybrid approach. The design and implementation of our framework are based on the evaluation of various existing machine learning techniques. Our approach was tested using a dataset of real-world ransomware attacks on IoT devices and achieved high accuracy (90%) and low false-positive rates, demonstrating its effectiveness in detecting and preventing ransomware attacks on IoT devices running PureOS.

Keywords: ransomware detection; machine learning; malware analysis; feature extraction; Internet of Things (IoT)

MSC: 68M25

1. Introduction

1.1. Background on Ransomware Attacks

The Internet of Things (IoT) is causing a significant transformation in the way people live and work. The prevalence of internet-connected devices in households is rising, including but not limited to smart thermostats, light bulbs, speakers, and virtual assistants, which can be remotely controlled through mobile devices. IoT devices are used extensively across various industries, e.g., mining, utilities, agriculture, automotive, discrete manufacturing, etc., to collect data at various stages of operations to leverage artificial intelligence (AI) and predictive analytics [1]. Incorporating these sensors enables monitoring and control of a process or environment in real-time, resulting in faster and more rational decision-making.

Although IoT devices have immense potential, their vulnerability to network attacks remains a significant concern. Network threats, such as data theft, phishing attempts, spoofing, and denial of service, can affect IoT devices. These attacks can lead to additional cybersecurity risks, such as ransomware, which can be incredibly expensive and time-consuming to fix for enterprises. The number of ransomware attacks has surged in recent years. One notable incident was the WannaCry ransomware attack in 2017, which affected a large number of computers globally, including many IoT devices [2]. Another incident in 2019 targeted a smart building in Finland, which caused considerable damage [3]. In 2020, a German hospital was also affected by ransomware that targeted an IoT device, resulting in the shutdown of critical systems, including emergency services. A report recently published by Sonic Wall highlighted a 77% increase in malware attacks on IoT devices during the first half of 2022 [4]. According to the report, ransomware attacks had decreased by 23%, whereas cryptojacking attacks had increased by 30%, and intrusion attempts had increased by 19%. These numbers point to the growing threat of ransomware attacks on IoT devices and underscore the need for more robust security measures to handle such attacks.

1.2. The Need for Effective Defense Mechanisms against Ransomware Attacks

We assert that IoT devices require effective protection measures due to their characteristics as well as their applications. The following are some of the reasons that support our assertion:

(a) Due to their compact and low-cost form factors, many devices in the IoT suffer from processing power and memory constraints. They may not have the resources to run computer-intensive security programs or communicate at a high bandwidth. Therefore, they become increasingly susceptible to ransomware anomalies as the number of linked devices grows.
(b) Because of a lack of robust security measures and standards, many IoT devices are vulnerable to attacks. This is a real concern, especially for older devices that were not always built with safety in mind.
(c) Sensitive information, such as medical records, financial records, and personal preferences, is frequently collected by IoT devices. These sensors' data could be stolen and utilized for nefarious purposes if they were hacked.
(d) The hardware, software, and network architecture that make up an IoT system can be rather complicated. Because of this complexity, proactively spotting and preventing ransomware is challenging. Due to heterogeneous operational and functional requirements, integrating IoT equipment into older, less secure systems is widespread. Therefore, it could be challenging to protect these systems without causing operational disruptions.

Despite all these challenges, putting security first is essential for the IoT devices to realize a secure IoT paradigm.

1.3. The Role of Machine Learning in Ransomware Defense

Machine learning (ML) can play an important role in ransomware defense in IoT by helping to detect and prevent ransomware attacks before they can cause significant damage. For example, ML algorithms can be trained to recognize patterns in IoT network traffic that may indicate that a malware attack is potentially underway. This can include detecting unusual network behavior, such as a sudden surge in traffic or a large number of requests for a particular type of data. ML models can be trained on the existing attacks data and be used to predict/identify similar attacks in the future. Several predictive modeling systems have been developed for malware detection such as:

(a) Random Forest algorithm with an ensemble of decision trees was used to classify malware samples in [4].
(b) Support Vector Machine (SVM) is a supervised learning algorithm that has been used for classification and regression analysis [5,6].
(c) In probability theory, Bayes' theorem is the basis for the Naive Bayes algorithm and has been used in spam detection to identify malware [6].
(d) Decision trees [7] are another ML technique that has been frequently employed in combination with other supportive algorithms for malware detection.
(e) Logistic regression [8] is a statistical method used to figure out how likely a binary outcome is to happen. It has been used successfully in programs that look for malware.
(f) Neural Networks [9] have also been used successfully in malware detection applications.

Traditionally, researchers use various features to train machine learning models to identify the signatures or behaviors of malware. These models are then used to create a framework that could identify and mitigate specific anomalies such as ransomware. The following are some of the widely used factors that are used to train ML models for malware-detecting systems:

(a) Unusual or high-volume network traffic [10], as well as traffic from unknown sources, ports, or protocols, are just some of the indicators that were uncovered by ML models monitoring network activity.
(b) System calls are used by malware to communicate with the operating system and were a telltale sign of malicious software [11]. Models trained with ML were very vigilant on system calls for signs of malicious activity.
(c) Resource use anomalies [12] caused by malware, such as high central processing unit (CPU) or memory usage, were easily detectable by ML models.
(d) Anomalous activity, such as changes to system settings [13] or user behavior that does not make sense, might be a telltale sign of malware and was detected using ML models.
(e) The software on IoT devices was analyzed by ML models for the presence of recognized malware signatures or dangerous patterns.

1.4. PureOS

PureOS is an open-source operating system based on the Linux kernel and includes pre-installed privacy-enhancing tools, such as the Tor Browser and hypertext transfer protocol secure (HTTPS-Everywhere) and has strong default encryption for user data. PureOS has a built-in feature. "PureBoot", that uses a "Heads" firmware payload to enable a user to boot the system from a trusted source and check the integrity of the system's firmware and boot process. PureBoot is a great way to establish an effective measure for preventing malware installation on a device.

Like any operating system, PureOS is also a target of "unpatched security flaws", "misconfigured settings", "weak authentication", "social engineering vulnerabilities (e.g., fake software updates, etc.)", and "supply-chain attack (e.g., inserting backdoors or other malicious code during the manufacturing or distribution process)". Ultimately, any successful anomalous attempt can trigger an enterprise-wide impact that may reflect the horrific consequences of ransomware.

The main objective of this paper is to put forward and investigate solutions to mitigate the impact of ransomware vulnerabilities on IoT devices that run PureOS [14]. The following are the main contributions of this work:

i. We investigated 15,000 samples (i.e., ransomware and benign) instances, detailing hitherto unreported facets of ransomware attacks with an emphasis on shared traits amongst malware families.
iii. We outlined the design process behind the fundamental components of ransomware samples and discussed how this knowledge can be leveraged to prevent future intrusion. In devastating ransomware cyberattacks of varying degrees of complexity, our research demonstrated that aberrant control efforts should be reliably monitored.
iii. We proposed methods to counter the widespread threat of dissimilar ransomware attacks. We have suggested a generic approach to detecting such risks, one that makes no presumptions about the specific methods through which user records are maliciously made unavailable.

The rest of the paper is organized as follows. Section 2 is dedicated to presenting a comprehensive literature review, while Section 3 delves into the intricate details of data collection, augmentation, balancing, and processing techniques. In Section 4, we present our approach, while Section 5 expounds upon the practical implementation and rigorous testing of our proposed ransomware analysis and identification architecture. Ultimately, the paper culminates in Section 6, where a conclusion is reached.

2. Literature Review

The NIST 2018 framework [15] proposes the adoption of a Framework Core consisting of five fundamental functions, i.e., Identify, Protect, Detect, Respond, and Recover, to structure cybersecurity activities optimally. These elements aid organizations in formulating their cybersecurity risk management strategy by arranging data, supporting risk management decisions, reducing risks, and enhancing performance through the integration of previous experiences.

Organizations are mandated by the NIST guidelines to implement targeted strategies to combat malware effectively. These strategies encompass various aspects, including the timely identification and characterization of incidents, the swift dissemination of pertinent information, evaluation of actions that may hinder recovery efforts, reinforcement of information sharing within network environments, implementation of corrective measures to prevent a recurrence, monitoring of precursor events or indicators for future incident detection, and the acquisition of supplementary tools and resources for incident detection, analysis, and mitigation. By proactively adopting these measures, organizations can fortify their systems against potential threats and maintain their resilience in the face of cyber-attacks. From the earliest extensive analyses of ransomware behavior [16,17], scholars have advanced diverse perspectives and multifarious tools and techniques to detect ransomware behavior, including but not limited to filesystem activity monitoring and application programming interface (API) hooking. It is significant to note that while static analysis, particularly signature-based detection, retains its status as a conventional method for detecting malware in general, it is not as widely utilized in the context of ransomware detection. Despite many antivirus tools incorporating ransomware signatures into their databases, current research primarily accentuates the significance of behavioral approaches, potentially in response to the ubiquitous adoption of ransomware-as-a-service (RaaS) and the inclination of ransomware authors to imitate one another, resulting in the emergence of a profusion of dissimilar and transient variations.

The increasing prevalence of ransomware among attackers has led to a surge in its popularity within the realm of cybersecurity research. Upadhyaya et al. [18] conducted a comprehensive analysis of the anatomy and features of ransomware, a type of malicious software that frequently blocks access to task manager, command prompts, and other executable files, rendering the infected system unusable. Nevertheless, the present study focuses exclusively on CTB Locker, a specific type of ransomware, and explores its modus operandi in terms of infiltration, its process of generating a Bitcoin wallet for each target, and its payment system facilitated through the Tor network. Meanwhile, certain physicists have suggested the implementation of quantum cryptography systems that are impervious to loopholes, which have been compared to illusory mirages. Conversely, others advocate taking proactive measures such as safeguarding digital assets and maintaining routine backups in preparation for any future attacks. In Gagneja's [19] analysis, several methods are identified by which ransomware infiltrates a system by exploiting security vulnerabilities within outdated applications on a victim's computer. As a consequence of such an attack, backup files and directories are deliberately removed to obstruct the system's restoration process, leading to the eventual encryption of vital system files. To counteract these malicious activities, it was recommended to provide comprehensive training to personnel on all matters related to system security, ensuring the timely installation of patches to address any potential security weaknesses, implementing firewall protection, conducting regular email scanning, and employing only licensed operating systems as preventative measures against the possibility of ransomware attacks.

Celdrán and Moon, in their respective works [20,21], present an evaluation of the impact of various techniques such as hash-coded string extraction, file format analysis, file fingerprinting, packer detection, and disassembly on the efficacy of static and dynamic analysis. The primary objective of this analysis was to yield two critical advantages. The first advantage is the safety that static analysis affords during the evaluation process, given that there is no need to execute the malware. Secondly, the method provides more profound insights into the execution pathways of malware, enabling a more comprehensive understanding of its operations. Furthermore, the research illustrated that in the realm of binary analysis, two primary methodologies can be employed for malware analysis: static analysis and dynamic analysis. Static analysis involves scrutinizing the binary without execution as a preliminary step. This approach does not necessarily necessitate the utilization of a virtual environment and can be challenging to utilize with packed binaries unless they are unpacked manually. However, static analysis is capable of rendering an extensive and all-encompassing view of the code coverage with a low false positive rate. Conversely, dynamic analysis requires the binary to be executed first before being analyzed. To start the analysis process, a virtual environment must be configured, and packed binaries are automatically unpacked. While dynamic analysis provides insight into the path of execution of running modules, its false positive rate is notably high.

Dargahi et al. [22] formulated a systematic classification of the distinguishing attributes of ransomware from the perspective of cybercriminals using the Cyber Kill Chain (CKC) model. This work explores the interconnectedness between various ransomware characteristics and the different stages of the Cyber Kill Chain (CKC). It focuses on how factors such as payload delivery and access prevention play a role throughout the CKC, starting from the weaponization phase and progressing until the desired objectives are achieved. Although Dargahi et al.'s approach is innovative, its scope was narrow. The authors solely analyzed crypto-ransomware that targets desktop systems and its malevolent attributes, such as the potentiality of botnet deployments. The authors did not assess the efficacy or feasibility of alternative strategies nor explore mobile or IoT platforms, which can be susceptible to ransomware attacks.

Furthermore, it is essential to note that the taxonomy proposed by Dargahi et al. [22] is only one of several approaches to categorizing ransomware. Other researchers have proposed alternative taxonomies that focus on different aspects of ransomware behavior, such as the analysis of network traffic or the identification of ransomware families based on code similarities. While Dargahi et al.'s method was valuable in identifying the objectives and motives of ransomware attackers, it did not provide insights into the best practices for preventing or mitigating ransomware attacks.

Table 1 provides a comprehensive overview of different ransomware detection techniques, presented in existing works, and their respective features, advantages, and disadvantages. Signature-based techniques are well-established and effective against known ransomware variants, but can be ineffective against new or polymorphic variants. Heuristic-based techniques can detect new or unknown variants, but may have a higher false-negative rate and limited ability to differentiate between benign and malicious activity. Machine-learning-based techniques offer the ability to learn and adapt to new variants, but require significant amounts of representative data and may produce false positives. Hybrid approaches provide a combination of signature and machine-learning-based techniques for improved accuracy, but can be resource-intensive. It's important to note that the effectiveness of each technique may vary depending on the specific implementation, the ransomware being targeted, and the context in which the detection is taking place.

Overall, we have reviewed 298 research papers that were searched with the keyword "Ransomware" on Google Scholar that were published from the year 2010 to April 2023, and we have found a few issues that have not been properly covered in existing research. The first issue we encountered pertains to the widespread and interchangeable usage of the term "ransomware" and "crypto-ransomware", which may indicate a lack of consensus among researchers as to whether these two terms are technically equivalent or whether non-crypto-ransomware can be classified as ransomware at all.

Another issue we identified is the lack of a universal standard for defining benign or malicious (ransomware-like) behaviors. Ransomware is a type of malware that is primarily designed to extort ransom payments from users, and while it is generally agreed that different variants of ransomware share two common features, namely, blocking user access to resources (often files) and attempting to extort ransom payments, researchers have divergent views on which additional features or feature combinations are indicative of malicious behavior.

Table 1. Comparison of ransomware detection techniques and their features, advantages, and isadvantages.

Detection Technique	Features	Advantages	Disadvantages
Signature-based	Hash values, file names, behavior patterns	High accuracy, low false positive rate	Inability to detect new, unknown ransomware variants, ineffective against polymorphic ransomware
Heuristic-based	Behavior patterns, file access patterns, network traffic	Ability to detect new, unknown ransomware variants, low false positive rate, effective against polymorphic ransomware	Higher false negative rate, limited ability to differentiate between benign and malicious activity
Machine learning-based	Dynamic behavior analysis, system calls, network traffic, entropy, header information	Ability to detect new, unknown ransomware variants, ability to differentiate between benign and malicious activity, high accuracy, effective against polymorphic ransomware	Requires large, representative datasets for training, may be susceptible to adversarial attacks, may produce false positives due to benign software with similar behavior
Hybrid approach	Combination of signature-based and machine-learning-based techniques	Improved accuracy and ability to detect new, unknown ransomware variants, effective against polymorphic ransomware	May be more complex and resource-intensive, may still miss new, unknown ransomware variants

Furthermore, we observed a lack of uniform usage of terminologies in the context of mitigation strategies, which could potentially lead to confusion and misunderstandings. Finally, we found that there is no universally accepted standard for evaluating and comparing the effectiveness of different strategies, further underscoring the need for additional research in this area.

3. Data Collection and Preparation

3.1. Data Collection and Processing Techniques

In this section, we discuss our procedure for selecting ransomware samples, which played a vital role in our study's malware dataset collection. To assemble the ransomware datasets, we utilized the widely used malware analyzer Anubis and ESET NOD32 [23], as well as a plethora of publicly available malware archives and anecdotal research in online security forums. We compiled and analyzed a dataset comprising more than 15,000 ransomware samples. Our analysis aimed to uncover novel insights into previously undocumented aspects of ransomware attacks and identify commonalities among different malware families. To ensure the validity and precision of the dataset, we conducted a rigorous examination of multiple factors. These included assessing the reliability and diversity of the data sources, evaluating the size and diversity of the dataset, verifying the accuracy of pre-labeled ransomware classifications, performing meticulous data preprocessing and normalization, ensuring the integrity of the data, and considering the timeframe during which the data were collected. The validation process involved meticulous checks for inconsistencies, errors, and biases within the dataset. Furthermore, we compared our dataset with other publicly available datasets or ground truth data to further validate its reliability.

We have adopted the dynamic analysis technique that involved running ransomware in a controlled environment such as a sandbox and virtual machine to observe its behavior and capture relevant data such as system calls, network traffic, and registry modifications. The dynamic analysis helped us understand the dissimilar characteristics of the ransomware dataset. Ransomware characteristics include, but are not limited to, metadata, behavior logs, network traffic, malware landscape, representativeness (i.e., ransomware families, types, and variants), transferability of threat models, imbalance (i.e., data noise and errors), and temporality (i.e., time-period and frequency of malware sample collection).

3.2. Preprocessing and Feature Engineering

For data preprocessing and feature engineering of ransomware, we have removed duplicate and irrelevant data, handled missing values, and scaled the ransomware log data to ensure that features are comparable. Effective data preprocessing and feature engineering improve the accuracy of ransomware detection and facilitate the development of a robust security framework. Feature engineering involved the examination of file size, file type, file entropy, API calls, code obfuscation, code analysis, sandbox analysis, and evaluation of digital signatures if files are digitally signed by the creator for feature detection of malware.

3.3. Data Augmentation and Balancing Techniques

For ransomware data augmentation, we applied two techniques: (a) random noise (i.e., adding random noise (e.g., irrelevant features, redundant features, missing codes, and significantly different data points) to the malware samples to make them more robust to variations in the data), and (b) random cropping (i.e., cropping the malware samples to a smaller size). The purpose of data augmentation for ransomware was to increase the size and variability of the malware dataset used to train the applied machine learning model. By generating new samples from the existing dataset through data augmentation techniques, we were able to create a more diverse and representative training set, which led to the proposed method to improve model performance and generalization.

Consequently, data augmentation helped to address the problem of imbalanced datasets, where the number of samples in each class was not equal. We employed the Synthetic Minority Over-sampling Technique (SMOTE) to balance the dataset, by generating synthetic samples that increased the number of minority class samples. This helped us tackle the problem of class imbalance, where there were significantly fewer samples in the minority class compared to the benign class. SMOTE also prevented overfitting, as it increased the size of the minority class, leading to a better generalization of the model to new data. Consequently, SMOTE was instrumental in accurately classifying new malware samples.

Table 2 exhibits the pseudocode that outlines how Synthetic Minority Over-sampling Technique (SMOTE) can be applied to identify ransomware in a dataset.

Table 2. Assessing the feasibility of SMOTE for ransomware detection in a dataset.

SMOTE Applicability to Identify Ransomware in a Dataset
(1) Load the ransomware dataset.
(2) Split the dataset into training and testing sets.
(3) Determine the minority class (i.e., ransomware samples).
(4) Apply SMOTE to the training set to generate synthetic samples for the minority class:
(a) Determine the number of synthetic samples to generate based on the desired ratio of minority to majority samples.
(b) Select a random minority sample.
(c) Identify its k nearest neighbors.
(d) Randomly select one of the k nearest neighbors and use it to create a new synthetic sample by interpolating between the selected sample and its neighbor.
(e) Repeat steps b–d until the desired number of synthetic samples is generated.
(5) Combine the original training set with the generated synthetic samples to create a new, balanced training set.
(6) Train a machine learning model on the new training set.
(7) Evaluate the model's performance on the testing set, using metrics such as precision, recall, and F1-score.
If the model's performance is satisfactory, use it to predict whether new samples are ransomware or not.

3.4. Focused Ransomware Variants

To evaluate the effectiveness of our proposed ransomware detection framework in a real-world scenario, we needed to test it on actual ransomware samples. However, the ransomware variants we had access to were not compatible with the PureOS operating environment. Therefore, we re-implemented the ransomware variants to make them suitable for the PureOS environment. This process involved analyzing the following ransomware code and modifying it to ensure that it could be executed and studied within the PureOS environment.

i. The **Kryptik** [24] ransomware is a type of malware that is often disseminated through email phishing campaigns and exploit kits. This advanced form of ransomware uses encryption algorithms to lock down the victim's files, rendering them inaccessible. Kryptik ransomware was re-designed to evade detection by antivirus software (i.e., Virus Chaser [25]) and uses command-and-control (C&C) servers to obtain instructions from the attacker. It employs encryption algorithms (i.e., RSA-2048 and AES-256) to encrypt the victim's files, rendering them inaccessible. It utilizes obfuscation techniques to conceal its activities. The impact of Kryptik ransomware can be catastrophic, resulting in critical data loss and disrupting business operations.

ii. We have re-implemented the **Cloud Snooper** [26] ransomware to target cloud-based systems and services (i.e., Tonido cloud platform [27] through the Nautilus file manager plugin). It exploited the weaknesses in cloud infrastructure to gain unauthorized access to the victim's network. Some of the notable features of Cloud Snooper ransomware include its ability to bypass firewalls and intrusion detection systems and encrypt files. It operated covertly to evade detection and caused severe damage to the victim (i.e., sandbox experimental setup. The impact of Cloud Snooper ransomware was particularly devastating, as it resulted in the loss of sensitive information and disruption of normal OS operations (i.e., encrypting or locking files, modifying system settings, and interfering with the normal functioning of applications and system processes).

iii. The **WannaCry** [28] ransomware was first identified in May 2017. It spread rapidly, infecting over 230,000 computers in over 150 countries within just a few days. Originally, the ransomware used a vulnerability in Microsoft Windows known as EternalBlue to spread from one computer to another, making it particularly dangerous. Key features of WannaCry were as follows:

   a. It encrypts files on the infected system using the AES encryption algorithm, making them inaccessible to the user.
   b. It can spread rapidly across a network, infecting other vulnerable computers without any user interaction.
   c. A "kill switch" was built into the code of WannaCry, allowing researchers to halt the spread of the ransomware by registering a domain name that the malware checked before encrypting files.

   WannaCry was altered and reprogrammed to accommodate the PureOS functional requirements that were originally implemented to specifically targeted systems running Microsoft Windows operating systems, with a particular focus on older, unsupported versions such as Windows Server 2003 and Server 2022. The ransomware payload was delivered as a PureOS executable file disguised as a software update. Once the file was executed, it installed ransomware on the system and began encrypting files. We have used AES encryption to encrypt files on the infected system, with a unique key generated for each system. The re-implemented ransomware also encrypted the key itself using RSA encryption, making it intolerable to decrypt the files without the private key presumably held by the attackers.

iv. **LockBit** [29] is a file-encrypting ransomware that uses a combination of RSA and AES encryption algorithms to encrypt the victim's files. Once the files are encrypted, the ransomware displays a ransom note, demanding payment in exchange for the decryption key. We re-designed the malware by granting it the ability to spread across a network and infect multiple devices connected to it. Revised implementation was equipped with a timer feature that deletes files after a set amount of time, which means that the anomaly must be counter-measured to diminish the impact. This ransomware was keen to target critical files, such as documents, images, and databases.

v. Re-programmed Black Basta [30] ransomware used AES-256 encryption to encrypt files on the victim's PureOS mounted computer (i.e., including desktops, laptops, and servers). It appended a unique extension to encrypted files, making them unusable until they are decrypted. The encryption process took several minutes or in some iterations even hours, depending on the size of the files.

vi. **Revised Hive** [31] ransomware used a combination of RSA and AES encryption algorithms to lock the victim's files (i.e., experimental setup). It entered the system through an exploit kit and could spread to other connected devices on the sandbox network. The ransomware could erase shadow copies and backup files to obstruct the victim's efforts to recover their encrypted data.

vii. **ALPHV**, **BlackCat**, and **Noberus** [31] are three distinct ransomware families with their own unique features, system and network targets, technical details, and impact. Common features included its use of double extortion tactics, which involve not only encrypting a victim's files (i.e., AES-256, and RSA), but also stealing sensitive data. We re-implemented these ransomware variants by using multiple techniques to evade detection, including code obfuscation, anti-debugging techniques, and process injection. During certain experimental iterations, we appended the ".noberus" extension to encrypted files. We have observed that ransomware typically appends a unique extension to encrypted files as a way to differentiate them from their original unencrypted state.

viii. PureOS-focused **AvosLocker** [32] used strong encryption algorithms (such as AES-256 and RSA) to encrypt files on a victim's computer or network. AvosLocker targeted the honeypot computer and network that was vulnerable to its distribution method (such as outdated Remote Desktop Protocol (RDP)) and contains vulnerabilities that can be exploited. In the revised implementation, AvosLocker generated a unique encryption key for each infected computer, which was stored on the attacker's (i.e., anomaly) server. The impact of this ransomware was severe, as it caused the victim to lose access to important files and data.

ix. The **Conti** [33] ransomware is a highly advanced and complex malware that uses a sophisticated encryption algorithm to encrypt files on a victim's computer system. It can spread through a network, infecting other connected systems. The vulnerabilities that Conti exploits in PureOS include exploiting weaknesses in the RDP protocol to gain access to internet-connected systems, exploiting vulnerabilities in VPN and remote access software such as Pulse Secure VPN, Fortinet VPN, and Citrix ADC, and exploiting vulnerabilities in web servers such as Apache and Nginx to gain unauthorized access to victims' systems. To achieve our goal, we have ensured that Conti ransomware uses a combination of symmetric and asymmetric encryption techniques to encrypt the files of its victims (i.e., random 256-bit ChaCha symmetric key for each file's encryption and an asymmetric encryption algorithm RSA cryptography for the encryption of the ChaCha key). Furthermore, it communicated with its C&C server using an encrypted channel, making it difficult to track its activities.

x. We implemented **REvil** [34] ransomware more powerfully by using stronger encryption algorithms such as RSA-2048 and AES-256. This allowed the ransomware to encrypt not only local files but also files on network shares and mapped drives. As a result, any PureOS-based computing system, including the Librem Server, workstations (such as the Librem 14 and Librem Mini), and cellular devices (such as the Librem 5) could potentially be targeted [35]. After infecting a victim's computer, the ransomware was designed to remain there by creating a scheduled task or modifying the registry. Furthermore, we made the ransomware even more malicious by adding the ability to exfiltrate sensitive data before encrypting it.

xi. We implemented **DarkSide** [35] ransomware by enforcing strong encryption algorithms, such as RSA and AES, to encrypt files on a victim's computer and prevent them from being accessed without meeting the adversary criteria. Various obfuscation techniques (i.e., (a) code encryption and obfuscation, (b) applying the polymorphic code, (c) applying the dynamically linked to system libraries, (d) malware code compression, and (e) equipping it with an anti-debugging capacity to detect when it is being analyzed or debugged and takes actions to evade or disable the analysis) were introduced to evade detection.

xii. The **Babuk** [36] ransomware was re-designed to use a combination of symmetric and asymmetric encryption algorithms to encrypt data on the target system. It used a per-file random 256-bit ChaCha symmetric key for each file's encryption, and an asymmetric encryption algorithm such as RSA cryptography for the encryption of the ChaCha key. The asymmetric encryption algorithm is used to securely transmit the ChaCha key to the ransomware operator, allowing them to decrypt the files. Babuk's feature allowed it to steal data from infected systems. These data were then encrypted and sent to the ransomware operator (i.e., adversarial process). It was also capable of terminating running processes, deleting shadow volume copies, and disabling the PureOS System Restore feature.

xiii. To satisfy the experimental requirement, we redesigned the **Egregor** [37] ransomware that enabled it to use a mix of symmetric and asymmetric encryption algorithms to encrypt files on the targeted computer. The process involved generating a unique 256-bit ChaCha symmetric key for each file and using the RSA algorithm to encrypt the ChaCha key for secure transmission to the attacker (i.e., automated process), which could then decrypt the files. Moreover, the ransomware had various capabilities such as appending a random extension to the encrypted files, exploiting vulnerabilities in RDP connections and exploit kits, stealing data from infected computers, terminating processes, removing shadow volume copies, and disabling the PureOS System Restore function. Upon infecting the computer, the ransomware compressed the encrypted files into a single archive using an encryption and compression technique (i.e., "Lossless" and "Huffman coding" [35] compression).

xiv. The updated/re-designed version of the **Avaddon** [37] ransomware had numerous functions, such as employing both symmetric and asymmetric encryption methods to encrypt files. It used the RSA algorithm to encrypt files and used an exclusive AES-256 key for each file, making it challenging to decrypt without the key. The ransomware also added a distinct extension to each encrypted file, making it hard to recognize and retrieve the files. Moreover, the malware was equipped with an extended capacity to extract sensitive data from the infected system and forward it to the attacker node (i.e., an automated process). It could terminate ongoing processes and deactivate various operating system security features, including PureBoot [38].

4. Applied Machine Learning Models for Ransomware Defense

4.1. Overview of Different Machine Learning Models

Detecting malware using machine learning is a complex undertaking that has been a focus of research for many years. With the increasing sophistication of ransomware, there is a constant race between security researchers and malware creators to stay ahead of each other. This means that research in this field will always remain important and relevant. Even if a new machine learning method is developed that is capable of identifying all types of ransomwares, it is likely that malware creators will eventually develop new techniques to evade detection. As a result, the pursuit of improving malware detection methods is an ongoing process that requires continuous innovation and adaptation to keep up with the evolving threat landscape.

Our study aimed to identify the most effective ML approach(es) for detecting ransomware and benign executable files. To achieve this, we have adopted a three-step methodology.

Firstly, we conducted a thorough review of state-of-the-art machine learning methods (random forest, support vector machine (SVM), decision tree, naïve Bayes, AdaBoost, etc.) and examined the datasets and data collection methods used in recent research to identify the most promising techniques.

Secondly, we re-implemented and trained the three most effective methods identified in the first step using our collected dataset. By re-implementing and training these methods, we aimed to assess their performance on our specific dataset and compare their accuracy in detecting malicious software.

Ultimately, by using real-world samples, we evaluated the effectiveness of each method in identifying malware and determining which approach offers the best performance for detecting malicious software. Overall, our research endeavored to contribute to the development of a more accurate and reliable ransomware detection method that can enhance cybersecurity and protect against evolving threats.

To accomplish our goal of achieving the desired impact, we performed a comparative analysis of a hybrid-supervised learning approach in three different scenarios. These scenarios were designed to represent different levels of stringency when it came to the samples considered.

(a) The first scenario was very strict, and only a very well-characterized set of samples were included.
(b) The second scenario was less strict and included a broader range of well-studied samples.
(c) The third scenario was the most realistic, representing the actual conditions faced by vendors of ransomware detection solutions.

By designing these three scenarios, we gained insight into how the use of a smaller, more distinct dataset compared to a larger, more varied one can impact the proposed framework. This analysis helped us understand the effects of the framework in a more nuanced way, leading to a better accomplishment of our goal. Overall, our comparative analysis and experimental outcome provided valuable information that helped us make more informed decisions when it comes to implementing supervised learning approaches in real-world scenarios.

4.2. Selection of Appropriate Machine Learning Models

(a) We wanted to find the best machine-learning model for detecting ransomware. Therefore, we created a set of criteria for our search. The criteria are not exhaustive but include the following: the selected model should have high accuracy in detecting ransomware and be able to minimize false positives and false negatives.
(b) The model should be scalable and perform well even when dealing with small or large datasets.
(c) It should be able to generalize well to new and unseen ransomware samples.
(d) The model should be robust and able to perform well in the presence of noise, adversarial attacks, and other anomalies.
(e) The model should provide clear and interpretable explanations for its decisions and predictions.
(f) It should be efficient in terms of computation time, memory usage, and power consumption.
(g) The model should be flexible and easily adaptable to changing ransomware attack patterns with the ability to incorporate new data.

We have explored the relevance of using regression models for detecting ransomware, as they possess the capability to estimate the likelihood of a file or behavior being malicious. This is important, especially because conventional techniques such as signature-based detection may not be effective in detecting new or unknown malware variants. The regression model (XGBoost (i.e., useful for dealing with large datasets and is known for its speed and scalability) [39], and ElasticNet (i.e., to achieve a balance between sparsity and accuracy)) [40] was trained on a dataset of labeled instances, where each example was a file or behavior that was either "malicious" or "benign". By analyzing the features of these instances, the model could then predict the probability of a new file or behavior being malicious. Some of the initial features that were leveraged for ransomware detection included file size and entropy, the presence of specific strings or signatures, API calls and their arguments, and network traffic patterns. It is worth noting that both XGbBoost and ElasticNet regression have been proven to be useful in machine learning applications where the input data have many features and some of them are correlated. By identifying the key features that are essential for predicting the target outcome, the process of feature selection enhances the practicality of the application.

Referring to Figure 1, in the pseudocode provided above (Table 3), the functions **collect_data()** and **preprocess_data(data)** serve the purposes of data collection and data preprocessing, respectively. The function **split_data(preprocessed_data, test_size = 0.2)** splits the preprocessed data into training and testing sets, **perform_elasticnet(train_data)** identifies the most important features for predicting ransomware using ElasticNet, and **select_features(data, important_features)** selects only the important features from the data. Similarly, the function **train_xgboost(train_data_selected)** trains the XGBoost model on the selected features and **validate_model(model, test_data_selected)** validates the model's performance on the testing data. We used **tune_hyperparameters(model, train_data_selected)** to fine-tune the model's hyperparameters and **evaluate_model_performance(tuned_model_performance)** to obtain the performance evaluation of the tuned model. Finally, **deploy_model(tuned_model)** is used to deploy the tuned model for use in a production environment.

Table 3. Detecting ransomware using XGBoost and ElasticNet.

Pseudocode for Detecting Ransomware Using XGBoost and ElasticNet
(1) Collect and preprocess the data: 　(a)　data = collect_data() 　(b)　preprocessed_data = preprocess_data(data)
(2) Split the data: 　(a)　train_data, test_data = split_data(preprocessed_data, test_size = 0.2)
(3) Feature selection: 　(a)　important_features = perform_elasticnet(train_data) 　(b)　train_data_selected = select_features(train_data, important_features) 　(c)　test_data_selected = select_features(test_data, important_features)
(4) Train the model: 　(a)　model = train_hybrid_xgboost_elasticnet(train_data_selected) 　(b)　model_performance = validate_model(model, test_data_selected)
(5) Tune the model: 　(a)　tuned_model = tune_hyperparameters(model, train_data_selected) 　(b)　tuned_model_performance = validate_model(tuned_model, test_data_selected)
(6) Evaluate the model: 　(a)　evaluate_model_performance(tuned_model_performance)
(7) Deploy the model: 　(a)　deploy_model(tuned_model)

Thus, detecting ransomware using XGBoost involved training a machine learning model using features that helped to distinguish between normal and ransomware behavior. Data related to "file access patterns" was formulated as:

$$XGBoost(Ransomware) = w_1 * num\_of\_files\_created + w_2 * num\_of\_files\_deleted \\ + w_3 * num\_of\_files\_renamed + w_4 * num\_of\_files\_read + b \quad (1)$$

where w_1, w_2, w_3, and w_4 are the weights assigned to the number of files created, deleted, renamed, and read, respectively, and "b" is the bias term.

Data related to "network traffic patterns" was formulated as:

$$XGBoost(Ransomware) = w_1 * num\_of\_outgoing\_connections + w_2 * \\ num\_of\_incoming\_connections + w_3 * num\_of\_data\_packets\_sent + w_4 * \\ num\_of\_data\_packets\_received + b \quad (2)$$

where w_1, w_2, w_3, and w_4 are the weights assigned to the number of outgoing connections, incoming connections, data packets sent, and data packets received, respectively, and b is the bias term. Data related to "system call patterns" was formulated as:

$$XGBoost(Ransomware) = w_1 * num\_of\_system\_calls + w_2 * \\ num\_of\_suspicious\_system\_calls + b \quad (3)$$

where w_1 and w_2 are the weights assigned to the total number of system calls and suspicious system calls, respectively, and b is the bias term.

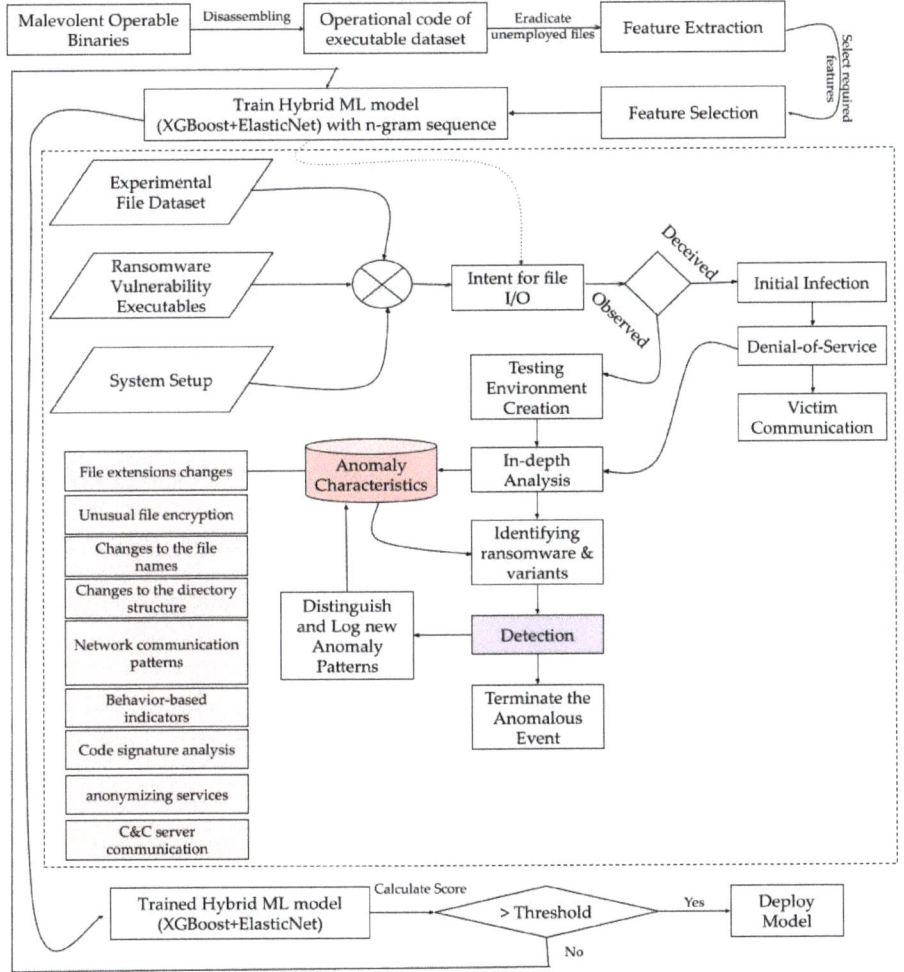

Figure 1. Flow diagram of ransomware detection criteria using XGBoost and ElasticNet.

The experiment was revised with a unique dataset using ElasticNet methodology by following conventional steps (i.e., collection of an indicative dataset, processing the data for feature normalization, splitting data into training and testing sets, training the ML model, and testing the model using a metric such as accuracy, precision, or recall.

ElasticNet loss function was evaluated as:

$$\min\left(1/\left(2*n_{samples}\right)||y - Xw||_2^2 + alpha * l4_{ratio} * ||w| + 0.5 * alpha * (1 - l4_{ratio}) * ||w||_2^2\right) \quad (4)$$

where

i. "n_samples" is the number of samples in the dataset.
ii. "y" is the target variable in the dataset.
iii. "X" is the matrix of features in the dataset.
iv. "W" is the vector of coefficients that are learned by the model.
v. "l4_ratio" is a hyperparameter that controls the balance between purportedly L_1 and L_2 regularization. As asserted, the L_1 regularization promotes sparsity in the learned coefficients, while L_2 regularization promotes small, non-zero coefficients.
vi. "Alpha" is a hyperparameter that controls the strength of the regularization. Higher values of alpha lead to more regularization.

In this scenario, the ElasticNet loss function is referred to as a combination of L_1 and L_2 regularization. The L_1 regularization term is given by $alpha * l4_{ratio} * ||w||_1$, which is the sum of the absolute values of the coefficients multiplied by a scaling factor $alpha * l4\_ratio$. The L_2 regularization term is given by $0.5 * alpha * (1 - l4_{ratio}) * ||w||_2^2$, which is the sum of the squares of the coefficients multiplied by a scaling factor $0.5 * alpha * (1 - l4_{ratio})$. The L_1 scaling factors are designed to balance the strength of the two regularization terms.

4.3. Feature Selection and Model Tuning

To develop effective ransomware detection methods, it was necessary to extract relevant features from the ransomware. This process involved closely analyzing the ransomware's code and behavior to identify specific characteristics or patterns that can distinguish it from other types of malwares. Reimplemented ransomware possesses distinct features that are useful in identifying and detecting them. These features are unique to ransomware and can differentiate it from other types of malwares. Some of the essential ransomware features include, but are not limited to:

i. Atypical network activity that is not typical for the system.
ii. Alterations to file extensions are not typical for the system.
iii. Suspicious processes with names that are random or located in unusual directories.
iv. Changes to the registry.
v. Unusual CPU or disk usage that is not typical for the system.
vi. Pop-up messages or warnings.
vii. Atypical system crashes or errors.
viii. Encryption key generation by malware.
ix. Usage of non-standard encryption algorithms.
x. Unusual behavior, such as modification of file timestamps or the creation of decoy files to deceive the victim.
xi. Atypical file access patterns that are not typical for the system.
xii. Large numbers of file deletions.
xiii. Changes to file permissions that are not typical for the system.
xiv. Random file names on large file datasets, all at once.
xv. Large numbers of failed login attempts.
xvi. Unusual file sizes that are not typical for the system.

Once the relevant features were extracted, they were used to train the machine learning model for detecting and classifying ransomware in real-world scenarios. This approach allowed for more effective ransomware detection, as it leverages the unique characteristics of ransomware to identify and mitigate threats. Furthermore, by continually updating the feature extraction process, the detection model was adapted to the evolving threat landscape of ransomware attacks.

4.4. Evaluation of Model Performance

To evaluate the performance of our model for detecting ransomware using XGBoost and ElasticNet, we used well-known ML model evaluation metrics, i.e., accuracy, precision, recall, and F1-score. The followings are the main steps performed for the performance evaluation:

1. Split the data into training and testing sets.
2. Perform feature selection using ElasticNet to identify the most important features for predicting ransomware.
3. Train an XGBoost model on the selected features using the training set.
4. Predict the labels of the test set using the trained model.
5. Evaluate the performance of the model.

Table 4 depicts the model code in which **X** and **y are** the features and labels of the data, respectively. **train_test_split()** was used to split the data into training and testing sets. **perform_elasticnet()** identifies the important features using ElasticNet. **select_features()** selects the important features from the data. **train_xgboost()** trains the XGBoost model on the selected features. **predict()** predicts the labels of the test set. Ultimately, the evaluation metrics are computed using the appropriate functions from scikit-learn (**accuracy_score()**, **precision_score()**, **recall_score()**. It is worth highlighting that the importance of employing parameters test_size and random_state is as follows:

i. The test_size parameter specifies the proportion of the data that will be used for testing, while the remaining data are used for training. For example, a test_size of 0.2 means that 20% of the data will be used for testing, and 80% will be used for training.
ii. The random_state parameter is used to set the seed for the random number generator, which ensures that the results are reproducible. This is important because the random sampling of data for training and testing can affect the performance metrics of the model. By setting the random_state parameter to a specific value, the same random sampling will occur every time the code is run, ensuring that the results are consistent and reproducible.

Table 4. Algorithmic outline for assessing model performance.

Pseudocode for Evaluating the Performance of the Model
 # Split the data into training and testing sets X_train, X_test, y_train, y_test = train_test_split(X, y, test_size = 0.2, random_state = 42) *# Perform feature selection using ElasticNet* important_features = perform_elasticnet(X_train, y_train) *# Select the important features* X_train_selected = select_features(X_train, important_features) X_test_selected = select_features(X_test, important_features) *# Train an XGBoost model on the selected features* model = train_xgboost(X_train_selected, y_train) *# Predict the labels of the test set* y_pred = model.predict(X_test_selected) *# Compute the evaluation metrics* accuracy = accuracy_score(y_test, y_pred) precision = precision_score(y_test, y_pred) recall = recall_score(y_test, y_pred) f1 = f1_score(y_test, y_pred)

To compute the accuracy, precision, recall, and F1-score for detecting ransomware using XGBoost and ElasticNet, it was necessary to obtain a set of true positive (TP), true negative (TN), false positive (FP), and false negative (FN) values for the proposed model. These values were obtained by comparing the predictions made by the XGBoost and ElasticNet models to the actual labels of the data.

Once the model had the TP, TN, FP, and FN values, it calculated the following metrics:

$$\text{Accuracy} = (TP+TN)/(TP+TN+FP+FN). : The proportion of correctly classified instances among instances. \tag{5}$$

$$\text{Precision} = TP/(TP+FP). : The proportion of correctly identified positive instances among all positive instances. \tag{6}$$

$$\text{Recall} = TP/(TP+FP). : The proportion of correctly identified positive instances among all actual positive instances. \tag{7}$$

$$\text{F1-score} = 2*(Precision*Recall)/(Precision+Recall). : The harmonic means of precision and recall, which gives a balanced measure of both metrics. \tag{8}$$

Table 5 presents the performance of the ransomware detection model in accurately identifying distinct types of ransomware. The table also shows the model's ability to minimize false positives and false negatives. False positives refer to cases when the model indicates that a system or file has ransomware, when in fact it does not, while false negatives occur when the model fails to detect the presence of ransomware that is there. By providing this information, the dataset enabled us to assess the model's ability to accurately identify diverse types of ransomwares. Furthermore, the dataset includes key performance metrics such as Accuracy, Precision, Recall, and F-Score, which were frequently employed to gauge the effectiveness of the model. These metrics enabled us to compare the effectiveness of various ransomware detection variables in terms of their accuracy in identifying different types of ransomware while minimizing the number of false positives and false negatives.

Table 5. Testing the proposed method on a limited dataset of ransomware anomalies to determine its average performance.

Ransomware	False/Positive	False/Negative	Accuracy	Precision	Recall	F-Score
Kryptik	3.21	1.95	85	0.823	0.853	0.869
Cloud Snooper	1.67	2.84	92	0.882	0.830	0.863
WannaCry	0.95	2.18	81	0.854	0.818	0.861
LockBit	3.53	3.34	88	0.801	0.846	0.832
Black Basta	2.47	1.17	84	0.888	0.839	0.854
Revised Hive	1.92	2.53	89	0.820	0.817	0.829
ALPHV/BlackCat/Noberus	2.99	2.28	95	0.847	0.856	0.844
AvosLocker	1.42	1.11	83	0.897	0.824	0.819
Conti	3.76	3.89	87	0.876	0.811	0.876
REvil	1.08	3.48	80	0.815	0.857	0.877
DarkSide	2.27	1.73	91	0.809	0.814	0.816
Babuk	0.85	3.29	94	0.865	0.847	0.823
Egregor	3.94	3.747	82	0.839	0.819	0.881
Avaddon	2.04	1.09	90	0.896	0.862	0.858

The effectiveness of our feature selection criteria was evaluated by comparing information gain and chi-square methods using the Naïve Bayes classifier. The feature sets were created using 28, 56, 84, 122, and 140 features. Table 6 presents the similarities between the two approaches and their classification performance using four metrics: True Positive, False Positive, Precision, and F-Score. The Bayesian predictor with attributes selected via information gain and chi-square techniques was used to generate the results of the detection process. The results indicated a positive correlation between the number of features used and anomaly detection in both methods, suggesting that accuracy improved when the features were optimized.

Table 6. The level of accuracy achieved by the hybrid "XGBoost and ElasticNet" method in detecting a specific ransomware variant.

Feature Optimization	Applied Feature Count	TP Rate (%)	FP Rate	Precision	F-Score
Information Gain	140	82.96	2.74	0.928	0.844
	112	86.02	2.12	0.867	0.804
	84	81.75	3.14	0.923	0.823
	56	85.14	2.58	0.849	0.862
	28	83	1.98	0.882	0.818
Chi-Square	140	91.94	2.54	0.798	0.844
	112	92.13	3.10	0.826	0.804
	84	91.56	2.28	0.771	0.823
	56	92.01	3.30	0.793	0.862
	28	92.32	1.99	0.810	0.818

We have also used Information Gain as a metric to measure the usefulness of a feature in splitting the data into different classes. It calculated the reduction in entropy achieved by splitting the data on a particular feature. The higher the Information Gain, the more useful the feature is in the classification process. Similarly, Chi-Square is used to determine whether there was a significant association between two categorical variables. In the context of feature selection, Chi-Square was employed to identify features that were significantly associated with the target variable. The higher the Chi-Square score, the more significant the association between the feature and the target variable.

To use these metrics to detect ransomware, we selected the features with the highest Information Gain or Chi-Square score and used them to train the projected model. The selected features were able to distinguish between ransomware and non-ransomware samples with high accuracy. Furthermore, to select the best feature count and metric for detecting ransomware, we compared the TP rate, FP rate, Precision, and F-Score for each combination of feature count and metric. We plotted the results to visualize the performance of each combination.

We have formulated Information Gain as:

$$\text{Information Gain} = \text{Entropy}(S) - \sum [p(v) \times \text{Entropy}(S_v)] \qquad (9)$$

where,
- S is the original dataset.
- v is a specific value of the feature being considered.
- p(v) is the proportion of the number of elements in S that have the value v to the number of elements in S.
- S_v is the subset of S where the feature has the value v.

- Entropy(S) is the entropy of the original dataset S.
- Entropy(Sv) is the entropy of the subset Sv.

The entropy Entropy(S) for the original dataset S is calculated using the following principle:

$$\text{Entropy}(S) = -\sum [p(c) \times \log 2(p(c))]. \qquad (10)$$

where c is a class label in S, and p(c) is the proportion of the number of elements in S that belong to class c to the number of elements in S. This formula gives the entropy of the original dataset S based on the class labels in the dataset.

Once the entropy of the original dataset S is calculated, we then used the formula for information gain to determine the importance of each feature in S. The information gain measures the reduction in entropy achieved by splitting the data based on a particular feature.

To estimate the Chi-Square, the following formula was employed:

$$\chi^2 = \sum [(O - E)^2/E] \qquad (11)$$

where,
- O is the observed frequency for a given feature and the presence of ransomware.
- E is the expected frequency for the same feature and ransomware presence.
- $\sum$ is the summation over all possible values of the feature and ransomware presence.

The expected frequency was calculated based on the assumption that the feature and the presence of ransomware were independent. If the observed frequency significantly differs from the expected frequency, it suggests that there was a correlation between the feature and the presence of ransomware. In the proposed ransomware detection, Chi-Square was used to identify features that are significantly correlated with ransomware. These features were then used as input for the applied machine learning model (i.e., hybrid XGBoost and ElasticNet) to detect ransomware.

5. Implementation and Testing

Our model was trained using different configurations:

1. The first one involved a Librem 14 laptop equipped with an Intel Core i7 10710U processor with 6 cores and 12 threads, DDR4 RAM of 64 GB, Intel UHD Graphics 620 GPU, M.2 SSD storage of 2 TB (NVMe), PureBoot firmware, and a PureOS operating system.
2. The second configuration used a Librem 5 smartphone, which had an NXP® i.MX 8M Quad core Cortex A53 processor with 64-bit ARM architecture running at a maximum of 1.5 GHz (along with an auxiliary Cortex M4), Vivante GC7000Lite GPU, 3 GB of RAM, 32 GB eMMC internal storage, and a PureOS operating system.

The model was trained with 15,000 instances obtained from an experimental setup. The dataset comprised 27% legitimate instances, 15% crypto miners, 13% memory dumps, 4% RAT-rated files, and 41% ransomware samples, which were customized versions of Kryptik, Cloud Snooper, WannaCry, LockBit, Black Basta, Hive, ALPHV/BlackCat/Noberus, AvosLocker, Conti, REvil, DarkSide, Babuk, and Avaddon. The data were updated as of 23 March 2023. We utilized a simulation model in the VMware NSX sandbox [41] to generate ransomware sample strings. By employing Full-system Mirroring alongside NSX Sandbox, we ensured precise detection capabilities. To gain a deeper understanding of the sandbox's configurations, we additionally executed our script in the Cuckoo Sandbox [42]. This allowed us to observe the behavior of the file within a practical and isolated environment. The decision was made to trust the actual behavior of the files, monitored by the sandbox, allowing us to identify specific features extracted through the sandbox's monitoring.

To identify the necessary prerequisites for a specific action, we employed two separate testing environments. The feature set comprised 140 characteristics, with 30 of them consisting of calls to API packages that encompassed all PureOS application programming interfaces. An outline of the ransomware versions employed in the evaluation stage is provided in Table 7.

Table 7. A high-level view of the analyzed ransomware variants.

Ransomware	Encoding	Lock	Remote Access Trojan	Sample Size (%)
Kryptik	✔	✔	✔	4
Cloud Snooper	✔	✔	✔	9
WannaCry	✔	-	-	7
LockBit	✔	✔	-	5
Black Basta	✔	-	-	11
Revised Hive	✔	✔	-	8
ALPHV/BlackCat/Noberus	✔	-	-	10
AvosLocker	✔	✔	✔	6
Conti	✔	-	✔	12
REvil	✔	-	✔	3
DarkSide	✔	-	✔	8
Babuk	✔	✔	-	2
Egregor	✔	✔	✔	9
Avaddon	✔	✔	-	6

Cuckoo sandbox was capable of analyzing a wide range of file extensions including .js, .hta, .psi, .pdf, .ppt, .ps1, .python, .vbs, .zip, etc. Furthermore, applets, classes (e.g., bin, cpl, dll, etc.), functions (e.g., DllMain, arguments, loader, etc.), dumps (e.g., memory.dump, dump.pcap, tlsmaster.txt, and files.json for metadata extraction), .bson, shots, and more were also examined.

The APIs that were used to facilitate or trigger ransomware operations included a variety of types from various categories. These include, but are not limited to, ShellExecute, CreateProcess, WriteProcessMemory, VirtualAllocEx, RegOpenKey, RegCreateKey, RegSetValue, HttpSendRequest, and LoadLibrary. These APIs belong to a range of different categories such as system calls, networking, input/output, file system, cryptography, and user interface. It is important to note that these APIs were utilized maliciously by threat actors (i.e., pre-fabricated anomalies) to carry out ransomware attacks.

The ransomware we used for encrypting the data (i.e., files of varying sizes ranging from 100KB to 1GB) on the hacked system employed RSA-2048, AES-256, and ChaCha-256 encryption algorithms. We carried out a thorough investigation of the time taken by these algorithms and found that the ChaCha-256 had the fastest encryption speed among the three, making it a more efficient option for use in ransomware attacks. The time-based encryption comparison is shown in Figure 2 and can be summarized as:

(a) Ransomware attackers are using advanced encryption algorithms such as RSA-2048, AES-256, and ChaCha-256 to encrypt victim data, making it inaccessible without the decryption key.
(b) The speed at which encryption algorithms operate can impact the success of a ransomware attack. In this case, ChaCha-256 was found to be the fastest among the three encryption algorithms, making it a potentially more effective choice for attackers.
(c) As a result of the faster encryption speed, ChaCha-256 may become more prevalent in future ransomware attacks.

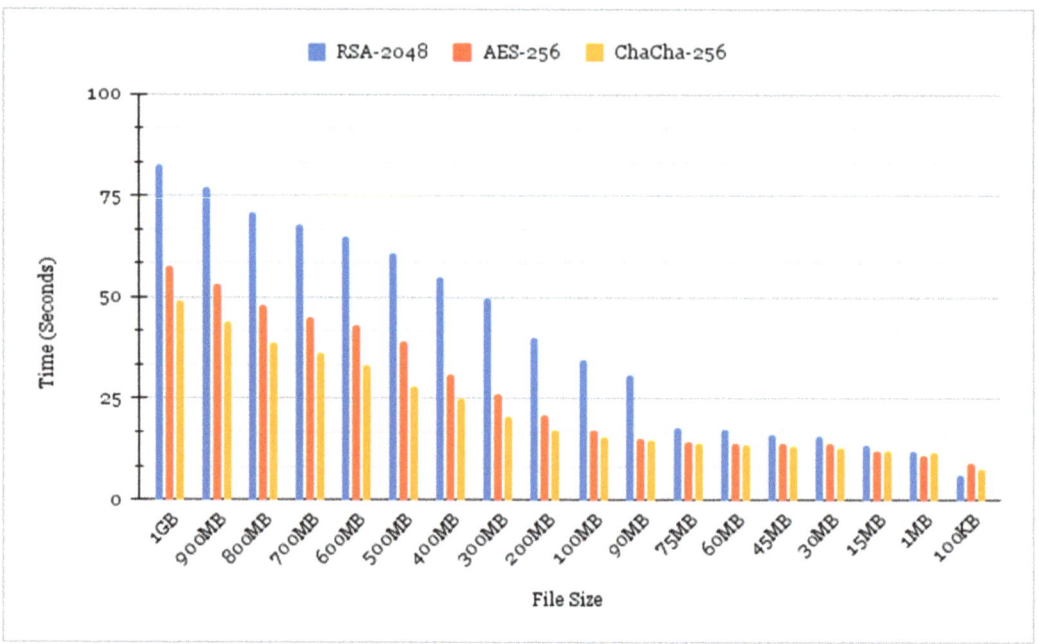

Figure 2. The use of RSA-2048, AES-256, and ChaCha-256 for time-based encryption comparisons.

Figure 3 shows the effect of selecting a subset of features from a dataset of ransomware characteristics based on their variance. The variance threshold is a value that is set to determine the minimum variance a feature must have to be included in the subset. During the optimization process, we noticed that by varying the variance threshold, it is possible to select different numbers of features for the subset. By setting a variance threshold for each feature, only those that significantly differ across the dataset will be included in the subset. If the variance threshold is set high, only features with high variance are included in the subset, leading to a smaller number of ransomware features. In contrast, if the variance threshold is set low, more features with lower variance are included, resulting in a larger number of ransomware features.

It is important to note that the number of ransomware features selected for the subset can have a significant impact on the performance of applied machine learning models (i.e., XGBoost and ElasticNet). Therefore, selecting the optimal number of ransomware features with varying variance thresholds is a crucial step in developing effective ransomware detection and prevention systems.

The study conducted tests on the entire dataset, using a cross-validation technique that involved 25 folds, and splitting the data into training and testing subsets randomly, with 60% of the data used for training and 40% for testing. Table 8 presents the performance of six different machine learning algorithms in detecting and preventing ransomware attacks. The metrics (i.e., accuracy, precision, recall, and F-score) were evaluated using both a 25-fold cross-validation technique and a 60% split training/test set approach. The proposed algorithm, the hybrid XGBoost and ElasticNet, has the highest routine across evaluation techniques, indicating that it outperforms the other algorithms. The results highlight the potential of machine learning algorithms in detecting and preventing ransomware attacks and provide insights into which algorithms perform better in this context.

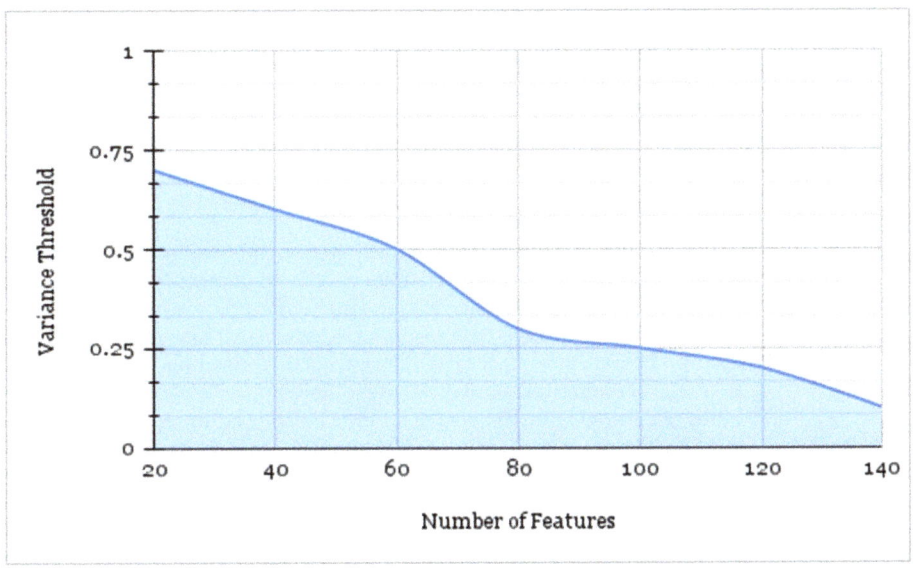

Figure 3. Dimensionality in the number of characteristics with various thresholds for variance.

Table 8. The outcomes of the Accuracy, Precession, Recall, and F-Score.

Sr#	ML Algorithm	Accuracy		Precession		Recall		F-Score	
		25 Folds	60% Split	25 Folds	60% Split	25 Folds	60% Split	25 Folds	60% Split
1	Reinforcement learning (Markovic Decision Process + Q-Learning) [43]	0.867	0.865	0.867	0.865	0.845	0.842	0.874	0.872
2	K-Nearest Neighbors Algorithm [44]	0.872	0.870	0.872	0.871	0.855	0.853	0.880	0.882
3	Support Vector Machine [45]	0.845	0.846	0.846	0.842	0.803	0.806	0.845	0.842
4	Stochastic Gradient Descent [46]	0.811	0.816	0.813	0.817	0.733	0.725	0.804	0.818
5	Naive Bayes [44]	0.512	0.532	0.672	0.666	0.551	0.533	0.865	0.847
6	Hybrid XGBoost and ElasticNet	0.901	0.907	0.921	0.917	0.920	0.933	0.921	0.927

Limitations

The proposed research has primarily focused on exploring the robustness of classifiers that solely examine the structure of binary programs (i.e., of benign and ransomware samples). However, the methods (i.e., hybrid XGBoost and ElasticNet) we have applied would not affect classifiers that consider the execution of such programs, and extract features such as the sequence of system calls. The reason for this limitation is that the data we introduce and modify are not executed during the program runtime. To deal with active features, an attacker would have to resort to using binary rewriting techniques, which are practical modifications specifically designed for this purpose. These alterations involve manipulating the program's anomalous code by adding new branches or replacing semantically equivalent instructions, which can be used to encode ransomware in a way that has broad applicability.

6. Conclusions and Future Work

It can be asserted with a high degree of certainty that machine learning algorithms have proven to be efficacious tools in identifying and detecting malicious software. However, designing such systems is often difficult because they involve complex features that can make it hard to understand how the models learn and accurately identify the real characteristics of malware. Consequently, systems that have these weaknesses can unintentionally incorporate false patterns, which may make them more vulnerable to attacks from malicious actors.

The focal point of this article is the detection of PureOS-specific ransomware, a pernicious and insidious threat that has proliferated with unprecedented velocity in recent years. We conducted a comprehensive examination of the efficacy of various single feature type sets in identifying this type of ransomware, while also considering the customary tactics employed by malevolent actors to camouflage their nefarious activities.

To further refine and optimize these techniques, we exploited hybrid machine learning methodologies, such as XGBoost and ElasticNet, to scrutinize and assess the strength and validity of the developed systems. The ultimate goal was to propose effective methodologies for the judicious implementation of these techniques. Accordingly, experimental work was conducted to evaluate the potential impact of these methodologies on the detection of ransomware and to enhance the design process of hybrid machine-learning-based systems.

It is clear from the results that our approach performs exceptionally well in detecting ransomware patterns with high accuracy and a low false-negative rate. This work shows that ML techniques can be used to significantly improve the effectiveness and efficiency of cybersecurity defenses against ransomware attacks.

We assert that combining multiple machine learning models can improve the overall detection accuracy and reduce false positives. This work might provide a boost to ensemble learning techniques, especially in the area of cyber security.

Author Contributions: Conceptualization, U.T. and T.A.A.; methodology, F.D., U.T. and S.A.C.; software, U.T. and Y.M.; validation, U.T. and T.A.A.; formal analysis, U.T.; investigation, S.A.C. and U.T.; resources, U.T. and T.A.A.; data curation, Y.M. and U.T.; writing—original draft preparation, T.A.A., U.T. and F.D.; writing—review and editing, Y.M., U.T. and S.A.C..; visualization, Y.M. and U.T.; supervision, T.A.A.; project administration, S.A.C. and Y.M.; funding acquisition, S.A.C. All authors have read and agreed to the published version of the manuscript.

Funding: The authors extend their appreciation to the Deputyship for Research and Innovation, Ministry of Education in Saudi Arabia for funding this research work through project number 2022/01/22636.

Institutional Review Board Statement: The study was conducted according to the guidelines of the Declaration of Deanship of Scientific Research, Prince Sattam Bin Abdulaziz University, Saudi Arabia.

Informed Consent Statement: Not applicable.

Data Availability Statement: Not applicable.

Acknowledgments: This study is supported via funding from Prince Sattam Bin Abdulaziz University.

Conflicts of Interest: The authors declare no conflict of interest.

References

1. Lawal, K.; Rafsanjani, H.N. Trends, benefits, risks, and challenges of IoT implementation in residential and commercial buildings. *Energy Built Environ.* **2022**, *3*, 251–266. [CrossRef]
2. Ransomware at Colorado IT Provider Affects 100+ Dental Offices—Krebs on Security. 7 December 2019. Available online: https://krebsonsecurity.com/2019/12/ransomware-at-colorado-it-provider-affects-100-dental-offices/ (accessed on 27 March 2023).
3. NATO Countries Hit with Unprecedented Cyber Attacks. GovTech. 4 September 2022. Available online: https://www.govtech.com/blogs/lohrmann-on-cybersecurity/nato-countries-hit-with-unprecedented-cyber-attacks (accessed on 28 March 2023).
4. Cui, J. Malware Detection Algorithm for Wireless Sensor Networks in a Smart City Based on Random Forest. *J. Test. Eval.* **2022**, *51*, 20220100. [CrossRef]

5. Singh, T.; Di Troia, F.; Corrado, V.A.; Austin, T.H.; Stamp, M. Support Vector Machines and Malware Detection. *J. Comput. Virol. Hacking Tech.* **2015**, *12*, 203–212. [CrossRef]
6. Yilmaz, A.B.; Taspinar, Y.S.; Koklu, M. Classification of Malicious Android Applications Using Naive Bayes and Support Vector Machine Algorithms. *Int. J. Intell. Syst. Appl. Eng.* **2022**, *10*, 269–274. Available online: https://ijisae.org/index.php/IJISAE/article/view/2010 (accessed on 29 March 2023).
7. Abu Al-Haija, Q.; Odeh, A.; Qattous, H. PDF Malware Detection Based on Optimizable Decision Trees. *Electronics* **2022**, *11*, 3142. [CrossRef]
8. Gao, Y.; Hasegawa, H.; Yamaguchi, Y.; Shimada, H. Malware Detection Using LightGBM with a Custom Logistic Loss Function. *IEEE Access* **2022**, *10*, 47792–47804. [CrossRef]
9. Xie, N. Andro_MD: Android Malware Detection based on Convolutional Neural Networks. *Int. J. Perform. Eng.* **2018**, *14*, 547–558. [CrossRef]
10. Liu, T.; Li, Z.; Long, H.; Bilal, A. NT-GNN: Network Traffic Graph for 5G Mobile IoT Android Malware Detection. *Electronics* **2023**, *12*, 789. [CrossRef]
11. Manoharan, S.; Sugumaran, P.; Kumar, K. Multichannel Based IoT Malware Detection System Using System Calls and Opcode Sequences. *Int. Arab. J. Inf. Technol.* **2022**, *19*, 261–271. [CrossRef]
12. Sun, H.; Wang, X.; Buyya, R.; Su, J. CloudEyes: Cloud-based malware detection with reversible sketch for resource-constrained internet of things (IoT) devices. *Softw. Pract. Exp.* **2016**, *47*, 421–441. [CrossRef]
13. Ahmed, U.; Lin, J.C.W.; Srivastava, G. Mitigating adversarial evasion attacks of ransomware using ensemble learning. *Comput. Electr. Eng.* **2022**, *100*, 107903. [CrossRef]
14. Ibrahim, A.; Tariq, U.; Ahamed Ahanger, T.; Tariq, B.; Gebali, F. Retaliation against Ransomware in Cloud-Enabled PureOS System. *Mathematics* **2023**, *11*, 249. [CrossRef]
15. Barrett, M.P. Framework for Improving Critical Infrastructure Cybersecurity Version 1.1. NIST. 16 April 2018. Available online: https://www.nist.gov/publications/framework-improving-critical-infrastructure-cybersecurity-version-11 (accessed on 27 March 2023).
16. Hull, G.; Jhon, H.; Arief, B. Ransomware deployment methods and analysis: Views from a predictive model and human responses. *Crime Sci.* **2019**, *8*, 2. [CrossRef]
17. Kharraz, A.; Robertson, W.; Kirda, E. Protecting against Ransomware: A New Line of Research or Restating Classic Ideas? *IEEE Secur. Priv.* **2018**, *16*, 103–107. [CrossRef]
18. Upadhyaya, R.; Jain, A. Cyber ethics and cyber crime: A deep dwelved study into legality, ransomware, underground web and bitcoin wallet. In Proceedings of the 2016 International Conference on Computing, Communication and Automation (ICCCA), Greater Noida, India, 29–30 April 2016; pp. 143–148. [CrossRef]
19. Gagneja, K.K. Knowing the ransomware and building defense against it—Specific to healthcare institutes. In Proceedings of the 2017 Third International Conference on Mobile and Secure Services (MobiSecServ), Miami Beach, FL, USA, 11–12 February 2017; pp. 1–5. [CrossRef]
20. Celdrán, A.H.; Sánchez, P.M.S.; Castillo, M.A.; Bovet, G.; Pérez, G.M.; Stiller, B. Intelligent and behavioral-based detection of malware in IoT spectrum sensors. *Int. J. Inf. Secur.* **2022**, *22*, 541–561. [CrossRef]
21. Moon, D.; Lee, J.; Yoon, M. Compact feature hashing for machine learning based malware detection. *ICT Express* **2022**, *8*, 124–129. [CrossRef]
22. Dargahi, T.; Dehghantanha, A.; Bahrami, P.N.; Conti, M.; Bianchi, G.; Benedetto, L. A Cyber-Kill-Chain based taxonomy of crypto-ransomware features. *J. Comput. Virol. Hacking Tech.* **2019**, *15*, 277–305. [CrossRef]
23. ESET: Threat Report Q2 2020. *Comput. Fraud. Secur.* **2020**, *2020*, 4. [CrossRef]
24. Yang, W.; Gao, M.; Chen, L.; Liu, Z.; Ying, L. RecMaL: Rectify the malware family label via hybrid analysis. *Comput. Secur.* **2023**, *128*, 103177. [CrossRef]
25. VirusChaser: A Comprehensive Antivirus Solution Equipped with Powerful System Protection Features. VirusChaser. 18 February 2023. Available online: https://www.ncloud.com/marketplace/viruschaser (accessed on 16 April 2023).
26. FKIE, F. Cloud Snooper (Malware Family). Cloud Snooper (Malware Family). 21 December 2020. Available online: https://malpedia.caad.fkie.fraunhofer.de/details/elf.cloud_snooper (accessed on 1 March 2023).
27. Tonido—Run Your Personal Cloud. A Free Private Cloud Server. (n.d.). Tonido—Run Your Personal Cloud. A Free Private Cloud Server. Available online: https://www.tonido.com/ (accessed on 2 March 2023).
28. Ghafur, S.; Kristensen, S.; Honeyford, K.; Martin, G.; Darzi, A.; Aylin, P. A retrospective impact analysis of the WannaCry cyberattack on the NHS. *npj Digit. Med.* **2019**, *2*, 98. [CrossRef]
29. Eliando, E.; Purnomo, Y. LockBit 2.0 Ransomware: Analysis of infection, persistence, prevention mechanism. *CogITo Smart J.* **2022**, *8*, 232–243. [CrossRef]
30. Kajave, A.; Nismy, S.A.H. How Cyber Criminal Use Social Engineering to Target Organizations. *arXiv* **2022**, arXiv:2212.12309. [CrossRef]
31. Tanner, D.A.; Hinchliffe, A.; Santos, D. Threat Assessment: Blackcat Ransomware. 2022. Available online: https://shorturl.at/cdV37 (accessed on 2 March 2023).
32. Kara, I.; Aydos, M. The rise of ransomware: Forensic analysis for windows based ransomware attacks. *Expert Syst. Appl.* **2022**, *190*, 116198. [CrossRef]

33. Umar, R.; Riadi, I.; Kusuma, R.S. Analysis of Conti Ransomware Attack on Computer Network with Live Forensic Method. *IJID Int. J. Inform. Dev.* **2021**, *10*, 53–61. [CrossRef]
34. Datta, P.M.; Acton, T. From disruption to ransomware: Lessons from hackers. *J. Inf. Technol. Teach. Cases* **2022**. [CrossRef]
35. Purism Products. Available online: https://puri.sm/products/ (accessed on 3 March 2023).
36. Zou, S.; Zhang, J.; Jiang, S.; Cheng, Y.; Ji, X.; Xu, W. OutletGuarder: Detecting DarkSide Ransomware by Power Factor Correction Signals in an Electrical Outlet. In Proceedings of the 2022 IEEE 28th International Conference on Parallel and Distributed Systems (ICPADS), Nanjing, China, 10–12 January 2023; pp. 419–426. [CrossRef]
37. Lin, C.; Kimberly, G.; Daniel, R.; Henry, U. Blockchain Forensics and Crypto-Related Cybercrimes. *SSRN* **2023**. [CrossRef]
38. PureBoot & Ndash; Purism. (n.d.). Purism. Available online: https://puri.sm/projects/pureboot/ (accessed on 1 March 2023).
39. Palša, J.; Ádám, N.; Hurtuk, J.; Chovancová, E.; Madoš, B.; Chovanec, M.; Kocan, S. MLMD—A Malware-Detecting Antivirus Tool Based on the XGBoost Machine Learning Algorithm. *Appl. Sci.* **2022**, *12*, 6672. [CrossRef]
40. Srinivasan, S.; Deepalakshmi, P. ENetRM: ElasticNet Regression Model based malicious cyber-attacks prediction in real-time server. *Meas. Sens.* **2023**, *25*, 100654. [CrossRef]
41. VMware. NSX Sandbox I VMware. Available online: https://www.vmware.com/products/nsx-sandbox.html (accessed on 4 March 2023).
42. Wahidin, G.W.; Syaifuddin, S.; Sari, Z. Analisis Ransomware Wannacry Menggunakan Aplikasi Cuckoo Sandbox. *J. Repos.* **2022**, *4*, 83–94. [CrossRef]
43. Lee, C.; Han, S.M.; Chae, Y.H.; Seong, P.H. Development of a cyberattack response planning method for nuclear power plants by using the Markov decision process model. *Ann. Nucl. Energy* **2022**, *166*, 108725. [CrossRef]
44. Sahin, D.O.; Akleylek, S.; Kilic, E. LinRegDroid: Detection of Android Malware Using Multiple Linear Regression Models-Based Classifiers. *IEEE Access* **2022**, *10*, 14246–14259. [CrossRef]
45. Singh, P.; Borgohain, S.K.; Kumar, J. Performance Enhancement of SVM-based ML Malware Detection Model Using Data Preprocessing. In Proceedings of the 2022 2nd International Conference on Emerging Frontiers in Electrical and Electronic Technologies (ICEFEET), Patna, India, 24–25 June 2022; pp. 1–4. [CrossRef]
46. Mowri, R.A.; Siddula, M.; Roy, K. Interpretable Machine Learning for Detection and Classification of Ransomware Families Based on API Calls. *arXiv* **2022**, arXiv:2210.11235. [CrossRef]

Disclaimer/Publisher's Note: The statements, opinions and data contained in all publications are solely those of the individual author(s) and contributor(s) and not of MDPI and/or the editor(s). MDPI and/or the editor(s) disclaim responsibility for any injury to people or property resulting from any ideas, methods, instructions or products referred to in the content.

Article

Multi-Country and Multi-Horizon GDP Forecasting Using Temporal Fusion Transformers †

Juan Laborda [1,*], Sonia Ruano [2] and Ignacio Zamanillo [2]

1. Department of Business Administration, Universidad Carlos III, Getafe, 28903 Madrid, Spain
2. Banco de España, C/Alcalá 48, 28014 Madrid, Spain; sonia.ruano@bde.es (S.R.); ignacio.zamanillo@bde.es (I.Z.)
* Correspondence: jlaborda@emp.uc3m.es; Tel.: +34-655-019-700
† The opinions and analyses expressed in this paper are the responsibility of the authors and, therefore, do not necessarily reflect those of the Banco de España or the Eurosystem.

Abstract: This paper applies a new artificial intelligence architecture, the temporal fusion transformer (TFT), for the joint GDP forecasting of 25 OECD countries at different time horizons. This new attention-based architecture offers significant advantages over other deep learning methods. First, results are interpretable since the impact of each explanatory variable on each forecast can be calculated. Second, it allows for visualizing persistent temporal patterns and identifying significant events and different regimes. Third, it provides quantile regressions and permits training the model on multiple time series from different distributions. Results suggest that TFTs outperform regression models, especially in periods of turbulence such as the COVID-19 shock. Interesting economic interpretations are obtained depending on whether the country has domestic demand-led or export-led growth. In essence, TFT is revealed as a new tool that artificial intelligence provides to economists and policy makers, with enormous prospects for the future.

Keywords: GDP; deep learning; time fusion transformers; multi-horizon forecasting; interpretability

MSC: 37M10

Citation: Laborda, J.; Ruano, S.; Zamanillo, I. Multi-Country and Multi-Horizon GDP Forecasting Using Temporal Fusion Transformers. *Mathematics* 2023, 11, 2625. https://doi.org/10.3390/math11122625

Academic Editor: Wei Fang

Received: 3 May 2023
Revised: 2 June 2023
Accepted: 7 June 2023
Published: 8 June 2023

Copyright: © 2023 by the authors. Licensee MDPI, Basel, Switzerland. This article is an open access article distributed under the terms and conditions of the Creative Commons Attribution (CC BY) license (https://creativecommons.org/licenses/by/4.0/).

1. Introduction

The Great Recession, the COVID-19 pandemic, and the war in Ukraine increased the uncertainty surrounding the economic cycle. Preceding these crises, the world economy underwent a process of financialization over the preceding two decades, characterized by a broad range of shifts in the relationship between the financial and real sectors. This phenomenon elevated the significance of financial actors in the economy ([1]). It altered the aspects of micro and macro dynamics. This translated the dynamics of financial markets, in particular, nonlinearities and long-term dependencies ([2,3]), into features of different business cycle indicators, including real GDP. Consequently, forecasting macroeconomic data, such as real GDP growth, became a more complex task.

The effect of an explanatory variable on real GDP depends on how it is interrelated with other explanatory variables, which, in addition, can vary over time. An example of that is the evidence that we obtain in this study on the loss of the predictive power of the slope of the yield curve to anticipate the business cycle. In different previous studies, the yield curve was revealed as an extremely powerful predictor of recessions ([4–9]).

The existence of long-range dependence and non-linearities in a business cycle time series ([10–13]) opens the door to the use of artificial intelligence (AI) techniques to forecast real GDP. AI is the development of computer-based algorithms that can perform tasks similar to human intelligence being able to modify their actions, thus maximizing their chances of success. Such algorithms are increasingly capable of solving extremely complex problems, such as helping in decision-making processes; including the classification and evaluation of large amounts of data.

This paper contributes to the real GDP forecasting literature by proposing the application of temporal fusion transformers (TFTs). This state-of-the-art time series model, developed by [14], is encompassed within deep neural networks (DNNs). This new attention-based architecture offers significant comparative advantages over regression models and other deep learning methods. First, it can be applied to univariate and multivariate time series. Second, three types of explanatory variables can be used: temporal data known only up to the present, temporal data with known inputs into the future, and/or exogenous static/categorical variables. Third, it allows working with heterogeneous time series, so that it can train on multiple time series from different distributions. Fourth, the TFT architecture splits processing into local preprocessing and global processing. The first one captures specific events and the second one the common features of all the time series. Fifth, the results are interpretable since the impact of each explanatory variable on each forecast can be calculated by analysing the variable selection weights. Sixth, it allows for visualizing persistent temporal patterns and identifying significant events and different regimes. Finally, it provides quantile regressions and permits computing simulations based on a known input into the future. This feature is especially valuable to evaluate macroeconomic policies.

We apply TFTs for the joint GDP forecasting of 25 OECD countries using macroeconomic and financial variables. Since TFTs allow multi-horizon forecasts, we will forecast at different time horizons: one, two, three, and four quarters. It requires the data sample to be partitioned into three datasets: the training dataset, the validation dataset, and finally the test dataset. The obtained results are compared with those of a benchmark ARIMA model using two standard metrics, mean absolute error (MAE) and root mean square error (RMSE).

TFT outperforms the standard ARIMA in the two proposed metrics, MAE and RMSE. The performance of TFT forecasts was compared to that of the ARIMA model separately, in recession and expansion sub-periods, in order to give greater robustness to the results obtained at a global level. TFT outperforms ARIMA in periods of economic slowdown or global recession as well as in periods of stable growth; in this case, the improvement is marginal. Results suggest that TFTs outperform regression models, especially in periods of turbulence, such as the COVID-19 shock. Interesting economic interpretations are obtained depending on whether the country has domestic demand-led or export-led growth. The obtained results show that the TFT forecasts improvements are significantly greater in demand-driven growth countries.

The use of TFTs to predict real GDP yields very interesting results regarding the importance of the explanatory variables. While the slope of the curve has limited predictive power, it is worth noting that the variable measuring the indebtedness of the non-financial private sectors demonstrates a remarkable ability to anticipate future trends. This variable played a catalytic role in the Great Recession once the value of collateral began to deteriorate, in accordance with Hyman Minsky's financial instability hypothesis ([15,16]). In this regard, recent studies show the high persistence of the ratio of private debt to GDP for different OECD countries, and the key importance of macroprudential policy, as one of the pillars of macroeconomic policy ([17]). Finally, it should be noted that the importance of the explanatory variables in predicting real GDP might vary somewhat depending on the phase of the economic cycle or the forecast time horizon. TFTs are capable of capturing this.

The rest of the paper is organized as follows: Section 2 discusses the theoretical framework that allows us to use financial variables, composite leading indicators, the credit cycle, and international trade as predictors of economic growth. Section 3 reviews the literature on forecasting economic growth using deep learning and regression models. Section 4 formulates the methodology designed, using TFTs, for the joint forecasting of the GDPs of a substantial number of countries, and details the description of the sample and the variables used. Section 5 discusses the empirical results obtained. Finally, Section 6 presents the conclusions, pointing out future lines of research.

2. Predictors of GDP Growth: A Literature Review

Over decades, economists devoted a substantial amount of effort to model economic growth. There exists a wide literature that supports the importance of different kinds of variables to predict the evolution of GDP. Throughout this section, we review a list of variables from a broad array of candidates and describe how they are related to the business cycle.

2.1. Financial Variables and Leading Indicators

Financial variables, such as the prices of financial instruments, interest rates, interest rate spreads, stock price indexes, and monetary aggregates, have significant predictive content for economic activity since they are forward-looking variables, and therefore, are useful indicators in macroeconomic prediction. For a comprehensive literature review, see [18].

1. The Yield Curve. The spreads between interest rates for different maturities tend to be interpreted as the market expectations of future rates corresponding to the period between the two maturities. Intuitively, long-term rates incorporate the expectations of financial markets on future short-term rates. Consequently, a negative-sloped or flat curve means that markets' prospects involve a decrease in future real interest rates, which is associated with weak economic activity or downturn.

Evidence on the predictive power of the spread between long-term and short-term government bond rates, called the slope of the yield curve, for inflation and real economic activity is wide and robust across countries and time periods ([4,5,19–23]).

Ref. [6] provides the theoretical basis for this statistical evidence. In particular, the main implication of the analytical rational expectations model is that the relationships are not structural since they are influenced by the monetary policy regime. In other words, the extent to which the yield curve is a good predictor depends on the form of the monetary policy reaction function, which, in turn, may depend on explicit policy objectives. The yield curve has predictive power, for example, if the monetary authority follows strict or flexible inflation targeting or if policy follows the [24] rule.

We hypothesize that the impact of the yield curve on economic growth will depend on how it interacts non-linearly with the global credit spread cycle and the official interest rates.

2. Corporate Bond Spreads. Asset purchase programs, forward guidance, and other unconventional monetary policies can lower long-term interest rates, altering the information content of the yield curve. However, even in such circumstances, the behavior of the corporate bond credit spread curve varies over the business cycle, potentially containing more information about the future.

Many studies focused on corporate bond spreads ([25–31]), providing strong evidence for the link between this spread and the economic activity.

We include in our model the ratio of the Moody's U.S. Baa corporate bond yields to that of Aaa as a global proxy for credit spread.

3. The Composite Leading Indicator. The combination of multiple leading variables in composite leading indicators (CLIs) pursues a more accurate prediction of the development of the reference series. CLIs are designed to predict the development of the business cycle, focusing on the identification of turning points that occur when the growth rate moves from an expansion period to a contraction period or vice versa. Empirical evidence supporting the usefulness of the CLI, both in-sample and out-of-sample real-time, in a real time context, is wide. Some examples are [4,32–35].

We include in our model the CLI built by OECD (see [36]), which captures fluctuations of the economic activity around its long-term potential level. This CLI shows short-term economic movements in qualitative rather than quantitative terms. A CLI reading above (below) 100 precedes levels of GDP above (below) its long-term trend.

4. The Industrials Commodity Price Index. The CRB Raw Industrials Spot Index, drawn from Bloomberg, is a synthetic measure of price movements of 13 sensitive basic commodities whose markets are presumed to be among the first to be influenced by changes in economic conditions. As such, it serves as one early indication of imminent changes in business activity.

The criteria for the selection of commodities are: (i) wide use for further processing (basic); (ii) freely traded in an open market; (iii) sensitive to changing conditions significant in those markets; and (iv) sufficiently homogeneous or standardized so that uniform and representative price quotations can be obtained over a period of time.

Then, the Spot Market Index is defined as the unweighted geometric mean of the individual commodity price relatives (i.e., the ratios of the current prices to the base period prices).

Different papers empirically examine the interactions between commodity prices, money, interest rates, goods, and economic growth ([37–41]). In particular, Ref. [41] explores how the commodity market can predict GDP growth for countries worldwide, rather than a few specific countries or regions. They find commodity returns significantly predict the next quarter's GDP growth, and thus can be considered as leading indicators of economic growth.

2.2. The Credit Cycle

The credit cycle and the economic cycle are closely related. Many studies provide empirical evidence supporting that endogenous credit supply expansions precede a decline in real GDP (see [42], for a review). The intuition is that, in the supply side of financial markets, risk appetite and the debt accumulation evolve over the business cycle following a regular process, and ultimately, this credit cycle translates to the real economy through defaults that materialize credit risk, and the end, financial constraints affecting the real economy. In particular, the Minsky's financial instability hypothesis ([15,16,43,44]) predicts that, for a given microeconomic condition, the likelihood of facing credit constraints decreases in periods of GDP expansion and increases in periods of contraction.

We include in our model the measurement of private indebtedness at the country level developed and published by the Bank for International Settlements (BIS). Specifically, it is defined as the ratio of the total debt of non-financial private sectors at market value of one country over its nominal GDP.

2.3. World Trade and Economic Integration across Countries

As was first stressed by the classics, Adam Smith and David Ricardo, trade promotes growth by allowing the optimal use of resources. Empirical evidence is profuse and supports that trade tends to favor development, given that it stimulates technical progress, which is spread across countries through the importation of capital goods that incorporate innovations (for a survey, see [45]).

Particularly, exports promote economic growth through several channels: they enhance a better allocation of resources through specialization on goods that have an improved comparative advantage, favoring productivity gains through economies of scale, spillover effects, and learning-by-doing. In this sense, trade integration enables a higher external demand that increases the probability and/or intensity of exporting, and therefore, of economic growth, especially in periods where domestic demand is under pressure ([46–48]).

International trade was also identified as a channel through which shocks are internationally transmitted, contributing to the synchronization in business cycles across countries. In particular, countries joining a currency union may lose their ability to stabilize cyclical fluctuations through independent counter-cyclical monetary policy. In general, empirical research found that pairs of countries with relatively strong economic linkages, not only in terms of trade intensity, but also in terms of financial and institutional integration, tend to have highly correlated business cycles. For example, Refs. [49–51] find that the closer the trade linkages are, the higher the correlation in countries' business cycles are as well. Similarly, Ref. [52] shows that more financially integrated countries display more correlated business cycles.

We incorporate in our model the World Trade Volume Index that is monthly computed by the Netherlands Bureau for Economic Policy Analysis. This index, defined as the arithmetic average of world exports and imports of goods, constitutes an indicator of global economic activity. It covers the United States, Japan, EU, and four groups of emerging countries: Asian countries (excluding Japan), Eastern Europe and CIS countries, Latin America, and Africa and the Middle East.

Here, we have to emphasize the ability of the temporal fusions transformers methodology to capture cross-country business cycle co-movements, even if the drivers of this synchronization are not explicitly introduced in the list of explanatory variables.

3. Forecasting Economic Growth Using Deep Learning and Regression Models: Literature Review

The Great Recession (2007–2009) and the COVID-19 pandemic increased the uncertainty surrounding the economic cycle. This indetermination occurs in a context of the financialization of the global economy in recent decades, understood as a broad set of changes in the relationship between the financial sector and the real sector, which gave greater weight than before to financial motives and actors, consequently affecting the different relationships between macroeconomic and/or financial variables.

The influence of macroeconomic and/or financial variables on the business cycle was extensively detailed in the previous section. In this one, we collect the different technical contributions to the forecasting of the business cycle, measured by GDP in real terms, from advanced regression models, especially in time series analysis, for the use of AI techniques.

3.1. The Use of Regression Models for Business Cycle Forecasting

There is a wide variety of regression models used in macroeconomic research in order to forecast economic activity. They range from the early ARIMA ([53–55]), or VAR models ([56,57]) to those more complex ones that analyze the cycle from an explicit non-linear perspective. VAR models are particularly useful for forecasting purpose but suffer from a major drawback, as they require the estimation of many potentially non-significant parameters. This over-parametrization problem, resulting in multicollinearity and loss of degrees of freedom, leads to inefficient estimates and large out-of-sample forecast errors. To face this problem, there are two main approaches. The first one consist in identifying non-significant lags through statistical tests and estimating the restricted version of the model that incorporates the identified restrictions on the parameters of the model. The second approach uses quasi-VAR models, which specify an unequal number of lags for the different equations.

Alternatively, some authors ([58,59]) propose a Bayesian VAR or BVAR model. Instead of eliminating the longest lags, the Bayesian method imposes restrictions on the coefficients of the model, assuming that these coefficients are more likely to approach zero than the coefficients of the shortest lags. Within the VAR family, in order to capture the systemic dimension while retaining the advantage of estimating a single equation, structural vector autoregressive (SVAR) models emerged ([60,61]). Finally, it is worth mentioning the time-varying parameter VAR models, which successfully model regime-switching time series ([62–64]).

Within business cycle modeling from an explicit nonlinear perspective, the range is very broad. They include, for example, smooth transition regression (STR) models, which are a general class of reduced-form, state-dependent, nonlinear time series models in which the transition between states is, generally, generated endogenously, and where smooth transition autoregression (STAR) models are a particular case. See [65–67].

Ref. [68] shows that the STR models include particular cases, in addition to the STAR, the exponential autoregressive (EAR), the threshold autoregressive (TAR), and the SETAR models. TAR and SETAR models are those which, maintaining the idea that the level and time structure in an economic phenomenon depend on the cyclical phase in which it is found, provide a relatively simple way of introducing non-linear elements in the econometric analysis of time series. See [69–71].

Finally, within the nonlinear modeling of the business cycle, we distinguish those models where the state of the cycle can be represented by a binary state variable whose evolution is explicitly characterized by a Markov chain. This state variable conditions the parameters of a linear model that completes the representation of the observed dynamics. We refer to Markov-switching autoregression (MS-AR) models, see [57,72–79], and further generalize the MS-AR model to a MS-VAR time series model.

Ref. [80] use a small set of variables (real GDP, the inflation rate, and the short-term interest rate) to analyze atheoretical (time series) and theoretical (structural) regression models, as well as linear and nonlinear, to test whether the decline in U.S. real GDP during the Great Recession had the potential to be predicted. Their results suggest that structural (theoretical) models, especially the nonlinear model, perform well on average at all forecast horizons in ex post, out-of-sample forecasts, although at certain forecast horizons, certain nonlinear atheoretical models perform better. The nonlinear theoretical model also dominates in the ex ante, out-of-sample forecasts of the Great Recession.

3.2. Forecasting Real GDP Using Artificial Intelligence Models

Forecasting real GDP growth, such as with other macroeconomic data, is a far from straightforward process. Starting from the causal relationship between dependent and independent variables, traditional economic models use predetermined relevant variables to make predictions, adopting top-down and theory-driven approaches ([81]). This process, in relation to the data and methods used, is founded on economic intuition and forecasters' judgment. If any of the forecasters' assumptions are not met, the models will produce inaccurate predictions.

The effect of an explanatory variable on real GDP depends on how it is interrelated with other explanatory ones, which, in addition, can vary over time. This feature cannot be modeled using the conventional regression framework, opening the door to the use of AI techniques. AI is the development of computer-based algorithms that can perform tasks similar to human intelligence, being able to modify their actions to maximize their chances of success. Such algorithms are increasingly capable of solving extremely complex problems, and can assist in decision-making, including the classification and evaluation of large amounts of data.

Unlike many traditional economic forecasting models, AI machine learning models focus on pure prediction ([82]). Being more flexible than traditional economic forecasting models, they produce predictions without predetermined assumptions or judgments. Therefore, thanks to the development of new algorithms and the increase in computing power, machine learning models were actively applied in various fields, from forecasting transportation, traffic or electricity flows ([14,83,84]), to forecasting housing prices ([85]) or financial market volatility ([14,86]). In most of the fields analyzed, machine learning methods perform better than traditional econometric models, including cases with low-frequency data. Looking at their application to economics, such as the inflation forecasting studies of [87,88], they produce robust predictions.

Ref. [89] divides AI learning methods into four major groups: unsupervised, supervised, semi-supervised, and reinforcement learning.

Almost all the AI models applied for business cycle forecasting fall within the supervised learning models, although elements of reinforcement learning can also be incorporated. For real GDP forecasting, different AI models are used: K-nearest neighbor ([90–92]); decision trees, boosted trees, gradient boosting and/or random forest ([91,93–98]); artificial neural networks and their deep learning extensions ([99–101]); ordinary and alternative support vector machines ([91,101–103]); and Boltzmann machines ([101]). These papers find that all these learning algorithms can outperform traditional statistical models, thus offering a relevant addition to the field of economic forecasting.

It is important to remark that most machine learning techniques, such as random forest or gradient boosting algorithms, are not ideal for time series forecasting since they ignore the time order of the features. They assume that the value of each feature at a certain time step is independent of the value of the same feature at the previous time step. This is violated in time series data, where serial correlations are essential.

Because of this, recurrent neural networks (RNNs), such as gated recurrent units (GRUs) and long short-term memory networks (LSTMs), are extensively used to solve time series forecasting problems since they are capable of capturing the dependencies between time steps. The problem with these DNNs is that they cannot correctly capture long-range dependencies. This issue is solved in the transformer architecture, initially presented in [104].

This paper is a contribution to the real GDP forecasting literature based on the application of AI. It proposes the application of TFTs, recently developed by [14], which are encompassed within DNNs. TFTs provide considerable advantages that will be detailed in the next section.

4. Methodology and Database

We will apply a new deep learning model, the temporal fusion transformers, for forecasting jointly the real GDP on a quarterly basis for 25 OECD countries at different time horizons. We will detail the main features of TFTs, explaining both the attributes that make them very suitable for forecasting macroeconomic variables and the different blocks of their architecture. We will then explain in detail the methodology we designed for the joint forecasting of the GDPs of a substantial number of countries.

4.1. Temporal Fusion Transformers for Forecasting Real GDP

TFT ([14]) is the state-of-the-art model for interpretable, multi-horizon time series forecasting. This attention-based architecture is specifically designed for time series prediction and provides several advantages over other deep learning models (Figure 1).

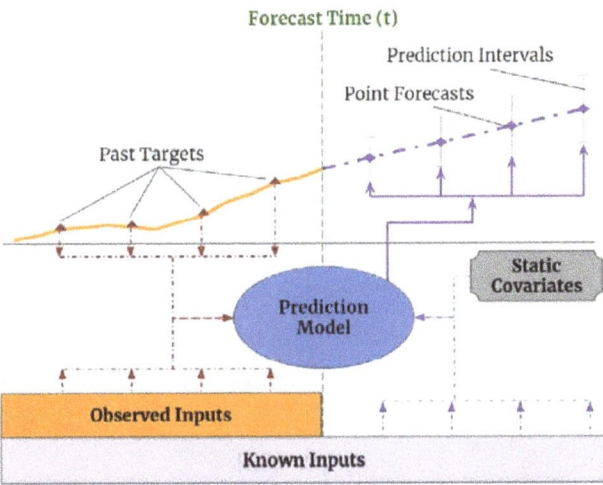

Figure 1. The TFT advantages. Source: [14].

First, TFTs support different types of variables as inputs: time series that are only known up to the present (this is the type of data that most models work with); time series with known values in the future; and static or time-invariant variables. All these variables can be categorical or continuous. Due to its ability to process static variables, TFTs permit training on multiple time series, from different distributions. This is extremely important because it enabled us to train the model with data from different countries, significantly increasing the size of the dataset, something essential for machine learning models.

Most models are not able to work with known future values and this is essential for certain time series problems. For example, from the perspective of a central bank, the model's ability to work with known future values of a given explanatory variable will allow for an analysis of the impact of monetary policy (interest rates and/or quantitative easing) on a given macroeconomic variable under study, be it inflation and/or real GDP.

Secondly, TFTs allow multi-horizon quantile prediction through multi-step forecasts by calculating prediction intervals using the quantile loss function. The user can define these forecasting intervals.

Finally, one main property of TFTs is their interpretability. Most deep learning architectures are "black box" models and their predictions cannot be explained. Generally, AI explanatory methods obtain interpretability measures in a differentiated process from the estimation one. Common post hoc machine learning explanatory techniques, such as SHAP or LIME, do not take into account the temporal order of the inputs, ignoring dependencies between time steps that are essential in time series. TFTs address this weakness by incorporating variable selection networks (VSN) that provide variable selection weights, which quantify the importance of each feature in the prediction of each observation in the dataset. Then, selection weights are collected for each variable across the entire test set to compute any statistic that characterizes each sampling distribution. In addition to quantifying the importance of each input variable in prediction, TFTs permit us to visualize persistent temporal patterns, different regimes, and significant events. For this purpose, TFTs employ a self-attention mechanism that estimates the attention weights that measure the importance of each period.

Having already explained the capabilities that make the TFT ideal for economic forecasting, we will now briefly explain its architecture before detailing the methodology we designed for the joint forecasting of real GDP for a considerable number of countries. See Figure 2.

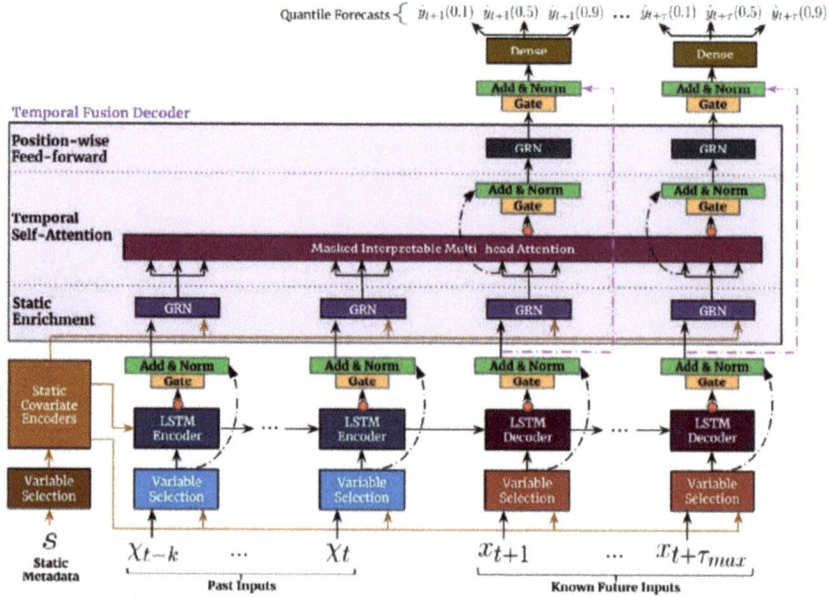

Figure 2. TFT architecture. Source: [14].

TFT has a complex architecture, which gives it enormous flexibility and computing potential, the main blocks being:

1-Gating mechanisms: Gating mechanisms give TFTs the ability to skip unused parts of the architecture. This is especially important in small or noisy datasets, where a simpler model can enhance performance (as the problem solved in this paper). This gated residual network (GRN) is one of the main blocks of TFTs. The GRN takes in the main input and a context vector and decides whether additional dense layers are useful or these layers can be skipped through the residual connection. See Figure 3.

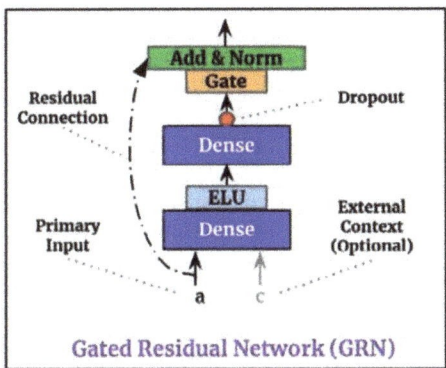

Figure 3. GRN Scheme. Source: [14].

2-Variable selection networks (VSN): In most prediction problems, we have variables that do not increase the prediction ability of the model. TFT introduced variable selection networks: this part of the architecture removes irrelevant inputs that decrease the algorithm performance and provides information about the most relevant variables just by analyzing the weights assigned to each one.

3-Static covariate encoders: TFT is able to use information from static data thanks to separate GRN encoders that produce different context vectors that are connected to several parts of the architecture. These kinds of encoders are especially important for our problem since they allow the model to train with data from different countries.

4-LSTM Encoder-Decoder: This sequence-to-sequence layer is used for local processing; it captures short-term time dependencies. Known future inputs are directly connected to the decoder.

5-Interpretable multi-head self-attention: TFT has a self-attention mechanism that makes the model capable of learning long-term relationships: it integrates information from any time step. This transformer architecture presents some changes in comparison to standard transformers ([104]); these modifications allow for conducting interpretability studies by the analysis of attention weights.

6-Dense layers: Several dense layers are part of the model; these layers learn through different non-linear transformations. The final dense layer generates prediction intervals in addition to point forecasts.

7-Loss function: TFT is trained by minimizing the quantile loss of all quantile outputs. We use the following quantiles: {0.02, 0.1, 0.25, 0.5, 0.75, 0.9, and 0.98}. The following equation represents the loss function:

$$\mathcal{L}(\Omega, W) = \sum_{y_t \in \Omega} \sum_{q \in Q} \sum_{\tau=1}^{\tau_{max}} \frac{QL(y_t, \hat{y}(q, t-\tau, \tau), q)}{M\tau_{max}} \qquad (1)$$

$$QL(y_t, \hat{y}, q) = q(y-\hat{y})_+ + (1-q)(\hat{y}-y)_+ \qquad (2)$$

4.2. Methodology

In this section, we provide a brief explanation of the data used in the training, validation, and test datasets, the hyperparameter configuration, and the model specifications for each forecast horizon.

The target value (y) of our neural network is the GDP logarithmic growth rate, expressed as:

$$y = \log \frac{GDP_{(t+s)}}{GDP_{(t)}}, \quad s = 1, 2, 3 \text{ or } 4 \tag{3}$$

where s denotes the number of quarters. For example, in the case of the annual growth rate forecast, it would be:

$$y = \log \frac{GDP_{(t+4)}}{GDP_{(t)}}. \tag{4}$$

This means that we will train our network with four different target values and different hyperparameters settings depending on the forecast horizon. We will measure the performance of the models using two different metrics, the RMSE and the MAE. For each date, the dataset is composed of the data from 25 OECD selected countries. Thus, we will simultaneously train and forecast for all of them.

The main disadvantage of machine learning models for macroeconomic forecasting is the lack of available data. We used the Python library PyTorch Forecasting to implement the TFT; this package does not have stochastic gradient descent available. Because of this, we need to refit the model for each forecast to incorporate the data from the latest available observation. This is critical to forecast the GDP since the economic paradigm can change suddenly.

As shown in Figure 4, the first observation that belongs to the test dataset is the first quarter of 2009 and the last one is the third quarter of 2021. PyTorch Forecasting uses the last available quarter as the validation dataset; therefore, the validation and test datasets will contain one observation per country in each forecast.

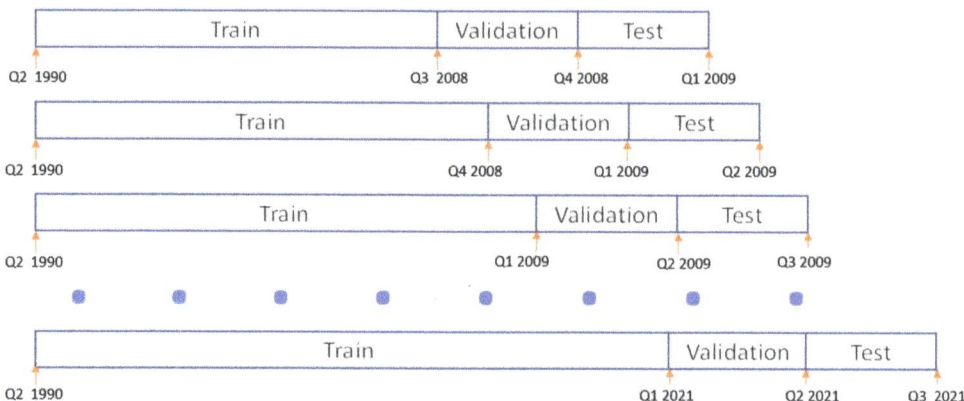

Figure 4. Quarterly prediction methodology.

When we make predictions greater than one quarter (s = 2, 3, or 4 quarters), the test dataset contains the GDP logarithmic growth rate that corresponds to those s periods. The forecast that we will use to check the model performance is the last one, in order to avoid overlapping data. We can see in Figure 5 how we may predict Q4 2009 when the last data available are Q4 2008. Even though our test dataset contains four annual growth rates, we only use the last one since it is the first prediction that does not contain any information from the test dataset.

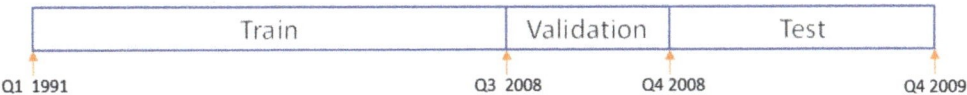

Figure 5. Annual prediction methodology.

The hyperparameters used to forecast at different time horizons are the same, with the only exception being the number of epochs. The main hyperparameters are shown in Table 1.

Table 1. Main hyperparameters.

Main Hyperparameters	Forecast Horizon			
	1Q	2Q	3Q	4Q
Epochs	13	17	19	20
Learning rate	0.03			
Dropout	0.1			
Number of heads	1			
State size	16			
Batch size	64			
Quantiles	0.02, 0.1, 0.25, 0.5, 0.75, 0.9, 0.98			
Normalized	GroupNormalizer			

The GroupNormalizer scales by groups (in this application, countries). It means that for each group, a scaler is fitted and applied.

In Appendix B, we added the code for annual predictions and how we compute the RMSE and the MAE for the whole dataset.

4.3. Sample Data and Variables

The database used in this paper comes from different combined sources corresponding to the period 1990–2021 for 25 OECD countries (See Table 2). (i) The Organization for Economic Co-operation and Development (OECD) for GDP in volume index, and main economic indicators; (ii) The Bank for International Settlements (BIS) for the Total Debt Non Financial Private Sectors over GDP; (iii) Federal Reserve Economic Data (FRED), Federal Reserve Bank of St. Louis for Credit Spreads; (iv) Netherlands Bureau for Economic Policy Analysis (CPB) for World Trade data; and (v) Bloomberg for CRB Raw Industrials Spot Index. Table 3 shows detailed information about the variables, the reason for use, and the sources.

Table 2. Selected countries.

Australia	Italy	United Kingdom
Austria	Japan	United States
Belgium	Korea	South Africa
Canada	Mexico	
Denmark	Netherlands	
Finland	New Zealand	
France	Norway	
Germany	Portugal	
Greece	Spain	
Iceland	Sweden	
Ireland	Switzerland	

Table 3. Variables description.

Variable	Definition	Reason of Use	Source
Dependent variable			
GDP logarithmic growth rate$_{it}$	GDP in volume index, hundredths, 2015 = 100, of every country i in year t.	Dependent variable for the country's economic growth.	OECD
Independent variables			
Idiosyncratic variables			
Yield curve (YC$_{it}$)	It is the ratio of long-term interest rates on sovereign debt to short-term interest rates.	The slope of the yield curve was shown empirically to be a significant predictor of inflation and real economic activity. Quite a few academic studies suggested that the slope of the yield curve seems to be extremely promising as a predictor of recessions. See [4–9]. We hypothesize that its impact on economic growth will depend on how it interacts non-linearly with the global credit spread cycle and official interest rates.	OECD
Debt non-financial private sectors/GDP (private debt/GDP)$_{it}$	Ratio of the total debt of non-financial private sectors at market value of one country over its nominal GDP. It is developed, calculated and updated by the Bank for International Settlements (BIS). This index is regularly updated.	It captures the progression of risk appetite and the debt accumulation process. During an economic expansion investors' risk appetite tends to increase; the longer the expansion, without any major setback, the higher the risk appetite, indebtedness, and economic growth—exactly the opposite during periods of deleveraging and private balance sheet recessions ([15,16,43,44,48,105–107]). Ref. [108] found an increase in the household debt to GDP ratio predicts lower GDP growth and higher unemployment in the medium run for an unbalanced panel of 30 countries from 1960 to 2012. Ref. [17] found for almost all of the 43 OECD countries analyzed that the private debt-to-GDP ratio is highly persistent. These results suggest long-lived effects of shocks to the private debt-to-GDP ratio, which require appropriate policy actions.	BIS
OECD composite leading indicator (CLI$_{it}$)	The OECD Composite Leading Indicator (CLI) is an aggregate time series displaying a reasonably consistent leading relationship with the reference series for the business cycle of a country (GDP). A CLI reading above (below) 100 is always an indication that anticipates levels of GDP above(below) long-term trend.	The composite leading indicator (CLI) is designed to provide early signals of turning points in business cycles showing fluctuation in the economic activity around its long term potential level. Different research found that the composite leading indicators (CLI) are useful for forecasting gross demand product (GDP), both in sample and in an out-of-sample real-time exercise ([4,32–34,38]).	OECD
Common variables			

Table 3. Cont.

Variable	Definition	Reason of Use	Source
Global Credit spread cycle (GCSC$_t$)	The ratio of the Moody's U.S. BAA corporate bond yields to that of AAA is taken as a proxy for the global credit spread cycle.	Much research indicates the usefulness of credit curve information to predict economic activity ([25–29,31]). Most unconventional monetary policies, such as asset purchase programs and forward guidance, aim to lower long-term rates, significantly affecting the information content of the yield curve. However, even in such circumstances, the behaviour of the corporate bond credit spread curve varies over the business cycle, potentially containing more information about the future economy. More recently, research ([30]) found credit spread curve information in higher deciles (implying low credit quality) is statistically significant and economically important for predicting the business cycle.	FRED, Federal Reserve Bank of St. Louis
CRB RIND Index (CRBRIND$_t$)	CRB Raw Industrials Spot Index	It is a measure of the price movements of 13 sensitive basic commodities whose markets are presumed to be among the first to be influenced by changes in economic conditions. As such, it serves as one early indication of impending changes in business activity.	Bloomberg
World Trade volume Index (WTVI$_t$)	The monthly world trade volume index is computed by the CPB (Netherlands Bureau for Economic Policy Analysis) and is defined as arithmetic average of world exports and world imports of goods. The series covers United States, Japan and EU and four groups of emerging countries: OPEC, Asian newly industrialised countries (Taiwan, Hong Kong, Singapore and South Korea), transition countries (central and eastern European countries including Turkey and ex-Soviet Union's countries) and other emerging economies	It is an indicator of global economic activity. Although, after the financial crisis in 2008, the growth rate in world trade is unusually low relative to growth in world GDP ([109]), a higher external demand increases the probability and/or intensity of exporting, and therefore, of economic growth, especially in periods where domestic demand is under pressure ([46–48]).	CPB

5. Results and Discussion

The TFT model is estimated for the 25 OECD countries listed in Table 2, focusing the analysis of the results of 10 representative countries that were selected taking into account their heterogeneity in terms of size, growth pattern (demand-led or export-led growth), and monetary sovereignty.

In this section, we present and discuss the most important results. First, in Section 5.1 we will discuss the results obtained over the entire test period for all forecast horizons and differentiating them across the 10 representative countries. Second, in Section 5.2, we will present the results across different sub-periods defined to observe differences in performance, depending on the stage of the business cycle. Finally, we will provide some concrete examples of TFT forecasts and their interpretability.

5.1. Performance over the Entire Period

Table 4 shows how TFT outperforms the standard ARIMA over the entire test period for the selected countries in two metrics: mean absolute error (MAE) and root mean square error (RMSE). Percentages reflect the error excess of ARIMA relative to TFT. For example, for an annual forecast, ARIMA RMSE is 188.27% higher than that of TFT. Improvements occur for all forecast time horizons.

Table 4. Improvement of the MAE and RMSE of TFT relative to ARIMA.

Metric	t + 1	t + 2	t + 3	t + 4
MAE	8.38%	33.89% ***	47.98% ***	48.53% ***
RMSE [a]	12.44%	88.80% ***	151.85% ***	157.07% ***

[a] RMSE is the average of the RMSEs calculated at country level. Note: *** significant coefficient at 1%.

To evaluate the statistical significance of the results, we perform a one-tailed hypothesis tests on the TFT error metrics. We compute the 99th percentile of the bootstrap distribution of the TFT error metrics and compare this critical value against the error metrics of the benchmark model. For the two metrics and across all forecast horizons', except for one quarter, ARIMA error measures are higher than the 99th percentile of the TFT error metric distribution, confirming that TFT error metrics are statistically lower than the ARIMA ones, at the 1% significance level (see Appendix A).

Table 5 shows the increases in the two considered error metrics (MAE and RMSE), for the ARIMA model with respect to the TFT in the 10 selected countries for the 1-quarter and 1-year forecasts. It shows that the TFT forecasts are usually more accurate than ARIMA, being that these improvements greater in demand-driven growth countries.

Table 5. Improvement of the MAE and RMSE of TFT relative to ARIMA by country.

		CAN	GER	DNK	SPA	FRA	GBR	ITA	JPN	POR	USA
MAE	t + 1	3.0%	−8.0%	11.0%	23.3%	20.8%	25.0%	−5.8%	5.0%	1.1%	−2.1%
	t + 4	17.0%	4.2%	12.0%	113.8%	78.3%	103.5%	41.6%	1.8%	49.1%	36.8%
RMSE	t + 1	9.1%	−19.1%	16.9%	21.1%	20.6%	45.4%	−0.7%	−1.1%	1.4%	2.4%
	t + 4	63.3%	12.3%	7.6%	327.2%	205.2%	416.5%	92.0%	2.7%	127.1%	128.2%

One of TFT's most interesting features is its interpretability. Figure 6 shows the encoder variables importance for one quarter (LHS) and annual (RHS) forecasts.

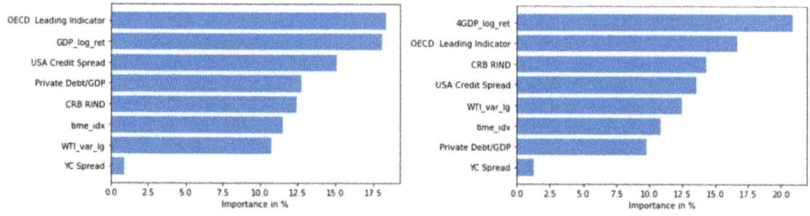

Figure 6. Encoder variables importance for one quarter (**left** hand side) and annual predictions (**right** hand side).

As expected, the most important predictor is the nearest lag of real GDP growth, which reflects the autoregressive behavior of the time series. Likewise, the OECD Leading Indicator Index provides early signals of turning points in business cycles ([4,32–34,109]). The CRB Raw Industrial Spot Index's relevance confirms it serves as an early indicator of impending changes in global business activity ([41]). The change in the World Trade Volume Index is an indicator of the global external demand, and its importance depicts how it affects countries' business activity.

It is remarkable the predictive capacity of the variable that captures the indebtedness of the non-financial private sectors as a percentage of GDP, which played a catalytic role in the Great Recession once the value of collateral began to deteriorate in accordance with Hyman Minsky's financial instability hypothesis ([15,16]). Recent studies provide evidence on the high persistence of the ratio of private debt to GDP for different OECD countries and the key importance of macroprudential policy in this area ([17]).

Related to this variable, our proxy of global credit spread cycle (USA Credit Spread) is economically important for predicting the business cycle ([25–31]). In contrast, the limited forecasting capacity of the yield curve in TFT suggests that the slope of the sovereign debt interest rate curve diminished its predictive power, compared to previous work ([4–9]), in anticipating the evolution of the business cycle. This loss of forecasting accuracy occurs in a context where quantitative easing policies gained importance. More research is needed to understand the effects of quantitative easing on the yield curve's predictive power.

5.2. Performance over Expansive and Recessive Periods

A comparison of TFT versus ARIMA was performed in both recession and expansion sub-periods in order to give greater robustness to the results obtained at a global level. Table 6 shows how TFT clearly outperforms the standard ARIMA during the COVID-19 pandemic and behaves almost equally in the rest of sub-periods. The difference in performance between both models increases in long-term forecasts due to the TFT ability to capture nonlinearities.

Table 6. Improvement of the MAE and RMSE [a] of TFT relative to ARIMA by period.

Period	Metric	t + 1	t + 2	t + 3	t + 4
2008–2011	MAE	13.82%	10.04%	−3.54%	−5.85%
	RMSE [a]	10.96%	5.31%	−3.52%	−4.14%
2012–2015	MAE	0.18%	−2.42%	8.01%	26.59%
	RMSE [a]	−2.76%	−0.99%	4.35%	21.72%
2016–2019	MAE	−4.85%	6.56%	−10.54%	0.67%
	RMSE [a]	−6.20%	4.83%	−6.85%	0.01%
2020–2021 (Q3)	MAE	9.43%	56.12%	116.82%	115.92%
	RMSE [a]	12.47%	94.64%	190.81%	204.09%

[a] RMSE is the average of the RMSEs calculated at country level.

Table 7 exhibits the increases in the two considered error metrics (MAE and RMSE), for the ARIMA model with respect to the TFT, in the 10 selected countries for 1-year forecasts over the different sub-periods. In general, TFT forecasts are more accurate than those of the ARIMA, being that these improvements are greater in periods of economic slowdown or recession, in particular, in demand-driven growth countries.

Table 7. Improvement of the MAE and RMSE of TFT relative to ARIMA by period and country in annual forecast.

Period	Metric	CAN	DEU	DNK	ESP	FRA	GBR	ITA	JPN	POR	USA
2008–2011	MAE	−13.4%	−14.2%	10.0%	9.0%	−20.8%	−31.0%	−1.7%	−2.1%	19.9%	−7.4%
	RMSE	−0.7%	−13.0%	5.3%	−0.2%	−10.2%	−18.5%	1.0%	−2.2%	5.3%	−5.9%
2012–2015	MAE	15.8%	−10.2%	27.4%	49.4%	34.3%	−27.8%	100.2%	3.2%	81.0%	−17.7%
	RMSE	6.4%	−5.8%	21.6%	32.9%	29.5%	−26.6%	70.2%	−2.3%	74.1%	7.4%
2016–2019	MAE	−15.8%	80.5%	6.5%	−11.7%	40.0%	−24.0%	−21.3%	−17.2%	−29.0%	40.2%
	RMSE	−11.0%	77.6%	−2.4%	−21.0%	38.3%	−23.3%	−18.7%	−22.5%	−23.0%	41.8%
2020–2021 (Q3)	MAE	61.6%	19.1%	11.6%	201.3%	140.6%	237.5%	68.6%	18.4%	79.1%	111.8%
	RMSE	94.9%	41.6%	12.3%	363.3%	219.7%	476.6%	105.7%	16.2%	149.7%	190.8%

5.3. Forecast Examples

In order to provide a better understanding of the TFT, in this section, we present concrete examples of its predictions and their interpretability. We show the quantile forecast for Spain and the United States for two years, 2011 and 2017. The first year displays how the model works in a period of turbulence, while the second presents its performance in a period of stable growth.

Figure 7 represents the quantile forecast for Spain (LHS) and the USA (RHS) for the year 2011. In addition to the point forecasts (orange line), the confidence intervals for different significance levels (2%, 10%, 25%, 50%, 75%, 90%, and 98%) are plotted. The primary y-axis represents the accumulated logarithmic growth rate, while the secondary y-axis provides information of which of the previous periods has more importance in each prediction. This aspect is obtained by analyzing the attention weights. As expected, the Great Recession has a great importance.

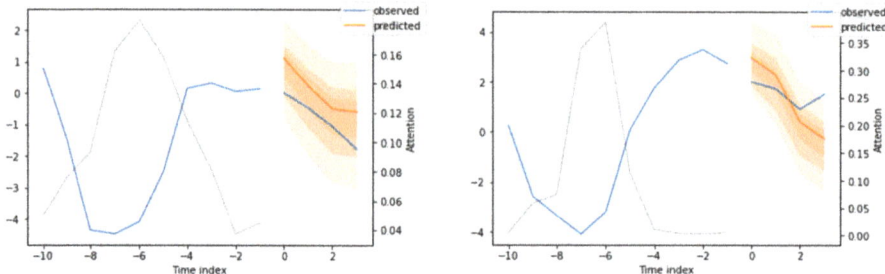

Figure 7. 2011 quantile forecast for Spain (**left** hand side) and the USA (**right** hand side).

Figure 8 shows the encoder variables importance for the 2011 forecast. Variable time_idx, which represents the temporal sequence, is the most important one, followed by the World Trade Volume Index, the autoregressive component, the OECD Leading Indicator, and the CRB Raw Industrial Spot Index. Otherwise, the private debt to GDP ratio and our proxy of global credit spread cycle (USA Credit Spread) are not as relevant, as most of private deleveraging process already occurred. Finally, the yield curve spread predictive power is almost insignificant.

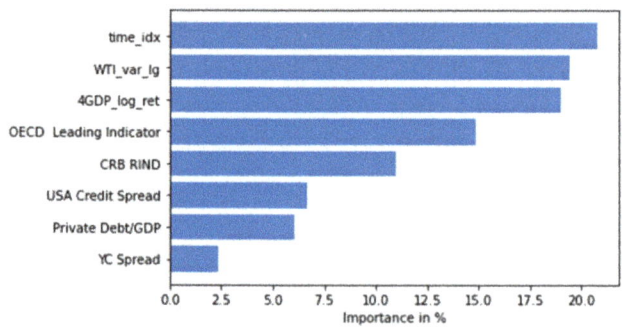

Figure 8. Encoder variables importance for the year 2011 forecast.

Figure 9 displays the quantile forecasting results for Spain (LHS) and the USA (RHS) in 2017, including the predicted values compared to the observed ones, the prediction intervals, and the relative importance of each lag in the forecast (grey line).

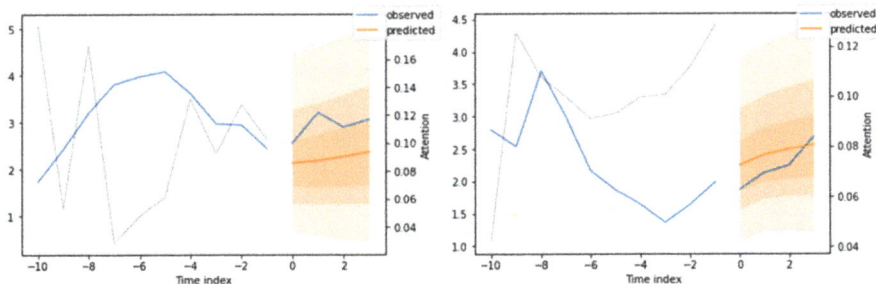

Figure 9. 2017 quantile forecast for Spain (**left** hand side) and USA (**right** hand side).

Figure 10 depicts the encoder variables importance for the 2017 forecast. The variable that captures the temporal sequence (time_idx) is revealed as the most important one, followed by the autoregressive component and the OECD leading indicator.

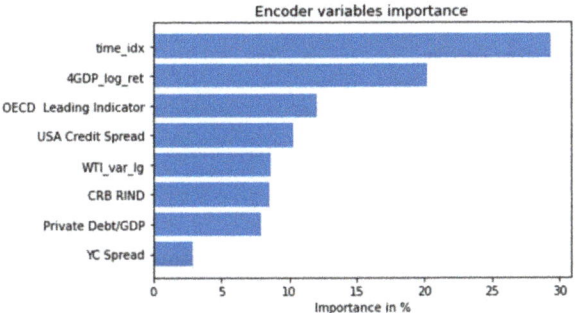

Figure 10. Encoder variables importance for the 2017 forecast.

6. Concluding Remarks

The main contribution of this paper is that it is the first to apply a new artificial intelligence architecture, TFTs, recently developed by [14], to the joint forecasting of GDP growth for a large number of OECD countries at different time horizons. Its relevance lies in the fact that this AI architecture offers important comparative advantages over regression models and other deep learning methods in a context where the time series characteristics of business cycle indicators are affected by long-run non-linearities. Mainly, it enables the training of the model on multiple time series from different distributions; it allows for visualizing persistent temporal patterns and identifying significant events and different regimes, providing quantile regressions for forecasts and interpretable results since the impact of each explanatory variable is quantified.

Future research aims to reinforce and improve the results obtained, incorporating additionally countries and more explanatory variables. Furthermore, it will be necessary to compare their results with models that are much richer than baseline ARIMA models, both regression models (dynamic factor models [110]) and deep learning models, especially state-of-the-art methods such as the sample convolution and interaction network (SCINet) [111], Informer [112], DeepAR [84], or frequency improved legendre memory model (FiLM) [113].

The results of the joint GDP forecasting of 25 OECD countries at different time horizons—one, two, three, and four quarters—using macroeconomic and financial variables outperform those obtained with the benchmark (ARIMA) in terms of both the MAE and the RMSE, especially in periods of turbulence, such as the COVID-19 shock. The obtained results show that TFT forecasts improvements are greater in the demand-driven growth countries than in export-led growth ones.

The use of TFTs to predict real GDP yields very interesting results regarding the importance of the explanatory variables. The relative importance of variables might vary somewhat, depending on the phase of the economic cycle or the forecast time horizon. It is remarkable the predictive capacity of the autoregressive component and the OECD composite leading indicator, in addition to the CRB Raw Industrial Spot Index, as well as the variable that captures the indebtedness of the non-financial private sectors, which is related to our proxy of global credit spread cycle (USA Credit Spread), and the world trade indicator. On the opposite side, it is worth highlighting the low predictive power of the slope of the yield curve.

Future research should exploit the one main ability of TFTs, which is the possibility of incorporating the effects of known future inputs in the predictions. It allows policymakers to perform the impact assessment of changes in instrumental economic variables, such as interest rates, taxes, etc. Given that one of the findings in this paper are the importance of private debt in forecasting real GDP, this framework could be used to simulate the effects of credit tightening measures.

Finally, it would be very interesting to exploit one of the most outstanding features of TFTs, the possibility of identifying different economic regimes. Several studies ([114–116]) suggest the hypothesis that, in the last decades, the only source of growth in the western countries is bubble generation (financial or real estate). This new AI architecture would be useful to identify the blow-up periods and the subsequent bursting ones.

In short, TFTs are revealed as a new AI tool available to economists and policymakers, with enormous potential in the prediction of economic cycles.

Author Contributions: All authors have contributed equally. All authors have read and agreed to the published version of the manuscript.

Funding: This research received no external funding.

Data Availability Statement: Data available on request.

Conflicts of Interest: The authors declare no conflict of interest.

Appendix A. One Sided Tests for the Outperforming of TFT GDP Forecast with Respect the Benchmark ARIMA

We formally test the improvement of the MAE and RMSE metrics of TFT relative to ARIMA using the bootstrap one-sided test. The null hypothesis is that the difference between the metrics of both estimation procedures is not significant against the alternative hypothesis of the metric, for the TFT is lower than that for the ARIMA. We compute the 99% critical value of the distribution of the TFT metric (MAE or RMSE) using bootstrap resampling. Then, we calculate the percentage difference of the ARIMA metric (MAE or RMSE, respectively) relative to this bootstrap critical value. As shown in Table A1, for both metrics, all the test-statistics for periods greater than one quarter are positive. Therefore, we can conclude that TFT outperforms ARIMA at the 99% significance level for most prediction horizons.

Table A1. Percentage difference of the ARIMA performance metric (MAE and RMSE) of ARIMA relative to the 99% critical value of the bootstrap distribution for the TFT metric.

Metric	t + 1	t + 2	t + 3	t + 4
MAE	−18.59%	8.21%	25.02%	26.22%
RMSE [a]	−20.05%	60.46%	118.43%	120.20%

[a] RMSE is the average of the RMSE calculated at country level.

Appendix B. Code for Annual Forecast

```python
import copy
from pathlib import Path
import warnings
import numpy as np
import pandas as pd
import pytorch_lightning as pl
from pytorch_lightning.callbacks import EarlyStopping, LearningRateMonitor
from pytorch_lightning.loggers import TensorBoardLogger
import torch
from pytorch_forecasting import Baseline, TemporalFusionTransformer, TimeSeriesDataSet
from pytorch_forecasting.data import GroupNormalizer, EncoderNormalizer
from pytorch_forecasting.metrics import SMAPE, PoissonLoss, QuantileLoss
from pytorch_forecasting.models.temporal_fusion_transformer.tuning import optimize_hyperparameters
from pytorch_forecasting.metrics import RMSE
import tensorflow as tf
import tensorboard as tb
tf.io.gfile = tb.compat.tensorflow_stub.io.gfile


Df = pd.read_excel('Pruebas/PRUEBAS_4T/Completed_25_14052022.xlsx', header=0, parse_dates=['Date'])
Df['4GDP_log_ret'] = Df['4GDP_log_ret'].replace(0, np.NaN)
Df = Df.dropna(subset=['4GDP_log_ret'])


"""     1-Function creation      """
def Create_Model(Df_train, max_encoder_length, max_prediction_length, Variable_to_predict):
    # DEFINE PARAMETERS
    batch_size = 64 # set this between 32 to 128
    training = TimeSeriesDataSet(
        Df_train,
        time_idx="time_idx",
```

```python
    target=Variable_to_predict,
    group_ids=["Country"],
    min_encoder_length=max_encoder_length // 2,  # keep encoder length long (as it is in the validation set)
    max_encoder_length=max_encoder_length,
    min_prediction_length=1,
    max_prediction_length=max_prediction_length,
    static_categoricals=["Country"],
    time_varying_known_reals=["time_idx"],
    time_varying_unknown_reals=[
        "#GDP_log_ret",
        'USA Credit Spread',
        'CRB RIND',
        'WTI_var_1Q',
        'YC Spread',
        'Private Debt/GDP',
        'OECD Leading Indicator',
    ],
    target_normalizer=GroupNormalizer(groups=["Country"], transformation="softplus"),
    add_relative_time_idx=False,
    add_target_scales=True,
    add_encoder_length=True,
    allow_missing_timesteps=False,
)
pl.seed_everything(42)
# create dataloaders for model
train_dataloader = training.to_dataloader(train=True, batch_size=batch_size, num_workers=0)
validation = TimeSeriesDataSet.from_dataset(training, Df_train, predict=True, stop_randomization=True)
val_dataloader = validation.to_dataloader(train=False, batch_size=batch_size * 10, num_workers=0)

"""                 MODEL CREATION              """
# configure network and trainer
early_stop_callback = EarlyStopping(monitor="val_loss", min_delta=1e-4, patience=10, verbose=False, mode="min")
lr_logger = LearningRateMonitor()  # log the learning rate
logger = TensorBoardLogger("lightning_logs")  # logging results to a tensorboard
trainer = pl.Trainer(
    max_epochs=20,
    gpus=0,
    weights_summary="top",
    gradient_clip_val=0.1,
    limit_train_batches=45,  #
    callbacks=[lr_logger, early_stop_callback],
    logger=logger,
```

```python
    )

    tft = TemporalFusionTransformer.from_dataset(
        training,
        learning_rate=0.03,
        hidden_size=16,  # most important hyperparameter apart from learning rate
        attention_head_size=1,
        dropout=0.1,
        hidden_continuous_size=8,
        output_size=7,
        loss=QuantileLoss(),
        reduce_on_plateau_patience=4,
    )
    print(f"Number of parameters in network: {tft.size()/1e3:.1f}k")
    return (train_dataloader, val_dataloader, tft, trainer)
Nper = 52  # number of periods to predict
max_prediction_length = 4
max_encoder_length = 10
Date_inicial = "2008-03-01"  # first date to predict
Variable_to_predict = "dGDP_log_ret"
idx_first_pred = (Df.loc[(Df['Date'] == Date_inicial), "time_idx"][:1].to_numpy()[0])
# first idx
Country_List = ['CAN', 'DEU', 'DNK', 'ESP', 'FRA', 'GBR', 'ITA', 'JPN', 'POR', 'USA']
Country_U_Dict = {
    "CAN": {}, "DEU": {}, "DNK": {}, "ESP": {}, "FRA": {},
    "GBR": {}, "ITA": {}, "JPN": {}, "POR": {}, "USA": {}
}

for i in range(idx_first_pred, (idx_first_pred + Nper)):
    Df_train = Df[Df["time_idx"] < i]
    train_dataloader, val_dataloader, tft, trainer = Create_Model(Df_train, max_encoder_length,
max_prediction_length, Variable_to_predict)
    pl.seed_everything(42)

    # fit network
    trainer.fit(tft, train_dataloaders=train_dataloader, val_dataloaders=val_dataloader)
    # load the best model according to the validation loss
    # (given that we use early stopping, this is not necessarily the last epoch)
    best_model_path = trainer.checkpoint_callback.best_model_path
    best_tft = TemporalFusionTransformer.load_from_checkpoint(best_model_path)

    #       DEFINE PREDICTION DATASET
    Dfpred = Df[((Df["time_idx"] >= (i - max_encoder_length)) & (Df["time_idx"] < (i + max_prediction_length)))]
```

```python
    prediction, prediction_index_df = best_tft.predict(Dfpred, return_index=True)
    prediction2 = prediction.numpy()  # pick first prediction after encoding
    Prediction2 = np.transpose(prediction2)
    Prediction_Df = pd.DataFrame(data=Prediction2, columns=prediction_index_df["Country"].to_numpy())
    for j in Country_List:
        U = 0
        Prediction_Values_Selected_Country = Prediction_Df[j].to_numpy()
        Real_Values = Df[Df["time_idx"] >= i]
        Real_Values_Selected_Country = Real_Values[Real_Values["Country"] == j]
        Real_Values_Selected_Country_Period = Real_Values_Selected_Country[Variable_to_predict][
            :max_prediction_length].to_numpy()
        U = Real_Values_Selected_Country_Period - Prediction_Values_Selected_Country
        Country_U_Dict[j].append(U)

"""              WHOLE DATASET        """
#                         MAE
Country_U_Dict_Copy = Country_U_Dict.copy()  # we generate a copy so we can keep the original data
Country_U_Dict_row_mean = {
    "CAN": [], "DEU": [], "DNK": [], "ESP": [], "FRA": [],
    "GBR": [], "ITA": [], "JPN": [], "POR": [], "USA": []}
# We generate an empty dictionary to save the final values
Um = []
U_mae_todos_paises_TFT = []
for j in Country_List:
    # j="DNK"
    Country_U_Dict_Copy[j] = np.array(Country_U_Dict_Copy[j])
    Country_U_Dict_Copy[j] = np.transpose(Country_U_Dict_Copy[j])
    Country_U_Dict_Copy[j] = np.abs(Country_U_Dict_Copy[j])
    U_mae_todos_paises_TFT.append(Country_U_Dict_Copy[j])
    Country_U_Dict_row_mean[j] = np.mean(Country_U_Dict_Copy[j], axis=1)
    Um.append(Country_U_Dict_row_mean[j])
Um = np.array(Um)
Um = np.transpose(Um)
Umbis = np.mean(Um, axis=1)
UmDf = pd.DataFrame(data=Um, columns=Country_List)

#                         RMSE
Country_U_Dict_Copy_R = Country_U_Dict.copy()
Country_U_Dict_row_mean_R = {
    "CAN": [], "DEU": [], "DNK": [], "ESP": [], "FRA": [],
    "GBR": [], "ITA": [], "JPN": [], "POR": [], "USA": []}
# We generate an empty dictionary to save the final values
```

References

1. Stockhammer, E. Financialisation and the slowdown of accumulation. *Camb. J. Econ.* **2004**, *28*, 719–741. [CrossRef]
2. Christodoulou-Volos, C.; Siokis, F.M. Long-range dependence in stock market returns. *Appl. Financ. Econ.* **2006**, *16*, 1331–1338. [CrossRef]
3. Murialdo, P.; Ponta, L.; Carbone, A. Long-range dependence in financial markets: A moving average cluster entropy approach. *Entropy* **2020**, *22*, 634. [CrossRef] [PubMed]
4. Estrella, A.; Mishkin, F.S.; Predicting, U.S. recessions: Financial variables as leading indicators. *Rev. Econ. Stat.* **1998**, *80*, 45–61. [CrossRef]
5. Chauvet, M.; Potter, S. Forecasting recessions using the yield curve. *J. Forecast.* **2005**, *24*, 77–103. [CrossRef]
6. Estrella, A. Why does the yield curve predict output and inflation? *Econ. J.* **2005**, *11*, 722–744. [CrossRef]
7. Kauppi, H.; Saikkonen, P. Predicting US recessions with dynamic binary response models. *Rev. Econ. Stat.* **2008**, *90*, 777–791. [CrossRef]
8. Katayama, M. *Improving Recession Probability Forecasts in the US Economy*; Working Paper; Louisiana State University: Baton Rouge, LA, USA, 2009.
9. Hamilton, J.D. Calling recessions in real time. *Int. J. Forecast.* **2011**, *27*, 1006–1026. [CrossRef]
10. Van Dijk, D.; Franses, P.H.; Paap, R. A nonlinear long memory model, with an application to US unemployment. *J. Econom.* **2002**, *110*, 135–165. [CrossRef]
11. Cuestas, J.C.; Garratt, D. Is real GDP per capita a stationary process? Smooth transitions, nonlinear trends and unit root testing. *Empir. Econ.* **2011**, *41*, 555–563. [CrossRef]
12. Choudhry, T.; Papadimitriou, F.I.; Shabi, S. Stock market volatility and business cycle: Evidence from linear and nonlinear causality tests. *J. Bank. Financ.* **2016**, *66*, 89–101. [CrossRef]
13. Cerra, M.V.; Fatás, A.; Saxena, M.S.C. *Hysteresis and Business Cycles*; International Monetary Fund: Washington, DC, USA, 2020.
14. Lim, B.; Arık, S.Ö.; Loeff, N.; Pfister, T. Temporal Fusion Transformers for Interpretable Multi-Horizon Time Series Forecasting. *Int. J. Forecast.* **2021**, *37*, 1748–1764. [CrossRef]
15. Minsky, H.P. *Stabilizing an Unstable Economy*; Yale University Press: New Haven, CT, USA, 1986.
16. Minsky, H.P. *The financial Instability Hypothesis*; Working Paper 74; The Jerome Levy Economics Institute of Bard College: Annandale-On-Hudson, NY, USA, 1992.
17. Caporale, G.M.; Gil-Alana, L.A.; Malmierca, M. Persistence in the private debt-t-GDP ratio: Evidence from 43 OECD countries. *Appl. Econ.* **2021**, *53*, 5018–5027. [CrossRef]
18. Stock, J.H.; Watson, M.W. Forecasting output and inflation: The role of asset prices. *J. Econ. Lit.* **2003**, *41*, 788–829. [CrossRef]
19. Harvey, C. The real term structure and consumption growth. *J. Financ. Econ.* **1988**, *22*, 305–333. [CrossRef]
20. Laurent, R.D. An interest rate-based indicator of monetary policy. *Econ. Perspect.* **1988**, *12*, 3–14.
21. Estrella, A.; Hardouvelis, G. The term structure as a predictor of real economic activity. *J. Financ.* **1991**, *46*, 555–576. [CrossRef]
22. Estrella, A.; Mishkin, F.S. The term structure of interest rates and its role in monetary policy in Europe and the United States: Implications for the European Central Bank. *Eur. Econ. Rev.* **1997**, *41*, 1375–1401. [CrossRef]
23. Bernard, H.; Gerlach, S. Does the term structure predict recessions? The international evidence. *Int. J. Financ. Econ.* **1998**, *3*, 195–215. [CrossRef]
24. Taylor, J.B. Discretion versus policy rules in practice. *J. Monet. Econ.* **1993**, *39*, 195–214. [CrossRef]
25. Gilchrist, S.; Yankov, V.; Zakrajšek, E. Credit market shocks and economic fluctuations: Evidence from corporate bond and stock markets. *J. Monet. Econ.* **2009**, *56*, 471–493. [CrossRef]
26. Gilchrist, S.; Zakrajšek, E. Credit spreads and business cycle fluctuations. *Am. Econ. Rev.* **2012**, *102*, 1692–1720. [CrossRef]

27. Faust, J.; Gilchrist, S.; Wright, J.H.; Zakrajšek, E. Credit spreads as predictors of real-time economic activity: A Bayesian model-averaging approach. *Rev. Econ. Stat.* **2013**, *95*, 1501–1519. [CrossRef]
28. Bleaney, M.; Mizen, P.; Veleanu, V. Bond spreads and economic activity in eight European economies. *Econ. J.* **2016**, *126*, 2257–2291. [CrossRef]
29. Okimoto, T.; Takaoka, S. The term structure of credit spreads and business cycle in Japan. *J. Jpn. Int.* **2017**, *45*, 27–36. [CrossRef]
30. Okimoto, T.; Takaoka, S. The credit spread curve distribution and economic fluctuations in Japan. *J. Int. Money Financ.* **2022**, *122*, 102582. [CrossRef]
31. Gilchrist, S.; Mojon, B. Credit risk in the Euro area. *Econ. J.* **2018**, *128*, 118–158. [CrossRef]
32. Hamilton, J.D.; Pérez-Quirós, G. Do the Leading Indicators Lead? *J. Bus.* **1996**, *69*, 27–49. [CrossRef]
33. Banerjee, T.; Marcellino, M. Are there any reliable leading indicators for US inflation and GDP growth? *Int. J. Forecast.* **2006**, *22*, 137–151. [CrossRef]
34. Kulendran, N.; Wong, K.F. Determinants versus Composite Leading Indicators in Predicting Turning Points in Growth Cycle. *J. Travel Res.* **2011**, *50*, 417–430. [CrossRef]
35. Tkacova, A.; Gavurova, B.; Behun, M. The Composite Leading Indicator for German Business Cycle. *J. Compet.* **2017**, *9*, 114–133. [CrossRef]
36. OECD. Composite Leading Indicator (CLI). 2023. Available online: https://data.oecd.org/leadind/composite-leading-indicator-cli.htm (accessed on 2 May 2023).
37. Hanson, M.S. The "price puzzle" reconsidered. *J. Monet. Econ.* **2004**, *51*, 1385–1413. [CrossRef]
38. Beckmann, J.; Belke, A.; Czudaj, R. Does global liquidity drive commodity prices? *J. Bank. Financ.* **2014**, *48*, 224–234. [CrossRef]
39. Belke, A.; Bordon, I.; Hendricks, T.W. Monetary policy, global liquidity and commodity price dynamics. *N. Am. J. Econ. Financ.* **2014**, *28*, 1–16. [CrossRef]
40. Yardeni, E. *Predicting the Markets*; YRI Press: Brookville, NY, USA, 2018.
41. Ge, Y.; Tang, K. Commodity prices and GDP growth. *Int. Rev. Financial Anal.* **2020**, *71*, 101512. [CrossRef]
42. Mian, A.R.; Sufi, A. Finance and business cycles: The credit-driven household demand channel. *J. Econ. Perspect.* **2018**, *32*, 31–58. [CrossRef]
43. Minsky, H.P. *Can It Happen Again?* M.E. Sharpe: New York, NY, USA, 1984.
44. Minsky, H.P. *The Financial Instability Process: A Restatement*; Post Keynesian Economic Theory; Arestis, P., Shouras, T., Eds.; Wheatsheaf Books: Sussex, UK, 1985.
45. Singh, T. Does International Trade Cause Economic Growth? A Survey. *World Econ.* **2010**, *33*, 1517–1564. [CrossRef]
46. Esteves, P.S.; Rua, A. Is there a role for domestic demand pressure on export performance? *Empir. Econ.* **2015**, *49*, 1173–1189. [CrossRef]
47. Bobeica, E.; Esteves, P.S.; Rua, A.; Staehr, K. Exports and domestic demand pressure: A dynamic panel data model for the euro area countries. *Rev. World Econ.* **2016**, *152*, 107–125. [CrossRef]
48. Laborda, J.; Salas, V.; Suárez, C. Manufacturing firms' export activity: Business and financial cycles overlaps! *Int. Econ.* **2020**, *162*, 1–14. [CrossRef]
49. Frankel, J.A.; Rose, A.K. The endogeneity of the optimum currency area criteria. *Econ. J.* **1998**, *108*, 1009–1025. [CrossRef]
50. Clark, T.E.; Van Wincoop, E. Borders and business cycle. *J. Int. Econ.* **2001**, *55*, 59–85. [CrossRef]
51. De Soyres, F.; Gaillard, A. Global trade and GDP comovement. *J. Econ. Dyn. Control* **2022**, *138*, 104353. [CrossRef]
52. Imbs, J. Trade, finance, specialization and synchronization. *Rev. Econ. Stat.* **2004**, *86*, 723–734. [CrossRef]
53. Box, G.; Jenkins, G.M. *Time Series Analysis; Forecasting and Control*; Holden-Day: San Francisco, CA, USA, 1970.
54. Kirchgässner, G.; Wolters, J.; Hassler, U. Univariate stationary processes. In *Introduction to Modern Time Series Analysis*; Springer: Berlin/Heidelberg, Germany, 2013; pp. 27–93. [CrossRef]
55. Chatfield, C. *The Analysis of Time Series: An Introduction*; CRC Press: Boca Raton, FL, USA, 2016.
56. Sims, C.A. Macroeconomics and reality. *Econometrica* **1980**, *48*, 1–48. [CrossRef]
57. Hamilton, J.D. A new approach to the economic analysis of nonstationary time series and the business cycle. *Econometrica* **1989**, *57*, 357–384. [CrossRef]
58. Litterman, R.B. Forecasting with bayesian vector autoregressions-Five years of experience. *J. Bus. Econ. Stat.* **1986**, *4*, 25–38. [CrossRef]
59. Spencer, D.E. Developing a bayesian vector autoregression forecasting model. *Int. J. Forecast.* **1993**, *9*, 407–421. [CrossRef]
60. Bernanke, B.; Blinder, A. The Federal funds rate and the channels of monetary transmission. *Am. Econ. Rev.* **1992**, *82*, 901–921.
61. Sims, C.A. Interpreting the macroeconomic time series facts: The effects of monetary policy. *Eur. Econ. Rev.* **1992**, *36*, 975–1000. [CrossRef]
62. D'Agostino, A.; Gambetti, L.; Giannone, D. Macroeconomic forecasting and structural change. *J. Appl. Econ.* **2013**, *28*, 82–101. [CrossRef]
63. Korobilis, D. VAR forecasting using bayesian variable selection. *J. Appl. Econ.* **2013**, *28*, 204–230. [CrossRef]
64. Koop, G.; Korobilis, D. Large time-varying parameter VARs. *J. Econom.* **2013**, *177*, 185–198. [CrossRef]
65. Terasvirta, T.; Anderson, H.M. Characterizing nonlinearities in business cycles using smooth transition autoregressive models. *J. Appl. Econ.* **1992**, *7*, S119–S136. [CrossRef]

66. Granger, C.W.; Teräsvirta, T.; Anderson, H.M. Modeling nonlinearity over the business cycle. In *Business Cycles, Indicators and Forecasting*; University of Chicago Press: Chicago, IL, USA, 1993; pp. 311–326.
67. Granger, C.W.; Terasvirta, T. *Modelling Non-Linear Economic Relationships*; OUP Catalogue: Oxford, UK, 1993.
68. Escribano, A.; Jorda, O. *Improved Testing and Specification of Smooth Transition Regression Models*; Nonlinear Time Series Analysis of Economic and Financial Data; Springer: Boston, MA, USA, 1999; pp. 289–319.
69. Tsay, R.S. Testing and modelling threshold autoregressive processes. *J. Am. Stat. Assoc.* **1989**, *84*, 231–240. [CrossRef]
70. Tiao, G.C.; Tsay, R.S. Some advances in non-linear and adaptive modelling in time series. *J. Forecast.* **1994**, *13*, 109–131. [CrossRef]
71. Chen, R.; Langnau, A. Turning Points Detection of Business Cycles: A Model Comparison. 2010. Available online: https://ssrn.com/abstract=1680828 (accessed on 1 May 2023). [CrossRef]
72. Hamilton, J.D. Specification testing in Markov-switching time-series models. *J. Econom.* **1996**, *70*, 127–157. [CrossRef]
73. Filardo, A.J. Business-cycle phases and their transitional dynamics. *J. Bus. Econ. Stat.* **1994**, *12*, 299–308. [CrossRef]
74. McCulloch, R.E.; Tsay, R.S. Statistical analysis of economic time series via Markov switching models. *J. Time Ser. Anal.* **1994**, *15*, 523–539. [CrossRef]
75. Filardo, A.J.; Gordon, S.F. Business cycle durations. *J. Econom.* **1998**, *85*, 99–123. [CrossRef]
76. Kim, C.J.; Nelson, C.R. *State Space Models with Regime Switching: Classical and Gibbs-Sampling Approaches with Applications*; MIT Press: Cambridge, MA, USA, 1999.
77. Camacho, M.; Perez-Quiros, G.; Poncela, P. *Extracting Nonlinear Signals from Several Economic Indicators*; Bank of Spain Working Paper 1202; Bank of Spain: Madrid, Spain, 2012.
78. Camacho, M.; Perez-Quiros, G.; Poncela, P. *Markov-Switching Dynamic Factor Models in Real Time*; Bank of Spain Working Paper 1205; Bank of Spain: Madrid, Spain, 2012.
79. Krolzig, H.M. *Markov-Switching Vector Autoregressions: Modelling, Statistical Inference, and Application to Business Cycle Analysis*; Springer Science & Business Media: Berlin, Germany, 2013; Volume 454.
80. Balcilar, M.; Gupta, R.; Majumdar, A.; Miller, S.M. Was the recent downturn in US real GDP predictable? *Appl. Econ.* **2015**, *47*, 2985–3007. [CrossRef]
81. Mullainathan, S.; Spiess, J. Machine learning: An applied econometric approach. *J. Econ. Perspect.* **2017**, *31*, 87–106. [CrossRef]
82. Varian, H.R. Big data: New tricks for econometrics. *J. Econ. Perspect.* **2014**, *28*, 3–28. [CrossRef]
83. Yu, H.F.; Rao, N.; Dhillon, I.S. Temporal regularized matrix factorization for high-dimensional time series prediction. In Proceedings of the Advances in Neural Information Processing Systems NeurIPS Proceedings, Barcelona, Spain, 5–10 December 2016.
84. Salinas, D.; Flunkert, V.; Gasthaus, J.; Januschowski, T. DeepAR: Probabilistic forecasting with autoregressive recurrent networks. *Int. J. Forecast.* **2020**, *36*, 1181–1191. [CrossRef]
85. Plakandaras, V.; Gupta, R.; Gogas, P.; Papadimitriou, T. Forecasting the US real house price index. *Econ. Model.* **2015**, *45*, 259–267. [CrossRef]
86. Heber, G.; Lunde, A.; Shephard, N.; Sheppard, K. *Oxford-Man Institute's Realized Library*; Version 0.1; University Of Oxford: Oxford, UK, 2009.
87. Medeiros, M.C.; Vasconcelos, G.F.R.; Veiga, Á.; Zilberman, E. Forecasting inflation in a data-rich environment: The benefits of machine learning methods. *J. Bus. Econ. Stat.* **2019**, *39*, 98–119. [CrossRef]
88. Inoue, A.; Kilian, L. How useful is bagging in forecasting economic time series? A Case study of US consumer price inflation. *J. Am. Stat. Assoc.* **2008**, *103*, 511–522. [CrossRef]
89. Rahmani, A.M.; Yousefpoor, E.; Yousefpoor, M.S.; Mehmood, Z.; Haider, A.; Hosseinzadeh, M.; Ali Naqvi, R. Machine Learning (ML) in medicine: Review, applications, and challenges. *Mathematics* **2021**, *9*, 2970. [CrossRef]
90. Jönsson, K. Machine Learning and Nowcasts of Swedish GDP. *J. Bus. Cycle Res.* **2020**, *16*, 123–134. [CrossRef]
91. Cicceri, G.; Inserra, G.; Limosani, M. A machine learning approach to forecast economic recessions—An Italian case study. *Mathematics* **2020**, *8*, 241. [CrossRef]
92. Maccarrone, G.; Morelli, G.; Spadaccini, S. GDP forecasting: Machine learning, linear or autoregression? *Front. Artif. Intell.* **2021**, *4*, 757864. [CrossRef] [PubMed]
93. Biau, O.; D'Elia, A. *Euro Area GDP Forecast Using Large Survey Dataset—A Random Forest Approach*; Euroindicators Working Paper 2011/002; European Commission: Brussels, Belgium, 2011.
94. Tiffin, M.A. *Seeing in the Dark: A Machine-Learning Approach to Nowcasting in Lebanon*; International Monetary Fund: Washington, DC, USA, 2016.
95. Behrens, C.; Pierdzioch, C.; Risse, M. A test of the joint efficiency of macroeconomic forecasts using multivariate random forests. *J. Forecast.* **2018**, *37*, 560–572. [CrossRef]
96. Prüser, J. Forecasting with many predictors using bayesian additive regression trees. *J. Forecast.* **2019**, *38*, 621–631. [CrossRef]
97. Foltas, A.; Pierdzioch, C. On the efficiency of German growth forecasts: An empirical analysis using quantile random forests and density forecasts. *Appl. Econ. Lett.* **2021**, *29*, 1644–1653. [CrossRef]
98. Yoon, J. Forecasting of real GDP growth using machine learning models: Gradient boosting and random forest approach. *Comput. Econ.* **2021**, *57*, 247–265. [CrossRef]
99. Chai, S.H.; Lim, J.S. Forecasting business cycle with chaotic time series based on neural network with weighted fuzzy membership functions. *Chaos Solitons Fractals* **2016**, *90*, 118–126. [CrossRef]

100. Jung, J.K.; Patnam, M.; Ter-Martirosyan, A. *An Algorithmic Crystal Ball: Forecasts-Based on Machine Learning*; International Monetary Fund: Washington, DC, USA, 2018.
101. Alaminos, D.; Salas, M.B.; Fernández-Gámez, M.A. Quantum computing and deep learning methods for GDP growth forecasting. *Comput. Econ.* **2022**, *59*, 803–829. [CrossRef]
102. Emsia, E.; Coskuner, C. Economic growth prediction using optimized support vector machines. *Comput. Econ.* **2016**, *48*, 453–462. [CrossRef]
103. Kouziokas, G.N. A new W-SVM kernel combining PSO-neural network transformed vector and bayesian optimized SVM in GDP forecasting. *Eng. Appl. Artif. Intell.* **2020**, *92*, 103650. [CrossRef]
104. Vaswani, A.; Shazeer, N.; Parmar, N.; Uszkoreit, J.; Jones, L.; Gomez, A.N.; Polosukhin, I. Attention is all you need. Advances in Neural Information Processing Systems NeurIPS Proceedings. In Proceedings of the 31st Conference on Neural Information Processing Systems, Long Beach, CA, USA, 4–9 December 2017.
105. Koo, R. *Balance Sheet Recession: Japan's Struggle with Uncharted Economics and Its Global Implications*; John Wiley & Sons: Singapore, 2003.
106. Koo, K. *The Holy Grail of Macroeconomics: Lessons from Japan's Great Recession*; John Wiley & Sons: Singapore, 2009.
107. Laborda, J.; Salas, V.; Suárez, C. Financial constraints on R&D projects and Minsky moments: Containing the credit cycle. *J. Evol. Econ.* **2021**, *31*, 1089–1111. [CrossRef]
108. Mian, A.; Straub, L.; Sufi, A. Indebted demand. *Q. J. Econ.* **2021**, *136*, 2243–2307. [CrossRef]
109. Armelius, H.; Belfrage, C.J.; Stenbacka, H. The mystery of the missing world trade growth after the global financial crisis. *Sver. Riksbank Econ. Rev.* **2014**, *3*, 7–22.
110. Barhoumi, K.; Darné, O.; Ferrara, L. Dynamic factor models: A review of the literature. *OECD J. J. Bus. Cycle Meas. Anal.* **2013**, *2*. [CrossRef]
111. Liu, M.; Zeng, A.; Chen, M.; Xu, Z.; Lai, Q.; Ma, L.; Xu, Q. Scinet: Time series modeling and forecasting with sample convolution and interaction. *Adv. Neural Inf. Process. Syst.* **2022**, *35*, 5816–5828.
112. Zhou, H.; Zhang, S.; Peng, J.; Zhang, S.; Li, J.; Xiong, H.; Zhang, W. Informer: Beyond efficient transformer for long sequence time-series forecasting. In Proceedings of the AAAI Conference on Artificial Intelligence, Virtually, 2–9 February 2021; Volume 35, pp. 11106–11115.
113. Zhou, T.; Ma, Z.; Wen, Q.; Sun, L.; Yao, T.; Yin, W.; Jin, R. Film: Frequency improved Legendre memory model for long-term time series forecasting. *Adv. Neural Inf. Process. Syst.* **2022**, *35*, 12677–12690.
114. Gordon, R.J. *Is US Economic Growth Over? Faltering Innovation Confronts the Six Headwinds*; National Bureau of Economic Research: Cambridge, MA, USA, 2012; p. w18315.
115. Summers, L.H. US economic prospects: Secular stagnation, hysteresis, and the zero lower bound. *Bus. Econ.* **2014**, *49*, 65–73. [CrossRef]
116. Summers, L.H. Demand side secular stagnation. *Am. Econ. Rev.* **2015**, *105*, 60–65. [CrossRef]

Disclaimer/Publisher's Note: The statements, opinions and data contained in all publications are solely those of the individual author(s) and contributor(s) and not of MDPI and/or the editor(s). MDPI and/or the editor(s) disclaim responsibility for any injury to people or property resulting from any ideas, methods, instructions or products referred to in the content.

Article

NSNet: An N-Shaped Convolutional Neural Network with Multi-Scale Information for Image Denoising

Yifen Li [1] and Yuanyang Chen [2,*]

[1] School of Economics and Management, Changsha University, Changsha 410022, China
[2] School of Automation, Central South University, Changsha 410083, China
* Correspondence: 204612129@csu.edu.cn

Abstract: Deep learning models with convolutional operators have received widespread attention for their good image denoising performance. However, since the convolutional operation prefers to extract local features, the extracted features may lose some global information, such as texture, structure, and color characteristics, when the object in the image is large. To address this issue, this paper proposes an N-shaped convolutional neural network with the ability to extract multi-scale features to capture more useful information and alleviate the problem of global information loss. The proposed network has two main parts: a multi-scale input layer and a multi-scale feature extraction layer. The former uses a two-dimensional Haar wavelet to create an image pyramid, which contains the corrupted image's high- and low-frequency components at different scales. The latter uses a U-shaped convolutional network to extract features at different scales from this image pyramid. The method sets the mean-squared error as the loss function and uses the residual learning strategy to learn the image noise directly. Compared with some existing image denoising methods, the proposed method shows good performance in gray and color image denoising, especially in textures and contours.

Keywords: image denoising; wavelet transform; Unet; image pyramid; multi-scale features

MSC: 68U10

Citation: Li, Y.; Chen, Y. NSNet: An N-Shaped Convolutional Neural Network with Multi-Scale Information for Image Denoising. *Mathematics* 2023, 11, 2772. https://doi.org/10.3390/math11122772

Academic Editor: Jakub Nalepa

Received: 4 June 2023
Revised: 15 June 2023
Accepted: 18 June 2023
Published: 19 June 2023

Copyright: © 2023 by the authors. Licensee MDPI, Basel, Switzerland. This article is an open access article distributed under the terms and conditions of the Creative Commons Attribution (CC BY) license (https://creativecommons.org/licenses/by/4.0/).

1. Introduction

Image denoising is one of the basic tasks of computer vision and is of wide interest to academia and industry, as it can effectively improve image quality. The purpose of image denoising is to remove noise from a corrupted image and restore its original content as much as possible. In many computer vision tasks, image denoising is often used as a preprocessing method to improve the practical performance of advanced computer vision tasks [1]. Over the past few decades, many outstanding image denoising methods, as shown in Figure 1, have been proposed, including filtering-based [2,3], sparse-representation-based [4–8], external-prior-based [9–12], low-rank-representation-based [13,14], and deep-learning-based methods [15–18].

Filtering-based methods were the first techniques to be applied to image denoising and rely on the self-similarity of images. Well-known approaches include Gaussian filtering, mean filtering, and median filtering. These three methods assume that the pixels in an image do not exist in isolation and have connections to other pixels. However, Buades et al. [2] found that similar pixels are not limited to local areas, and making full use of the redundant information in an image can improve the image denoising performance. Hence, they proposed a nonlocal mean filtering method (NLM) based on existing smoothing filtering methods. Although NLM can achieve good denoising performance, it needs to find a sufficient number of similar blocks when computing each pixel, which gives it high computational complexity. To solve this problem, Kostadin et al. [3] proposed a block-matching and 3D filtering (BM3D) method, which has a good denoising performance and fast computational speed.

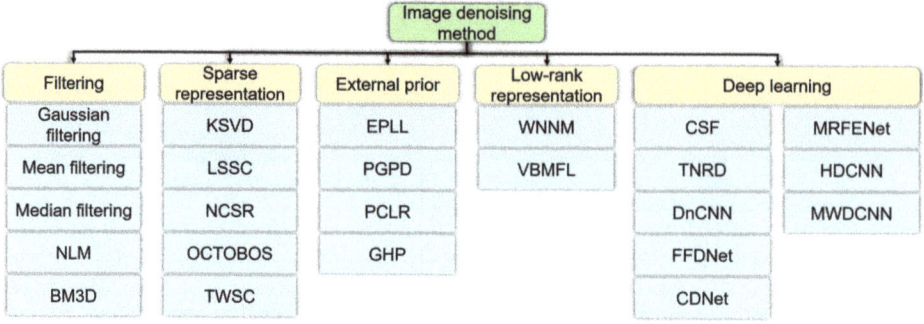

Figure 1. Classification of image denoising methods.

Sparse-representation-based methods are based on image sparsity and achieve image denoising by training an over-complete dictionary. A more representative case is the K-singular value decomposition (KSVD) method using sparse representation [4]. Inspired by KSVD, Mairal et al. [5] combined image self-similarity with sparse coding to decompose similar patches using similar sparse patterns, thus forming a Learned Simultaneous Sparse Coding (LSSC) method. Although sparse representation models have shown good results in image denoising, the sparse representation of traditional models may not be accurate enough due to the degradation of the observed images. To further improve the performance of image denoising based on sparse representation, Dong et al. [6] proposed a nonlocally centralized sparse representation (NCSR), which transformed the denoising problem into a problem of suppressing sparse coding noise. In addition, because the sparse coding of images using a single transform can limit performance, Wen et al. [7] proposed a structured over-complete sparsifying transform model with block cosparsity (OCTOBOS). These methods [4–7] have exhibited good results in denoising additive Gaussian white noise (AWGN); however, it is difficult to obtain good performance in real image denoising. To achieve better denoising of real images, Xu et al. [8] proposed a trilateral weighted sparse coding scheme (TWSC).

External-prior-based methods realize image denoising by using the statistical properties of natural images. A representative method is the denoising method based on expected patch log likelihood (EPLL) proposed by Zoran and Weiss [9]. This method applies the Gaussian mixture model to learn prior knowledge from a large number of natural image blocks and applies it to the denoising of other natural images. Similar to EPLL, Xu et al. [10] proposed a patch group prior-based denoising method (PGPD) to learn the self-similar features of natural images from groups of similar patches using the Gaussian mixture distribution. Inspired by EPLL, Chen et al. [11] proposed an external patch prior-guided internal clustering approach by combining an image external prior and an internal self-similarity prior, which is named PCLR. To improve the texture restoration capability of the image denoising method, Zou et al. [12] proposed a gradient histogram preservation method (GHP) based on texture enhancement. GHP improves texture recovery by preserving the gradient distribution of the corrupted image.

Low-rank representation-based methods exploit the low-rank properties of natural images and achieve denoising by extracting their low-rank components. A typical case is the Weighted Nuclear Norm Minimization (WNNM) proposed by Gu et al. [13]. Low-rank matrix factorization is also a method used to extract low-rank components from a dataset and is often applied in cases where the image size is large and its rank is much smaller than the length and width of the dataset. The most well-known method is the low-rank matrix factorization based on variational Bayesian (VBMFL), which was proposed by Zhao et al. [14]. This method improves the robustness of the model to outliers by using a Laplace distribution to establish a noise model.

Deep-learning-based denoising methods are currently the most popular. They usually learn the direct mapping from the corrupted image to the clean image or the noise. Since deep-learning-based denoising methods do not rely on image priori (e.g., self-similarity, sparsity, gradient, statistical properties, and low-rank properties), they do not have to spend much time finding and processing similar blocks in the images. Thus, they not only achieve a good denoising performance but also have a fast inference speed. Schmidt et al. [15] proposed a method based on a cascade of shrinkage fields (CSF) to improve the denoising performance while considering computational efficiency. Chen et al. [16] extended conventional nonlinear reaction–diffusion models with several parametrized linear filters as well as several parametrized influence functions and proposed a trainable nonlinear reaction–diffusion method (TNRD). Although CSF and TNRD show good denoising performance, they can only provide the best denoising results at known noise levels. To solve the problem of blind image denoising, Zhang et al. [17] proposed a deep learning method using a denoising convolutional neural network (DnCNN), which was the first application of residual learning to general image denoising. The application of residual learning to image denoising has greatly improved the denoising performance of networks and inspired many outstanding denoising methods based on deep learning [17–22]. In addition, Zhang et al. [18] further improved the DnCNN and proposed a fast and flexible denoising convolutional neural network (FFDNet), which achieves a good trade-off between the inference speed and denoising performance by downsampling and manually inputting a noise estimation map. Binh et al. [23] combined DnCNN with ResNet and proposed a convolutional denoising neural network called FlashLight CNN. A complex-valued deep convolutional neural network called CDNet was proposed by Quan et al. [24], and it effectively improved the denoising performance of the network. Guan et al. [25] proposed an image denoising method for remote sensing images called MRFENet. It demonstrated good denoising performance and preserved the edge details of the images. Zhang et al. [26] utilized dilated convolutions to capture more contextual information and then proposed a hybrid denoising neural network called HDCNN to enhance the denoising performance of CNN networks in complex application scenarios. Tian et al. [27] combined dynamic convolution, wavelet transform, and discriminative learning to propose a convolutional neural network based on the wavelet transform called Multi-stage Image Denoising CNN with the Wavelet Transform (MWDCNN). To reduce the parameter size and training burden of deep denoising networks, Tang et al. [28] employed a cascaded residual network and proposed a lightweight, multi-scale, efficient convolutional neural network.

The results of most denoising methods are obtained directly from the fusion of high-level features, while low-level features containing texture and contour information are ignored, resulting in the loss of some important information. Furthermore, since the convolutional operation prefers to extract local features, it is difficult to extract global information such as textures and contours when the objects in the image are relatively large. To solve these problems, an N-shaped convolutional neural network, named NSNet, using multi-scale features is proposed in this paper. In this model, a 2D Haar wavelet is used to construct an image pyramid that contains high- and low-frequency components of the corrupted image at different scales. The multi-scale features are extracted from the image pyramid by a U-shaped convolutional network [29], and the low- and high-level features are fused by skip connections in the U-shaped network. The 2D Haar wavelet is widely used in image denoising, and many scholars have achieved excellent denoising performance with it [30–33]. To verify the denoising performance of NSNet, the denoising of gray and color images was carried out at different noise levels and compared with existing denoising methods. The contributions of this work are summarized as follows:

(1) An N-shaped convolutional neural network for extracting multi-scale information is proposed. The network exploits multi-scale information to compensate for the

drawbacks of convolutional operations in extracting global features, which effectively improves the network's ability to recover textures and contours.

(2) A scheme for constructing image pyramids using a 2D Haar wavelet is proposed. The image pyramid is obtained by using a multi-scale 2D Haar wavelet, and each layer of the pyramid contains one low-frequency component and three high-frequency components. In image denoising, the high-frequency components can be used as an estimate of the noise level to facilitate denoising.

(3) NSNet shows good denoising performance for AWGN at a noise level range of (0, 55) and good recovery of textures and contours. It provides a solution for applications that need not only denoising but also texture and contour recovery.

The rest of this paper is organized as follows. Section 2 presents the techniques involved in the proposed model. Section 3 describes the proposed NSNet and the construction of the image pyramid in detail. Section 4 presents the results of experiments, and Section 5 concludes the paper.

2. Theoretical Aspects

2.1. The 2D Haar Wavelet

The process of decomposing an image using the 2D Haar wavelet is shown in Figure 2. The blocks with five-pointed stars in the figure are the finite impulse response filter. $h_\varphi = \{1/\sqrt{2}, 1/\sqrt{2}\}$ denotes a low-pass filter, and $h_\psi = \{-1/\sqrt{2}, 1/\sqrt{2}\}$ denotes a high-pass filter. The down arrow ($\downarrow$) indicates downsampling, which means adding two adjacent pixels in the column or row direction.

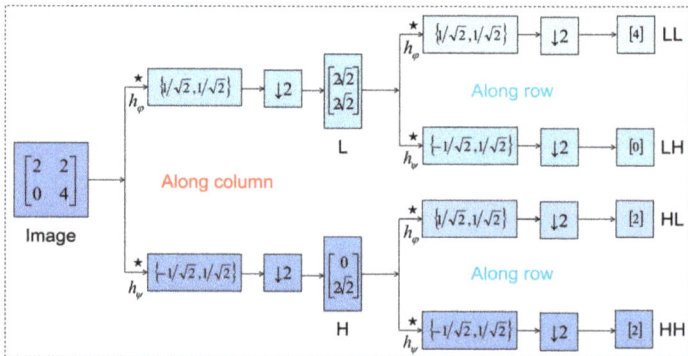

Figure 2. The 2D Haar wavelet transform.

The image is first processed with the two filters separately and is compressed in the column direction to obtain a low-frequency component L and a high-frequency component H. The two components are then processed with low- and high-pass filters in turn and compressed in the row direction to obtain the low-frequency component LL, the high-frequency component LH in the vertical direction, the high-frequency component HL in the horizontal direction, and the high-frequency component HH in the diagonal direction. According to the principle of 2D Haar wavelets, assuming that the corrupted image is $X \in R^{m \times n}$, the formulas for the components of the image can be simplified as

$$A_{ij} = X(2i, 2j), \quad B_{ij} = X(2i+1, 2j) \tag{1}$$

$$C_{ij} = X(2i, 2j+1), \quad D_{ij} = X(2i+1, 2j+1) \tag{2}$$

$$LL_{ij} = \frac{1}{2}(A_{ij} + B_{ij} + C_{ij} + D_{ij}), \quad HL_{ij} = \frac{1}{2}(B_{ij} + D_{ij} - A_{ij} - C_{ij}) \tag{3}$$

$$LH_{ij} = \frac{1}{2}(C_{ij} + D_{ij} - A_{ij} - B_{ij}), \quad HH_{ij} = \frac{1}{2}(A_{ij} + D_{ij} - B_{ij} - C_{ij}) \tag{4}$$

where $\{i|0 \leq i \leq m/2\}$ and $\{j|0 \leq j \leq n\}$. The two-scale 2D Haar wavelet applied to the image "Monarch" is shown in Figure 3. Through the 2D Haar wavelet, the image is decomposed into three high-frequency components (LH, HL, HH) and a low-frequency component (LL).

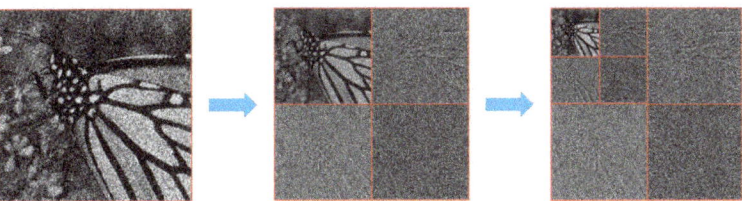

Figure 3. Two-scale 2D Haar wavelet processing results on the image "Monarch".

2.2. U-Shaped Convolutional Network

The U-shaped convolutional network was first proposed by Ronneberger et al. [29]. The network has been widely used in various fields for its powerful encoding and decoding capabilities [34,35]. The U-shaped convolutional network includes four downsampling operators and four upsampling operators and uses skip connections at the same stage, which not only gives the network the ability to extract multi-scale features but also ensures that the output integrates more low-level features [21]. The structure of the U-shaped convolutional network with batch normalization (BN) is shown in Figure 4.

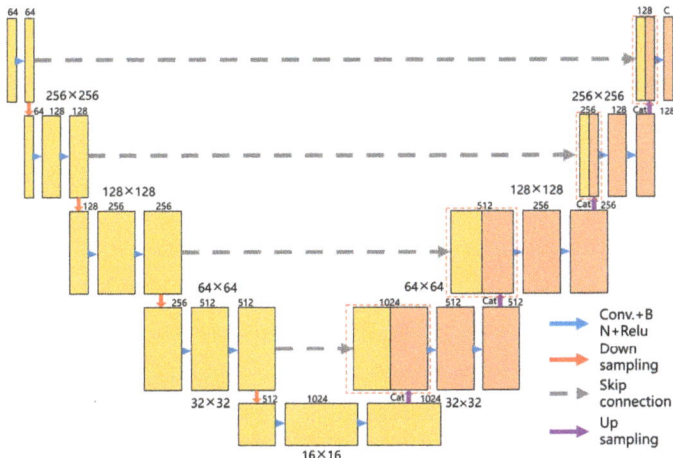

Figure 4. Network structure of the U-shaped network with BN.

When the neural network becomes very deep, an internal covariate offset may occur, which can lead to two problems: (1) it affects the learning efficiency and makes the learning process unstable, and (2) it makes the input data of the later layers too large or small, thus falling into the saturation area of the activation function and causing the learning process to stop prematurely. To solve the problem of the internal covariate offset, a general approach is to add BN, as proposed by Ioffe and Szegedy [36], to the U-shaped convolutional network.

The BN layer is usually placed between the convolutional operation and the Rectified Linear Unit (ReLU), and the parameters of the BN layer are adjusted by training. Supposing that there is a mini-batch $B = \{X_{1 \dots m}\}$ of size m, and the parameters to be learned are γ and β, the BN process can be expressed as

$$\gamma = \sqrt{Var[x]}, \ \beta = E[x], \tag{5}$$

$$\mu_B = \frac{1}{m}\sum_{i=1}^{m} x_i, \quad \delta_B^2 = \frac{1}{m}\sum_{i=1}^{m}(x_i - \mu_B)^2, \tag{6}$$

$$\hat{x}_i = \frac{x_i - \mu_B}{\sqrt{\delta_B^2 + \varepsilon}}, \quad y_i = \gamma \hat{x}_i + \beta, \tag{7}$$

where ε is a constant added to the mini-batch variance for numerical stability.

2.3. Residual Learning

When the network becomes very deep, some convolutional layers may appear to have identity mapping, resulting in degradation problems and vanishing and exploding gradients. To solve this problem, He et al. [37] proposed a residual network with the residual block shown in Figure 5. It connects the input and output directly through a shortcut connection, allowing $F(x)$ to learn small changes. This not only allows the convolutional layer to maintain identity mapping but also avoids vanishing and exploding gradients. The relationship between the input x and output x^* of the residual block is

$$x^* = F(x) + x. \tag{8}$$

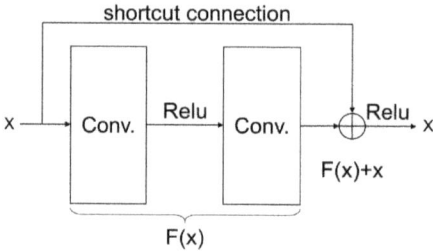

Figure 5. Basic structure of a residual block.

In image denoising, when the noise level is low, the mapping from the noisy image to the clean image is close to an identity mapping, which is not conducive to the training of the network. To solve this problem, Zhang et al. [17] first applied residual learning to image denoising. Assuming that the input image is $Input$ and the output image is $Output$, their relationship is

$$F(x) = Output - Input. \tag{9}$$

It can be seen from (9) that residual learning for image denoising uses noise as the training target, which is a valuable technique for improving the denoising performance of the model.

3. The Proposed NSNet Model

In this section, the proposed NSNet model is introduced in detail; its architecture is shown in Figure 6. It mainly consists of a multi-scale input layer and a multi-scale feature extraction layer. The multi-scale input layer uses a 2D Haar wavelet to create an image pyramid, which decomposes the corrupted image into high- and low-frequency components at different scales. The multi-scale feature extraction layer uses a U-shaped convolutional network to extract features at different scales from the image pyramid. Additionally, NSNet sets the mean-squared error as the loss function and uses the residual learning strategy to learn the noise directly.

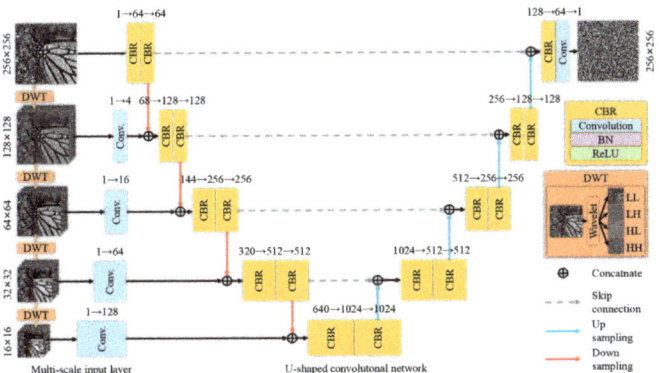

Figure 6. Architecture of NSNet.

The 2D Haar wavelet can decompose the image into four sub-images, each with a size half that of the original image. By using a 2D Haar wavelet to decompose the image, we can obtain

$$LL_1, (LH_1, HL_1, HH_1) = dwt(y), \qquad (10)$$

where $dwt(\cdot)$ represents the 2D Haar wavelet, y is the corrupted image, LL_1 is the low-frequency component, and LH_1, HL_1, and HH_1 are the high-frequency components. Then, the 2D Haar wavelet is applied once again to the low-frequency component LL_1 to obtain

$$LL_2, (LH_2, HL_2, HH_2) = dwt(LL_1), \qquad (11)$$

Finally, to obtain the image pyramid shown in Figure 7, the same operation is repeated twice, resulting in

$$LL_3, (LH_3, HL_3, HH_3) = dwt(LL_2), \qquad (12)$$

$$LL_4, (LH_4, HL_4, HH_4) = dwt(LL_3). \qquad (13)$$

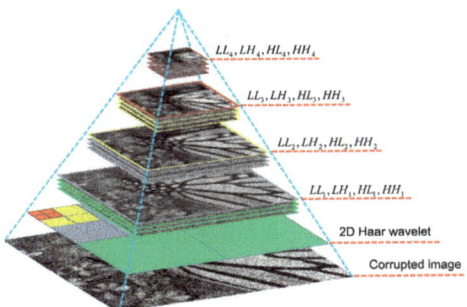

Figure 7. Image pyramid constructed by a 2D Haar wavelet.

The image pyramid contains images at five different scales, each of which corresponds to a different stage of the U-shaped convolutional network. In addition to the original scale, each scale contains a low-frequency component LL and three high-frequency components LH, HL, and HH. As shown in Figure 7, the low-frequency component is close to the corrupted input image, while the high-frequency components contain a lot of noise and some textures, which can be considered an estimate of the noise level.

The image degradation model is established as $y = x + v$, where y denotes the corrupted image, x denotes the clean image, and v denotes the noise. The proposed model inputs the corrupted image y into the network to predict the noise $v \approx F(y)$ and finally obtains the clean image $x = y - v$ through simple subtraction. The mean-squared error is used as the loss function:

$$L(\theta) = \frac{1}{2N}\sum_{i=1}^{N}||F(y_i;\theta) - (y_i - x_i)||_F^2, \tag{14}$$

where θ represents the parameter set of the model, N is the total number of images, and x_i and y_i represent the *ith* clean image and noisy image, respectively.

For convenience, the proposed model trained at a known noise level is named NSNet-S, and the model trained at an unknown noise level is named NSNet-B. The pseudo-code of the proposed method is shown in Algorithm 1.

Algorithm 1 The algorithm of NSNet

Input: All training images D from the observed dataset, denoising mode (B or S), noise level $noiseL$, range of noise level $noiseR$, maximum epoch $Mepoch$.
Output: The trained network f.
1:    Initialing model parameters θ and learning rate η;
2:    Sampling m patches $(x_1, \cdots, x_m)$ from D;
3:    **for** epoch = 1 to $Mepoch$ **do**
4:       **if** epoch > 30 **then**
5:          $\eta \leftarrow \eta/10$;
6:       **end if**
7:       Set $\hat{g} = 0$;
8:       **for** $i = 1$ to m **do**
9:          **if** mode == "B" **then**
10:            Setting $noiseL$ as an integer at the range $noiseR$ randomly;
11:          **end if**
12:          Adding Gaussian noise with the noise level of $noiseL$ to x_i:
$$y_i = x_i + noise_i;$$
13:          Performing multi-scale wavelet transform on y_i to obtain $y_i^1, y_i^2, y_i^3, y_i^4$:
$y_i^1 = \{LL_1, LH_1, HL_1, HH_1\} = dwt(y_i), y_i^2 = \{LL_2, LH_2, HL_2, HH_2\} = dwt(LL_1),$
$y_i^3 = \{LL_3, LH_3, HL_3, HH_3\} = dwt(LL_2), y_i^4 = \{LL_4, LH_4, HL_4, HH_4\} = dwt(LL_3);$
14:          Predicting noise using the network f with parameter θ:
$$out_i \leftarrow f(y_i, y_i^1, y_i^2, y_i^3, y_i^4; \theta);$$
15:          Calculating the loss according to Equation (14);
16:          Computing the gradient: $\hat{g} \leftarrow \hat{g} + \frac{1}{m}\nabla_\theta L(\theta)$;
17:       **end for**
18:       Updating θ: $\theta \leftarrow \theta - \eta \times \hat{g}$;
19:    **end for**

---

4. Experimental Results

Gray image denoising and color image denoising were carried out to compare the denoising performance of the proposed NSNet with those of existing models, including NLM [2], BM3D [3], KSVD [4], NCSR [6], OCTOBOS [7], TWSC [8], GHP [9], EPLL [10], PGPD [11], PCLR [12], WNNM [13], CSF [15], TNRD [16], and FFDNet [18]. Moreover, two different types of DnCNNs [17] were also selected as the compared models. They are DnCNN-S and DnCNN-B, which are trained at known and unknown noise levels, respectively.

4.1. Evaluation Metrics

The results of all denoising methods were analyzed quantitatively in terms of the peak signal-to-noise ratio (PSNR) and structural similarity (SSIM).

(1) Supposing that the recovered image is $I \in R^{m \times n}$ and the corrupted image is $K \in R^{m \times n}$, the PSNR is calculated as

$$MSE = \frac{1}{mn} \sum_{i=0}^{m-1} \sum_{j=0}^{n-1} [I(i,j) - K(i,j)]^2, \quad (15)$$

$$PSNR = 10 \cdot \log_{10}\left(\frac{MAX_I^2}{MSE}\right), \quad (16)$$

where MSE is the mean-squared error, and MAX_I denotes the maximum value of the pixels in the image. In general, $MAX_I = 255$ if each pixel is represented in 8-bit binary form or 1 if it is represented in 1-bit binary.

(2) The SSIM is calculated as

$$SSIM(I,K) = \frac{(2\mu_I \mu_K + c_1)(\sigma_{IK} + c_2)}{(\mu_I^2 + \mu_K^2 + c_1)(\sigma_I^2 + \sigma_K^2 + c_2)} \quad (17)$$

where μ_I and μ_K denote the means of I and K, respectively, and σ_I and σ_K denote their standard deviations, while σ_{IK} denotes the covariance of I and K, and c_1 and c_2 are constants.

4.2. Experimental Setting

For the ablation experiment, NSNet, NSNet without BN, Unet, and Unet without BN were compared. All compared methods were trained using 400 images of size 180 × 180 pixels, as mentioned in [17]. The test sets were Set12, which is widely used in the evaluation of denoising methods, and BSD68 [38]. In training the model, the size of the patch was set to 48 × 48, and 128 × 618 patches were cropped from the 400 images. Four denoising methods were trained at noise levels of 15, 25, 35, 45, and 50. For a noise level of α, the noise was generated by a Gaussian distribution with a mean of zero and a variance of α.

For the denoising of gray images, the 400 images were still used as the training set, and 128 × 2934 patches of size 48 × 48 were cropped from them. Since most image denoising methods can only obtain the best denoising performance at a known noise level, to achieve a fair comparison, the proposed method was trained at an unknown noise level and at noise levels of 15, 25, and 50. The test sets were Set12 and BSD68, neither of which participated in model training.

For color image denoising, 432 images were selected from the color image dataset CBSD500 [39] as training samples, and the remaining 68 images (CBSD68) were used as the test set. The test set also included Kodak24 [40] and McMaster [41]. In this experiment, 96 × 3900 patches were cropped from the 432 images to train the color image denoising model. The other settings were largely consistent with the settings used for gray image denoising. The specific settings of NSNet are shown in Table 1.

Table 1. Specific settings of NSNet used in all experiments.

Experiment	Model	Noise Level	Patch Size	Number of Patches
Ablation experiment	NSNet-S	15, 25, 35, 45, 50	48 × 48	128 × 618
Gray image denoising	NSNet-S	15, 25, 50	48 × 48	128 × 2934
Gray image denoising	NSNet-B	(0, 55)	48 × 48	128 × 2934
Color image denoising	NSNet-B	(0, 55)	48 × 48	96 × 3900

When training NSNet-S, each clean image input to the model was corrupted by the same level of noise. When training NSNet-B, each clean image input to the model was corrupted by noise at a level drawn randomly from the range (0, 55). The Adam optimizer was used to tune the model with an initial learning rate of 0.001. The maximum training epoch was 50. After 30 epochs, the learning rate was adjusted to 0.0001. The size of each mini-batch was set to 128. The denoising network was trained in PyTorch, and all experiments were carried out in the pycharm environment running on a PC with an AMD Ryzen 9 5900HX with Radeon Graphics 3.30 GHz CPU and an NVIDIA GeForce RTX 3070 Laptop GPU.

4.3. Ablation Experiment

This section describes the ablation experiment that was carried out to demonstrate the effectiveness of the main components of the proposed model. The experiment tested the denoising performance of NSNet, Unet, NSNet without BN, and Unet without BN at noise levels of 15, 25, 35, 45, and 50. The denoising results on the Set12 dataset and the gray version of BSD68 are shown in Table 2, in which values with # and * represent the best and second-best denoising performance, respectively.

Table 2. Average PSNR/SSIM of four denoising methods in the ablation experiment.

Model	Nosie Level	Method			
		NSNet	Unet	NSNet(-BN)	Unet(-BN)
Set12	$\sigma = 15$	32.90 #/0.9040 #	32.75/0.9017	32.76 */0.9025 *	31.81/0.8835
	$\sigma = 25$	30.50 #/0.8643 #	30.48 */0.8640 *	30.33/0.8610	30.28/0.8602
	$\sigma = 35$	28.95 #/0.8319 #	28.89 */0.8300 *	28.65/0.8243	28.77/0.8270
	$\sigma = 45$	27.81 #/0.8041 #	27.80 */0.8029 *	27.66/0.7993	26.52/0.7945
	$\sigma = 50$	27.32 #/0.7910 #	27.32 */0.7901 *	26.93/0.7737	26.90/0.7724
BSD68	$\sigma = 15$	31.79 #/0.8927 #	31.71 */0.8912 *	31.70/0.8916 *	31.04/0.8748
	$\sigma = 25$	29.31 #/0.8322 #	29.29 */0.8321 *	29.20/0.8294	29.18/0.8288
	$\sigma = 35$	27.82 #/0.7849 #	27.76 */0.7810 *	27.65/0.7779	27.71/0.7788
	$\sigma = 45$	26.78 #/0.7446 #	26.77 */0.7442 *	26.70/0.7413	26.63/0.7364
	$\sigma = 50$	26.35 #/0.7267 #	26.34 */0.7260 *	26.10/0.7101	26.11/0.7106

Note: NSNet(-BN) means NSNet without BN, and Unet(-BN) means Unet without BN. # The best denoising performance. * The second-best denoising performance.

The denoising performance of NSNet is better than that of Unet at all noise levels, which shows that multi-scale input can improve the denoising performance. The results for NSNet and NSNet without BN show that the denoising performance of NSNet is greatly improved after adding the BN layer. As mentioned in [29], the BN layer can improve the denoising performance of the neural network. At all noise levels, NSNet without BN achieves better denoising than Unet without BN, and its denoising performance is close to that of Unet at low noise levels, which indicates that the multi-scale input greatly improved the denoising performance of the model at low noise levels. With increases in the noise level, the structure of the compressed image is increasingly corrupted; thus, it cannot provide accurate information for the network. In this case, the performance of NSNet is similar to that of Unet. For example, the denoising performance of NSNet is similar to that of Unet at a noise level of 50.

4.4. Gray Image Denoising

In this experiment, AWGN was added to Set12 and the gray version of BSD68, and the noise levels were set to 15, 25, and 50. The denoising results of all methods on Set12 are shown in Tables 3–5. Due to insufficient parameters, CSF cannot be tested at a noise level of 50.

Table 3 shows the denoising results of all methods at a noise level of 15. NSNet-S has a better denoising performance than other methods and obtained the first-ranked denoising performance on ten images. NSNet-S ranked a very close second in terms of denoising the image "House". In this case, the denoising performance of NSNet-S is 1.86 dB higher than that of the worst method, NLM, on average, and 0.1 dB higher than that of DnCNN-S, on average, in terms of PSNR. The average results of all methods show that there is little difference in the denoising performance of most methods at a noise level of 15. At a low noise level, the self-similarity, sparsity, and low-rank properties of the image are still relatively complete, and the traditional denoising methods (e.g., BM3D, NCSR, TWSC, PCLR, WNNM) also achieve a good denoising performance.

Table 3. PSNRs of all methods on Set12 at a noise level of 15.

Model	C.man	House	Pappers	Starfish	Monar.	Airpl.	Parrot	Lena	Barbara	Boat	Man	Couple	Average
NLM	30.05	33.23	31.59	30.30	30.47	29.42	30.07	33.16	31.33	31.25	31.27	30.97	31.09
BM3D	31.92	34.95	32.70	31.15	31.86	31.08	31.38	34.27	33.11	32.14	31.93	32.11	32.38
KSVD	31.46	34.24	32.20	30.70	31.41	30.75	30.95	33.71	32.42	31.76	31.53	31.47	31.89
NCSR	32.01	35.04	32.66	31.50	32.25	31.19	31.37	34.12	33.06	32.08	31.98	32.00	32.44
OCTOBOS	31.91	34.32	32.49	31.04	31.72	30.98	31.29	33.91	32.59	31.87	31.74	31.77	32.14
TWSC	32.01	35.11 [#]	32.83	31.64	32.47	31.14	31.52	34.39	33.64 [#]	32.24	32.09	32.15	32.60
EPLL	31.82	34.14	32.58	31.08	32.03	31.16	31.40	33.87	31.34	31.91	31.97	31.91	32.10
GHP	31.48	34.07	32.40	31.09	31.63	30.77	31.16	33.54	32.01	31.72	31.62	31.54	31.92
PCLR	32.23	35.07	33.00	31.75	32.63	31.45	31.62	34.27	33.12	32.25	32.16	32.14	32.64
PGPD	31.83	34.79	32.61	31.25	32.15	31.19	31.32	34.04	32.74	32.03	31.99	32.07	32.33
WNNM	32.18	35.15	32.97	31.83	32.72	31.40	31.61	34.38	33.61 [*]	32.28	32.12	32.18	32.70
CSF	31.95	34.40	32.83	31.56	32.34	31.34	31.36	34.07	31.93	32.01	32.09	31.99	32.32
TNRD	32.19	34.55	33.03	31.76	32.57	31.47	31.63	34.25	32.14	32.15	32.24	32.11	32.51
DnCNN-S	32.59 [*]	34.99	33.24 [*]	32.13 [*]	33.25 [*]	31.67 [*]	31.88 [*]	34.58	32.61	32.42 [*]	32.43 [*]	32.43 [*]	32.85 [*]
DnCNN-B	32.14	34.96	33.09	31.92	33.08	31.54	31.64	34.52	32.03	32.36	32.37	32.38	32.67
FFDnet	32.37	35.05	33.01	31.95	32.92	31.55	31.79	34.60 [*]	32.48	32.36	32.37	32.43 [*]	32.74
NSNet-S	32.67 [#]	35.09 [*]	33.33 [#]	32.29 [#]	33.32 [#]	31.79 [#]	31.97 [#]	34.69 [#]	32.80	32.50 [#]	32.48 [#]	32.52 [#]	32.95 [#]
NSNet-B	32.02	34.63	32.74	32.08	32.87	31.31	31.60	34.42	30.59	32.29	32.18	32.20	32.41

Note: [#] The best denoising performance. [*] The second-best denoising performance.

Table 4. PSNRs of all methods on Set12 at a noise level of 25.

Model	C.man	House	Pappers	Starfish	Monar.	Airpl.	Parrot	Lena	Barbara	Boat	Man	Couple	Average
NLM	29.97	30.38	29.02	27.82	28.07	27.33	27.98	30.38	28.59	28.74	28.80	28.32	28.61
BM3D	29.45	32.86	30.16	28.56	29.25	28.43	28.93	32.08	30.72	29.91	29.62	29.72	29.98
KSVD	28.90	32.10	29.65	28.19	28.81	28.16	28.46	31.36	29.58	29.32	29.11	28.88	29.38
NCSR	29.43	32.89	30.05	28.77	29.43	28.45	28.86	31.92	30.62	29.77	29.58	29.49	29.94
OCTOBOS	29.25	32.08	29.78	28.24	28.78	28.28	28.67	31.56	29.88	29.51	29.26	29.23	29.54
TWSC	29.54	33.05	30.32	28.98	29.71	28.55	29.08	32.22	31.26 [#]	29.99	29.71	29.79	30.18
EPLL	29.24	32.04	30.07	28.43	29.30	28.56	28.91	31.62	28.55	29.69	29.63	29.48	29.63
GHP	29.28	32.50	30.04	28.66	29.02	28.28	28.87	31.69	30.29	29.71	29.49	29.37	29.77
PCLR	29.67	32.98	30.46	28.87	29.75	28.77	29.13	32.17	30.65	30.00	29.77	29.73	30.16
PGPD	29.26	32.79	30.07	28.49	29.29	28.54	28.80	31.93	30.28	29.82	29.66	29.68	29.88
WNNM	29.64	33.23	30.40	29.03	29.85	28.70	29.13	32.25	31.24 [*]	30.03	29.77	29.82	30.26
CSF	29.47	32.40	30.28	28.80	29.62	28.72	28.89	31.80	29.03	29.77	29.72	29.53	29.84
TNRD	29.71	32.54	30.55	29.02	29.86	28.89	29.18	32.01	29.41	29.92	29.88	29.71	30.06
DnCNN-S	30.21 [#]	33.10	30.82 [*]	29.36	30.41 [*]	29.08 [*]	29.44 [*]	32.41	30.01	30.20	30.08	30.08	30.43 [*]
DnCNN-B	30.03	33.04	30.73	29.24	30.37	29.06	29.35	32.40	29.67	30.19	30.06	30.05	30.35
FFDnet	30.05	33.26 [*]	30.72	29.28	30.29	29.01	29.42	32.57 [*]	29.98	30.23 [*]	30.07 [*]	30.15 [*]	30.42
NSNet-S	30.12 [*]	33.30 [#]	31.05 [#]	29.90 [#]	30.48 [#]	29.24 [#]	29.45 [#]	32.64 [#]	30.39	30.27 [#]	30.14 [#]	30.22 [#]	30.60 [#]
NSNet-B	30.05	33.05	30.62	29.62 [*]	30.33	28.97	29.39	32.57 [*]	27.54	30.23 [*]	29.99	30.05	30.20

Note: [#] The best denoising performance. [*] The second-best denoising performance.

Table 5. PSNRs of all methods on Set12 at a noise level of 50.

Model	C.man	House	Pappers	Starfish	Monar.	Airpl.	Parrot	Lena	Barbara	Boat	Man	Couple	Average
NLM	24.26	25.69	24.79	23.88	24.16	23.60	24.35	25.97	24.31	24.80	25.06	24.41	24.61
BM3D	26.13	29.69	26.68	25.04	25.82	25.10	25.90	29.05	27.23	26.78	26.81	26.46	26.73
KSVD	25.68	27.97	26.09	24.53	25.30	24.61	25.38	27.86	25.47	25.95	26.10	25.30	25.85
NCSR	26.15	29.62	26.53	25.09	25.77	24.93	25.71	28.90	26.99	26.67	26.67	26.19	26.60
OCTOBOS	25.62	28.59	26.15	24.57	25.04	24.86	25.39	28.37	26.17	26.30	26.27	25.82	26.10
TWSC	26.46	30.17	26.88	25.41	26.27	25.38	26.11	29.08	27.54 *	26.88	26.82	26.48	26.96
EPLL	26.03	28.77	26.63	25.04	25.78	25.24	25.84	28.42	24.82	26.65	26.72	26.24	26.35
GHP	25.91	28.51	26.38	24.39	25.53	24.76	25.71	27.43	25.44	25.99	25.92	25.46	25.95
PCLR	26.56	29.77	27.03	25.32	26.24	25.50	26.15	29.11	27.11	26.99	26.94	26.55	26.94
PGPD	26.40	29.73	26.69	25.10	25.89	25.34	25.84	29.00	26.84	26.82	26.84	26.47	26.75
WNNM	26.42	30.33	26.91	25.43	26.32	25.42	26.09	29.25	27.79 #	26.97	26.94	26.64	27.04
CSF	-	-	-	-	-	-	-	-	-	-	-	-	-
TNRD	26.61	29.49	27.08	25.42	26.32	25.59	26.16	28.94	25.70	26.94	26.99	26.50	26.81
DnCNN-S	27.26	29.96	27.35	25.64	26.83	25.83	26.42	29.34	26.15	27.19	27.19	26.86	27.17
DnCNN-B	27.26	29.91	27.35	25.60	26.84	25.82	26.48	29.34	26.32	27.18	27.17	26.87	27.18
FFDnet	27.24	30.36 *	27.41	25.68	26.92	25.79	26.57 #	29.63	26.41	27.30 *	27.26 *	27.04 *	27.30 *
NSNet-S	27.38 #	30.43 #	27.54 #	26.24 *	26.93 *	25.96 #	26.50	29.74 #	27.04	27.38 #	27.31 #	27.14 #	27.47 #
NSNet-B	27.35 *	30.24	27.47 *	26.17 #	26.94 #	25.89 *	26.54 *	29.70 *	25.46	27.30 *	27.19	27.01	27.27

Note: # The best denoising performance. * The second-best denoising performance.

Table 4 shows the denoising results obtained by all methods at a noise level of 25. With increases in the noise level, the best and second-best denoising performance was obtained with the deep-learning-based methods, which shows the superiority of deep learning in image denoising. As the noise level increases, the self-similarity and other features of the image are increasingly corrupted, which leads to the fact that the traditional image-prior-based denoising methods are no longer advantageous. The deep-learning-based denoising methods learn the potential noise directly from the corrupted image and rely less on the prior knowledge of the image. This allows them to achieve a good denoising performance, even at high noise levels. In this case, NSNet-S is ranked first in terms of denoising performance on ten images and second on one image. NSNet-B is ranked second in terms of denoising performance on three images. The denoising performance of NSNet-S is 1.99 dB higher than that of the worst method, NLM, and 0.17 dB higher than that of the second-best method, DnCNN-S, in terms of PSNR. Compared with the traditional denoising methods BM3D, NCSR, TWSC, and WNNM, NSNet-B is close to WNNM and outperforms BM3D, NCSR, and TWSC at a noise level of 25.

Table 5 shows the denoising results obtained by all methods at a noise level of 50. In this case, NSNet-S is ranked first in terms of denoising performance on eight images and second on two images. NSNet-B is ranked first in terms of denoising performance on two images and second on six images. Compared with other methods, NSNet-B provides a better denoising performance at a high noise level. The reason for this may be that an image with high noise will cause a greater deviation than one with low noise, and the network will pay more attention to the restoration of images with high noise when training NSNet-B. In this case, NSNet-S is 2.86 dB higher than the worst method, NLM, and 0.17 dB higher than the second-best method, FFDNet. NSNet-B also has an outstanding performance; its denoising performance surpasses that of DnCNN-B and WNNM and differs from that of FFDNet by only 0.03 dB.

In the above three experiments, NSNet shows a good denoising performance in most cases, although that of NSNet on the image "Barbara" is not as good as that of traditional methods (e.g., TWSC, WNNM). "Barbara" has similar rich textures, and the method based on image self-similarity can effectively use them to achieve better denoising. Both texture and noise are high-frequency information; therefore, image denoising methods that use residual learning tend to treat texture as noise, which makes the denoising performance of the proposed model poor. In addition, the same experiments were conducted on the dataset BSD68 to better demonstrate the denoising performance of NSNet. The average PSNRs and SSIMs of all methods on Set12 and BSD68 are shown in Table 6. Compared with other methods, the average denoising performance of NSNet-S on the two datasets is the best, and NSNet-B has a better denoising performance at a high noise level.

Table 6. Average PSNRs/SSIMs of all methods on datasets Set12 and BSD68.

Model	Set 12			BSD68		
	$\sigma = 15$	$\sigma = 25$	$\sigma = 50$	$\sigma = 15$	$\sigma = 25$	$\sigma = 50$
NLM	31.09/0.8594	28.62/0.7711	24.61/0.5695	29.82/0.8322	27.56/0.7296	24.01/0.5212
BM3D	32.38/0.8957	29.98/0.8510	26.73/0.7681	31.08/0.8722	28.57/0.8017	25.62/0.6869
KSVD	31.89/0.8847	29.38/0.8308	25.85/0.7260	30.86/0.8677	28.29/0.7889	25.18/0.6548
NCSR	32.44/0.8958	29.94/0.8501	26.60/0.7673	31.19/0.8770	28.61/0.8045	25.59/0.6864
OCTOBOS	32.14/0.8889	29.54/0.8378	26.10/0.7433	31.08/0.8744	28.46/0.7989	25.33/0.6705
TWSC	32.60/0.8989	30.18/0.8549	26.96/0.7731	31.28/0.8782	28.76/0.8077	25.77/0.6903
EPLL	32.10/0.8936	29.63/0.8444	26.35/0.7475	31.19/0.8825	28.68/0.8123	25.68/0.6877
GHP	31.92/0.8693	29.77/0.8415	25.95/0.7562	30.83/0.8513	28.49/0.8039	24.94/0.6809
PCLR	32.64/0.8979	30.16/0.8542	26.94/0.7763	31.38/0.8799	28.84/0.8106	25.88/0.6970
PGPD	32.33/0.8900	29.88/0.8447	26.75/0.7602	31.14/0.8705	28.64/0.8019	25.76/0.6877
WNNM	32.70/0.8982	30.26/0.8557	27.04/0.7775	31.32/0.8766	28.80/0.8029	24.43/0.6838
CSF	32.32/0.8923	29.84/0.8450	-/-	31.24/0.8746	28.73/0.8055	-/-
TNRD	32.51/0.8967	30.06/0.8520	26.81/0.7666	31.42/0.8825	28.91/0.8155	25.96/0.7024
DnCNN-S	32.85 */0.9025 *	30.43 */0.8616	27.17/0.7828	31.74 */0.8907 *	29.23 */0.8279	26.24/0.7189
DnCNN-B	32.67/0.9000	30.35/0.8599	27.18/0.7816	31.62/0.8868	29.16/0.8244	26.23/0.7164
FFDnet	32.74/0.9024	30.42/0.8631 *	27.30 */0.7900 *	31.64/0.8902	29.19/0.8828	26.29/0.7239
NSNet-S	32.95 #/0.9054 #	30.59 #/0.8662 #	27.47 #/0.7956 #	31.81 #/0.8936 #	29.33 #/0.8339 #	26.42 #/0.7316 #
NSNet-B	32.41/0.8943	30.20/0.8595	27.27/0.7895	31.46/0.8870	29.18/0.8304 *	26.32 */0.7242 *

Note: # The best denoising performance. * The second-best denoising performance.

Figures 8 and 9 show the denoising performance of all compared methods on gray images at noise levels of 25 and 50, respectively. In order to facilitate the comparison of the denoising performance, the results were transformed into pseudo-color images. The red box in Figure 8 shows the restoration effect of all compared methods on the "grass". It can be seen that NSNet's recovery of the "grass" is closer to the clean image than the other compared methods and results in sharper and clearer edges and textures. The red box in Figure 9 further demonstrates the advantages of NSNet in edge and texture restoration. As shown in Figure 9, compared to other methods, NSNet can not only make the edges and textures sharper but also restore more image details.

4.5. Color Image Denoising

The previous section compared the denoising performance of the methods on gray images, where BM3D, DnCNN, and FFDnet had the better denoising performance and computational speed. In the experiment described in this subsection, these methods were selected for a further comparative test of the denoising ability of the proposed model with color images. The datasets used here are the color versions of CBSD68, Kodak24, and McMaster.

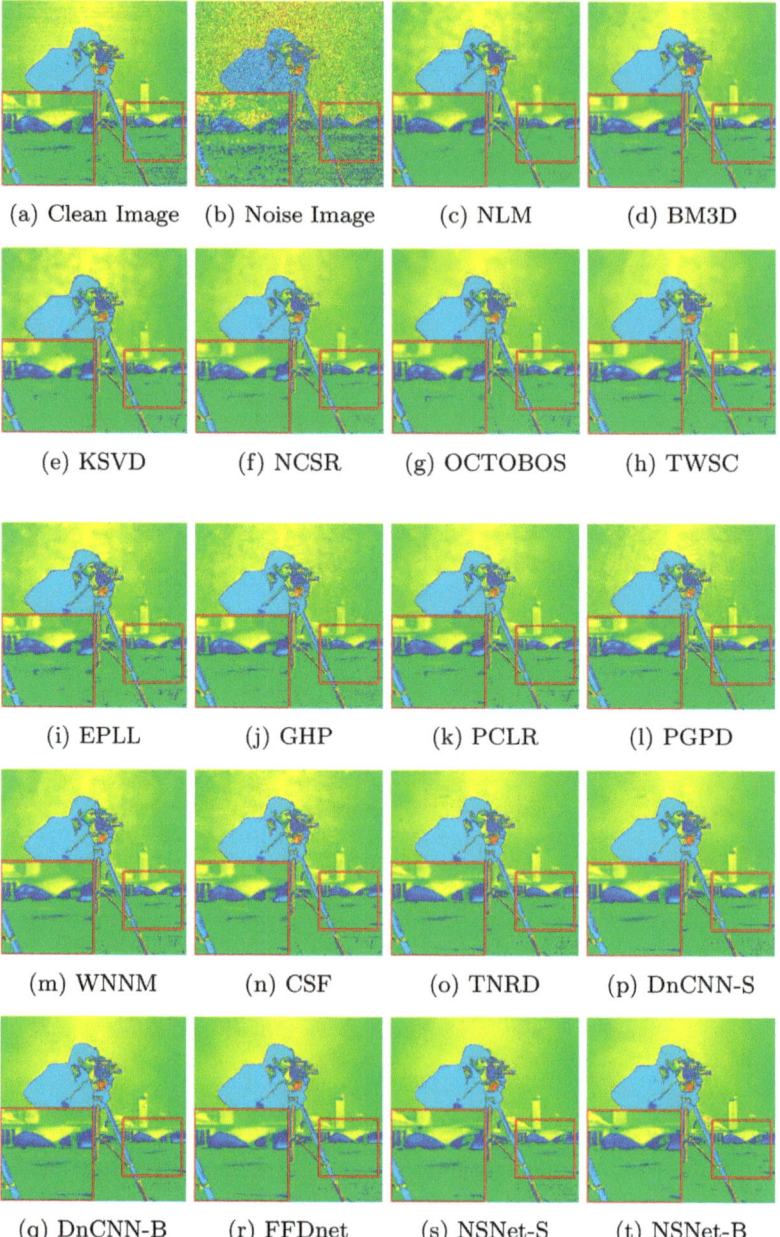

Figure 8. Results of some denoising methods at a noise level of 25.

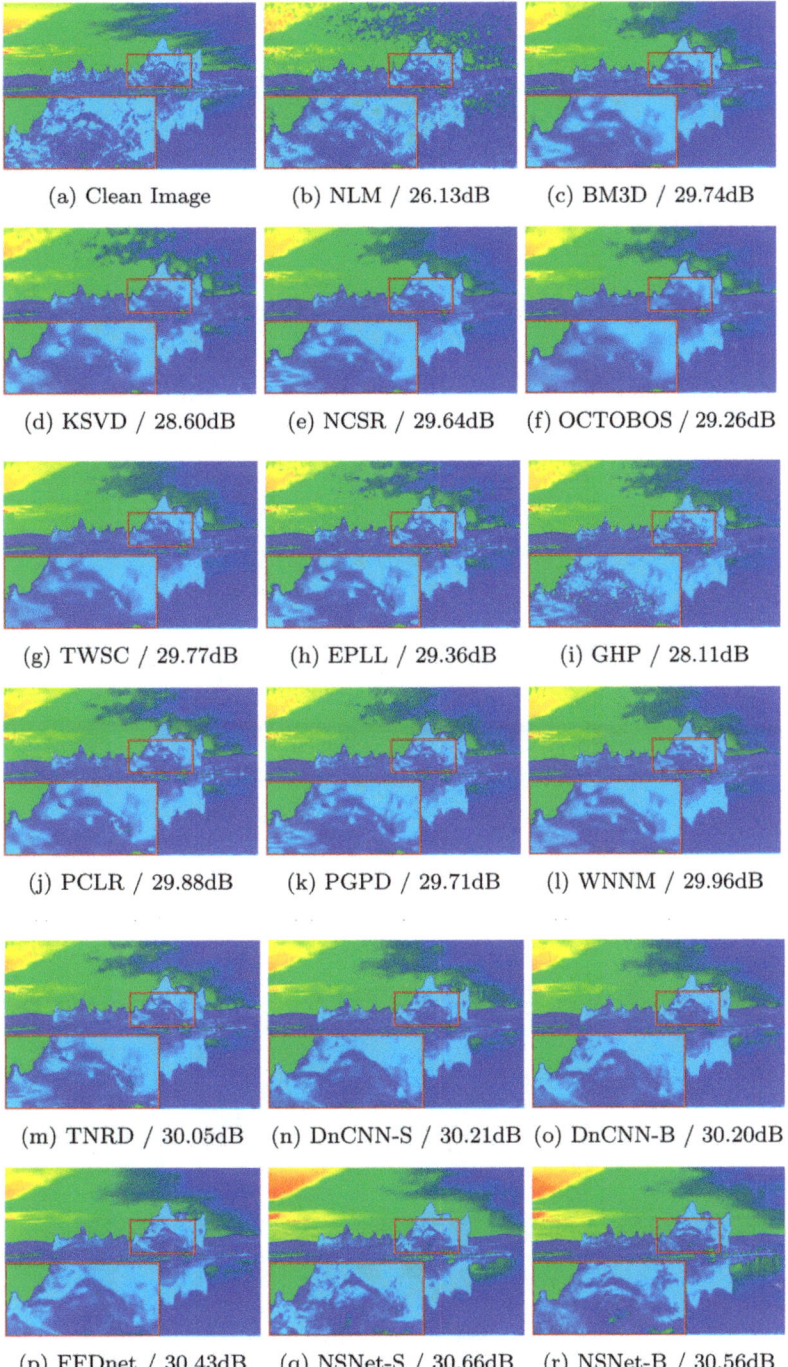

Figure 9. Results of some denoising methods at a noise level of 50.

The denoising performance of four methods (BM3D, DnCNN, FFDNet, and NSNet) at noise levels of 35, 45, and 55 is shown in Table 7. The proposed NSNet is the best model in the denoising experiments with CBSD68 and Kodak24, with McMaster ranked second.

Table 7. Average PSNRs/SSIMs of all methods on color images.

Dataset	Noise Level	Method			
		BM3D	DnCNN	FFDNet	NSNet
CBSD68	$\sigma = 35$	28.88/0.8160	29.60 */0.8422 *	29.59/0.8408	29.69 #/0.8481 #
	$\sigma = 45$	27.84/0.7793	28.43/0.8060 *	28.44 */0.8048	28.58 #/0.8150 #
	$\sigma = 55$	26.97/0.7468	27.50/0.7736	27.56 */0.7738 *	27.70 #/0.7854 #
Kodak24	$\sigma = 35$	29.89/0.8208	30.45/0.8387	30.56 */0.8405 *	30.67 #/0.8478 #
	$\sigma = 45$	28.91/0.7906	29.31/0.8057	29.44 */0.8083 *	29.59 #/0.8187 #
	$\sigma = 55$	28.06/0.7629	28.38/0.7753	28.57 */0.7811 *	28.72 #/0.7929 #
McMaster	$\sigma = 35$	29.93/0.8237	30.15/0.8392	30.83 #/0.8550 #	30.60 */0.8527 *
	$\sigma = 45$	29.00/0.7988	29.08/0.8116	29.68 #/0.8275 *	29.55 */0.8281 #
	$\sigma = 55$	28.13/0.7712	28.17/0.7832	28.76 #/0.8032 #	28.73 */0.8049 #

Note: # The best denoising performance. * The second-best denoising performance.

In the denoising experiment with the dataset CBSD68, NSNet performed 0.81 dB better than BM3D, 0.09 dB better than DnCNN, and 0.1 dB better than FFDNet at a noise level of 35. It was 0.74 dB better than BM3D, 0.15 dB better than DnCNN, and 0.14 dB better than FFDNet at a noise level of 45, and 0.73 dB better than BM3D, 0.2 dB better than DnCNN, and 0.14 dB better than FFDNet at a noise level of 55. In the denoising experiment with the dataset Kodak24, NSNet was 0.78 dB better than BM3D, 0.22 dB better than DnCNN, and 0.11 dB better than FFDNet at a noise level of 35. It was 0.68 dB better than BM3D, 0.28 dB better than DnCNN, and 0.15dB better than FFDNet at a noise level of 45, and 0.66 dB better than BM3D, 0.34 dB better than DnCNN, and 0.15 dB better than FFDNet at a noise level of 55. In the denoising experiment using the McMaster dataset, although the denoising performance of NSNet was not as good as that of FFDNet, the comparison of all methods in terms of SSIM shows that NSNet is able to recover the structure of the color image better.

Figure 10 shows the denoising results of four methods (BM3D, DnCNN, FFDNet, and NSNet) on one image of the public dataset CBSD68 at a noise level of 45. To better demonstrate the denoising performance of the proposed method, two representative parts are highlighted. These show that NSNet repairs the texture better than other methods. Figure 11 shows the denoising results of four methods at a noise level of 40. NSNet has a more significant repair effect on "stone" in the image, and its recovery of textures is better than those of other methods.

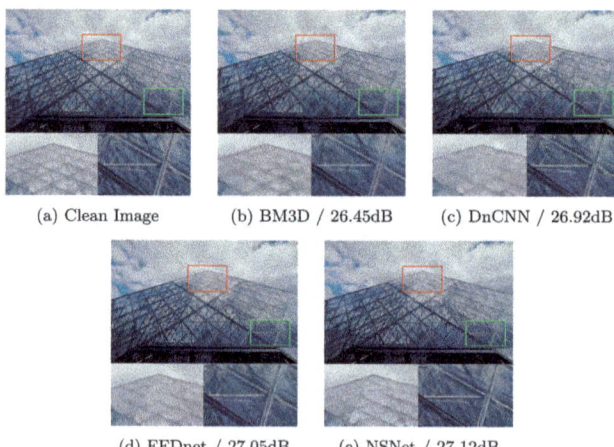

(a) Clean Image (b) BM3D / 26.45dB (c) DnCNN / 26.92dB
(d) FFDnet / 27.05dB (e) NSNet / 27.12dB

Figure 10. Comparison of denoising results on one color image of the public dataset CBSD68 [39] at a noise level of 45.

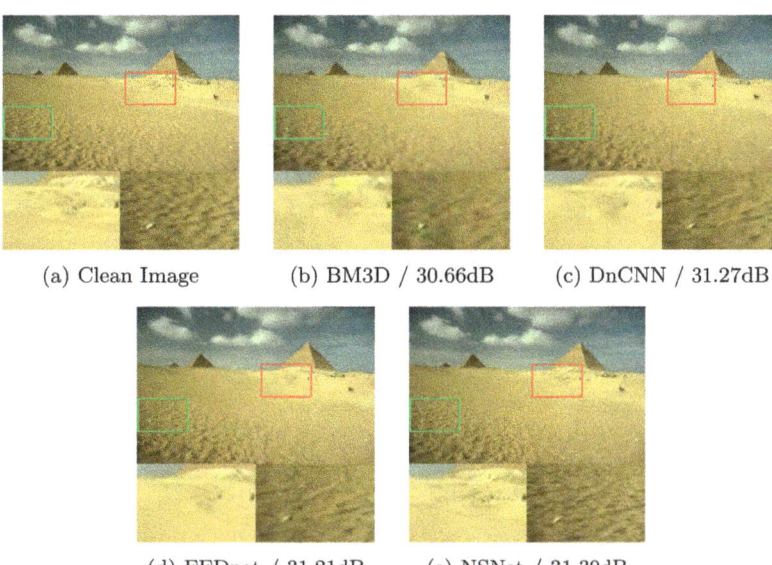

Figure 11. Comparison of denoising results on one color image of the public dataset CBSD68 [39] at a noise level of 40.

5. Conclusions

In this study, an N-shaped convolutional network that can extract multi-scale information is proposed. NSNet is able to extract multi-scale information from corrupted images and uses it to compensate for the drawbacks of convolutional operations in extracting global features, thus enhancing NSNet's ability to capture global information and reconstruct textures and contours. Ablation experiments demonstrate that extracting multi-scale information is beneficial to improving the denoising performance of the model at noise levels in the range of (0, 50). Gray and color image denoising experiments demonstrate that NSNet outperforms many existing image denoising methods at noise levels of 15, 25, and 50, especially at high noise levels. In addition, NSNet has a good blind denoising performance, where its performance at high noise levels is close to that at known noise levels.

Author Contributions: Conceptualization, writing—review and editing, visualization, supervision, and funding acquisition, Y.L. Methodology, software, validation, investigation, and writing—original draft preparation, Y.C. All authors have read and agreed to the published version of the manuscript.

Funding: This research was funded by the Changsha Municipal Natural Science Foundation under Grant kq2208432.

Data Availability Statement: Not applicable.

Conflicts of Interest: The authors declare no conflict of interest.

References

1. Chatterjee, P.; Milanfar, P. Is denoising dead? *IEEE Trans. Image Process.* **2009**, *19*, 895–911. [CrossRef] [PubMed]
2. Buades, A.; Coll, B.; Morel, J.-M. A non-local algorithm for image denoising. In Proceedings of the 2005 IEEE Computer Society Conference on Computer Vision and Pattern Recognition, San Diego, CA, USA, 20–25 June 2005; Volume 2, pp. 60–65.
3. Dabov, K.; Foi, A.; Katkovnik, V.; Egiazarian, K. Image denoising by sparse 3-D transform-domain collaborative filtering. *IEEE Trans. Image Process.* **2007**, *16*, 2080–2095. [CrossRef] [PubMed]
4. Elad, M.; Aharon, M. Image denoising via sparse and redundant representations over learned dictionaries. *IEEE Trans. Image Process.* **2006**, *15*, 3736–3745. [CrossRef] [PubMed]
5. Mairal, J.; Bach, F.; Ponce, J.; Sapiro, G.; Zisserman, A. Non-local sparse models for image restoration. In Proceedings of the 2009 IEEE 12th International Conference on Computer Vision, Kyoto, Japan, 29 September–2 October 2009; pp. 2272–2279.

6. Dong, W.; Zhang, L.; Shi, G.; Li, X. Nonlocally centralized sparse representation for image restoration. *IEEE Trans. Image Process.* **2013**, *22*, 1620–1630. [CrossRef] [PubMed]
7. Wen, B.; Ravishankar, S.; Bresler, Y. Structured overcomplete sparsifying transform learning with convergence guarantees and applications. *Int. J. Comput. Vis.* **2015**, *114*, 137–167. [CrossRef]
8. Xu, J.; Zhang, L.; Zhang, D. A trilateral weighted sparse coding scheme for real-world image denoising. In Proceedings of the European Conference on Computer Vision, Munich, Germany, 8–14 September 2018; pp. 20–36.
9. Zoran, D.; Weiss, Y. From learning models of natural image patches to whole image restoration. In Proceedings of the 2011 International Conference on Computer Vision, Barcelona, Spain, 6–13 November 2011; pp. 479–486.
10. Xu, J.; Zhang, L.; Zuo, W.; Zhang, D.; Feng, X. Patch group based nonlocal self-similarity prior learning for image denoising. In Proceedings of the 2015 IEEE International Conference on Computer Vision (ICCV), Santiago, Chile, 7–13 December 2015; pp. 244–252.
11. Chen, F.; Zhang, L.; Yu, H. External patch prior guided internal clustering for image denoising. In Proceedings of the 2015 IEEE International Conference on Computer Vision (ICCV), Santiago, Chile, 7–13 December 2015; pp. 603–611.
12. Zuo, W.; Zhang, L.; Song, C.; Zhang, D. Texture enhanced image denoising via gradient histogram preservation. In Proceedings of the 2013 IEEE Conference on Computer Vision and Pattern Recognition, Portland, OR, USA, 23–28 June 2013; pp. 1203–1210.
13. Gu, S.; Zhang, L.; Zuo, W.; Feng, X. Weighted nuclear norm minimization with application to image denoising. In Proceedings of the 2014 IEEE Conference on Computer Vision and Pattern Recognition, Columbus, OH, USA, 23–28 June 2014; pp. 2862–2869.
14. Zhao, Q.; Meng, D.; Xu, Z.; Zuo, W.; Yan, Y. L1-norm low-rank matrix factorization by variational bayesian method. *IEEE Trans. Neural Netw. Learn. Syst.* **2015**, *26*, 825–839. [CrossRef] [PubMed]
15. Schmidt, U.; Roth, S. Shrinkage fields for effective image restoration. In Proceedings of the 2014 IEEE Conference on Computer Vision and Pattern Recognition, Columbus, OH, USA, 23–28 June 2014; pp. 2774–2781.
16. Chen, Y.; Yu, W.; Pock, T. On learning optimized reaction diffusion processes for effective image restoration. In Proceedings of the 2015 IEEE Conference on Computer Vision and Pattern Recognition (CVPR), Boston, MA, USA, 7–12 June 2015; pp. 5261–5269.
17. Zhang, K.; Zuo, W.; Chen, Y.; Meng, D.; Zhang, L. Beyond a gaussian denoiser: Residual learning of deep cnn for image denoising. *IEEE Trans. Image Process.* **2017**, *26*, 3142–3155. [CrossRef] [PubMed]
18. Zhang, K.; Zuo, W.; Zhang, L. Ffdnet: Toward a fast and flexible solution for cnn-based image denoising. *IEEE Trans. Image Process.* **2018**, *27*, 4608–4622. [CrossRef] [PubMed]
19. Guo, S.; Yan, Z.; Zhang, K.; Zuo, W.; Zhang, L. Toward convolutional blind denoising of real photographs. In Proceedings of the 2019 IEEE/CVF Conference on Computer Vision and Pattern Recognition, Long Beach, CA, USA, 15–20 June 2019; pp. 1712–1722.
20. Ma, R.; Zhang, B.; Hu, H. Gaussian pyramid of conditional generative adversarial network for real-world noisy image denoising. *Neural Process. Lett.* **2020**, *51*, 2669–2684. [CrossRef]
21. Anwar, S.; Barnes, N. Real image denoising with feature attention. In Proceedings of the 2019 IEEE/CVF International Conference on Computer Vision (ICCV), Seoul, Republic of Korea, 27 October–2 November 2019; pp. 3155–3164.
22. Li, D.; Chen, H.; Jin, G.; Jin, Y.; Chen, E. A multiscale dilated residual network for image denoising. *Multim. Tools Appl.* **2020**, *79*, 34443–34458. [CrossRef]
23. Binh, P.H.T.; Cruz, C.; Egiazarian, K. Flashlight CNN image denoising. In Proceedings of the IEEE European Signal Processing Conference, Amsterdam, The Netherlands, 18–21 January 2021; pp. 670–674.
24. Quan, Y.; Chen, Y.; Shao, Y.; Teng, H.; Xu, Y.; Ji, H. Image denoising using complex-valued deep CNN. *Pattern Recognit.* **2021**, *111*, 107–113. [CrossRef]
25. Guan, X.; Hu, W.; Fu, H. Remote sensing image denoising algorithm with multi-receptive field feature fusion and enhancement. *Acta Photonica Sin.* **2022**, *51*, 365–377.
26. Zheng, M.; Zhi, K.; Zeng, J.; Tian, C.; You, L. A hybrid CNN for image denoising. *J. Artif. Intell. Technol.* **2022**, *2*, 93–99. [CrossRef]
27. Tian, C.; Zheng, M.; Zuo, W.; Zhang, B.; Zhang, Y.; Zhang, D. Multi-stage image denoising with the wavelet transform. *Pattern Recognit.* **2023**, *134*, 109050. [CrossRef]
28. Tang, Y.; Wang, X.; Zhu, J.; Gao, Y.; Jiang, A. LMENet: A lightweight multiscale efficient convolutional neural network for image denoising. In Proceedings of the IEEE Region 10 Conference 2022, Hong Kong, China, 1–4 November 2022; pp. 1–6.
29. Ronneberger, O.; Fischer, P.; Brox, T. U-net: Convolutional networks for biomedical image segmentation. In Proceedings of the International Conference on Medical Image Computing and Computer-assisted Intervention 2015, Munich, Germany, 5–9 October 2015; pp. 234–241.
30. Gungor, M.A.; Gencol, K. Developing a compression procedure based on the wavelet denoising and jpeg2000 compression. *Optik* **2020**, *218*, 164933. [CrossRef]
31. Liu, P.; Zhang, H.; Zhang, K.; Lin, L.; Zuo, W. Multi-level wavelet-CNN for image restoration. In Proceedings of the 2018 IEEE/CVF Conference on Computer Vision and Pattern Recognition Workshops, Salt Lake City, UT, USA, 18–22 June 2018; pp. 773–782.
32. Gungor, M.A. A comparative study on wavelet denoising for high noisy ct images of COVID-19 disease. *Optik* **2021**, *235*, 166652. [CrossRef] [PubMed]
33. Qian, Y.; Huang, Z.; Fang, H.; Zuo, Z. Wglfnets: Wavelet-based global-local filtering networks for image denoising with structure preservation. *Optik* **2022**, *261*, 169089. [CrossRef]

34. Fu, H.; Cheng, J.; Xu, Y.; Wong, D.W.K.; Liu, J.; Cao, X. Joint optic disc and cup segmentation based on multi-label deep network and polar transformation. *IEEE Trans. Med. Imaging* **2018**, *37*, 1597–1605. [CrossRef] [PubMed]
35. Liu, Y.; Cheng, M.-M.; Hu, X.; Wang, K.; Bai, X. Richer convolutional features for edge detection. In Proceedings of the 2017 Conference on Computer Vision and Pattern Recognition, Honolulu, HI, USA, 21–26 July 2017; pp. 5872–5881.
36. Ioffe, S.; Szegedy, C. Batch normalization: Accelerating deep network training by reducing internal covariate shift. In Proceedings of the 32nd International Conference on International Conference on Machine Learning, Lille, France, 6–11 July 2015; pp. 448–456.
37. He, K.; Zhang, X.; Ren, S.; Sun, J. Deep residual learning for image recognition. In Proceedings of the 2016 IEEE Conference on Computer Vision and Pattern Recognition (CVPR), Las Vegas, NV, USA, 27–30 June 2016; pp. 770–778.
38. Roth, S.; Black, M.J. Fields of experts: A framework for learning image priors. In Proceedings of the 2005 IEEE Computer Society Conference on Computer Vision and Pattern Recognition, San Diego, CA, USA, 20–25 June 2005; Volume 2, pp. 860–867.
39. Martin, D.; Fowlkes, C.; Tal, D.; Malik, J. A database of human segmented natural images and its application to evaluating segmentation algorithms and measuring ecological statistics. In Proceedings of the Eighth IEEE International Conference on Computer Vision, Vancouver, BC, Canada, 7–14 July 2001; Volume 2, pp. 416–4232.
40. Franzen, R. Kodak Lossless True Color Image Suite. 1999. Available online: http://r0k.us/graphics/kodak (accessed on 1 January 2022).
41. Zhang, L.; Wu, X.; Buades, A.; Li, X. Color demosaicking by local directional interpolation and nonlocal adaptive thresholding. *J. Electron. Imaging* **2011**, *20*, 23016.

Disclaimer/Publisher's Note: The statements, opinions and data contained in all publications are solely those of the individual author(s) and contributor(s) and not of MDPI and/or the editor(s). MDPI and/or the editor(s) disclaim responsibility for any injury to people or property resulting from any ideas, methods, instructions or products referred to in the content.

Article

An Analysis of Climate Change Based on Machine Learning and an Endoreversible Model

Sebastián Vázquez-Ramírez [1], Miguel Torres-Ruiz [1,*], Rolando Quintero [1], Kwok Tai Chui [2] and Carlos Guzmán Sánchez-Mejorada [1]

[1] Instituto Politécnico Nacional, CIC, UPALM-Zacatenco, Mexico City 07320, Mexico; svazquezr1102@alumno.ipn.mx (S.V.-R.); rquintero@ipn.mx (R.Q.); cmejora@ipn.mx (C.G.S.-M.)
[2] Department of Electronic Engineering and Computer Science, School of Science and Technology, Hong Kong Metropolitan University, Hong Kong, China; jktchui@hkmu.edu.hk
* Correspondence: mtorresru@ipn.mx; Tel.: +52-(55)-5729-6000 (ext. 56590)

Abstract: Several Sun models suggest a radioactive balance, where the concentration of greenhouse gases and the albedo effect are related to the Earth's surface temperature. There is a considerable increment in greenhouse gases due to anthropogenic activities. Climate change correlates with this alteration in the atmosphere and an increase in surface temperature. Efficient forecasting of climate change and its impacts could be helpful to respond to the threat of c.c. and develop sustainably. Many studies have predicted temperature changes in the coming years. The global community has to create a model that can realize good predictions to ensure the best way to deal with this warming. Thus, we propose a finite-time thermodynamic (FTT) approach in the current work. FTT can solve problems such as the faint young Sun paradox. In addition, we use different machine learning models to evaluate our method and compare the experimental prediction and results.

Keywords: clustering; machine learning; greenhouse gas; finite-time thermodynamics; climate change

MSC: 68U01

Citation: Vázquez-Ramírez, S.; Torres-Ruiz, M.; Quintero, R.; Chui, K.T.; Guzmán Sánchez-Mejorada, C. An Analysis of Climate Change Based on Machine Learning and an Endoreversible Model. *Mathematics* **2023**, *11*, 3060. https://doi.org/10.3390/math11143060

Academic Editor: Wei Fang

Received: 15 June 2023
Revised: 8 July 2023
Accepted: 9 July 2023
Published: 11 July 2023

Copyright: © 2023 by the authors. Licensee MDPI, Basel, Switzerland. This article is an open access article distributed under the terms and conditions of the Creative Commons Attribution (CC BY) license (https://creativecommons.org/licenses/by/4.0/).

1. Introduction

The issue of climate change stands as one of the most significant obstacles that humanity must confront. Thus, extensive scientific evidence demonstrates that the altering climate has significantly impacted societies throughout history and in the present, posing severe effects for the future. Modern advancements in quantitative empirical studies have shed light on the crucial interconnections within the interconnected climate–human system [1]. Various statistical studies have explored the cause-and-effect relationship between particular climate conditions and their influence on social interaction, agriculture, economics, migratory flows, and health [2].

The emergence of scientific efforts in different fields has created a consensus concerning the sustainable development of initiatives and strategies to mitigate climate change. The most severe consequences of climate change directly affect the health of citizens due to human activities causing the proliferation of greenhouse gases in the atmosphere, which induces the increase in temperatures and alteration of the hydrologic cycle [3]. The analysis of the climate change situation is very timely, because secondary effects are associated with the negative impact on agriculture, the geographic distribution of infectious diseases, large-scale migrations, clean water access, and others [4].

Machine learning techniques have recently successfully employed statistical downscaling methods for global climate models. According to Nourani et al. [5], a diverse range of machine learning models have been developed and used in groundwater modeling and other prediction tasks within the field of environmental engineering [6]. Prediction models focused on machine learning to analyze climate variables such as precipitation and temperature have been proposed in other studies to improve accuracy [7]. The support vector regression model, the adaptive neurofuzzy inference system, and the feedforward neural network (FFNN) are the most frequently employed machine learning models to analyze climate change and particular groundwater levels [8,9]. Other approaches are based on Gaussian models, which are suitable methods for global climate modeling [10].

Recently, there has been a growing emergence of deep learning models that have garnered significant attention across various engineering disciplines due to their ability to extract features from data. Among these models, the long short-term memory (LSTM) neural network stands out as a powerful deep learning model capable of capturing sequential characteristics from time series data. LSTM has already been successfully applied in groundwater-level modeling, as demonstrated by Nourani et al. [11]. According to the literature review, decision trees, random forests, and artificial neural networks are the most commonly applied machine algorithms to analyze climate change risk assessment. They have enabled the identification, classification, and detection of targets and environmental and structural features, particularly flood and landslide risk events [12].

In the same context, analyzing changes in hydrological systems directly impacts global climate change, in which classic machine learning algorithms could be limited to quantifying events related to the climate variability in those hydrological systems. However, the Gaussian process regression method has been demonstrated to improve the analysis concerning nonlinear climate variables [13].

On the other hand, the literature reports a crucial synergy between the physics-based models and machine-learning techniques to develop hybrid approaches to climate change analysis [14]. Thus, Chukwujindu et al. [15] revealed a crucial relationship between physics and artificial intelligence to understand better the climate change caused by solar radiation.

According to the development and integration of multidisciplinary fields, the last years have involved applying physics theories to analyze various Earth phenomena. Now, physicists and computer scientists have demonstrated enormous interest in studying the aforementioned secondary effects of climate change. In this sense, Jusup et al. [16] considered "social physics" an essential tool to quantify social and environmental phenomena. Moreover, this approach is oriented toward analyzing different issues in which this discipline can explicitly explain each phenomenon. For instance, in addressing the climate change topic, the use of network area to describe the complex problem of Earth's climate system evidences how physics methods are suitable to work in a multidisciplinary way with other fields to face this issue quantitatively.

Addressing the risks associated with climate change, Steffen et al. [17] recognized the relationship between the social community and climate. Therefore, this strategy extends beyond solely understanding the physical aspects, and requires mobilizing human action. Scientists are striving to meet this challenge by integrating climate science, social sciences, computer science, and humanities, resulting in a new field called earth system science, which aims to foster a holistic understanding of the Earth's complex dynamics.

On the other hand, global warming is a visible consequence of the heightened intensity and frequency of extreme weather and climate events, which encompass a range of phenomena, including heatwaves, droughts, wildfires, floods, and hurricanes. These extreme events pose a substantial risk to human lives and livelihoods, evident through consequences such as fresh and clean water scarcity and diminished food production. Such extreme events are characterized by the climatic variable surpassing a critical threshold. It is worth noting that some extreme events may arise from natural climate variability and are not directly linked to human-induced forces [18].

There is a high degree of confidence that the anthropogenic rise in greenhouse gas concentrations and other human-induced factors is responsible for more than 50% of the reported global average surface temperature accumulation between 1951 and 2010 [16].

Thus, considering the theoretical foundations presented in [16,19], we propose a finite-time thermodynamic approach to model and predict Earth's global warming, comparing the results of the model with the implementation of machine learning techniques to assess the predictions.

Finite-time thermodynamics (FTT) has been developed by placing realistic limits on irreversible processes through various properties, such as power, efficiency, and dissipation. FTT can be considered an extension of classical equilibrium thermodynamics (CET), in which thermodynamic models more similar to the real world are sought compared to those given by CET. So, these models consider the irreversibilities of the system [20,21]. The approach incorporates the constraints of finite-time operation; constraints on system variables; and generic models for the sources of irreversibility, and thus the production of entropy such as finite rate, heat transfer, friction, and heat leakage, among others [22]. Moreover, an extreme or optimum of a thermodynamically significant variable is calculated, such as minimizing entropy production, maximizing energy or availability, and maximizing power and efficiency [22]. The pioneering work of the FTT corresponds to Curzon and Ahlborn [20,22], in which the fundamental limits of a power plant used a *machine endoreversible* model. This is made up of an endoreversible Carnot cycle, where the irreversible processes involve the exchange of heat between the thermal reservoirs and the active substance.

The thermal engine is composed of two temperature stores, T_1 and T_2, where $T_1 > T_2$, two irreversible components that are the two thermal resistances, which produce thermal flows towards the reversible Carnot engine with intermediate temperatures T_{1w} and T_{2w}, with $T_{1w} > T_{2w}$, placed between the intermediate stores. The model considers a linear heat transfer between two irreversible components (thermal conductances α and β) conductances (see Figure 1).

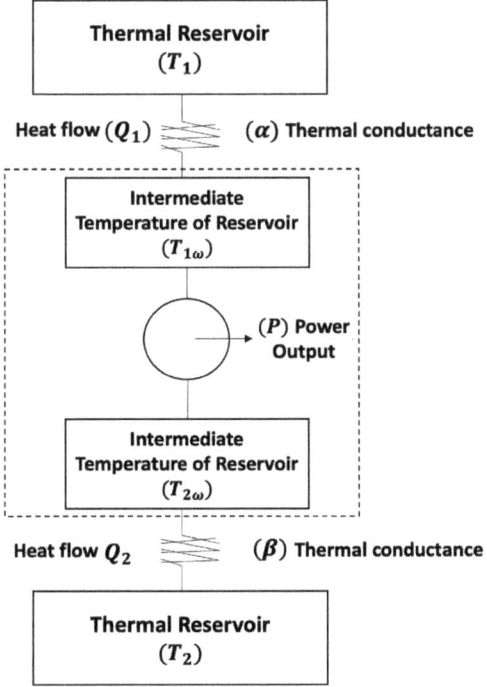

Figure 1. Scheme of a endoreversible model proposed by De Vos [23].

Summing up, Figure 1 shows a schematic representation of the endoreversible Curzon–Ahlborn engine. It is built by two reservoirs of temperatures T_1 and T_2, respectively: α and β, which denote thermal conductance constants, and a reversible Carnot engine represented by T_{1w} and T_{1w}, where P is the power output of the cycle.

A problem solved by finite-time thermodynamics efficiently is the so-called weak young Sun paradox proposed by Sagan and Mullen [24]. This study presents a drawback for understanding the early stages of planet Earth, since the Sun's luminosity about 4.5 Gyr ago was between 70–80% of its value to operate [24–26]. So, it represents a terrestrial temperature below the water freezing point. The planet's surface temperature is controlled by the solar radiation it acquires and its interchange with the gases in the atmosphere. We consider a blackbody radiative equilibrium between the young Sun and the Earth obtained in a surface temperature T = 255K, low enough to keep most of the planet's surface frozen down to 1–2 Gyr [24]. However, several studies, together with sedimentary records, suggest the existence of an average surface temperature capable of having liquid water for almost the entire history of the planet [24]. So, to resolve such a paradox, the first assumption is taken that solar radiation has increased in the Sun's lifetime due to the increase in density of the solar nucleus [24]. The luminosity of the young Sun has been estimated to be 30% less than the actual value received from the Sun, according to what was said by Gough [24], where I_{sc} is the present luminosity of the Sun and $t_0 \approx 4.56$ Gyr, which is the present age of the Sun. Equation (1) shows the evolution of the Sun's luminosity, and this equation affects the amount of average solar radiation $\bar{q}_s = I_{sc}(1-\rho)/4$ received by the planet. The equation of the luminosity of Gough is expressed in the following way:

$$I(t) = \left[1 + 0.4\left(1 - \frac{t}{t_0}\right)\right]^{-1} I_{sc} \qquad (1)$$

Based on the foundation, the problem of thermodynamic equilibrium between the solar system's planets depends on the influx of solar incident I_{sc}, the Earth's albedo ρ, and the effect of greenhouse γ. Thus, the issue of the thermal equilibrium among solar system planets and a correct temperature estimation is solved based on the atmosphere's physical characteristics. Curzon and Ahlborn [22] introduced the finite-time thermodynamics concept. They achieved this using a Carnot cycle model, incorporating limited heat transfer between the heat reservoir and the working substance, all within a maximum-power operating regime. Following its initial introduction, finite-time thermodynamics underwent further development to encompass various operating regimes, including—but not limited to—efficiency power, ecological function, and more. Using the FTT-based approach in creating models for power converters results in more accurate representations of their operational levels in real-world scenarios. In [20], an atmospheric convection model, known as the Gordon–Zarmi (GZ) model, was introduced to estimate the temperature of the Earth's lowest atmospheric layer and establish an upper limit for average wind power. The GZ model incorporates a convection cell, an endoreversible Carnot cycle, and two external thermal reservoirs, such as air, surrounding the active substance.

The study presented in [27] examined the endoreversible model and recognized that there is a dissipation of wind energy. The authors proposed to derive an upper limit for the efficiency of converting solar energy into wind energy, which is approximately 8.3%, assuming the atmospheric "heat engine" is fully powered by a complete power engine.

On the other hand, Van der Wel improved a new efficiency of the solar energy upper bound $w_{max} \approx 10.23\%$ with another endoreversible model based on convective Hadley cells [24,28]. The peculiarity of the GZ models is that they offer a potential resolution to the paradox known as the "young and weak Sun", which was initially introduced by Carl Sagan and George Mullen in 1972 [25,26]. The GZ and Gough models examine the evolution of the solar constant, enabling the investigation of potential future scenarios for Earth's temperature. These models employ various objective functions, including maximum power, efficient power, and ecological function, to analyze and assess these scenarios.

Hence, the present research study aims to investigate the planet's surface temperatures resulting from the escalating levels of greenhouse gases. The approach involves analyzing the thermodynamic behavior of the atmosphere within a finite-time regime. We decided to employ this methodology, considering the good results in predicting climate change in several geologic eras in the past. So, it is possible to modify and set the endoreversible machine model to forecast temperatures derived from climate change in the coming years.

The remaining paper is organized as follows: The subsequent section consists of comprehensive state-of-the-art climate change models based on different approaches. Section 3 describes the preliminary foundations concerning finite-time thermodynamics; Section 4 outlines the methods related to the proposed endoreversible model; and Section 5 describes the proposed model and its peculiarities. Section 6 shows the experimental results, and the discussion of the outcomes and findings are included in Section 7, and the last section involves the conclusion and future works.

2. Related Work

Global warming caused by human activities represents one of the most significant challenges of the present time. The classical approaches concerning climate change have studied complex systems such as differential equations and developments in chaos theory. Nevertheless, the large amount of data available allows us to use artificial intelligence techniques, which are more straightforward than those used by the areas of complexity science, resulting in the prediction of future scenarios due to climate change.

According to Houghton [29], global warming is a climate system where several variables are responsible for raising global average temperatures. Most of these effects are related to the radiative balance of the planetary atmosphere: water vapor feedback, cloud radiation feedback, and ocean circulation feedback. In consequence, all of them refer to the albedo and greenhouse effects. Therefore, to forecast global warming, a set of characteristics that affect the global emission of greenhouse gases must be taken. These gases have had a notable increase due to anthropogenic behavior and activity. Development projections of global average temperature changes for the present century are in the range of 0.15–0.6 °C per decade. Understanding this problem allows us to consider humans' and ecosystems' impacts and adaptive capacity [29].

One of the major consequences of global warming is the melting of ice bodies on the Earth. The Arctic Sea is one of the leading indicators of the increase in average temperature. The study of the ice concentration and the rise in sea level has various approaches, one of which that is widely used is deep learning techniques to predict how the ice concentration changes with the increase in average temperature [30]. In the same way that the Arctic layers and their melting show the effect of climate change, all oceans experience the same significant warming and a rising sea level, so it is necessary to generate diagnostic and prognostic prediction models to elucidate these increases and their risks, since they are associated with other adverse events such as the propagation of cycles, lack of rain, and the growth and spread of diseases. According to diverse authors, the combination of machine learning and deep learning techniques can give us entirely accurate predictions for the future [31–34].

In the study carried out by Sidhu et al. [35], the use of machine learning is analyzed to understand the impact of climate change on different types of crops, taking into account climate–yield relationships. The authors compared the usual linear regression technique for estimating historical data to approximate yield against climate change and using boosted regression trees. The conclusions suggested that interpreting results based on a single model can generate biases in the information obtained.

On the other hand, due to the high economic and social impacts associated with climate change, it is essential to understand the causes and identify the patterns of the obtained data to make correct predictions. According to Zheng et al. [36], the construction of a reliable model based on experimental data and the relationship between temperature and the concentration of gases in the atmosphere such as carbon dioxide (CO_2), nitrous oxide (N_2O) and methane (CH_4), is the first challenge to address the climate change problem. Zheng's study used various learning techniques, such as linear regression, support vector machines, and random forests to build an accurate model that would identify changes in the atmosphere's increasing temperature, dominated mainly by the increase in the temperature of CO_2 due to its higher concentration within greenhouse gases.

Different authors argue that the construction of a reliable model combined with the temperature dataset and machine learning prediction tools will help us to have a better understanding of the phenomenon, and thus be able to make a good forecast that allows us to face the risks of climate change. The thermal equilibrium model was studied by De Vos and Flater [28], who analyzed solar radiation as an energy converter used to examine the average temperature of a planet. It is carried out by the radiation from the planet's surface and the irradiance reaching Earth. This analysis takes into account the physical characteristics of the atmosphere, such as friendliness and the albedo effect [22,27,28]. Thus, the total flux Q appears as shown in Equation (2).

$$Q = 4\pi R^2 \sigma \left((1-\rho)\frac{f}{4}T_s^4 - (1-\gamma)T_p^4 \right) \quad (2)$$

It is the first thermodynamic model that allows for a dynamic study of the different layers of the atmosphere, with the lowest layer corresponding to the temperature on the planetary surface. This development can analyze various scenarios where greenhouse gases and albedo concentrations are modified. The feasibility of the model was tested in the study of geological eras, and several authors carried out the solution of the faint young Sun paradox [24,25]. The study of the solar converters under the regime of finite-time thermodynamics was analyzed in this work, changing the parameters to current time, considering the increase in CO_2 main greenhouse gas [36]; its relationship with albedo was developed too. In addition, a dissipation of energy in the system has realistic results at the current time.

According to the state of the art, there are several proposals related to analyzing global climate change based on prediction models developed with deep learning approaches, using specifically convolutional and recurrent neural networks. In [37], a method to efficiently predict weather forecasting was proposed by designing a model based on a convolutional neural network (CNN). Thus, Miloshevich et al. [38] proposed a methodology to create forecasting artifacts trained with data of 8000-year models, considering an infrastructure defined by a set of various CNNs, which was primarily focused on describing extreme heatwave datasets.

On the other hand, the CNN architecture has been widely employed to assess predictions between the hourly soil temperature and the subsurface depth. Thus, ref. [39] described a one-dimensional CNN prediction model to demonstrate that the air temperature and surface thermal radiation directly impact the soil temperature prediction model, affecting global warming.

Diverse studies have revealed that climate change rushes the increasing global temperature, causing a rise in the international sea level. Consequently, Hassan [40] implemented a set of different multivariable prediction models based on the principal deep learning techniques: recurrent neural networks (RNN), long short-term memory networks (LSTM), gated recurrent unit networks (GRU), and WaveNet as a particular case of CNN. The models used 29 years of data with multiple variables such as changes in the ocean heat content, level of carbon dioxide, mass variation in the Greenland and Antarctica regions, and global temperature anomalies.

According to Ghimire et al. [41], the use of a convolutional neural network with a multilayer perceptron (MLP) generates efficient forecasts of global solar radiation (GSR). The outcomes of their model achieved a relative error of less than 10%, generating a model with very high performance compared to climate models, especially in models developed with convective cells, such as Gordon and Zarmi-type models. Therefore, using CNN enriches the predictions of the climate models, inducing better forecasts that detect extreme weather events caused by climate change.

In consequence, the impact of climate change is reflected in the manifestation of extreme weather events such as droughts, floods, and heat waves. So, improving the methods for predicting global warming and its effects allows for adapting as a society to the planet's dynamic environment. An issue to analyze with climate change is its correlation with the hydroclimatic systems of the Earth. Larson et al. [42] proposed a deep convolutional residual regressive neural network to determine river basins' response to the water cycle's flows. The analysis revealed that this architecture and the catchment flow data exhibited satisfactory prediction performance for various locations at different time scales.

Natural disasters are related to climate change; some examples of these events include flash floods, droughts, and hurricanes. Thus, the Pacific Ocean weather phenomenon known as El Niño-Southern Oscillation (ENSO) is caused by cyclical changes in sea surface temperature (SST) and temperatures in the atmosphere near the tropics. The ENSO impact generates temperature variations, making them slightly warmer or colder up to extreme temperatures, inducing natural disasters. As claimed by Jonnalagadda and Hashemi [43], the use of the adaptive graph convolutional recurrent neural network (AGCRNN) can capture the temporal relationships of features with the Oceanic Niño Index (ONI), increasing the prediction time from three months to eighteen months, surpassing the current dynamic and statistical models.

In recent years, it has been observed that the automated detection of extreme weather events has increased. Therefore, it is required to improve the prediction performance to deal with these weather anomalies. Current research has shown that new convolutional neural network architectures enhance meteorological event detection. According to Lacombe et al. [44], the use of weighted loss functions counteracting the class imbalance in the data together with a correct architecture could show a significant improvement of the prediction up to 39.2% concerning events as natural cyclones. Due to the high impacts of extreme weather events, an energy transition that does not depend on the burning of fossil fuels, the main generator of greenhouse gases, is urgent. Photovoltaic power production is a good power generation option. However, this type of energy production is sensitive to weather, and can generate variations depending on weather conditions. To make realistic energy production forecasts, Ramakrishnan et al. [45] suggested a combined CNN and LSTM model, obtaining a better percentage of photovoltaic yield prediction, considering slow climate fluctuations and substantial climatic variations.

On the other hand, among the most significant consequences of climate change is related to the solar energy generation of power systems. Recently, the accuracy of intrahour solar forecasting has been a crucial topic to be analyzed in the field due to two critical aspects: (1) the accuracy of prediction models considering the dynamic coverage of clouds, and (2) the short forecast horizon for a minimal time window [46]. Thus, different proposals and methods to face these aspects have been proposed. Caldas and Alonso-Suárez [47] designed a hybrid model to predict solar irradiance, merging sky (cloud status) data provided by images and irradiance measures. The outcomes revealed that the model is efficient in preserving solar energy resources. In this sense, Pedro et al. [48] presented a study to compare machine learning algorithms such as k-nearest neighbors and gradient boosting in tasks to classify data based on intrahour forecasting and irradiance, taking information from sky images. Moreover, solar energy is the most favorable renewable source of electricity, employing a system based on a photovoltaic power supply. In [49], an artificial neural model was designed to predict solar irradiance values without using the detection of clouds.

3. Preliminary

3.1. Finite-Time Thermodynamics

The endoreversible Carnot machine is not in thermodynamic equilibrium with the reservoirs and the active substance. There is a separation between the internally reversible processes and the irreversibilities at the system boundaries, where internal processes with fast relaxation times can be considered reversible and the entropy change for the thermodynamic universe ΔS_u of the machine is positive, the entropy being of our null working substance $\Delta S_w = 0$. This definition is known as the endoreversibility hypothesis; when the model proposed by Curzon and Ahlborn [22] evolves in finite time, the model's power is nonzero, unlike that given by CET [50].

3.2. Curzon and Ahlborn Engine

The engine has thermal conductances that comply with Fourier's law for heat conduction ($\dot{Q} = -\lambda \nabla T$). In the present work, we will use the following notation to refer to the heat flows $Q = \dot{Q}$, such that:

$$Q_1 = \alpha(T_1 - T_{1w}) \tag{3}$$

$$Q_2 = \beta(T_{2w} - T_2) \tag{4}$$

A form of solution to the Curzon and Ahlborn [22] engine and the machine schematic was proposed in [27]. From the conservation of energy, we have the heat flow Q_1 from the upper reservoir, towards the reversible machine with power P to the output flow Q_2 [51]. By the entropic conservation of the system, $\Sigma S = 0$. Therefore, the production of entropy must be zero, whereas for the reversible internal machine, we assume that its entropy changes are zero (*endoreversibility hypothesis*) [23,28,51,52].

$$\sigma = \frac{Q_1}{T_{1w}} - \frac{Q_2}{T_{2w}} = 0 \tag{5}$$

From Equation (5) with the second law of thermodynamics, we have the following relationship for thermal conductors T_{1w} and T_{2w}.

$$T_{1w} = \frac{\alpha}{\alpha + \beta} T_1 + \frac{\beta}{\alpha + \beta} \frac{1}{1 - \eta} T_2 \tag{6}$$

$$T_{2w} = \frac{\alpha}{\alpha + \beta}(1 - \eta) T_1 + \frac{\beta}{\alpha + \beta} T_2 \tag{7}$$

Substituting T_{1w} in Equation (6) and T_{2w} in Equation (7) with our flow Q_1 and Q_2, we obtain Equations (8) and (9).

$$Q_1 = \gamma \frac{T_1 - T_2 - T_1 \eta}{1 - \eta} \tag{8}$$

$$Q_2 = T_2 \left(\frac{\beta(T_1(1 - \eta) - T_2)}{\gamma(1 - \eta)T_1 + \beta T_2} \right) \tag{9}$$

with the expression:

$$\gamma = \frac{\alpha \beta}{\alpha + \beta}$$

Thus, from the definition of efficiency, we can obtain an expression for the power given by:

$$P = \gamma \frac{\eta(T_1 - T_2 - T_1 \eta)}{1 - \eta} \tag{10}$$

Resulting in efficiency at maximum power for the Curzon–Ahlborn machine known in finite-time thermodynamics as η_{ca} that satisfies $0 < \eta_{ca} < \eta_c$.

$$\eta_{CA} = 1 - \sqrt{\frac{T_2}{T_1}} \tag{11}$$

In the endoreversible Curzon–Ahlborn model, the dissipation will be given by formulas that have been derived that show the efficiency of an engine under maximum power conditions [20,21].

$$\Phi_{rb} = Q_2 - \frac{T_2}{T_1} Q_1 \tag{12}$$

4. Materials and Methods

4.1. Gordon and Zarmi (GZ) Model

The atmospheric convection model proposed by GZ consists of a cell as an endoreversible Carnot cycle between two thermal reservoirs of extreme temperatures: the temperature T_1 is the working fluid (atmosphere) temperature at the lowest altitude in the system, related to the temperature of Earth's surface; the temperature in the highest part of the working fluid is the cold reservoir in the GZ model, and the temperature is related to the cosmic background radiation $T_2 = 3K$ (see Figure 2) [20]. The input energy is solar radiation, the active substance is the atmosphere, and the work performed by the fluid of the thermal machine is the mean power of the winds. The GZ convection cell consists of several components, including two isothermal branches where the atmosphere absorbs heat at lower altitudes. Additionally, two intermediate adiabatic branches are assumed to be instantaneous, and the remaining branch releases heat at higher altitudes into the universe [53]. The GZ maximizes the work per cycle W, subject to thermodynamic restrictions and the average solar radiation flux q_s [20,53].

$$\bar{q}_s = \frac{I_{sc}(1-\rho)}{4} \qquad (13)$$

The GZ model works with a Sun–Earth–wind system as an endoreversible engine, in which the input heat is the solar radiation, the active substance is the atmosphere, and the labor produced by this cycle is the mean power of the winds. The cold store for this machine is outer space, with the temperature of the cosmic background radiation of 3K [20].

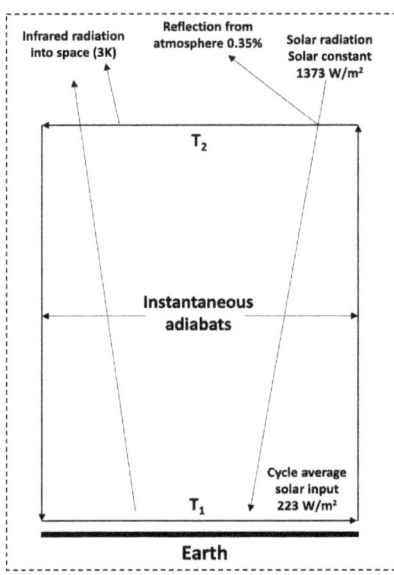

Figure 2. Simplified schema proposed by the GZ diagram of a cyclic heat engine driven by solar energy, the heat input is the solar radiation per area q_s, and the working fluid is the atmosphere. In contrast, the work output is the maximum wind energy. The model can obtain maximum and minimum temperatures of the atmosphere without considering any other effect on the Earth apart from the one already described in the convective cell [20].

Figure 2 shows a schematic view of the simplified system, including its isothermal and adiabatic branches. In addition, this diagram is a simplified version of a thermal engine driven by solar energy. The description of this figure is denoted as follows:

1. The atmosphere absorbs solar radiation at low altitudes through two isothermal branches. At the same time, heat is pushed out at high altitudes through another branch, in which the atmosphere rejects the excess heat.
2. There are two intermediate adiabats characterized by ascending and descending air currents, which occur instantaneously.

The temperatures associated with the four-cycle branches are as follows:

1. T_1 represents the temperature of the working fluid in the isothermal branch situated at the lowest altitude. Here, the working fluid absorbs solar radiation during every half cycle.
2. In the second half of the cycle, heat is released from the working fluid at temperature T_2 (at the highest altitude of the cell) through blackbody radiation, which is directed towards the cold reservoir at temperature T_{ex} (representing the 3K background radiation of the universe) [20,54].

The objective of this model is to maximize the work per cycle, equivalent to maximizing the average power output, according to certain thermodynamic restrictions. From the first law of thermodynamics for this model, we have the following:

$$\Delta U = -W + \int_{t=0}^{t=t_c} q_s(t) - \sigma[T^4(t) - T_e x^4(t)] dt = 0 \qquad (14)$$

where ΔU is the change in internal energy of the active substance, σ is the Stefan–Boltzman constant ($5.67 \times 10^{-8} \frac{W}{m^2 K^4}$), t_c is the cycle time, and T is the temperature of the active substance. The entropy change is subject to the endoreversibility restriction.

$$\Delta S = \int_{t=0}^{t=t_c} \left(\frac{q_s(t) - \sigma[T^4(t) - T_{ex}^4(t)]}{T(t)} \right) dt = 0 \qquad (15)$$

The variables T, T_{ext} are functions associated with the time.

$$T(t) = \begin{cases} T_1 & 0 \le t \le t_c/2 \\ T_2 & t_c/2 \le t \le t_c \end{cases} \qquad (16)$$

$$T_{ex}(t) = 3k \quad 0 \le t \le t_c \qquad (17)$$

The variable q_s is a function of time, I_{sc} is the average solar constant over the Earth's surface (1372.7 W/m^2), the average albedo $\rho = 0.35$, and the average values are as follows:

$$q_s(t) = \begin{cases} I_{sc}(1-\rho)/2 & 0 \le t \le t_c/2 \\ 0 & t_c/2 \le t \le t_c \end{cases} \qquad (18)$$

$$\bar{T} = (T_1 + T_2)/2 \qquad (19)$$

$$\bar{T}^n = (T_1^n + T_2^n)/2 \qquad (20)$$

The mean power of the winds is obtained by:

$$P = \frac{W}{t_0} = \bar{q}_s + \sigma T_{ex}^4 - \sigma \bar{T}^4 \qquad (21)$$

The model used by GZ considers the following approximation $\bar{q}_s \gg \sigma T_{ex}^4$; we have the following Equation:

$$P = \bar{q}_s - \sigma \bar{T}^4 \qquad (22)$$

From the endoreversibility condition, the variables T, T_{ex} and the mean values we obtained are:

$$\Delta S_{int} = \frac{\bar{q}_s}{T_1} - \frac{\sigma}{2}(T_1^3 + T_2^3) \qquad (23)$$

To maximize P subject to the endoreversibility condition, the Lagrangian is defined in terms of the Lagrange multiplier λ and the thermodynamic constraint given by $L = P - \lambda \Delta S$, so that:

$$L = T^4(t) + \lambda[q_s(t)/T(t) - \sigma T^3(t)] \tag{24}$$

For finding the extreme of L, that is, solving $\frac{\partial L(t)}{\partial T(t)} = 0$, we have the following system of equations:

$$T_1^5(t) + 3\sigma\lambda T_1^4/4 - \lambda q_s(t)/4 = 0 \tag{25}$$

$$T_2^5(t) + 3\sigma\lambda T_2^4/4 = 0 \tag{26}$$

GZ found the following temperature values for the lowest and highest layers of the Earth's atmosphere $T_1 = 277K$, $T_2 = 192K$ and $P_{max} = 17.1 \frac{W}{m^2}$. These values are not far from the literature $P_{max} = 7\frac{W}{m^2}$, $T_1 = 290K$ (on the surface) and $T_2 = 195K$ (between 75 and 90 km). Gordon and Zarmi [20] stated that their mean power of winds should be taken as an upper limit.

4.2. Nonendoreversibility Parameter in G-Z

In recent studies, the nonendoreversibility parameter R has been used to investigate the thermal machines of TTF. This parameter was introduced from the Clausius inequality, considering a clearance measure in the endoreversible regime [55].

$$\Delta S_{w1} + \Delta S_{w2} \leq 0 \tag{27}$$

ΔS_{w1} changes in the hot isotherm and ΔS_{w2} in the cold compression isotherm, in the endoreversible case. Thus, this inequality becomes equality in the following equation.

$$\Delta S_{w1} + R\Delta S_{w2} = 0, \tag{28}$$

where R is given by:

$$R = \frac{\Delta S_{w1}}{\|\Delta S_{w2}\|} \tag{29}$$

where $R = \frac{\Delta S_{w1}}{\|\Delta S_{w2}\|}$; the parameter of non-endoreversibility is in the interval $0 \leq R \leq 1$, where $R = 1$ is the endoreversible limit [51]. The previous GZ convection cell process is enriched using the parameter R. Thus, to maximize P subject to the endorreversibility condition plus the parameter R, the Lagrangean $L = P - \lambda \Delta S$ to occupy is given as follows:

$$L = \frac{\sigma}{2}(T_1^4 + T_2^4) + \lambda\left[\frac{q_s}{T_1} - \frac{R\sigma(T_1^3 + T_2^3)}{2}\right] \tag{30}$$

Solving $\frac{\partial L(t)}{\partial T(t)} = 0$ to find the extrema of the Lagrangian; solving the system numerically, it is found that for a nonendoreversibility parameter $R = 0.953$ [55] for $\rho = 0.35$, $I_{sc} = 1372.7 \, W/m^2$. GZ found the following temperature values for the lowest and highest layers of the Earth's atmosphere $T_1 = 280.562K$, $T_2 = 194.293K$.

5. The Proposed Model

5.1. Greenhouse Factor

The planet's surface temperature computation is modified by adding the greenhouse parameter γ. Therefore, it is necessary to add the greenhouse effect to the equations proposed by the thermodynamics of finite times, to obtain the temperatures of the lower and upper layers of our active substance (in this case, the air). Thus, the equations for entropy and internal energy are also changed.

$$\Delta U = -w + \int_{t=0}^{t=t_c} q_s(t) - \sigma(1-\gamma)[T^4(t) - T_e x^4(t)]dt = 0 \tag{31}$$

Equation (15) is expressed in terms of the nonendoreversibility parameter and the greenhouse factor, giving as a result the following expression:

$$\Delta S = \int_{t=0}^{t=t_c} \left(\frac{q_s(t) - R(1-\gamma)\sigma[T^4(t) - T_{ex}^4(t)]}{T(t)} \right) dt = 0 \tag{32}$$

From the G-Z section, the average power of the winds $P = \frac{w_c}{t}$, in which $\bar{q}_s \gg \sigma T_{ex}^4$, the power expression output for the case of the greenhouse effect is of the form:

$$P = \bar{q}_s - \frac{\sigma}{2}(1-\gamma)[T_1^4 + T_2^4] \tag{33}$$

Equations (31) and (32) show us a greenhouse factor acting on the two layers of the atmosphere with temperatures T_1 and T_2. To maximize P subject to the endoreversibility condition, we defined the Lagrangian in terms of the Lagrange multiplier λ and the thermodynamic constraint given by $L = P - \lambda \Delta S$, so that:

$$L = \bar{q}_s - \frac{\sigma}{2}(1-\gamma)[T_1^4 + T_2^4] - \lambda \left\{ \frac{\bar{q}_s}{T_1} - \frac{\sigma}{2}(1-\gamma)[T_1^3 + T_2^3] \right\} \tag{34}$$

where λ is a Lagrange multiplier. By solving the Euler–Lagrange equations $\frac{\partial L(t)}{\partial T(t)} = 0$, a system of equations is obtained, which allows us to calculate the extremes of the power.

For $\frac{\partial L(t)}{\partial T_1(t)} = 0$:

$$T_1^5 - \frac{3}{4}R\lambda T_1^4 - \frac{\bar{q}_s}{2\sigma(1-\gamma)} = 0 \tag{35}$$

For the case $\frac{\partial L(t)}{\partial T_2(t)} = 0$:

$$T_2 = \frac{3R}{4}\lambda \tag{36}$$

Finally, for $\frac{\partial L(t)}{\partial \lambda} = 0$ we have:

$$\frac{\bar{q}_s}{T_1} - \frac{\sigma}{2}(1-\gamma)[T_1^3 + T_2^3] = 0 \tag{37}$$

Eliminating λ and giving the value of $q_s \approx 229$ W/m^2 [50], we have two equations whose numerical solution provides the highest and lowest layer surface temperatures. The low of the Earth's atmosphere is under a regime of maximum power in terms of the nonendoreversibility parameter R, the albedo ρ, the greenhouse effect γ, and the current solar constant $I_s c$.

$$T_1^5 - T_2 T_1^4 - \frac{2q_s}{3R\sigma(1-\gamma)} T_2 = 0 \tag{38}$$

$$T_1^4 + T_2^3 T_1 - \frac{2\bar{q}_s}{R\sigma(1-\gamma)} = 0 \tag{39}$$

5.2. Greenhouse Factor in the Lowest Layer of the Atmosphere Average Surface Temperature

The power for the G-Z model is given by $P = \frac{w_c}{t}$, where for $T_{ex} = 3K \bar{q}_s >> \sigma T_{ex}^4$, the output power expression with the greenhouse effect in the lower part is the following:

$$P = \bar{q}_s - \frac{\sigma R}{2}[(1-\gamma)T_1^4 + T_2^4] \tag{40}$$

It is necessary to maximize P subject to the endoreversibility condition and the greenhouse effect at the bottom. Then, the Lagrangian is defined in terms of the Lagrange multiplier λ and the constraint on thermodynamics showing the following Lagrangian expression:

$$L = \bar{q}_s - \frac{\sigma}{2}[(1-\gamma)T_1^4 + T_2^4] - \lambda\left\{\frac{\bar{q}_s}{T_1} - \frac{\sigma}{2}[(1-\gamma)T_1^3 + T_2^3]\right\} \tag{41}$$

Solving the Euler–Lagrange equations $\frac{\partial L(t)}{\partial T(t)} = 0$, we obtain the following equations:

For $\frac{\partial L(t)}{\partial T_1(t)} = 0$:

$$T_1^5 - \frac{3}{4}R\lambda T_1^4 - \frac{\bar{q}_s}{2\sigma(1-\gamma)} = 0 \tag{42}$$

For $\frac{\partial L(t)}{\partial T_2(t)} = 0$:

$$T_2 = \frac{3R}{4}\lambda \tag{43}$$

For $\frac{\partial L(t)}{\partial \lambda} = 0$, we have:

$$\frac{\bar{q}_s}{T_1} - \frac{\sigma}{2}[(1-\gamma)T_1^3 + T_2^3] = 0 \tag{44}$$

Removing the λ parameters from Equations (42)–(44), we obtain:

$$T_1^5 - T_2 T_1^4 - \frac{2\bar{q}_s}{3R\sigma(1-\gamma)}T_2 = 0 \tag{45}$$

$$T_1^4 + \frac{1}{(1-\gamma)}T_2^3 T_1 - \frac{2q_s}{R\sigma(1-\gamma)} = 0 \tag{46}$$

The FTT models are developed as engines that use the conversion of solar energy into wind energy; the hypothesis is that atmospheric work as a "heat engine" provides reasonable values for the average power of winds and extreme temperatures in specific layers of the atmosphere. To compute the efficiency of the energy converter, it is necessary to take the average power output associated with the yearly average solar radiation flux q_s expressed per unit area of the Earth's surface (see Equation (47)). Therefore, solar energy efficiency or performance is defined as $w = P/q_s$.

$$w = \frac{(1-\gamma)(R-1) + R^4(1-\eta)^3[1 - R(1-\eta)]}{R[(1-\gamma) + R^3(1-\eta)^3]} \tag{47}$$

Thus, for the endoreversible case $R = 1$:

$$w = \frac{\eta(1-\eta)^3}{(1-\gamma) + (1-\eta)^3} \tag{48}$$

Equation (48) shows us that even for an endoreversible case, the efficiency of solar energy depends on the greenhouse effect. For a regime at maximum power for $\gamma = 0$, 7.67% of the solar energy q_s can be converted into energy, regardless of the planet and the solar system.

Nevertheless, it does not represent a realistic model of the atmosphere of the planets. The model can be extended by considering other thermodynamic regimes, such as the ecological and efficient power regimes. Other conditions, such as physical and geometric issues about the planet, improve our thermal engine, which implies more accurate predictions. According to the model developed by De Vos and Flatter [27], they obtained a value $\omega = 9.64\%$ whereas a Hadley-type considers a convection cell and divides the planet into two hemispheres, thus generating different heat exchanges where radiation is received or emitted from their surface areas.

The models proposed by De Vos as well as Gordon and Zarmi [20,27] can compute the temperatures of the atmosphere of some past or future periods of the Earth, as was carried out in the study by Angulo and Barranco-Jiménez [24], where the temperatures of early age were calculated with enough accuracy. In the present work, we worked similarly, but for a future time of the atmosphere (prediction event), we considered the atmosphere's physical characteristics, such as the albedo greenhouse effect. The model created by De Vos shows an excellent relationship between the theoretical and experimental data. Our proposed work approximated the albedo dependent on the greenhouse effect with $a = 0.072$, $b = 0.4955$, and $c = 0.1527$.

$$\rho = a\gamma^2 + b\gamma + c \tag{49}$$

The GZ-type models with the greenhouse factor and the albedo condition above, and the atmosphere represented by Equations (45) and (46), allow us to obtain temperatures of the highest and lowest layers of the atmosphere. It is necessary to determine the atmospheric characteristics of the GZ-type models. According to the solution of the faint young Sun paradox presented in [24], the finite-time thermodynamics models efficiently resolve the paradox, calculating the planet's average surface temperature from different geological stages. Using scenarios where the luminosity of the Sun is taken into account through the Gough Equation (1), it is necessary to modify this equation to actual luminosity, as represented in Equation (50).

$$I(t) = \left[1 + 0.4\left(1 - \frac{t + t_0}{t_0}\right)\right]^{-1} I_{sc} \tag{50}$$

Using the albedo ρ (Equation (49)), the average solar radiation flux, and greenhouse coefficient γ, we modified the scheme proposed by Angulo and Barranco to determine the effects of climate change due to the increase in greenhouse gas, taking the relationship proposed in our work. That relationship between the albedo and greenhouse effect is represented in Equation (49), including the present-day values for average luminosity, its variation per year (Equation 50), and the changes directly proportional to the flux q_s expressed in Equation (13). Nevertheless, it is necessary to consider the dissipation in the maximum power regime to obtain realistic results. This modification allows results to be obtained to predict the effects of climate change in future years. Thus, the average temperature of the surface (T_s) at present will be based on the existing relationship in the dissipation (Equation (12)) of the system in maximum-power conditions in the GZ-type model with Equations (45) and (46).

$$T_s = T_1 + T_2\left(\frac{\beta(T_1(1 - \eta_{CA}) - T_2)}{\gamma(1 - \eta_{CA})T_1 + \beta T_2}\right) - \frac{T_2\gamma(T_1 - T_2 - T_1\eta_{CA})}{T_1(1 - \eta_{CA})} \tag{51}$$

Simplifying:

$$T_s = T_1 + T_2\left(\frac{T_1(1 - \eta_{CA}) - T_2}{(1 - \eta_{CA})T_1 + T_2}\right) - \frac{T_2}{T_1}\left(\frac{(T_1 - T_2 - T_1\eta_{CA})}{(1 - \eta_{CA})}\right) \tag{52}$$

6. Experimental Results

It is necessary to determine possible and future scenarios for the growth of greenhouse gases. Most of the concentration of gases in the atmosphere has presented a significant increase since the 1970s due to industrial activities. According to the Mauna Loa laboratory in Hawaii [53,56], the data show a massive rise in CO_2 by the empirical formula concentration for the interval $1975 \leq t \leq 2100$ [53]. So, the expression obtained by Wubbles concerning the trace gas trends and their potential role in climate change is valid for this methodology [53].

$$[CO_2] = 330 e^{0.0056(t-1975)} \tag{53}$$

According to Equation (49), the albedo and the greenhouse effect are related. For the Earth, the value of the greenhouse effect can be defined as $\gamma = (E_s - F)/E_s$, where E_s is the surface emission and F is the outgoing radiation [24]. Moreover, it is noticed that the increase in greenhouse gases rises over time, according to Wubbles and different experimental measurements. With all these characteristics, the natural average temperature (T_s) and its possible evolution in the coming years can be determined with reasonable accuracy. To test the GZ model, a dissipation ϕ_{rb}, developed in this work, is considered, solving numerically with $R = 1$ and different values of γ are related to the year. It is a data compilation by Berkeley Earth. The study shows the temperature of the Earth's surface, and the experimentally measured temperatures T_{obs} were compared against our theoretically calculated temperatures T_s to use a forecasting technique later to determine the future of temperatures.

On the other hand, the comparison was made using machine learning techniques such as linear regression, Ridge regression, and artificial neural networks. Concerning the implementation, we used the Scikit-learn framework for regression methods and the TensorFlow package with Keras for designing the artificial neural network. The parameters for the artificial intelligence-based approach were described according to the formalism of Scikit-learn and TensorFlow Keras. Thus, the setup parameters and configuration were established as follows:

- **Linear regression**: `train_size = X_train, X_test, y_train, y_test = train_test_split(X, y, train_size = 0.8)`
- **Ridge regression**: `train_size = X_train, X_test, y_train, y_test = train_test_split(X, y, train_size = 0.8)`
- **Neural network optimizer** was implemented by applying Adam's algorithm. The regression loss was defined by `MeanSquaredError`. Moreover, four layers were established with the activation functions: `linear, linear, relu, linear`.

Data Preprocessing

To analyze the complexity of climate change, the terrestrial and oceanic temperatures of the planet were measured. The used data are a compilation of a dataset provided by Berkeley Laboratory. Other widely used datasets are MLOST NOAA Land-Ocean Surface Temperature and GISTEM from NASA [57–59]. The data compilation by Berkeley records land average temperatures in the format yyyy/mm/dd. So, a split was made by year, month, and day, taking the temperature of each month, and the mean temperature per year was computed. It was observed that there is a correlation with a value of 0.89 between the variables of the year and the land average temperature from the year 1975 to 2015 [57–59]. Figure 3 shows the climatology of the average annual terrestrial temperature between 1951 and 1980 from the Berkeley Earth Data with a global mean of 9.17 Celsius. In our work, the mean experimental temperature of each year was compared with the obtained data from our theoretical model.

The results of the data and the surface temperatures T_s obtained from the model expressed in Equation (52) that was developed in this work are shown in Table 1. All the results regarding data are presented in degrees Celsius.

Table 1. Average temperatures observed and computed by the GZ-type model.

Year	T_{obs}	T_s
1975	8.74	8.41
1976	8.34	8.44
1977	8.85	8.48
1978	8.69	8.51
1979	8.73	8.55
1980	8.98	8.58
1981	9.16	8.62
1982	8.63	8.65
1983	9.02	8.69
1984	8.65	8.73
1985	8.65	8.77
1986	8.83	8.80
1987	8.99	8.84
1988	9.20	8.88
1989	8.922	8.92
1990	9.23	8.96
1991	9.17	9.00
1992	8.83	9.04
1993	8.86	9.08
1994	9.03	9.12
1995	9.34	9.16
1996	9.03	9.21
1997	9.20	9.24
1998	9.52	9.29
1999	9.28	9.33
2000	9.20	9.37
2001	9.41	9.38
2002	9.57	9.46
2003	9.52	9.50
2004	9.32	9.48
2005	9.70	9.59
2006	9.53	9.64
2007	9.73	9.73
2008	9.43	9.74
2009	9.50	9.78
2010	9.703	9.82
2011	9.51	9.87
2012	9.507	9.92
2013	9.606	9.97
2014	9.570	10.02
2015	9.831	10.07

The temperature increase due to greenhouse gas growth has been analyzed since 1975. It was fixed this year because of the significant increase in the concentration of CO_2, as shown by the experimental development of Wubbles in Equation (53), when seeing the correlations of the observational variables of the temperature of the Berkeley database. We can notice a high correlation between the year and the land's average temperature, and the correlation is equal to 0.89. Therefore, a linear regression model is sufficient in this case to make a future prediction of the temperature. In the following plot (Figure 4, average temperatures observed and calculated by the GZ-type model), we can observe a relationship between the average temperature per year measured against the temperature of the modified GZ model.

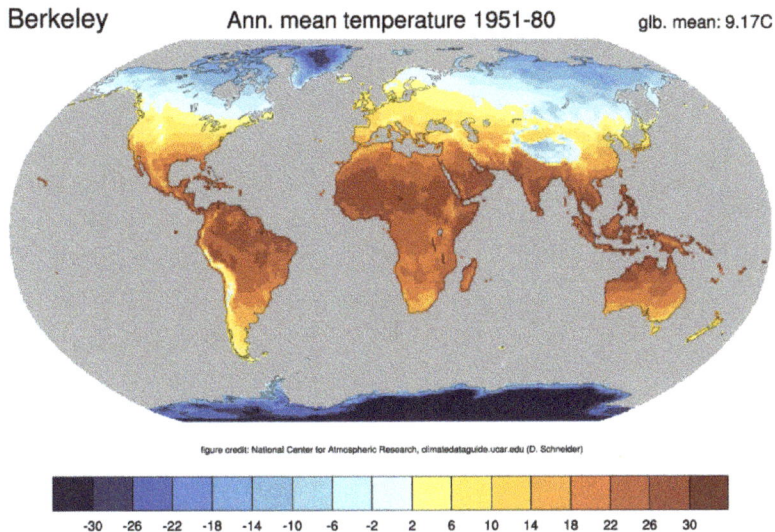

Figure 3. Climatology of annual mean land temperature. NCAR, Climate Data Guide [59].

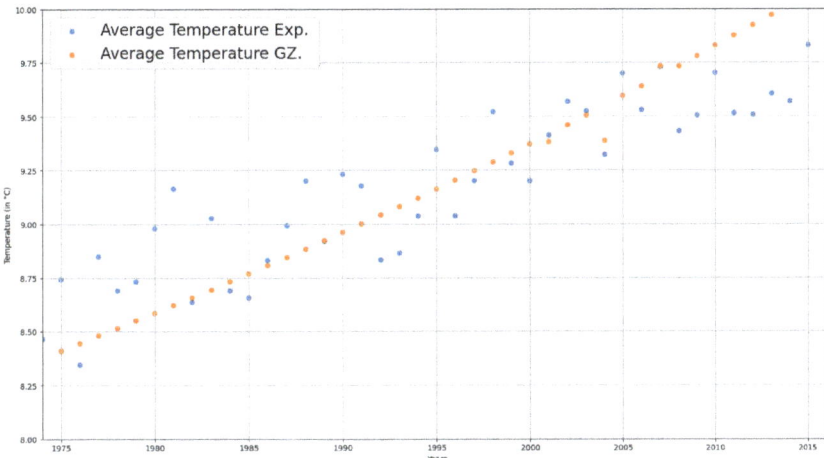

Figure 4. Average temperatures observed and computed by the GZ-type model compared with the average measured yearly temperature.

Thus, (Figure 5, average temperatures observed since 1975 with linear regression) shows how a linear regression adjusts perfectly to predict the evolution of the temperature from the year 1975. It is possible to infer how the temperature change will be towards the year 2100 thanks to this type of modeling.

On the other hand, Table 2 presents the future prediction of the temperatures using linear regression (LR), ridge regression (RR), and an artificial neural network (ANN). Thus, the ANN has five layers: an input layer with a linear activation function; three layers with a rectified linear activation function, or *Relu* or *ReLU* for short; and an output layer with a linear activation function. All techniques were applied to the observed temperatures (T_{obs}) and the models' temperatures used in the present work. In the same way, the third column shows the temperatures computed (T_s) from our model of Gordon and Zarmi (GZM) without applying a linear regression, where the physical characteristics of the atmosphere are taken into account and what theoretical temperature would be reached. In addition, Table 2 depicts the entire prediction made up to 2100, starting in 2016.

Table 2. Average temperatures observed and computed by the GZ type model.

Year	T_{obs} with LR	T_s with LR	T_{obs} with RR	T_{obs} with NN	T_s with GZM
2016	9.839	10.049	9.845	10.089	10.121
2017	9.842	10.094	9.860	10.094	10.176
2018	9.845	10.135	9.869	10.099	10.228
2019	9.860	10.178	9.884	10.105	10.281
2020	9.885	10.219	9.907	10.110	10.334
2021	9.913	10.251	9.937	10.115	10.387
2022	9.941	10.292	9.967	10.120	10.440
2023	9.969	10.333	9.996	10.125	10.495
2024	9.997	10.374	10.026	10.130	10.550
2025	10.025	10.426	10.056	10.135	10.606
2026	10.053	10.456	10.086	10.140	10.663
2027	10.081	10.497	10.116	10.144	10.720
2028	10.109	10.538	10.146	10.149	10.777
2029	10.137	10.579	10.175	10.154	10.836
2030	10.165	10.620	10.205	10.159	10.895
2031	10.193	10.661	10.235	10.164	10.954
2032	10.221	10.702	10.265	10.169	11.014
2033	10.249	10.743	10.295	10.174	11.018
2034	10.277	10.784	10.325	10.179	11.138
2035	10.305	10.825	10.354	10.184	11.200
2036	10.333	10.866	10.384	10.189	11.263
2037	10.361	10.907	10.414	10.194	11.327
2038	10.389	10.948	10.444	10.199	11.392
2039	10.417	10.989	10.474	10.204	11.456
2040	10.445	11.030	10.504	10.209	11.524
2041	10.473	11.071	10.533	10.213	11.591
2042	10.501	11.112	10.563	10.218	11.659
2043	10.529	11.153	10.593	10.223	11.728
2044	10.557	11.194	10.623	10.233	11.798
2045	10.585	11.235	10.653	10.238	11.868
2046	10.613	11.276	10.683	10.243	11.939
2047	10.641	11.317	10.713	10.246	12.012
2048	10.669	11.358	10.742	10.248	12.085
2049	10.697	11.399	10.772	10.253	12.159
2050	10.725	11.440	10.802	10.258	12.234
2051	10.753	11.481	10.832	10.263	12.311
2052	10.781	11.522	10.862	10.268	12.388
2053	10.809	11.563	10.892	10.272	12.465
2054	10.837	11.604	10.921	10.277	12.545
2055	10.865	11.645	10.951	10.282	12.625
2056	10.893	11.686	10.981	10.287	12.707
2057	10.921	11.727	11.011	10.292	12.789
2058	10.949	11.768	11.041	10.297	12.872
2059	10.977	11.809	11.071	10.302	12.957
2060	11.005	11.850	11.100	10.307	13.043
2061	11.033	11.891	11.130	10.312	13.129
2062	11.061	11.932	11.160	10.317	13.218
2063	11.089	11.973	11.190	10.322	13.308
2064	11.117	12.014	11.220	10.327	13.398
2065	11.145	12.055	11.250	10.332	13.490
2066	11.173	12.096	11.279	10.336	13.584
2067	11.201	12.137	11.309	10.341	13.659
2068	11.229	12.178	11.339	10.346	13.775
2069	11.257	12.219	11.369	10.351	13.872

Table 2. Cont.

Year	T_{obs} with LR	T_s with LR	T_{obs} with RR	T_{obs} with NN	T_s with GZM
2070	11.285	12.260	11.399	10.356	13.972
2071	11.313	12.301	11.429	10.361	14.072
2072	11.341	12.342	11.458	10.366	14.174
2073	11.369	12.383	11.488	10.371	14.277
2074	11.397	12.424	11.518	10.376	14.383
2075	11.425	12.465	11.548	10.381	14.490
2076	11.453	12.506	11.578	10.386	14.599
2077	11.481	12.547	11.608	10.390	14.709
2078	11.509	12.588	11.637	10.396	14.820
2079	11.537	12.629	11.667	10.401	14.935
2080	11.565	12.670	11.697	10.405	15.050
2081	11.593	12.711	11.727	10.410	15.168
2082	11.621	12.752	11.757	10.415	15.287
2083	11.649	12.793	11.787	10.420	15.408
2084	11.677	12.834	11.816	10.425	15.533
2085	11.705	12.875	11.846	10.430	15.658
2086	11.733	12.916	11.876	10.435	15.786
2087	11.761	12.957	11.906	10.440	15.916
2088	11.789	12.998	11.936	10.445	16.048
2089	11.817	13.039	11.966	10.450	16.183
2090	11.845	13.080	11.995	10.455	16.320
2091	11.873	13.121	12.025	10.460	16.460
2092	11.901	13.162	12.055	10.465	16.601
2093	11.929	13.203	12.085	10.469	16.746
2094	11.957	13.244	12.115	10.474	16.894
2095	11.985	13.285	12.145	10.479	17.043
2096	12.013	13.326	12.174	10.484	17.196
2097	12.041	13.367	12.204	10.489	17.352
2098	12.069	13.408	12.234	10.494	17.511
2099	12.097	13.449	12.264	10.499	17.673
2100	12.125	13.490	12.294	10.504	17.838

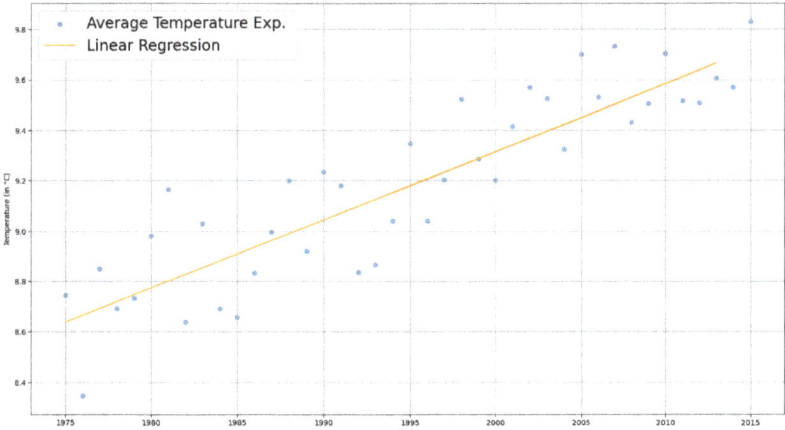

Figure 5. Average temperatures observed since 1975 with linear regression adjusted to predict the rise of mean temperature.

Moreover, Figure 6 shows the evolution of the surface temperature (T_s), according to the predictions made by the model proposed in our work with the initials GZM and the temperature prediction from the experimental data (T_{obs}). Thus, T_S and T_{obs} were forecasted using machine learning techniques.

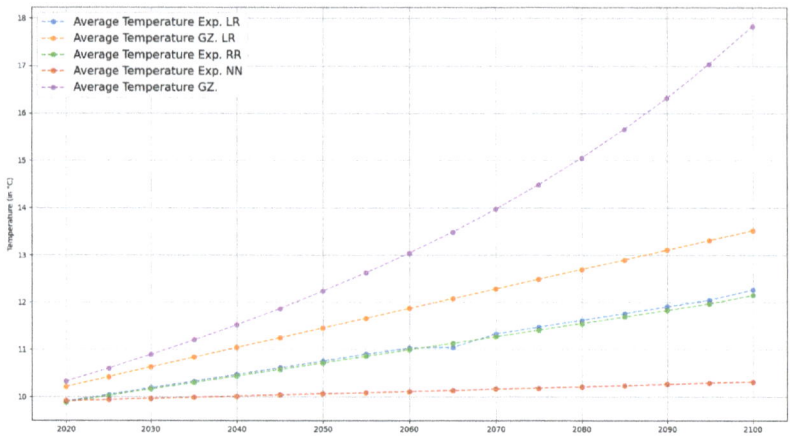

Figure 6. Comparison of the evolution of temperature from the year 2020 to 2100 through theoretical and experimental models.

From a correlation analysis between the temperature variables under different machine learning techniques, such as linear regression (LR), ridge regression (RR), artificial neural network (ANN), and the proposed endoreversible model (GZM), it can be observed that the GZM model is more suitable with a linear relationship (see Figure 7).

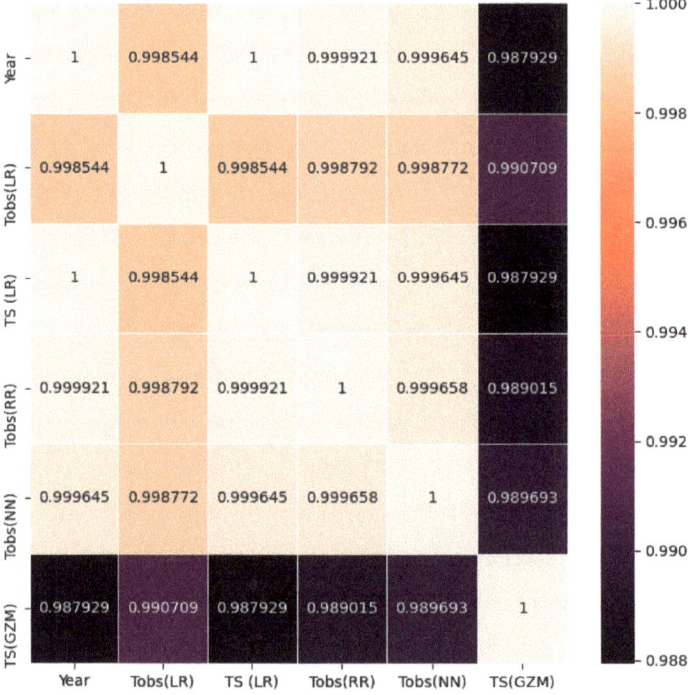

Figure 7. Comparison of the correlation between year variables and observed temperatures with the theoretical model.

7. Discussion

According to several authors, the changes in the concentration of gases in the atmosphere, mainly greenhouse gases, in addition to their directed relationship with the albedo effect, are related to climate change [24,29,60,61].

Climate model development and the implications in a model's prediction reliability can be difficult, because the climate is a complex system with many variables and factors. The models are fully coupled when studying a complete interaction among the global radiation budget, different layers of the atmosphere, physical and chemical atmospheric processes, and their implications in the biosphere. The models are considered partially coupled and developed in a system of Sun–atmosphere–ocean. Differential equations represent the governing equations that describe atmospheric and ocean circulation, geophysical fluid dynamics, continuity equations, the input of solar radiation, and physical thermodynamic processes [29,61–65]. Therefore, global climate models can have many degrees of freedom.

Nevertheless, these models are very complex and expensive to solve through analytical and computational methods. Thus, the nonlinearity leads to multiple solutions that must be carefully analyzed to find physically acceptable results and predictions. A method used to work with these chaotic systems is the use of approximations or attractors, the use and development of simplified climate models, or the linearization of global climate models [29,65–67].

In this work, we used a climate model based on the Gordon–Zarmi approach, where the system is represented like a heat engine that describes an Earth–atmosphere–Sun system, providing reasonable values of extreme temperatures in the layers of the atmosphere. The model solved the paradox of the young and weak Sun, proposing a series of scenarios with the different greenhouse effect and albedo values, taking into account the luminosity of the Sun and the evolution of these values over time. These variables are responsible for generating global warming, and the obtained prediction is correlated with the estimated warming values from experimental data.

According to Houghton et al. [29], it is essential to note that since the climate is a chaotic system, its predictions become very complicated, so using climate models and predictions made from experimental data through numerical techniques or machine learning help to provide robustness to future predictions.

In this analysis of climate change, an endoreversible modeling of the Gordon and Zarmi type was carried out. Unlike other finite-time thermodynamic studies for studying the atmosphere, adjustments were made to give the model realistic results if applied. As for the climatic analysis of geological eras, as observed in other works, it is noticed that the results do not correspond to what is reported by observations of the current temperature. According to Levario et al. [21], for a correct thermodynamic optimization of power plants, it is necessary to consider the system's variations. Therefore, the modeling was performed considering those variations, the change in luminosity per year, the increase in greenhouse gas, and its relationship with the terrestrial albedo, thus adapting it to our model of winds at maximum power. In this way, the family from Equation (45) to Equation (53) complements the system to calculate climate change due to atmospheric conditions and the increase in greenhouse gases by anthropogenic conditions.

From Table 1, an increase in the average temperature of the Earth's surface can be seen from 1975 to 2015, both in the observational (experimental) model and the theoretical model developed in our work. The rise in temperature in both cases is related to the increase in greenhouse gases in the atmosphere.

In Figure 2, we can appreciate the differences between the points obtained experimentally (observation and measures in the laboratory) and the modeling proposed in our work. Suppose we observe Figure 3 and correlation analysis; in that case, the experimental points in blue show a high linear tendency, so linear or ridge regression is an excellent technique for correctly predicting temperature increases.

On the other hand, the points of our previously mentioned modeling of the GZM would seem to show the same linear trend, so in Table 2, two comparisons were made, taking into account a linear regression with T_s **LR** and an analysis obtained directly from our modeling with T_s **GZM**. As a result, we obtained a difference between the analysis with LR and GZM. This is explained considering that the temperature observations only recorded points in our vector. In contrast, the modeling records these points, and the physical information of the atmosphere is saved, as well as the thermodynamic variables of the system, which gives us results of the mean temperature increase with more value than those obtained by an analysis of experimental points.

Moreover, Figure 4 shows a plot of the predictions made from the experimental data T_{obs} and the modeling of the GZM system. It is important to note that in future scenarios with forecasting by GZM, the average temperature is higher than that obtained by the data of the evolution of the observed temperatures T_{obs} from various machine learning techniques. Nevertheless, the rate of temperature increase is in the range per decade, according to [29]. The plot shows that the temperature evolution in the case of the construction of an ANN, LR, and RR grows in a widespread gradual way compared with our proposed model. The GZM model saves the atmosphere's physical characteristics, such as entropic relationships, radiation conditions, and irradiance. It helps to present more realistic behavior in the data, unlike the other forecasting, which only shows us a regression of the linear type without considering the evolution of the physical parameters caused by the alterations in the Earth's atmosphere.

The most significant challenge for developing a sun model is establishing a critical finite-time thermodynamics condition. Developing objective functions that characterize the "optimal" modes of operation is not a trivial task. However, there are no established criteria to set the objective functions, so the objective of the modeling itself is the one that affects the construction of the "heat engine", in addition to affecting its behavior in the energy converter and its performance [68].

Solar energy converters under the branch of FTT have been developed to create models with better coupled experimental and theoretical results. These energy converters are focused on entropy minimization and output power maximization, among others. According to De Vos [28], the Curzon and Ahlborn engine is valid when the heat transfer is linear or Newtonian, so another challenge related to these modeling types is to work the heat transfer linearly.

8. Conclusions and Future Work

In this article, we proposed a new finite-time thermodynamics approach to predict changes in surface temperature in the lowest layer of the atmosphere that corresponds to the average temperature. The proposed approach considers the evolution in albedo and greenhouse gases, the change in luminosity per year, and the system's dissipation in the regime of maximum-power conditions. Our model achieves predictions in the range of future projections, obtaining better results than the machine learning techniques used in the experiments. Another area for improvement is that it performs a simple climate model, avoiding the complexity of modeling the climate as a chaotic system. The current modeling is a modification of previous models of the GZ type that, in addition to obtaining realistic values of the extreme temperatures of the system, also allows us to carry out the evolution of temperatures according to the modifications of the physical processes of the planet in a rate of change of time.

Thus, an increase in temperature is linked to physical conditions such as irradiance and radiation. Moreover, a comparison with different machine learning techniques showed a rise in temperature in all these methods. It is crucial to notice that machine learning algorithms do not preserve atmospheric information in the period studied. Therefore, the forecasting could present a *bias* in the prediction because these are trained only with experimental data without considering the variables that generate climate change. The comparison gives robustness to the model when comparing the experimental data with the theoretical ones. As mentioned previously, due to the high degrees of freedom of the climate model, interdisciplinary works are necessary to face new challenges in climate warming. All the techniques and our modeling demonstrated an increase in temperature. We can conclude the success of our model by comparing it with our experimental data. In addition, according to Houghton [29], the projections of global average temperature changes are in the range of 0.15 °C–0.6 °C per decade, which is in the threshold of the obtained values.

In the present work, the endoreversible engines of FTT deal with the problem of the radiative thermal balance between planets, generating a Sun–Earth–wind system through an atmospheric heat engine that allows for the optimization of the extreme values of the model to find the maximum output power and entropy minimization, among others. Thus, these values allow us to work under different thermal regimes of the FTT, namely the maximum power regime (MPR), maximum ecological regime (MER), and maximum efficiency power (MEPR). This model was created under the MER regime. According to several authors, to fully model, it is necessary to generalize various cases and verify experimental data due to climate variability as a subject of study. Therefore, an extension of our research work would be to analyze the other thermodynamic regimes. We have to propose several cases of increases in greenhouse gases and the albedo effect, compare them with the experimental data, and complement them with deep learning techniques. All theoretical predictions will always be compared against experimental data to face climate change in the best way.

On the other hand, it is necessary to conduct studies concerning the atmosphere and consider a wind engine the most common control in obtaining the maximum power as it works, collecting data from these experiments and generating machine learning models to characterize the phenomenon. In this paper, studying other regimes will allow us to analyze the whole spectrum of our modeling (wind engine) and thus observe all cases of global warming.

Author Contributions: Conceptualization, S.V.-R. and M.T.-R.; methodology, R.Q.; software, C.G.S.-M. and K.T.C.; validation, S.V.-R. and M.T.-R.; formal analysis, R.Q. and S.V.-R.; investigation, M.T.-R.; resources, K.T.C.; data curation, C.G.S.-M.; writing—original draft preparation, S.V.-R.; writing—review and editing, M.T.-R.; visualization, K.T.C.; supervision, M.T.-R.; project administration, C.G.S.-M.; funding acquisition, K.T.C. All authors have read and agreed to the published version of the manuscript.

Funding: This work was partially sponsored by the Instituto Politécnico Nacional and the Consejo Nacional de Ciencia y Tecnología under grants 20230655, 20231372, and SECTEI-2023, respectively.

Institutional Review Board Statement: Not applicable.

Informed Consent Statement: Not applicable.

Data Availability Statement: Not applicable.

Acknowledgments: We are thankful to the reviewers for their time and their invaluable and constructive feedback that helped improve the quality of the paper.

Conflicts of Interest: The authors declare no conflict of interest.

References

1. Kirilenko, A.P.; Sedjo, R.A. Climate change impacts on forestry. *Proc. Natl. Acad. Sci. USA* **2007**, *104*, 19697–19702. [CrossRef] [PubMed]
2. Carleton, T.A.; Hsiang, S.M. Social and economic impacts of climate. *Science* **2016**, *353*, aad9837. [CrossRef] [PubMed]
3. Wheeler, T.; Von Braun, J. Climate change impacts on global food security. *Science* **2013**, *341*, 508–513. [CrossRef] [PubMed]
4. Louis, M.E.S.; Hess, J.J. Climate change: Impacts on and implications for global health. *Am. J. Prev. Med.* **2008**, *35*, 527–538. [CrossRef] [PubMed]
5. Nourani, V.; Tapeh, A.H.G.; Khodkar, K.; Huang, J.J. Assessing long-term climate change impact on spatiotemporal changes of groundwater level using autoregressive-based and ensemble machine learning models. *J. Environ. Manag.* **2023**, *336*, 117653. [CrossRef]
6. Yeganeh-Bakhtiary, A.; EyvazOghli, H.; Shabakhty, N.; Kamranzad, B.; Abolfathi, S. Machine learning as a downscaling approach for prediction of wind characteristics under future climate change scenarios. *Complexity* **2022**, *2022*, 8451812.

7. Rajaee, T.; Ebrahimi, H.; Nourani, V. A review of the artificial intelligence methods in groundwater level modeling. *J. Hydrol.* **2019**, *572*, 336–351. [CrossRef]
8. Sattari, M.T.; Mirabbasi, R.; Sushab, R.S.; Abraham, J. Prediction of groundwater level in Ardebil plain using support vector regression and M5 tree model. *Groundwater* **2018**, *56*, 636–646. [CrossRef]
9. Zare, M.; Koch, M. Groundwater level fluctuations simulation and prediction by ANFIS-and hybrid Wavelet-ANFIS/Fuzzy C-Means (FCM) clustering models: Application to the Miandarband plain. *J. Hydro-Environ. Res.* **2018**, *18*, 63–76. [CrossRef]
10. Donnelly, J.; Abolfathi, S.; Pearson, J.; Chatrabgoun, O.; Daneshkhah, A. Gaussian process emulation of spatio-temporal outputs of a 2D inland flood model. *Water Res.* **2022**, *225*, 119100. [CrossRef]
11. Nourani, V.; Khodkar, K.; Paknezhad, N.J.; Laux, P. Deep learning-based uncertainty quantification of groundwater level predictions. *Stoch. Environ. Res. Risk Assess.* **2022**, *36*, 3081–3107. [CrossRef]
12. Zennaro, F.; Furlan, E.; Simeoni, C.; Torresan, S.; Aslan, S.; Critto, A.; Marcomini, A. Exploring machine learning potential for climate change risk assessment. *Earth-Sci. Rev.* **2021**, *220*, 103752. [CrossRef]
13. Kalu, I.; Ndehedehe, C.E.; Okwuashi, O.; Eyoh, A.E.; Ferreira, V.G. Identifying impacts of global climate teleconnection patterns on land water storage using machine learning. *J. Hydrol. Reg. Stud.* **2023**, *46*, 101346. [CrossRef]
14. Nwokolo, S.C.; Obiwulu, A.U.; Ogbulezie, J.C. Machine learning and analytical model hybridization to assess the impact of climate change on solar PV energy production. *Phys. Chem. Earth Parts A/B/C* **2023**, *130*, 103389. [CrossRef]
15. Nwokolo, S.C.; Ogbulezie, J.C.; Obiwulu, A.U. Impacts of climate change and meteo-solar parameters on photosynthetically active radiation prediction using hybrid machine learning with Physics-based models. *Adv. Space Res.* **2022**, *70*, 3614–3637. [CrossRef]
16. Jusup, M.; Holme, P.; Kanazawa, K.; Takayasu, M.; Romić, I.; Wang, Z.; Geček, S.; Lipić, T.; Podobnik, B.; Wang, L.; et al. Social physics. *Phys. Rep.* **2022**, *948*, 1–148. [CrossRef]
17. Steffen, W.; Richardson, K.; Rockström, J.; Schellnhuber, H.J.; Dube, O.P.; Dutreuil, S.; Lenton, T.M.; Lubchenco, J. The emergence and evolution of Earth System Science. *Nat. Rev. Earth Environ.* **2020**, *1*, 54–63. [CrossRef]
18. Seneviratne, S.; Nicholls, N.; Easterling, D.; Goodess, C.; Kanae, S.; Kossin, J.; Luo, Y.; Marengo, J.; McInnes, K.; Rahimi, M.; et al. Changes in Climate Extremes and Their Impacts on the Natural Physical Environment. 2012. Available online: https://library.harvard.edu/sites/default/files/static/collections/ipcc/docs/AR5_WG2_n_SREX_chapters_and_review/ii_SREX/c_Final_draft_SREX/SREX-Chap3_FINAL.pdf (accessed on 12 March 2023).
19. Wang, Z.; Jusup, M.; Guo, H.; Shi, L.; Geček, S.; Anand, M.; Perc, M.; Bauch, C.T.; Kurths, J.; Boccaletti, S.; et al. Communicating sentiment and outlook reverses inaction against collective risks. *Proc. Natl. Acad. Sci. USA* **2020**, *117*, 17650–17655. [CrossRef]
20. Gordon, J.M.; Zarmi, Y. Wind energy as a solar-driven heat engine: A thermodynamic approach. *Am. J. Phys.* **1989**, *57*, 995–998. [CrossRef]
21. Levario-Medina, S.; Valencia-Ortega, G.; Arias-Hernandez, L. Optimizacion Termodinámica de Algunas Plantas Generadoras de Energia Mediante la k-Potencia Eficiente. 2021. Available online: https://www.esfm.ipn.mx/assets/files/esfm/docs/RNAFM/articulos-2020/XXVRNAFM013.pdf (accessed on 23 April 2023).
22. Curzon, F.L.; Ahlborn, B. Efficiency of a Carnot engine at maximum power output. *Am. J. Phys.* **1975**, *43*, 22–24. [CrossRef]
23. Arias-Hernandez, L.A.; Angulo-Brown, F. A general property of endoreversible thermal engines. *J. Appl. Phys.* **1997**, *81*, 2973–2979. [CrossRef]
24. Angulo-Brown, F.; Rosales, M.A.; Barranco-Jimenez, M.A. The faint young Sun paradox: A simplified thermodynamic approach. *Adv. Astron.* **2012**, *2012*, 478957. [CrossRef]
25. Sagan, C.; Mullen, G. Earth and Mars: Evolution of atmospheres and surface temperatures. *Science* **1972**, *177*, 52–56. [CrossRef]
26. Kasting, J.F.; Grinspoon, D.H. The faint young Sun problem. In *The Sun in Time*; University of Arizona Press: Tucson, AZ, USA, 1991; pp. 447–462.
27. De Vos, A.; Flater, G. The maximum efficiency of the conversion of solar energy into wind energy. *Am. J. Phys.* **1991**, *59*, 751–754. [CrossRef]
28. De Vos, A.; Van der Wel, P. The efficiency of the conversion of solar energy into wind energy by means of Hadley cells. *Theor. Appl. Climatol.* **1993**, *46*, 193–202. [CrossRef]
29. Houghton, J. Global warming reports on progress. *Physics* **2005**, *68*, 1340–1403.
30. Wang, R.; Li, L.; Gentine, P.; Zhang, Y.; Chen, J.; Chen, X.; Chen, L.; Ning, L.; Yuan, L.; Lü, G. Recent increase in the observation-derived land evapotranspiration due to global warming. *Environ. Res. Lett.* **2022**, *17*, 024020. [CrossRef]
31. Chi, J.; Kim, H.c. Prediction of arctic sea ice concentration using a fully data driven deep neural network. *Remote Sens.* **2017**, *9*, 1305. [CrossRef]
32. Asthana, T.; Krim, H.; Sun, X.; Roheda, S.; Xie, L. Atlantic hurricane activity prediction: A machine learning approach. *Atmosphere* **2021**, *12*, 455. [CrossRef]
33. Nieves, V.; Radin, C.; Camps-Valls, G. Predicting regional coastal sea level changes with machine learning. *Sci. Rep.* **2021**, *11*, 7650. [CrossRef]
34. Khasnis, A.A.; Nettleman, M.D. Global warming and infectious disease. *Arch. Med. Res.* **2005**, *36*, 689–696. [CrossRef] [PubMed]
35. Sidhu, B.S.; Mehrabi, Z.; Ramankutty, N.; Kandlikar, M. How can machine learning help in understanding the impact of climate change on crop yields? *Environ. Res. Lett.* **2023**, *18*, 024008. [CrossRef]
36. Zheng, H. Analysis of global warming using machine learning. *Comput. Water Energy Environ. Eng.* **2018**, *7*, 127. [CrossRef]

37. Cheremisin, G.; Egorov, D.; Kravchenko, O.; Dev, A. Deep convolutional neural network for reconstructing the cloud phase distribution from level-1b MODIS data. *Proc. AIP Conf. Proc.* **2023**, *2819*, 030005.
38. Miloshevich, G.; Cozian, B.; Abry, P.; Borgnat, P.; Bouchet, F. Probabilistic forecasts of extreme heatwaves using convolutional neural networks in a regime of lack of data. *Phys. Rev. Fluids* **2023**, *8*, 040501. [CrossRef]
39. Farhangmehr, V.; Cobo, J.H.; Mohammadian, A.; Payeur, P.; Shirkhani, H.; Imanian, H. A Convolutional Neural Network Model for Soil Temperature Prediction under Ordinary and Hot Weather Conditions: Comparison with a Multilayer Perceptron Model. *Sustainability* **2023**, *15*, 7897. [CrossRef]
40. Hassan, K.M.A. Predicting Future Global Sea Level Rise From Climate Change Variables Using Deep Learnin. *Int. J. Comput. Digit. Syst.* **2023**. [CrossRef]
41. Ghimire, S.; Nguyen-Huy, T.; Prasad, R.; Deo, R.C.; Casillas-Perez, D.; Salcedo-Sanz, S.; Bhandari, B. Hybrid convolutional neural network-multilayer perceptron model for solar radiation prediction. *Cogn. Comput.* **2023**, *15*, 645–671. [CrossRef]
42. Larson, A.; Hendawi, A.; Boving, T.; Pradhanang, S.M.; Akanda, A.S. Discerning Watershed Response to Hydroclimatic Extremes with a Deep Convolutional Residual Regressive Neural Network. *Hydrology* **2023**, *10*, 116. [CrossRef]
43. Jonnalagadda, J.; Hashemi, M. Long Lead ENSO Forecast Using an Adaptive Graph Convolutional Recurrent Neural Network. *Eng. Proc.* **2023**, *39*, 5.
44. Lacombe, R.; Grossman, H.; Hendren, L.; Lüdeke, D. Improving extreme weather events detection with light-weight neural networks. *arXiv* **2023**, arXiv:2304.00176.
45. Raman, R.; Mewada, B.; Meenakshi, R.; Jayaseelan, G.; Sharmila, K.S.; Taqui, S.N.; Al-Ammar, E.A.; Wabaidur, S.M.; Iqbal, A. Forecasting the PV Power Utilizing a Combined Convolutional Neural Network and Long Short-Term Memory Model. *Electr. Power Components Syst.* **2023**, 1–17. [CrossRef]
46. Lin, F.; Zhang, Y.; Wang, J. Recent advances in intra-hour solar forecasting: A review of ground-based sky image methods. *Int. J. Forecast.* **2023**, *39*, 244–265. [CrossRef]
47. Caldas, M.; Alonso-Suárez, R. Very short-term solar irradiance forecast using all-sky imaging and real-time irradiance measurements. *Renew. Energy* **2019**, *143*, 1643–1658. [CrossRef]
48. Pedro, H.T.; Coimbra, C.F.; David, M.; Lauret, P. Assessment of machine learning techniques for deterministic and probabilistic intra-hour solar forecasts. *Renew. Energy* **2018**, *123*, 191–203. [CrossRef]
49. Kamadinata, J.O.; Ken, T.L.; Suwa, T. Sky image-based solar irradiance prediction methodologies using artificial neural networks. *Renew. Energy* **2019**, *134*, 837–845. [CrossRef]
50. Barranco-Jimenez, M.A.; Chimal-Eguia, J.C.; Angulo-Brown, F. The Gordon and Zarmi model for convective atmospheric cells under the ecological criterion applied to the planets of the solar system. *Rev. Mex. Fis.* **2006**, *52*, 205–212.
51. Ocampo-Garcia, A. Optimizacion Termodinamica y Termoeconomica de Modelos Extendidos de Maquinas Endorreversibles. Ph.D. Thesis, Instituto Politecnico Nacional, Mexico City, Mexico, 2020.
52. Angulo-Brown, F.; Arias-Hernandez, L.A.; Santillan, M. On some connections between first order irreversible thermodynamics and finite-time thermodynamics. *Rev. Mex. Fis.* **2002**, *48*, 182–192.
53. Norma Sanchez, F.; Angulo-Brown, M.B.J. Posibles futuros escenarios de la temperatura superficial de la Tierra con la evolucion de la constante solar. In Proceedings of the XXII Congreso Nacional de Termodinamica, Sociedad Mexicana de Termodinamica A.C., Mexico City, Mexico, 10–12 September 2007.
54. Barranco-Jimenez, M.A.; Angulo-Brown, F. A simple model on the influence of the greenhouse effect on the efficiency of solar-to-wind energy conversion. *Il Nuovo Cimento C* **2003**, *26*, 535–552.
55. Barranco-Jimenez, M.A.; Angulo-Brown, F. A nonendoreversible model for wind energy as a solar-driven heat engine. *J. Appl. Phys.* **1996**, *80*, 4872–4876. [CrossRef]
56. National Oceanic and Atmospheric Administration. Trends in Atmospheric Carbon Dioxide. 2023. Available online: https://gml.noaa.gov/ccgg/trends/ (accessed on 3 July 2023).
57. Berkeley Earth. Global Warming Data Overview. 2023. Available online: https://berkeleyearth.org/data/ (accessed on 3 July 2023).
58. National Center for Atmosferic Research. Global Surface Temperatures: BEST: Berkeley Earth Surface Temperatures. 2023. Available online: https://climatedataguide.ucar.edu/climate-data/global-surface-temperatures-best-berkeley-earth-surface-temperatures (accessed on 3 June 2023).
59. National Aeronautics and Space Administration. GISS Surface Temperature Analysis (GISTEMP v4). 2023. Available online: https://data.giss.nasa.gov/gistemp/ (accessed on 3 June 2023).
60. Pierrehumbert, R.T. Infrared radiation and planetary temperature. *Phys. Today* **2011**, *64*, 33–38. [CrossRef]
61. Curry, J.A.; Webster, P.J. *Thermodynamics of Atmospheres and Oceans*; Elsevier: Amsterdam, The Netherlands, 1998.
62. von Paris, P.; Rauer, H.; Grenfell, J.L.; Patzer, B.; Hedelt, P.; Stracke, B.; Trautmann, T.; Schreier, F. Warming the early Earth—CO2 reconsidered. *Planet. Space Sci.* **2008**, *56*, 1244–1259. [CrossRef]
63. Krasnopolsky, V.M.; Fox-Rabinovitz, M.S. Complex hybrid models combining deterministic and machine learning components for numerical climate modeling and weather prediction. *Neural Netw.* **2006**, *19*, 122–134. [CrossRef] [PubMed]
64. Schmidt, G.A.; Sherwood, S. A practical philosophy of complex climate modelling. *Eur. J. Philos. Sci.* **2015**, *5*, 149–169. [CrossRef]
65. Knutti, R.; Rugenstein, M.A. Feedbacks, climate sensitivity and the limits of linear models. *Philos. Trans. R. Soc. A Math. Phys. Eng. Sci.* **2015**, *373*, 20150146. [CrossRef] [PubMed]

66. Visconti, G. *Fundamentals of Physics and Chemistry of the Atmosphere*; Springer: Berlin/Heidelberg, Germany, 2001.
67. North, G.R.; Cahalan, R.F.; Coakley, J.A., Jr. Energy balance climate models. *Rev. Geophys.* **1981**, *19*, 91–121. [CrossRef]
68. Levario Medina, S. Estudio de Algunas Funciones Compromiso y Sus Efectos en la Optimización Termodinámica en los Modelos de Convertidores de Energía. Ph.D. Thesis, Escuela Superior de Física y Matemáticas, Instituto Politécnico Nacional, Mexico City, Mexico, 2021.

Disclaimer/Publisher's Note: The statements, opinions and data contained in all publications are solely those of the individual author(s) and contributor(s) and not of MDPI and/or the editor(s). MDPI and/or the editor(s) disclaim responsibility for any injury to people or property resulting from any ideas, methods, instructions or products referred to in the content.

Article

ACMKC: A Compact Associative Classification Model Using K-Modes Clustering with Rule Representations by Coverage

Jamolbek Mattiev [1,*], Monte Davityan [2] and Branko Kavsek [3,4]

1 Computer Science Department, Urgench State University, Khamid Alimdjan 14, Urgench 220100, Uzbekistan
2 Computer Science Department, California State University of Fullerton, 2555 Nutwood Avenue, Fullerton, CA 92831, USA; monte@csu.fullerton.edu
3 Department of Information Sciences and Technologies, University of Primorska, Glagoljaška 8, 6000 Koper, Slovenia; branko.kavsek@upr.si
4 AI Laboratory, Jožef Stefan Institute, Jamova Cesta 39, 1000 Ljubljana, Slovenia
* Correspondence: jamolbek.mattiev@famnit.upr.si or mattiev.jamolbek@urdu.uz; Tel.: +998-99-5854223

Abstract: The generation and analysis of vast amounts of data have become increasingly prevalent in diverse applications. In this study, we propose a novel approach to address the challenge of rule explosion in association rule mining by utilizing the coverage-based representations of clusters determined by K-modes. We utilize the FP-Growth algorithm to generate class association rules (CARs). To further enhance the interpretability and compactness of the rule set, we employ the K-modes clustering algorithm with a distance metric that binarizes the rules. The optimal number of clusters is determined using the silhouette score. Representative rules are then selected based on their coverage within each cluster. To evaluate the effectiveness of our approach, we conducted experimental evaluations on both UCI and Kaggle datasets. The results demonstrate a significant reduction in the rule space (71 rules on average, which is the best result among all state-of-the-art rule-learning algorithms), aligning with our goal of producing compact classifiers. Our approach offers a promising solution for managing rule complexity in association rule mining, thereby facilitating improved rule interpretation and analysis, while maintaining a significantly similar classification accuracy (ACMKC: 80.0% on average) to other rule learners on most of the datasets.

Keywords: class association rules; clustering; representative rule; model coverage; classification

MSC: 90C90

1. Introduction

In the modern era of data-driven applications, there has been a significant increase in the gathering and retention of large amounts of data. Extracting association rules from these extensive datasets and reducing their complex combinations has become a crucial method for uncovering valuable insights [1]. However, a major hurdle lies in the sheer number of rules discovered in real-world datasets, which requires the crucial task of pruning and clustering rules to create classifiers that are concise, precise, and easy to understand.

Association rule (AR) mining [2] seeks to create all relevant rules in a database, adhering to user-defined thresholds for minimum support and confidence. On the other hand, classification rule mining focuses on extracting a subset of rules to develop precise and effective models for predicting labels of ambiguous objects. Combining these two crucial data-mining methods in Associative Classification (AC) allows for the creation of a cohesive framework [3,4]. Association rules utilize many of the AC techniques presented by researchers to create efficient and accurate classifiers [5–12]. Although their effectiveness depends on user-defined factors like minimum support and confidence, research investigations have shown that AC methods can be more accurate than conventional categorization systems. Unsupervised learning techniques like clustering [13–15] also play a significant part. Partitional clustering or hierarchical clustering are two categories of clustering techniques. In partitional clustering [16,17], objects are divided into distinct clusters to ensure that objects inside a cluster are more similar than those in other clusters. On the other hand, nested partitions make up a hierarchy in hierarchical clustering [18]. While the top–down method starts with a single cluster that contains all items and then splits them into smaller clusters, the bottom–up method joins smaller clusters to create bigger ones.

Our research focuses on generating strong class association rules (CARs) using the "FP-Growth" algorithm for frequent itemsets, satisfying minimum support and confidence requirements. Additionally, we propose an approach to associative classification utilizing K-modes clustering with a novel distance metric built on direct measurements like rule items to reduce the rule space. Our method represents rules as binary vectors of itemsets, enabling efficient similarity calculation and making it compatible with clustering techniques like K-modes. We explore the benefits and methodology of K-modes clustering, which reveals hidden patterns in itemsets and provides computational efficiency for large datasets compared to other clustering approaches. Moreover, we introduce a two-step process using the silhouette score to determine the optimal number of clusters, ensuring a balance between cohesion and separation. After clustering the CARs, we select a representative CAR for each cluster using two approaches based on dataset coverage and rules similarity, aiming to enhance coverage and classification accuracy.

In order to assess the effectiveness of our proposed techniques, we carried out experiments on 13 meticulously chosen datasets sourced from the UCI Machine Learning Database Repository [19] and Kaggle. A comparative evaluation was conducted, comparing our methods against seven well-known associative and classical classification algorithms. These algorithms include Decision Table and Naïve Bayes (DTNB) [20], Decision Table (DT) [21], Classification Based on Predictive Association rules (CPAR) [22], Classification based on Multiple Association Rules (CMAR) [18], C4.5 [23], Classification-Based Association (CBA) [3], and Simple Associative Classifier (SA) [24].

Experimental results showed that ACMKC achieved the best result when comparing the average number of classification rules while maintaining the similar classification accuracy with other models. The ACMKC model showed great advantage to produce statistically smaller classifiers on bigger datasets, which was the primary goal of the study.

The following sections of the paper are structured as follows: Section 2 includes past works related to our research. Section 3 presents a comprehensive explanation of our proposed methodology. Section 4 focuses on the experimental evaluation. Section 5 outlines the conclusion and future plans. The paper concludes with the Acknowledgement and References sections.

2. Related Work

Our proposed approach introduces innovation in the selection of "strong" class association rules, the clustering process, and the determination of a "representative" class association rule for each cluster. Other relevant studies also address the concept of clustering CARs, but they employ various approaches. This section discusses these related approaches to clustering CARs, highlighting both the similarities and differences compared to our proposed approach.

To the best of our knowledge, and due to the lack of information relating to the combination of class association rules and clustering, our approach serves as a coalescence of these two to create a method of determining representative class association rules for clusters. While there are methods that employ associative classification and clustering to accomplish a similar feat, ours differs in that it uses CARS instead of associative classification.

The techniques used in [25] involve Association Rule Classification and Clustering units. In the Association Rule Classification unit, the Apriori Algorithm is applied to identify regularities between flow parameters; it is used for the finer classification and prediction of IPs and ports for future application servicing. This approach focuses on deriving association rules to enhance classification accuracy. On the other hand, in the Clustering unit, both K-Mean and Model-based clustering algorithms are compared to determine the optimum performance. Unsupervised clustering techniques group datasets with similar characteristics together, aiding the classification process. K-Mean partitions data into k groups to minimize the Euclidean distance of cluster centers. Model-Based Clustering assumes a data model and utilizes the Mclust package with Expectation–Maximization (EM) for parameter estimation and hierarchical clustering. These techniques differ from K-modes and class association rules by exploring distinct approaches to data representation, rule generation, and clustering strategies for classification tasks.

A new method researchers propose utilizes K-means (partitional) clustering to cluster association rules [26]. The primary objective of this research is to cluster discovered association rules to facilitate user selection of the most suitable rules. Four steps make up the algorithm: (1) The "Apriori" algorithm is used to extract ARs from frequent patterns; (2) Lift, Cosinus, Conviction, and Information Gain are computed for all rules generated in step 1; (3) Using the K-means algorithm, a set of association rules is divided into disjoint clusters; they attempt to cluster the rules that share the fewest similarities. Euclidean and degree of similarity distances are used; (4) Finally, the group of rules is ranked from best to worst based on the centroid of each cluster.

The CPAR algorithm is introduced by Yin and Han as a fusion of associative classification and traditional rule-based classification methods. CPAR employs a greedy algorithm and draws inspiration from the First-Order Inductive Learner (FOIL) [27] technique to directly generate rules from the training dataset, deviating from the generation of a vast number of candidate rules derived from frequent itemsets in other associative classification approaches. CPAR evaluates each rule using expected accuracy to address overfitting and employs a distinct classification process. Firstly, it selects all rules whose bodies match the testing example; then, it extracts the best k rules for each class among the selected rules. Finally, CPAR compares the average expected accuracy of the best k rules per class from step 2 and predicts the class label associated with the highest expected accuracy.

CMAR, an associative classification method, employs multiple association rules for classification. It extends the efficient FP-Growth algorithm [28] to mine large datasets and introduces a novel data structure called a CR-tree. The CR-tree aims to store and retrieve a large number of rules compactly and efficiently by utilizing a prefix tree structure that explores rule sharing, resulting in significant compactness. Additionally, the CR-tree acts as an index structure for rules, enabling efficient rule retrieval. In the rule selection phase, CMAR identifies highly confident and related rules by considering dataset coverage and analyzing their correlation. For each rule R, all examples covered by R are identified, and if R correctly classifies an example, it is selected for inclusion in the final classifier. The cover count of examples covered by R is incremented by 1, with a cover count threshold C initially applied. If the cover count of an example exceeds C, that example is removed. This iterative process continues until both the training dataset and rule set are empty.

Liu, Hsu, and Ma developed the heuristic technique known as CBA [3] in 1998. Its structure is similar to associative classification algorithms and includes steps for rule development and selection. CBA uses an iterative process for rule creation comparable to the Apriori algorithm [2]. CBA detects frequent rule-items and creates strong class association rules from these frequent itemsets by repeatedly examining the data. A pruning technique based on a pessimistic error rate is used in the rule-generation phase. Rules are extracted depending on dataset coverage during the rule-selection step. A rule qualifies as a prospective classifier candidate if it accurately classifies at least one example. Finally, based on the assessment of total error, rules are added to the final classifier.

In reference [29], a classifier named J&B was developed through a thorough exploration of the complete example space, resulting in a straightforward and accurate classifier. Our selection of strong class association rules was based on their contribution to enhancing the coverage of the learning set. J&B incorporates a stopping criterion in the rule-selection process, which relies on the coverage of the training dataset. In the representative CAR-selection process of this study, we employed the J&B approach without using a stopping condition. There is no need to use a stopping criterion in this method because the size of the classifier, which is decided by the number of clusters, is determined using a separate strategy.

Conditional market-basket difference (CMBP) and conditional market-basket log-likelihood (CMBL) approaches are two further strategies suggested in [30]. This method groups association rules using a new normalized distance metric. Agglomerative clustering is used to group the rules based on distance. In addition, the rules are clustered using self-organizing maps and multi-dimensionally scaled in a vector space. This approach is relatively similar to ours, but instead of using "indirect" measurements based on CAR support and coverage, we suggest a new normalized distance metric based on "direct" and "combined" distances between class association rules.

Another related strategy is mining clusters with ARs [31]. The FP-Growth algorithm generates the rules in this case. However, a unique distance metric (based on K-modes) is afterward applied to identify similarities between rules. Provided is the list of products purchased by each client, and rules are clustered using a top–down hierarchical clustering algorithm to identify clusters in a population of customers. After clustering the rules, we introduce a specific distance metric to assess the effectiveness of the clustering process.

3. Methodology

Our approach (Compact, Accurate and Descriptive Associative Classifier) is divided into 3 main actions outlined in the preceding section. The following subsections go into further depth about each of these steps.

3.1. Class Association Rule Generation

In this subsection, we address the method of finding the strong CARs from frequent itemsets. The process of creating ARs typically consists of two primary stages: first, all frequent itemsets from the training dataset are found using the least support; then, we use these frequent itemsets along with minimum confidence to create strong association rules. The identical process used for AR creation is also followed in the discovery of CARs. The main distinction is that in the rule-generation phase, the rule's result in CAR generation comprises just the class label, whereas the rule's result in AR generation might contain any frequent itemset. In the first step, the "FP-Growth" algorithm is employed to discover frequent itemsets. The "FP-Growth" algorithm uses a "growth" technique to decrease the number of itemset candidates at each level, therefore speeding up the search process. To create the 2-frequent itemset and beyond, it starts by determining the 1-frequent itemset. Since they cannot add to frequent itemsets, any infrequent itemsets found during the procedure are discarded. By completing this trimming step before calculating the support at each level, the temporal complexity of the algorithm is decreased. After obtaining every frequent itemset from the training datasets, creating strong class association rules (CARs) that meet the minimal support and minimum confidence requirements is a simple process. The frequent itemsets found in the first stage serve as the basis for these rules. The confidence of a rule can be calculated using the following formula:

$$confidence(A \to B) = \frac{support\_count(A \cup B)}{support\_count(A)} \quad (1)$$

In Equation (1), the support count of an itemset is used, where A represents the premise (itemset on the left-hand side of the rule), B represents the consequence (class label on the right-hand side of the rule), $support\_count(A \cup B)$ represents the number of transactions that contain both itemsets A and B, and $support\_count(A)$ represents the number of transactions that contain itemset A. On the basis of the prior equation, the following procedures can be used to build strong class association rules that satisfy the minimum confidence threshold:

- Generate all nonempty subsets S for each frequent itemset L and a class label C.
- For each nonempty subset S of L, output the strong rule R in the form of "$S \rightarrow C$" if $\frac{support\_count(R)}{support\_count(S)} \leq min\_conf$, where min_conf represents the minimum confidence threshold.

3.2. Clustering

Clustering algorithms put comparable examples together into clusters, where the examples in each cluster differ from the examples in other clusters and share commonalities with each other. Among the different clustering techniques, K-modes is a noteworthy one. Because of its unique benefits in some situations, such as efficiently managing datasets with discrete qualities or categorical variables, like the suggested distance matrix we use to describe association rules, the K-modes technique is used.

3.2.1. Distance Metric

We suggest a new distance metric in this part that is based on direct measurements for rule items. Our main objective is to decrease the rule space by using direct distance measurements for clustering.

The encoding of rules as a binary vector of itemsets is one of our work's contributions. With this structure, calculating similarities across rules is quick and easy, and our binary governed dataset is a perfect fit for clustering methods like K-modes.

The antecedent, or left side of the rule, is taken into consideration when we are calculating the distance between the rules that have the same class value.

Let $R = \{r_1, r_2, \ldots, r_n\}$ be a rule set, and each rule is denoted as follows: $r = \{a_1, a_2, \ldots, a_k\} \rightarrow \{c\}$, where $\{a_1, a_2, \ldots, a_k\}$ are values of the attribute and c is a class value. We first transfer the rule items a_i into a binary vector. The existing attribute's value is replaced with 1 and the remaining attribute's values (which were not present in a rule) are replaced with 0.

Example: Let us assume that attribute Windy has two values: "T" and "F", and attribute Temperature has three values: "Hot", "Mild" and "Cool". An antecedent of the example rule is as follows: Windy = T and Temp = Cool; a subsetted example of the represented rule is shown below.

Rule	Windy = T	Windy = F	Temp = Hot	Temp = Mild	Temp = Cool
{Windy=T, Temp=Cool}	1	0	0	0	1

After transferring the rules into binary vectors, we use a simple method of computing the distance between two rules as follows:

Given two rules ($rule1$, $rule2$):

$$rule1 = \{y_1, y_2, \ldots, y_k\} \rightarrow \{c\}$$

$$rule2 = \{z_1, z_2, \ldots, z_k\} \rightarrow \{c\}$$

where $\{y_1, y_2, \ldots, y_k$ and $z_1, z_2, \ldots, z_k\} \subseteq 0, 1$, and $c \in C$. We compute the similarity between $rule1$ and $rule2$ as follows:

$$distance(rule1, rule2) = \sum_{i=1}^{k} |y_i - z_i| \qquad (2)$$

3.2.2. K-Modes

In K-modes, the clustering process involves iteratively assigning examples to clusters, considering the modes (the most frequent values) of the categorical attributes. This approach seeks to identify groups of examples that share similar modes across all categorical variables, ensuring that the resulting clusters are internally cohesive. By employing K-modes, we can achieve several benefits. Firstly, it allows us to capture the inherent structure within the itemsets contained in the rules, revealing patterns and associations that might be hidden in numerical-based clustering methods. Secondly, K-modes offers computational efficiency and scalability for large datasets with categorical variables. It can handle high-dimensional data and handle a large number of categories within each attribute, making it suitable for real-world applications with diverse and complex categorical data. The K-modes algorithm is described in Algorithm 1.

Algorithm 1 The K-modes algorithm for partitioning, where each cluster's center is represented by the median value of the objects in the cluster.

Input: k: the number of clusters, D: a dataset containing n rules
Output: A set of k clusters
1: Arbitrarily choose k rules from D as the initial cluster centers;
2: **repeat**
3:    (Re)assign each rule to the cluster to which the rule is the most similar based on the median value of the rules in the cluster;
4:    Update the cluster medians, i.e., calculate the median value of the rules for each cluster;
5: **until** no change.

We run the K-modes method twice. Since Algorithm 1 takes the number of clusters in advance, we initially run the algorithm to determine the optimal number of clusters. Then, the algorithm is run again with the determined optimal clusters. When determining the optimal number of clusters in K-modes, the silhouette score can be utilized as a metric. The silhouette score assists in identifying the "natural" number of clusters by evaluating the cohesion and separation of examples within the clusters.

To calculate the silhouette score, each example is assigned to a cluster, and the following values are computed:

- The average dissimilarity (distance) between an example i and all other examples within the same cluster. This value measures how well an example fits within its assigned cluster with lower values indicating better cohesion.
- The average dissimilarity (distance) between an example i and all examples in the nearest neighboring cluster. This value captures the separation or dissimilarity between an example and other clusters with higher values indicating greater dissimilarity.

By computing the silhouette scores for all examples across a range of cluster numbers, the optimal number of clusters can be identified. The "natural" number of clusters corresponds to the point where the silhouette score is highest, indicating the configuration with the best balance of cohesion and separation. The algorithm that identifies the "natural" number of clusters is presented in Algorithm 2.

Algorithm 2 Computing the optimal number of clusters.

Input: D: a dataset containing n rules; $max\_clusters$: the maximum number of clusters to search for
Output: Optimal number of clusters
1:    $Opt\_number\_of\_cluster = 1$;
2:    $Best\_score = 1$;
3: **for** $(k = 2; k \leq max\_clusters; k++)$ **do**
4:    Run K-modes with dataset D and number of clusters as k;
5:    Calculate *silhouette_score*;
6:    **if** *silhouette_score* $>=$ *Best_score* **then**
7:       $Best\_score = silhouette\_score$;
8:       $Opt\_number\_of\_cluster = k$;
9:    **end if**
10: **end for**
11: **return** $Opt\_number\_of\_clusters$

3.3. Extracting the Representative CAR

After locating each cluster, the last step is to separate the representative CARs from each cluster to create a descriptive, compact, and useful associative classifier. In this work, we extracted representative rules based on dataset coverage while considering the rules similarity.

The decision was made to utilize this approach in order to raise the classification accuracy and overall coverage. It is not necessary to consider the outer-class overlapping problem—which indicates that some samples from different classes have similar characteristics—because we are clustering similar rules with the same class value. However, we should avoid the inter-class overlapping problem, which arises when multiple rules from the same class cover the same samples. By choosing the representative CARs according to database coverage, we work around this issue. When the coverage of the rules is the same, we take into account how similar the rules are to each other. This means that we select the CAR that is closest to the cluster center (it has the lowest average distance to all other rules). The steps are described in Algorithm 3.

Algorithm 3 A Representative CAR based on Dataset Coverage and Minimum Distance.

Input: A set of class association rules in *CARs* array, a training dataset D and *covered_traindata* array
Output: Three representative class association rules
1: *CARs* = sort(*CARs*, *coverage*, *minimum_distance*);
2: Representative_CARs. add (CARs[1]):
3: **for** $(i = 2; i \leq CARs.length; i++)$ **do**
4:   **for** $(j = 1; j \leq D.length; j++)$ **do**
5:     **if** *covered_traindata*$[j]$ = **false then**
6:       **if** *CARs[i]* covers *D[j]* **then**
7:         *covered_traindata*$[j]$ = **true**;
8:         increment *contribution* of CARs[i] by 1;
9:       **end if**
10:    **end if**
11:   **end for**
12:   **if** *contribution* of CARs[i] > 0 **then**
13:     Representative_CARs. add (CARs[i]);
14:     **break**;
15:   **end if**
16:   **if** Representative_CARs. length = 3 **then**
17:     **return** *Representative_CARs*;
18:   **end if**
19: **end for**

Firstly, class association rules within the cluster are sorted (line 1) by *coverage* and *minimum_distance* in descending order by the following criteria: Given two rules R_1 and R_2, R_1 is said to have a higher rank than R_2, which is denoted as $R_1 > R_2$,

- If and only if, $coverage(R_1) > coverage(R_2)$; or
- If $coverage(R_1) = coverage(R_2)$ but, $minimum_distance(R_1) > minimum_distance(R_2)$;
- If the entire set of parameters of the rules is equal, we may choose any of one of them.

After sorting the rules based on coverage and minimum distance, we extracted the top three rules for each cluster. We selected three rules as optimal according to experiments. Each potential rule is checked (Lines 3–19); if it covers at least one new example (Lines 12–15), then we add it to the representative CARs array and remove all the examples covered by that rule; otherwise, we continue.

Associative Classification Model

After extracting the representative class association rules, we produce our explainable, compact and descriptive model which is represented in Algorithm 4.

Algorithm 4 Compact and Explainable Associative Classification Model.

Input: A distance matrix d and number of clusters S
Output: Cluster heights (AHCCLH), Cluster of CARs (AHCCLC)
  1: **Initialization:** *minimum support* and *minimum confidence* thresholds are set to generate the CARs;
  2: **Generate:** The frequent itemsets are generated from the dataset by using the FP-Growth algorithm and used to produce strong class association rules, which are sorted based on confidence and support. Cars are then groupped according to class label;
  3: **Cluster:** For each group of CARs, the K-modes clustering algorithm is utilized to cluster them. For this purpose, the newly developed distance metric (Section 3.2.1) is used to find the similarity between CARs, and the optimal number of clusters is identified based on the silhouette score (Algorithm 2);
  4: **Extract representative rules:** Three representative rules are extracted for each cluster according to Algorithm 3:
  5: **Producing final model:** For each class value, all the rules extracted from each cluster are collected to produce the final compact and explainable associative classification model.
---

4. Results

Experimental assessment supported the accomplishment of the scientific goals. Thirteen real-world datasets from Kaggle and the UCI Machine Learning Database Repository were used to test our models. By comparing our classifier's classification accuracy and rule count to those of eight well-known rule-based classification algorithms (DTNB, DT, C4.5, CPAR, CMAR, CBA, and SA), we were able to assess its performance. A paired *t*-test was used to determine the statistical significance of each difference (with a 95% level of significance).

Associative classifiers were run with default parameters at *minimum support* = 1% and *minimum confidence* = 50%. We utilized their WEKA workbench implementation with default parameters for the other classification models. The description of the datasets is shown in Table 1.

An evaluation methodology that uses 10-fold cross-validation was used to achieve all experimental outcomes. Table 2 displays the experimental findings for classification accuracy (mean values throughout the 10-fold cross-validation with standard deviations).

Table 2 shows that the ACMKC model achieved the best accuracies on the "Abalone", "Adult", "Connect4" and "Diabetes" datasets among all classification models and obtained comparable accuracies on other datasets. Our proposed model attained the third highest result on average accuracy with 80.0%, which was slightly lower than the results of the C4.5 (82.7%) and CMAR (82.4%) models. Rule-based models DTNB, DT, and C4.5 obtained better accuracies on the "Car.Evn" and "Nursery" datasets than associative classifications CPAR, CMAR, CBA, SA, and ACMKC. The main reason is that those datasets are imbalanced, which causes a problem in the rule-generation part of AC models (AC models were not able to produce enough class association rules for each class value with imbalanced datasets). Interestingly, CPAR and CMAR achieved over 99% accuracy on the "Mushroom" dataset, which was 15–25% higher than other rule learners.

Table 1. Datasets description.

Dataset	Attributes	Classes	Records	Analyzed Rules
Car.Evn	7	4	1728	10,000
Tic-Tac-Toe	10	2	958	10,000
Nursery	9	5	12,960	20,000
Mushroom	23	2	8124	20,000
Abalone	9	3	4177	10,000
Adult	15	2	45,221	20,000
Laptop	11	3	1303	10,000
Chess	37	2	3196	10,000
Connect4	43	3	67,557	10,000
Airplane	17	2	103,904	20,000
Airline Reviews	8	2	129,455	20,000
Diabetes	13	2	70,692	10,000
Recruitment	7	2	215	1000

Table 2. Evaluation of classification models on accuracy.

Dataset	DTNB	DT	C4.5	CPAR	CMAR	CBA	SA	ACMKC
Car.Evn	**95.4 ± 0.8**	91.3 ± 1.7	92.1 ± 1.7	78.1 ± 2.5	86.7 ± 2.1	91.2 ± 3.9	86.2 ± 2.1	83.0 ± 3.0
Tic-Tac-Toe	69.9 ± 2.7	74.4 ± 4.4	85.2 ± 2.7	70.5 ± 1.6	**95.3 ± 1.8**	73.1 ± 0.8	91.7 ± 1.5	74.4 ± 3.7
Nursery	94.0 ± 1.5	93.6 ± 1.2	**95.4 ± 1.4**	78.9 ± 1.2	91.7 ± 2.2	92.1 ± 2.4	91.6 ± 1.2	85.6 ± 1.3
Mushroom	75.0 ± 7.2	53.4 ± 8.3	78.7 ± 8.4	99.1 ± 0.0	**99.4 ± 0.0**	75.6 ± 10.9	73.1 ± 6.0	83.0 ± 0.9
Abalone	62.1 ± 1.3	61.8 ± 1.5	62.3 ± 1.2	60.2 ± 1.1	58.3 ± 1.7	61.1 ± 1.0	61.0 ± 0.9	**66.9 ± 5.3**
Adult	73.0 ± 4.1	82.0 ± 2.3	82.4 ± 4.7	77.4 ± 2.9	80.2 ± 2.4	81.8 ± 3.4	80.8 ± 2.6	**82.8 ± 4.5**
Laptop	**75.7 ± 2.6**	72.9 ± 2.9	75.3 ± 2.3	70.9 ± 2.7	72.8 ± 1.0	75.4 ± 2.0	72.0 ± 1.4	71.5 ± 3.3
Chess	93.7 ± 3.0	97.3 ± 3.1	**98.9 ± 3.6**	93.7 ± 3.2	93.8 ± 2.9	95.4 ± 2.9	92.2 ± 3.8	95.7 ± 2.7
Connect4	78.8 ± 5.9	76.7 ± 7.7	80.0 ± 6.8	68.6 ± 4.4	68.8 ± 4.7	80.9 ± 8.1	78.7 ± 6.0	**82.4 ± 4.4**
Airplane	89.6 ± 0.9	93.2 ± 0.3	**95.7 ± 0.2**	88.2 ± 1.3	91.7 ± 2.2	75.7 ± 6.9	77.4 ± 8.1	83.2 ± 0.8
Airline Reviews	94.0 ± 1.0	94.0 ± 1.9	93.8 ± 1.4	**96.0 ± 0.9**	94.2 ± 1.2	74.2 ± 1.8	76.2 ± 2.6	92.1 ± 2.1
Diabetes	72.9 ± 0.6	73.1 ± 0.5	72.9 ± 0.4	69.9 ± 1.7	70.9 ± 0.6	71.7 ± 2.4	70.0 ± 1.7	**74.2 ± 1.5**
Recruitment	65.1 ± 5.2	**67.5 ± 5.9**	63.0 ± 6.4	63.8 ± 3.4	67.2 ± 2.8	64.4 ± 2.5	61.6 ± 4.1	65.3 ± 5.5
Average (%):	79.9 ± 2.8	79.3 ± 3.2	82.7 ± 3.2	78.8 ± 2.1	82.4 ± 2.0	77.8 ± 3.8	77.9 ± 3.2	80.0 ± 3.0

Table 3 displays statistically significant testing (wins/losses counts) on accuracy between ACMKC and other classification methods. The following represent the results displayed below: **W**: our approach was significantly better than the algorithms being compared; **L**: the selected rule-learning algorithm significantly outperformed our algorithm; **N**: no significant difference has been detected in the comparison.

It can be seen from Table 3 that our proposed model outperformed SA (8/3/2) and CPAR (7/3/3) methods based on win/losses counts. Although ACMKC statistically lost to the C4.5 model on 6 datasets out of 13, it achieved comparable results with DTNB, DT and CMAR algorithms and had a slightly better result than CBA (5/3/5) in terms of win/losses counts.

In our goal to develop an association rule-based model that significantly reduces the required number of rules, we find our model uses far less rules that many other common rule-based and associative classification models, which is shown in Table 4. On average, for the datasets we tested, our model produced 71 rules with the other two closest algorithms being CPAR at 90 rules and CBA at 95 rules. Our method beats the other compared methods for seven out of thirteen datasets and performs in the top two for the least amount of rules for ten of the thirteen tested datasets. The other models in comparison produced far more rules on average.

Table 3. Comparison of classification models on accuracy based on statistically significant wins/losses counts.

	DTNB	DT	C4.5	CPAR	CMAR	CBA	SA
W	5	3	3	7	4	5	8
L	4	3	6	3	5	3	3
N	4	7	4	3	4	5	2

Table 4. Evaluation of classification models based on number of rules.

Dataset	DTNB	DT	C4.5	CPAR	CMAR	CBA	SA	ACMKC
Car.Evn	144	432	123	40	567	72	160	**21**
Tic-Tac-Toe	258	121	88	**11**	166	23	60	48
Nursery	1240	804	301	**60**	1935	141	175	132
Mushroom	50	50	26	19	100	15	70	**12**
Abalone	165	60	49	**17**	834	132	155	36
Adult	737	1571	279	120	3411	126	130	**101**
Laptop	101	101	72	41	783	**39**	75	45
Chess	507	101	31	14	282	14	120	**12**
Connect4	3826	952	3973	657	6877	349	600	**267**
Airplane	3201	4444	772	**41**	391	104	660	120
Airline Reviews	186	890	259	117	3218	121	140	**99**
Diabetes	160	244	221	37	3572	95	160	**24**
Recruitment	20	**8**	13	10	106	15	14	12
Average:	773	1060	477	90	1710	95	184	71

The main advantage of our model is producing noticeably smaller classifiers on bigger datasets comparing to other rule-based and associative classification models (illustrated in Figure 1).

When the size of the dataset increases, the number of rules in the DTNB, DT, C4.5 and CMAR models also rises. However, ACMKC is not sensitive to the dataset size, which can be proven on selected datasets in Figure 1. Figure 1 illustrates the huge advantage of our proposed model compared to other classification models in terms of classifier size. Table 5 provides detailed information on the statistically significant win/loss counts of our methods when compared to other classification models for the number of rules.

Table 5 shows that ACMKC statistically outperformed all the models on the number of rules according to the win/losses counts. Although ACMKC achieved slightly worse results than the C4.5 and CMAR algorithms on accuracy, it produced statistically smaller classifiers than those models in all datasets. Our proposed model achieved statistically better results than DTNB on every dataset and DT on 12 datasets out of 13 in terms of classifier size. Our model had a statistically worse result than CBA on three datasets and CPAR on four datasets, and there were no statistical differences between those methods on three datasets out of 13.

As displayed in Figure 2, our method provides competitive accuracies against the other classification models while utilizing significantly less rules. Only the CPAR algorithm provides a similar result when trading accuracy and number of rules; yet, on average, our method utilizes far less rules.

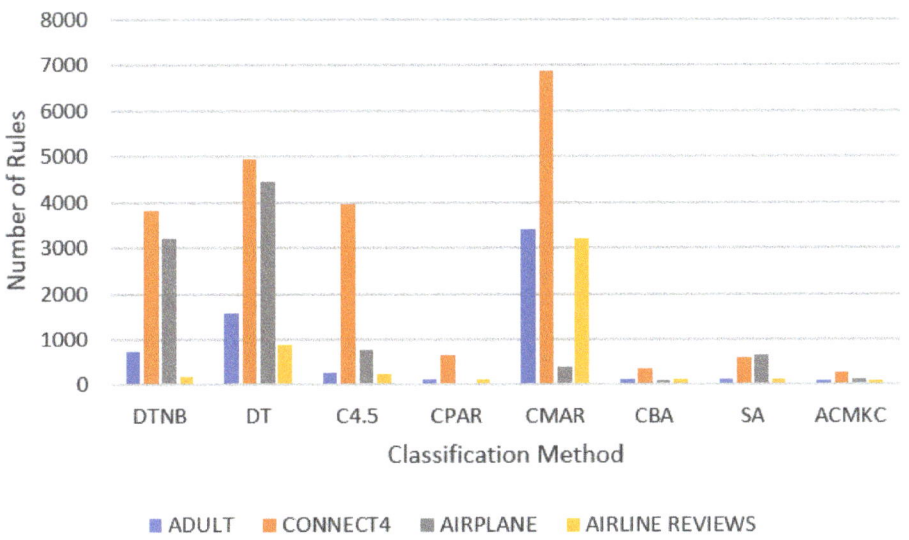

Figure 1. Comparison of classification models on bigger datasets based on classifier size.

Table 5. Comparison of classification models on rules based on statistically significant wins/losses counts.

	DTNB	DT	C4.5	CPAR	CMAR	CBA	SA
W	13	12	12	6	13	7	12
L	0	1	0	4	0	3	0
N	0	0	1	3	0	3	1

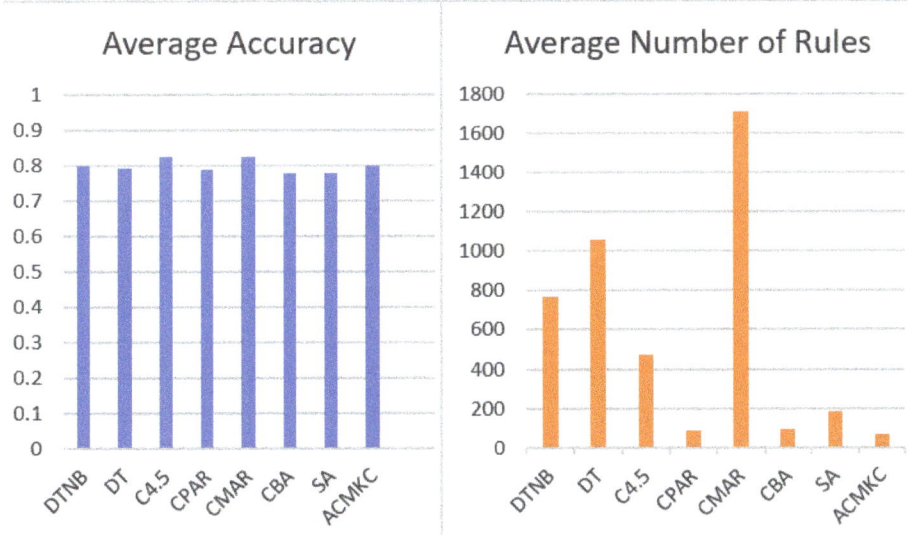

Figure 2. Comparison of classification models in terms of average accuracy and number of rules.

It is of note that not only does our method perform comparably and sometimes better in regard to accuracy, it also has better precision, recall and F-measure scores when comparing our method to other class association rule algorithms used in classification tasks (shown in Figure 3). As mentioned above, it does this while producing significantly fewer rules than other methods, which was the main goal of this research.

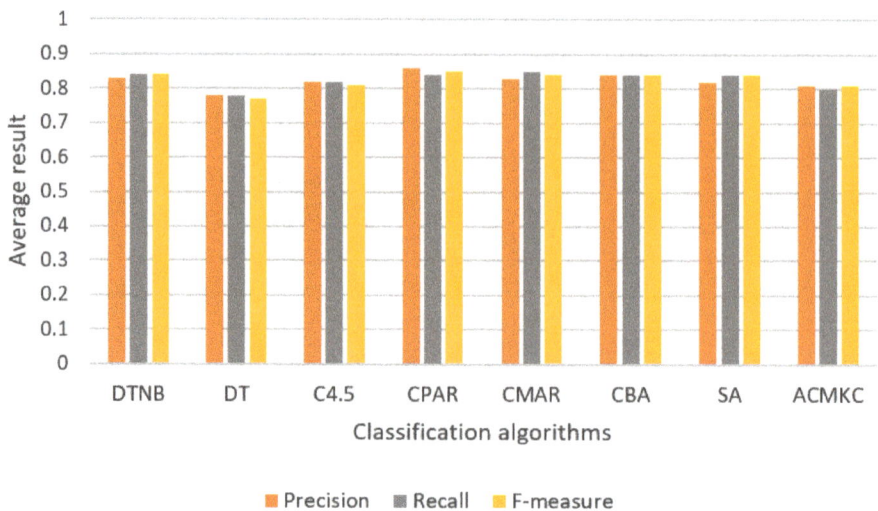

Figure 3. Comparison of classification models on "precision", "recall" and "F-measure".

5. Conclusions

By exhaustively searching the whole example space utilizing constraints and clustering, the fundamental goal of this research is to produce a compact and meaningful yet accurate classifier. According to experimental findings, ACMKC greatly decreased the number of classification rules while retaining classification accuracy, which was the major objective of this study. More specifically, the ACMKC method outperformed all other models in terms of average number of rules with 71 rules, which was ten times better than the results of the DTNB, DT, and CMAR algorithms. The proposed model's overall accuracy was on par with that of all other models, and it was the third highest between all classification models.

The advantage of the proposed model over previous rule-based and associative classification models was demonstrated experimentally by the fact that it produced smaller classifiers on larger datasets.

In future work, we plan to optimize our model ACMKC to improve its time complexity, which is a major drawback of our method. We also would like to investigate ways of including numeric attributes into the associative classification models, as using clustering on class association rules with numeric attributes may reveal new interesting perspectives on the subject.

Author Contributions: Conceptualization, J.M., M.D. and B.K.; methodology, J.M. and M.D.; software, J.M. and M.D.; validation, J.M. and M.D.; formal analysis, J.M., M.D. and B.K.; writing—original draft preparation, J.M. and M.D.; writing—review and editing, J.M. and B.K. All authors have read and agreed to the published version of the manuscript.

Funding: Jamolbe Mattiev acknowledges funding by the Ministry of "Innovative Development" of the Republic of Uzbekistan, grant: UZ-N47.

Data Availability Statement: The dataset used in this paper can be found at https://www.kaggle.com/datasets?tags=13302-Classification and https://archive.ics.uci.edu/ (accessed on 27 June 2023).

Acknowledgments: The Slovenian Research Agency ARRS provided financing for the project J2-2504, which the first and third authors recognize. They also express their gratitude to the Republic of Slovenia (Investment funding of the Republic of Slovenia and the European Union of the European

Regional Development Fund) and the European Commission for supporting the InnoRenewCoE project through the Horizon2020 Widespread-Teaming program, respectively (Grant Agreement #739574). The Ministry of "Innovative Development" of the Republic of Uzbekistan, which provided money for this study, is also acknowledged and sincerely thanked by the first author. The second author was partially funded by the National Science Foundation (NSF) grant of the Californian State University (grant number #1826490).

Conflicts of Interest: The authors declare no conflict of interest.

References

1. Lent, B.; Swami, A.; Widom, J. Clustering association rules. In Proceedings of the 13th International Conference on Data Engineering, Birmingham, UK, 7–11 April 1997; pp. 220–231. [CrossRef]
2. Agrawal, R.; Srikant, R. Fast algorithms for mining association rules. In Proceedings of the 20th International Conference on Very Large Data Bases, VLDB, Santiago, Chile, 12–15 September 1994; Volume 1215, pp. 487–499.
3. Liu, B.; Hsu, W.; Ma, Y. Integrating Classification and Association Rule Mining. In Proceedings of the Fourth International Conference on Knowledge Discovery and Data Mining, New York, NY, USA, 27–31 August 1998; KDD'98; AAAI Press: Washington, DC, USA, 1998; pp. 80–86.
4. Mattiev, J.; Kavšek, B. CMAC: Clustering Class Association Rules to Form a Compact and Meaningful Associative Classifier. In *Machine Learning, Optimization, and Data Science, Proceedings of the 6th International Conference, LOD 2020, Siena, Italy, 19–23 July 2020*; Springer: Berlin/Heidelberg, Germany, 2020; pp. 372–384. [CrossRef]
5. Hu, L.Y.; Hu, Y.H.; Tsai, C.F.; Wang, J.S.; Huang, M.W. Building an associative classifier with multiple minimum supports. *SpringerPlus* **2016**, *5*, 528. [CrossRef] [PubMed]
6. Deng, H.; Runger, G.; Tuv, E.; Bannister, W. CBC: An Associative Classifier with a Small Number of Rules. *Decis. Support Syst.* **2014**, *59*, 163–170. [CrossRef]
7. Rajab, K. New Associative Classification Method Based on Rule Pruning for Classification of Datasets. *IEEE Access* **2019**, *7*, 157783–157795. [CrossRef]
8. Mattiev, J.; Kavšek, B. Coverage-Based Classification Using Association Rule Mining. *Appl. Sci.* **2020**, *10*, 7013. [CrossRef]
9. Thabtah, F.; Cowling, P.; Peng, Y. MCAR: Multi-class Classification based on Association Rule. In Proceedings of the 3rd ACS/IEEE International Conference onComputer Systems and Applications, Cairo, Egypt, 6 January 2005; Volume 2005, p. 33. [CrossRef]
10. Thabtah, F.; Cowling, P.; Peng, Y. MMAC: A new multi-class, multi-label associative classification approach. In Proceedings of the Fourth IEEE International Conference on Data Mining (ICDM'04), Brighton, UK, 1–4 November 2004; pp. 217–224. [CrossRef]
11. Mattiev, J.; Kavsek, B. Distance based clustering of class association rules to build a compact, accurate and descriptive classifier. *Comput. Sci. Inf. Syst.* **2021**, *18*, 791–811. [CrossRef]
12. Chen, G.; Liu, H.; Yu, L.; Wei, Q.; Xing, Z. A new approach to classification based on association rule mining. *Decis. Support Syst.* **2006**, *42*, 674–689. [CrossRef]
13. Kaufman, L.; Rousseeuw, P. *Finding Groups in Data: An Introduction to Cluster Analysis*; John Wiley & Sons: Hoboken, NJ, USA, 1990. [CrossRef]
14. Zaït, M.; Messatfa, H. A comparative study of clustering methods. *Future Gener. Comput. Syst.* **1997**, *13*, 149–159. [CrossRef]
15. Arabie, P.; Hubert, L.J. An Overview of Combinatorial Data Analysis. In *Clustering and Classification*; Arabie, P., Hubert, L.J., Soete, G.D., Eds.; World Scientific Publishing: Hackensack, NJ, USA, 1996; pp. 5–63.
16. Ng, T.R.; Han, J. Efficient and Effective Clustering Methods for Spatial Data Mining. In Proceedings of the 20th Conference on Very Large Data Bases (VLDB), Santiago, Chile, 12–15 September 1994; pp. 144–155.
17. Zhang, T.; Ramakrishnan, R.; Livny, M. BIRCH: An Efficient Data Clustering Method for Very Large Databases. In Proceedings of the 1996 ACM SIGMOD International Conference on Management of Data, New York, NY, USA, 22–27 June 2013 1996; SIGMOD'96; pp. 103–114. [CrossRef]
18. Theodoridis, S.; Koutroumbas, K. *Chapter 13. Clustering Algorithms II: Hierarchical Algorithms*; Academic Press: San Diego, CA, USA, 2009; pp. 653–700. [CrossRef]
19. Dua, D.; Graff, C. *UCI Machine Learning Repository*; University of California: Irvine, CA, USA, 2019.
20. Hall, M.; Frank, E. Combining Naive Bayes and Decision Tables. In Proceedings of the Twenty-First International Florida Artificial Intelligence Research Society Conference, Coconut Grove, FL, USA, 15–17 May 2008; AAAI Press: Washington, DC, USA, 2008
21. Kohavi, R. The Power of Decision Tables. In *European Conference on Machine Learning*; Springer: Berlin/Heidelberg, Germany, 1995; pp. 174–189.
22. Yin, X.; Han, J. CPAR: Classification Based on Predictive Association Rules. In Proceedings of the 2003 SIAM International Conference on Data Mining. Society for Industrial and Applied Mathematics, San Francisco, CA, USA, 1–3 May 2003; Volume 3. [CrossRef]
23. Salzberg, S.L. *C4.5: Programs for Machine Learning by J. Ross Quinlan*; Springer: Berlin/Heidelberg, Germany, 1994; Volume 16, pp. 235–240. [CrossRef]

24. Mattiev, J.; Kavšek, B. Simple and Accurate Classification Method Based on Class Association Rules Performs Well on Well-Known Datasets. In *Machine Learning, Optimization, and Data Science, Proceedings of the 5th International Conference, LOD 2019, Siena, Italy, 10–13 September 2019*; Springer: Berlin/Heidelberg, Germany, 2019; pp. 192–204. [CrossRef]
25. Chaudhary, U.; Papapanagiotou, I.; Devetsikiotis, M. Flow classification using clustering and association rule mining. In Proceedings of the 2010 15th IEEE International Workshop on Computer Aided Modeling, Analysis and Design of Communication Links and Networks (CAMAD), Miami, FL, USA, 3–4 December 2010. [CrossRef]
26. Dahbi, A.; Mohammed, M.; Balouki, Y.; Gadi, T. Classification of association rules based on K-means algorithm. In Proceedings of the 2016 4th IEEE International Colloquium on Information Science and Technology (CiSt), Tangier, Morocco, 24–26 October 2016; pp. 300–305. [CrossRef]
27. Quinlan, J.R.; Cameron-Jones, R.M. FOIL: A midterm repor. In *Machine Learning: ECML-93, Proceedings of the European Conference on Machine Learning Vienna, Austria, 5–7 April 1993*; Springer: Berlin/Heidelberg, Germany, 1993; Volume 667, pp. 3–20. [CrossRef]
28. Han, J.; Pei, J.; Yin, Y. *Mining Frequent Patterns without Candidate Generation*; Association for Computing Machinery: New York, NY, USA, 2000; pp. 1–12.
29. Mattiev, J.; Kavšek, B. A compact and understandable associative classifier based on overall coverage. *Procedia Comput. Sci.* **2020**, *170*, 1161–1167. [CrossRef]
30. Gupta, K.G.; Strehl, A.; Ghosh, J. Distance based clustering of association rules. In Proceedings of the Artificial Neural Networks in Engineering Conference, St. Louis, MI, USA, 7–10 November 1999; pp. 759–764.
31. Kosters, W.A.; Marchiori, E.; Oerlemans, A.A.J. Mining Clusters with Association Rules. In Proceedings of the Advances in Intelligent Data Analysis, Amsterdam, The Netherlands, 9–11 August 1999; Hand, D.J., Kok, J.N., Berthold, M.R., Eds.; Springer: Berlin/Heidelberg, Germany, 1999; pp. 39–50.

Disclaimer/Publisher's Note: The statements, opinions and data contained in all publications are solely those of the individual author(s) and contributor(s) and not of MDPI and/or the editor(s). MDPI and/or the editor(s) disclaim responsibility for any injury to people or property resulting from any ideas, methods, instructions or products referred to in the content.

MDPI
St. Alban-Anlage 66
4052 Basel
Switzerland
www.mdpi.com

Mathematics Editorial Office
E-mail: mathematics@mdpi.com
www.mdpi.com/journal/mathematics

Disclaimer/Publisher's Note: The statements, opinions and data contained in all publications are solely those of the individual author(s) and contributor(s) and not of MDPI and/or the editor(s). MDPI and/or the editor(s) disclaim responsibility for any injury to people or property resulting from any ideas, methods, instructions or products referred to in the content.

www.ingramcontent.com/pod-product-compliance
Lightning Source LLC
LaVergne TN
LVHW070504100526
838202LV00014B/1786